Peterson's
CULINARY SCHOOLS

Peterson's

Culinary SCHOOLS

11th Edition

PETERSON'S

A ℮elnet COMPANY

PETERSON'S

A **nelnet** COMPANY

About Peterson's, a Nelnet company

Peterson's (www.petersons.com) is a leading provider of education information and advice, with books and online resources focusing on education search, test preparation, and financial aid. Its Web site offers searchable databases and interactive tools for contacting educational institutions, online practice tests and instruction, and planning tools for securing financial aid. Peterson's serves 110 million education consumers annually.

For more information, contact Peterson's, 2000 Lenox Drive, Lawrenceville, NJ 08648; 800-338-3282; or find us on the World Wide Web at www.petersons.com/about.

Editor: Fern A. Oram; Production Editor: Mark D. Snider; Research Project Manager: Steve Sauermelch; Programmer: Alex Lin; Manufacturing Manager: Ray Golaszewski; Composition Manager: Linda M. Williams; Client Relations Representatives: Janet Garwo, Mimi Kaufman, Danielle Vreeland

ISBN-13: 978-0-7689-2410-7
ISBN-10: 0-7689-2410-3

Printed in Canada

10 9 8 7 6 5 4 3 2 1   10 09 08

Eleventh Edition

CONTENTS

A NOTE FROM THE PETERSON'S EDITORS

For more than ten years, Peterson's has given students and parents the most comprehensive, up-to-date information on culinary institutions in the United States and abroad. *Peterson's Culinary Schools* features advice and tips on the culinary school search and selection process, such as how to choose and pay for a cooking school and how to then make the most of your culinary career.

Opportunities abound for culinary students, and this guide can help you find what you want in a number of ways:

- For advice and guidance in the culinary school search and selection process, just turn the page to our **So You Want a Career in the Culinary Arts** section. Providing insight into how to know which school is right for you and why, "Get Cooking!" explains the increasingly important role a cooking school education has in a cooking career. Wondering how you'll pay? "Paying for Your Culinary Education" has all the tips and answers so that you'll wonder no more! "Charting a Successful Culinary Career" answers that burning question: What else can I do with a cooking degree besides open a restaurant? Finally, "Culinary Apprenticeships" outlines the benefits of this exciting training option.

- You'll then want to read through "How to Use This Guide," which explains the information presented in the individual culinary school profiles, lists culinary degree and certificate acronyms, and defines how we collect our data.

- Up next is the **Quick-Reference Chart**, where programs are listed geographically, and you can see at-a-glance the areas of spcialization (culinary arts, baking and pastry, management) and credentials they offer.

- Following that are the **Profiles of Professional Programs** and **Profiles of Apprenticeship Programs.** Here you'll find our unparalleled culinary program descriptions, arranged alphabetically by state and by country. They provide a complete picture of need-to-know information about culinary schools and apprenticeship programs, including program affiliation, areas of study, facilities, student and faculty profiles, expenses, and financial aid and housing availability. All the information you need to apply is placed together at the conclusion of each profile.

- If you already have specifics in mind, turn to the **Indexes.** Here you can search for a culinary school based on the certificate, diploma, or degree programs it offers. If you already have schools in mind that pique your interest, you can use the **Alphabetical Listing of Schools and Programs** to search for these schools.

Peterson's publishes a full line of resources to help guide you and your family through the culinary school admissions process. Peterson's publications can be found at your local bookstore, library, and high school guidance office—or visit us on the Web at www.petersons.com.

We welcome any comments or suggestions you may have about this publication and invite you to complete our online survey at **www.petersons.com/booksurvey.** Or you can fill out the survey at the back of this book, tear it out, and mail it to us at:

Publishing Department
Peterson's, a Nelnet company
2000 Lenox Drive
Lawrenceville, NJ 08648

Your feedback will help us make your educational dreams possible.

Schools will be pleased to know that Peterson's helped you in your selection. Admissions staff members are more than happy to answer questions, address specific problems, and help in any way they can. The editors at Peterson's wish you great success in your culinary school search!

So You Want a Career in the Culinary Arts

GET COOKING!

Selecting the finest ingredients. Combining them into a symphony of flavor. Presenting a culinary masterpiece. When preparing a meal feels less like work and more like a labor of love, you've found your calling.

And so have millions of like-minded culinary artists in the foodservice industry. According to the National Restaurant Association, foodservice employs 12.8 million people, making it the second-largest employer in the United States, behind the U.S. Government. That number is projected to grow to 14.8 million by 2017. Given its size, the industry can offer a substantial number of jobs, including a variety of positions in food preparation. But only the crème de la crème can snag the most coveted slots.

So how can you rise to the top?

It takes more than just talent and passion to make a good chef great. Much like stock forms the basis of any good soup, a formal culinary education provides a solid foundation of knowledge on which to build your career. You'll find that what you learn in cooking school you can use throughout your life, whether you graduated fifteen years, fifteen months, or 15 minutes ago.

Lots of successful chefs have built culinary empires without the help of institutional training. But even the most seasoned professionals who didn't attend cooking school recommend that aspiring chefs enroll in a culinary program. And if you're already a foodservice professional, a culinary education will complement your experience in the industry.

In an increasingly competitive field, you need all the advantages you can get and culinary education provides the knowledge that experience alone doesn't give you. With the rigors of daily restaurant life, you'll have little time to learn a lot on the job. When you enroll in a cooking school, however, you can tailor your curriculum to a narrow focus, so you can spend your time gaining expertise in the area where your interests lie.

Culinary school exposes you to a wide variety of relevant information, such as theory, international cuisine, and techniques. You'll get to apply what you learn in the classroom to what you do in the kitchen, working with experienced chefs and state-of-the-art equipment. You'll repeat basic and advanced cooking skills until you've mastered them, an opportunity that the real world can't always offer you. Then, you'll get to use your skills in professional kitchens; most cooking-school programs require hands-on training, usually in partnership with local restaurants.

Just by completing a program, you show potential employers that you're dedicated and hard working. Best of all, you'll get to spend time doing what you love to do—namely, express your creative culinary self.

FINDING THE RIGHT FIT

Some institutes offer programs leading to associate or bachelor's degrees in such fields as culinary arts, pastry and baking arts, and culinary management, to name a few. Completing a degree program normally takes between two and four years. Although it can be an investment in both time and money, you do earn college-level credit in a degree program. Other institutions offer certificates and diplomas, which take less time to finish, usually between two and ten months, but do not grant you college credit.

Discovering your options and narrowing the field are essential to getting into the program that's best for you. First, figure out what you want to do. Is baking your calling, or do you prefer contemporary French cuisine? Find schools that offer your specialty. A great place to start your search is by asking chefs in your area for recommendations. The Internet also provides an easy way to gather copious amounts of information on programs that fit your needs.

Once you've compiled your list of schools, gather as much information as you can from their Web sites, brochures, viewbooks, and other materials. Talk to faculty members and students at each institution to see whether you'd be a good fit with

Courtesy The French Culinary Institute/Matthew Septhimus

the program. If you can, spend a day—and even sit in on a class or two—at your top prospective schools.

Now that you've got your short list of programs, how do you choose? It's important to keep these factors in mind:

- Is the school accredited? By whom?
- Where is it located?
- Does the program suit your interests?
- What are the curriculum's requirements? What kind of classes will you take?
- When are classes held? Are there flexible scheduling options?
- Must students get practical experience, for example, in an externship? If so, do students earn credit for it?
- Are study-abroad opportunities offered?
- What facilities—classrooms, libraries, computers, and, most important, kitchen equipment—are available for student use?

- What are the current students like?
- How big are the classes? What is the student-faculty ratio?
- Are there job-placement and other career services available?
- Where do the program's alumni work? Are they successful?
- How much does the program cost?

Culinary programs can range between $15,000 and $30,000, depending on the school and type of program. The total cost, however, includes more than just tuition; you'll have to figure in fees, room and board, books and other supplies, and travel expenses. But don't be intimidated by the price tag—need- and merit-based financial aid can help you manage the cost. If you're willing to do a little digging, you can find several culinary scholarship opportunities online and through schools, businesses, and charitable foundations, among other places. As with most scholarships, it's best to apply for them as soon as possible. Contact the financial aid departments at your prospective schools to find out what aid opportunities are available to you and how and when to apply.

ENTRÉE

Admission requirements vary widely, depending on the program. Some schools simply ask you to fill out an application form and pay a fee, while others will also require you to have an interview and submit high school and/or college transcripts, test scores, essays, a resume, letters of recommendation, and a work sample. Typically, degree programs have more demanding application requirements than certificate or diploma programs.

Application questions might try to determine your background; whether you've traveled and, if so, where; what research you've conducted on the industry (e.g., through attending lectures or reading literature); why you're interested in the culinary arts; and, perhaps most revealing, why you've chosen to apply to a particular school. Be sure to answer honestly yet succinctly and show that you've done your homework. This is your chance to demonstrate your commitment to the program.

If you're interested in a competitive school, remember that not everyone gets in, so find ways to set yourself apart. Stick closely to application requirements, especially the deadlines. Get some work experience before you apply, even if it's just a summer stint at a neighborhood cafe. Play up your experience in other fields as well, since it can show that you're ready for the demands of education.

Don't forget that having some work experience before applying to any school can never hurt; it can be helpful in finding out whether this is truly what you want to do—and whether you're cut out for it.

As with financial aid opportunities, it is imperative to apply to any program as early as possible. A timely application can't hurt your chances of getting in.

EARNING YOUR TOQUE BLANCHE

Your hard work may have paid off once your acceptance letter finally arrives, but you've only really just started. School can be rigorous and rewarding. You'll quickly learn that the glamorous image of the chef so often portrayed in pop culture isn't entirely accurate—if your work experience hasn't already showed you this reality. After all, only those who have actually sweated, served, and survived in an actual kitchen know just how intense it can be. Yet you'll find that your sacrifices are worth it if you get to do what you love every day.

Take advantage of every opportunity you come across at school. Read as much as you can so you can stay up-to-date with the latest industry trends. Ask many questions, not just of faculty members, but of your peers as well. Learn as much as possible, especially outside the classroom. Volunteer whenever you can. And get to know your instructors; you can make lasting connections that can help you throughout your professional life.

It's likely you won't have the time—or the energy—to work full-time while you're enrolled in a program, but you should complement your education with more work experience. There are several reasons for this:

- You'll reinforce classroom lessons and apply them in real-world settings.
- You'll retain more of what you're learning.
- You'll see what you're not learning.
- You can pursue other related interests as you discover them.

You don't have to work at the most prestigious place to learn the best lessons. As is true of most anything, what you get out of your experience depends on what you make of it.

Many culinary programs require students to complete an externship, in which they work in a restaurant for a short time to get practical experience. Like internships, externships may be paid or unpaid. Unlike internships, they are much shorter, often only a few weeks. An externship student might do less actual work and more shadowing.

Courtesy The French Culinary Institute/Matthew Septhimus

Apply the same research skills you used in your culinary program search to obtaining an internship. Scout out several externship possibilities; you can generate leads by speaking to your professors and to chefs. To get the experience you want, offer to work for free if you can afford to do so. Although any work experience is valuable, land an externship at the best place you can. Not only will you gain indispensable knowledge, but also you'll have an addition to your resume that can help you nab a great job after graduation. Be sure to demonstrate your solid work ethic while you're on the job—come in early, stay late, get along with your coworkers, and take direction well from your boss. Even if your externship doesn't immediately lead to a post-graduation position, you could still earn glowing recommendations to help you in your job search.

CONTINUALLY REFINING YOUR PALATE

You may find that you discover the most important lessons outside the classroom. And working in foodservice means you'll never stop learning. Graduation is only the beginning. To stay ahead of the curve, you'll need to be proactive about continuing your culinary education, whether with more schooling, more work experience, or both.

For busy adults, many institutions offer for- and non-credit continuing education classes; a few culinary schools have continuing education programs for the working chef. In addition, seminars, lectures, and the like—many given by world-renown chefs—can be found everywhere, even in your neighborhood. Check out places like local libraries and schools for more information. Some national associations, such as the American Culinary Federation, have local chapters that can point you in the right direction. If you still can't find anything in your neck of the woods, online education is always an option. Some culinary artists have online tutorials to help you refine your skills, or you can take a formal class through distance learning.

To get the most from your education, say some culinary experts, don't take a chef position right after graduation—although it's highly unlikely that you'll land such a prestigious position as a newly minted graduate. You'll still have a lot to learn, and your time will be better spent working your way up in the best places possible. Try to work for chefs you admire. Absorb all the information you can. And remember that, even though you don't (and won't) know everything, your talent, passion, and culinary education will blend together nicely in the recipe for your continuing success.

PAYING FOR YOUR CULINARY EDUCATION

Madge Griswold

Culinary training can be expensive—nearly as expensive as attending a private university and sometimes more expensive than attending a public university. Few prospective students can simply pay the bills from their own savings. Some depend on their parents' generosity to fund their studies. Fortunately, help is available through loans and other financial aid programs and also in the form of scholarships.

Once you have decided which schools are most appealing to you, contact the financial aid office at each to determine exactly what kind of assistance is available. Some schools

Finding and Applying for Scholarships

even have work-study arrangements that allow students to work part-time and study as well.

Financial aid offices at culinary schools administer financial aid programs of various kinds and also provide basic advice about securing educational loans. You should consider this advice to be an integral part of your overall career planning. Financing your degree should be viewed as a long-term investment in your professional career. You should understand how this complex system works to be sure you are getting the best deal possible.

You may be eligible for grant assistance if financial need is proved. A grant is an outright award of money, whereas a loan must be paid back. Financial aid officers are more than happy to counsel you about these options.

Scholarship awards are usually based on talent and potential. Financial need may or may not be considered when a scholarship is awarded. Requirements for scholarship candidates are established by the donors of specific scholarships. Scholarships are awarded by culinary schools themselves and also by a number of professional culinary associations. A serious applicant in need of substantial financial assistance should explore all of these avenues. Additional information is provided later in this article, but you should also do your own research using the Web. A good place to start is at Peterson's (www. petersons.com) or at www.finaid.org.

When you plan for your culinary education, you'll want to find the best mix of grants, scholarships, loans, and work-study opportunities. In many cases, loans for education can be used to support a student's whole educational experience, including tuition, room and board, books, tools, and transportation. The financial aid office will put together the best aid "package" to meet your needs. If you feel this aid "package" is not sufficient, you should meet with the aid office either to reexamine your current situation or investigate other alternatives.

Many local community colleges have established fine culinary programs that are considerably cheaper than traditional programs at private institutions. You may want to consider programs at some of the community schools described in this guide. Many schools have excellent reputations locally and offer generous financial aid packages and scholarship assistance. And remember, culinary education is only part of preparing for a career in the culinary field. The rest is *you*—your knowledge, your talents, your creativity, and your overall work experience.

Financial Assistance at a Glance

Grants—*outright awards based on financial need. Ask the financial aid advisers at the schools you are interested in for details.*

Scholarships—*awards for culinary study based on talent or potential for excellence in the culinary field. Scholarships are awarded by both schools and organizations related to the culinary field. If you are interested in applying for culinary scholarships, ask about them when discussing options with the financial aid advisers.*

Loans—*available to persons who qualify for them. Loans, unlike grants and scholarships, must be paid back once you graduate. Ask the financial aid advisers at the schools you are interested in for details or ask about student loans at your local bank.*

Work-Study Programs—*programs that allow students to work while studying. Ask the financial aid advisers at the schools you are interested in whether such programs exist at their institutions and how you can be considered for these worthwhile programs.*

APPLYING FOR SCHOLARSHIPS

Almost all culinary schools award scholarships to truly promising students, so remember to ask for information about each school's requirements. In addition, many organizations associated with the culinary field award scholarships. You will want to begin addressing the scholarship application process even before you send in your admission application because the scholarship process can take longer than the admission process.

Each organization that provides scholarship aid has its own criteria for making awards, its own application process, and its own time frame. Many of these organizations evaluate applications only once a year. Some do it two or three times a year. Some organizations offer scholarships only for specialized kinds of study or to students with specific talents and characteristics. Others administer a broad range of scholarships.

Scholarships awarded by organizations (other than schools) are of two kinds:

1. **Awards for specific schools.** These awards are usually for tuition credit, although occasionally some aid is given for room and board, books, uniforms, or tools.

2. **Awards of a specific cash value that can be used at a variety of institutions.** Awards like these are usually designated by the donors to be applied only against tuition. They cannot be used to help pay for room and board, books, tools, uniforms, or getting to and from school. Cash-value awards generally are paid by the awarding organization directly to the chosen institution. Rarely, if ever, is money paid directly to a student to use as he or she wishes.

Since decisions about scholarship aid are based on the promise of achievement in the culinary field and not just financial need, it's a good idea to think through what kind of impression you want to make on the person or committee who will be evaluating your application. Here are some pointers from an experienced scholarship committee judge:

- Check your spelling carefully. If you are unsure of how to spell a word, look it up in a dictionary. Spelling errors detract from the message you are trying to communicate.

- Fill in all the information and submit all materials requested. You could be disqualified for not following directions.

- Be sure that all materials requested to be sent separately *are* sent separately. Frequently, letters of recommendation are requested separately to give some privacy to the referees and to ensure that they actually are the authors of the letters.

- List all work experience in the culinary field. Culinary work often demands long hours and considerable physical and mental effort. The fact that you have worked in the culinary field and understand the demands of your chosen career is important to judges. If you have done volunteer work in the culinary field, be sure to list that as well.

- Throughout the evaluation process, be prepared to explain your goals in life and your plans for the next few years. Lofty ambitions may be lauded but unrealistic plans are not.

- If you are asked to write an essay, write it yourself. This should be obvious; it's cheating if someone else writes your essay. A reviewer who suspects that you have not written your own essay may disqualify your entire application. Don't try to impress reviewers with flowery language or French culinary terms unless you actually have worked in a French kitchen and need to describe a station or task in French because of it. Don't list impossible or outrageous goals. If you are 18, it's unlikely that in five years you will be the executive chef in a prominent hotel or own your own restaurant. Remember that the readers of your application are food professionals who are well aware of how long it takes to achieve a position in the field and how much it costs to start a restaurant.

- Make your essay original. If you have had unique experiences that have influenced you to become involved in the culinary profession, by all means include them, but don't say that ever since you were a little child you have wanted to go into the culinary field. It may be true, but it's trite. Tell the reader what is unique and special about you, why you deserve the scholarship, and what it will enable you to do with your life.

THE SCHOLARSHIP INTERVIEW

These interviews can be fun because you may find that you and your interviewer have many experiences and ideas in common. Your interviewer will probably put you at ease quickly. Your interviewer is interested in learning how well you speak and how well you present yourself. Conversation with you will convey to the interviewer how committed you are to your culinary goals and something about yourself other than your culinary side. You might be asked "what do you do when you are not cooking?" Your interviewer will also try to make sure you really understand just what the scholarship can and cannot do for you. Often interviewers act as advisers to candidates, pointing out opportunities they may have overlooked. An interview can be an excellent opportunity for you to present what is unique about you and why you deserve to be given a specific award. Look forward to this opportunity.

SCHOLARSHIP OPPORTUNITIES

In addition to the schools themselves, a number of organizations award scholarships for culinary education. Some organizations give scholarships only for very specific purposes. Others give scholarships only for management training or for graduate work.

American Culinary Federation (ACF)

This long-established association of professional cooks has a membership of more than 19,000 and more than 230 chapters in many cities. In addition to its apprenticeship program, which provides an excellent alternate approach to culinary training, the ACF awards some scholarships on the national level. Contacts at the local level will be able to provide information about any scholarships awarded by a local chapter. For information about a local chapter, contact the ACF at 800-624-9458. Information about scholarships at the national level may be obtained by calling this number or by writing to:

American Culinary Federation
180 Center Place Way
St. Augustine, FL 32095
Phone: 904-824-4468 or
        800-624-9458 (toll-free)
Fax: 904-825-4758
E-mail: educate@acfchefs.net
www.acfchefs.org

American Dietetic Association (ADA)

This organization is made up of more than 67,000 members, 75 percent of whom are registered dietitians. It only awards scholarships for registered dietitians working toward master's degrees. If you think you are eligible, contact them at:

American Dietetic Association
120 South Riverside Plaza, Suite 2000
Chicago, IL 60606-6995
Phone: 800-877-1600 (toll-free)
www.eatright.org

The American Institute of Wine & Food (AIWF)

A nonprofit organization created to promote appreciation of wine and food and encourage scholarly education in gastronomy, this more than 4,000-member organization has twenty-five chapters in U.S. cities. Only certain chapters of the AIWF give scholarships for culinary education. Some are administered by the individual chapters; others are administered through the facilities of the International Association of Culinary Professionals (IACP) Foundation scholarship committee. You can reach AIWF at:

> The American Institute of Wine & Food
> 213–37 39th Avenue
> Box 216
> Bayside, NY 11361
> Phone: 800-274-2493 (toll-free)
> Fax: 718-522-0204
> E-mail: info@aiwf.org
> www.aiwf.org

Careers through Culinary Arts Program, Inc. (C-CAP)

A school-to-work program, established in a number of major metropolitan areas, C-CAP integrates culinary training at the high school level with work and business experience. C-CAP provides awards and scholarships ranging from $1000 to full tuition and assists students in making college and career choices. If you are a high school student, ask your guidance counselor if there is a C-CAP program in your area and how you might participate.

> Careers through Culinary Arts
> Program, Inc.
> 250 West 57th Street, Suite 2015
> New York, NY 10107
> Phone: 212-974-7111

> Fax: 212-974-7117
> E-mail: info@ccapinc.org
> www.ccapinc.org

Confrérie de la Chaîne des Rôtisseurs

A long-established organization for promoting appreciation of fine food and wine, this society has members in more than seventy countries and has granted more than $2 million dollars in scholarships to more than sixty qualifying schools since 1996. Scholarships are established directly with culinary schools. Interested candidates should ask financial aid officers at specific schools about these awards.

> Confrérie de la Chaîne des Rôtisseurs
> Chaîne House at Fairleigh Dickinson
> University
> 285 Madison Avenue
> Madison, NJ 07940-1099
> Phone: 973-360-9200
> Fax: 973-360-9330
> E-mail: chaine@chaineus.org
> www.chaineus.org

The Culinary Trust

This charitable and educational affiliate of the International Association of Culinary Professionals has, as one of its functions, the administration of scholarships that provide either tuition-credit assistance at specific institutions or financial assistance that can be applied to a variety of institutions. The Culinary Trust scholarship committee awards scholarships on an annual cycle, with an application deadline of December 15 for scholarships beginning the following July 1. Interested applicants should consult The Culinary Trust office, since deadlines sometimes change. Contact them at:

> The Culinary Trust
> 304 West Liberty Street, Suite 201

Louisville, KY 40202
Phone: 502-581-9786 Ext. 264
Fax: 502-589-3602
E-mail: tgribbins@hqtrs.com
www.theculinarytrust.com

International Foodservice Editorial Council (IFEC)

Dedicated to the improvement of media communications quality in the food field, this small organization of food service magazine editors and public relations executives awards between four and six scholarships annually to persons seeking careers that combine food service and communications.

IFEC
P.O. Box 491
Hyde Park, NY 12538
Phone: 845-229-6973
Fax: 845-229-6993
E-mail: info@ifeconline.com
www.ifec-is-us.com

International Food Service Executives Association (IFSEA)

A long-established educational and community service association, this group provides some scholarships of its own and also provides information about scholarships offered by other organizations.

IFSEA
2609 Surfwood Drive
Las Vegas, NV 89128
Phone: 702-430-9217
Fax: 702-430-9223
www.ifsea.com

The James Beard Foundation

This prominent organization of food professionals, devoted to the ideals and principles of legendary American cook and writer James Beard, awards a number of substantial scholarships each year. The application deadline is usually in May.

Diane Harris Brown
Educational and Community
Programming
The James Beard Foundation
6 West 18th Street, 10th Floor
New York, NY 10011
Phone: 212-627-1128
Fax: 212-627-1064
E-mail: scholarships@jamesbeard.org
www.jamesbeard.org

Les Dames d'Escoffier (LDEI)

This association has chapters in many major cities. One of its major purposes is the creation and awarding of scholarships to assist women with culinary training. These scholarships are awarded directly by the chapters. Women who are interested in applying for such scholarships should contact LDEI's executive director, Greg Jewell, at gjewell@aecmanagement.com, or visit their Web site at www.ldei.org.

National Restaurant Association Educational Foundation

An educational organization that produces a variety of courses, video training sessions, seminars, and other educational opportunities for persons in the hospitality industry, this group also offers scholarships.

National Restaurant Association
Educational Foundation
175 West Jackson Boulevard, Suite 1500
Chicago, IL 60604-2702
Phone: 312-715-1010 (Chicagoland) or
800-765-2122 (toll-free)
E-mail: info@nraef.org
www.nraef.org

Women Chefs & Restaurateurs (WCR)

An association specifically designed to promote the education and advancement of women in the culinary profession and to promote the industry overall, the WCR distributes more than $100,000 to its members for professional development. For further information, contact them at:

Women Chefs & Restaurateurs
455 South Fourth Street, Suite 650
Louisville, KY 40202
Phone: 877-927-7787
Fax: 502-589-3602
E-mail: wcr@hqtrs.com
www.womenchefs.org

Madge Griswold, CCP, is an author and culinary historian, past Chairman of the Board of Trustees of the International Association of Culinary Professionals Foundation, founding Chairman of the American Institute of Wine & Food's Baja Arizona chapter, and a member of the James Beard Foundation. Among her publications are two sections of Culinaria: The United States, A Culinary Discovery, *Cologne: Könemann. She is a member of the editorial advisory board of the journal* Gastronomica.

CHARTING A SUCCESSFUL CULINARY CAREER

Barbara Sims-Bell

What Else Can You Do with a Cooking Degree (besides open a restaurant)?

You love to cook; garlic essence smells better to you than an expensive French perfume; your friends and family say you should have a restaurant (well, maybe not your family); and right now you're seriously studying the choice of the best culinary training you can afford to allow you to live your dream. But it is never too early to contemplate the future, to think about opportunities that will come along after culinary training.

Chef, caterer, pastry cook, and restaurant cook are merely the most familiar four; there are hundreds of jobs in the food industry. You may want to consider preparing for positions in management as executive chef, or sales as catering director, or administration in food and beverage management. Maybe you'll want to explore developing specialty products—a line of sauces, dressings, or convenience foods, for example—for retail or wholesale markets. There are also teaching opportunities in professional cooking schools (possibly even the one you choose to attend). Others set out to become a restaurant consultant to entrepreneurs who want to start a restaurant or improve the one they own. Still another option is food writing and editing for magazines and books devoted to food and cooking.

For any of these career directions, you'll find the best and the broadest preparation in an accredited school program. You will come out with a certificate or a degree, and forever after when you are asked, "Where did you get your training?" you can refer to an accepted and respected credential in professional cooking. This training provides you with a lifelong basis for understanding quality raw ingredients, creating balance and pleasure in combined flavors, and presenting a beautiful plate to the diner.

Yes, you keep learning, but culinary school gives you a base of knowledge to test and compare to new trends, new ingredients, and your own creativity.

WHERE CAN I GO FROM HERE?

When most culinary students start their training, they believe they have found the work they want to do for the rest of their lives—and many are right. But some are surprised when they find so much routine and boredom and repetitive tasks. You haven't seen appetizers until you've assembled 3,000 identical stuffed puffs for a hotel reception. House salad? You'll clean and prep cases of the same greens and garnishes day after day. And the signature white chocolate mousse and meringue dacquoise layers you always wanted to perfect? You'll be preparing untold orders for it every evening. You have to love it.

If managerial positions are more to your liking, you'll need skills in addition to cooking. Managers create the working environment for the staff, often developing a sixth sense to recognize problems before they erupt. They are the motivational force that drives the staff. They must understand finance and business reports and their implications. They must have highly sensitive character judgment and the ability to manage people from hiring to mentoring to firing.

If your interests take you into catering and sales, think about these skills: You'll need to be able to research a product and explore your market. You'll need to really enjoy being with people. You'll need to draw on strong self-esteem to hear "no" and not take it personally. You'll need internal discipline to keep the work flowing. You'll need communication skills to persuade people that your product is best. And you'll need to be strongly motivated to make a sale.

WHERE DO I FIT?

To choose a career path that seems right for you, you'll need to define your own personality profile, whether it gives you the skills you need if you want to move higher or take a detour and move sideways. Or do you need to add some skills that you haven't yet developed?

One approach is to see a qualified career counselor for an evaluation of your strengths and weaknesses. Even if you reject or overrule the findings, you may gain an understanding of yourself that you didn't have before. Career testing extracts from us an inventory of our preferences.

Professional career counselors have the training, experience, and credentials to help you explore some of the possible choices that tempt you. They use finely tuned tests, such as Myers-Briggs, Holland, and Strong Interest. Then they interpret the test reports to give you additional guidance, either to follow your obvious bent or to stretch yourself into other areas with training and exploration. As in everything, there are quacks and there are bona fide wizards. The best course is to check the credentials of anyone you're considering.

Whether or not you seek outside career guidance, you should do some soul-searching on your own. Take stock of who you are. What are your best skills? Break them down into culinary, service, finance, research, communication, and management. Some of the categories will be longer than others; that tells you where you've placed your learning emphasis and where you'll have to work a bit harder. Think about your lifestyle and workplace values. Is independence something you seek, or do routine and stability matter more? Are you aiming for wealth or is leisure time now more important? Another significant list is what leisure activities you enjoy the most, then rating them by cost, whether they are solitary or social activities, and whether you've been able to fit them into your life lately. Are you a risk taker or do you proceed with caution? Even the most cautious of us can be successful entrepreneurs, but your own slant between these two types is important for you to know.

GETTING THE WHOLE CULINARY PICTURE

An easy and enjoyable way to learn about the spectrum of food-related jobs is by joining one or more professional organizations. Among the largest are the American Culinary Federation (ACF) and the International Association of Culinary Professionals (IACP). There are regional culinary groups—guilds, societies, alliances—in many large urban areas, and if the school you choose doesn't have the information, someone at IACP headquarters will be able to give you a current name and address near you to contact. Even if you are not yet a bona fide culinarian, as soon as you are enrolled in a professional program, you can usually join in the student-member category—at a lower annual dues rate. Most organizations allow guests to come to their meetings and pro-

grams—a good way to get connected and see if you feel comfortable in the group before joining.

Among the rewards of joining a local culinary group are friendships; meeting potential mentors; learning from varied guest speakers; job leads; customer referrals when another member is too booked to take the work; learning unrelated skills when you volunteer to work on program, membership, and communication committees; contributing to the community when you volunteer to work on a food-related benefit; and the lifelong asset of connections.

Take an inventory of "Whom do I know who I can call about this?" Culinary groups provide a wealth of leads and good food and wine to enjoy. Get the name and phone number, call to find out when and where the next meeting will be, and ask if they welcome guests. When you get there tell the greeter "I'm new here; who can I talk to about (baking, catering kitchens, ethnic ingredient stores, this organization, volunteering)"—pick a topic and start listening. Bring your business cards (not having them is unforgivable), give them out, and be sure to take cards from members you meet. Write the date of the meeting and what you talked about on the back before you go to sleep that night. Thus begins the building of a personal network, the invaluable channel to your peers.

The first time I met a friend of mine she was working as a waitress at a sort-of-Italian café where our Roundtable for Women in Foodservice chapter was having a program titled "Networking." I was moderating the panel, and the waitress was mesmerized by the dynamic group of professional women who were the audience. I noticed her enthusiasm, talked to her a bit, and encouraged her to join our chapter.

Stephanie Hersh

Stephanie Hersh defined her career goal of being a pastry chef at the age of 6 with the gift of a Betty Crocker Easy-Bake Oven. It was simplistic cause and effect: She produced the sweet offerings from batters, and everyone fluttered around telling her she was "terrific." She figured this could last her whole lifetime if she just kept on making cake. Her granny lived nearby and regularly let the diminutive yet determined youngster bake alongside her, making family desserts and good, sweet stuff.

Her parents were a harder nut to crack, insisting on scholastic accomplishment, first in her private high school, then in a four-year college. Looking back, she thinks it was the best for her because "I needed to grow up before going to culinary school." She worked part-time in restaurants, both front of the house and back, making some headway in the cooking hierarchy as she became more experienced. The work was everything she dreamed: It gave her pleasure, satisfaction, self-esteem, self-confidence. Her personality drove her to "always be the best," and she knew that to be best she had to have professional training. The restaurant business was changing at that time, and she knew it would no longer be possible to work up in kitchens from dishwasher to executive chef. Restaurant owners were hiring the applicant with the best culinary education. In 1985, Stephanie graduated from The Culinary Institute of America in Hyde Park, New York.

Her first professional job as a hotel pastry chef in Boston was a rude awakening. For the first time, pastries became work to do and get done, and it wasn't fun. She still had her pastry shop dream, and to feed her savings faster she devised a dual plan, based on her new goals—"I just wanted to cook and enjoy it and make money." Stephanie took a job as a private chef, live-in, for a small family with 2 professional working parents and 2 children. With her daytimes freed up, she enrolled at Katharine Gibbs School, figuring she could still be a private chef and work days as a secretary, with almost no living expenses. Then something happened.

Julia Child phoned the school asking if they had a graduate to recommend, commenting that it would be nice if the person knew something about cooking. When they described Stephanie's culinary background, she turned her down, saying that she really wanted a secretary, not a chef. Stephanie was in the school office when it happened and asked permission to call Julia back so she could press her case for herself. There was serious persuasion involved on Stephanie's part, but the statement was repeated: "I just want a secretary; I don't need anyone to work in my kitchen." Stephanie agreed that she just wanted to be a secretary. The next morning, minutes after arriving at the Cambridge house, Stephanie was in the kitchen prepping three recipes for demonstration stages and cooking aromatic fish stew for serving. Julia had forgotten she had agreed to a television taping/interview and greeted Stephanie with a fistful of recipe copies and almost no instruction except "just wiggle a finger at me when you've got it all ready," while she went back to the camera crew.

Suddenly Stephanie Hersh was an administrator, a facilitator, an essential sidekick, and accepted—smack, dab, in the center of the high-profile food industry. She loved her job. Her schooling continued, and, with Julia's encouragement, Stephanie was the first graduate in Boston University's master's program in gastronomy. She later ran her own business, Chef Steph, through which she sold cakes and pastries and organized cooking parties for children. An active member of IACP, Hersh lives and works in New Zealand.

With a university degree in soils science, she was working as a server "because that is what I like to do more than anything else"—and her people skills were what I continued to notice as she joined the chapter, came to meetings, and changed jobs a few times. Within a year, she was hired by the oldest established winery in our region as Tasting Room Manager and then became its local Sales Manager. Her education in soils and geology gave her a head start in understanding wine production for her job. "Who you know" only opens the door, but "what you know" gets you the job.

TRAVEL STAGES FOR A CAREER

If you have already identified some role models in the food industry and have learned a little about their lives and careers, you know that a long stretch of steady, hard work is the story of their success. We can divide that stretch into sections, though, and understand ways that your own success can be realized.

Beginner

Focus on a career plan for yourself as early as you can. You will make changes, take detours, and acquire unrelated skills that you want to use, but having a predetermined route tells you whether you're lost or just on a scenic loop. Use the professional network you are gathering right away. At first that may be primarily your fellow students and your teachers, but they are an important network for you to maintain. How do you use them? As questions arise in your mind, ask "Whom do I know who might answer this?" Make contact with the person, ask your questions, strengthen your bond. Ask your teachers and your mentors about industry conferences and trade shows you can attend, and make an effort to go. The more you know what is going on in the food industry, the better you can steer yourself to success. Donate your time and skills to publicized events—does your school or your restaurant put on fund-raisers for community projects? Volunteer to assist, to cook, to serve, or to do

Courtesy The French Culinary Institute/Matthew Septhimus

whatever is needed and talk to your peers at the event. Remember, always take your business cards and give them out as you are collecting new ones. Write on the backs! As soon as you become a "head chef"—whether in your own restaurant or as an employee—create some public appearance opportunities for yourself. Participate in community benefits that feature a group of local chefs providing the food. If you are developing a product through the restaurant or on your own, find opportunities to have guests taste it at local events. If you author a cookbook, offer to do book signings at local bookstores. Work closely with your culinary peers, participate in public events as much as possible, and barter your services for product. Keep your name out there, and it will become your billboard.

Intermediate

This is the stage to position yourself for publicity. The first step is to run your business (whether self-owned or profit-sharing status) so well you can be absent on tour. Go to Beard House dinners in New York City, and talk to them about scheduling you to cook one. Contact the nearest chapter of the American Institute of Wine & Food and ask if it will set up a program using you as a guest chef. Develop your public speaking skills; if you need help with public speaking, contact your local adult education program for workshops and local coaches. The better you can hold your audience's attention while you speak (and this includes table side in your restaurant), the more you will promote your success. As soon as you are confident speaking to medium-size groups (50 to 200 people) and have something to talk about, offer to be a speaker at professional conferences: the American Culinary Federation, the International Association of Culinary Professionals, and regional culinary organizations. After a few more experiences, and when word of your entertainment value gets around, you will be paid travel and lodging expenses to be a speaker (and in time you'll be paid an honorarium, as well). At this midcareer stage, you can search out ways to market your name, and offers will come to you unsolicited: consider allowing your name to be used on aprons or chef's clothing labels (this can be either your own merchandise line or the use of your name). Newcomers to the restaurant business looking for help and advice may turn to you, and you can decide whether to give it freely or charge as a consultant (probably a little of both, depending on the circumstances). By now, you recognize the need for a support network to help you manage some of these outside activities: a lawyer, an accountant, a marketing assistant, and possibly a booking agent. Don't sit back thinking that when you need them they will be there. As with everything, you have to look ahead and look out for yourself.

Advanced

If you're doing it right, now is the stage to get paid for having fun. If you still want to cook, you'll be doing it, probably with one or two trained cooks behind you so you can take care of the peripheral business you've created. Here are some ways you'll find to stimulate your creative juices and make money at the same time: You'll be paid an honorarium and expenses as a speaker. You'll be recruited to head business development teams for other culinary start-ups. You'll be paid for product and service endorsements. You may spin off your name or your label on merchandise for royalties. You'll attract potential investors and/or buyers for expansion or retirement from your own restaurant or company. If this is fun for you, you'll find the time to do it.

Graduate

This is the time to be a mentor and a philanthropist within your culinary community. When you were a beginner in professional training, your school probably brought in the best local chefs to inspire you. You may have received a culinary scholarship from one of the professional organizations. Now it's your turn to be on the giving side. You'll still get requests to speak and be paid well for most of the gigs, but consider giving some time to smaller groups of the next generation of chefs. The appearances you'll get paid for will be keynoter, industry spokesperson, and expert; consider being on a panel or a roundtable to answer questions one-on-one. You will be offered an investment position in food companies solely as an adviser. The fee you get for endorsements will be higher than ever. To truly be a graduate in this career field, you will consciously find, promote, and mentor promising individuals who can advance the industry in the future. Well done!

KEEPING YOUR OPTIONS OPEN

The future of any career, say, ten or twenty years ahead, is excruciatingly difficult to focus in on. Whether you look through a camera's viewer or through eyeglasses customized to your needs, you make physical adjustments to bring a faraway object into focus.

Once you have chosen a culinary school for your training and started instruction, it's already time to start asking about future opportunities. Bombard your chefs at school with questions about what you need to know for jobs that sound enticing to you. You may not act on that information for several years, but you've started to adjust your focus whenever you gather more knowledge about future opportunities.

The speck on the horizon that is your future career is barely visible now, but as you move toward it or look for it through a magnifier, you will develop your own vision, and it will become excitingly clear to you. Good luck to every one of you.

Barbara Sims-Bell was the founder of and primary instructor at the Santa Barbara Cooking School from 1979 to 1985. She is the author of two books about careers and jobs in the culinary field, Career Opportunities in the Food and Beverage Industry, *New York: Facts on File, 1995, and* FoodWork—Jobs in the Food Industry and How to Get Them, *Santa Barbara, Calif.: Advocacy Press, 1994.*

CULINARY APPRENTICESHIPS

American Culinary Federation

*C*ulinary apprenticeships are on-the-job training programs reinforced by related instruction from educational institutions. Many successful apprenticeship programs offer an associate degree. Apprentices receive years of documented work experience while also receiving an education that is specific to the industry, and apprentice graduates can confidently accept a job based on the experience received during their apprenticeship program. These graduates also receive Certified Cook status through the American Culinary Federation (ACF) National Certification Program. The ultimate designation of Chef comes through additional experience and education.

Experience and Education

The success of apprenticeship comes from the commitment made by the industry chef and management, the education institution, and the American Culinary Federation (local and national). Each of these entities is responsible for maintaining high-quality standards.

Employers of apprentices enjoy the benefit of committed and loyal culinarians who enhance the enthusiasm and positive attitudes of the entire staff. Apprentices enter a kitchen starting at the beginning, giving the supervising chef the unique opportunity to develop a mentorship relationship with the apprentice. The *Training Log* cultivates this relationship by requiring a weekly entry by the apprentice. The supervising chef periodically reviews these entries.

The ACF Apprenticeship Program offers a unique connection between industry and education. The standard curriculum and competencies are delivered by the supervising chef in tandem with the educational institution. An apprenticeship can strengthen many ACF chapters by providing chefs with a purpose: to share their culinary knowledge and expertise.

The ACF Apprenticeship Program began in 1976 with a grant from the United States government. Today, it is one of two programs remaining from that training initiative and is the seventh-largest apprenticeship program in the United States.

_____

Reprinted with the permission of the American Culinary Federation.

HOW TO USE THIS GUIDE

Find the Right Culinary School for You

*P*eterson's Culinary Schools is a comprehensive guide to culinary schools in the United States and abroad. The guide provides detailed descriptions of hundreds of professional degree and apprenticeship programs.

QUICK-REFERENCE CHART

The **Quick-Reference Chart** lists programs by state and country, indicates what degrees or awards are offered, and notes if the program offers degree specializations in the areas of culinary arts, baking and pastry, or management. Please be aware that there are other degree specializations, and you will have to refer to individual profiles to discover what an individual program may offer beyond these popular ones.

PROFILES OF PROFESSIONAL PROGRAMS

Peterson's Culinary Schools profiles are organized into two main sections, each arranged alphabetically by state within the United States and by country. The first section includes profiles of professional programs and the second, profiles of apprenticeship programs.

Professional programs offer formalized instruction in a class setting. A diploma, degree, or certificate is awarded to the student at the end of successful completion of a predetermined curriculum of courses and a minimum number of credit hours. Workplace training in the form of an externship or work-study program may be an option but is not usually required. An apprenticeship is essentially an on-the-job training program. Typical apprenticeship programs entail completion of a specific term of full-time employment for wages in a food service kitchen under a qualified chef. Classroom culinary instruction is usually required in addition to the scheduled work, and a certificate may be awarded.

General Information. Indicates private or public institution, coeducational or single-sex, type of institution, and the campus setting.

The founding year of the institution is also listed, as is institutional accreditation information.

Program Information. Indicates the year the program started offering classes, program accreditation, the program calendar (semester, quarter, etc.), the type of degrees and awards offered, degree and award specializations, and the length of time needed to complete the degree or award.

Program Affiliation. Lists those organizations to which the school or program belongs.

Areas of Study. Includes the courses available.

Facilities. Lists the number and types of facilities available to students.

(Typical) Student Profile. Provides the total number of students enrolled in the program and the number who are full-time and part-time and the age range of students.

Faculty. Provides the total number of faculty members, the number who are full-time and part-time, and the number who are culinary accredited, industry professionals, master bakers, or master chefs. The names of prominent faculty members and their degree or certificate level are listed if provided. The faculty-student ratio is also listed.

Prominent Alumni and Current Affiliation. Provides information on notable alumni and the restaurant/hotel/facility with which they are affiliated.

Special Programs. Notes special educational opportunities offered by the program.

Typical Expenses. Includes information on full-time, part-time, in-state, and out-of-state tuition costs; special program-related fees;

and application fees. Dollar signs without further notation refer to U.S. currency.

Financial Aid. Provides information on the number and amount of program-specific loans and scholarships awarded during the 2004–05, 2005–06, or 2006–07 academic year and unique financial aid opportunities available to students. (This section covers only culinary-related financial aid and does not include types of financial aid that are open to all students, such as Pell Grants and Stafford Loans.)

Housing. Indicates the type of on-campus housing available, as well as the typical cost of off-campus housing in the area.

Application Information. Provides information on application deadlines, the number of students who applied for admission to the program, and the number of students accepted to the program for the 2004–05, 2005–06, or 2006–07 academic year, and application materials that are required.

Contact. Includes the name, address, telephone and fax numbers, and e-mail address (if provided) of the contact person for the program and the Web address of the program or institution.

PROFILES OF APPRENTICESHIP PROGRAMS

Program Information. Indicates if the apprenticeship program is directly sponsored by a college, university, or culinary institute; if the program is approved by the American Culinary Federation; if an apprentice is eligible to receive a degree from a college or university upon successful completion of the program; and if any special apprenticeships are available.

Placement Information. Provides the number and types of locations where apprentices may be placed and lists the most popular placement locations of participants.

(Typical) Apprentice Profile. Indicates the number of participants, the age range of participants, and the application materials a prospective apprentice must submit.

Typical Expenses. Provides information on the basic costs of participating in the program as well as the application fee and special program-related fees.

Entry-Level Compensation. Indicates the typical salary for an apprentice at the beginning of the apprenticeship program.

Contact. Includes the name, address, telephone and fax numbers, and e-mail address (if provided) of the contact person for the apprenticeship program and the Web address of the program or institution.

INDEXES

Two indexes are available at the end of the book. The first, **Certificate, Diploma, and Degree Programs**, lists programs by whether they offer a certificate or diploma or a degree (associate, bachelor's, master's, or doctoral). The second index, **Alphabetical Listing of Schools and Programs**, is an alphabetical list by name of the program or institution.

CULINARY DEGREES AND CERTIFICATES

Below is a list of degrees and certificates common to the culinary and hospitality industries. You'll often see these acronyms

following the names of faculty members to indicate their level of education and certification.

AA	Associate of Arts
AAC	American Academy of Chefs
AAS	Associate of Applied Science
BA	Bachelor of Arts
BS	Bachelor of Science
CAGS	Certificate of Advanced Graduate Study
CC	Certified Culinarian
CCC	Certified Chef de Cuisine
CCE	Certified Culinary Educator
CCM	Certified Club Manager
CCP	Certified Culinary Professional
CDM	Certified Dietary Manager
CDN	Certified Dietetics Nutritionist
CEC	Certified Executive Chef
CEPC	Certified Executive Pastry Chef
CFBE	Certified Food and Beverage Executive
CFBM	Certified Food and Beverage Manager
CFE	Certified Food Executive
CFSC	Certified Food Service Consultant
CFSM	Certified Food Service Manager
CHA	Certified Hotel Administrator
CHAE	Certified Hospitality Accounting Executive
CHE	Certified Hospitality Educator
CHM	Certified Hospitality Manager
CMB	Certified Master Baker
CMC	Certified Master Chef
CMPC	Certified Master Pastry Chef
CPC	Certified Pastry Culinarian
CPCE	Certified Professional Catering Executive
CRDE	Certified Rooms Division Executive
CSC	Certified Sous Chef
CWC	Certified Working Chef
CWPC	Certified Working Pastry Chef
DFS	Doctor of Food Service
DTR	Dietetic Technician, Registered
EdD	Doctor of Education

EPC	Executive Pastry Chef
FADA	Fellow of the American Dietetic Association
FMP	Food Service Management Professional
FCSI	Foodservice Consultants Society International
HRTA	Hotel, Restaurant, and Travel Administration
LD	Licensed Dietitian
LRD	Licensed Registered Dietician
MA	Master of Arts
MBA	Master of Business Administration
MEd	Master of Education
MHRIM	Master of Hotel, Restaurant, and Institutional Management
MOF	Meilleur Ouvrier de France
MPC	Master Pastry Chef
MPH	Master of Public Health
MPS	Master of Professional Studies
MS	Master of Science
MSA	Master of Science in Administration
MSEd	Master of Science in Education
PhD	Doctor of Philosophy
RD	Registered Dietitian
REHS	Registered Environmental Health Specialist

DATA COLLECTION PROCEDURES

Information in this book was collected between summer 2005 and summer 2007 using questionnaires. Changes may occur after publication, so be sure to contact the institutions directly for the most current information on their programs.

QUICK-REFERENCE CHART

CULINARY PROGRAMS AT-A-GLANCE—U.S.

State/School	Credentials Offered	Culinary Arts	Baking and Pastry	Management	Apprenticeship Programs
Alabama					
ACF Greater Montgomery Chapter					■
Alabama Agricultural and Mechanical University	B, M			■	
CULINARD–The Culinary Institute of Virginia College	D, A, B	■	■	■	
The Gulf Coast Culinary Institute	C, A	■	■	■	
Tuskegee University	B			■	
The University of Alabama	C, B			■	
Alaska					
Alaska Vocational Technical Center/Alaska Culinary Academy	C	■	■		
University of Alaska Anchorage	A, B	■		■	
University of Alaska Fairbanks	C, A	■	■		
Arizona					
Arizona Culinary Institute	D	■	■	■	
Arizona Western College	C, A	■		■	
The Art Institute of Phoenix	D, A, B	■	■		
The Art Institute of Tucson	A, B	■			
Central Arizona College	C, A	■		■	
Chefs Association of Southern Arizona, Tucson					■

Credentials: *C* = Certificate; *D* = Diploma; *A* = Associate Degree; *B* = Bachelor's Degree; *M* = Master's Degree; **Ph.D.** = Doctorate

State/School	Credentials Offered	Culinary Arts	Baking and Pastry	Management	Apprenticeship Programs
Arizona *(continued)* Maricopa Skill Center	C				
Northern Arizona University	C, B	■		■	
Pima Community College	C, A	■			
Scottsdale Community College	C, A	■		■	
Scottsdale Culinary Institute	C, A, B	■	■	■	
Arkansas					
Ozarka College	C, A	■			
Pulaski Technical College Arkansas Culinary School	C, A	■	■		
University of Arkansas at Pine Bluff	B			■	
California					
American River College	C, A	■	■	■	
The Art Institute of California–Inland Empire	A, B	■		■	
The Art Institute of California–Los Angeles	D, A, B	■	■	■	
The Art Institute of California–Orange County	D, A, B	■	■	■	
The Art Institute of California–Sacramento	A, B	■		■	
The Art Institute of California–San Diego	A, B	■	■	■	
The Art Institute of California–San Francisco	A, B	■		■	
Barona Valley Ranch Resort & Casino					■
Bauman College: Holistic Nutrition & Culinary Arts–Berkeley	C				

*Credentials: **C** = Certificate; **D** = Diploma; **A** = Associate Degree; **B** = Bachelor's Degree; **M** = Master's Degree; **Ph.D.** = Doctorate*

State/School	Credentials Offered	Culinary Arts	Baking and Pastry	Management	Apprenticeship Programs
Bauman College: Holistic Nutrition & Culinary Arts–Penngrove	C				
Bauman College: Holistic Nutrition & Culinary Arts–Santa Cruz	C				
California Culinary Academy	C, A	■	■	■	
California School of Culinary Arts	D, A	■	■	■	
California State Polytechnic University, Pomona	B			■	
Chef Eric's Culinary Classroom	C	■	■		
City College of San Francisco	A	■		■	
College of the Canyons	A			■	
Contra Costa College	C, A	■	■		
The Culinary Institute of America	C, A	■	■		
Epicurean School of Culinary Arts	C		■		
Institute of Technology	C, D	■	■		
Institute of Technology–Modesto	C, D	■	■		
Institute of Technology–Roseville	C, D	■	■		
JobTrain	C	■			
Kitchen Academy	D	■			
Kitchen Academy–Sacramento	D	■			
Lake Tahoe Community College	C, A	■	■		
Long Beach City College	C, A	■	■	■	
Mission College	C, A			■	

State/School	Credentials Offered	Culinary Arts	Baking and Pastry	Management	Apprenticeship Programs
California *(continued)* Modesto Junior College	C, A	■			
Monterey Peninsula College	C, A		■	■	
Mt. San Antonio College	C, A			■	
Napa Valley College	C	■			
National Culinary and Bakery School	C	■	■		
The New School of Cooking	D	■	■		
Orange Coast College	C, A	■		■	
Oxnard College	C, A	■		■	
Professional Culinary Institute	D, A	■	■	■	
Quality College of Culinary Careers	C, A	■	■		
Richardson Researches, Inc.	D				
Riverside Community College	C, A	■			
San Diego Mesa College	C, A	■		■	
San Francisco Culinary/Pastry Program					■
Santa Barbara City College	C, A	■		■	
Tante Marie's Cooking School	C	■	■		
University of San Francisco	B			■	
Westlake Culinary Institute	C	■	■		
Colorado					
ACF Colorado Chefs Association					■

*Credentials: **C** = Certificate; **D** = Diploma; **A** = Associate Degree; **B** = Bachelor's Degree; **M** = Master's Degree; **Ph.D.** = Doctorate*

State/School	Credentials Offered	Culinary Arts	Baking and Pastry	Management	Apprenticeship Programs
The Art Institute of Colorado	D, A, B	■	■	■	
Colorado Mountain College	C, A	■			
Colorado Mountain College					■
Cook Street School of Fine Cooking	D	■			
Culinary School of the Rockies	D	■	■		
Front Range Community College	C, A	■		■	
Johnson & Wales University–Denver Campus	A, B	■	■	■	
Mesa State College	C, A	■			
Metropolitan State College of Denver	C, B	■		■	
Pikes Peak Community College	C, A	■	■	■	
School of Natural Cookery	C				
Connecticut					
Briarwood College	A			■	
Center for Culinary Arts	D	■			
Center for Culinary Arts	D	■			
Connecticut Culinary Institute	D	■	■		
Connecticut Culinary Institute-Suffield	D	■	■		
Gateway Community College	C, A	■		■	
International College of Hospitality Management	C, A	■		■	
Naugatuck Valley Community College	C, A	■		■	

State/School	Credentials Offered	Culinary Arts	Baking and Pastry	Management	Apprenticeship Programs
Delaware					
Delaware State University	B			■	
Delaware Technical and Community College	D, A	■		■	
Delaware Technical and Community College	A	■			
University of Delaware	B, M			■	
District of Columbia					
Howard University	B			■	
Florida					
ACF Treasure Coast Chapter					■
The Art Institute of Fort Lauderdale	D, A, B	■	■	■	
The Art Institute of Jacksonville	D, A, B	■		■	
The Art Institute of Tampa	D, A, B	■	■	■	
Atlantic Technical Center	C	■			
Bethune-Cookman University	B			■	
Charlotte Technical Center	C	■			
First Coast Technical College	C	■	■		
Florida Culinary Institute A Division of Lincoln College of Technology	D, A, B	■	■	■	
Fort Lauderdale ACF Inc.					■
Gulf Coast Community College	A	■		■	
Hillsborough Community College	C, A	■		■	

*Credentials: **C** = Certificate; **D** = Diploma; **A** = Associate Degree; **B** = Bachelor's Degree; **M** = Master's Degree; **Ph.D.** = Doctorate*

State/School	Credentials Offered	Culinary Arts	Baking and Pastry	Management	Apprenticeship Programs
Indian River Community College	C, A	■		■	
Indian River Community College					■
Johnson & Wales University–North Miami	A, B	■	■	■	
Keiser University	A	■			
Keiser University	A	■			
Keiser University	A	■	■		
Le Cordon Bleu College of Culinary Arts	D, A	■	■		
Manatee Technical Institute	C	■			
Northwood University, Florida Campus	A, B			■	
Notter School of Pastry Arts	C, D		■		
Orlando Culinary Academy	D, A	■	■	■	
Palm Beach Community College	A			■	
Pensacola Junior College	A	■		■	
Pinellas Technical Education Center–Clearwater Campus	C	■			
St. Thomas University	B			■	
University of Central Florida	B, M, Ph.D.			■	
Valencia Community College	C, A	■	■	■	
Webber International University	A, B			■	
Georgia					
The Art Institute of Atlanta	D, A, B	■	■	■	

State/School	Credentials Offered	Culinary Arts	Baking and Pastry	Management	Apprenticeship Programs
Georgia *(continued)* Augusta Technical College	D	■			
Chattahoochee Technical College	D, A	■			
Coastal Georgia Community College	C	■			
Georgia Southern University	B			■	
Georgia State University	C, B, M			■	
Le Cordon Bleu College of Culinary Arts, Atlanta	C, A	■	■		
North Georgia Technical College	C, D, A	■			
North Georgia Technical College, Blairsville Campus	C, D, A	■			
Ogeechee Technical College	C, D, A	■			
Savannah Technical College	D, A	■			
West Georgia Technical College	C, D	■			
Hawaii					
Leeward Community College	C, A		■	■	
Maui Community College	C, A	■	■	■	
Travel Institute of the Pacific	D	■	■		
University of Hawaii–Kapiolani Community College	C, A	■	■		
Idaho					
Boise State University	C, A	■			
Idaho State University	C, A	■		■	

*Credentials: **C** = Certificate; **D** = Diploma; **A** = Associate Degree; **B** = Bachelor's Degree; **M** = Master's Degree; **Ph.D.** = Doctorate*

State/School	Credentials Offered	Culinary Arts	Baking and Pastry	Management	Apprenticeship Programs
Illinois					
Black Hawk College	A	■			
College of DuPage	C, A	■	■	■	
College of Lake County	C, A	■		■	
The Cooking and Hospitality Institute of Chicago	C, A	■	■		
Elgin Community College	C, A	■	■	■	
The Illinois Institute of Art–Chicago	A, B	■		■	
Joliet Junior College	C, A	■	■	■	
Kendall College	C, A, B	■	■	■	
Lexington College	A, B			■	
Lincoln Land Community College	C, A	■	■	■	
Parkland College	C, A			■	
Robert Morris College	A, B	■		■	
Southwestern Illinois College	C, A	■		■	
Triton College	C, A	■	■	■	
University of Illinois at Urbana–Champaign	B			■	
Washburne Culinary Institute	C, A	■	■		
Indiana					
The Art Institute of Indianapolis	C, A, B	■	■	■	
Ball State University	A, B			■	
Indiana Business College	A	■	■		

State/School	Credentials Offered	Culinary Arts	Baking and Pastry	Management	Apprenticeship Programs
Indiana *(continued)*					
Indiana University–Purdue University Fort Wayne	A, B			■	
Ivy Tech Community College–Central Indiana	C, A	■	■	■	
Ivy Tech Community College–North Central	A	■	■	■	
Ivy Tech Community College–Northeast	A	■	■		
Ivy Tech Community College–Northwest	C, A	■	■	■	
Iowa					
Des Moines Area Community College	A	■		■	
Iowa Lakes Community College	D, A			■	
Iowa State University of Science and Technology	B, M, Ph.D.			■	
Kirkwood Community College	C, D, A	■	■	■	
Kansas					
American Institute of Baking	C		■		
Johnson County Community College	C, A		■	■	
Johnson County Community College					■
Kansas City Kansas Area Technical School	C			■	
Kentucky					
Elizabethtown Community and Technical College	C, D	■		■	
Sullivan University	D, A, B	■	■	■	
Western Kentucky University	B			■	

*Credentials: **C** = Certificate; **D** = Diploma; **A** = Associate Degree; **B** = Bachelor's Degree; **M** = Master's Degree; **Ph.D.** = Doctorate*

State/School	Credentials Offered	Culinary Arts	Baking and Pastry	Management	Apprenticeship Programs
Louisiana					
Delgado Community College	C, A	■	■	■	
Delgado Community College					■
Grambling State University	B			■	
Louisiana Culinary Institute, LLC	D, A	■		■	
Louisiana Technical College–Baton Rouge Campus	C, D	■			
Nicholls State University	A, B	■			
Sclafani Cooking School, Inc.	C				
Southern University at Shreveport	C, A			■	
University of Louisiana at Lafayette	B			■	
Maine					
Eastern Maine Community College	C, A	■		■	
Southern Maine Community College	A	■			
York County Community College	C, A	■		■	
Maryland					
Allegany College of Maryland	A	■	■		
Anne Arundel Community College	C, A	■	■	■	
Baltimore International College	C, A, B, M	■	■	■	
L'Academie de Cuisine	C	■	■		
Lincoln Tech	D	■			

State/School	Credentials Offered	Culinary Arts	Baking and Pastry	Management	Apprenticeship Programs
Maryland (*continued*) Wor-Wic Community College	C, A	■		■	
Massachusetts					
Branford Hall Career Institute	C	■			
Bristol Community College	A	■	■		
Bunker Hill Community College	C, A	■			
The Cambridge School of Culinary Arts	C, D	■	■		
Endicott College	B			■	
International Institute of Culinary Arts	C, D	■	■	■	
Massasoit Community College	C, A	■			
Middlesex Community College	C, A	■		■	
Newbury College	C, A, B	■	■	■	
University of Massachusetts Amherst	C, B, M			■	
Michigan					
ACF Blue Water Chefs Association					■
ACF Michigan Chefs de Cuisine Association					■
The Art Institute of Michigan	C, A, B	■	■	■	
Baker College of Muskegon	C, A, B	■	■	■	
Central Michigan University	B			■	
Grand Rapids Community College	C, A	■	■	■	
Grand Valley State University	B			■	

*Credentials: **C** = Certificate; **D** = Diploma; **A** = Associate Degree; **B** = Bachelor's Degree; **M** = Master's Degree; **Ph.D.** = Doctorate*

State/School	Credentials Offered	Culinary Arts	Baking and Pastry	Management	Apprenticeship Programs
Great Lakes Culinary Institute at Northwestern Michigan College	C, A	■			
Henry Ford Community College	C, A	■	■	■	
Macomb Community College	C, A	■	■	■	
Michigan State University	B, M			■	
Mott Community College	A	■	■	■	
Northern Michigan University	A, B			■	
Northwood University	A, B			■	
Oakland Community College	C, A	■	■	■	
Schoolcraft College	C, A	■	■		
Washtenaw Community College	C, A	■	■	■	
Minnesota					
The Art Institutes International Minnesota	C, A, B	■	■	■	
Hennepin Technical College	C, D, A	■			
Hibbing Community College	D, A	■		■	
Le Cordon Bleu Minneapolis/St. Paul	C, A	■	■		
South Central College	D, A	■		■	
Mississippi					
Coahoma Community College	C, A	■		■	
Meridian Community College	A			■	
Mississippi Gulf Coast Community College	D			■	

State/School	Credentials Offered	Culinary Arts	Baking and Pastry	Management	Apprenticeship Programs
Mississippi *(continued)* Mississippi University for Women	B	■			
Missouri					
Chefs de Cuisine of St. Louis Association					■
College of the Ozarks	B			■	
Columbia Missouri Chapter ACF					■
Jefferson College	C, A	■			
Penn Valley Community College	A				
St. Louis Community College	C, A	■	■	■	
University of Missouri–Columbia	B, M			■	
Montana					
Flathead Valley Community College	A	■			
The University of Montana–Missoula	C, A	■		■	
Nebraska					
ACF Professional Chefs and Culinarians of the Heartland					■
Central Community College–Hastings Campus	D, A	■		■	
Metropolitan Community College	A	■	■	■	
Southeast Community College, Lincoln Campus	A	■		■	
Nevada					
The Art Institute of Las Vegas	A, B	■	■	■	

*Credentials: **C** = Certificate; **D** = Diploma; **A** = Associate Degree; **B** = Bachelor's Degree; **M** = Master's Degree; **Ph.D.** = Doctorate*

State/School	Credentials Offered	Culinary Arts	Baking and Pastry	Management	Apprenticeship Programs
Le Cordon Bleu College of Culinary Arts, Las Vegas	C, A	■	■		
University of Nevada, Las Vegas	B	■		■	
New Hampshire					
McIntosh College	A	■			
New Hampshire Community Technical College	C, D, A	■	■		
Southern New Hampshire University	C, A, B, M	■	■	■	
University of New Hampshire	A			■	
New Jersey					
Atlantic Cape Community College	C, A	■	■	■	
Bergen Community College	C, A	■		■	
Brookdale Community College	C, A	■		■	
Burlington County College	C, A	■	■	■	
Hudson County Community College	C, A	■	■	■	
Mercer County Community College	C, A	■	■	■	
Middlesex County College	C, A	■		■	
Technical Institute of Camden County	D	■			
Thomas Edison State College	B			■	
Union County College	A			■	
New Mexico					
Culinary Business Academy	C				

State/School	Credentials Offered	Culinary Arts	Baking and Pastry	Management	Apprenticeship Programs
New Mexico *(continued)* Luna Community College	C, A	■			
New Mexico State University	B			■	
The Roswell Job Corps Center	C	■			
New York					
The Art Institute of New York City	C, A	■	■	■	
Broome Community College	A			■	
Career Academy of New York	C	■	■	■	
Culinary Academy of Long Island	C	■	■	■	
The Culinary Institute of America	A, B	■	■	■	
Erie Community College, City Campus	C, A	■	■		
Erie Community College, North Campus	A	■		■	
The French Culinary Institute at The International Culinary Center	C, D	■	■	■	
Genesee Community College	C, A			■	
The Institute of Culinary Education	D	■	■	■	
Julie Sahni's School of Indian Cooking	D	■			
Mohawk Valley Community College	C, A	■		■	
Monroe College	A, B	■	■	■	
Monroe Community College	C, A	■		■	
Nassau Community College	C, A			■	

Credentials: **C** = *Certificate;* **D** = *Diploma;* **A** = *Associate Degree;* **B** = *Bachelor's Degree;* **M** = *Master's Degree;* **Ph.D.** = *Doctorate*

State/School	Credentials Offered	Culinary Arts	Baking and Pastry	Management	Apprenticeship Programs
The Natural Gourmet Institute for Health and Culinary Arts	D	■			
New York City College of Technology of the City University of New York	A, B			■	
New York Institute of Technology	C, A, B	■	■	■	
New York University	B, M, Ph.D.			■	
Niagara County Community College	C, A	■	■	■	
Niagara University	B			■	
Onondaga Community College	C, A	■		■	
Paul Smith's College of Arts and Sciences	C, A, B	■	■	■	
Plattsburgh State University of New York	B			■	
Rochester Institute of Technology	B, M			■	
St. John's University	B			■	
State University of New York College at Cobleskill	C, A, B	■		■	
State University of New York College at Oneonta	B			■	
State University of New York College of Agriculture and Technology at Morrisville	A, B			■	
State University of New York College of Technology at Alfred	A	■	■		
State University of New York College of Technology at Delhi	A, B	■		■	
Sullivan County Community College	C, A	■	■	■	
Syracuse University	B			■	

State/School	Credentials Offered	Culinary Arts	Baking and Pastry	Management	Apprenticeship Programs
New York (*continued*) Tompkins Cortland Community College	A			■	
Westchester Community College	A	■		■	
Wilson Technological Center	C	■			
North Carolina					
The Art Institute of Charlotte	C, A, B	■		■	
Asheville-Buncombe Technical Community College	A	■	■	■	
Central Piedmont Community College	C, D, A	■	■	■	
East Carolina University	B, M			■	
Johnson & Wales University–Charlotte	A, B	■	■	■	
Southwestern Community College	C, A	■			
The University of North Carolina at Greensboro	B, M, Ph.D.			■	
Wake Technical Community College	C, A	■	■	■	
Wilkes Community College	C, A	■	■		
North Dakota					
North Dakota State College of Science	D, A			■	
Ohio					
ACF Columbus Chapter					■
The Art Institute of Ohio–Cincinnati	A	■			
Ashland University	B			■	

*Credentials: **C** = Certificate; **D** = Diploma; **A** = Associate Degree; **B** = Bachelor's Degree; **M** = Master's Degree; **Ph.D.** = Doctorate*

State/School	Credentials Offered	Culinary Arts	Baking and Pastry	Management	Apprenticeship Programs
Cincinnati State Technical and Community College	C, A	■		■	
Columbus State Community College	C, A		■	■	
Cuyahoga Community College, Metropolitan Campus	C, A	■		■	
The International Culinary Arts & Sciences Institute (ICASI)	C, D	■	■		
Owens Community College	C, A	■		■	
Sinclair Community College	C, A	■		■	
The University of Akron	C, A	■		■	
Zane State College	C, A	■			
Oklahoma					
Metro Area Vocational Technical School District 22	C			■	
Oklahoma State University, Okmulgee	A	■			
Oregon					
Central Oregon Community College	C, A	■		■	
Chemeketa Community College	C, A			■	
Culinary Awakenings	C	■			
International School of Baking	C		■		
Lane Community College	C, A	■		■	
Linn-Benton Community College	A			■	
Oregon Coast Culinary Institute	A	■	■	■	

State/School	Credentials Offered	Culinary Arts	Baking and Pastry	Management	Apprenticeship Programs
Oregon *(continued)* Oregon Culinary Institute	C, D, A	■	■		
Southern Oregon University	B			■	
Western Culinary Institute	D, A	■	■	■	
Pennsylvania					
ACF Laurel Highlands Chapter					■
The Art Institute of Philadelphia	D, A, B	■	■	■	
The Art Institute of Pittsburgh	D, A, B	■		■	
The Art Institute Online	B	■		■	
Bucks County Community College	C, A	■	■	■	
Bucks County Community College					■
Butler County Community College	C, A			■	
Cheyney University of Pennsylvania	B			■	
Commonwealth Technical Institute	D, A	■			
Delaware Valley College	A, B	■		■	
Drexel University	B	■		■	
East Stroudsburg University of Pennsylvania	B			■	
Greater Altoona Career and Technology Center	D	■	■		
Harrisburg Area Community College	C, D, A	■	■	■	
Indiana University of Pennsylvania	C, B	■	■	■	
JNA Institute of Culinary Arts	D, A	■		■	

Credentials: *C* = *Certificate;* *D* = *Diploma;* *A* = *Associate Degree;* *B* = *Bachelor's Degree;* *M* = *Master's Degree;* **Ph.D.** = *Doctorate*

State/School	Credentials Offered	Culinary Arts	Baking and Pastry	Management	Apprenticeship Programs
Keystone Technical Institute		■			
Lehigh Carbon Community College	A			■	
Mercyhurst College	A, B	■		■	
Northampton County Area Community College	D, A	■		■	
Pennsylvania College of Technology	A, B	■	■	■	
Pennsylvania Culinary Institute	D, A	■	■	■	
The Pennsylvania State University–University Park Campus	A, B, M, Ph.D.			■	
The Restaurant School at Walnut Hill College	A, B	■	■	■	
Seton Hill University	B			■	
Westmoreland County Community College	C, A	■	■	■	
Widener University	B, M			■	
Winner Institute of Arts & Sciences Culinary Education	A	■			
Yorktowne Business Institute	C, D, A	■	■	■	
YTI Career Institute	D, A	■	■	■	
Rhode Island					
Johnson & Wales University	A, B	■	■	■	
South Carolina					
The Art Institute of Charleston	A, B	■	■	■	
The Culinary Institute of Charleston	C, D, A	■	■	■	
Greenville Technical College	C, A	■	■	■	

State/School	Credentials Offered	Culinary Arts	Baking and Pastry	Management	Apprenticeship Programs
South Carolina *(continued)* Horry-Georgetown Technical College	C, A	■	■		
South Dakota					
Mitchell Technical Institute	D, A	■			
South Dakota State University	B, M, Ph.D.			■	
Tennessee					
The Art Institute of Tennessee–Nashville	D, A, B	■	■	■	
Nashville State Technical Community College	C, A	■			
Pellissippi State Technical Community College	C, A			■	
Walters State Community College	C, A	■		■	
Texas					
Aims Academy	D	■			
AIMS Academy School of Culinary Arts	D	■			
The Art Institute of Dallas	C, A	■		■	
The Art Institute of Houston	D, A, B	■	■	■	
Austin Community College	C, A	■		■	
Central Texas College	C, A	■		■	
Culinary Academy of Austin, Inc.	D	■	■		
Culinary Institute Alain and Marie LeNôtre	D, A	■	■		
Del Mar College	C, A	■	■	■	
El Paso Community College	C, A	■	■	■	

Credentials: ***C*** *= Certificate;* ***D*** *= Diploma;* ***A*** *= Associate Degree;* ***B*** *= Bachelor's Degree;* ***M*** *= Master's Degree;* ***Ph.D.*** *= Doctorate*

State/School	Credentials Offered	Culinary Arts	Baking and Pastry	Management	Apprenticeship Programs
Galveston College	C, A	■		■	
Houston Community College System	C, A	■	■	■	
Lamar University	C, B, M	■		■	
Le Cordon Bleu Institute of Culinary Arts	D	■			
Northwood University, Texas Campus	A, B			■	
Remington College–Dallas Campus	A	■			
San Jacinto College–Central Campus	C, A	■		■	
Texas Culinary Academy	C, A	■	■		
University of Houston	B, M			■	
University of North Texas	B, M			■	
Utah					
The Art Institute of Salt Lake City	D, A, B	■	■	■	
Utah Valley State College	A	■			
Vermont					
Champlain College	C, B			■	
Johnson State College	B			■	
New England Culinary Institute	C, A, B	■	■	■	
Virginia					
The Art Institute of Washington	D, A, B	■	■	■	
James Madison University	B			■	
J. Sargeant Reynolds Community College	C, A	■	■	■	

State/School	Credentials Offered	Culinary Arts	Baking and Pastry	Management	Apprenticeship Programs
Virginia *(continued)* Northern Virginia Community College	C, A	■		■	
Stratford University	D, A, B	■	■	■	
Tidewater Community College	C, A	■		■	
Virginia State University	B			■	
Virgin Islands (U.S.)					
University of the Virgin Islands	A			■	
Washington					
The Art Institute of Seattle	D, A	■	■		
Bellingham Technical College	C, A	■	■		
Olympic College	C, A			■	
Seattle Central Community College	C, A	■			
South Puget Sound Community College	C, A	■			
West Virginia					
West Virginia Northern Community College	C, A	■			
Wisconsin					
Blackhawk Technical College	C, A	■	■		
Chefs of Milwaukee					■
Fox Valley Technical College	C, D, A	■	■	■	
Madison Area Technical College	D, A	■	■	■	
Milwaukee Area Technical College	D, A	■	■	■	

*Credentials: **C** = Certificate; **D** = Diploma; **A** = Associate Degree; **B** = Bachelor's Degree; **M** = Master's Degree; **Ph.D.** = Doctorate*

State/School	Credentials Offered	Culinary Arts	Baking and Pastry	Management	Apprenticeship Programs
Moraine Park Technical College	C, D, A	■	■	■	
Nicolet Area Technical College	C, D, A	■	■	■	
Southwest Wisconsin Technical College	D, A	■		■	
University of Wisconsin–Stout	B, M			■	
Wyoming					
Sheridan College	C, A	■		■	

CULINARY PROGRAMS AT-A-GLANCE—CANADA

School	Credentials Offered	Culinary Arts	Baking and Pastry	Management	Apprenticeship Programs
The Art Institute of Vancouver (Dubrulle Culinary Arts Location)	C, D	■	■	■	
Canadore College of Applied Arts & Technology	C, D	■		■	
Culinary Institute of Canada	C, D	■	■	■	
George Brown College	C, D	■	■	■	
Georgian College of Applied Arts and Technology	D	■			
Humber Institute of Technology and Advanced Learning	C, D	■		■	
Le Cordon Bleu, Ottawa Culinary Arts Institute	C, D	■	■		
Liaison College	D			■	
Malaspina University–College	C, D	■	■		
Mount Saint Vincent University	C, D, B			■	
Niagara College Canada	C, D, B	■		■	
Northern Alberta Institute of Technology	C, D	■	■	■	
Northwest Culinary Academy of Vancouver	C, D	■	■		
Pacific Institute of Culinary Arts	C, D	■	■	■	
St. Clair College of Applied Arts and Technology	C, D	■		■	
SAIT-Polytechnic School of Hospitality and Tourism	C, D	■	■	■	
Stratford Chefs School	D	■			
University of Guelph	B, M			■	

Credentials: ***C*** = Certificate; ***D*** = Diploma; ***A*** = Associate Degree; ***B*** = Bachelor's Degree; ***M*** = Master's Degree; ***Ph.D.*** = Doctorate

School	Credentials Offered	Culinary Arts	Baking and Pastry	Management	Apprenticeship Programs	
University of New Brunswick, Saint John Campus	B			■		

■ CULINARY PROGRAMS AT-A-GLANCE—INTERNATIONAL ■

Country/School	Credentials Offered	Culinary Arts	Baking and Pastry	Management	Apprenticeship Programs
Australia					
Le Cordon Bleu Australia	C, D, B, M	■	■	■	
Le Cordon Bleu Sydney Culinary Arts Institute	D	■	■	■	
Finland					
Haaga-Helia University of Applied Sciences	B, M			■	
France					
Ecole des Arts Culinaires et de l'Hôtellerie de Lyon	C, D, B, M	■		■	
Ecole Supérieure de Cuisine Française Groupe Ferrandi	C	■	■		
Le Cordon Bleu	C, D	■	■		
Ritz–Escoffier Paris	C, D, M	■	■	■	
Italy					
APICIUS–The Culinary Institute and School of Hospitality	C	■	■	■	
The International Cooking School of Italian Food and Wine	C	■			
Italian Culinary Institute for Foreigners–USA	C, D	■			
Italian Food Artisans, LLC	C	■			
Italian Institute for Advanced Culinary and Pastry Arts	C	■			

*Credentials: **C** = Certificate; **D** = Diploma; **A** = Associate Degree; **B** = Bachelor's Degree; **M** = Master's Degree; **Ph.D.** = Doctorate*

Country/School	Credentials Offered	Culinary Arts	Baking and Pastry	Management	Apprenticeship Programs
Japan					
Le Cordon Bleu Japan	C	■	■		
Le Cordon Bleu Kobe	C	■	■		
Lebanon					
Le Cordon Bleu Liban					
Mexico					
Le Cordon Bleu Mexico	C, D	■	■		
New Zealand					
New Zealand School of Food and Wine	C	■		■	
Peru					
Le Cordon Bleu Peru	D	■	■	■	
Philippines					
Center for Culinary Arts, Manila	C, D	■	■	■	
Republic of Korea					
Le Cordon Bleu Korea	C, D, B, M	■		■	
South Africa					
Christina Martin School of Food and Wine	C, D	■		■	
Spain					
Le Cordon Bleu Madrid					

Country/School	Credentials Offered	Culinary Arts	Baking and Pastry	Management	Apprenticeship Programs
Switzerland					
DCT Hotel and Culinary Arts School, Switzerland	C, D	■	■	■	
Thailand					
Le Cordon Bleu Dusit Culinary School	C, D	■	■	■	
United Kingdom					
Cookery at the Grange	C	■			
Le Cordon Bleu–London Culinary Institute	C, D	■	■		
Leith's School of Food and Wine	C, D	■			
Rosie Davies	C	■			
Tante Marie School of Cookery	C, D	■			

*Credentials: **C** = Certificate; **D** = Diploma; **A** = Associate Degree; **B** = Bachelor's Degree; **M** = Master's Degree; **Ph.D.** = Doctorate*

PROFILES OF PROFESSIONAL PROGRAMS

ALABAMA

ALABAMA AGRICULTURAL AND MECHANICAL UNIVERSITY

Nutrition and Hospitality Management

Normal, Alabama

GENERAL INFORMATION
Public, coeducational, university. Urban campus. Founded in 1875. Accredited by Southern Association of Colleges and Schools.

PROGRAM INFORMATION
Offered since 1985. Accredited by American Dietetic Association. Program calendar is divided into semesters. 2-year master's degree in nutrition and hospitality management. 4-year bachelor's degree in hospitality management. 4-year bachelor's degree in general dietetics.

PROGRAM AFFILIATION
American Dietetic Association.

AREAS OF STUDY
Hospitality management; nutrition.

FACILITIES
Catering service; 2 laboratories; 2 lecture rooms; student lounge; teaching kitchen; delicatessen; kiosk breakfast.

STUDENT PROFILE
46 total: 43 full-time; 3 part-time.

FACULTY
5 total: 3 full-time; 2 part-time. 1 is a master baker; 1 is a culinary-certified teacher. Prominent faculty: Ann Warren, RD, LD; Dr. Johnson Kamalu; Nahid Sistani, PhD, RD, LD; Dr. Ola Goode Sanders. Faculty-student ratio: 1:12.

TYPICAL EXPENSES
Application fee: $10. In-state tuition: $2039 per 12 hours ($143 for each additional hour) full-time (in district), $143 per credit hour part-time. Out-of-state tuition: $3755 per 12 hours ($288 for additional hour) full-time, $286 per credit hour part-time. Tuition for international students: $3755 per 12 hours ($478 per semester for mandatory insurance) full-time, $286 per credit hour part-time. Program-related fee includes $20 for lab fees per course.

FINANCIAL AID
In 2006, 1 scholarship was awarded (award was $750). Employment placement assistance is available. Employment opportunities within the program are available.

HOUSING
Apartment-style and single-sex housing available. Average off-campus housing cost per month: $400–$665.

APPLICATION INFORMATION
Students may begin participation in January, June, and August. Application deadline for fall is July 15. Application deadline for spring is December 1. Application deadline for summer is May 15. In 2006, 5 applied; 5 were accepted. Applicants must have high school diploma.

CONTACT
Ann D. Warren, Coordinator, Nutrition and Hospitality Management, PO Box 232, Normal, AL 35762. Telephone: 256-858-4103. Fax: 256-858-5433. E-mail: ann.warren@email.aamu.edu. World Wide Web: http://www.aamu.edu.

CULINARD–THE CULINARY INSTITUTE OF VIRGINIA COLLEGE

Culinary Arts

Birmingham, Alabama

GENERAL INFORMATION
Private, coeducational, culinary institute. Urban campus. Founded in 1989. Accredited by Accrediting Council for Independent Colleges and Schools.

PROGRAM INFORMATION
Offered since 2000. Accredited by American Culinary Federation Accrediting Commission. Program calendar is divided into quarters. 24-month occupational associate in pastry, baking, and confectionery arts. 36-week diploma in culinary arts. 4-year bachelor's degree in culinary arts management.

PROGRAM AFFILIATION
American Culinary Federation; American Institute of Baking; American Institute of Wine & Food; Chefs Collaborative 2000; Confrerie de la Chaine des Rotisseurs; Council on Hotel, Restaurant, and Institutional Education; International Association of

CULINARD–The Culinary Institute of Virginia College *(continued)*

Culinary Professionals; International Food Service Executives Association; James Beard Foundation, Inc.; National Restaurant Association; National Restaurant Association Educational Foundation; Research Chefs Association; Retailer's Bakery Association; Southern Foodways Alliance; The Bread Bakers Guild of America; U.S. Pastry Alliance; Women Chefs and Restaurateurs; Women's Foodservice Forum.

AREAS OF STUDY
Baking; beverage management; buffet catering; confectionery show pieces; controlling costs in food service; culinary skill development; food preparation; food purchasing; food service communication; food service math; garde-manger; international cuisine; introduction to food service; kitchen management; meal planning; meat cutting; meat fabrication; menu and facilities design; nutrition; nutrition and food service; patisserie; restaurant opportunities; sanitation; saucier; seafood processing; soup, stock, sauce, and starch production; wines and spirits.

FACILITIES
Bake shop; bakery; catering service; 10 classrooms; 5 computer laboratories; demonstration laboratory; food production kitchen; garden; gourmet dining room; learning resource center; 10 lecture rooms; library; public restaurant; student lounge; 5 teaching kitchens.

STUDENT PROFILE
400 full-time. 160 are under 25 years old; 197 are between 25 and 44 years old; 43 are over 44 years old.

FACULTY
18 total: 15 full-time; 3 part-time. 17 are industry professionals; 1 is a culinary-certified teacher; 1 is a certified sanitarian; 1 registered dietitian. Prominent faculty: Antony Osborne. Faculty-student ratio: 1:16.

SPECIAL PROGRAMS
Student hot food competitions, student Knowledge Bowl competitions, student externships.

TYPICAL EXPENSES
Application fee: $100. Tuition: $19,500 per culinary arts program; $38,450 per pastry, baking, and confectionary arts degree.

FINANCIAL AID
In 2006, 5 scholarships were awarded (average award was $1000). Employment placement assistance is available. Employment opportunities within the program are available.

HOUSING
Average off-campus housing cost per month: $450.

APPLICATION INFORMATION
Students may begin participation in January, February, April, May, July, August, October, and November. Applications are accepted continuously. Applicants must interview; submit a formal application.

CONTACT
Mr. Chris Moore, Director of Admissions, Culinary Arts, 65 Bagby Drive, Birmingham, AL 35209. Telephone: 205-802-1200. Fax: 205-802-7045. E-mail: chris.moore@vc.edu or admissions@vc.edu. World Wide Web: http://www.culinard.com.

See color display following page 90.

THE GULF COAST CULINARY INSTITUTE

James H. Faulkner State Community College Hospitality Management Services

Gulf Shores, Alabama

GENERAL INFORMATION
Public, coeducational, two-year college. Urban campus. Founded in 1965. Accredited by Southern Association of Colleges and Schools.

PROGRAM INFORMATION
Offered since 1994. Accredited by American Culinary Federation Accrediting Commission, Council on Hotel, Restaurant and Institutional Education. Program calendar is divided into semesters. 1-year certificate in dietary management. 1-year certificate in pastry/baking. 1-year certificate in condominium/resort management. 1-year certificate in hotel/restaurant management. 1-year certificate in culinary arts. 2-year associate degree in dietary management. 2-year associate degree in pastry/baking. 2-year associate degree in condominium/resort management. 2-year associate degree in hotel/restaurant management. 2-year associate degree in food service management. 2-year associate degree in culinary arts. 3-year associate degree in pastry/baking apprenticeship. 3-year associate degree in culinary arts apprenticeship.

PROGRAM AFFILIATION
American Culinary Federation; American Institute of Baking; American Wine Society; Confrerie de la Chaine des Rotisseurs; Council on Hotel, Restaurant, and Institutional Education; National Restaurant Association; National Restaurant Association Educational Foundation; Retailer's Bakery Association; Society of Wine Educators.

AREAS OF STUDY

Baking; beverage management; cake decorating; confectionery show pieces; controlling costs in food service; culinary French; culinary skill development; food preparation; food purchasing; food service math; garde-manger; international cuisine; introduction to food service; management and human resources; meal planning; meat cutting; meat fabrication; menu and facilities design; nutrition; patisserie; sanitation; saucier; seafood processing; soup, stock, sauce, and starch production; spices and aromatics; wines and spirits.

FACILITIES

Bakery; 4 classrooms; computer laboratory; 2 demonstration laboratories; food production kitchen; garden; gourmet dining room; 2 laboratories; learning resource center; 2 lecture rooms; library; 2 student lounges; teaching kitchen.

STUDENT PROFILE

155 total: 120 full-time; 35 part-time.

FACULTY

12 total: 3 full-time; 9 part-time. 7 are industry professionals; 5 are culinary-certified teachers. Prominent faculty: Ron Koetter, CEC, CCE, AAC; Jim Hurtubise, CWPC; Edward Bushaw, CHA, CFBE. Faculty-student ratio: 1:15.

SPECIAL PROGRAMS

Culinary competitions, 2-year paid internship.

TYPICAL EXPENSES

In-state tuition: $93 per semester hour. Out-of-state tuition: $186 per semester hour. Program-related fees include $200 for cutlery; $80 for uniform.

FINANCIAL AID

In 2006, 6 scholarships were awarded (average award was $1000). Program-specific awards include American Culinary Federation scholarship $5000, Alabama Hospitality Association $5000. Employment placement assistance is available. Employment opportunities within the program are available.

HOUSING

Coed housing available. Average on-campus housing cost per month: $380. Average off-campus housing cost per month: $400.

APPLICATION INFORMATION

Students may begin participation in January, May, and August. Applications are accepted continuously. In 2006, 75 applied; 75 were accepted. Applicants must submit a formal application.

The Gulf Coast Culinary Institute

Enjoy the pristine beaches of the Gulf of Mexico as you study to be a chef with a program accredited by the American Culinary Federation and the Council on Hotel/Restaurant and Institutional Education. State-of-the-art facilities, outstanding faculty, and required, paid internships all at a fraction of the cost of most culinary schools.

www.gulfcoastculinaryinstitute.com

The Gulf Coast Culinary Institute *(continued)*

CONTACT
Edward Bushaw, Director, James H. Faulkner State Community College Hospitality Management Services, 3301 Gulf Shores Parkway, Gulf Shores, AL 36542. Telephone: 251-968-3103. Fax: 251-968-3120. E-mail: ebushaw@faulknerstate.edu. World Wide Web: http://www.gulfcoastculinaryinstitute.com.

TUSKEGEE UNIVERSITY

Tuskegee, Alabama

GENERAL INFORMATION
Private, coeducational, comprehensive institution. Small-town setting. Founded in 1881. Accredited by Southern Association of Colleges and Schools.

PROGRAM INFORMATION
Accredited by American Dietetic Association. Program calendar is divided into semesters. 4-year bachelor's degree in hospitality management.

PROGRAM AFFILIATION
American Dietetic Association.

AREAS OF STUDY
Nutrition.

FACILITIES
Bake shop; bakery; cafeteria; catering service; classroom; coffee shop; computer laboratory; demonstration laboratory; food production kitchen; garden; gourmet dining room; laboratory; learning resource center; lecture room; library; public restaurant; snack shop; student lounge; teaching kitchen; vineyard.

STUDENT PROFILE
20 full-time.

FACULTY
2 total: 2 full-time. 2 are culinary-certified teachers. Faculty-student ratio: 1:7.

TYPICAL EXPENSES
Tuition: $6760 per semester full-time, $555 per credit hour part-time. Program-related fees include $150 for technology (per semester); $240 for health insurance (per year); $30 for I.D. card activation (per semester).

FINANCIAL AID
Employment placement assistance is available.

HOUSING
Apartment-style and single-sex housing available. Average on-campus housing cost per month: $400.

APPLICATION INFORMATION
Students may begin participation in January, June, and August. Applications are accepted continuously. Applicants must interview; submit a formal application and an essay.

CONTACT
Robert L. Laney, Vice President/Director of Admissions and Enrollment Management, Old Administration Building, Suite 101, Tuskegee, AL 36088-1920. Telephone: 334-727-8500. Fax: 334-727-4402. E-mail: admissions@tuskegee.edu. World Wide Web: http://www.tuskegee.edu.

THE UNIVERSITY OF ALABAMA

Restaurant, Hotel and Meetings Management

Tuscaloosa, Alabama

GENERAL INFORMATION
Public, coeducational, university. Suburban campus. Founded in 1831. Accredited by Southern Association of Colleges and Schools.

PROGRAM INFORMATION
Offered since 1986. Accredited by American Association of Family and Consumer Sciences. National Restaurant Association Educational Foundation ManageFirst certificates available. Program calendar is divided into semesters. 1-semester certificate in ServSafe certification. 4-year bachelor's degree in restaurant and hospitality management. 4-year certificate in American Hotel & Lodging Association operations.

PROGRAM AFFILIATION
American Dietetic Association; American Hotel and Lodging Association; Council on Hotel, Restaurant, and Institutional Education; National Restaurant Association; National Restaurant Association Educational Foundation.

AREAS OF STUDY
Baking; beverage management; buffet catering; controlling costs in food service; convenience cookery; food preparation; food purchasing; food service communication; food service math; introduction to food service; kitchen management; management and human resources; meal planning; menu and facilities design; nutrition and food service; restaurant opportunities; sanitation; soup, stock, sauce, and starch production; wines and spirits.

FACILITIES
2 classrooms; computer laboratory; learning resource center; food science laboratory; 2 multimedia rooms.

FACULTY

12 total: 4 full-time; 8 part-time. 12 are industry professionals. Prominent faculty: Roy Maize, RD, FADA, PhD; Mildred Switzer, RD; Alvin Niuh, RD, FMP; Kim Boyle. Faculty-student ratio: 1:17.

PROMINENT ALUMNI AND CURRENT AFFILIATION

Trey Jackson, Epiphany Cafe; Emily Thornton, Riverview Plaza Hotel.

SPECIAL PROGRAMS

Practicum in hospitality management (1000 hours) or internship in hospitality management (400–600 hours).

TYPICAL EXPENSES

In-state tuition: $5700 per year. Out-of-state tuition: $16,518 per year. Program-related fees include $5 for processing (per credit hour); $35 for paper application fee, $30 apply on-line.

FINANCIAL AID

In 2006, 15 scholarships were awarded (average award was $2000). Employment placement assistance is available.

HOUSING

Coed, apartment-style, and single-sex housing available.

APPLICATION INFORMATION

Students may begin participation in January and August. Applications are accepted continuously. Applicants must submit a formal application.

CONTACT

Dr. Roy Maize, Director, Restaurant, Hotel & Meetings Management, Restaurant, Hotel and Meetings Management, Box 870158, Tuscaloosa, AL 35487. Telephone: 205-348-9147. Fax: 205-348-3789. E-mail: rmaize@ches.ua.edu. World Wide Web: http://www.ches. ua.edu/RHM/.

ALASKA

ALASKA VOCATIONAL TECHNICAL CENTER/ALASKA CULINARY ACADEMY

Culinary Arts and Sciences Department

Seward, Alaska

GENERAL INFORMATION

Public, coeducational, culinary institute. Rural campus. Founded in 1969. Accredited by Council on Occupational Education.

PROGRAM INFORMATION

Offered since 1972. Accredited by American Culinary Federation Accrediting Commission. Program calendar is continuous. 212-training day certificate in professional baking. 212-training day certificate in professional cooking. 302-training day certificate in professional cooking and baking.

PROGRAM AFFILIATION

American Culinary Federation; National Restaurant Association; National Restaurant Association Educational Foundation.

AREAS OF STUDY

Baking; beverage management; buffet catering; confectionery show pieces; controlling costs in food service; culinary skill development; food preparation; food purchasing; food service math; garde-manger; international cuisine; introduction to food service; kitchen management; management and human resources; meal planning; meat cutting; meat fabrication; menu and facilities design; nutrition; nutrition and food service; patisserie; sanitation; saucier; soup, stock, sauce, and starch production; wines and spirits.

FACILITIES

Bakery; cafeteria; classroom; computer laboratory; food production kitchen; gourmet dining room; learning resource center; library; public restaurant; snack shop; student lounge; teaching kitchen.

STUDENT PROFILE

30 full-time.

FACULTY

5 total: 3 full-time; 2 part-time. Prominent faculty: Robert E. Wilson, CEC, CCE, FMP; Kevin Lane, CEC; Elizabeth Fackler, CEPC, CCE. Faculty-student ratio: 1:8.

TYPICAL EXPENSES

Application fee: $25. Tuition: $2087 per program. Program-related fees include $1000 for books/supplies (sold by AVTEC); $310 for tools/supplies (not sold by AVTEC).

FINANCIAL AID

In 2006, 2 scholarships were awarded (average award was $700). Employment placement assistance is available. Employment opportunities within the program are available.

HOUSING

Coed and apartment-style housing available. Average off-campus housing cost per month: $500.

Alaska Vocational Technical Center/Alaska Culinary Academy *(continued)*

APPLICATION INFORMATION

Students may begin participation in January, August, and October. Applications are accepted continuously. Applicants must have high school diploma or GED, be 18 years of age, and meet physical requirements for program.

CONTACT

Kim Kain, Admissions Head, Culinary Arts and Sciences Department, PO Box 889, 518 3rd Avenue, Seward, AK 99664. Telephone: 800-478-5389. Fax: 907-224-4143. E-mail: kim.kain@avtec.edu. World Wide Web: http://avtec.labor.state.ak.us/.

UNIVERSITY OF ALASKA ANCHORAGE

Culinary Arts and Hospitality

Anchorage, Alaska

GENERAL INFORMATION

Public, coeducational, comprehensive institution. Suburban campus. Founded in 1954. Accredited by Northwest Commission on Colleges and Universities.

PROGRAM INFORMATION

Offered since 1972. Accredited by American Dietetic Association. Program calendar is divided into semesters. 2-year associate degree in culinary arts. 4-year bachelor's degree in hospitality and restaurant management.

PROGRAM AFFILIATION

American Culinary Federation; American Dietetic Association; Council on Hotel, Restaurant, and Institutional Education; Dietary Managers Association; Foodservice Educators Network International; Institute of Food Technologists; International Association of Culinary Professionals; National Association of Catering Executives; National Restaurant Association; National Restaurant Association Educational Foundation.

AREAS OF STUDY

Baking; beverage management; buffet catering; controlling costs in food service; culinary skill development; food preparation; food purchasing; food service math; garde-manger; international cuisine; kitchen management; management and human resources; meal planning; meat cutting; meat fabrication; menu and facilities design; nutrition; patisserie; restaurant opportunities; sanitation; saucier; seafood processing; soup, stock, sauce, and starch production; wines and spirits.

FACILITIES

Bake shop; 3 classrooms; computer laboratory; demonstration laboratory; 2 food production kitchens; garden; gourmet dining room; learning resource center; lecture room; library; public restaurant; 3 teaching kitchens.

STUDENT PROFILE

455 total: 390 full-time; 65 part-time.

FACULTY

11 total: 6 full-time; 5 part-time. 4 are industry professionals; 1 is a culinary-certified teacher; 5 are registered dietitians. Prominent faculty: Timothy Doebler, CCE; Dr. Anne Bridges, RD; Carrie King, RD, LD; Naomi Everett. Faculty-student ratio: 1:20.

SPECIAL PROGRAMS

2 semesters of study at either University of Nevada, Las Vegas or Northern Arizona University for students in bachelor's program (required).

TYPICAL EXPENSES

Application fee: $40. In-state tuition: $128 per credit. Out-of-state tuition: $427 per credit. Program-related fees include $350 for cutlery, uniforms; $50 for lab fee; $50 for meat fabrication course; $90 for grocery items.

FINANCIAL AID

In 2006, 10 scholarships were awarded. Program-specific awards include in-house scholarship opportunities. Employment placement assistance is available. Employment opportunities within the program are available.

HOUSING

Coed, apartment-style, and single-sex housing available. Average off-campus housing cost per month: $900.

APPLICATION INFORMATION

Students may begin participation in January and August. Application deadline for fall is June 1. Application deadline for spring is September 1. In 2006, 72 applied; 72 were accepted. Applicants must submit a formal application and have high school diploma or GED; must be 18 years of age.

CONTACT

Timothy Doebler, Director, Culinary Arts and Hospitality, 3211 Providence Drive, Cuddy Hall, Anchorage, AK 99508. Telephone: 907-786-4728. Fax: 907-786-1402. E-mail: aftwd@uaa.alaska.edu. World Wide Web: http://www.uaa.alaska.edu.

UNIVERSITY OF ALASKA FAIRBANKS

Culinary Arts

Fairbanks, Alaska

GENERAL INFORMATION
Public, coeducational, university. Suburban campus. Founded in 1917. Accredited by Northwest Commission on Colleges and Universities.

PROGRAM INFORMATION
Offered since 1986. Accredited by Northwest Comission on Colleges and Universities. National Restaurant Association Educational Foundation ManageFirst certificates available. Program calendar is divided into semesters. 1-year certificate in culinary arts. 1-year certificate in cooking. 1-year certificate in baking. 2-year associate degree in culinary arts.

PROGRAM AFFILIATION
American Culinary Federation; American Institute of Wine & Food; International Association of Culinary Professionals; International Food Service Executives Association; National Restaurant Association; National Restaurant Association Educational Foundation; The Bread Bakers Guild of America.

AREAS OF STUDY
Baking; buffet catering; confectionery show pieces; controlling costs in food service; convenience cookery; culinary French; culinary skill development; food preparation; food purchasing; food service math; garde-manger; international cuisine; introduction to food service; kitchen management; meal planning; meat cutting; meat fabrication; nutrition; patisserie; sanitation; saucier; seafood processing; soup, stock, sauce, and starch production; wines and spirits.

FACILITIES
Bake shop; bakery; cafeteria; catering service; 2 classrooms; computer laboratory; demonstration laboratory; food production kitchen; learning resource center; lecture room; library; student lounge; teaching kitchen.

STUDENT PROFILE
158 total: 18 full-time; 140 part-time.

FACULTY
11 total: 3 full-time; 8 part-time. 2 are industry professionals; 1 is a culinary-certified teacher; 2 are certified executive chefs. Prominent faculty: Frank Davis, Jr.; Ruiz Anne Rozell; Jakub Esop; Louis Martines. Faculty-student ratio: 1:10.

PROMINENT ALUMNI AND CURRENT AFFILIATION
James Scullion, Sysco.

TYPICAL EXPENSES
Application fee: $40. In-state tuition: $90 per credit hour. Out-of-state tuition: $281 per credit hour. Program-related fee includes $250 for uniforms and uniform maintenance.

FINANCIAL AID
In 2006, 3 scholarships were awarded (average award was $500). Employment placement assistance is available. Employment opportunities within the program are available.

HOUSING
Coed housing available.

APPLICATION INFORMATION
Students may begin participation in January and September. Applications are accepted continuously. In 2006, 36 applied; 22 were accepted. Applicants must submit a formal application.

CONTACT
Frank U. Davis, Coordinator, Culinary Arts, 604 Barnette Street, Fairbanks, AK 99701. Telephone: 907-455-2809. Fax: 907-455-2828. E-mail: fffud@uaf.edu. World Wide Web: http://www.tvc.uaf.edu.

ARIZONA

ARIZONA CULINARY INSTITUTE

Scottsdale, Arizona

GENERAL INFORMATION
Private, coeducational, culinary institute. Suburban campus. Founded in 2001. Accredited by Accrediting Commission of Career Schools and Colleges of Technology.

PROGRAM INFORMATION
Offered since 2001. Program calendar is continuous. 9-month diploma in culinary arts, baking, and restaurant management.

PROGRAM AFFILIATION
American Culinary Federation; American Institute of Wine & Food; International Association of Culinary Professionals; National Association of Catering Executives; National Restaurant Association; National Restaurant Association Educational Foundation; Society of Wine Educators.

AREAS OF STUDY
Baking; beverage management; confectionery show pieces; controlling costs in food service; culinary French; culinary skill development; food preparation; food purchasing; food service math; garde-manger;

international cuisine; introduction to food service; kitchen management; management and human resources; meat cutting; meat fabrication; menu and facilities design; nutrition; patisserie; restaurant opportunities; sanitation; saucier; soup, stock, sauce, and starch production; wines and spirits.

FACILITIES
2 bakeries; 3 classrooms; computer laboratory; 3 food production kitchens; gourmet dining room; learning resource center; 2 lecture rooms; library; public restaurant; student lounge; 5 teaching kitchens.

STUDENT PROFILE
210 full-time. 95 are under 25 years old; 86 are between 25 and 44 years old; 29 are over 44 years old.

FACULTY
12 total: 11 full-time; 1 part-time. 10 are industry professionals; 2 are culinary-certified teachers. Prominent faculty: Jennifer Sedig; Glenn Humphrey, CEC, CCE; Michael Dudley; Jason Warden. Faculty-student ratio: 1:8.

SPECIAL PROGRAMS
3-month paid internship.

TYPICAL EXPENSES
Application fee: $25. Tuition: $23,800 per diploma. Program-related fee includes $1805 for knives, books, uniforms, supplies.

FINANCIAL AID
In 2006, 15 scholarships were awarded (average award was $500); 170 loans were granted (average loan was $25,000). Employment placement assistance is available. Employment opportunities within the program are available.

HOUSING
Average off-campus housing cost per month: $400–$700.

APPLICATION INFORMATION
Students may begin participation in January, February, April, May, July, August, September, and November. Applications are accepted continuously. In 2006, 225 applied; 210 were accepted. Applicants must submit a formal application and high school diploma/GED.

CONTACT
Admissions Director, 10585 North 114th Street, Suite 401, Scottsdale, AZ 85259. Telephone: 480-603-1066. Fax: 480-603-1067. E-mail: info@azculinary.com. World Wide Web: http://www.azculinary.com.

See display on page 72.

ARIZONA WESTERN COLLEGE

Culinary Arts/Dietary Management/Hotel and Restaurant Management

Yuma, Arizona

GENERAL INFORMATION
Public, coeducational, two-year college. Rural campus. Founded in 1962. Accredited by North Central Association of Colleges and Schools.

PROGRAM INFORMATION
Offered since 1996. Accredited by Dietary Manager Program accredited by Dietary Managers Association. Program calendar is divided into semesters. 2-semester certificate in dietary manager. 2-semester certificate in culinary arts. 2-year associate degree in hotel/restaurant management.

PROGRAM AFFILIATION
Dietary Managers Association.

AREAS OF STUDY
Baking; food preparation; food purchasing; garde-manger; international cuisine; management and human resources; meal planning; nutrition; restaurant opportunities; sanitation; soup, stock, sauce, and starch production.

FACILITIES
Classroom; computer laboratory; food production kitchen; gourmet dining room; learning resource center; lecture room; library.

STUDENT PROFILE
17 total: 12 full-time; 5 part-time. 12 are under 25 years old; 3 are between 25 and 44 years old; 2 are over 44 years old.

FACULTY
4 total: 1 full-time; 3 part-time. 3 are industry professionals; 1 is a registered dietitian. Prominent faculty: Nancy L. Meister, RD, MPH; Ross Smith; Bill Pike; Valerie Cook, CDM. Faculty-student ratio: 1:17.

SPECIAL PROGRAMS
Placement in local restaurants for field experience, placement in local extended-care facilities for institutional food experience.

TYPICAL EXPENSES
In-state tuition: $540 per semester full-time (in district), $45 per credit hour part-time. Out-of-state tuition: $2932 per semester full-time, $244 per credit hour part-time. Program-related fees include $340 for lab food fees; $800 for books; $60 for uniforms.

FINANCIAL AID
Employment placement assistance is available.

Arizona Western College *(continued)*

HOUSING
Coed housing available. Average off-campus housing cost per month: $500.

APPLICATION INFORMATION
Students may begin participation in January and August. Application deadline for spring is January 15. Application deadline for fall is August 15. In 2006, 17 applied; 17 were accepted. Applicants must submit a formal application.

CONTACT
Nancy L. Meister, Coordinator, Culinary Arts/Dietary Management/Hotel and Restaurant Management, PO Box 929, Yuma, AZ 85366. Telephone: 928-344-7779. Fax: 928-317-6119. E-mail: nancy.meister@azwestern.edu. World Wide Web: http://www.azwestern.edu.

THE ART INSTITUTE OF PHOENIX

The International Culinary School at The Art Institute of Phoenix

Phoenix, Arizona

GENERAL INFORMATION
Private, coeducational institution.

PROGRAM INFORMATION
Associate degree in Culinary Arts. Bachelor's degree in Culinary Arts. Diploma in Baking and Pastry. Diploma in The Art of Cooking.

CONTACT
Office of Admissions, The International Culinary School at The Art Institute of Phoenix, 2233 West Dunlap Avenue, Phoenix, AZ 85021-2859. Telephone: 602-331-7500. World Wide Web: http://www.artinstitutes.edu/phoenix/.
See color display following page 186.

THE ART INSTITUTE OF TUCSON

The International Culinary School at The Art Institute of Tucson

Tucson, Arizona

GENERAL INFORMATION
Private, coeducational institution.

PROGRAM INFORMATION
Associate degree in Culinary Arts. Bachelor's degree in Culinary Arts.

CONTACT
Office of Admissions, The International Culinary School at The Art Institute of Tucson, 1030 North Alvernon Way, Tucson, AZ 85711. Telephone: 520-881-2900. Fax: 520-881-4234. World Wide Web: http://www.artinstitutes.edu/tucson.
See color display following page 186.

CENTRAL ARIZONA COLLEGE

Hotel and Restaurant Management/Culinary Arts/Nutrition and Dietetics

Coolidge, Arizona

GENERAL INFORMATION
Public, coeducational, two-year college. Rural campus. Founded in 1970. Accredited by North Central Association of Colleges and Schools.

PROGRAM INFORMATION
Offered since 1990. Accredited by American Culinary Federation Accrediting Commission, Council on Hotel, Restaurant and Institutional Education. Program calendar is divided into semesters. 1-year certificate in dietary manager. 17-credit certificate in restaurant management. 17- to 19-credit certificate in cook's level I. 18-credit certificate in hotel/lodging management. 2-year associate degree in hotel and restaurant management. 2-year associate degree in dietetic technician. 2-year associate degree in cook level 2-culinary apprenticeship.

PROGRAM AFFILIATION
American Culinary Federation; American Dietetic Association; Council on Hotel, Restaurant, and Institutional Education; National Restaurant Association; National Restaurant Association Educational Foundation.

AREAS OF STUDY
Baking; beverage management; controlling costs in food service; culinary skill development; food preparation; food purchasing; food service math; garde-manger; hotel management; introduction to food service; management and human resources; nutrition; nutrition and food service; restaurant management; sanitation.

STUDENT PROFILE
60 total: 40 full-time; 20 part-time. 40 are under 25 years old; 20 are between 25 and 44 years old.

FACULTY

4 total: 2 full-time; 2 part-time. 1 is a culinary-certified teacher; 2 are registered dietetic technicians; several registered dietitians. Prominent faculty: Gayle K. Haro, CCE, ACF, MEd, CHE; Lisa Koering, MS, RD; Janice Pratt, CHA, CHE, MBA, MEd. Faculty-student ratio: 1:10.

SPECIAL PROGRAMS

Apprenticeship program (ACF Resort and Country Club Chefs).

TYPICAL EXPENSES

In-state tuition: $55 per credit full-time (in district), $55 per credit part-time. Out-of-state tuition: $80 per credit full-time, $80 per credit part-time. Program-related fee includes $50 for uniform.

FINANCIAL AID

Employment opportunities within the program are available.

HOUSING

Coed housing available.

APPLICATION INFORMATION

Students may begin participation in January and August. Applications are accepted continuously. Applicants must submit a formal application, letters of reference, and an essay.

CONTACT

Gayle Haro, Culinary Arts Instructor, Hotel and Restaurant Management/Culinary Arts/Nutrition and Dietetics, 8470 North Overfield Road, Coolidge, AZ 85228. Telephone: 520-426-4403. Fax: 520-426-4259. E-mail: gayle_haro@centralaz.edu. World Wide Web: http://www.centralaz.edu.

MARICOPA SKILL CENTER

Food Preparation Program

Phoenix, Arizona

GENERAL INFORMATION

Public, coeducational, adult vocational school. Urban campus. Founded in 1962. Accredited by North Central Association of Colleges and Schools.

PROGRAM INFORMATION

Offered since 1977. Program calendar is year-round, year-round. 14-week certificate in pantry goods maker (salad maker). 18-week certificate in baker's helper. 18-week certificate in kitchen helper. 27-week certificate in cook's apprentice.

PROGRAM AFFILIATION

National Restaurant Association; National Restaurant Association Educational Foundation.

AREAS OF STUDY

Baking; food preparation; food service math; introduction to food service; meat cutting; restaurant opportunities; soup, stock, sauce, and starch production.

FACILITIES

Cafeteria; catering service; classroom; demonstration laboratory; food production kitchen; learning resource center; lecture room; public restaurant; student lounge; teaching kitchen.

TYPICAL STUDENT PROFILE

40 full-time.

FINANCIAL AID

Employment placement assistance is available.

APPLICATION INFORMATION

Students may begin participation year-round. Applications are accepted continuously. Applicants must submit student information form and make financial arrangements; complete TABE assessment.

CONTACT

Director of Admissions, Food Preparation Program, 1245 East Buckeye Road, Phoenix, AZ 85034. Telephone: 602-238-4331. Fax: 602-238-4307. World Wide Web: http://www.maricopaskillcenter.com/.

NORTHERN ARIZONA UNIVERSITY

School of Hotel and Restaurant Management

Flagstaff, Arizona

GENERAL INFORMATION

Public, coeducational, university. Small-town setting. Founded in 1899. Accredited by North Central Association of Colleges and Schools.

PROGRAM INFORMATION

Offered since 1987. Accredited by Council on Hotel, Restaurant and Institutional Education, Accreditation Commission for Programs in Hospitality Administration. Program calendar is divided into semesters. Certificate in managing customer service. 15-credit hour certificate in international tourism management. 15-credit hour certificate in restaurant management. 15-week certificate in culinary arts for management. 4-year bachelor's degree in international hospitality management. 4-year bachelor's degree in hotel and restaurant management.

Northern Arizona University *(continued)*

PROGRAM AFFILIATION

American Hotel and Lodging Association; Council on Hotel, Restaurant, and Institutional Education; International Food Service Executives Association; National Restaurant Association; National Restaurant Association Educational Foundation.

AREAS OF STUDY

Beverage management; controlling costs in food service; event planning; food preparation; food purchasing; introduction to food service; management and human resources; restaurant opportunities; sanitation; wines and spirits.

FACILITIES

Classroom; coffee shop; computer laboratory; demonstration laboratory; food production kitchen; gourmet dining room; learning resource center; lecture room; public restaurant; student lounge; teaching kitchen.

STUDENT PROFILE

877 total: 777 full-time; 100 part-time.

FACULTY

23 total: 16 full-time; 7 part-time. Prominent faculty: Dr. Matt Casado; Dr. Galen Collins; Dr. Claudia Jurowski; Allen Z. Reich, PhD. Faculty-student ratio: 1:20 labs; 1:35 lecture.

PROMINENT ALUMNI AND CURRENT AFFILIATION

Bruce Turner, National Director of Development for Sodecho Sports & Leisure; Lana Trevisan, Director of Operations/Partner for B.R. Guest Restaurants.

SPECIAL PROGRAMS

Paid internships, summer program in Europe, International Student Exchange program.

TYPICAL EXPENSES

Application fee: $25. In-state tuition: $2273 per semester full-time, 1-6 credits $245 per credit per semester; 7 hours or more $2250 per semester part-time. Out-of-state tuition: $6744 per semester full-time, semester part-time. Tuition for international students: $26,000 per academic year. Program-related fees include $20 for computer supplies; $40 for food production materials and supplies; $40 for bar and beverage; $20 for hospitality leadership; $10 for introduction to property management.

FINANCIAL AID

In 2006, 110 scholarships were awarded (average award was $1200). Employment placement assistance is available. Employment opportunities within the program are available.

HOUSING

Coed, apartment-style, and single-sex housing available. Average on-campus housing cost per month: $467. Average off-campus housing cost per month: $600–$700.

APPLICATION INFORMATION

Students may begin participation in January, May, and August. Application deadline for fall is March 1. Application deadline for spring is December 1. In 2006, 900 applied. Applicants must submit a formal application and ACT or SAT scores; have a high school diploma.

CONTACT

Kim Knowles, Coordinator of Advisement, School of Hotel and Restaurant Management, NAU Box 5638, Building 33A, Flagstaff, AZ 86011-5638. Telephone: 928-523-9050. Fax: 928-523-1711. E-mail: kim.knowles@nau.edu. World Wide Web: http://www.nau.edu/hrm.

PIMA COMMUNITY COLLEGE

Culinary Arts Program

Tucson, Arizona

GENERAL INFORMATION

Public, coeducational, two-year college. Urban campus. Founded in 1966. Accredited by North Central Association of Colleges and Schools.

PROGRAM INFORMATION

Offered since 1970. Program calendar is divided into semesters. 1-year certificate in culinary arts. 2-year associate degree in culinary arts.

PROGRAM AFFILIATION

Chefs Association of Southern Arizona; Slow Food International.

AREAS OF STUDY

Baking; beverage management; controlling costs in food service; culinary skill development; food preparation; food service math; garde-manger; international cuisine; management and human resources; meal planning; meat cutting; meat fabrication; menu and facilities design; nutrition; nutrition and food service; sanitation; saucier; seafood processing; soup, stock, sauce, and starch production; wines and spirits.

FACILITIES

Cafeteria; catering service; 4 classrooms; computer laboratory; demonstration laboratory; food production kitchen; learning resource center; library; public restaurant; teaching kitchen.

STUDENT PROFILE
72 full-time. 15 are under 25 years old; 45 are between 25 and 44 years old; 12 are over 44 years old.

FACULTY
9 total: 1 full-time; 8 part-time. 5 are industry professionals; 1 is a master baker; 1 is a culinary-certified teacher. Prominent faculty: Barry Infuso, CEC, CCE, AAC; Jan Osipowitcz, CEC; Rohan Warishani, CPC. Faculty-student ratio: 1:12.

SPECIAL PROGRAMS
Culinary Club, culinary team, apprenticeship (2 or 3 years).

TYPICAL EXPENSES
In-state tuition: $47 per credit hour. Out-of-state tuition: $75 per credit hour. Program-related fees include $250 for textbooks/notebooks; $150 for knives/supplies; $100 for uniforms; $450 for lab fees.

FINANCIAL AID
Program-specific awards include Culinary Club Scholarship, Chef's Association Scholarship. Employment placement assistance is available. Employment opportunities within the program are available.

HOUSING
Average off-campus housing cost per month: $300.

APPLICATION INFORMATION
Students may begin participation in January and August. Applications are accepted continuously. In 2006, 220 applied; 72 were accepted. Applicants must interview and submit an application, placement test scores, or academic transcripts.

CONTACT
Barry Infuso, Director, Culinary Arts Program, 5901 South Calle Santa Cruz, Tucson, AZ 85709-6080. Telephone: 520-206-5164. Fax: 520-206-5143. E-mail: barry.infuso@pima.edu. World Wide Web: http://www.pima.edu.

SCOTTSDALE COMMUNITY COLLEGE

Culinary Arts Program

Scottsdale, Arizona

GENERAL INFORMATION
Public, coeducational, two-year college. Suburban campus. Founded in 1969. Accredited by North Central Association of Colleges and Schools.

PROGRAM INFORMATION
Offered since 1984. Accredited by American Culinary Federation Accrediting Commission. Program calendar is divided into semesters. 1-semester certificate in culinary fundamentals. 2-semester certificate in professional culinary arts. 2-semester certificate in culinary arts. 2-year associate degree in culinary fundamentals. 2-year associate degree in professional culinary arts. 2-year associate degree in culinary arts. 2-year associate degree in hospitality management.

PROGRAM AFFILIATION
American Culinary Federation; National Restaurant Association; Women Chefs and Restaurateurs.

AREAS OF STUDY
Baking; beverage management; buffet catering; controlling costs in food service; culinary skill development; dining room service; food preparation; food purchasing; food service communication; food service math; garde-manger; international cuisine; introduction to food service; kitchen management; management and human resources; meal planning; meat cutting; meat fabrication; menu and facilities design; nutrition; nutrition and food service; patisserie; restaurant opportunities; sanitation; saucier; seafood processing; soup, stock, sauce, and starch production.

FACILITIES
Bake shop; 3 classrooms; computer laboratory; demonstration laboratory; 2 food production kitchens; gourmet dining room; learning resource center; lecture room; library; 2 public restaurants; student lounge; teaching kitchen.

STUDENT PROFILE
72 full-time. 29 are under 25 years old; 36 are between 25 and 44 years old; 7 are over 44 years old.

FACULTY
14 total: 4 full-time; 10 part-time. 6 are industry professionals; 4 are culinary-certified teachers. Prominent faculty: Dominic O'Neill, AAS; Karen Chalmers, BA; Tom Greenwalt, AAS, CCE, CEPC; Michael Wheelan, BA. Faculty-student ratio: 1:12.

PROMINENT ALUMNI AND CURRENT AFFILIATION
Aaron May, Sol y Sombra; Tracy Dempsey, Cowboy Ciao.

SPECIAL PROGRAMS
Culinary competitions.

TYPICAL EXPENSES
In-state tuition: $4200 per certificate; $6060 per degree. Out-of-state tuition: $8400 per certificate; $10,200 per degree. Program-related fees include $475 for lab/food purchase fee (per semester); $350 for uniforms; $525 for knives/bakery supplies.

Scottsdale Community College *(continued)*

FINANCIAL AID
In 2006, 5 scholarships were awarded (average award was $1000); 25 loans were granted (average loan was $2000). Employment placement assistance is available.

APPLICATION INFORMATION
Students may begin participation in January and August. Applications are accepted continuously. In 2006, 300 applied; 72 were accepted. Applicants must interview and submit a formal application and placement scores in English, reading, and math.

CONTACT
Karen Chalmers, Program Director, Culinary Arts Program, 9000 East Chaparral Road, Scottsdale, AZ 85256. Telephone: 480-423-6241. Fax: 480-423-6091. E-mail: karen.chalmers@sccmail.maricopa.edu. World Wide Web: http://www.scottsdalecc.edu/culinary.

SCOTTSDALE CULINARY INSTITUTE

Le Cordon Bleu

Scottsdale, Arizona

GENERAL INFORMATION
Private, coeducational, culinary institute. Suburban campus. Founded in 1986. Accredited by Accrediting Commission of Career Schools and Colleges of Technology.

PROGRAM INFORMATION
Offered since 1986. Accredited by American Culinary Federation Accrediting Commission. Program calendar is divided into six-week cycles. 15-month associate degree in Le Cordon Bleu Patisserie and Baking. 15-month associate degree in Le Cordon Bleu Hospitality and Restaurant Management. 15-month associate degree in Le Cordon Bleu Culinary Arts. 29-month bachelor's degree in Le Cordon Bleu Hospitality and Restaurant Management. 30-month bachelor's degree in Le Cordon Bleu Culinary Management. 8-month certificate in Le Cordon Bleu Culinary Arts. 9-month certificate in Le Cordon Bleu Patisserie and Baking.

PROGRAM AFFILIATION
American Culinary Federation; American Institute of Wine & Food; Council on Hotel, Restaurant, and Institutional Education; International Association of Culinary Professionals; International Wine & Food Society; James Beard Foundation, Inc.; National Restaurant Association; Phoenix Restaurant Association; Women Chefs and Restaurateurs.

AREAS OF STUDY
Baking; beverage management; buffet catering; confectionery show pieces; controlling costs in food service; culinary skill development; food preparation; food purchasing; food service communication; food service math; garde-manger; international cuisine; introduction to food service; management and human resources; meal planning; meat cutting; meat fabrication; menu and facilities design; nutrition; nutrition and food service; patisserie; restaurant opportunities; sanitation; saucier; seafood processing; soup, stock, sauce, and starch production; wines and spirits.

FACILITIES
2 bake shops; 2 catering services; 5 classrooms; computer laboratory; demonstration laboratory; 2 food production kitchens; garden; 2 gourmet dining rooms; learning resource center; 3 lecture rooms; library; 2 public restaurants; snack shop; student lounge; 10 teaching kitchens.

STUDENT PROFILE
1200 full-time.

FACULTY
55 total: 45 full-time; 10 part-time. 34 are culinary-certified teachers; 1 is a registered dietitian. Prominent faculty: Philip Sayre; Tracy Flowers; Garry Waldie; Michael Adessa. Faculty-student ratio: 1:16.

SPECIAL PROGRAMS
Paid externships, culinary competitions, participation in community and resort events.

TYPICAL EXPENSES
Application fee: $95.

FINANCIAL AID
In 2006, 30 scholarships were awarded (average award was $2000); 250 loans were granted (average loan was $2611). Employment placement assistance is available. Employment opportunities within the program are available.

HOUSING
Average off-campus housing cost per month: $500.

APPLICATION INFORMATION
Students may begin participation in January, February, March, April, May, July, August, September, October, November, and December. Applications are accepted continuously. Applicants must submit a formal application, essay, academic transcripts and have a high school diploma or GED.

CONTACT
Lee Griffith, Director of Admissions, Le Cordon Bleu, 8100 East Camelback Road, Suite 1001, Scottsdale, AZ 85251. Telephone: 800-848-2433. Fax: 480-990-0351. E-mail: lgriffith@scichefs.com. World Wide Web: http://www.chefs.com.

ARKANSAS

OZARKA COLLEGE

Culinary Arts

Melbourne, Arkansas

GENERAL INFORMATION
Public, coeducational, two-year college. Small-town setting. Founded in 1973. Accredited by North Central Association of Colleges and Schools.

PROGRAM INFORMATION
Offered since 1973. Accredited by Arkansas Hospitality Association. Program calendar is divided into semesters. 2-semester certificate in culinary arts. 4-semester associate degree in general technology (culinary arts emphasis).

PROGRAM AFFILIATION
American Culinary Federation; American Dietetic Association; National Restaurant Association; National Restaurant Association Educational Foundation.

AREAS OF STUDY
Baking; buffet catering; controlling costs in food service; culinary skill development; food preparation; food purchasing; food service math; garde-manger; international cuisine; introduction to food service; kitchen management; management and human resources; meal planning; nutrition; nutrition and food service; patisserie; sanitation; saucier; seafood processing; soup, stock, sauce, and starch production.

FACILITIES
Catering service; classroom; computer laboratory; demonstration laboratory; food production kitchen; gourmet dining room; laboratory; learning resource center; lecture room; library; public restaurant; student lounge; teaching kitchen.

STUDENT PROFILE
16 total: 15 full-time; 1 part-time. 7 are under 25 years old; 4 are between 25 and 44 years old; 5 are over 44 years old.

FACULTY
2 total: 2 full-time. 2 are culinary-certified teachers. Prominent faculty: Linda Taylor; Miriam "Mimi" Newsome. Faculty-student ratio: 1:15.

PROMINENT ALUMNI AND CURRENT AFFILIATION
Sean T. Reynolds, Sean's Restaurant; Clint Stevens, Executive Chef, Lyon College; Rhonda Hammond, Purdue University.

SPECIAL PROGRAMS
Skills USA culinary competitions, Disney World intern opportunities, student participation in corporate food shows.

TYPICAL EXPENSES
In-state tuition: $55 per credit hour part-time. Out-of-state tuition: $168 per credit hour part-time. Program-related fee includes $50 for consumables used in program.

FINANCIAL AID
In 2006, 2 scholarships were awarded (average award was $1000). Program-specific awards include off-campus catering opportunities. Employment placement assistance is available. Employment opportunities within the program are available.

HOUSING
Average off-campus housing cost per month: $375.

APPLICATION INFORMATION
Students may begin participation in August. Application deadline for fall is May 31. In 2006, 25 applied; 15 were accepted. Applicants must interview; submit a formal application, letters of reference, and an essay.

CONTACT
Linda Taylor, Chef Instructor, Culinary Arts, PO Box 10, Melbourne, AR 72556. Telephone: 870-368-7371. Fax: 870-368-2091. E-mail: ltaylor@ozarka.edu. World Wide Web: http://www.ozarka.edu.

PULASKI TECHNICAL COLLEGE ARKANSAS CULINARY SCHOOL

Little Rock, Arkansas

GENERAL INFORMATION
Public, coeducational, two-year college. Urban campus. Founded in 1995. Accredited by North Central Association of Colleges and Schools.

PROGRAM INFORMATION
Offered since 1995. Accredited by Arkansas State Department of Higher Education. National Restaurant Association Educational Foundation ManageFirst certificates available. Program calendar is divided into

Pulaski Technical College Arkansas Culinary School
(continued)

semesters. 1-year certificate in culinary arts. 1-year certificate in baking and pastry arts. 2-year associate degree in culinary arts.

PROGRAM AFFILIATION
American Culinary Federation; National Restaurant Association; National Restaurant Association Educational Foundation.

AREAS OF STUDY
Baking; beverage management; buffet catering; confectionery show pieces; controlling costs in food service; convenience cookery; culinary French; culinary skill development; food preparation; food purchasing; food service communication; food service math; garde-manger; international cuisine; introduction to food service; kitchen management; management and human resources; meal planning; meat cutting; meat fabrication; menu and facilities design; nutrition; nutrition and food service; patisserie; restaurant opportunities; sanitation; saucier; seafood processing; soup, stock, sauce, and starch production; wines and spirits.

FACILITIES
Bakery; 4 classrooms; computer laboratory; demonstration laboratory; food production kitchen; laboratory; learning resource center; library; student lounge; teaching kitchen.

STUDENT PROFILE
93 total: 83 full-time; 10 part-time. 30 are under 25 years old; 40 are between 25 and 44 years old; 23 are over 44 years old.

FACULTY
14 total: 4 full-time; 10 part-time. 7 are industry professionals; 7 are culinary-certified teachers. Prominent faculty: Cynthia East, AOS; Todd Gold, CEC, CCA; Jamie McAfee, CEC; Katie Tumlison, RD. Faculty-student ratio: 1:18.

SPECIAL PROGRAMS
Culinary competitions, culinary anthropology, summer credit in Italy, practicum.

TYPICAL EXPENSES
Tuition: $2500 per semester (average) full-time (in district), $80 per credit hour (plus $500-$740 lab fees) part-time.

FINANCIAL AID
In 2006, 20 scholarships were awarded.

HOUSING
Average off-campus housing cost per month: $400–$600.

APPLICATION INFORMATION
Students may begin participation in January, June, and August. Applications are accepted continuously. In 2006, 100 applied; 85 were accepted. Applicants must interview; submit a formal application, letters of reference, an essay, transcripts, GRE/high school diploma.

CONTACT
Renee Jeffery, Assistant Director, 4901 Asher Avenue, Little Rock, AR 72204. Telephone: 866-804-CHEF(2433). Fax: 501-570-4095. E-mail: info@ arkansaschef.com. World Wide Web: http://www. pulaskitech.edu/programs_of_study/culinary/default.asp.

UNIVERSITY OF ARKANSAS AT PINE BLUFF

Food Service Restaurant Management

Pine Bluff, Arkansas

GENERAL INFORMATION
Public, coeducational, comprehensive institution. Urban campus. Founded in 1873. Accredited by North Central Association of Colleges and Schools.

PROGRAM INFORMATION
Offered since 1957. Accredited by American Dietetic Association. Program calendar is divided into semesters. 4-year bachelor's degree in food service and restaurant management. 4-year bachelor's degree in dietetics and nutrition.

PROGRAM AFFILIATION
American Dietetic Association; Council on Hotel, Restaurant, and Institutional Education.

AREAS OF STUDY
Food service management; nutrition; nutrition and food service; restaurant management.

FACILITIES
Cafeteria; 2 computer laboratories; food production kitchen; 3 laboratories; learning resource center; 2 lecture rooms; 3 libraries; student lounge; teaching kitchen.

STUDENT PROFILE
16 full-time. 16 are under 25 years old.

FACULTY
3 total: 3 full-time. 2 are registered dietitians. Faculty-student ratio: 1:10.

TYPICAL EXPENSES

In-state tuition: $110 per credit hour. Out-of-state tuition: $257 per credit hour. Program-related fees include $6.75 for technology fee (per hour); $35 for laboratory fee.

FINANCIAL AID

Employment placement assistance is available.

HOUSING

Single-sex housing available.

APPLICATION INFORMATION

Students may begin participation in January and August. Applications are accepted continuously. In 2006, 6 applied; 6 were accepted. Applicants must submit a formal application.

CONTACT

Dr. Valerie Colyard, Chairperson, Food Service Restaurant Management, Department of Human Sciences, 1200 North University Drive, Mail Slot 4971, Pine Bluff, AR 71601. Telephone: 870-575-8807. Fax: 870-575-4684. E-mail: colyardv@uapb.edu. World Wide Web: http://www.uapb.edu.

CALIFORNIA

AMERICAN RIVER COLLEGE

Hospitality Management Program

Sacramento, California

GENERAL INFORMATION

Public, coeducational, two-year college. Suburban campus. Founded in 1955. Accredited by Western Association of Schools and Colleges.

PROGRAM INFORMATION

Offered since 1975. Program calendar is divided into semesters. 1-year certificate in introductory baking. 1.5-year certificate in restaurant management. 1.5-year certificate in culinary arts. 2-year associate degree in culinary arts.

PROGRAM AFFILIATION

American Culinary Federation; National Restaurant Association.

AREAS OF STUDY

Baking; dining room management; food preparation; kitchen management; restaurant management.

FACILITIES

Bake shop; classroom; gourmet dining room; laboratory; lecture room.

STUDENT PROFILE

330 total: 220 full-time; 110 part-time.

FACULTY

11 total: 5 full-time; 6 part-time. Prominent faculty: Brian Knirk, MBA, CEC, CCE; Teresa Urkofsky, CEC; Judy Parks, CEC. Faculty-student ratio: 1:22.

SPECIAL PROGRAMS

Culinary competitions, student-run fine dining restaurant open to public.

TYPICAL EXPENSES

In-state tuition: $20 per unit full-time (in district), $20 per unit part-time. Out-of-state tuition: $125 per unit full-time, $125 per unit part-time.

APPLICATION INFORMATION

Students may begin participation in January, June, and August. Applications are accepted continuously.

CONTACT

Brian Knirk, Director, Hospitality Management Program, 4700 College Oak Drive, Sacramento, CA 95841-4286. Telephone: 916-484-8656. Fax: 916-484-8880. E-mail: knirkb@arc.losrios.edu. World Wide Web: http://www.arc.losrios.edu/chef.

THE ART INSTITUTE OF CALIFORNIA–INLAND EMPIRE

The International Culinary School at The Art Institute of California–Inland Empire

San Bernardino, California

GENERAL INFORMATION

Private, coeducational institution.

PROGRAM INFORMATION

Associate degree in Culinary Arts. Bachelor's degree in Culinary Management.

CONTACT

Office of Admissions, The International Culinary School at The Art Institute of California–Inland Empire, 630 East Brier Drive, San Bernardino, CA 92408-2800. Telephone: 909-915-2100. World Wide Web: http://www.artinstitutes.edu/inlandempire/.

See color display following page 186.

THE ART INSTITUTE OF CALIFORNIA–LOS ANGELES

The International Culinary School at The Art Institute of California–Los Angeles

Santa Monica, California

GENERAL INFORMATION
Private, coeducational institution.

PROGRAM INFORMATION
Associate degree in Culinary Arts. Bachelor's degree in Culinary Management. Diploma in The Art of Cooking. Diploma in Baking and Pastry.

CONTACT
Office of Admissions, The International Culinary School at The Art Institute of California–Los Angeles, 2900 31st Street, Santa Monica, CA 90405-3035. Telephone: 310-752-4700. World Wide Web: http://www.artinstitutes.edu/losangeles/.

See color display following page 186.

THE ART INSTITUTE OF CALIFORNIA–ORANGE COUNTY

The International Culinary School at The Art Institute of California–Orange County

Santa Ana, California

GENERAL INFORMATION
Private, coeducational institution.

PROGRAM INFORMATION
Associate degree in Culinary Arts. Bachelor's degree in Culinary Management. Diploma in Baking and Pastry. Diploma in Art of Cooking.

CONTACT
Office of Admissions, The International Culinary School at The Art Institute of California–Orange County, 3601 West Sunflower Avenue, Santa Ana, CA 92704-7931. Telephone: 714-830-0200. World Wide Web: http://www.artinstitutes.edu/orangecounty/.

See color display following page 186.

THE ART INSTITUTE OF CALIFORNIA–SACRAMENTO

The International Culinary School at The Art Institute of California–Sacramento

Sacramento, California

GENERAL INFORMATION
Private, coeducational institution.

PROGRAM INFORMATION
Associate degree in Culinary Arts. Bachelor's degree in Culinary Management.

CONTACT
Office of Admissions, The International Culinary School at The Art Institute of California–Sacramento, 2850 Gateway Oaks Drive, Suite 100, Sacramento, CA 95833. Telephone: 916-830-6320. World Wide Web: http://www.artinstitutes.edu/sacramento/.

See color display following page 186.

THE ART INSTITUTE OF CALIFORNIA–SAN DIEGO

The International Culinary School at The Art Institute of California–San Diego

San Diego, California

GENERAL INFORMATION
Private, coeducational institution.

PROGRAM INFORMATION
Associate degree in Baking and Pastry. Associate degree in Culinary Arts. Bachelor's degree in Culinary Management.

CONTACT
Office of Admissions, The International Culinary School at The Art Institute of California–San Diego, 7650 Mission Valley Road, San Diego, CA 92108-4423. Telephone: 858-598-1200. World Wide Web: http://www.artinstitutes.edu/sandiego/.

See color display following page 186.

THE ART INSTITUTE OF CALIFORNIA–SAN FRANCISCO

The International Culinary School at The Art Institute of California–San Francisco

San Francisco, California

GENERAL INFORMATION
Private, coeducational institution.

PROGRAM INFORMATION
Associate degree in Culinary Arts. Bachelor's degree in Culinary Management.

CONTACT
Office of Admissions, The International Culinary School at The Art Institute of California–San Francisco, 1170 Market Street, San Francisco, CA 94102-4928. Telephone: 415-865-0198. World Wide Web: http://www.artinstitutes.edu/sanfrancisco/.

See color display following page 186.

BAUMAN COLLEGE: HOLISTIC NUTRITION & CULINARY ARTS–BERKELEY

Natural Chef Training Program

Berkeley, California

GENERAL INFORMATION
Private, coeducational, culinary institute. Founded in 1984.

PROGRAM INFORMATION
Offered since 1997. Program calendar is divided into semesters. 5-month certificate in natural chef.

PROGRAM AFFILIATION
Sonoma County Culinary Guild; World Association of Chefs and Cooks.

AREAS OF STUDY
Baking; buffet catering; controlling costs in food service; culinary French; culinary skill development; ethnic cuisine; food preparation; food purchasing; food service math; healthy professional cooking; international cuisine; kitchen management; meal planning; menu and facilities design; nutrition; nutrition and food service; organic gardening; sanitation; saucier; soup, stock, sauce, and starch production; therapeutic cooking; vegetarian cooking.

FACILITIES
Classroom; computer laboratory; demonstration laboratory; food production kitchen; learning resource center; lecture room; library; teaching kitchen.

STUDENT PROFILE
125 full-time. 50 are under 25 years old; 50 are between 25 and 44 years old; 25 are over 44 years old.

FACULTY
9 total: 9 full-time. 9 are culinary-certified teachers; 1 is a gardening teacher. Prominent faculty: Ed Bauman, PhD, NC; Marcella Friel, Natural Chef Instructor; Denise Jardine, Natural Chef Instructor; Kathy Cummins, Natural Chef Instructor. Faculty-student ratio: 1:14.

SPECIAL PROGRAMS
French intensive organic gardening, classes in herbal remedies and cooking for a variety of health problems, personal chef focus.

TYPICAL EXPENSES
Tuition: $8500 per 5 months. Program-related fees include $395 for class materials (including books, chef's coat, apron, and knives), software, thermometer; $100 for registration; $20 for STRF fee.

FINANCIAL AID
Employment placement assistance is available. Employment opportunities within the program are available.

HOUSING
Average off-campus housing cost per month: $500.

APPLICATION INFORMATION
Students may begin participation in March and September. Applications are accepted continuously. In 2006, 125 applied; 125 were accepted. Applicants must interview; submit a formal application, letters of reference, an essay, resume, photo.

CONTACT
Lori Cottrell, Admissions Advisor, Natural Chef Training Program, PO Box 940, Penngrove, CA 94951. Telephone: 800-987-7530. Fax: 707-795-3375. E-mail: inquiry@baumancollege.org. World Wide Web: http://www.iet.org/cai.html.

BAUMAN COLLEGE: HOLISTIC NUTRITION & CULINARY ARTS–PENNGROVE

Natural Chef Training Program

Penngrove, California

GENERAL INFORMATION
Private, coeducational, culinary institute. Small-town setting.

PROGRAM INFORMATION
Program calendar is divided into semesters. 5-month certificate in natural chef.

PROGRAM AFFILIATION
Sonoma County Culinary Guild; World Association of Chefs and Cooks.

AREAS OF STUDY
Baking; buffet catering; controlling costs in food service; culinary French; culinary skill development; ethnic cuisine; food preparation; food purchasing; food service math; healthy professional cooking; international cuisine; kitchen management; meal planning; menu and facilities design; nutrition; nutrition and food service; organic gardening; sanitation; saucier; soup, stock, sauce, and starch production; therapeutic cooking; vegetarian cooking.

FACILITIES
Classroom; computer laboratory; demonstration laboratory; food production kitchen; learning resource center; lecture room; library; teaching kitchen.

STUDENT PROFILE
125 full-time. 50 are under 25 years old; 50 are between 25 and 44 years old; 25 are over 44 years old.

FACULTY
9 total: 9 full-time. 9 are culinary-certified teachers; 1 is a gardening teacher. Prominent faculty: Ed Bauman, PhD, NC; Marcella Friel, Natural Chef Instructor; Denise Jardine, Natural Chef Instructor; Kathy Cummins, Natural Chef Instructor. Faculty-student ratio: 1:14.

SPECIAL PROGRAMS
French intensive organic gardening, classes in herbal remedies and cooking for a variety of health problems, personal chef focus.

TYPICAL EXPENSES
Tuition: $8500 per 5 months. Program-related fees include $395 for class materials (including books, chef's coat, apron, and knives), software, thermometer; $100 for registration; $20 for STRF fee.

FINANCIAL AID
Employment placement assistance is available. Employment opportunities within the program are available.

HOUSING
Average off-campus housing cost per month: $500.

APPLICATION INFORMATION
Students may begin participation in March and September. Applications are accepted continuously. In 2006, 125 applied; 125 were accepted. Applicants must interview; submit a formal application, letters of reference, an essay, resume, photo.

CONTACT
Lori Cottrell, Admissions Advisor, Natural Chef Training Program, PO Box 940, Penngrove, CA 94951. Telephone: 800-987-7530. Fax: 707-795-3375. E-mail: inquiry@baumancollege.org. World Wide Web: http://www.baumancollege.org.

BAUMAN COLLEGE: HOLISTIC NUTRITION & CULINARY ARTS–SANTA CRUZ

Natural Chef Training Program

Santa Cruz, California

GENERAL INFORMATION
Private, coeducational, culinary institute. Small-town setting.

PROGRAM INFORMATION
Program calendar is divided into semesters. 5-month certificate in natural chef.

PROGRAM AFFILIATION
Sonoma County Culinary Guild; World Association of Chefs and Cooks.

AREAS OF STUDY
Baking; buffet catering; controlling costs in food service; culinary French; culinary skill development; ethnic cuisine; food preparation; food purchasing; food service math; healthy professional cooking; international cuisine; kitchen management; meal planning; menu and facilities design; nutrition; nutrition and food service; organic gardening; sanitation; saucier; soup, stock, sauce, and starch production; therapeutic cooking; vegetarian cooking.

FACILITIES

Classroom; computer laboratory; demonstration laboratory; food production kitchen; learning resource center; lecture room; library; teaching kitchen.

STUDENT PROFILE

125 full-time. 50 are under 25 years old; 50 are between 25 and 44 years old; 25 are over 44 years old.

FACULTY

9 total: 9 full-time. 9 are culinary-certified teachers; 1 is a gardening teacher. Prominent faculty: Ed Bauman, PhD, NC; Marcella Friel, Natural Chef Instructor; Denise Jardine, Natural Chef Instructor; Kathy Cummins, Natural Chef Instructor. Faculty-student ratio: 1:14.

SPECIAL PROGRAMS

French intensive organic gardening, classes in herbal remedies and cooking for a variety of health problems, personal chef focus.

TYPICAL EXPENSES

Tuition: $8500 per 5 months. Program-related fees include $395 for class materials (including books, chef's coat, apron, and knives), software, thermometer; $100 for registration; $20 for STRF fee.

FINANCIAL AID

Employment placement assistance is available. Employment opportunities within the program are available.

HOUSING

Average off-campus housing cost per month: $500.

APPLICATION INFORMATION

Students may begin participation in March and September. Applications are accepted continuously. In 2006, 125 applied; 125 were accepted. Applicants must interview; submit a formal application, letters of reference, an essay, resume, photo.

CONTACT

Lori Cottrell, Admissions Advisor, Natural Chef Training Program, PO Box 940, Penngrove, CA 94951. Telephone: 800-987-7530. Fax: 707-795-3375. E-mail: inquiry@baumancollege.org. World Wide Web: http://www.baumancollege.org.

CALIFORNIA CULINARY ACADEMY

San Francisco, California

GENERAL INFORMATION

Private, coeducational, culinary institute. Urban campus. Founded in 1977. Accredited by Accrediting Commission of Career Schools and Colleges of Technology.

PROGRAM INFORMATION

Offered since 1977. Accredited by American Culinary Federation Accrediting Commission. Program calendar is continuous. 30-week certificate in baking and pastry arts. 45-week associate degree in Le Cordon Bleu Hospitality and Restaurant Management. 60-week associate degree in Le Cordon Bleu culinary arts.

PROGRAM AFFILIATION

American Culinary Federation; American Institute of Wine & Food; California Restaurant Association; International Association of Culinary Professionals; National Restaurant Association.

AREAS OF STUDY

Baking; beverage management; buffet catering; casino and gaming; confectionery show pieces; controlling costs in food service; culinary French; culinary skill development; food preparation; food purchasing; food service math; garde-manger; global cuisine; international cuisine; introduction to food service; kitchen management; management and human resources; meat cutting; meat fabrication; menu and facilities design; nutrition; nutrition and food service; patisserie; restaurant opportunities; sanitation; saucier; seafood processing; soup, stock, sauce, and starch production; wines and spirits.

FACILITIES

Bake shop; 6 bakeries; cafeteria; 10 classrooms; coffee shop; 2 computer laboratories; 6 demonstration laboratories; 8 food production kitchens; gourmet dining room; 5 laboratories; learning resource center; library; 2 public restaurants; snack shop; student lounge; 3 teaching kitchens; retail shop; mixology laboratory; casino.

STUDENT PROFILE

950 full-time.

FACULTY

66 total: 66 full-time. Prominent faculty: Michael Weller; Tim Grable; Rocco Lamanna; Larry Michael. Faculty-student ratio: 1:32 lecture; 1:16 lab.

PROMINENT ALUMNI AND CURRENT AFFILIATION

Ron Siegel, Ritz Carlton, San Francisco; Justine Miner, RNM, San Francisco; Jose Calvo-Perez, Fresca, San Francisco.

California Culinary Academy *(continued)*

SPECIAL PROGRAMS
Externships for all programs (as of January 2008), culinary competitions, 3 Le Cordon Bleu certified programs (as of January 2008).

TYPICAL EXPENSES
Application fee: $65. Tuition: $46,951 for culinary arts program; $26,314 for baking/pastry program; $37,446 for hospitality and restaurant management program. Program-related fees include $3386 for student supply package (culinary arts); $2749 for student supply package (baking and pastry); $5381 for student supply package (hospitality and restaurant management).

FINANCIAL AID
In 2006, 25 scholarships were awarded (average award was $1775); 56 loans were granted (average loan was $14,120). Program-specific awards include Career Education Scholarship Fund, Future Chef of America high school competitions. Employment placement assistance is available. Employment opportunities within the program are available.

HOUSING
Coed housing available. Average on-campus housing cost per month: $600–$1000. Average off-campus housing cost per month: $1000.

APPLICATION INFORMATION
Students may begin participation in January, February, April, May, July, August, September, and November. Applications are accepted continuously. Applicants must interview; submit a formal application and application fee, entrance exam; have proof of high school graduation or GED.

CONTACT
Sanjay Ketty, Director of Admissions, 625 Polk Street, San Francisco, CA 94102. Telephone: 800-229-2433. Fax: 415-771-2194. E-mail: admissions@baychef.com. World Wide Web: http://www.baychef.com.

CALIFORNIA SCHOOL OF CULINARY ARTS

Le Cordon Bleu Programs

Pasadena, California

GENERAL INFORMATION
Private, coeducational, culinary institute. Urban campus. Founded in 1994. Accredited by Accrediting Council for Independent Colleges and Schools.

PROGRAM INFORMATION
Offered since 1994. 1-year diploma in Le Cordon Bleu Patisserie and Baking. 15-month associate degree in Le Cordon Bleu Culinary Arts. 42-week diploma in Le Cordon Bleu Patisserie and Baking (weeknight and Saturday classes). 60-week associate degree in Le Cordon Bleu Hospitality and Restaurant Management.

PROGRAM AFFILIATION
American Culinary Federation.

FINANCIAL AID
Employment placement assistance is available. Employment opportunities within the program are available.

APPLICATION INFORMATION
Applications are accepted continuously. Applicants must interview; submit a formal application, pre-enrollment exam, high school diploma or equivalent.

CONTACT
Admissions Department, Le Cordon Bleu Programs, 521 East Green Street, Pasadena, CA 91101. Telephone: 866-230-9450. World Wide Web: http://www.csca.edu.

CALIFORNIA STATE POLYTECHNIC UNIVERSITY, POMONA

The Collins School of Hospitality Management

Pomona, California

GENERAL INFORMATION
Public, coeducational, comprehensive institution. Suburban campus. Founded in 1938. Accredited by Western Association of Schools and Colleges.

PROGRAM INFORMATION
Offered since 1973. Accredited by Council on Hotel, Restaurant and Institutional Education. Program calendar is divided into quarters. 4-year bachelor's degree in hotel and restaurant management.

PROGRAM AFFILIATION
American Culinary Federation; Council on Hotel, Restaurant, and Institutional Education; International Association of Culinary Professionals; National Restaurant Association; National Restaurant Association Educational Foundation; Society of Wine Educators.

AREAS OF STUDY
Beverage management; beverage marketing; club management; controlling costs in food service; culinary product development; food preparation; food purchasing; food service math; hotel management; introduction to food service; kitchen management;

management and human resources; meal planning; menu and facilities design; restaurant management; restaurant opportunities; sanitation; soup, stock, sauce, and starch production; wines and spirits.

FACILITIES
10 classrooms; computer laboratory; food production kitchen; gourmet dining room; laboratory; 5 lecture rooms; library; public restaurant; student lounge; 2 demonstration auditoriums.

FACULTY
24 total: 20 full-time; 4 part-time. 22 are industry professionals; 1 is a culinary-certified teacher. Faculty-student ratio: 1:29.

SPECIAL PROGRAMS
Participation at national trade shows.

TYPICAL EXPENSES
In-state tuition: $3102 per year full-time (in district), $700 per quarter part-time. Out-of-state tuition: $3102 per year, plus $226 per unit full-time, $700 per quarter, plus $226 per unit part-time. Program-related fees include $45 for kitchen uniform/knives; $45 for food and beverage operations I; $10 for beverage management course lab fee; $20 for healthy American cuisine lab fee; $40 for wines and spirits class; $75 for wines of the world class.

FINANCIAL AID
In 2006, 23 scholarships were awarded (average award was $1500).

HOUSING
Coed housing available.

APPLICATION INFORMATION
Students may begin participation in January, March, June, and September. Application deadline for spring is August 31. Application deadline for summer is February 28. Application deadline for fall is November 30. Application deadline for winter is June 30. In 2006, 496 applied; 262 were accepted. Applicants must submit a formal application.

CONTACT
Ms. Lucy Miranda, Administrative Assistant, The Collins School of Hospitality Management, 3801 West Temple Avenue, Pomona, CA 91768-2557. Telephone: 909-869-2275. Fax: 909-869-4805. E-mail: lymiranda@csupomona.edu. World Wide Web: http://www.csupomona.edu/~cshm/collins_school/index.shtml.

CHEF ERIC'S CULINARY CLASSROOM
Professional and Recreational Cooking School

Los Angeles, California

GENERAL INFORMATION
Private, coeducational, culinary institute. Urban campus. Founded in 2003.

PROGRAM INFORMATION
Offered since 2003. Program calendar is continuous. 10-week certificate in baking II -advanced. 10-week certificate in comprehensive baking I. 10-week certificate in advanced meal preparation/presentation. 10-week certificate in International cuisines of the world. 20-week certificate in comprehensive culinary arts program.

AREAS OF STUDY
Baking; buffet catering; controlling costs in food service; convenience cookery; culinary French; culinary skill development; food preparation; food purchasing; food service communication; food service math; garde-manger; international cuisine; introduction to food service; meal planning; meat cutting; meat fabrication; nutrition; nutrition and food service; plating and presentation; restaurant opportunities; sanitation; seafood processing; soup, stock, sauce, and starch production; special events management.

FACILITIES
Classroom; demonstration laboratory; food production kitchen; gourmet dining room; lecture room; library; student lounge; teaching kitchen; special event room.

STUDENT PROFILE
750 total: 150 full-time; 600 part-time. 100 are under 25 years old; 400 are between 25 and 44 years old; 250 are over 44 years old.

FACULTY
6 total: 2 full-time; 4 part-time. 4 are industry professionals; 2 are culinary-certified teachers. Prominent faculty: Eric J. Crowley; Wendy Jacobs-Riche; Deena Fiske. Faculty-student ratio: 1:6.

SPECIAL PROGRAMS
Over 40 special recreational classes (3 hours each on nights and weekends), Children's Culinary Academy 1,2,3 (summers only), 4-week introduction to culinary arts program.

TYPICAL EXPENSES
Tuition: $1200–$2200 per 10 week programs; $2200 for 20 week program (includes jacket, apron and CIA text book) full-time, $75–$90 per recreational individual classes part-time.

Chef Eric's Culinary Classroom *(continued)*

FINANCIAL AID
In 2006, 2 scholarships were awarded (average award was $2200). Program-specific awards include payment plans available. Employment placement assistance is available.

APPLICATION INFORMATION
Students may begin participation year-round. Applications are accepted continuously.

CONTACT
Chef Eric J. Crowley, President, Professional and Recreational Cooking School, 2366 Pelham Avenue, Los Angeles, CA 90064. Telephone: 310-470-2640. Fax: 310-470-2642. E-mail: cheferic@culinaryclassroom.com. World Wide Web: http://www.culinaryclassroom.com.

CITY COLLEGE OF SAN FRANCISCO

Culinary Arts and Hospitality Studies Department

San Francisco, California

GENERAL INFORMATION
Public, coeducational, two-year college. Urban campus. Founded in 1935. Accredited by Western Association of Schools and Colleges.

PROGRAM INFORMATION
Offered since 1936. Accredited by American Culinary Federation Accrediting Commission. Program calendar is divided into semesters. 4-semester associate degree in hotel management. 4-semester associate degree in food service management. 4-semester associate degree in culinary arts.

PROGRAM AFFILIATION
American Culinary Federation; American Institute of Wine & Food; California Hotel and Motel Association; California Restaurant Association; Council on Hotel, Restaurant, and Institutional Education; Gastronomic Club; National Restaurant Association; National Restaurant Association Educational Foundation; Women Chefs and Restaurateurs.

AREAS OF STUDY
Baking; beverage management; buffet catering; confectionery show pieces; controlling costs in food service; culinary French; culinary skill development; food preparation; food purchasing; food service communication; food service math; garde-manger;

hospitality accounting; hospitality law; hospitality marketing; international cuisine; introduction to food service; kitchen management; management and human resources; meat cutting; meat fabrication; menu and facilities design; nutrition; nutrition and food service; orientation to hospitality; patisserie; restaurant opportunities; sanitation; saucier; seafood processing; soup, stock, sauce, and starch production; wines and spirits.

FACILITIES
Bake shop; cafeteria; catering service; 3 classrooms; computer laboratory; demonstration laboratory; 3 food production kitchens; gourmet dining room; 3 lecture rooms; library; public restaurant; snack shop; 5 teaching kitchens.

STUDENT PROFILE
250 total: 220 full-time; 30 part-time. 50 are under 25 years old; 150 are between 25 and 44 years old; 50 are over 44 years old.

FACULTY
19 total: 11 full-time; 8 part-time. 11 are industry professionals. Faculty-student ratio: 1:15.

PROMINENT ALUMNI AND CURRENT AFFILIATION
Sean O'Brien, Chef/Owner, Myth Restaurant; Belinda Leong, Restaurant Gary Danko, Pastry Chef; Maggie Pond, Cesar, Chef/Partner.

SPECIAL PROGRAMS
240-hour internship at one of 100 hotels/restaurants in Bay Area.

TYPICAL EXPENSES
In-state tuition: $300 per semester (15 units). Out-of-state tuition: $2550 per semester (15 units). Tuition for international students: $2850 per semester (15 units). Program-related fees include $150 for uniforms; $240 for kitchen tools; $250 for books (per semester).

FINANCIAL AID
In 2006, 40 scholarships were awarded (average award was $1000). Program-specific awards include Hotel and Restaurant Foundation scholarships. Employment placement assistance is available. Employment opportunities within the program are available.

HOUSING
Average off-campus housing cost per month: $1000.

APPLICATION INFORMATION
Students may begin participation in January and August. Application deadline for spring is November 13. Application deadline for fall is April 10. In 2006, 200 applied; 180 were accepted. Applicants must submit a formal application, an essay; international students must submit TOEFL scores (minimum 475).

CONTACT
Lynda Hirose, Program Advisor, Culinary Arts and Hospitality Studies Department, 50 Phelan Avenue, SW156, San Francisco, CA 94112-1821. Telephone: 415-239-3152. Fax: 415-239-3913. E-mail: cahs@ccsf.edu. World Wide Web: http://www.ccsf.edu/cahs.

COLLEGE OF THE CANYONS

Hotel and Restaurant Management

Santa Clarita, California

GENERAL INFORMATION
Public, coeducational, two-year college. Suburban campus. Founded in 1969. Accredited by Western Association of Schools and Colleges.

PROGRAM INFORMATION
Offered since 1990. Program calendar is divided into semesters. 2-year associate degree in hotel management. 2-year associate degree in restaurant management. 2-year associate degree in combined hotel and restaurant management.

AREAS OF STUDY
Beverage management; controlling costs in food service; hospitality law; hotel operations; kitchen management; management and human resources; nutrition and food service; restaurant opportunities; sales/marketing; sanitation.

FACILITIES
Classroom; computer laboratory; learning resource center; library.

STUDENT PROFILE
100 full-time.

FACULTY
4 total: 1 full-time; 3 part-time. 1 is an industry professional; 1 is a culinary-certified teacher. Prominent faculty: Kevin Anthony; Laura Karp; Dimaggio Washington; Gevork Kazanclann. Faculty-student ratio: 1:14.

SPECIAL PROGRAMS
Internships, wine tasting appreciation class.

TYPICAL EXPENSES
Tuition: $18 per unit. Program-related fee includes $75 for NRA Food Handlers certificate.

FINANCIAL AID
In 2006, 2 scholarships were awarded (average award was $500). Employment placement assistance is available.

College of the Canyons *(continued)*

APPLICATION INFORMATION
Students may begin participation in January, June, and August. Applications are accepted continuously. In 2006, 54 applied; 54 were accepted. Applicants must submit a formal application.

CONTACT
Kevin Anthony, Department Chair, Hotel and Restaurant Management, 26455 Rockwell Canyon Road, Santa Clarita, CA 91355. Telephone: 661-362-3712. Fax: 661-259-8302. E-mail: kevin.anthony@canyons.edu. World Wide Web: http://www.coc.cc.ca.us/.

CONTRA COSTA COLLEGE

Culinary Arts

San Pablo, California

GENERAL INFORMATION
Public, coeducational, two-year college. Urban campus. Founded in 1948. Accredited by Western Association of Schools and Colleges.

PROGRAM INFORMATION
Offered since 1964. Program calendar is divided into semesters. 2-year certificate in cooking. 2-year certificate in baking. 3-year associate degree in culinary arts.

PROGRAM AFFILIATION
National Restaurant Association.

AREAS OF STUDY
Baking; buffet catering; confectionery show pieces; controlling costs in food service; culinary French; culinary skill development; food preparation; food purchasing; food service communication; food service math; garde-manger; international cuisine; introduction to food service; kitchen management; management and human resources; meal planning; meat cutting; meat fabrication; menu and facilities design; nutrition; patisserie; sanitation; saucier; seafood processing; soup, stock, sauce, and starch production; wines and spirits.

FACILITIES
Bakery; cafeteria; 2 classrooms; 4 computer laboratories; gourmet dining room; 2 laboratories; library; public restaurant; 2 teaching kitchens.

STUDENT PROFILE
180 total: 100 full-time; 80 part-time.

FACULTY
6 total: 2 full-time; 4 part-time. 6 are industry professionals; 2 are culinary-certified teachers. Prominent faculty: Nader Sharkes, CEC. Faculty-student ratio: 1:14.

SPECIAL PROGRAMS
Related internships, culinary competitions.

TYPICAL EXPENSES
In-state tuition: $11 per unit. Out-of-state tuition: $155 per unit. Tuition for international students: $169 per unit. Program-related fees include $150–$200 for cutlery; $50–$100 for uniforms.

FINANCIAL AID
In 2006, 3 scholarships were awarded (average award was $500). Program-specific awards include California Restaurant Association scholarships. Employment placement assistance is available. Employment opportunities within the program are available.

HOUSING
Average off-campus housing cost per month: $800.

APPLICATION INFORMATION
Students may begin participation in January and August. Applications are accepted continuously. In 2006, 100 applied; 100 were accepted. Applicants must submit a formal application.

CONTACT
Joyce Edwards, Instructional Assistant, Culinary Arts, 2600 Mission Bell Drive, San Pablo, CA 94806-3195. Telephone: 510-235-7800 Ext. 4409. Fax: 510-236-6768. E-mail: jedwards@contracosta.edu. World Wide Web: http://www.contracosta.cc.ca.us.

THE CULINARY INSTITUTE OF AMERICA

The Culinary Institute of America at Greystone

St. Helena, California

GENERAL INFORMATION
Private, coeducational, culinary institute. Rural campus. Founded in 1946. Accredited by Accrediting Commission of Career Schools and Colleges of Technology, Middle States Association of Colleges and Schools.

PROGRAM INFORMATION
Offered since 1946. Program calendar is divided into semesters. 21-month associate degree in culinary arts. 30-week certificate in accelerated culinary arts. 30-week certificate in baking and pastry arts.

PROGRAM AFFILIATION
American Culinary Federation; American Dietetic Association; American Institute of Baking; American Institute of Wine & Food; Confrerie de la Chaine des Rotisseurs; Council on Hotel, Restaurant, and Institutional Education; International Association of Culinary Professionals; International Foodservice Editorial Council; James Beard Foundation, Inc.; Napa Valley Wine Library Association; National Association for the Specialty Food Trade, Inc.; National Restaurant Association; Oldways Preservation and Exchange Trust; Society of Wine Educators; Sommelier Society of America; The Bread Bakers Guild of America; Women Chefs and Restaurateurs.

AREAS OF STUDY
Baking; beverage management; buffet catering; confectionery show pieces; controlling costs in food service; culinary skill development; food preparation; food service math; garde-manger; international cuisine; introduction to food service; management and human resources; meat cutting; meat fabrication; menu and facilities design; nutrition; nutrition and food service; patisserie; restaurant opportunities; sanitation; saucier; seafood processing; soup, stock, sauce, and starch production; wines and spirits.

FACILITIES
2 bake shops; cafeteria; 7 classrooms; computer laboratory; 2 demonstration laboratories; garden; library; public restaurant; student lounge; 6 teaching kitchens; amphitheater.

STUDENT PROFILE
125 full-time. 105 are under 25 years old; 20 are between 25 and 44 years old.

FACULTY
16 total: 13 full-time; 3 part-time. 12 are industry professionals; 1 is a master chef; 1 is a master baker; 5 are culinary-certified teachers. Prominent faculty: Robert Jörin, CEPC, CCE, CHE, CMB; Adam Busby, CHE, CMC; Stephen Durkee, CHE, CMPC. Faculty-student ratio: 1:18.

PROMINENT ALUMNI AND CURRENT AFFILIATION
Duff Goldman, Charm City Cakes, Baltimore, MD; En-Ming Hsu, Pastry Consultant, Las Vegas, NV.

SPECIAL PROGRAMS
21-week paid externship (associate's only).

TYPICAL EXPENSES
Application fee: $50. Tuition: $10,640 per semester. Program-related fees include $360 for general fee; $915 for books and supplies; $1120 for board (mandatory).

FINANCIAL AID
Program-specific awards include ACAP Dean's Scholarship ($2000), Classic Residences by Hyatt Scholarship ($5,000). Employment placement assistance is available. Employment opportunities within the program are available.

HOUSING
Coed housing available. Average on-campus housing cost per month: $750. Average off-campus housing cost per month: $750.

APPLICATION INFORMATION
Students may begin participation in January, March, April, July, September, and October. Applications are accepted continuously. Applicants must interview; submit a formal application, letters of reference, an essay, academic transcripts; pass math and writing competency exams.

CONTACT
CIA Greystone Inquiries, The Culinary Institute of America at Greystone, Admissions Officer, 1946 Campus Drive, Hyde Park, NY 12538. Telephone: 800-CULINARY. E-mail: admissions@culinary.edu. World Wide Web: http://www.prochef.com.
See display on page 242.

EPICUREAN SCHOOL OF CULINARY ARTS
Los Angeles, California

GENERAL INFORMATION
Private, coeducational, culinary institute. Urban campus. Founded in 1985.

PROGRAM INFORMATION
Offered since 1985. Program calendar is continuous. Certificate in baking II. Certificate in baking I. 10-session certificate in baking III. 10-week certificate in professional chef II. 25-week certificate in professional chef I.

FACULTY
Prominent faculty: Teri Appleton; Suzanne Griswold; Roxannn Jullatot.

FINANCIAL AID
Employment placement assistance is available.

APPLICATION INFORMATION
Students may begin participation year-round. Applications are accepted continuously. Applicants must submit an informal application.

Epicurean School of Culinary Arts *(continued)*

CONTACT
Director, 8500 Melrose Avenue, Los Angeles, CA 90069. Telephone: 310-659-5990. Fax: 310-659-0302. E-mail: epicurean20@gmail.com. World Wide Web: http://EpicureanSchool.com.

INSTITUTE OF TECHNOLOGY

Clovis, California

GENERAL INFORMATION
Private institution.

PROGRAM INFORMATION
Certificate in culinary arts specialist. Certificate in baking and pastry specialist. Diploma in culinary arts professional.

CONTACT
Admissions, 731 W. Shaw, Clovis, CA 93612. Telephone: 800-696-6146. World Wide Web: http://www.it-colleges.edu.

INSTITUTE OF TECHNOLOGY– MODESTO

Modesto, California

GENERAL INFORMATION
Coeducational institution.

PROGRAM INFORMATION
Certificate in culinary arts professional. Certificate in baking and pastry specialist. Diploma in culinary arts professional.

APPLICATION INFORMATION
Applications are accepted continuously.

CONTACT
Admissions Department, 5737 Stoddard Road, Modesto, CA 95356. Telephone: 800-696-6146. World Wide Web: http://www.it-colleges.edu/modesto.php.

INSTITUTE OF TECHNOLOGY– ROSEVILLE

Roseville, California

GENERAL INFORMATION
Coeducational institution.

PROGRAM INFORMATION
Certificate in culinary arts professional. Certificate in baking and pastry specialist. Diploma in culinary arts professional.

APPLICATION INFORMATION
Applications are accepted continuously.

CONTACT
Admissions, 333 Sunrise Avenue, Suite 400, Roseville, CA 95661. Telephone: 800-696-6146. World Wide Web: http://www.it-colleges.edu/roseville.php.

JOBTRAIN

Culinary Arts Program

Redwood City, California

GENERAL INFORMATION
Private, coeducational, adult vocational school. Suburban campus. Founded in 1965. Accredited by Western Association of Schools and Colleges.

PROGRAM INFORMATION
Offered since 1965. Accredited by Western Association of Schools and Colleges. Program calendar is continuous, year-round. 3-month certificate in culinary arts.

PROGRAM AFFILIATION
National Restaurant Association; National Restaurant Association Educational Foundation.

AREAS OF STUDY
Baking; buffet catering; controlling costs in food service; culinary French; culinary skill development; food preparation; food purchasing; food service communication; food service math; garde-manger; international cuisine; introduction to food service; kitchen management; management and human resources; meal planning; meat cutting; menu and facilities design; nutrition; nutrition and food service; patisserie; restaurant opportunities; sanitation; saucier; seafood processing; soup, stock, sauce, and starch production; wines and spirits.

FACILITIES
Catering service; classroom; food production kitchen; learning resource center; lecture room; library; public restaurant.

TYPICAL STUDENT PROFILE
70 total: 45 full-time; 25 part-time.

SPECIAL PROGRAMS
Two-week externship (unpaid).

FINANCIAL AID
Program-specific awards include opportunity to work with caterers. Employment placement assistance is available. Employment opportunities within the program are available.

APPLICATION INFORMATION
Students may begin participation year-round. Applications are accepted continuously. Applicants must submit a formal application.

CONTACT
Director of Admissions, Culinary Arts Program, 1200 O'Brien Drive, Menlo Park, CA 94025. Telephone: 650-330-6429. Fax: 650-324-3419. World Wide Web: http://www.jobtrainworks.org/jobtrain/index.html.

KITCHEN ACADEMY

Hollywood, California

GENERAL INFORMATION
Coeducational, culinary institute. Urban campus.

PROGRAM INFORMATION
30-week diploma in professional culinary arts.

FACULTY
Faculty-student ratio: 1:16.

FINANCIAL AID
Employment placement assistance is available.

APPLICATION INFORMATION
Applications are accepted continuously. Applicants must interview; submit a formal application and Wonderlic Exam.

CONTACT
Director of Admissions, 6370 West Sunset Boulevard, Hollywood, CA 90028. Telephone: 888-807-7222. World Wide Web: http://www.kitchenacademy.com.

KITCHEN ACADEMY–SACRAMENTO

Sacramento, California

GENERAL INFORMATION
Coeducational, culinary institute. Urban campus.

PROGRAM INFORMATION
30-week diploma in professional culinary arts.

FINANCIAL AID
Employment placement assistance is available.

APPLICATION INFORMATION
Applications are accepted continuously. Applicants must interview; submit a formal application and Wonderlic Exam.

CONTACT
Director of Admissions, 2450 Del Paso Road, Sacramento, CA 95834. Telephone: 888-807-7222. World Wide Web: http://www.kitchenacademy.com.

LAKE TAHOE COMMUNITY COLLEGE

Culinary Arts Department

South Lake Tahoe, California

GENERAL INFORMATION
Public, coeducational, two-year college. Small-town setting. Founded in 1975. Accredited by Western Association of Schools and Colleges.

PROGRAM INFORMATION
Offered since 2000. Program calendar is divided into quarters. Certificate of specialization in cooking. 1-year certificate of achievement in culinary arts. 1-year certificate of specialization in global cuisine. 1-year certificate of specialization in whole life foods. 1-year certificate of specialization in wine. 1-year certificate of specialization in baking and pastry. 1- to 2-year advanced certificate in culinary arts. 2-quarter certificate in culinary arts. 2- to 3-year associate degree in culinary arts.

PROGRAM AFFILIATION
American Center for Wine, Food and the Arts; American Culinary Federation; Chefs Collaborative 2000; Copia; National Restaurant Association Educational Foundation; Oldways Preservation and Exchange Trust.

AREAS OF STUDY
Baking; beverage management; buffet catering; controlling costs in food service; culinary skill development; food preparation; food purchasing; food service math; garde-manger; history of food and

Lake Tahoe Community College *(continued)*

cooking; ice carving; international cuisine; introduction to food service; kitchen management; management and human resources; nutrition; patisserie; restaurant opportunities; sanitation; soup, stock, sauce, and starch production; wines and spirits.

FACILITIES
Bake shop; cafeteria; catering service; classroom; computer laboratory; demonstration laboratory; food production kitchen; garden; gourmet dining room; lecture room; public restaurant; teaching kitchen.

STUDENT PROFILE
450 total: 50 full-time; 400 part-time. 80 are under 25 years old; 200 are between 25 and 44 years old; 170 are over 44 years old.

FACULTY
11 total: 1 full-time; 10 part-time. 7 are industry professionals; 3 are master bakers; 1 is a culinary-certified teacher. Prominent faculty: Stephen C. Fernald, CCC; Stephen Moise; Ryan Payne; Chris Drake. Faculty-student ratio: 1:10.

SPECIAL PROGRAMS
Field trips and classes in Napa Valley and San Francisco Bay area, paid externships in Lake Tahoe and regional restaurants and resorts, membership in Tahoe Epicurean Club.

TYPICAL EXPENSES
Tuition: $13 per unit. Program-related fee includes $150 for knives and uniform.

FINANCIAL AID
In 2006, 1 scholarship was awarded (award was $1000). Program-specific awards include Foundation Scholarship for advanced classes at CIA Greystone, Lenore Fahey Memorial Scholarship. Employment placement assistance is available. Employment opportunities within the program are available.

HOUSING
Average off-campus housing cost per month: $500.

APPLICATION INFORMATION
Students may begin participation in January, April, July, and September. Applications are accepted continuously. Applicants must submit a formal application.

CONTACT
Stephen Fernald, Instructor, Culinary Arts, Culinary Arts Department, One College Drive, South Lake Tahoe, CA 96150. Telephone: 530-541-4660 Ext. 334. Fax: 530-541-7852. E-mail: fernald@ltcc.edu. World Wide Web: http://www.ltcc.edu.

LONG BEACH CITY COLLEGE

Culinary Arts

Long Beach, California

GENERAL INFORMATION
Public, coeducational, two-year college. Urban campus. Founded in 1927. Accredited by Western Association of Schools and Colleges.

PROGRAM INFORMATION
Offered since 1949. Accredited by American Dietetic Association. Program calendar is divided into semesters. 0.5-year certificate in food handlers certification. 1-year certificate in dietetic service supervisor. 1.5-year associate degree in restaurant management. 1.5-year associate degree in catering management. 1.5-year associate degree in commercial baking and pastry. 1.5-year associate degree in hotel/restaurant management. 1.5-year certificate in dietetic technician. 1.5-year certificate in restaurant management. 1.5-year certificate in catering management. 1.5-year certificate in commercial baking and pastry. 1.5-year certificate in culinary arts. 2-year associate degree in dietetic technician. 2-year associate degree in dietetic service supervisor. 2-year associate degree in culinary arts.

PROGRAM AFFILIATION
Academic Culinaire Paris; American Culinary Federation; American Dietetic Association; American Institute of Baking; Confrerie de la Chaine des Rotisseurs; French Chefs Association of California; National Restaurant Association; National Restaurant Association Educational Foundation; Société Culinaire Philanthropique; The Bread Bakers Guild of America; Toques Blanches.

AREAS OF STUDY
Baking; beverage management; buffet catering; controlling costs in food service; culinary French; culinary skill development; food preparation; food purchasing; food service communication; food service math; garde-manger; international cuisine; introduction to food service; kitchen management; meal planning; meat cutting; meat fabrication; menu and facilities design; nutrition; nutrition and food service; patisserie; restaurant opportunities; sanitation; saucier; seafood processing; soup, stock, sauce, and starch production; wines and spirits.

FACILITIES
2 bake shops; 2 cafeterias; 2 catering services; 4 classrooms; coffee shop; 2 computer laboratories; 4 demonstration laboratories; 4 food production kitchens;

garden; gourmet dining room; 2 learning resource centers; 4 lecture rooms; 2 libraries; 2 public restaurants; 2 snack shops; 2 student lounges; 3 teaching kitchens.

TYPICAL STUDENT PROFILE
155 total: 37 full-time; 118 part-time. 63 are under 25 years old; 64 are between 25 and 44 years old; 28 are over 44 years old.

SPECIAL PROGRAMS
Culinary set competitions, food expositions and field trips (produce, meat, and seafood processing companies).

FINANCIAL AID
Program-specific awards include home economics and dietetics scholarships.

APPLICATION INFORMATION
Students may begin participation in January, June, and August. Applications are accepted continuously. Applicants must submit a formal application.

CONTACT
Director of Admissions, Culinary Arts, 4901 East Carson Street, Long Beach, CA 90808. Telephone: 562-938-4502. Fax: 562-938-4334. World Wide Web: http://www.lbcc.edu.

MISSION COLLEGE
Hospitality Management Program

Santa Clara, California

GENERAL INFORMATION
Public, coeducational, two-year college. Urban campus. Founded in 1967. Accredited by Western Association of Schools and Colleges.

PROGRAM INFORMATION
Offered since 1967. Accredited by American Culinary Federation Accrediting Commission, Council on Hotel, Restaurant and Institutional Education. National Restaurant Association Educational Foundation ManageFirst certificates available. Program calendar is divided into semesters. 2-semester certificate in food service fundamentals. 3-semester certificate in food service. 4-semester associate degree in food service management.

PROGRAM AFFILIATION
American Culinary Federation; California Restaurant Association; Council on Hotel, Restaurant, and Institutional Education; Hospitality Sales and Marketing Association International; National Association of Catering Executives; National Association of College and University Food Service; National Restaurant Association; National Restaurant Association Educational Foundation; The Bread Bakers Guild of America.

AREAS OF STUDY
Baking; beverage management; buffet catering; controlling costs in food service; culinary skill development; food preparation; food purchasing; food service math; international cuisine; introduction to food service; kitchen management; management and human resources; meal planning; meat cutting; meat fabrication; menu and facilities design; nutrition; nutrition and food service; restaurant operation; restaurant opportunities; sanitation; saucier; seafood processing; soup, stock, sauce, and starch production; wines and spirits.

FACILITIES
Catering service; 3 classrooms; computer laboratory; demonstration laboratory; food production kitchen; garden; gourmet dining room; laboratory; 2 lecture rooms; 2 public restaurants; teaching kitchen.

STUDENT PROFILE
275 total: 175 full-time; 100 part-time.

FACULTY
8 total: 2 full-time; 6 part-time. Prominent faculty: W. Haze Dennis; Brian Estrada; Daniel Anras; Lurraine Rees.

PROMINENT ALUMNI AND CURRENT AFFILIATION
David Cash, Sodexho; Margaret Choy, Bon Apetite.

SPECIAL PROGRAMS
Attendance at national conferences and NRA show, culinary competitions, on-site visits to industry segments, one-day wine tours, hands-on catering opportunities.

TYPICAL EXPENSES
Tuition: $20 per unit full-time (in district), $20 per unit part-time. Tuition for international students: $173 per unit full-time, $173 per unit part-time. Program-related fees include $90 for lab fee for baking and healthy cuisine classes; $45 for uniforms; $90–$100 for all hands-on electives; $5 for online application fee.

FINANCIAL AID
In 2006, 4 scholarships were awarded (average award was $250). Program-specific awards include industry-sponsored awards. Employment placement assistance is available. Employment opportunities within the program are available.

HOUSING
Average off-campus housing cost per month: $700–$1300.

Mission College *(continued)*

APPLICATION INFORMATION
Students may begin participation in January, May, and August. Application deadline for fall is September 4. Application deadline for spring is February 4. Application deadline for summer is June 7. Applicants must submit a formal application and have high school diploma or GED.

CONTACT
W. Haze Dennis, Department Chair, Hospitality Management Program, 3000 Mission College Boulevard, Santa Clara, CA 95050. Telephone: 408-855-5252. Fax: 408-855-5452. E-mail: haze_dennis@wvm.edu. World Wide Web: http://www.missioncollege.org/.

MODESTO JUNIOR COLLEGE

Culinary Arts

Modesto, California

GENERAL INFORMATION
Public, coeducational, two-year college. Urban campus. Founded in 1921. Accredited by Western Association of Schools and Colleges.

PROGRAM INFORMATION
Offered since 1998. Program calendar is divided into semesters. 1-year certificate in culinary arts. 2-year associate degree in culinary arts.

AREAS OF STUDY
Baking; beverage management; buffet catering; controlling costs in food service; culinary French; culinary skill development; food preparation; food purchasing; food service communication; food service math; garde-manger; international cuisine; introduction to food service; kitchen management; management and human resources; meal planning; meat cutting; meat fabrication; menu and facilities design; nutrition; nutrition and food service; patisserie; restaurant opportunities; sanitation; saucier; soup, stock, sauce, and starch production; wines and spirits.

FACILITIES
Bake shop; catering service; classroom; 3 computer laboratories; demonstration laboratory; food production kitchen; 2 learning resource centers; lecture room; library.

STUDENT PROFILE
30 full-time.

FACULTY
6 total: 1 full-time; 5 part-time. 4 are industry professionals; 1 is a culinary-certified teacher. Faculty-student ratio: 1:30.

TYPICAL EXPENSES
Tuition: $364 per semester full-time (in district), $26 per unit part-time. Program-related fee includes $125 for lab fee.

FINANCIAL AID
In 2006, 8 scholarships were awarded (average award was $125). Employment placement assistance is available. Employment opportunities within the program are available.

APPLICATION INFORMATION
Students may begin participation in August. Applications are accepted continuously. In 2006, 30 were accepted. Applicants must go through a regular community college application/registration process.

CONTACT
Bob Glatt, Instructor, Culinary Arts, 435 College Avenue, Modesto, CA 95350-5800. Telephone: 209-575-6975. Fax: 209-575-6989. E-mail: glattb@yosemite.cc.ca.us. World Wide Web: http://mjc.yosemite.cc.ca.us/.

MONTEREY PENINSULA COLLEGE

Hospitality Program

Monterey, California

GENERAL INFORMATION
Public, coeducational, two-year college. Small-town setting. Founded in 1947. Accredited by Western Association of Schools and Colleges.

PROGRAM INFORMATION
Offered since 1975. Program calendar is divided into semesters. 1-year certificate in hospitality operations. 2-semester certificate of completion in baking and pastry arts. 2-semester certificate of completion in food service management. 2-semester certificate of completion in line cook. 2-year associate degree in restaurant management.

PROGRAM AFFILIATION
American Hotel and Lodging Association; Council on Hotel, Restaurant, and Institutional Education; Monterey County Hospitality Association.

AREAS OF STUDY
Baking; beverage management; culinary skill development; food purchasing; garde-manger; nutrition; sanitation; special events management.

FACILITIES
2 classrooms; laboratory; teaching kitchen.

STUDENT PROFILE
70 total: 40 full-time; 30 part-time.

FACULTY
10 total: 1 full-time; 9 part-time. 3 are industry professionals; 3 are master chefs; 1 is a master baker. Prominent faculty: Paul Lee, CEC; Sylvia Langland, RD; Kay Covert, RD; André Adam. Faculty-student ratio: 1:15.

TYPICAL EXPENSES
In-state tuition: $20 per unit. Out-of-state tuition: $130 per unit.

FINANCIAL AID
Program-specific awards include local scholarships provided by Hospitality Association.

HOUSING
Average off-campus housing cost per month: $800.

APPLICATION INFORMATION
Students may begin participation in January and August. Applications are accepted continuously. Applicants must submit a formal application and application prior to start date.

CONTACT
Mary Nelson, Director, Hospitality Program, 980 Fremont Street, Monterey, CA 93940. Telephone: 831-646-4134. Fax: 831-759-9675. E-mail: mnelson@mpc.edu. World Wide Web: http://www.mpchospitalityprogram.com.

MT. SAN ANTONIO COLLEGE

Hospitality and Restaurant Management

Walnut, California

GENERAL INFORMATION
Public, coeducational, two-year college. Suburban campus. Founded in 1946. Accredited by Western Association of Schools and Colleges.

PROGRAM INFORMATION
Offered since 1946. Program calendar is divided into semesters. 1-year certificate in hospitality: restaurant management: Level II. 1-year certificate in hospitality: restaurant management: Level I. 1-year certificate in hospitality management: Level II. 1-year certificate in hospitality management: Level I. 1-year certificate in food services. 1-year certificate in catering. 2-year associate degree in hospitality and restaurant management.

PROGRAM AFFILIATION
National Restaurant Association.

AREAS OF STUDY
Accounting; controlling costs in food service; food preparation; food service math; garde-manger; introduction to food service; management and human resources; menu and facilities design; nutrition; nutrition and food service; patisserie; restaurant opportunities; sanitation; saucier; seafood processing; soup, stock, sauce, and starch production.

FACILITIES
Classroom; computer laboratory; demonstration laboratory; food production kitchen; lecture room; teaching kitchen.

STUDENT PROFILE
175 total: 67 full-time; 108 part-time. 125 are under 25 years old; 44 are between 25 and 44 years old; 6 are over 44 years old.

FACULTY
2 total: 1 full-time; 1 part-time. 2 are industry professionals. Prominent faculty: Dr. Fawaz Al-Malood. Faculty-student ratio: 1:19.

SPECIAL PROGRAMS
Job internships (paid/unpaid).

TYPICAL EXPENSES
In-state tuition: $240 per semester full-time (in district), $60 per 3 units part-time. Out-of-state tuition: $2076 per semester full-time, $519 per 3 units part-time. Tuition for international students: $2364 per semester full-time, $591 per 3 units part-time. Program-related fee includes $15 for health services fee.

FINANCIAL AID
Employment placement assistance is available. Employment opportunities within the program are available.

APPLICATION INFORMATION
Students may begin participation in January, February, June, and August. Applications are accepted continuously. Applicants must submit a formal application.

CONTACT
Dr. Fawaz Al-Malood, Professor, Hospitality and Restaurant Management, 1100 North Grand Avenue, Walnut, CA 91789-1399. Telephone: 909-594-5611 Ext. 4139. Fax: 909-468-3936. E-mail: falmaloo@mtsac.edu. World Wide Web: http://www.mtsac.edu.

Napa Valley College

Napa Valley Cooking School

St. Helena, California

GENERAL INFORMATION
Public, coeducational, culinary institute. Suburban campus. Founded in 1996. Accredited by Western Association of Schools and Colleges.

PROGRAM INFORMATION
Offered since 1996. Program calendar is divided into semesters. 14-month certificate in culinary arts.

PROGRAM AFFILIATION
American Culinary Federation.

AREAS OF STUDY
Baking; buffet catering; controlling costs in food service; culinary French; culinary skill development; food preparation; food purchasing; food service math; garde-manger; international cuisine; introduction to food service; kitchen management; meat cutting; meat fabrication; menu and facilities design; nutrition; nutrition and food service; patisserie; restaurant opportunities; sanitation; saucier; seafood processing; soup, stock, sauce, and starch production; vegetarian cookery; wine and food; wines and spirits.

FACILITIES
Classroom; computer laboratory; food production kitchen; garden; lecture room; library; student lounge; teaching kitchen; vineyard.

TYPICAL STUDENT PROFILE
18 full-time. 3 are under 25 years old; 14 are between 25 and 44 years old; 1 is over 44 years old.

SPECIAL PROGRAMS
Tours of wineries and local farms, 5-month externship.

FINANCIAL AID
Program-specific awards include 2 Culinary Institute of America scholarships ($1000), various culinary association scholarships ($1000–$5000). Employment placement assistance is available.

APPLICATION INFORMATION
Students may begin participation in August. Applications are accepted continuously. Applicants must interview; submit a formal application, letters of reference, high school diploma/GED, academic transcripts, and 200-word essay describing career interest.

CONTACT
Director of Admissions, Napa Valley Cooking School, 1088 College Avenue, St. Helena, CA 94574. Telephone: 707-967-2930. Fax: 707-967-2909. World Wide Web: http://www.napavalley.edu/apps/comm.asp?Q=29.

National Culinary and Bakery School

La Mesa, California

GENERAL INFORMATION
Private, coeducational, culinary institute. Suburban campus. Founded in 1993.

PROGRAM INFORMATION
Offered since 1993. Program calendar is continuous. 10-week certificate in pastry. 10-week certificate in bakery. 4-month certificate in culinary arts.

PROGRAM AFFILIATION
American Culinary Federation; National Restaurant Association; National Restaurant Association Educational Foundation.

AREAS OF STUDY
Baking; confectionery show pieces; controlling costs in food service; culinary French; culinary skill development; food preparation; food purchasing; food service math; garde-manger; international cuisine; introduction to food service; kitchen management; meal planning; meat cutting; meat fabrication; menu and facilities design; nutrition; patisserie; restaurant opportunities; sanitation; saucier; seafood processing; soup, stock, sauce, and starch production.

FACILITIES
Bake shop; bakery; catering service; classroom; demonstration laboratory; food production kitchen; lecture room; library.

STUDENT PROFILE
75 full-time.

FACULTY
5 total: 5 full-time. Prominent faculty: Dal Smith; Margaret Patt. Faculty-student ratio: 1:6.

SPECIAL PROGRAMS
Field trips to places of work, catering events for internships, organic mushroom farms.

TYPICAL EXPENSES
Application fee: $100. Tuition: $9800 for culinary; $6000 for bakery program. Program-related fee includes $250 for culinary knife set (optional).

FINANCIAL AID
Program-specific awards include in-house private financing. Employment placement assistance is available.

HOUSING
Average off-campus housing cost per month: $400.

APPLICATION INFORMATION
Applications are accepted continuously. Application deadline for for each session: 2 weeks prior to start. In 2006, 75 applied; 75 were accepted. Applicants must interview and demonstrate the desire and passion to become a professional chef.

CONTACT
Dal Smith or Margaret Pott, Owner, 8400 Center Drive, La Mesa, CA 91942. Telephone: 619-461-2800. Fax: 619-461-2881. E-mail: natlschools@nationalschools.com. World Wide Web: http://www.nationalschools.com.

THE NEW SCHOOL OF COOKING

Culver City, California

GENERAL INFORMATION
Private, coeducational institution. Urban campus. Founded in 1999.

PROGRAM INFORMATION
Offered since 1999. Program calendar is continuous. 10-week diploma in professional baking. 10-week diploma in culinary arts advanced. 20-week diploma in culinary arts.

PROGRAM AFFILIATION
American Culinary Federation; International Association of Culinary Professionals; James Beard Foundation, Inc.; Women Chefs and Restaurateurs.

AREAS OF STUDY
Baking; culinary French; culinary skill development; food preparation; meal planning; patisserie; sanitation; seafood processing; soup, stock, sauce, and starch production.

FACILITIES
Classroom; demonstration laboratory; food production kitchen; teaching kitchen.

STUDENT PROFILE
72 part-time. 5 are under 25 years old; 55 are between 25 and 44 years old; 12 are over 44 years old.

FACULTY
9 total: 3 full-time; 6 part-time. 3 are industry professionals; 4 are culinary-certified teachers. Prominent faculty: Carol Cotner Thompson; Cindy Mushet; May Parich; Jet Tila. Faculty-student ratio: 1:12.

SPECIAL PROGRAMS
Regional ethnic series, vegetarian series and individual classes, wine education.

TYPICAL EXPENSES
Tuition: $2400 for culinary arts; $1200 for culinary arts advanced; $1200 for professional baking full-time, $2500 for 20 week professional cooking (once a week), $1300 for 10 week professional baking (once a week) part-time.

FINANCIAL AID
Employment placement assistance is available.

APPLICATION INFORMATION
Students may begin participation year-round. Applications are accepted continuously.

CONTACT
Anne Smith, Owner, 8690 Washington Boulevard, Culver City, CA 90232. Telephone: 310-842-9702. E-mail: annesmith@newschoolofcooking.com. World Wide Web: http://www.newschoolofcooking.com.

ORANGE COAST COLLEGE

Hospitality Department

Costa Mesa, California

GENERAL INFORMATION
Public, coeducational, two-year college. Suburban campus. Founded in 1947. Accredited by Western Association of Schools and Colleges.

PROGRAM INFORMATION
Offered since 1964. Accredited by American Culinary Federation Accrediting Commission. Program calendar is semester plus summer session. 1-year certificate in institutional dietetic service supervisor. 1-year certificate in fast food service. 1-year certificate in culinary arts. 1-year certificate in child nutrition programs. 1-year certificate in catering. 2-year associate degree in hotel management. 2-year associate degree in culinary arts. 2-year associate degree in food service management. 2-year certificate in restaurant supervision. 2-year certificate in institutional dietetic technician. 3-year certificate in cook apprentice. 30-month certificate in institutional dietetic service manager.

PROGRAM AFFILIATION
American Culinary Federation; American Dietetic Association; California Restaurant Association; Confrerie de la Chaine des Rotisseurs; International Food Service Executives Association; National Association of College and University Food Service; Retailer's Bakery Association.

Orange Coast College *(continued)*

AREAS OF STUDY

Baking; beverage management; buffet catering; controlling costs in food service; convenience cookery; culinary skill development; dining room management; food preparation; food purchasing; food service communication; food service math; garde-manger; hotel and restaurant law; international cuisine; introduction to food service; kitchen management; management and human resources; meal planning; meat cutting; meat fabrication; menu and facilities design; nutrition; nutrition and food service; patisserie; restaurant opportunities; sanitation; saucier; seafood processing; soup, stock, sauce, and starch production.

FACILITIES

Bake shop; bakery; cafeteria; catering service; 4 classrooms; computer laboratory; 2 food production kitchens; gourmet dining room; lecture room; library; public restaurant; student lounge.

STUDENT PROFILE

400 total: 200 full-time; 200 part-time. 90 are under 25 years old; 250 are between 25 and 44 years old; 60 are over 44 years old.

FACULTY

20 total: 6 full-time; 14 part-time. 6 are industry professionals; 1 is a master baker; 7 are culinary-certified teachers. Prominent faculty: Bill Barber, CWC. Faculty-student ratio: 1:15.

SPECIAL PROGRAMS

Food show seminar (3 three-hour sessions), student hot food team.

TYPICAL EXPENSES

Tuition: $18 per unit. Program-related fees include $20–$45 for materials (per culinary preparation class); $80 for uniform; $100 for cutlery.

FINANCIAL AID

In 2006, 30 scholarships were awarded. Employment placement assistance is available. Employment opportunities within the program are available.

HOUSING

Average off-campus housing cost per month: $500–$700.

APPLICATION INFORMATION

Students may begin participation in January and August. Applications are accepted continuously. Applicants must submit a formal application.

CONTACT

Bill Barber, Program Coordinator, Hospitality Department, 2701 Fairview Road, PO Box 5005, Costa Mesa, CA 92628-5005. Telephone: 714-432-5835. Fax: 714-432-5609. World Wide Web: http://www.orangecoastcollege.com.

OXNARD COLLEGE

Hotel and Restaurant Management

Oxnard, California

GENERAL INFORMATION

Public, coeducational, two-year college. Suburban campus. Founded in 1975. Accredited by Western Association of Schools and Colleges.

PROGRAM INFORMATION

Offered since 1985. National Restaurant Association Educational Foundation ManageFirst certificates available. Program calendar is divided into semesters. 2-year associate degree in restaurant management. 2-year associate degree in culinary arts. 2-year certificate in restaurant management. 2-year certificate in culinary arts.

PROGRAM AFFILIATION

American Culinary Federation; Council on Hotel, Restaurant, and Institutional Education; National Restaurant Association Educational Foundation.

AREAS OF STUDY

Baking; beverage management; buffet catering; controlling costs in food service; convenience cookery; culinary French; culinary skill development; food preparation; food purchasing; food service communication; food service math; garde-manger; international cuisine; introduction to food service; kitchen management; management and human resources; meal planning; menu and facilities design; nutrition; nutrition and food service; restaurant opportunities; sanitation; saucier; soup, stock, sauce, and starch production; wines and spirits.

FACILITIES

Bake shop; cafeteria; catering service; 2 classrooms; computer laboratory; demonstration laboratory; 2 food production kitchens; gourmet dining room; laboratory; learning resource center; lecture room; library; public restaurant; teaching kitchen.

STUDENT PROFILE

140 total: 70 full-time; 70 part-time.

FACULTY
6 total: 1 full-time; 5 part-time. Prominent faculty: Frank Haywood; Richard Harnden; Joe Carabajal; Henri Patey, CEC, CCE. Faculty-student ratio: 1:15.

SPECIAL PROGRAMS
Sanitation certification (ServSafe Education Foundation NRA).

TYPICAL EXPENSES
In-state tuition: $600 per 30 units full-time (in district), $20 per unit part-time. Out-of-state tuition: $5220 per 30 units full-time, $175 per unit part-time. Program-related fees include $400–$500 for tools and uniforms; $85 for textbooks (per class); $50 for application fee (for international students only).

FINANCIAL AID
In 2006, 13 scholarships were awarded (average award was $500); 10 loans were granted (average loan was $300). Program-specific awards include loan/voucher program for tools and uniforms. Employment placement assistance is available. Employment opportunities within the program are available.

HOUSING
Average off-campus housing cost per month: $700.

APPLICATION INFORMATION
Students may begin participation in January, June, and August. Application deadline for fall is August 18. Application deadline for spring is January 5. Application deadline for summer is May 15. In 2006, 100 applied; 100 were accepted.

CONTACT
Frank Haywood, Instructor, Hotel and Restaurant Management, 4000 South Rose Avenue, Oxnard, CA 93033. Telephone: 805-986-5869. Fax: 805-986-5806. E-mail: fhaywood@vcccd.net. World Wide Web: http://www.oxnardcollege.edu/programs/culinary/index.asp.

PROFESSIONAL CULINARY INSTITUTE
Campbell, California

GENERAL INFORMATION
Private, coeducational, culinary institute. Suburban campus. Founded in 2004.

PROGRAM INFORMATION
Offered since 2005. Program calendar is continuous. 1-year associate degree in hospitality management. 11-week diploma in certified sommelier. 8-month diploma in baking and pastry arts. 8-month diploma in culinary arts.

PROGRAM AFFILIATION
American Culinary Federation; Court of Master Sommeliers; National Restaurant Association.

AREAS OF STUDY
Baking; beverage management; buffet catering; culinary French; culinary skill development; food preparation; garde-manger; international cuisine; introduction to food service; management and human resources; meat fabrication; menu and facilities design; nutrition; nutrition and food service; patisserie; sanitation; saucier; seafood processing; soup, stock, sauce, and starch production; wines and spirits.

FACILITIES
Bakery; catering service; 7 classrooms; 2 computer laboratories; 2 demonstration laboratories; library; 2 student lounges; 5 teaching kitchens.

STUDENT PROFILE
220 total: 120 full-time; 100 part-time. 30 are under 25 years old; 180 are between 25 and 44 years old; 10 are over 44 years old.

FACULTY
16 total: 11 full-time; 5 part-time. 3 are industry professionals; 2 are master chefs; 1 is a master baker; 7 are culinary-certified teachers; 1 is a MBA. Prominent faculty: Bo Friberg, CMPC; Mial Parker, CEC; Randy Torres, CEC. Faculty-student ratio: 1:16.

SPECIAL PROGRAMS
Graduate Enhancement program (1-4 day seminar per year for 2 years after graduation), tours of local vineyards and breweries, paid externships.

TYPICAL EXPENSES
Tuition: $23400–$30,000 per 8 months–1 year. Tuition for international students: $24,200 per 8 months. Program-related fees include $50 for enrollment fee; $55 for student tuition refund fund (CA state residents only); $1200 for supply kit fee (culinary and baking); $2600 for supply kit fee (hospitality management).

FINANCIAL AID
In 2006, 2 scholarships were awarded (average award was $7500); 6 loans were granted (average loan was $15,000). Employment placement assistance is available.

HOUSING
Average off-campus housing cost per month: $850.

APPLICATION INFORMATION
Students may begin participation in January, April, July, and October. Applications are accepted continuously. In 2006, 250 applied; 220 were accepted. Applicants must interview; submit a formal application, letters of reference, high school transcript and diploma or GED.

Professional Culinary Institute *(continued)*

CONTACT
Nancy Pruitt, Director of Admissions, 700 West Hamilton Avenue, Suite 300, Campbell, CA 95008. Telephone: 408-370-9190. Fax: 408-370-9186. E-mail: nbp@pcichef.com. World Wide Web: http://www. pcichef.com/.

QUALITY COLLEGE OF CULINARY CAREERS

Fresno, California

GENERAL INFORMATION
Private, coeducational, culinary institute. Urban campus. Founded in 1994. Accredited by Accrediting Commission of Career Schools and Colleges of Technology.

PROGRAM INFORMATION
Program calendar is continuous. 14-week certificate in culinary arts. 2-year associate degree in professional baking and pastry chef. 2-year associate degree in professional cooking and culinary arts. 30-week certificate in culinary chef. 40-week certificate in food and beverage manager.

SPECIAL PROGRAMS
Culinary competitions.

APPLICATION INFORMATION
Applicants must interview; submit a formal application, letters of reference, and an essay.

CONTACT
Admissions Office, 1776 North Fine Avenue, Fresno, CA 93726. Telephone: 559-497-5050. E-mail: admissions@ qualitycollege.edu.

RICHARDSON RESEARCHES, INC.

Davis, California

GENERAL INFORMATION
Private, coeducational, confectionery food consultancy company. Urban campus. Founded in 1972.

PROGRAM INFORMATION
Offered since 1977. 1-week diploma in chocolate technology. 1-week diploma in confectionery technology.

PROGRAM AFFILIATION
Institute of Food Technologists; National Confectioners Association of the US; Retail Confectioners International.

AREAS OF STUDY
Confectionery and chocolate technologies.

FACILITIES
Computer laboratory; demonstration laboratory; laboratory; lecture room.

STUDENT PROFILE
18 full-time.

FACULTY
3 total: 2 full-time; 1 part-time. 3 are industry professionals. Prominent faculty: Terry Richardson; Peter Dea.

TYPICAL EXPENSES
Tuition: $1350–$1825 per diploma.

APPLICATION INFORMATION
Applications are accepted continuously. Applicants must submit a formal application.

CONTACT
Terry Richardson, President, 5445 Hilltop Crescent, Oakland, CA 94618. Telephone: 510-653-4385. Fax: 510-653-4865. E-mail: info@richres.com. World Wide Web: http://www.richres.com.

RIVERSIDE COMMUNITY COLLEGE

Culinary Academy

Riverside, California

GENERAL INFORMATION
Public, coeducational, two-year college. Suburban campus. Founded in 1916. Accredited by Western Association of Schools and Colleges.

PROGRAM INFORMATION
Offered since 1997. Program calendar is divided into semesters. 1-year certificate in culinary arts. 60-unit associate degree in culinary arts.

PROGRAM AFFILIATION
American Culinary Federation; California Restaurant Association.

AREAS OF STUDY
Baking; culinary skill development; food preparation; food purchasing; kitchen management; meal planning; restaurant opportunities; sanitation; saucier; soup, stock, sauce, and starch production.

FACILITIES
Bake shop; bakery; catering service; 2 classrooms; coffee shop; computer laboratory; 3 demonstration laboratories; food production kitchen; gourmet dining room; 3 laboratories; learning resource center; 2 lecture rooms; library; public restaurant; 3 teaching kitchens.

STUDENT PROFILE
146 total: 25 full-time; 121 part-time.

FACULTY
5 total: 4 full-time; 1 part-time. Prominent faculty: Bobby Moghaddam; David Avalos; Maria Williams; Robert Baradan. Faculty-student ratio: 1:22.

SPECIAL PROGRAMS
Field trips, food competitions, Skills USA/VICA Club.

TYPICAL EXPENSES
In-state tuition: $200 per semester full-time (in district), $20 per unit part-time. Out-of-state tuition: $1730 per semester full-time, $173 per unit part-time. Tuition for international students: $1920 per semester full-time, $192 per unit part-time. Program-related fees include $228.21 for uniforms; $186.35 for tools (cutlery); $375 for books; $40 for hat fee.

FINANCIAL AID
In 2006, 3 scholarships were awarded. Employment placement assistance is available. Employment opportunities within the program are available.

APPLICATION INFORMATION
Students may begin participation in January and August. Application deadline for winter is October 3. Application deadline for fall is May 22. In 2006, 300 applied; 121 were accepted. Applicants must interview; submit a formal application and take aptitude test.

CONTACT
Mr. Bobby Moghaddam, Director, Culinary and Hospitality Program, Culinary Academy, 1533 Spruce Street, Riverside, CA 92507. Telephone: 951-955-3311. Fax: 951-222-8095. E-mail: bobby.moghaddam@rcc.edu. World Wide Web: http://www.rcc.edu/academicprograms/culinary/index.cfm.

SAN DIEGO MESA COLLEGE

Hospitality Management

San Diego, California

GENERAL INFORMATION
Public, coeducational, two-year college. Urban campus. Founded in 1964. Accredited by Western Association of Schools and Colleges.

PROGRAM INFORMATION
Offered since 1964. Accredited by American Dietetic Association. Program calendar is divided into semesters. 1-year certificate in destination and event management. 1-year certificate in hotel management. 1-year certificate in culinary arts/culinary management. 1-year certificate in dietetic supervision. 2-year associate degree in destination and event management. 2-year associate degree in hotel management. 2-year associate degree in culinary arts/culinary management.

PROGRAM AFFILIATION
American Culinary Federation; American Dietetic Association.

AREAS OF STUDY
Baking; buffet catering; confectionery show pieces; controlling costs in food service; culinary French; culinary skill development; food preparation; food purchasing; garde-manger; introduction to food service; kitchen management; management and human resources; meal planning; meat cutting; meat fabrication; menu and facilities design; nutrition; nutrition and food service; restaurant opportunities; sanitation; saucier; seafood processing; soup, stock, sauce, and starch production.

FACILITIES
Bake shop; bakery; cafeteria; catering service; classroom; 2 computer laboratories; 2 demonstration laboratories; food production kitchen; garden; gourmet dining room; laboratory; learning resource center; lecture room; library; public restaurant; snack shop; student lounge; teaching kitchen.

STUDENT PROFILE
300 total: 200 full-time; 100 part-time.

FACULTY
12 total: 2 full-time; 10 part-time. Prominent faculty: Michael Fitzgerald; Karl Engstron; Peter Robson, CEC; Andrea Luoma, PhD. Faculty-student ratio: 1:30 theory; 1:20 lab.

SPECIAL PROGRAMS
Culinary competitions.

TYPICAL EXPENSES
In-state tuition: $20 per unit full-time (in district), $20 per unit part-time. Out-of-state tuition: $182 per unit full-time, $182 per unit part-time. Program-related fees include $150 for knives; $150 for uniforms.

FINANCIAL AID
In 2006, 8 scholarships were awarded (average award was $500). Employment opportunities within the program are available.

HOUSING
Average off-campus housing cost per month: $850.

San Diego Mesa College *(continued)*

APPLICATION INFORMATION
Students may begin participation in January and August. Application deadline for fall is August 20. Application deadline for spring is January 15. In 2006, 150 applied; 150 were accepted. Applicants must have a high school diploma.

CONTACT
Michael Fitzgerald, Assistant Professor, Hospitality Management, 7250 Mesa College Drive, San Diego, CA 92111. Telephone: 619-388-2240. Fax: 619-388-2677. E-mail: mfitzger@sdccd.edu. World Wide Web: http://www.sdmesa.edu/.

SANTA BARBARA CITY COLLEGE

Hotel, Restaurant, and Culinary Program

Santa Barbara, California

GENERAL INFORMATION
Public, coeducational, two-year college. Suburban campus. Founded in 1908. Accredited by Western Association of Schools and Colleges.

PROGRAM INFORMATION
Offered since 1970. Accredited by American Culinary Federation Accrediting Commission. Program calendar is divided into semesters. 4-semester certificate in restaurant management. 4-semester certificate in hotel management. 4-semester certificate in culinary arts. 5-semester associate degree in restaurant management. 5-semester associate degree in hotel management. 5-semester associate degree in culinary arts.

PROGRAM AFFILIATION
American Culinary Federation; American Institute of Wine & Food; California Restaurant Association; Confrerie de la Chaine des Rotisseurs; Council on Hotel, Restaurant, and Institutional Education; International Association of Culinary Professionals; National Restaurant Association; National Restaurant Association Educational Foundation; The Bread Bakers Guild of America.

AREAS OF STUDY
Baking; bartending; beverage management; buffet catering; confectionery show pieces; controlling costs in food service; convenience cookery; culinary French; culinary skill development; food preparation; food purchasing; food service communication; food service math; garde-manger; international cuisine; introduction to food service; kitchen management; management and human resources; meal planning; meat cutting; meat fabrication; menu and facilities design; nutrition and

food service; patisserie; restaurant opportunities; restaurant ownership; sanitation; saucier; seafood processing; soup, stock, sauce, and starch production; wines and spirits.

FACILITIES
Bake shop; cafeteria; catering service; 3 classrooms; coffee shop; computer laboratory; demonstration laboratory; 5 food production kitchens; garden; gourmet dining room; laboratory; learning resource center; lecture room; library; 2 public restaurants; 2 snack shops; student lounge; 3 teaching kitchens; 2 food preparation laboratories.

STUDENT PROFILE
165 total: 150 full-time; 15 part-time. 116 are under 25 years old; 41 are between 25 and 44 years old; 8 are over 44 years old.

FACULTY
10 total: 4 full-time; 6 part-time. Prominent faculty: Dr. Dixie Budke; Randy Bublitz, CCE; Charles Fredricks; Stephen Rapp. Faculty-student ratio: 1:15.

SPECIAL PROGRAMS
Student-run food operation, culinary competitions.

TYPICAL EXPENSES
In-state tuition: $18 per credit hour. Out-of-state tuition: $147 per credit hour. Program-related fees include $280 for uniforms; $120 for tools and equipment.

FINANCIAL AID
In 2006, 60 scholarships were awarded (average award was $500). Program-specific awards include scholarships from private sources. Employment placement assistance is available. Employment opportunities within the program are available.

HOUSING
Average off-campus housing cost per month: $500.

APPLICATION INFORMATION
Students may begin participation in January and August. Application deadline for spring is November 1. Application deadline for fall is June 1. In 2006, 120 applied; 100 were accepted. Applicants must interview; submit a formal application.

CONTACT
Randall Bublitz, Department Chair, Hotel, Restaurant, and Culinary Program, 721 Cliff Drive, Santa Barbara, CA 93109-2394. Telephone: 805-965-0581 Ext. 2457. Fax: 805-962-0257. E-mail: bublitz@sbcc.net. World Wide Web: http://www.sbcc.net/.

TANTE MARIE'S COOKING SCHOOL

San Francisco, California

GENERAL INFORMATION
Private, coeducational, culinary institute. Urban campus. Founded in 1979.

PROGRAM INFORMATION
Offered since 1979. 6-month certificate in professional culinary program. 6-month certificate in professional pastry program.

PROGRAM AFFILIATION
American Institute of Wine & Food; International Association of Culinary Professionals; James Beard Foundation, Inc.; San Francisco Professional Food Society; Women Chefs and Restaurateurs.

AREAS OF STUDY
Baking; culinary French; culinary skill development; food preparation; food purchasing; garde-manger; international cuisine; introduction to food service; meal planning; meat cutting; nutrition; patisserie; restaurant opportunities; sanitation; saucier; seafood processing; soup, stock, sauce, and starch production; wines and spirits.

FACILITIES
Demonstration laboratory; garden; 2 teaching kitchens.

STUDENT PROFILE
29 total: 15 full-time; 14 part-time.

FACULTY
4 total: 2 full-time; 2 part-time. 1 is an industry professional; 1 is a master chef; 2 are culinary-certified teachers. Prominent faculty: Mary S. Risley; Francis Wilson; Jennifer Altmon. Faculty-student ratio: 1:14.

PROMINENT ALUMNI AND CURRENT AFFILIATION
Heidi Krahling, Insalatas, San Anselmo; Shelley Lindgren, A16, San Francisco; Tori Ritchie, CBS Morning Show.

SPECIAL PROGRAMS
1-month externship.

TYPICAL EXPENSES
Tuition: $8500 (pastry certificate); $19,500 (culinary certificate). Program-related fees include $200 for uniform and supplies (pastry program); $200–$500 for uniform and supplies (culinary program).

FINANCIAL AID
Employment placement assistance is available. Employment opportunities within the program are available.

HOUSING
Average off-campus housing cost per month: $2000.

APPLICATION INFORMATION
Students may begin participation in April and October. Applications are accepted continuously. Applicants must submit a formal application and an essay.

CONTACT
Peggy Lynch, Administrator, 271 Francisco Street, San Francisco, CA 94133. Telephone: 415-788-6699. Fax: 415-788-8924. E-mail: peggy@tantemarie.com. World Wide Web: http://www.tantemarie.com.

UNIVERSITY OF SAN FRANCISCO

Hospitality Management Program

San Francisco, California

GENERAL INFORMATION
Private, coeducational, university. Urban campus. Founded in 1855. Accredited by Western Association of Schools and Colleges.

PROGRAM INFORMATION
Offered since 1982. Accredited by The Association to Advance Collegiate Schools of Business (AACSB). Program calendar is divided into 4-1-4. 4-year bachelor's degree in hospitality industry management.

PROGRAM AFFILIATION
American Hotel and Lodging Association; California Restaurant Association; Golden Gate Restaurant Association; Hotel Council of San Francisco; International Foodservice Editorial Council; National Restaurant Association; National Restaurant Association Educational Foundation.

AREAS OF STUDY
Beverage management; controlling costs in food service; culinary skill development; events management; food preparation; food purchasing; food service communication; food service math; introduction to food service; kitchen management; management and human resources; meal planning; menu and facilities design; nutrition and food service; restaurant opportunities; sanitation; seafood processing; soup, stock, sauce, and starch production; wines and spirits.

FACILITIES
Classroom; demonstration laboratory; food production kitchen; gourmet dining room; lecture room; library; teaching kitchen.

STUDENT PROFILE
100 full-time. 97 are under 25 years old; 3 are between 25 and 44 years old.

University of San Francisco *(continued)*

FACULTY
7 total: 3 full-time; 4 part-time. 3 are industry professionals; 1 is a culinary-certifed teacher. Prominent faculty: Thomas Costello, FSCI; K. O. Odsather, CHA; Jean-Marc Fullsack; Jeff Scharosch. Faculty-student ratio: 1:30.

PROMINENT ALUMNI AND CURRENT AFFILIATION
Mark Dommen, Co-owner and Executive Chef, One Market; Rita Gonzalez, Four Seasons, Palo Alto; Jeff Mall/Scott Silva, Zin Restaurants & Wine Bar.

SPECIAL PROGRAMS
San Francisco Educational Symposium, wine trip to Napa/Sonoma, 800-hour industry related work experience requirement, 200-hour mentorship program.

TYPICAL EXPENSES
Application fee: $55. Tuition: $30,840 per year full-time, $1100 per unit part-time.

FINANCIAL AID
In 2006, 10 scholarships were awarded (average award was $2100); 5 loans were granted (average loan was $8174). Program-specific awards include Joseph Drown Scholarship and Loan Fund, various endowed scholarships, partial tuition to full-tuition scholarships for transfer students. Employment placement assistance is available. Employment opportunities within the program are available.

HOUSING
Coed, apartment-style, and single-sex housing available. Average off-campus housing cost per month: $800–$1500.

APPLICATION INFORMATION
Students may begin participation in January and August. Application deadline for fall is February 1. Application deadline for spring is December 15. Application deadline for for fall early action is November 15. In 2006, 81 applied; 63 were accepted. Applicants must submit a formal application, letters of reference, an essay, SAT scores, and high school and/or college transcripts.

CONTACT
Mike Hughes, Director, Undergraduate Admissions, Hospitality Management Program, 2130 Fulton Street, San Francisco, CA 94117-1046. Telephone: 415-422-6563. Fax: 415-422-2217. E-mail: admissions@usfca.edu. World Wide Web: http://www.usfca.edu/sobam/under/hosp/hospitality.html.

WESTLAKE CULINARY INSTITUTE
Let's Get Cookin'

Westlake Village, California

GENERAL INFORMATION
Private, coeducational, culinary institute. Founded in 1988.

PROGRAM INFORMATION
Offered since 1988. Certificate in catering, beginning course. 10-session certificate in baking. 24-session certificate in professional cooking.

PROGRAM AFFILIATION
International Association of Culinary Professionals.

SPECIAL PROGRAMS
Basic Techniques for Creative Cooking (twice a year).

TYPICAL EXPENSES
Tuition: $4295 (professional cooking); $1295 (baking).

FINANCIAL AID
Employment placement assistance is available.

APPLICATION INFORMATION
Applicants must submit a formal application.

CONTACT
Phyllis Vaccarelli, Owner/Director, Let's Get Cookin', 4643 Lakeview Canyon Road, Westlake Village, CA 91361. Telephone: 818-991-3940. Fax: 805-495-2554. E-mail: lgcookin@aol.com. World Wide Web: http://www.letsgetcookin.com.

COLORADO

THE ART INSTITUTE OF COLORADO
The International Culinary School at The Art Institute of Colorado

Denver, Colorado

GENERAL INFORMATION
Private, coeducational institution.

PROGRAM INFORMATION
Associate degree in Baking and Pastry. Associate degree in Culinary Arts. Bachelor's degree in Culinary Management. Diploma in Baking and Pastry. Diploma in The Art of Cooking.

CONTACT
Office of Admissions, The International Culinary School at The Art Institute of Colorado, 1200 Lincoln Street, Denver, CO 80203-2172. Telephone: 303-837-0825. World Wide Web: http://www.artinstitutes.edu/denver/.
See color display following page 186.

COLORADO MOUNTAIN COLLEGE

Culinary Institute

Keystone and Vail, Colorado

GENERAL INFORMATION
Public, coeducational, two-year college. Rural campus. Founded in 1967. Accredited by North Central Association of Colleges and Schools.

PROGRAM INFORMATION
Offered since 1993. Accredited by American Culinary Federation Accrediting Commission. Program calendar is divided into semesters. 1-year certificate in apprentice cook. 1-year certificate in garde manger. 3-year associate degree in culinary arts (with apprenticeship).

PROGRAM AFFILIATION
American Culinary Federation.

AREAS OF STUDY
Baking; beverage management; buffet catering; controlling costs in food service; convenience cookery; culinary French; culinary skill development; food preparation; food purchasing; food service communication; food service math; garde-manger; international cuisine; introduction to food service; kitchen management; management and human resources; meal planning; meat cutting; meat fabrication; menu and facilities design; nutrition; nutrition and food service; patisserie; restaurant opportunities; sanitation; saucier; seafood processing; soup, stock, sauce, and starch production.

FACILITIES
Bake shop; bakery; 6 cafeterias; 4 catering services; 10 classrooms; coffee shop; 2 computer laboratories; 4 demonstration laboratories; 12 food production kitchens; 5 gourmet dining rooms; learning resource center; 12 lecture rooms; library; 12 public restaurants; snack shop; teaching kitchen.

STUDENT PROFILE
75 full-time.

Colorado Mountain College *(continued)*

FACULTY
12 total: 2 full-time; 10 part-time. 8 are industry professionals; 2 are culinary-certified teachers. Prominent faculty: Kevin Clarke, CC, JD; Todd Rymer, CEC. Faculty-student ratio: 1:15.

SPECIAL PROGRAMS
ACF apprenticeships at resorts in Keystone and Vail, culinary competitions.

TYPICAL EXPENSES
In-state tuition: $1032 per year full-time (in district), $43 per credit hour part-time (in district), $1728 per year full-time (out-of-district), $72 per credit hour part-time (out-of-district). Out-of-state tuition: $5544 per year full-time, $231 per credit hour part-time. Program-related fee includes $850 for tools and texts.

FINANCIAL AID
In 2006, 6 scholarships were awarded (average award was $800). Employment placement assistance is available. Employment opportunities within the program are available.

HOUSING
Coed and apartment-style housing available. Average on-campus housing cost per month: $350–$450. Average off-campus housing cost per month: $1000.

APPLICATION INFORMATION
Students may begin participation in June and September. Application deadline for fall (Vail) is July 1. Application deadline for summer (Keystone) is January 15. In 2006, 100 applied; 30 were accepted. Applicants must interview; submit a formal application, letters of reference, an essay, academic transcripts, Accuplacer test scores or ACT/SAT scores.

CONTACT
Deborah Cutter, Central Admissions, Enrollment Specialist, Culinary Institute, 831 Grand Avenue, Glenwood Springs, CO 81601. Telephone: 800-621-8559. Fax: 970-947-8324. E-mail: dcutter@coloradomtn.edu. World Wide Web: http://www.coloradomtn.edu.

COOK STREET SCHOOL OF FINE COOKING

Professional Food and Wine Career Program

Denver, Colorado

GENERAL INFORMATION
Private, coeducational, culinary institute. Founded in 1999. Accredited by Accrediting Council for Continuing Education and Training.

PROGRAM INFORMATION
Offered since 1999. Accredited by State of Colorado Department of Higher Education, Veterans Administration. 18-week diploma in culinary arts.

PROGRAM AFFILIATION
American Culinary Federation; American Institute of Wine & Food; Chefs Collaborative; Colorado Chefs Association; Confrerie de la Chaine des Rotisseurs; Culinary Business Academy; International Association of Culinary Professionals; James Beard Foundation, Inc.; United States Personal Chef Association; Women Chefs and Restaurateurs.

FACULTY
Prominent faculty: Michael Comstedt, CEC, CCE; Peter Ryan, CC; Lexie Justice; Dale Eiden, CEC.

SPECIAL PROGRAMS
3-week culinary education tour in France and Italy.

TYPICAL EXPENSES
Application fee: $150. Tuition: $24,990 per full program with European culinary tour.

FINANCIAL AID
Employment placement assistance is available. Employment opportunities within the program are available.

APPLICATION INFORMATION
Students may begin participation in January, April, July, and October. Applications are accepted continuously. Applicants must interview; submit a formal application, letters of reference, an essay, high school/college transcripts.

CONTACT
Admissions Coordinator, Professional Food and Wine Career Program, 1937 Market Street, Denver, CO 80202. Telephone: 303-308-9300. Fax: 303-308-9400. E-mail: admissions@cookstreet.com. World Wide Web: http://www.cookstreet.com.

CULINARY SCHOOL OF THE ROCKIES

Professional Culinary Arts Program

Boulder, Colorado

GENERAL INFORMATION

Private, coeducational, culinary institute. Urban campus. Founded in 1991. Accredited by Accrediting Council for Continuing Education and Training.

PROGRAM INFORMATION

Offered since 1996. Program calendar is divided into semesters. 15-week diploma in chef track. 5-week diploma in pastry arts. 6-month diploma in culinary arts.

PROGRAM AFFILIATION

American Culinary Federation; American Institute of Wine & Food; Chefs Collaborative; Chefs Cooperative; International Association of Culinary Professionals; James Beard Foundation, Inc.; National Restaurant Association; Slow Food International; Women Chefs and Restaurateurs.

AREAS OF STUDY

Baking; controlling costs in food service; culinary French; culinary skill development; food preparation; food purchasing; fundamentals of sensory awareness; garde-manger; international cuisine; kitchen management; meal planning; meat cutting; meat fabrication; menu and facilities design; nutrition and food service; palate development and education; patisserie; restaurant opportunities; sanitation; saucier; seafood processing; soup, stock, sauce, and starch production; wines and spirits.

FACILITIES

Classroom; computer laboratory; demonstration laboratory; food production kitchen; garden; learning resource center; lecture room; library; teaching kitchen.

STUDENT PROFILE

113 total: 65 full-time; 48 part-time.

FACULTY

4 total: 3 full-time; 1 part-time. 4 are culinary-certified teachers. Prominent faculty: Jason Aili; Michael Scott; Bethany Milan; Marilyn Kakudo. Faculty-student ratio: 1:8.

Culinary School of the Rockies *(continued)*

PROMINENT ALUMNI AND CURRENT AFFILIATION
Sean Keeler, Bistro Zinc, Las Vegas, NV; Owen Clark, wd~50, New York; Jared Sippel, Frasca Food and Wine, Boulder, CO.

SPECIAL PROGRAMS
1-month study in Avignon, France (includes work in a French restaurant), 5-week farm to table curriculum, Colorado Farms.

TYPICAL EXPENSES
Application fee: $35. Tuition: $29,485 (6-month diploma); $7,950 (15-week diploma); $6750 (5-week diploma).

FINANCIAL AID
In 2006, 1 scholarship was awarded (award was $8000); 75 loans were granted (average loan was $15,000). Program-specific awards include Sallie Mae Career Training Loans. Employment placement assistance is available. Employment opportunities within the program are available.

HOUSING
Average off-campus housing cost per month: $750.

APPLICATION INFORMATION
Students may begin participation in January, February, May, July, and October. Applications are accepted continuously. In 2006, 150 applied; 112 were accepted. Applicants must interview; submit a formal application, letters of reference, an essay, copy of most recent school transcript.

CONTACT
Karen Barela, Assistant Director, Professional Culinary Arts Program, 637 South Broadway, Suite H, Boulder, CO 80305. Telephone: 303-494-7988. Fax: 303-494-7999. E-mail: admissions@culinaryschoolrockies.com. World Wide Web: http://www.culinaryschoolrockies.com.

FRONT RANGE COMMUNITY COLLEGE

Hospitality/Food Management

Fort Collins, Colorado

GENERAL INFORMATION
Public, coeducational, two-year college. Suburban campus. Founded in 1968. Accredited by North Central Association of Colleges and Schools.

PROGRAM INFORMATION
Offered since 1998. Program calendar is divided into semesters. 10-credit certificate in beginning culinary arts. 2-year associate degree in hospitality/food management. 6-credit certificate in restaurant operations. 6-credit certificate in hotel operations. 8-credit certificate in advanced culinary arts. 9-credit certificate in hospitality supervision.

PROGRAM AFFILIATION
Colorado Restaurant Association; Council on Hotel, Restaurant, and Institutional Education; National Restaurant Association; National Restaurant Association Educational Foundation.

AREAS OF STUDY
Baking; controlling costs in food service; culinary skill development; food preparation; food purchasing; food service management; garde-manger; hospitality management; introduction to food service; kitchen management; management and human resources; meal planning; menu and facilities design; nutrition; nutrition and food service; patisserie; restaurant opportunities; sanitation.

FACILITIES
Bake shop; classroom; computer laboratory; demonstration laboratory; food production kitchen; laboratory; learning resource center; lecture room; library.

STUDENT PROFILE
45 total: 20 full-time; 25 part-time.

FACULTY
4 total: 4 part-time. Prominent faculty: Marjorie Trinen, BS, CEC; Joe Babíarz, CEC. Faculty-student ratio: 1:7.

SPECIAL PROGRAMS
Culinary exhibitions, summer Rocky Mountain Resorts internships, three experiential internships.

TYPICAL EXPENSES
In-state tuition: $894.60 per semester full-time (in district), $223–$447 per 3 to 6 credit hours part-time. Out-of-state tuition: $4141.80 per semester full-time, $1035–$2070 per 3 to 6 credit hours part-time. Program-related fee includes $5.70 for high cost items (per credit).

FINANCIAL AID
Employment placement assistance is available. Employment opportunities within the program are available.

HOUSING
Average off-campus housing cost per month: $300–$500.

APPLICATION INFORMATION

Students may begin participation in January and August. Applications are accepted continuously. In 2006, 40 applied; 40 were accepted. Applicants must submit a formal application.

CONTACT

Larry Lucas, Program Director, Hospitality/Food Management, 4616 South Shields, Fort Collins, CO 80526. Telephone: 970-204-8196. Fax: 970-204-8440. E-mail: larry.lucas@frontrange.edu. World Wide Web: http://frontrange.edu.

JOHNSON & WALES UNIVERSITY–DENVER CAMPUS

College of Culinary Arts

Denver, Colorado

GENERAL INFORMATION

Private, coeducational, four-year college. Urban campus. Founded in 2000. Accredited by New England Association of Schools and Colleges.

PROGRAM INFORMATION

Accredited by American Dietetic Association. Program calendar is divided into quarters. Associate degree in baking and pastry arts. Associate degree in culinary arts. Bachelor's degree in culinary arts and food service management (joint degree with the College of Culinary Arts and The Hospitality College). Bachelor's degree in pastry arts and food service management (joint degree with the College of Culinary Arts and The Hospitality College). Bachelor's degree in restaurant, food and beverage management. Bachelor's degree in hotel and lodging management. Bachelor's degree in culinary nutrition.

PROGRAM AFFILIATION

American Culinary Federation; American Dietetic Association; American Institute of Baking; American Institute of Wine & Food; Confrerie de la Chaine des Rotisseurs; Council on Hotel, Restaurant, and Institutional Education; Institute of Food Technologists; International Association of Culinary Professionals; International Food Service Executives Association; James Beard Foundation, Inc.; National Restaurant Association; National Restaurant Association Educational Foundation; The Bread Bakers Guild of America.

AREAS OF STUDY

Baking; beverage management; buffet catering; food purchasing; garde-manger; management and human resources; meat cutting; nutrition; patisserie; sanitation.

FACILITIES

3 bake shops; bakery; cafeteria; catering service; 21 classrooms; 2 coffee shops; 5 computer laboratories; demonstration laboratory; 2 gourmet dining rooms; 8 laboratories; learning resource center; 6 lecture rooms; library; 2 public restaurants; snack shop; 5 student lounges; 7 teaching kitchens; storeroom; wine & beverage lab; University events center; nutrition lab; culinary computer lab; soups, stocks & sauce kitchen.

STUDENT PROFILE

826 total: 799 full-time; 27 part-time. 705 are under 25 years old; 115 are between 25 and 44 years old; 6 are over 44 years old.

FACULTY

19 total: 18 full-time; 1 part-time. 4 are industry professionals; 2 are culinary-certified teachers. Prominent faculty: John Johnson, CCC, CCE, AAC; Peter Henkel, CEC; Jerry Comar, CEPC; Carrie Stebbins, Certified Sommelier. Faculty-student ratio: 1:22.

SPECIAL PROGRAMS

Every culinary student gets a real-life, career-building work experience through internship or co-op, international study, ACF-certification and 1-year membership for all completing associates degree.

TYPICAL EXPENSES

Tuition: $20,478 per year. Program-related fees include $984 for general fee; $255 for orientation fee; $300 for reservation deposit; $984 for optional weekend meal plan.

FINANCIAL AID

In 2006, 796 scholarships were awarded (average award was $4239.76); 265 loans were granted (average loan was $3783.71). Employment placement assistance is available.

HOUSING

Coed housing available. Average on-campus housing cost per month: $1000.

APPLICATION INFORMATION

Students may begin participation in March, June, September, and December. Applications are accepted continuously. In 2006, 1221 applied; 973 were accepted. Applicants must submit a formal application.

CONTACT

Kim Ostrowski, Director of Admissions, College of Culinary Arts, 7150 Montview Boulevard, Denver, CO 80220. Telephone: 877-598-3368. Fax: 303-256-9333. E-mail: admissions.den@jwu.edu. World Wide Web: http://culinary.jwu.edu.

See color display following page 90.

MESA STATE COLLEGE

Colorado Culinary Academy

Grand Junction, Colorado

GENERAL INFORMATION
Public, coeducational, comprehensive institution. Urban campus. Founded in 1925. Accredited by North Central Association of Colleges and Schools.

PROGRAM INFORMATION
Offered since 1998. National Restaurant Association Educational Foundation ManageFirst certificates available. Program calendar is divided into semesters. 1-year certificate in culinary arts. 2-year associate degree in culinary arts.

PROGRAM AFFILIATION
American Culinary Federation; National Restaurant Association; National Restaurant Association Educational Foundation.

AREAS OF STUDY
Baking; beverage management; controlling costs in food service; culinary skill development; food preparation; food purchasing; food service math; food service supervision; garde-manger; international cuisine; introduction to food service; management and human resources; meat cutting; meat fabrication; menu and facilities design; nutrition and food service; sanitation; saucier; seafood processing; soup, stock, sauce, and starch production; wines and spirits.

FACILITIES
Bake shop; cafeteria; 4 classrooms; coffee shop; 2 computer laboratories; 2 demonstration laboratories; food production kitchen; gourmet dining room; learning resource center; library; public restaurant; teaching kitchen; baking kitchen.

STUDENT PROFILE
92 total: 80 full-time; 12 part-time. 74 are under 25 years old; 10 are between 25 and 44 years old; 8 are over 44 years old.

FACULTY
8 total: 3 full-time; 5 part-time. 6 are industry professionals; 2 are culinary-certified teachers. Prominent faculty: Daniel Kirby, CHE; Wayne Smith, CEC, CCE; Robert Clarke. Faculty-student ratio: 1:8.

SPECIAL PROGRAMS
Culinary competitions, seven week paid internships, tours of Colorado wineries.

TYPICAL EXPENSES
Application fee: $30. In-state tuition: $2315.72 per semester full-time (in district), $149.78 per semester credit hour part-time. Out-of-state tuition: $6548.90 per semester full-time, $441.26 per semester credit hour part-time. Program-related fees include $250 for cutlery; $75 for uniforms; $528 for lab fees.

FINANCIAL AID
In 2006, 3 scholarships were awarded (average award was $1500). Employment placement assistance is available. Employment opportunities within the program are available.

HOUSING
Coed, apartment-style, and single-sex housing available. Average on-campus housing cost per month: $580.

APPLICATION INFORMATION
Students may begin participation in January, June, and August. Application deadline for fall is August 23. Application deadline for spring is January 17. Applicants must interview; submit a formal application.

CONTACT
Daniel Kirby, Department Chair, Colorado Culinary Academy, 2508 Blichmann Avenue, Grand Junction, CO 81505. Telephone: 970-255-2632. Fax: 970-255-2626. E-mail: dkirby@mesastate.edu. World Wide Web: http://www.mesastate.edu.

METROPOLITAN STATE COLLEGE OF DENVER

Hospitality, Meeting, and Travel Administration Department

Denver, Colorado

GENERAL INFORMATION
Public, coeducational, four-year college. Urban campus. Founded in 1963. Accredited by North Central Association of Colleges and Schools.

PROGRAM INFORMATION
Offered since 1963. Accredited by North Central Association of Colleges and Schools. Program calendar is divided into semesters. Certificate in Sommelier Diploma. 4-year bachelor's degree in hotel administration. 4-year bachelor's degree in culinary arts administration. 4-year bachelor's degree in restaurant administration.

PROGRAM AFFILIATION
American Culinary Federation; American Hotel and Lodging Association; Council on Hotel, Restaurant, and Institutional Education; International Food Service Executives Association; Les Amis d'Escoffier Society; National Restaurant Association; National Restaurant Association Educational Foundation; Slow Food International; Tasters Guild International.

AREAS OF STUDY

Beers; healthy professional cooking; kitchen management; nutrition; restaurant opportunities; wines and spirits.

FACILITIES

Bake shop; catering service; 4 classrooms; computer laboratory; demonstration laboratory; food production kitchen; gourmet dining room; learning resource center; 4 lecture rooms; library; public restaurant; 5 student lounges; teaching kitchen.

TYPICAL STUDENT PROFILE

475 total: 250 full-time; 225 part-time.

SPECIAL PROGRAMS

Swiss Hotel School exchange, international culinary and wine tours for college credit, Certified Cellar Manager Program, International Sommelier Guild Diploma, Tips Program, Bar-Code Certificate.

FINANCIAL AID

Program-specific awards include 2 Super Value Club Foods scholarships ($2000); 10 Southern Wine and Spirits Scholarship ($2000), Colorado Restaurant Association scholarship ($1000), International Sommelier Guild (10 at $75), 5 Culinary ProStart scholarships ($1000), CO Lodging Association (5 at $1000). Employment placement assistance is available. Employment opportunities within the program are available.

HOUSING

Apartment-style housing available.

APPLICATION INFORMATION

Students may begin participation in January and August. Application deadline for fall is August 15. Application deadline for spring is January 15. Applicants must submit a formal application.

CONTACT

Director of Admissions, Hospitality, Meeting, and Travel Administration Department, Campus Box 60, PO Box 173362, Osner, CO 80217. Telephone: 303-556-3152. Fax: 303-556-8046. World Wide Web: http://www.mscd.edu.

PIKES PEAK COMMUNITY COLLEGE

Culinary Institute of Colorado Springs

Colorado Springs, Colorado

GENERAL INFORMATION

Public, coeducational, two-year college. Urban campus. Founded in 1968. Accredited by North Central Association of Colleges and Schools.

PROGRAM INFORMATION

Offered since 1986. Accredited by American Culinary Federation Accrediting Commission. National Restaurant Association Educational Foundation ManageFirst certificates available. Program calendar is divided into semesters. 1-year certificate in food service management. 1-year certificate in culinary arts. 1-year certificate in baking. 2-year associate degree in baking pastry arts. 2-year associate degree in culinary arts.

PROGRAM AFFILIATION

American Culinary Federation; National Restaurant Association; National Restaurant Association Educational Foundation.

AREAS OF STUDY

Baking; beverage management; buffet catering; confectionery show pieces; controlling costs in food service; convenience cookery; culinary French; culinary skill development; food preparation; food purchasing; food service communication; food service math; garde-manger; international cuisine; introduction to food service; kitchen management; management and human resources; meal planning; meat cutting; meat fabrication; menu and facilities design; nutrition; nutrition and food service; patisserie; restaurant opportunities; sanitation; saucier; seafood processing; soup, stock, sauce, and starch production; wines and spirits.

FACILITIES

Bake shop; bakery; catering service; classroom; coffee shop; 2 computer laboratories; demonstration laboratory; food production kitchen; laboratory; learning resource center; lecture room; library; 2 snack shops; student lounge; teaching kitchen.

STUDENT PROFILE

350 total: 150 full-time; 200 part-time. 150 are under 25 years old; 150 are between 25 and 44 years old; 50 are over 44 years old.

FACULTY

12 total: 3 full-time; 9 part-time. 7 are industry professionals. Prominent faculty: Robert Hudson, CEC, CCE; Richard Carpenter, CEPC; Michael Paradiso; Darrin Bristol, CEC. Faculty-student ratio: 1:17 lab; 1:24 lecture.

PROMINENT ALUMNI AND CURRENT AFFILIATION

Jacque Hamilton, CEC, United States Olympic Training Center; Domonic Tardy, Venetian Hotel, Las Vegas; Alania Miranda, Tulalip Resort and Casino, WA.

SPECIAL PROGRAMS

Culinary competitions, one-semester paid internship, guest speakers for local organizations.

Pikes Peak Community College *(continued)*

TYPICAL EXPENSES

In-state tuition: $831.30 per semester for degree; $831.30 per semester for certificate full-time, $100.60 per credit hour part-time. Out-of-state tuition: $355.95 per credit hour part-time. Program-related fee includes $100 for lab course.

FINANCIAL AID

In 2006, 15 scholarships were awarded (average award was $1500). Employment placement assistance is available. Employment opportunities within the program are available.

HOUSING

Average off-campus housing cost per month: $400–$800.

APPLICATION INFORMATION

Students may begin participation in January, June, and August. Applications are accepted continuously. In 2006, 150 applied. Applicants must interview; submit a formal application and take placement test.

CONTACT

Rob Hudson, Department Chair, Culinary Institute of Colorado Springs, 5675 South Academy Boulevard, Colorado Springs, CO 80906. Telephone: 719-502-3193. Fax: 719-502-3301. E-mail: rob.hudson@ppcc.edu. World Wide Web: http://www.ppcc.edu/.

SCHOOL OF NATURAL COOKERY

Boulder, Colorado

GENERAL INFORMATION

Private, coeducational, culinary institute. Small-town setting. Founded in 1983.

PROGRAM INFORMATION

Offered since 1983. Accredited by Colorado Department of Higher Education, Division of Private Occupational Schools. Program calendar is divided into semesters. 12-month certificate in teacher training. 4-month certificate in personal chef training.

AREAS OF STUDY

Baking; business plan development; controlling costs in food service; convenience cookery; culinary skill development; energetic nutrition; food preparation; food purchasing; food service communication; food service math; gardening; international cuisine; introduction to food service; kitchen management; management and human resources; meal planning; menu and facilities design; nutrition; nutrition and food service; performance dinners; personal chef repertoire; sanitation; soup, stock, sauce, and starch production; vegan gastronomy.

FACILITIES

Food production kitchen; garden; gourmet dining room; laboratory; library; student lounge; teaching kitchen.

STUDENT PROFILE

8 full-time. 2 are under 25 years old; 5 are between 25 and 44 years old; 1 is over 44 years old.

FACULTY

5 total: 2 full-time; 3 part-time. 4 are industry professionals; 1 is a culinary-certified teacher. Prominent faculty: Joanne Saltzman; Susan Jane Cheney; Michael Thibodeaux; Maia Cunningham. Faculty-student ratio: 1:10 lecture; 1:5 lab.

PROMINENT ALUMNI AND CURRENT AFFILIATION

Rachael Kelsey, Leaf Restaurant.

SPECIAL PROGRAMS

Internships for qualified graduates.

TYPICAL EXPENSES

Application fee: $75. Tuition: $8800 per semester. Program-related fee includes $5500 for supplies, books, uniforms (included in total program cost for Personal Chef Training-$11,200 tuition.

FINANCIAL AID

Program-specific awards include financial aid loan program for qualified applicants, work-study assistance.

HOUSING

Average off-campus housing cost per month: $400–$600.

APPLICATION INFORMATION

Students may begin participation in January and July. Application deadline for fall is April 30. Application deadline for spring is October 30. In 2006, 20 applied; 8 were accepted. Applicants must interview; submit a formal application, an essay, and letters of reference.

CONTACT

Student Admissions, PO Box 19466, Boulder, CO 80308. Telephone: 303-444-8068. E-mail: info@naturalcookery.com. World Wide Web: http://www.naturalcookery.com.

CONNECTICUT

BRIARWOOD COLLEGE

Southington, Connecticut

GENERAL INFORMATION
Private, coeducational, two-year college. Rural campus. Founded in 1966. Accredited by New England Association of Schools and Colleges.

PROGRAM INFORMATION
Offered since 1986. Program calendar is divided into semesters. 2-year associate degree in hotel/restaurant management.

PROGRAM AFFILIATION
Connecticut Restaurant Association; Council on Hotel, Restaurant, and Institutional Education; National Restaurant Association; National Restaurant Association Educational Foundation.

AREAS OF STUDY
Beverage management; food preparation; food purchasing; international cuisine; restaurant opportunities; sanitation.

FACILITIES
5 catering services; learning resource center; 4 lecture rooms; library; student lounge.

TYPICAL STUDENT PROFILE
13 total: 10 full-time; 3 part-time. 13 are under 25 years old.

FINANCIAL AID
Employment placement assistance is available. Employment opportunities within the program are available.

HOUSING
Apartment-style housing available.

APPLICATION INFORMATION
Students may begin participation in January and September. Applications are accepted continuously. Applicants must submit a formal application.

CONTACT
Director of Admissions, 2279 Mount Vernon Road, Southington, CT 06489. Telephone: 860-628-4751. Fax: 860-628-6444. World Wide Web: http://www.briarwood.edu.

CENTER FOR CULINARY ARTS

Culinary Arts

Cromwell, Connecticut

GENERAL INFORMATION
Private, coeducational, culinary institute. Founded in 1997. Accredited by Accrediting Commission of Career Schools and Colleges of Technology.

PROGRAM INFORMATION
Accredited by American Culinary Federation Accrediting Commission. 15-month diploma in culinary arts.

PROGRAM AFFILIATION
American Culinary Federation.

FACILITIES
3 teaching kitchens.

APPLICATION INFORMATION
Applicants must interview; submit a formal application.

CONTACT
Admissions Department, Culinary Arts, 106 Sebethe Drive, Cromwell, CT 06416. Telephone: 860-613-3350. Fax: 860-613-3353. World Wide Web: http://www.lincolnedu.com/campus/cromwell-ct.

CENTER FOR CULINARY ARTS

Shelton, Connecticut

GENERAL INFORMATION
Accredited by Accrediting Commission of Career Schools and Colleges of Technology.

PROGRAM INFORMATION
Diploma in culinary arts.

CONTACT
Admissions Department, 8 Progress Drive, Shelton, CT 06484. Telephone: 203-929-0592. World Wide Web: http://www.lincolnedu.com/campus/shelton-ct.

CONNECTICUT CULINARY INSTITUTE

Advanced Culinary Arts Program

Hartford, Connecticut

GENERAL INFORMATION
Private, coeducational, culinary institute. Suburban campus. Founded in 1987. Accredited by Accrediting Commission of Career Schools and Colleges of Technology.

PROGRAM INFORMATION
Offered since 1987. Program calendar is divided into quarters, year-round. 15-month diploma in advanced culinary arts. 35-week diploma in professional pastry and baking. 60-week diploma in advanced Italian culinary arts.

PROGRAM AFFILIATION
American Culinary Federation.

SPECIAL PROGRAMS
6-month paid externship, hands-on learning in on-site café, field trips to restaurants and casinos.

FINANCIAL AID
Employment placement assistance is available. Employment opportunities within the program are available.

APPLICATION INFORMATION
Students may begin participation in February, May, August, and November. Application deadline for 30 days prior to start. Applicants must interview; submit a formal application; achieve satisfactory score in school's pre-enrollment test of verbal and quantitative skills.

CONTACT
Admissions Department, Advanced Culinary Arts Program, 85 Sigourney Street, Hartford, CT 06105. Telephone: 800-762-4337. Fax: 860-676-0679. E-mail: admissions@ctculinary.com. World Wide Web: http://www.ctculinary.edu.

CONNECTICUT CULINARY INSTITUTE-SUFFIELD

Suffield, Connecticut

GENERAL INFORMATION
Private, coeducational, culinary institute.

PROGRAM INFORMATION
Accredited by American Culinary Federation Accrediting Commission. Program calendar is divided into quarters, year-round. 15-month diploma in advanced culinary arts. 35-week diploma in professional pastry and baking. 60-week diploma in advanced Italian culinary arts.

PROGRAM AFFILIATION
American Culinary Federation.

SPECIAL PROGRAMS
Paid externships, field trips to restaurants and casinos.

FINANCIAL AID
Employment placement assistance is available. Employment opportunities within the program are available.

APPLICATION INFORMATION
Students may begin participation in February, May, August, and November. Application deadline for 30 days prior to start. Applicants must interview; submit a formal application; achieve satisfactory score in school's pre-enrollment test of verbal and quantitative skills.

CONTACT
Admissions Office, 1760 Mapleton Avenue, Suffield, CT 06078. Telephone: 866-672-4337. E-mail: suffieldinfo@ctculinary.com.

GATEWAY COMMUNITY COLLEGE

Hospitality Management

New Haven, Connecticut

GENERAL INFORMATION
Public, coeducational, two-year college. Urban campus. Founded in 1968. Accredited by New England Association of Schools and Colleges.

PROGRAM INFORMATION
Offered since 1985. Accredited by Council on Hotel, Restaurant and Institutional Education. Program calendar is divided into semesters. 1-year certificate in culinary arts. 2-year associate degree in hotel management. 2-year associate degree in foodservice management.

PROGRAM AFFILIATION
Council on Hotel, Restaurant, and Institutional Education; Hospitality Sales and Marketing Association International.

AREAS OF STUDY
Baking; beverage management; buffet catering; confectionery show pieces; controlling costs in food service; convenience cookery; culinary skill development; food preparation; food purchasing; food service math; international cuisine; introduction to food service; kitchen management; management and human resources; meal planning; nutrition; nutrition and food service; restaurant opportunities; sanitation; seafood processing; soup, stock, sauce, and starch production; wines and spirits.

FACILITIES
Bake shop; 2 cafeterias; 2 catering services; 4 computer laboratories; demonstration laboratory; 2 food production kitchens; gourmet dining room; laboratory; 2 libraries; public restaurant; 2 student lounges; teaching kitchen.

STUDENT PROFILE
160 total: 110 full-time; 50 part-time. 56 are under 25 years old; 56 are between 25 and 44 years old; 48 are over 44 years old.

FACULTY
7 total: 2 full-time; 5 part-time. 5 are industry professionals; 1 is a master chef; 1 is a master baker. Prominent faculty: Stephen Fries; Andrew V. Randi. Faculty-student ratio: 1:15.

PROMINENT ALUMNI AND CURRENT AFFILIATION
Debbie Mele, Omni New Haven Hotel at Yale.

SPECIAL PROGRAMS
One-day visit to the International Hotel/Restaurant show in New York City, internships.

TYPICAL EXPENSES
Application fee: $20. In-state tuition: $1414 per semester full-time (in district), $377.50 per 3 credit hours part-time. Out-of-state tuition: $4222 per semester full-time, $1122.50 per 3 credit hours part-time. Program-related fees include $100 for uniforms; $400 for textbooks; $62 for lab fee for each lab course.

FINANCIAL AID
In 2006, individual loans were awarded at $1500. Employment placement assistance is available. Employment opportunities within the program are available.

HOUSING
Average off-campus housing cost per month: $450.

APPLICATION INFORMATION
Students may begin participation in January and September. Application deadline for fall is September 6. Application deadline for spring is January 16. In 2006, 140 applied; 140 were accepted. Applicants must submit a formal application.

Gateway Community College *(continued)*

CONTACT

Stephen Fries, Coordinator, Hospitality Management, 60 Sargent Drive, New Haven, CT 06511-5918. Telephone: 203-285-2175. Fax: 203-285-2180. E-mail: sfries@gwcc.commnet.edu. World Wide Web: http://www.gwctc.commnet.edu.

INTERNATIONAL COLLEGE OF HOSPITALITY MANAGEMENT

Suffield, Connecticut

GENERAL INFORMATION

Private, coeducational, two-year college. Small-town setting. Founded in 1992. Accredited by New England Association of Schools and Colleges.

PROGRAM INFORMATION

Offered since 1992. Program calendar is divided into quarters. 1-year certificate in hospitality management. 2-year associate degree in culinary arts management. 2-year associate degree in hospitality management.

PROGRAM AFFILIATION

Council on Hotel, Restaurant, and Institutional Education; International Food Service Executives Association; James Beard Foundation, Inc.; National Restaurant Association; National Restaurant Association Educational Foundation.

AREAS OF STUDY

Baking; beverage management; controlling costs in food service; culinary French; culinary skill development; food preparation; food purchasing; food service communication; food service math; garde-manger; hospitality management; international cuisine; introduction to food service; kitchen management; management and human resources; meal planning; meat fabrication; menu and facilities design; nutrition; nutrition and food service; patisserie; restaurant opportunities; sanitation; saucier; soup, stock, sauce, and starch production; travel and tourism; wines and spirits.

FACILITIES

Bake shop; cafeteria; classroom; computer laboratory; demonstration laboratory; food production kitchen; garden; gourmet dining room; laboratory; learning resource center; lecture room; library; snack shop; student lounge; teaching kitchen.

STUDENT PROFILE

50 full-time. 45 are under 25 years old; 5 are between 25 and 44 years old.

FACULTY

24 total: 8 full-time; 16 part-time. 20 are industry professionals; 2 are culinary-certified teachers; 2 with a PhD and 1 with a J.D.. Prominent faculty: David Greeman, CEC; Leroy Baldwin, MA; Kenneth Zane, MBA; Rosemarie Leon, MS. Faculty-student ratio: 1:14.

SPECIAL PROGRAMS

One 6-month paid internship, two career days per year attended by 4- and 5-star properties.

TYPICAL EXPENSES

Application fee: $40. Tuition: $16,900 per 2 terms or 1 academic year full-time, $725 per credit part-time. Program-related fees include $875 for books, uniforms, technology; $450 for general fee.

FINANCIAL AID

In 2006, 40 scholarships were awarded. Program-specific awards include Presidential Scholarship ($2500). Employment placement assistance is available.

HOUSING

Coed housing available. Average on-campus housing cost per month: $500. Average off-campus housing cost per month: $800.

APPLICATION INFORMATION

Students may begin participation in February, April, August, and November. Applications are accepted continuously. Applicants must interview; submit a formal application, letters of reference, official high school transcript.

CONTACT

Ms. Jacqueline Ocholla, Admissions Coordinator, 1760 Mapleton Avenue, Suffield, CT 06078. Telephone: 860-668-3515. Fax: 860-668-7369. E-mail: admissions@ichm.edu. World Wide Web: http://www.ichm.edu.

NAUGATUCK VALLEY COMMUNITY COLLEGE

Hospitality Management Programs

Waterbury, Connecticut

GENERAL INFORMATION

Public, coeducational, two-year college. Urban campus. Founded in 1967. Accredited by New England Association of Schools and Colleges.

PROGRAM INFORMATION

Offered since 1982. Program calendar is divided into semesters. 1-semester certificate in dietary supervisor. 1-year certificate in culinary arts. 2-year associate degree in foodservice management. 2-year associate degree in hotel management.

PROGRAM AFFILIATION

American Wine Society; Council on Hotel, Restaurant, and Institutional Education; Institute of Food Technologists; National Restaurant Association; National Restaurant Association Educational Foundation.

AREAS OF STUDY

Buffet catering; controlling costs in food service; culinary skill development; food preparation; food purchasing; food service communication; food service math; garde-manger; international cuisine; introduction to food service; kitchen management; management and human resources; meal planning; menu and facilities design; nutrition; nutrition and food service; restaurant opportunities; sanitation; soup, stock, sauce, and starch production; wines and viniculture.

FACILITIES

Catering service; 2 classrooms; 6 computer laboratories; demonstration laboratory; food production kitchen; gourmet dining room; laboratory; learning resource center; library; student lounge; teaching kitchen; vineyard.

TYPICAL STUDENT PROFILE

115 total: 77 full-time; 38 part-time.

SPECIAL PROGRAMS

Cooperative education/work experience, international trips with student catering and sommelier clubs.

FINANCIAL AID

Employment placement assistance is available. Employment opportunities within the program are available.

APPLICATION INFORMATION

Students may begin participation in January, May, and September. Applications are accepted continuously. Applicants must submit a formal application, high school transcript, immunization record.

CONTACT

Director of Admissions, Hospitality Management Programs, 750 Chase Parkway, Business Division, Waterbury, CT 06708. Telephone: 203-596-8739. Fax: 203-596-8767. World Wide Web: http://www.nvctc.commnet.edu.

DELAWARE

DELAWARE STATE UNIVERSITY

Dover, Delaware

GENERAL INFORMATION

Public, coeducational, comprehensive institution. Suburban campus. Founded in 1891. Accredited by Middle States Association of Colleges and Schools.

PROGRAM INFORMATION

Offered since 1982. Accredited by Accreditation Commission for Programs in Hospitality Administration (ACPHA). National Restaurant Association Educational Foundation ManageFirst certificates available. Program calendar is divided into semesters. 4-year bachelor's degree in hospitality and tourism management.

PROGRAM AFFILIATION

Council on Hotel, Restaurant, and Institutional Education; National Restaurant Association; National Restaurant Association Educational Foundation; National Society for Minorities in Hospitality.

FACILITIES

Classroom; laboratory; public restaurant.

STUDENT PROFILE

56 total: 52 full-time; 4 part-time.

FACULTY

3 total: 1 full-time; 2 part-time. 1 is a master chef; 2 are certified food service executives. Prominent faculty: Dr. Cynthia R. Mayo; Dr. Clarice Thomas-Haysbert. Faculty-student ratio: 1:15.

PROMINENT ALUMNI AND CURRENT AFFILIATION

George Fhionile, Dover Downs Hotel and Casino; Shelly Dunkley, Dover Downs.

SPECIAL PROGRAMS

Paid internships, networking opportunities with hospitality/tourism industry.

TYPICAL EXPENSES

Application fee: $15. In-state tuition: $3956 per year full-time (in district), $154 per credit hour part-time. Out-of-state tuition: $8752 per year full-time, $346 per credit hour part-time. Program-related fee includes $200 for lab uniforms and supplies.

FINANCIAL AID

In 2006, individual scholarships were awarded at $1000. Program-specific awards include American Hotel and Lodging Association Award ($1000), NSMH award

Delaware State University *(continued)*

($1500), Hyatt, Delaware Lodging Association award ($1000). Employment placement assistance is available. Employment opportunities within the program are available.

HOUSING
Coed and apartment-style housing available.

APPLICATION INFORMATION
Students may begin participation in January and September. Application deadline for fall is June 1. Application deadline for spring is December 1. In 2006, 20 applied; 8 were accepted. Applicants must submit a formal application.

CONTACT
Dr. Cynthia Mayo, Program Director, 1200 North Dupont Highway, Dover, DE 19901. Telephone: 302-887-7992. Fax: 302-857-6983. E-mail: cmayo@dsc.edu. World Wide Web: http://www.desu.edu/som/hospitalityandtourism.php.

DELAWARE TECHNICAL AND COMMUNITY COLLEGE

Culinary Arts Technology

Dover, Delaware

GENERAL INFORMATION
Public, coeducational, two-year college. Suburban campus. Founded in 1967. Accredited by Middle States Association of Colleges and Schools.

PROGRAM INFORMATION
Offered since 1993. Program calendar is divided into semesters. 2-year associate degree in culinary arts.

PROGRAM AFFILIATION
American Culinary Federation; National Restaurant Association; National Restaurant Association Educational Foundation.

FACILITIES
Bake shop; cafeteria; catering service; classroom; computer laboratory; demonstration laboratory; food production kitchen; laboratory; library; teaching kitchen.

FACULTY
5 total: 1 full-time; 4 part-time. 1 is a culinary-certified teacher. Prominent faculty: Ed Hennessy, CEC. Faculty-student ratio: 1:15.

TYPICAL EXPENSES
Application fee: $15. In-state tuition: $1035 per semester full-time (in district), $86.25 per credit hour part-time. Out-of-state tuition: $2587.80 per semester full-time, $215.65 per credit hour part-time.

FINANCIAL AID
In 2006, 2 scholarships were awarded (average award was $1000). Employment placement assistance is available. Employment opportunities within the program are available.

APPLICATION INFORMATION
Students may begin participation in January and August. Applications are accepted continuously.

CONTACT
Ed Hennessy, Chair, Culinary Arts, Culinary Arts Technology, 100 Campus Drive, Dover, DE 19904. Telephone: 302-857-1706. Fax: 302-857-1798. E-mail: hennessy@dtcc.edu. World Wide Web: http://www.dtcc.edu.

DELAWARE TECHNICAL AND COMMUNITY COLLEGE

Culinary Arts/Food Service Management

Newark, Delaware

GENERAL INFORMATION
Public, coeducational, two-year college. Suburban campus. Founded in 1967. Accredited by Middle States Association of Colleges and Schools.

PROGRAM INFORMATION
Offered since 1993. Accredited by American Culinary Federation Accrediting Commission. National Restaurant Association Educational Foundation ManageFirst certificates available. Program calendar is divided into semesters. 1-year diploma in food service management. 2-year associate degree in culinary arts. 2-year associate degree in food service management.

PROGRAM AFFILIATION
American Culinary Federation; National Restaurant Association; National Restaurant Association Educational Foundation.

AREAS OF STUDY
Baking; beverage management; buffet catering; controlling costs in food service; convenience cookery; culinary skill development; food preparation; food purchasing; food service communication; food service math; garde-manger; international cuisine; introduction to food service; kitchen management; management and human resources; meal planning; meat cutting; meat

fabrication; menu and facilities design; nutrition; nutrition and food service; patisserie; restaurant opportunities; sanitation; saucier; seafood processing; soup, stock, sauce, and starch production.

FACILITIES
Cafeteria; 10 classrooms; 20 computer laboratories; food production kitchen; gourmet dining room; learning resource center; lecture room; library; student lounge; teaching kitchen.

STUDENT PROFILE
125 total: 75 full-time; 50 part-time.

FACULTY
6 total: 3 full-time; 3 part-time. 5 are industry professionals; 1 is a culinary-certified teacher. Prominent faculty: David Nolker, CCE; Thomas Howell, CEC; Ron Leounes; Andrea Brandli. Faculty-student ratio: 1:12.

TYPICAL EXPENSES
Application fee: $10. In-state tuition: $1086 per semester full-time (in district), $90.50 per credit part-time. Out-of-state tuition: $2715 per semester full-time, $226.25 per credit part-time. Program-related fees include $4.50 for materials; $65 for lab fees (per credit hour).

FINANCIAL AID
In 2006, 3 scholarships were awarded. Employment placement assistance is available. Employment opportunities within the program are available.

APPLICATION INFORMATION
Students may begin participation in January, June, and August. Application deadline for fall is April 15. Application deadline for spring is November 15. In 2006, 53 applied; 24 were accepted. Applicants must submit a formal application and letters of reference.

CONTACT
Admission Department, Culinary Arts/Food Service Management, 400 Christiana-Stanton Road, Newark, DE 19713-2197. Telephone: 302-454-3954. Fax: 302-368-6620. E-mail: dnolker@dtcc.edu. World Wide Web: http://www.dtcc.edu/stanton-wilmington/.

UNIVERSITY OF DELAWARE

Hotel, Restaurant, and Institutional Management
Newark, Delaware

GENERAL INFORMATION
Public, coeducational, university. Urban campus. Founded in 1743. Accredited by Middle States Association of Colleges and Schools.

PROGRAM INFORMATION
Offered since 1988. Program calendar is divided into semesters. 2-year master's degree in hospitality information management. 4-year bachelor's degree in hotel, restaurant, and institutional management.

PROGRAM AFFILIATION
Council on Hotel, Restaurant, and Institutional Education.

AREAS OF STUDY
Beverage management; culinary skill development; food preparation; food purchasing; food service communication; introduction to food service; management and human resources; meal planning; menu and facilities design; restaurant opportunities.

FACILITIES
Gourmet dining room; public restaurant; hotel.

STUDENT PROFILE
400 full-time.

FACULTY
18 total: 14 full-time; 4 part-time. Faculty-student ratio: 1:20.

TYPICAL EXPENSES
In-state tuition: $5577 per year. Out-of-state tuition: $16,060 per year.

FINANCIAL AID
Employment placement assistance is available. Employment opportunities within the program are available.

HOUSING
Coed and single-sex housing available.

APPLICATION INFORMATION
Students may begin participation in February and August. Application deadline for fall is January 15. Application deadline for spring is November 15. Applicants must submit a formal application.

CONTACT
Dr. Robert R. Nelson, Chair, Hotel, Restaurant, and Institutional Management, 14 West Main Street, Raub Hall, Newark, DE 19716. Telephone: 302-831-6077. Fax: 302-831-6395. E-mail: hrim-dept@udel.edu. World Wide Web: http://www.udel.edu/HRIM.

DISTRICT OF COLUMBIA

HOWARD UNIVERSITY

Center for Hospitality Management Education

Washington, District of Columbia

GENERAL INFORMATION
Private, coeducational, university. Urban campus. Founded in 1867. Accredited by Middle States Association of Colleges and Schools.

PROGRAM INFORMATION
Offered since 1970. Program calendar is divided into semesters. 4-year bachelor's degree in hospitality management.

AREAS OF STUDY
Bed & Breakfast; catering; food service; Individual Entrepreneur Options; lodging; meeting and event planning.

FACILITIES
Classroom; computer laboratory; learning resource center; lecture room; library; student lounge.

STUDENT PROFILE
50 total: 48 full-time; 2 part-time. 45 are under 25 years old; 5 are between 25 and 44 years old.

FACULTY
16 total: 16 full-time. Prominent faculty: Charles Murphy; Gwynette Lacy; Gadis Norrell; Subodh P. Kulkami. Faculty-student ratio: 1:3.

SPECIAL PROGRAMS
Internships, field trips, theoretical experiences.

TYPICAL EXPENSES
Application fee: $45. Tuition: $13,215 per year full-time, $551 per credit hour part-time.

FINANCIAL AID
Program-specific awards include corporate support. Employment placement assistance is available. Employment opportunities within the program are available.

HOUSING
Coed and apartment-style housing available. Average on-campus housing cost per month: $400. Average off-campus housing cost per month: $750.

APPLICATION INFORMATION
Students may begin participation in January and August. Application deadline for fall is March 1. Application deadline for spring is November 1. Application deadline for summer session is April 1. Applicants must submit a formal application and letters of recommendation (helpful).

CONTACT
Ms. Linda Sanders-Hawkins, Director, Admissions, Center for Hospitality Management Education, 2400 Sixth Street, NW, Administration Building, Washington, DC 20059. Telephone: 202-806-1535. Fax: 202-806-4465. E-mail: admission@howard.edu. World Wide Web: http://www.bschool.howard.edu/Programs/undergradprograms/management/management.htm.

FLORIDA

THE ART INSTITUTE OF FORT LAUDERDALE

The International Culinary School at The Art Institute of Fort Lauderdale

Fort Lauderdale, Florida

GENERAL INFORMATION
Private, coeducational institution.

PROGRAM INFORMATION
Associate degree in Baking and Pastry. Associate degree in Culinary Arts. Bachelor's degree in Culinary Management. Diploma in Art of Cooking.

CONTACT
Office of Admissions, The International Culinary School at The Art Institute of Fort Lauderdale, 1799 S.E. 17th Street, Fort Lauderdale, FL 33316-3013. Telephone: 954-463-3000. World Wide Web: http://www.artinstitutes.edu/fortlauderdale/.

See color display following page 186.

THE ART INSTITUTE OF JACKSONVILLE

The International Culinary School at The Art Institute of Jacksonville

Jacksonville, Florida

GENERAL INFORMATION
Private, coeducational institution.

PROGRAM INFORMATION
Associate degree in Culinary Arts. Bachelor's degree in Culinary Management. Diploma in Culinary Arts: SKILLS.

CONTACT
Office of Admissions, The International Culinary School at The Art Institute of Jacksonville, 8775 Baypine Road, Jacksonville, FL 32256-8528. Telephone: 904-486-3186. World Wide Web: http://www.artinstitutes.edu/jacksonville/.
See color display following page 186.

THE ART INSTITUTE OF TAMPA

The International Culinary School at The Art Institute of Tampa

Tampa, Florida

GENERAL INFORMATION
Private, coeducational institution.

PROGRAM INFORMATION
Associate degree in Wines, Spirits and Beverage Management. Associate degree in Culinary Arts. Bachelor's degree in Culinary Management. Bachelor's degree in Food and Beverage Management. Diploma in Baking and Pastry.

CONTACT
Office of Admissions, The International Culinary School at The Art Institute of Tampa, Parkside at Tampa Bay Park, 4401 North Himes Avenue, Suite 150, Tampa, FL 33614-7086. Telephone: 813-873-2112. World Wide Web: http://www.artinstitutes.edu/tampa/.
See color display following page 186.

ATLANTIC TECHNICAL CENTER

Coconut Creek, Florida

GENERAL INFORMATION
Public, coeducational, technical institute. Suburban campus. Founded in 1970. Accredited by Council on Occupational Education.

PROGRAM INFORMATION
Offered since 1970. Accredited by American Culinary Federation Accrediting Commission. Program calendar is continuous. 1500-hour certificate in commercial foods/culinary arts.

PROGRAM AFFILIATION
American Culinary Federation; National Restaurant Association.

AREAS OF STUDY
Baking; beverage management; convenience cookery; culinary skill development; food preparation; food purchasing; food service math; garde-manger; international cuisine; introduction to food service; kitchen management; management and human resources; meal planning; meat cutting; nutrition; patisserie; restaurant opportunities; sanitation; saucier; seafood processing; soup, stock, sauce, and starch production; wines and spirits.

FACILITIES
Bakery; cafeteria; 3 classrooms; computer laboratory; demonstration laboratory; 2 food production kitchens; gourmet dining room; learning resource center; library; public restaurant.

TYPICAL STUDENT PROFILE
201 total: 96 full-time; 105 part-time.

SPECIAL PROGRAMS
Culinary competitions.

FINANCIAL AID
Employment placement assistance is available. Employment opportunities within the program are available.

APPLICATION INFORMATION
Students may begin participation in January, April, June, August, and November. Applications are accepted continuously. Applicants must interview and take Test of Adult Basic Education.

CONTACT
Director of Admissions, 4700 Coconut Creek Parkway, Coconut Creek, FL 33063. Telephone: 754-321-5100 Ext. 2046. Fax: 754-321-5134. World Wide Web: http://www.atlantictechcenter.com.

BETHUNE-COOKMAN UNIVERSITY

Hospitality Management Program

Daytona Beach, Florida

GENERAL INFORMATION
Private, coeducational, four-year college. Small-town setting. Founded in 1904. Accredited by Southern Association of Colleges and Schools.

Bethune-Cookman University *(continued)*

PROGRAM INFORMATION
Offered since 1982. Accredited by Council on Hotel, Restaurant and Institutional Education, Accreditation Commission for Programs in Hospitality Administration. Program calendar is divided into semesters. 4-year bachelor's degree in hospitality management (travel and tourism concentration). 4-year bachelor's degree in hospitality management (lodging concentration). 4-year bachelor's degree in hospitality management (food and beverage concentration). 4-year bachelor's degree in hospitality management.

PROGRAM AFFILIATION
American Culinary Federation; Council on Hotel, Restaurant, and Institutional Education; Multicultural Food Service and Hospitality Alliance; National Restaurant Association; National Restaurant Association Educational Foundation.

AREAS OF STUDY
Beverage management; culinary skill development; food preparation; kitchen management; management and human resources; menu and facilities design; nutrition and food service; restaurant opportunities.

FACILITIES
Classroom; computer laboratory; food production kitchen; gourmet dining room; learning resource center; 2 lecture rooms; teaching kitchen.

STUDENT PROFILE
73 total: 68 full-time; 5 part-time.

FACULTY
5 total: 3 full-time; 2 part-time. 2 are industry professionals; 1 is a culinary-certified teacher; 1 is a certified executive chef. Prominent faculty: Graham Bowcher, MIH, FBII; Ruth Smith, MIH. Faculty-student ratio: 1:15.

SPECIAL PROGRAMS
National Society for Minorities in Hospitality (NSMH), summer internships, regional and national conferences.

TYPICAL EXPENSES
Application fee: $25. Tuition: $5570 per semester full-time, $464 per credit hour part-time.

FINANCIAL AID
In 2006, 6 scholarships were awarded (average award was $1000). Program-specific awards include Ocean Waters, American Hotel and Lodging Association, Education Foundation, Marriott Scholarship Foundation. Employment placement assistance is available. Employment opportunities within the program are available.

HOUSING
Single-sex housing available. Average on-campus housing cost per month: $670. Average off-campus housing cost per month: $830.

APPLICATION INFORMATION
Students may begin participation in January, May, and August. Application deadline for fall is June 30. Application deadline for spring is November 30. Application deadline for summer is April 15. In 2006, 95 applied; 71 were accepted. Applicants must submit a formal application, letters of reference, high school transcript or GED, SAT or ACT scores.

CONTACT
Graham P. Bowcher, Interim Department Head, Hospitality Management Program, 640 Dr. Mary McLeod Bethune Boulevard, Daytona Beach, FL 32114-3099. Telephone: 386-481-2871. Fax: 386-481-2980. E-mail: bowcherg@cookman.edu. World Wide Web: http://www.cookman.edu.

CHARLOTTE TECHNICAL CENTER

Culinary Arts Program

Port Charlotte, Florida

GENERAL INFORMATION
Public, coeducational, technical college. Urban campus. Founded in 1980. Accredited by Council on Occupational Education.

PROGRAM INFORMATION
Offered since 1980. Program calendar is divided into quarters. 1500-hour certificate in commercial foods and culinary arts.

PROGRAM AFFILIATION
American Culinary Federation; International Foodservice Editorial Council.

AREAS OF STUDY
Baking; buffet catering; controlling costs in food service; convenience cookery; culinary French; culinary skill development; food preparation; food purchasing; food service communication; food service math; garde-manger; ice sculpture; international cuisine; introduction to food service; kitchen management; management and human resources; meal planning; menu and facilities design; nutrition; patisserie; restaurant opportunities; safety and first aid; sanitation; saucier; seafood processing; soup, stock, sauce, and starch production; wines and spirits.

FACILITIES

Bake shop; cafeteria; catering service; classroom;
computer laboratory; demonstration laboratory; food
production kitchen; gourmet dining room; laboratory;
learning resource center; library; public restaurant;
snack shop; teaching kitchen.

TYPICAL STUDENT PROFILE

61 total: 21 full-time; 40 part-time. 40 are under 25
years old; 13 are between 25 and 44 years old; 8 are
over 44 years old.

SPECIAL PROGRAMS

Annual tour and lecture at Ritz Carlton (Naples),
culinary competitions.

FINANCIAL AID

Program-specific awards include Florida Vocational
Tuition Assistant, Charlotte Technical Center
Scholarship. Employment placement assistance is
available. Employment opportunities within the
program are available.

APPLICATION INFORMATION

Students may begin participation in January, March,
July, and October. Application deadline for summer
term is July 30. Application deadline for fall term is
September 30. Application deadline for winter term is
December 30. Application deadline for spring term is
March 30. Applicants must be at least 16 years of age
and pass entrance exam.

CONTACT

Director of Admissions, Culinary Arts Program, 18150
Murdock Circle, Port Charlotte, FL 33948. Telephone:
941-255-7500 Ext. 115. Fax: 941-255-7509. World Wide
Web: http://charlottetechcenter.ccps.k12.fl.us/
CulinaryArts.cfm.

FIRST COAST TECHNICAL COLLEGE

School of Culinary Arts

St. Augustine, Florida

GENERAL INFORMATION

Public, coeducational, two-year college. Small-town
setting. Founded in 1969. Accredited by Council on
Occupational Education, Southern Association of
Colleges and Schools.

PROGRAM INFORMATION

Offered since 1969. Accredited by American Culinary
Federation Accrediting Commission. National
Restaurant Association Educational Foundation

ManageFirst certificates available. Program calendar is
divided into quarters. 18-month certificate in culinary
arts. 6-month certificate in baking and pastry.

PROGRAM AFFILIATION

American Culinary Federation; Association of Dining
Professionals; National Restaurant Association
Educational Foundation.

AREAS OF STUDY

Baking; buffet catering; convenience cookery; food
preparation; food purchasing; garde-manger;
international cuisine; introduction to food service;
kitchen management; management and human
resources; meat cutting; meat fabrication; nutrition and
food service; restaurant opportunities; sanitation;
seafood processing.

FACILITIES

Bake shop; cafeteria; catering service; 6 classrooms;
computer laboratory; demonstration laboratory; 3 food
production kitchens; gourmet dining room; public
restaurant.

STUDENT PROFILE

60 total: 50 full-time; 10 part-time.

FACULTY

8 total: 6 full-time; 2 part-time. Prominent faculty: Noel
Ridsdale, CEC, CCA, AAC; Anthony Lowman, CCC,
CCE; Daniel Lundberg; Sherry Gaynor, CEPC. Faculty-
student ratio: 1:15.

PROMINENT ALUMNI AND CURRENT AFFILIATION

Keith Zimmerman, Eurest Dining Services; Andrea
Estes, Personal Chef—A Chef's Cooking Studio; Thomas
O'Quinn, Kessler Resort Properties.

SPECIAL PROGRAMS

Culinary competitions (team)—ACF, culinary
competitions (individual)—Skills USA, Baking and
Pastry Competition (Individual)—Skills USA.

TYPICAL EXPENSES

Application fee: $25. Tuition: $7500 per program (7
quarters). Program-related fees include $125 for knife
kit; $20 for one time registration; $628.82 for Garde
Manger 1/Cold Pantry program; $76.05 for Quantity
Foods program, $85.99 for Bake Shop and Advanced
Arts program; $260.61 for Presenting Service program,
$34.65 for Advanced Skills (Ala Carte Buffet Catering)
program.

FINANCIAL AID

Program-specific awards include scholarships from
department (after 1 term in program). Employment
placement assistance is available. Employment
opportunities within the program are available.

First Coast Technical College *(continued)*

HOUSING
Average off-campus housing cost per month: $600–$650.

APPLICATION INFORMATION
Students may begin participation in January, March, August, and October. Applications are accepted continuously. In 2006, 60 applied; 55 were accepted. Applicants must submit a formal application.

CONTACT
Noel Ridsdale, Culinary Director, School of Culinary Arts, 2980 Collins Avenue, St. Augustine, FL 32084. Telephone: 904-829-1070. Fax: 904-829-1089. E-mail: ridsdan@fct1.org. World Wide Web: http://www.fcti.org.

FLORIDA CULINARY INSTITUTE A DIVISION OF LINCOLN COLLEGE OF TECHNOLOGY

West Palm Beach, Florida

GENERAL INFORMATION
Private, coeducational, culinary institute. Suburban campus. Founded in 1987. Accredited by Accrediting Council for Independent Colleges and Schools.

PROGRAM INFORMATION
Offered since 1987. Accredited by American Culinary Federation Accrediting Commission. Program calendar is divided into quarters. 12-month diploma in baking and pastry essentials. 12-month diploma in culinary essentials. 18-month associate degree in food and beverage management. 18-month associate degree in culinary arts. 18-month associate degree in international baking and pastry. 18-month diploma in food and beverage management. 18-month diploma in international baking and pastry. 18-month diploma in culinary arts. 36-month bachelor's degree in culinary management.

PROGRAM AFFILIATION
American Culinary Federation; Confrerie de la Chaine des Rotisseurs; Council on Hotel, Restaurant, and Institutional Education; International Association of Culinary Professionals; James Beard Foundation, Inc.; National Restaurant Association; National Restaurant Association Educational Foundation; Retailer's Bakery Association; U.S. Pastry Alliance.

AREAS OF STUDY
Baking; beverage management; buffet catering; confectionery show pieces; controlling costs in food service; convenience cookery; culinary French; culinary skill development; food preparation; food purchasing; food service communication; food service math; garde-manger; international cuisine; introduction to food service; kitchen management; management and human resources; meal planning; meat cutting; meat fabrication; menu and facilities design; nutrition; nutrition and food service; patisserie; restaurant opportunities; sanitation; saucier; seafood processing; soup, stock, sauce, and starch production; wines and spirits.

FACILITIES
2 bake shops; 9 classrooms; computer laboratory; garden; learning resource center; 2 lecture rooms; library; public restaurant; student lounge; 7 teaching kitchens.

STUDENT PROFILE
650 full-time.

FACULTY
17 total: 17 full-time. Prominent faculty: Manfred Schmidtke, CMC, CEPC; August Carreiro, CEC, CCE; Dan Birney CEC, CCE; Peter Bonet, CEPC, CMB.

SPECIAL PROGRAMS
Culinary competitions, field trips, junior chapter of ACF.

TYPICAL EXPENSES
Application fee: $25. Tuition: $30,000 per associate's degree.

FINANCIAL AID
In 2006, individual scholarships were awarded at $2000. Employment placement assistance is available.

HOUSING
Average off-campus housing cost per month: $350.

APPLICATION INFORMATION
Students may begin participation in January, February, April, July, August, October, and November. Applications are accepted continuously. Applicants must submit a formal application and either high school diploma/GED or take Test of Adult Basic Education.

CONTACT
Dave Conway, Associate Director of Admissions, 2410 Metrocentre Boulevard, West Palm Beach, FL 33407. Telephone: 561-842-8324. Fax: 561-842-9503. E-mail: info@floridaculinary.com. World Wide Web: http://www.floridaculinary.com.

Gulf Coast Community College

Culinary Management

Panama City, Florida

General Information
Public, coeducational, two-year college. Small-town setting. Founded in 1957. Accredited by Southern Association of Colleges and Schools.

Program Information
Offered since 1987. Accredited by American Culinary Federation Accrediting Commission. Program calendar is divided into semesters. 2-year associate degree in culinary management.

Program Affiliation
American Culinary Federation; Confrerie de la Chaine des Rotisseurs; Florida Restaurant Association; National Restaurant Association; Retailer's Bakery Association; The Bread Bakers Guild of America.

Areas of Study
Baking; beverage management; buffet catering; confectionery show pieces; controlling costs in food service; convenience cookery; culinary French; culinary skill development; food preparation; food purchasing; food service communication; food service math; garde-manger; international cuisine; introduction to food service; kitchen management; management and human resources; meal planning; meat cutting; meat fabrication; menu and facilities design; nutrition; nutrition and food service; patisserie; restaurant opportunities; sanitation; saucier; seafood processing; soup, stock, sauce, and starch production; wines and spirits.

Facilities
2 bake shops; 2 classrooms; 3 demonstration laboratories; 2 food production kitchens; gourmet dining room; learning resource center; lecture room; library; public restaurant; teaching kitchen.

Student Profile
139 total: 73 full-time; 66 part-time.

Faculty
8 total: 3 full-time; 5 part-time. 8 are culinary-certified teachers. Prominent faculty: Billy Redd, CEC; Paul Ashman. Faculty-student ratio: 1:16.

Prominent Alumni and Current Affiliation
Jimmy Patronio, Capt. Anderson's.

Special Programs
French exchange (8 weeks), American Culinary Federation competitions.

Typical Expenses
In-state tuition: $55.75 per credit hour. Out-of-state tuition: $223 per credit hour.

Financial Aid
In 2006, 8 scholarships were awarded (average award was $800). Employment placement assistance is available. Employment opportunities within the program are available.

Application Information
Students may begin participation in January and August. Applications are accepted continuously. Applicants must interview; submit a formal application, essay, academic transcripts; take placement test.

Contact
Richard Stewart, Coordinator, Culinary Management, 5230 West Highway 98, Panama City, FL 32401. Telephone: 850-872-3839. Fax: 850-747-3259. E-mail: rstewart@gulfcoast.edu. World Wide Web: http://culinary.gulfcoast.edu.

Hillsborough Community College

Hospitality Management

Tampa, Florida

General Information
Public, coeducational, two-year college. Urban campus. Founded in 1968. Accredited by Southern Association of Colleges and Schools.

Program Information
Offered since 1985. Accredited by American Culinary Federation Accrediting Commission. Program calendar is divided into semesters. 1-year certificate in food and beverage management. 2-year associate degree in dietetic technician. 2-year associate degree in hotel management. 2-year associate degree in restaurant management. 2-year associate degree in culinary arts.

Program Affiliation
American Culinary Federation; American Dietetic Association; International Food Service Executives Association; National Restaurant Association; National Restaurant Association Educational Foundation.

Areas of Study
Baking; beverage management; controlling costs in food service; culinary skill development; food preparation; food purchasing; food service math; garde-manger; international cuisine; introduction to food service; kitchen management; management and human

Hillsborough Community College *(continued)*

resources; meal planning; menu and facilities design; nutrition; nutrition and food service; sanitation; saucier; seafood processing; wines and spirits.

FACILITIES
Bake shop; cafeteria; 2 classrooms; computer laboratory; demonstration laboratory; food production kitchen; laboratory; learning resource center; lecture room; library; public restaurant; snack shop; student lounge; teaching kitchen.

STUDENT PROFILE
147 full-time. 91 are under 25 years old; 43 are between 25 and 44 years old; 13 are over 44 years old.

FACULTY
8 total: 2 full-time; 6 part-time. 5 are industry professionals; 3 are culinary-certified teachers. Prominent faculty: Frederick Jaeger; Stephen Gagnon. Faculty-student ratio: 1:12.

PROMINENT ALUMNI AND CURRENT AFFILIATION
Dr. Idel Suarez; Cheryl White; Jessie Jimenez.

SPECIAL PROGRAMS
2-year paid internship, culinary competitions.

TYPICAL EXPENSES
Application fee: $20. In-state tuition: $69.69 per credit hour full-time (in district), $66.69 per credit hour part-time. Out-of-state tuition: $248.95 per credit hour full-time, $248.95 per credit hour part-time. Program-related fees include $15 for food prep for managers class (FSS 1223); $15 for food specialties (baking) class (FSS 1246C); $15 for food specialties class (FSS 1248C); $15 for food specialties III class (FSS 1249C).

FINANCIAL AID
In 2006, 4 scholarships were awarded (average award was $500). Employment placement assistance is available. Employment opportunities within the program are available.

HOUSING
Apartment-style housing available.

APPLICATION INFORMATION
Students may begin participation in January, May, and August. Applications are accepted continuously. In 2006, 204 applied. Applicants must submit a formal application and high school diploma or GED.

CONTACT
Fred Jaeger, Program Manager, Hospitality Management, PO Box 30030, Tampa, FL 33630. Telephone: 813-253-7358. Fax: 813-253-7400. E-mail: fjaeger@hccfl.edu. World Wide Web: http://www.hccfl.edu.

INDIAN RIVER COMMUNITY COLLEGE

Culinary Institute of the Treasure Coast

Fort Pierce, Florida

GENERAL INFORMATION
Public, coeducational, two-year college. Small-town setting. Founded in 1960. Accredited by Southern Association of Colleges and Schools.

PROGRAM INFORMATION
Offered since 1994. Accredited by American Culinary Federation Accrediting Commission. Program calendar is divided into semesters. 2-year associate degree in restaurant management and culinary arts. 3-year certificate in commercial foods and culinary arts apprenticeship.

PROGRAM AFFILIATION
American Culinary Federation.

AREAS OF STUDY
Baking; buffet catering; controlling costs in food service; culinary French; food preparation; food purchasing; food service communication; food service math; garde-manger; introduction to food service; kitchen management; management and human resources; meal planning; meat cutting; meat fabrication; menu and facilities design; nutrition and food service; sanitation; saucier; seafood processing; soup, stock, sauce, and starch production.

FACILITIES
3 bake shops; 4 classrooms; 3 demonstration laboratories; 3 food production kitchens; 3 laboratories; learning resource center; 2 teaching kitchens.

STUDENT PROFILE
125 full-time. 62 are under 25 years old; 60 are between 25 and 44 years old; 3 are over 44 years old.

FACULTY
10 total: 3 full-time; 7 part-time. 1 is an industry professional; 1 is a master chef; 8 are culinary-certified teachers. Prominent faculty: Deborah Midkiff; William Soloman; Jack Fredericks. Faculty-student ratio: 1:15.

SPECIAL PROGRAMS
Tuition-free Apprenticeship Program, student trip to explore cultural cuisine.

TYPICAL EXPENSES
Application fee: $30. Tuition: $8400 per year. Program-related fee includes $600–$800 for tools, books, uniforms, and dues.

FINANCIAL AID
In 2006, 1 scholarship was awarded (award was $1000). Employment placement assistance is available. Employment opportunities within the program are available.

HOUSING
Apartment-style housing available. Average on-campus housing cost per month: $300. Average off-campus housing cost per month: $550.

APPLICATION INFORMATION
Students may begin participation in January, May, and August. Applications are accepted continuously. In 2006, 125 applied; 125 were accepted. Applicants must interview; submit a formal application, letters of reference, and an essay.

CONTACT
Lisa Velasquez, Academic Coordinator, Culinary Institute of the Treasure Coast, 3209 Virginia Avenue, Fort Pierce, FL 34981. Telephone: 772-226-2511. Fax: 772-226-2520. E-mail: lvelasqu@ircc.edu. World Wide Web: http://www.ircc.edu.

JOHNSON & WALES UNIVERSITY– NORTH MIAMI

College of Culinary Arts

North Miami, Florida

GENERAL INFORMATION
Private, coeducational, four-year college. Urban campus. Founded in 1992. Accredited by New England Association of Schools and Colleges.

PROGRAM INFORMATION
Offered since 1992. Program calendar is divided into quarters. Associate degree in baking and pastry arts. Associate degree in culinary arts. Bachelor's degree in culinary arts and food service management (joint degree with the College of Culinary Arts and The Hospitality College). Bachelor's degree in pastry arts and food service management (joint degree with the College of Culinary Arts and The Hospitality College). Bachelor's degree in restaurant, food and beverage management. Bachelor's degree in hotel and lodging management.

PROGRAM AFFILIATION
American Culinary Federation; American Dietetic Association; American Institute of Baking; American Institute of Wine & Food; Confrerie de la Chaine des Rotisseurs; Council on Hotel, Restaurant, and Institutional Education; Institute of Food Technologists; International Association of Culinary Professionals; International Food Service Executives Association; International Foodservice Editorial Council; James Beard Foundation, Inc.; National Restaurant Association; National Restaurant Association Educational Foundation; Oldways Preservation and Exchange Trust; Sommelier Society of America; Tasters Guild International.

AREAS OF STUDY
Baking; beverage management; buffet catering; confectionery show pieces; controlling costs in food service; convenience cookery; culinary French; culinary skill development; food preparation; food purchasing; food service communication; food service math; garde-manger; international cuisine; introduction to food service; kitchen management; management and human resources; meat cutting; meat fabrication; menu and facilities design; nutrition; nutrition and food service; patisserie; restaurant opportunities; sanitation; saucier; seafood processing; soup, stock, sauce, and starch production.

FACILITIES
Bake shop; cafeteria; 15 classrooms; 2 computer laboratories; 8 food production kitchens; 2 gourmet dining rooms; learning resource center; 6 lecture rooms; library; public restaurant; 2 student lounges; pastry shop; meatroom/butcher shop; beverage lab; garde-manger kitchen; 5 hot kitchens.

STUDENT PROFILE
975 total: 902 full-time; 73 part-time. 799 are under 25 years old; 158 are between 25 and 44 years old; 18 are over 44 years old.

FACULTY
22 total: 22 full-time. Prominent faculty: Drue Brandenburg, MS, CEC, CCE; Patricia Wilson, PhD; Felicia Pritchett; Todd Tonova, PhD. Faculty-student ratio: 1:20.

SPECIAL PROGRAMS
3-month internship (every culinary student gets a real life, career building work experience through internship/co-op), ACF certification and one year membership for all completing associate degrees.

TYPICAL EXPENSES
Tuition: $20,478 per year. Program-related fees include $984 for general fee; $255 for orientation fee; $987 for optional weekend meal plan; $300 for room and board reservation deposit.

FINANCIAL AID
In 2006, 914 scholarships were awarded (average award was $3557.40); 438 loans were granted (average loan was $4014.80). Employment placement assistance is available. Employment opportunities within the program are available.

Johnson & Wales University–North Miami *(continued)*

HOUSING

Coed and apartment-style housing available. Average on-campus housing cost per month: $1000. Average off-campus housing cost per month: $950.

APPLICATION INFORMATION

Students may begin participation in March, June, July, September, and December. Applications are accepted continuously. In 2006, 1891 applied; 1446 were accepted. Applicants must submit a formal application and official transcript from high school or college.

CONTACT

Jeffrey Greenip, Director of Admissions, College of Culinary Arts, 170 NE 127th Street, North Miami, FL 33181. Telephone: 800-BEA-CHEF. Fax: 305-892-7020. E-mail: admissions@jwu.edu. World Wide Web: http://culinary.jwu.edu.

See color display following page 90.

KEISER UNIVERSITY

Melbourne, Florida

GENERAL INFORMATION

Private, coeducational, two-year college. Urban campus. Founded in 1989. Accredited by Southern Association of Colleges and Schools.

PROGRAM INFORMATION

Offered since 2004. Program calendar is 3 semesters per year. 20-month associate degree in culinary arts.

AREAS OF STUDY

Baking; food preparation; food purchasing; food service math; garde-manger; international cuisine; meal planning; meat cutting; meat fabrication; nutrition; sanitation; soup, stock, sauce, and starch production.

FACILITIES

Bake shop; 3 classrooms; 2 computer laboratories; 3 food production kitchens; gourmet dining room; learning resource center; library; student lounge; teaching kitchen.

STUDENT PROFILE

48 full-time. 15 are under 25 years old; 33 are between 25 and 44 years old.

FACULTY

4 total: 4 full-time. Prominent faculty: Marjory Erixson, CEC; Darren Durham, CEC; Deborah Lindsay, CC; Luis A. Ortiz, CEC.

SPECIAL PROGRAMS

ACF sanctioned culinary competitions.

TYPICAL EXPENSES

Application fee: $50. Tuition: $43,000 per degree.

FINANCIAL AID

In 2006, 45 scholarships were awarded (average award was $1000); 51 loans were granted (average loan was $6228). Employment placement assistance is available.

HOUSING

Average off-campus housing cost per month: $700.

APPLICATION INFORMATION

Students may begin participation in January, April, and August. In 2006, 20 applied; 10 were accepted.

CONTACT

Chef Luis A. Ortiz, Department Chair, Culinary Arts, 900 South Babcock Street, Orlando, FL 32901. Telephone: 321-409-4800. Fax: 321-765-3766. E-mail: lortiz@keiserschools.org.

See display on page 131.

KEISER UNIVERSITY

Center for Culinary Arts

Tallahassee, Florida

GENERAL INFORMATION

Private, coeducational institution. Urban campus. Founded in 1977. Accredited by Southern Association of Colleges and Schools.

PROGRAM INFORMATION

Offered since 1998. Accredited by American Culinary Federation Accrediting Commission. Program calendar is 3 semesters per year. 20-month associate degree in baking and pastry arts. 20-month associate degree in culinary arts.

PROGRAM AFFILIATION

American Culinary Federation; International Association of Culinary Professionals; National Restaurant Association; Women Chefs and Restaurateurs.

AREAS OF STUDY

Baking; confectionery show pieces; culinary French; culinary skill development; food preparation; food purchasing; food service communication; food service math; garde-manger; international cuisine; management and human resources; meat cutting; meat fabrication; menu and facilities design; nutrition; patisserie; sanitation; saucier; seafood processing; soup, stock, sauce, and starch production; wines and spirits.

FACILITIES

Bake shop; classroom; 3 food production kitchens; gourmet dining room.

Your Chef's Career Starts Here

Earn your degree in Culinary Arts and begin your dream career in this creative and dynamic field

Keiser University Center for Culinary Arts provides:
- Practical experience in fully-equipped kitchens, plus solid academics
- Hands – on training in a professional environment by faculty with extensive industry experience

Culinary Arts, Associate of Science Degree

The A.S. Degree in Culinary Arts program has a comprehensive curriculum that includes of food service production, food service sanitation, nutrition, stock and sauces, American regional cuisine, dining room management, introduction to baking & pastry, storeroom operations, meat cutting, international cuisine, and French cuisine.

Baking & Pastry Arts, Associate of Science Degree

The Associate of Science degree in Baking and Pastry Arts provides instruction in the art and science of the baking profession. Students in this program will use a variety of tools and equipment to produce items such as quick breads, yeast breads, cakes, frozen desserts, centerpieces, candies, cookies and various pastries. - *offered at Tallahassee campus*

MONTHLY CLASS STARTS
For more information contact admissions at:

Tallahassee, 850-906-9494
Melbourne, 321-409-4800
Sarasota, 941-907-3900
or visit our website at
www.KeiserUniversity.edu/Culinary

Keiser University *(continued)*

STUDENT PROFILE
175 full-time.

FACULTY
16 total: 11 full-time; 5 part-time. Prominent faculty: Kevin Keating, CEC, CCE; Harold Hilliard, CEC, CCE; Pam Manley, CC; Mark Cross, CMB. Faculty-student ratio: 1:14.

PROMINENT ALUMNI AND CURRENT AFFILIATION
Chris Windus, Blue Zoo, Walt Disney World Dolphin; David Stroffolino, Alberts Provence Restaurant; Matrell Hawkins.

SPECIAL PROGRAMS
4-month paid externship, culinary competitions.

TYPICAL EXPENSES
Application fee: $55. Tuition: $6228 per semester. Program-related fees include $400 for cutlery set; $200 for uniforms.

FINANCIAL AID
Employment placement assistance is available.

APPLICATION INFORMATION
Students may begin participation in January, March, May, July, September, and November. Applications are accepted continuously. Applicants must interview; submit a formal application and entrance evaluation.

CONTACT
Christy Mantzanas, Director of Admissions, Center for Culinary Arts, 1700 Halstead Boulevard, Tallahassee, FL 32309. Telephone: 850-906-9494. Fax: 850-906-9497. E-mail: cmantzanas@keiseruniversity.edu. World Wide Web: http://www.keiseruniversity.edu/culinary.

See display on page 131.

KEISER UNIVERSITY

Center for Culinary Arts

Sarasota, Florida

GENERAL INFORMATION
Private, coeducational, four-year college. Founded in 1977. Accredited by Southern Association of Colleges and Schools.

PROGRAM INFORMATION
Offered since 2006. Program calendar is 3 semesters per year. 28-month associate degree in culinary arts.

PROGRAM AFFILIATION
American Culinary Federation; National Restaurant Association; National Restaurant Association Educational Foundation.

AREAS OF STUDY
Baking; controlling costs in food service; culinary French; culinary skill development; food preparation; food purchasing; garde-manger; international cuisine; introduction to food service; kitchen management; meal planning; meat cutting; meat fabrication; menu and facilities design; nutrition and food service; patisserie; sanitation; saucier; soup, stock, sauce, and starch production.

FACILITIES
Bake shop; 3 classrooms; 2 computer laboratories; 5 demonstration laboratories; 3 food production kitchens; gourmet dining room; 3 lecture rooms; library; student lounge.

STUDENT PROFILE
68 full-time.

FACULTY
6 total: 5 full-time; 1 part-time. Faculty-student ratio: 1:12.

SPECIAL PROGRAMS
4-month paid externship, culinary competitions.

TYPICAL EXPENSES
Application fee: $55. Program-related fee includes $145 for registration fee.

FINANCIAL AID
Employment placement assistance is available.

APPLICATION INFORMATION
Students may begin participation in January, February, March, April, May, June, July, August, September, October, and November. Applications are accepted continuously. Applicants must interview; submit a formal application, high school diploma or GED, entrance evaluation, and SAT/ACT scores.

CONTACT
Director of Admissions, Center for Culinary Arts, Admissions Department, 6151 Lake Osprey Drive, Sarasota, FL 34240. Telephone: 866-534-7372. Fax: 941-907-2016. E-mail: mimiller@keiseruniversity.edu. World Wide Web: http://www.keiseruniversity.edu/culinary.

See display on page 131.

LE CORDON BLEU COLLEGE OF CULINARY ARTS

Miramar, Florida

GENERAL INFORMATION
Coeducational, culinary institute.

PROGRAM INFORMATION
Associate degree in Le Cordon Bleu Culinary Arts. Diploma in Le Cordon Bleu Patisserie and Baking.

SPECIAL PROGRAMS
Externships.

FINANCIAL AID
Employment placement assistance is available.

APPLICATION INFORMATION
Applications are accepted continuously. Applicants must interview; submit a formal application and high school diploma or equivalent.

CONTACT
Admissions Office, 3221 Enterprise Way, Miramar, FL 33025. Telephone: 888-569-3222. World Wide Web: http://www.miamiculinary.com.

MANATEE TECHNICAL INSTITUTE

Commercial Foods and Culinary Arts

Bradenton, Florida

GENERAL INFORMATION
Public, coeducational, technical institute. Suburban campus. Founded in 1961. Accredited by Council on Occupational Education, Southern Association of Colleges and Schools.

PROGRAM INFORMATION
Offered since 1981. Accredited by American Culinary Federation Accrediting Commission. National Restaurant Association Educational Foundation ManageFirst certificates available. Program calendar is divided into quarters. 1440-hour certificate in commercial foods and culinary arts.

PROGRAM AFFILIATION
American Culinary Federation; National Restaurant Association; National Restaurant Association Educational Foundation; Retail Bakers of America.

AREAS OF STUDY
Baking; buffet catering; controlling costs in food service; convenience cookery; culinary French; culinary skill development; food preparation; food purchasing; food service communication; food service math; garde-manger; international cuisine; introduction to food service; kitchen management; meal planning; meat cutting; meat fabrication; menu and facilities design; nutrition; nutrition and food service; patisserie; restaurant opportunities; sanitation; saucier; seafood processing; soup, stock, sauce, and starch production.

FACILITIES
Bake shop; cafeteria; catering service; classroom; computer laboratory; demonstration laboratory; food production kitchen; learning resource center; 2 lecture rooms; library; 2 teaching kitchens.

STUDENT PROFILE
19 total: 17 full-time; 2 part-time.

FACULTY
4 total: 2 full-time; 2 part-time. 2 are industry professionals; 2 are culinary-certified teachers. Prominent faculty: Larry Colpitts, CEC; Suzette Marquette, CCC. Faculty-student ratio: 1:10.

PROMINENT ALUMNI AND CURRENT AFFILIATION
Dana Johnson, Pastry Chef, Long Boat Key Resort; Matt Schole, Ritz Carlton Hotel and Resort, Assistant Pastry Chef.

SPECIAL PROGRAMS
Culinary competition, Skills USA, ACF competitions, tours of various well-known kitchen operations, food irradiation facility.

TYPICAL EXPENSES
Application fee: $10. Tuition: $1891 per certificate. Program-related fees include $395 for lab fees; $72.12 for knife set; $87 for uniform.

FINANCIAL AID
In 2006, 3 scholarships were awarded (average award was $300). Program-specific awards include Kiwanis scholarship, culinary scholarship. Employment placement assistance is available. Employment opportunities within the program are available.

HOUSING
Average off-campus housing cost per month: $700.

APPLICATION INFORMATION
Students may begin participation in March, August, September, October, and December. In 2006, 30 applied; 25 were accepted. Applicants must interview, submit a formal application, and take the Test of Adult Basic Education.

CONTACT
Terrie Parrish, Counselor, Commercial Foods and Culinary Arts, 5603 34th Street, West, Bradenton, FL 34210. Telephone: 941-751-7900. World Wide Web: http://www.manateetechnicalinstitute.org/programs/career/culinary_arts.html.

NORTHWOOD UNIVERSITY, FLORIDA CAMPUS

Hotel, Restaurant, and Resort Management

West Palm Beach, Florida

GENERAL INFORMATION
Private, coeducational, four-year college. Urban campus. Founded in 1982. Accredited by North Central Association of Colleges and Schools.

PROGRAM INFORMATION
Offered since 1984. Program calendar is divided into quarters. 2-year associate degree in hotel, restaurant, resort management. 4-year bachelor's degree in hotel, restaurant, resort management.

PROGRAM AFFILIATION
Council on Hotel, Restaurant, and Institutional Education; National Restaurant Association; National Restaurant Association Educational Foundation; Palm Beach County Hotel and Lodging Association.

AREAS OF STUDY
Beverage management; food preparation; food purchasing; introduction to food service; management and human resources; menu and facilities design; restaurant opportunities; sanitation.

FACILITIES
Classroom; lecture room.

STUDENT PROFILE
47 full-time. 45 are under 25 years old; 2 are between 25 and 44 years old.

FACULTY
3 total: 1 full-time; 2 part-time. 2 are industry professionals. Prominent faculty: Dr. Janice Scarinci. Faculty-student ratio: 1:24.

SPECIAL PROGRAMS
400-hour paid internship, attendance at National Restaurant Association trade show in Chicago, participation in Palm Beach County Hotel and Lodging Association trade show and job fair.

TYPICAL EXPENSES
Tuition: $15,216 per year full-time, $330 per credit hour part-time. Program-related fee includes $25 for paper application fee, no fee to apply online.

FINANCIAL AID
In 2006, 8 scholarships were awarded (average award was $1000). Employment placement assistance is available. Employment opportunities within the program are available.

HOUSING
Single-sex housing available. Average on-campus housing cost per month: $430. Average off-campus housing cost per month: $1200.

APPLICATION INFORMATION
Students may begin participation in March, June, September, and December. Applications are accepted continuously. In 2006, 110 applied; 75 were accepted. Applicants must submit a formal application, official transcripts, SAT or ACT results.

CONTACT
Jack Letvinchuk, Director of Admissions, Hotel, Restaurant, and Resort Management, 2600 North Military Trail, West Palm Beach, FL 33409-2911. Telephone: 800-458-8325. Fax: 561-478-5500. E-mail: fladmit@northwood.edu. World Wide Web: http://www.northwood.edu.

NOTTER SCHOOL OF PASTRY ARTS

Orlando, Florida

GENERAL INFORMATION
Private, coeducational institution. Suburban campus. Founded in 1982.

PROGRAM INFORMATION
Offered since 1982. Accredited by American Culinary Federation Accrediting Commission. Program calendar is divided into weeks. 1-week certificate in cakes and desserts. 1-week certificate in wedding cake. 1-week certificate in advanced chocolate decoration. 1-week certificate in advanced sugar decoration. 1-week certificate in chocolate decoration. 1-week certificate in sugar blowing and pulling showplace class. 24-week diploma in European pastry and baking program.

AREAS OF STUDY
Confectionery show pieces; patisserie.

FACILITIES
Classroom; student lounge; teaching kitchen.

FACULTY
8 total: 8 full-time. 1 is a master chef; 6 are culinary-certified teachers. Prominent faculty: Chris Hanmes. Faculty-student ratio: 1:12.

FINANCIAL AID
Employment placement assistance is available. Employment opportunities within the program are available.

APPLICATION INFORMATION
Students may begin participation in January, February, March, April, May, June, July, August, September, October, and November.

CONTACT
Beverly Karshner, Owner, 8204 Crystal Clear Lane #1600, Orlando, FL 32809. Telephone: 407-240-9057. Fax: 407-240-9056. E-mail: info@notterschool.com. World Wide Web: http://www.notterschool.com/.

ORLANDO CULINARY ACADEMY
Orlando, Florida

GENERAL INFORMATION
Private, coeducational, culinary institute. Founded in 2002.

PROGRAM INFORMATION
Diploma in Le Cordon Bleu Hospitality and Restaurant Management. Diploma in Le Cordon Bleu Patisserie and Baking. 15-month associate degree in Le Cordon Bleu Culinary Arts.

FINANCIAL AID
Employment placement assistance is available.

APPLICATION INFORMATION
Applications are accepted continuously. Applicants must interview and have high school diploma or GED.

CONTACT
Director of Admissions, 8511 Commodity Circle, Suite 100, Orlando, FL 32819. Telephone: 888-793-3222. Fax: 407-888-4019. World Wide Web: http://www.orlandoculinary.com/.

PALM BEACH COMMUNITY COLLEGE
Hospitality Management
Lake Worth, Florida

GENERAL INFORMATION
Public, coeducational, two-year college. Urban campus. Founded in 1933. Accredited by Southern Association of Colleges and Schools.

PROGRAM INFORMATION
Program calendar is divided into semesters. 2-year associate degree in hospitality and tourism management.

PROGRAM AFFILIATION
American Hotel and Lodging Association.

AREAS OF STUDY
Beverage management; meal planning; menu and facilities design.

FACILITIES
Demonstration laboratory; food production kitchen; gourmet dining room; teaching kitchen.

STUDENT PROFILE
42 part-time.

FACULTY
6 total: 1 full-time; 5 part-time. Faculty-student ratio: 1:25.

TYPICAL EXPENSES
Application fee: $20. In-state tuition: $1596 per year full-time (in district), $66.50 per credit hour part-time. Out-of-state tuition: $5688 per year full-time, $237 per credit hour part-time. Tuition for international students: $237 per credit hour part-time.

HOUSING
Average off-campus housing cost per month: $1200.

APPLICATION INFORMATION
Students may begin participation in January, May, and August. Applications are accepted continuously.

CONTACT
Robin Johnson, Director of Outreach and Recruitment, Hospitality Management, 4200 Congress Avenue, Lake Worth, FL 33461-4796. Telephone: 561-868-3377. Fax: 561-868-3584. E-mail: johnsor@pbcc.edu. World Wide Web: http://www.pbcc.edu.

PENSACOLA JUNIOR COLLEGE
Hospitality and Tourism Management/Culinary Management
Pensacola, Florida

GENERAL INFORMATION
Public, coeducational, two-year college. Suburban campus. Founded in 1948. Accredited by Southern Association of Colleges and Schools.

PROGRAM INFORMATION
Offered since 1995. Accredited by American Culinary Federation Accrediting Commission. Program calendar is divided into semesters. 2-year associate degree in hospitality and tourism management. 2-year associate degree in culinary management.

PROGRAM AFFILIATION
American Culinary Federation; Council on Hotel, Restaurant, and Institutional Education.

Pensacola Junior College *(continued)*

AREAS OF STUDY

Baking; beverage management; buffet catering; confectionery show pieces; controlling costs in food service; culinary skill development; dining room management; food preparation; food purchasing; food service math; garde-manger; international cuisine; introduction to food service; kitchen management; management and human resources; meal planning; menu and facilities design; nutrition; patisserie; sanitation; saucier; soup, stock, sauce, and starch production.

FACILITIES

Bake shop; classroom; computer laboratory; food production kitchen; gourmet dining room; learning resource center; public restaurant; student lounge; teaching kitchen.

STUDENT PROFILE

62 full-time.

FACULTY

6 total: 4 full-time; 2 part-time. 2 are industry professionals; 4 are culinary-certified teachers. Faculty-student ratio: 1:14.

SPECIAL PROGRAMS

Mystery box competitions.

TYPICAL EXPENSES

Application fee: $30. In-state tuition: $65.87 per credit hour. Out-of-state tuition: $237.42 per credit hour. Program-related fees include $50 for lab fees (per class); $60 for uniforms.

FINANCIAL AID

Program-specific awards include private scholarships. Employment placement assistance is available. Employment opportunities within the program are available.

HOUSING

Average off-campus housing cost per month: $300.

APPLICATION INFORMATION

Students may begin participation in January, May, and August. Applications are accepted continuously. Applicants must submit a formal application.

CONTACT

Travis Herr, Professional Service Careers/Culinary, Hospitality and Tourism Management/Culinary Management, 1000 College Boulevard, Pensacola, FL 32504-8998. Telephone: 850-484-2506. Fax: 850-484-1543. E-mail: therr@pjc.edu. World Wide Web: http://www.pjc.edu.

PINELLAS TECHNICAL EDUCATION CENTER–CLEARWATER CAMPUS

Culinary Arts/Commercial Food

Clearwater, Florida

GENERAL INFORMATION

Public, coeducational, two-year college. Urban campus. Founded in 1969. Accredited by Council on Occupational Education.

PROGRAM INFORMATION

Offered since 1969. Accredited by American Culinary Federation Accrediting Commission. Program calendar is divided into quarters. 1500-hour certificate in culinary arts/commercial foods.

PROGRAM AFFILIATION

American Dietetic Association; Florida Restaurant Association; National Restaurant Association; National Restaurant Association Educational Foundation.

AREAS OF STUDY

Baking; buffet catering; convenience cookery; culinary skill development; food preparation; food purchasing; food service communication; food service math; garde-manger; international cuisine; introduction to food service; kitchen management; management and human resources; meal planning; meat fabrication; nutrition; nutrition and food service; sanitation; saucier; soup, stock, sauce, and starch production.

FACILITIES

Bake shop; bakery; cafeteria; catering service; 2 classrooms; computer laboratory; demonstration laboratory; 2 food production kitchens; gourmet dining room; 3 laboratories; learning resource center; lecture room; library; teaching kitchen.

TYPICAL STUDENT PROFILE

46 total: 28 full-time; 18 part-time.

SPECIAL PROGRAMS

Visits to industry, culinary competitions, field trips to food expositions.

FINANCIAL AID

Program-specific awards include American Culinary Federation scholarships, Andrew's Scholarship, Florida Restaurant Association scholarship. Employment placement assistance is available.

APPLICATION INFORMATION

Students may begin participation in January, April, August, and October. Applications are accepted continuously. Applicants must interview and submit a formal application.

CONTACT
Director of Admissions, Culinary Arts/Commercial Food, 6100 154th Avenue N, Clearwater, FL 33760. Telephone: 727-538-7167 Ext. 1140. Fax: 727-509-4246. World Wide Web: http://www.myptec.org/.

ST. THOMAS UNIVERSITY

Tourism and Hospitality Management

Miami Gardens, Florida

GENERAL INFORMATION
Private, coeducational, university. Urban campus. Founded in 1961. Accredited by Southern Association of Colleges and Schools.

PROGRAM INFORMATION
Program calendar is divided into semesters. 4-year bachelor's degree in tourism and hospitality management.

PROGRAM AFFILIATION
American Hotel and Lodging Association; Council on Hotel, Restaurant, and Institutional Education; Florida Restaurant Association; Greater Miami Conventions and Visitors Bureau; International Food Service Executives Association; International Society of Travel and Tourism Educators; National Restaurant Association.

AREAS OF STUDY
Beverage management; controlling costs in food service; convention, trade show and destination management; food preparation; food purchasing; introduction to food service; kitchen management; management and human resources; meal planning; menu and facilities design; restaurant opportunities; sanitation; sport tourism.

FACILITIES
Classroom; computer laboratory; garden; learning resource center; lecture room; library.

STUDENT PROFILE
32 total: 30 full-time; 2 part-time. 27 are under 25 years old; 5 are between 25 and 44 years old.

FACULTY
14 total: 10 full-time; 4 part-time. Prominent faculty: Paul-Michael Klein, MPS; Seok Ho Song, PhD; Jan Bell, EdD; Ted Abernethy, PhD. Faculty-student ratio: 1:15.

PROMINENT ALUMNI AND CURRENT AFFILIATION
Michael Basile, Marriott; Carol Ellis Cutler, Collier International; Gustaud Ustariz, Con Turismo.

SPECIAL PROGRAMS
Internships, experiential learning.

TYPICAL EXPENSES
Application fee: $40. Tuition: $19,680 per year full-time, $656 per credit part-time.

FINANCIAL AID
In 2006, 2 scholarships were awarded (average award was $9000). Program-specific awards include donor scholarships, PIT employment. Employment opportunities within the program are available.

HOUSING
Single-sex housing available.

APPLICATION INFORMATION
Students may begin participation in January and August. Applications are accepted continuously. In 2006, 24 applied. Applicants must submit a formal application, letters of reference, and an essay.

CONTACT
Andre Lightbourn, Director of Admissions, Tourism and Hospitality Management, 16401 NW 37th Avenue, Miami Gardens, FL 33054. Telephone: 305-628-6712. Fax: 305-628-6591. E-mail: alightbo@stu.edu. World Wide Web: http://www.stu.edu.

UNIVERSITY OF CENTRAL FLORIDA

Rosen College of Hospitality Management

Orlando, Florida

GENERAL INFORMATION
Public, coeducational, university. Suburban campus. Founded in 1963. Accredited by Southern Association of Colleges and Schools.

PROGRAM INFORMATION
Offered since 1983. Accredited by Council on Hotel, Restaurant and Institutional Education. Program calendar is divided into semesters. 2-year master's degree in hospitality management. 3-year doctoral degree in hospitality education. 4-year bachelor's degree in event management. 4-year bachelor's degree in restaurant management. 4-year bachelor's degree in hospitality management.

PROGRAM AFFILIATION
American Culinary Federation; Council on Hotel, Restaurant, and Institutional Education; National Restaurant Association; National Restaurant Association Educational Foundation.

University of Central Florida *(continued)*

AREAS OF STUDY
Beverage management; controlling costs in food service; food preparation; food purchasing; food service management; management and human resources; restaurant operations; restaurant opportunities; wines and spirits.

FACILITIES
Cafeteria; catering service; 23 classrooms; coffee shop; 3 computer laboratories; demonstration laboratory; 2 food production kitchens; gourmet dining room; lecture room; library; student lounge; teaching kitchen.

STUDENT PROFILE
2300 full-time. 2100 are under 25 years old; 200 are between 25 and 44 years old.

FACULTY
68 total: 46 full-time; 22 part-time. 20 are industry professionals; 2 are master chefs; 3 are culinary-certified teachers. Prominent faculty: Abraham Pizam, PhD; Stephen LeBruto, EdD, CPA, CHAE; William Fisher, PhD; Chris Muller, PhD. Faculty-student ratio: 1:16.

SPECIAL PROGRAMS
Semester study abroad in France, 3 semester cooperative work experience, distinguished lectures series.

TYPICAL EXPENSES
Application fee: $30. In-state tuition: $3324 per year full-time (in district), $118.72 per credit hour part-time. Out-of-state tuition: $16,579 per year full-time, $592.10 per credit hour part-time. Program-related fee includes $75 for laboratory fee (per semester).

FINANCIAL AID
In 2006, 100 scholarships were awarded (average award was $2500). Employment placement assistance is available. Employment opportunities within the program are available.

HOUSING
Coed and apartment-style housing available. Average on-campus housing cost per month: $660.

APPLICATION INFORMATION
Students may begin participation in January, May, June, and August. Application deadline for fall is May 1. Application deadline for spring is November 1. Application deadline for summer is March 1. Applicants must submit a formal application and SAT or ACT scores.

CONTACT
Robert Springall, Associate Director, Undergraduate Admissions, Rosen College of Hospitality Management, 9907 Universal Boulevard, Orlando, FL 32819.

Telephone: 407-903-8166. Fax: 407-903-8104. E-mail: rosenadmission@mail.ucf.edu. World Wide Web: http://www.hospitality.ucf.edu.

VALENCIA COMMUNITY COLLEGE

Culinary Management–Baking and Pastry Management

Orlando, Florida

GENERAL INFORMATION
Public, coeducational, two-year college. Urban campus. Founded in 1967. Accredited by Southern Association of Colleges and Schools.

PROGRAM INFORMATION
Offered since 1997. Program calendar is divided into semesters. 35-credit certificate in baking and pastry arts. 35-credit certificate in culinary arts. 64-credit associate degree in baking and pastry management. 64-credit associate degree in hospitality management. 64-credit associate degree in restaurant management. 64-credit associate degree in culinary management.

PROGRAM AFFILIATION
American Culinary Federation; Council on Hotel, Restaurant, and Institutional Education; Florida Restaurant Association; National Restaurant Association; National Restaurant Association Educational Foundation; The Bread Bakers Guild of America; Women Chefs and Restaurateurs.

AREAS OF STUDY
Baking; buffet catering; controlling costs in food service; convenience cookery; culinary French; culinary skill development; food preparation; food purchasing; food service communication; food service math; garde-manger; international cuisine; management and human resources; meal planning; meat cutting; meat fabrication; menu and facilities design; nutrition; nutrition and food service; patisserie; sanitation; saucier; seafood processing; soup, stock, sauce, and starch production; wines and spirits.

FACILITIES
Bakery; 6 classrooms; computer laboratory; 2 demonstration laboratories; food production kitchen; learning resource center; lecture room; library; teaching kitchen.

STUDENT PROFILE
530 total: 245 full-time; 285 part-time.

FACULTY

22 total: 2 full-time; 20 part-time. 20 are industry professionals; 3 are culinary-certified teachers. Prominent faculty: Pierre Pilloud, CEC, CHA; Marianne Hunnel, CEC; Steven Rujak, CPC; Kenneth Bourgoin, CEC. Faculty-student ratio: 1:24 lecture; 1:20 lab.

PROMINENT ALUMNI AND CURRENT AFFILIATION

Robert Young, Executive Chef, Marriott, Lake Mary, FL; Steven Richard, Executive Chef, Portabello Yacht Club, Lake Buena Vista, FL.

SPECIAL PROGRAMS

Participation in Florida Restaurant Association Southeast EXPO (assisting in culinary competitions), paid internship, participation in Walt Disney Food and Wine Festival at the Epcot Center.

TYPICAL EXPENSES

Application fee: $25. In-state tuition: $75 per credit. Out-of-state tuition: $250 per credit. Program-related fees include $100 for food cost (per lab course); $350 for knives, cutlery, and professional attire (chef coat, lab shoes, slacks).

FINANCIAL AID

In 2006, 1 scholarship was awarded (award was $709). Employment placement assistance is available. Employment opportunities within the program are available.

HOUSING

Average off-campus housing cost per month: $400.

APPLICATION INFORMATION

Students may begin participation in January, May, and August. Application deadline for fall is July 1. Application deadline for spring is November 1. Application deadline for summer is April 1. Applicants must submit a formal application and high school diploma or GED.

CONTACT

Pierre Pilloud, Program Director, Culinary Management–Baking and Pastry Management, PO Box 3028, Orlando, FL 32802-3028. Telephone: 407-532-1880. Fax: 407-582-1900. E-mail: ppilloud@valenciacc.edu. World Wide Web: http://www.valencia.cc.fl.us.

WEBBER INTERNATIONAL UNIVERSITY

Hospitality Business Management

Babson Park, Florida

GENERAL INFORMATION

Private, coeducational, comprehensive institution. Rural campus. Founded in 1927. Accredited by Southern Association of Colleges and Schools.

PROGRAM INFORMATION

Offered since 1972. Accredited by Council on Hotel, Restaurant and Institutional Education. National Restaurant Association Educational Foundation ManageFirst certificates available. Program calendar is divided into semesters. 2-year associate degree in hospitality business management. 4-year bachelor's degree in hospitality business management.

PROGRAM AFFILIATION

Council on Hotel, Restaurant, and Institutional Education; National Restaurant Association; National Restaurant Association Educational Foundation.

AREAS OF STUDY

Beverage management; controlling costs in food service; food purchasing; food service math; introduction to food service; kitchen management; management and human resources; meal planning; nutrition; restaurant opportunities.

FACILITIES

Cafeteria; 2 classrooms; 2 computer laboratories; food production kitchen; learning resource center; library; snack shop; student lounge.

STUDENT PROFILE

26 total: 25 full-time; 1 part-time. 25 are under 25 years old; 1 is between 25 and 44 years old.

FACULTY

2 total: 1 full-time; 1 part-time. 1 is an industry professional; 1 is a culinary-certified teacher. Prominent faculty: Ian David, CHA, AHMA, MSC, BSC. Faculty-student ratio: 1:20.

PROMINENT ALUMNI AND CURRENT AFFILIATION

Maria Chalmers, Disney Wilderness Resort; Cesar Solares, Hyatt, Miami, FL.

SPECIAL PROGRAMS

2 internship opportunities worldwide, trip to International Hotel and Lodging Show (New York), trip to National Restaurant Association Food Service Show (Chicago), field trip to Las Vegas.

Webber International University *(continued)*

TYPICAL EXPENSES
Application fee: $35. Tuition: $15,900 per year full-time, $200 per hour part-time.

FINANCIAL AID
Program-specific awards include Pro Start Scholarship-$2000 to graduate of high school culinary program who meets requirements, CFHLA Industry Scholarship-$1000. Employment placement assistance is available. Employment opportunities within the program are available.

HOUSING
Coed housing available. Average on-campus housing cost per month: $415. Average off-campus housing cost per month: $500.

APPLICATION INFORMATION
Students may begin participation in January, May, and September. Application deadline for fall is August 1. Application deadline for spring is December 1. Application deadline for summer is April 1. In 2006, 30 applied; 12 were accepted. Applicants must submit a formal application, letters of reference, an essay, SAT scores.

CONTACT
Ms. Julie Ragans, Director of Admissions, Hospitality Business Management, PO Box 96, Babson Park, FL 33827. Telephone: 800-741-1844. Fax: 863-638-1591. E-mail: admissions@webber.edu. World Wide Web: http://webber.edu.

GEORGIA

THE ART INSTITUTE OF ATLANTA

The International Culinary School at The Art Institute of Atlanta

Atlanta, Georgia

GENERAL INFORMATION
Private, coeducational institution.

PROGRAM INFORMATION
Associate degree in Wines, Spirits and Beverage Management. Associate degree in Culinary Arts. Bachelor's degree in Culinary Arts Management. Bachelor's degree in Food and Beverage Management. Diploma in Culinary Arts–Culinary Skills. Diploma in Culinary Arts–Baking and Pastry.

CONTACT
Office of Admissions, The International Culinary School at The Art Institute of Atlanta, 6600 Peachtree Dunwoody Road, NE, 100 Embassy Row, Atlanta, GA 30328-1635. Telephone: 770-394-8300. World Wide Web: http://www.artinstitutes.edu/atlanta/.
See color display following page 186.

AUGUSTA TECHNICAL COLLEGE

Culinary Arts

Augusta, Georgia

GENERAL INFORMATION
Public, coeducational, two-year college. Suburban campus. Founded in 1961. Accredited by Southern Association of Colleges and Schools.

PROGRAM INFORMATION
Offered since 1984. Program calendar is divided into quarters. 6-quarter diploma in culinary arts.

PROGRAM AFFILIATION
American Culinary Federation.

AREAS OF STUDY
Baking; buffet catering; food preparation; food purchasing; garde-manger; menu and facilities design; nutrition and food service; sanitation; soup, stock, sauce, and starch production.

FACILITIES
Bake shop; cafeteria; catering service; 2 classrooms; demonstration laboratory; food production kitchen; gourmet dining room; laboratory; learning resource center; library; teaching kitchen.

STUDENT PROFILE
15 are under 25 years old; 25 are between 25 and 44 years old; 20 are over 44 years old.

FACULTY
2 total: 2 full-time. Prominent faculty: Kathleen Fervan, CEC, CCE; Deborah Moreno. Faculty-student ratio: 1:20.

TYPICAL EXPENSES
Application fee: $15. Tuition: $26 per credit hour part-time. Program-related fees include $100 for uniforms; $225 for books; $200 for equipment.

FINANCIAL AID
In 2006, 6 scholarships were awarded (average award was $800). Program-specific awards include ProMgmt. scholarship, American Culinary Federation scholarship. Employment placement assistance is available.

HOUSING

Average off-campus housing cost per month: $600.

APPLICATION INFORMATION

Students may begin participation in March and September. Applications are accepted continuously. In 2006, 52 were accepted. Applicants must submit a formal application.

CONTACT

Kathleen A. Fervan, Department Head, Culinary Arts, 3200 Augusta Tech Drive, Augusta, GA 30906. Telephone: 706-771-4084. Fax: 706-771-4016. E-mail: kfervan@augusta.tech.ga.us. World Wide Web: http://www.augusta.tec.ga.us.

CHATTAHOOCHEE TECHNICAL COLLEGE

Culinary Arts

Marietta, Georgia

GENERAL INFORMATION

Public, coeducational, two-year college. Suburban campus. Founded in 1961. Accredited by Southern Association of Colleges and Schools.

PROGRAM INFORMATION

Offered since 2001. Accredited by American Culinary Federation Accrediting Commission. Program calendar is divided into quarters. 12-month diploma in culinary arts. 24-month associate degree in culinary arts.

PROGRAM AFFILIATION

American Culinary Federation; International Association of Culinary Professionals; James Beard Foundation, Inc.; National Restaurant Association; National Restaurant Association Educational Foundation.

AREAS OF STUDY

Baking; beverage management; buffet catering; controlling costs in food service; culinary skill development; food preparation; food purchasing; food service math; garde-manger; international cuisine; introduction to food service; kitchen management; management and human resources; meat fabrication; menu and facilities design; nutrition and food service; sanitation; soup, stock, sauce, and starch production; wines and spirits.

FACILITIES

Bake shop; catering service; classroom; computer laboratory; demonstration laboratory; food production kitchen; gourmet dining room; 2 lecture rooms; library; public restaurant; student lounge; teaching kitchen.

STUDENT PROFILE

170 total: 150 full-time; 20 part-time.

FACULTY

6 total: 3 full-time; 3 part-time. Prominent faculty: Michael P. Bologna, CEC, CCE, AAC; Kevin Walker, CMC; Hillary Gallagher; Gary Slivenik. Faculty-student ratio: 1:15.

SPECIAL PROGRAMS

Culinary competitions, twelve-day cooking tour of Italy.

TYPICAL EXPENSES

Application fee: $15. In-state tuition: $372 per quarter full-time (in district), $31 per credit hour part-time. Out-of-state tuition: $744 per quarter full-time, $62 per credit hour part-time. Tuition for international students: $1488 per quarter full-time, $124 per credit hour part-time. Program-related fees include $80 for uniforms; $350 for cutlery (knife kit).

FINANCIAL AID

In 2006, 6 scholarships were awarded (average award was $500). Employment placement assistance is available. Employment opportunities within the program are available.

HOUSING

Average off-campus housing cost per month: $650.

APPLICATION INFORMATION

Students may begin participation in January, March, July, and October. Applications are accepted continuously. In 2006, 100 applied; 75 were accepted. Applicants must interview; submit a formal application, letters of reference, an essay, official transcript from high school and/or college or original GED certificate.

CONTACT

Carolyn B. Hall, Dean, Culinary Arts, 2680 Gordy Parkway, Marietta, GA 30066. Telephone: 770-509-6310. Fax: 770-509-6345. E-mail: chall@chattcollege.com. World Wide Web: http://www.chattcollege.com.

COASTAL GEORGIA COMMUNITY COLLEGE

Culinary Arts

Brunswick, Georgia

GENERAL INFORMATION

Public, coeducational, two-year college. Small-town setting. Founded in 1961. Accredited by Southern Association of Colleges and Schools.

Coastal Georgia Community College *(continued)*

PROGRAM INFORMATION
Offered since 1994. Accredited by American Culinary Federation Accrediting Commission. National Restaurant Association Educational Foundation ManageFirst certificates available. Program calendar is divided into semesters. 18-month technical certificate in culinary arts. 24-month certificate in culinary arts.

PROGRAM AFFILIATION
American Culinary Federation; American Hotel and Lodging Association; Council on Hotel, Restaurant, and Institutional Education.

AREAS OF STUDY
Baking; beverage management; buffet catering; business math; controlling costs in food service; culinary French; culinary skill development; food preparation; food purchasing; food service math; garde-manger; introduction to food service; kitchen management; management and human resources; meal planning; menu and facilities design; nutrition; nutrition and food service; sanitation; soup, stock, sauce, and starch production; wines and spirits.

FACILITIES
3 classrooms; computer laboratory; demonstration laboratory; food production kitchen; 2 learning resource centers; 2 libraries; student lounge; teaching kitchen.

STUDENT PROFILE
80 total: 5 full-time; 75 part-time.

FACULTY
2 total: 2 full-time. 1 is an industry professional; 1 is a culinary-certified teacher. Prominent faculty: Walter Wright, CHA, CHE; Steven Ingersoll, CCC, CCE. Faculty-student ratio: 1:38.

PROMINENT ALUMNI AND CURRENT AFFILIATION
Leila Watson, Commanders Palace; Andy Leonard, Opal; Ahanda Draper, Sea Island Company.

SPECIAL PROGRAMS
Paid internships, culinary competitions.

TYPICAL EXPENSES
Application fee: $20. In-state tuition: $877 per semester full-time (in district), $68 per credit hour part-time. Out-of-state tuition: $3189 per semester full-time, $274 per credit hour part-time. Program-related fee includes $250 for uniforms and knives.

FINANCIAL AID
Employment placement assistance is available. Employment opportunities within the program are available.

HOUSING
Average off-campus housing cost per month: $700.

APPLICATION INFORMATION
Students may begin participation in January, May, and August. Applications are accepted continuously. In 2006, 75 applied; 75 were accepted. Applicants must submit a formal application and take COMPASS test.

CONTACT
Walter Wright, Assistant Professor, Hospitality and Culinary Programs, Culinary Arts, 3700 Altama Avenue, Brunswick, GA 31520. Telephone: 912-280-6899. Fax: 912-262-3283. E-mail: wwright@cgcc.edu. World Wide Web: http://www.cgcc.edu.

GEORGIA SOUTHERN UNIVERSITY

Department of Family and Consumer Sciences

Statesboro, Georgia

GENERAL INFORMATION
Public, coeducational, comprehensive institution. Small-town setting. Founded in 1906. Accredited by Southern Association of Colleges and Schools.

PROGRAM INFORMATION
Offered since 1989. Accredited by American Dietetic Association. Program calendar is divided into semesters. 4-year bachelor's degree in nutrition and food science (dietetics). 4-year bachelor's degree in hotel and restaurant management.

PROGRAM AFFILIATION
American Culinary Federation; American Dietetic Association; Confrerie de la Chaine des Rotisseurs; Council on Hotel, Restaurant, and Institutional Education; National Restaurant Association; National Restaurant Association Educational Foundation.

AREAS OF STUDY
Beverage management; buffet catering; controlling costs in food service; convenience cookery; culinary French; culinary skill development; food preparation; food purchasing; food service communication; food service math; international cuisine; introduction to food service; kitchen management; management and human resources; meal planning; menu and facilities design; nutrition; nutrition and food service; restaurant opportunities; saucier; soup, stock, sauce, and starch production.

FACILITIES
6 classrooms; computer laboratory; demonstration laboratory; food production kitchen; gourmet dining room; laboratory; learning resource center; 6 lecture rooms; library; public restaurant; teaching kitchen.

STUDENT PROFILE

317 total: 276 full-time; 41 part-time. 289 are under 25 years old; 27 are between 25 and 44 years old; 1 is over 44 years old.

FACULTY

3 total: 3 full-time. Prominent faculty: Dr. Larry Stalcup; Dr. Leslie Furr; Stephen Minton. Faculty-student ratio: 1:16.

SPECIAL PROGRAMS

New York Hotel Show (fall), Georgia Hotel Tourism Convention (fall/spring).

TYPICAL EXPENSES

Application fee: $30. In-state tuition: $2560 per year full-time (in district), $106 per semester hour part-time. Out-of-state tuition: $10,144 per year full-time, $423 per semester hour part-time.

FINANCIAL AID

In 2006, 4 scholarships were awarded (average award was $2500). Program-specific awards include Georgia Hospitality and Tourism Association Scholarship. Employment placement assistance is available.

HOUSING

Coed, apartment-style, and single-sex housing available. Average on-campus housing cost per month: $338.

APPLICATION INFORMATION

Students may begin participation in January and August. Application deadline for fall is August 1. Application deadline for spring is December 1. In 2006, 76 applied; 54 were accepted. Applicants must submit a formal application.

CONTACT

Mrs. Susan Braxton Davies, Director of Admissions, Department of Family and Consumer Sciences, PO Box 8024, Statesboro, GA 30460. Telephone: 912-681-5391. Fax: 912-486-7240. World Wide Web: http://chhs. georgiasouthern.edu/hospitality.

GEORGIA STATE UNIVERSITY

Cecil B. Day School of Hospitality Administration

Atlanta, Georgia

GENERAL INFORMATION

Public, coeducational, university. Urban campus. Founded in 1913. Accredited by Southern Association of Colleges and Schools.

PROGRAM INFORMATION

Offered since 1973. Accredited by Council on Hotel, Restaurant and Institutional Education. Program calendar is divided into semesters. 1-year certificate in hospitality. 2-year master of business administration in hotel real estate. 4-year bachelor's degree in hospitality administration.

PROGRAM AFFILIATION

American Hotel and Lodging Association; Council on Hotel, Restaurant, and Institutional Education; National Restaurant Association; National Restaurant Association Educational Foundation.

AREAS OF STUDY

Controlling costs in food service; food preparation; food purchasing; food service communication; kitchen management; management and human resources; meal planning; menu and facilities design; restaurant opportunities; sanitation.

FACILITIES

Food production kitchen; dedicated classroom.

STUDENT PROFILE

320 total: 260 full-time; 60 part-time.

FACULTY

10 total: 6 full-time; 4 part-time. 8 are industry professionals. Prominent faculty: David V. Pavesic, PhD, FMP, CHE; Debra Cannon, PhD, CHE; Raymond Ferreira, PhD; Deborah Robbe.

SPECIAL PROGRAMS

Student exchange program with European hospitality schools (semester), mentorship with industry executives (1 year), paid internships (semester).

TYPICAL EXPENSES

In-state tuition: $1960 per semester full-time (in district), $134 per credit hour part-time. Out-of-state tuition: $6672 per semester full-time, $535 per credit hour part-time.

FINANCIAL AID

In 2006, 15–20 scholarships were awarded (average award was $1000). Program-specific awards include scholarships from American Lodging Association, Days Inns, and GSU Foundation. Employment opportunities within the program are available.

HOUSING

Coed and apartment-style housing available.

APPLICATION INFORMATION

Students may begin participation in January, June, and August. Application deadline for fall is June 1. Application deadline for spring is November 15. Application deadline for summer is April 1. Applicants must submit a formal application, high school transcripts, SAT or ACT scores.

Georgia State University *(continued)*

CONTACT
Debra Cannon, Chairperson, Cecil B. Day School of Hospitality Administration, 35 Broad Street, Suite 220, Atlanta, GA 30303. Telephone: 404-413-7617. Fax: 404-413-7625. E-mail: hrtdfc@langate.gsu.edu. World Wide Web: http://robinson.gsu.edu/hospitality/index.htm.

LE CORDON BLEU COLLEGE OF CULINARY ARTS, ATLANTA

Tucker, Georgia

GENERAL INFORMATION
Private, coeducational, two-year college. Suburban campus. Founded in 2003. Accredited by Accrediting Commission of Career Schools and Colleges of Technology.

PROGRAM INFORMATION
Offered since 2003. Accredited by American Culinary Federation Accrediting Commission. Program calendar is continuous. 10-month certificate in Le Cordon Bleu Patisserie and Baking. 15-month associate degree in Le Cordon Bleu Culinary Arts.

PROGRAM AFFILIATION
American Culinary Federation; The Bread Bakers Guild of America.

AREAS OF STUDY
Baking; culinary French; culinary skill development; patisserie.

FACILITIES
4 classrooms; computer laboratory; 5 food production kitchens; library; public restaurant; student lounge; 4 teaching kitchens.

STUDENT PROFILE
887 full-time.

TYPICAL EXPENSES
Application fee: $50.

FINANCIAL AID
Employment placement assistance is available.

APPLICATION INFORMATION
Students may begin participation in January, February, April, May, July, August, October, and November. Applications are accepted continuously. Applicants must interview; submit a formal application.

CONTACT
Director of Admissions, Office of Admissions, 1927 Lakeside Parkway, Tucker, GA 30084. Telephone: 770-938-4711. Fax: 770-938-4571. World Wide Web: http://www.atlantaculinary.com.

NORTH GEORGIA TECHNICAL COLLEGE

Culinary Arts

Toccoa, Georgia

GENERAL INFORMATION
Public, coeducational, two-year college. Rural campus. Founded in 1907. Accredited by Council on Occupational Education.

PROGRAM INFORMATION
Offered since 2005. Accredited by American Culinary Federation Accrediting Commission. National Restaurant Association Educational Foundation ManageFirst certificates available. Program calendar is divided into quarters. 2-quarter technical certificate in food production assistant. 5-quarter diploma in culinary arts. 7-quarter associate degree in culinary arts.

PROGRAM AFFILIATION
American Culinary Federation; National Restaurant Association; National Restaurant Association Educational Foundation.

AREAS OF STUDY
Baking; buffet catering; controlling costs in food service; culinary skill development; food preparation; food purchasing; food service communication; food service math; garde-manger; international cuisine; introduction to food service; kitchen management; meal planning; meat cutting; meat fabrication; menu and facilities design; nutrition; nutrition and food service; patisserie; restaurant opportunities; sanitation; saucier; seafood processing; soup, stock, sauce, and starch production.

FACILITIES
Library.

STUDENT PROFILE
46 total: 39 full-time; 7 part-time. 28 are under 25 years old; 11 are between 25 and 44 years old; 7 are over 44 years old.

FACULTY
2 total: 2 full-time. Prominent faculty: Alexander Bladowski; Christopher Bladowski. Faculty-student ratio: 1:10.

TYPICAL EXPENSES

In-state tuition: $432 per quarter full-time (in district), $36 per credit hour part-time. Out-of-state tuition: $864 per quarter full-time, $52 per credit hour part-time. Tuition for international students: $1728 per quarter full-time, $144 per credit hour part-time. Program-related fees include $26 for registration fee; $25 for student activity fee; $35 for technology fee; $5 for parking fee; $4 for accident insurance fee.

FINANCIAL AID

Program-specific awards include Hope scholarship program (Georgia residents). Employment placement assistance is available. Employment opportunities within the program are available.

HOUSING

Coed housing available. Average off-campus housing cost per month: $450.

APPLICATION INFORMATION

Students may begin participation in January, April, July, and October. Applications are accepted continuously. In 2006, 63 applied; 43 were accepted. Applicants must submit a formal application and health certification form.

CONTACT

Erica Pickens, Student Service Director, Culinary Arts, 8989 Georgia Highway 17 South, Toccoa, GA 30577. Telephone: 706-779-8136. Fax: 706-779-8130. E-mail: epickens@northgatech.edu. World Wide Web: http://www.northgatech.edu.

NORTH GEORGIA TECHNICAL COLLEGE, BLAIRSVILLE CAMPUS

Culinary Arts

Blairsville, Georgia

GENERAL INFORMATION

Public, coeducational, two-year college. Rural campus. Founded in 1907. Accredited by Council on Occupational Education.

PROGRAM INFORMATION

Offered since 1998. Accredited by American Culinary Federation Accrediting Commission. National Restaurant Association Educational Foundation ManageFirst certificates available. Program calendar is divided into quarters. 2-quarter technical certificate in food production assistant. 3-quarter technical certificate in personal chef. 5-quarter diploma in culinary arts. 7-quarter technical associate degree in culinary arts.

PROGRAM AFFILIATION

American Culinary Federation; National Restaurant Association Educational Foundation; Research Chefs Association.

AREAS OF STUDY

Baking; buffet catering; controlling costs in food service; culinary skill development; food preparation; food purchasing; food service communication; food service math; garde-manger; international cuisine; introduction to food service; kitchen management; meal planning; meat cutting; meat fabrication; menu and facilities design; nutrition; nutrition and food service; patisserie; restaurant opportunities; sanitation; saucier; seafood processing; soup, stock, sauce, and starch production.

FACILITIES

Library; teaching kitchen.

STUDENT PROFILE

92 total: 55 full-time; 37 part-time. 31 are under 25 years old; 46 are between 25 and 44 years old; 15 are over 44 years old.

FACULTY

2 total: 2 full-time. Prominent faculty: David Drake; Jeff McKenna. Faculty-student ratio: 1:10.

TYPICAL EXPENSES

Application fee: $15. In-state tuition: $432 per quarter full-time (in district), $36 per credit hour part-time. Out-of-state tuition: $864 per quarter full-time, $52 per credit hour part-time. Tuition for international students: $1728 per quarter full-time, $144 per credit hour part-time. Program-related fees include $26 for registration fee; $25 for student activity fee; $35 for technology fee; $5 for parking fee; $4 for accident insurance fee.

FINANCIAL AID

Program-specific awards include Hope Scholarship program (Georgia residents). Employment placement assistance is available. Employment opportunities within the program are available.

HOUSING

Average off-campus housing cost per month: $450.

APPLICATION INFORMATION

Students may begin participation in January, April, July, and October. Applications are accepted continuously. In 2006, 93 applied; 74 were accepted. Applicants must submit a formal application and health certification form.

North Georgia Technical College, Blairsville Campus *(continued)*

CONTACT

Kristie Gibbs, Student Service Director, Culinary Arts, 434 Meeks Avenue, Blairsville, GA 30512. Telephone: 706-439-6316. Fax: 706-439-6302. E-mail: kgibbs@ northgatech.edu. World Wide Web: http://www. northgatech.edu.

OGEECHEE TECHNICAL COLLEGE

Culinary Arts Program

Statesboro, Georgia

GENERAL INFORMATION

Public, coeducational, two-year college. Small-town setting. Founded in 1986. Accredited by Council on Occupational Education.

PROGRAM INFORMATION

National Restaurant Association Educational Foundation ManageFirst certificates available. Program calendar is divided into quarters. 1-year diploma in culinary arts. 2-year associate degree in culinary arts. 9-month certificate in catering specialist.

PROGRAM AFFILIATION

National Restaurant Association Educational Foundation.

AREAS OF STUDY

Baking; buffet catering; confectionery show pieces; controlling costs in food service; culinary skill development; food preparation; food purchasing; food service communication; garde-manger; international cuisine; introduction to food service; kitchen management; management and human resources; meal planning; menu and facilities design; nutrition and food service; patisserie; sanitation.

FACILITIES

Classroom; computer laboratory; demonstration laboratory; food production kitchen; gourmet dining room; teaching kitchen.

FACULTY

2 total: 2 full-time.

PROMINENT ALUMNI AND CURRENT AFFILIATION

Larry O. March, Statesboro Inn; Daniel Clark, Blue Moon Café; Brad Bickford, Capital Grill.

SPECIAL PROGRAMS

Visits to food expos, culinary showcases, live work program.

TYPICAL EXPENSES

Application fee: $15. In-state tuition: $372 per quarter full-time (in district), $31 per credit hour part-time. Out-of-state tuition: $744 per quarter full-time, $62 per credit hour part-time. Tuition for international students: $1488 per quarter full-time, $124 per credit hour part-time. Program-related fees include $21 for student activity fee; $26 for registration fee; $4 for student accident insurance; $35 for technology fee; $1100 for books and supplies; $99 for knife kits; $11 for lab insurance, per year.

FINANCIAL AID

Program-specific awards include Stewart Scholarship. Employment placement assistance is available.

HOUSING

Average off-campus housing cost per month: $500.

APPLICATION INFORMATION

Students may begin participation in January, April, July, and October. Applicants must submit a formal application.

CONTACT

Ryan Foley, Director of Enrollment Services, Culinary Arts Program, 1 Joe Kennedy Boulevard, Statesboro, GA 30458. Telephone: 800-646-1316. Fax: 912-486-7704. E-mail: rfoley@ogeccheetech.edu. World Wide Web: http://www.ogeecheetech.edu.

SAVANNAH TECHNICAL COLLEGE

Culinary Institute of Savannah

Savannah, Georgia

GENERAL INFORMATION

Public, coeducational, two-year college. Urban campus. Founded in 1929. Accredited by Southern Association of Colleges and Schools.

PROGRAM INFORMATION

Offered since 1981. Accredited by American Culinary Federation Accrediting Commission. Program calendar is divided into quarters. 18-month associate degree in culinary arts. 18-month diploma in culinary arts.

PROGRAM AFFILIATION

American Culinary Federation; Savannah Tourism Leadership Council; Southeastern Retail Bakers Association.

AREAS OF STUDY

Baking; buffet catering; controlling costs in food service; culinary skill development; dining room/guest services; food preparation; food purchasing; food service math; garde-manger; international cuisine; introduction to food service; kitchen management; management and human resources; meal planning; meat fabrication; nutrition; restaurant opportunities; sanitation; saucier; soup, stock, sauce, and starch production.

FACILITIES
Bake shop; catering service; classroom; coffee shop; computer laboratory; demonstration laboratory; food production kitchen; garden; gourmet dining room; laboratory; learning resource center; lecture room; library; public restaurant; student lounge; teaching kitchen.

STUDENT PROFILE
135 total: 75 full-time; 60 part-time. 3 are under 25 years old; 132 are between 25 and 44 years old.

FACULTY
2 total: 2 full-time. 1 is an industry professional; 1 is a culinary-certified teacher. Faculty-student ratio: 1:20.

PROMINENT ALUMNI AND CURRENT AFFILIATION
Tony Espinoza, Ritz Carlton, Amelia Island; William Stevens, Pastry Passiono; Lorenzo Grant, Holiday Inn.

SPECIAL PROGRAMS
Field trips (restaurants, vendor warehouses, food processing plants), special food production presentations, culinary competitions.

TYPICAL EXPENSES
Application fee: $15. In-state tuition: $372 per quarter full-time (in district), $31 per credit hour part-time. Out-of-state tuition: $744 per quarter full-time, $62 per credit hour part-time. Tuition for international students: $1488 per quarter. Program-related fees include $265 for knives, other tools; $150 for uniforms; $300 for books (per quarter).

FINANCIAL AID
In 2006, 2 scholarships were awarded (average award was $1500). Program-specific awards include Hector Boiardi scholarship, Career Assistance Program, faculty and staff scholarships; Savannah Tourism Leadership Council Scholarships. Employment placement assistance is available.

HOUSING
Average off-campus housing cost per month: $600.

APPLICATION INFORMATION
Students may begin participation in April and October. Applications are accepted continuously. Application deadline for all sessions: 30 days prior to start of each quarter. In 2006, 150 applied; 150 were accepted. Applicants must submit a formal application and have a high school diploma or GED and ASSET or SAT scores.

CONTACT
Student Services, Culinary Institute of Savannah, 5717 White Bluff Road, Savannah, GA 31405-5521. Telephone: 912-443-5518. Fax: 912-303-1781. World Wide Web: http://www.savannahtech.edu.

WEST GEORGIA TECHNICAL COLLEGE

Culinary Arts

La Grange, Georgia

GENERAL INFORMATION
Public, coeducational, two-year college. Small-town setting. Founded in 1966. Accredited by Council on Occupational Education.

PROGRAM INFORMATION
Offered since 1996. Program calendar is divided into quarters. 18-month diploma in culinary arts. 6-month certificate in prep cook. 6-month certificate in food production worker I. 6-month certificate in basic culinary skills. 6-month certificate in assistant food purchasing agent.

AREAS OF STUDY
Beverage management; convenience cookery; food service communication; international cuisine; meat fabrication; menu and facilities design; nutrition; restaurant opportunities; wines and spirits.

FACILITIES
Classroom; library; student lounge; teaching kitchen.

STUDENT PROFILE
21 full-time. 10 are under 25 years old; 11 are between 25 and 44 years old.

FACULTY
1 total: 1 full-time. 1 is an industry professional; 1 is a culinary-certified teacher. Prominent faculty: L. Henry Menard, CEC, AAC. Faculty-student ratio: 1:21.

PROMINENT ALUMNI AND CURRENT AFFILIATION
Tulla White, Basil Leaf; Venucci's & Tulla's; Clenda Hollaway, Callaway Gardens Resort & Spa; Margaret Wright, Callaway Gardens Resort and Spa.

SPECIAL PROGRAMS
NRA ServSafe certification, Culinary Food and Equipment Show of Atlanta, Sysco/US Food Service (local) Food and Equipment Show.

TYPICAL EXPENSES
Application fee: $15. In-state tuition: $372 per quarter full-time (in district), $31 per credit hour part-time. Out-of-state tuition: $744 per quarter full-time, $62 per

West Georgia Technical College *(continued)*

credit hour part-time. Tuition for international students: $1488 per quarter full-time, $124 per credit hour part-time. Program-related fees include $113 for uniforms; $328 for tools; $480 for books; $81 for fees (per quarter).

FINANCIAL AID
Employment placement assistance is available.

APPLICATION INFORMATION
Students may begin participation in January, April, July, and October. Applications are accepted continuously. In 2006, 26 applied; 26 were accepted. Applicants must interview; submit a formal application.

CONTACT
Gill Ausman, Career Planner, Culinary Arts, 303 Fort Drive, La Grange, GA 30240. Telephone: 706-837-4246. Fax: 706-845-4340. E-mail: tausman@westgatech.edu. World Wide Web: http://www.westgatech.edu/.

HAWAII

LEEWARD COMMUNITY COLLEGE

Culinary Institute of the Pacific

Pearl City, Hawaii

GENERAL INFORMATION
Public, coeducational, two-year college. Suburban campus. Founded in 1968. Accredited by Western Association of Schools and Colleges.

PROGRAM INFORMATION
Offered since 1972. Accredited by American Culinary Federation Accrediting Commission. Program calendar is divided into semesters. 1-semester certificate of completion in food service. 1-semester certificate in prep cook. 1.5-semester certificate in dining room service. 1.5-semester certificate in baking. 2-semester certificate of achievement in food service. 2-year associate degree in food service.

PROGRAM AFFILIATION
American Culinary Federation.

AREAS OF STUDY
Baking; beverage management; controlling costs in food service; culinary skill development; food preparation; food purchasing; food service math; garde-manger; international cuisine; introduction to food service; management and human resources; nutrition and food service; sanitation; soup, stock, sauce, and starch production.

FACILITIES
Bake shop; cafeteria; 3 classrooms; coffee shop; 3 food production kitchens; gourmet dining room.

TYPICAL STUDENT PROFILE
150 total: 100 full-time; 50 part-time.

SPECIAL PROGRAMS
Taste of the Stars, Japan study-abroad course in nutrition, networking opportunities with Hawaii's best chefs.

FINANCIAL AID
Program-specific awards include Scholarship Branch Awards, industry scholarships. Employment placement assistance is available. Employment opportunities within the program are available.

APPLICATION INFORMATION
Students may begin participation in January and August. Application deadline for fall is July 15. Application deadline for spring is December 1. Applicants must submit a formal application.

CONTACT
Director of Admissions, Culinary Institute of the Pacific, 96-045 Ala Ike, Pearl City, HI 96782. Telephone: 808-455-0298. Fax: 808-455-0559. World Wide Web: http://www.lcc.hawaii.edu/.

MAUI COMMUNITY COLLEGE

Food Service Program

Kahului, Hawaii

GENERAL INFORMATION
Public, coeducational, two-year college. Small-town setting. Founded in 1967. Accredited by Western Association of Schools and Colleges.

PROGRAM INFORMATION
Offered since 1977. Accredited by American Culinary Federation Accrediting Commission. Program calendar is divided into semesters. 1-year certificate in culinary arts. 2-year associate degree in food service/restaurant supervision. 2-year associate degree in food service-culinary arts specialty. 2-year associate degree in food service-baking specialty.

PROGRAM AFFILIATION
American Culinary Federation; Confrerie de la Chaine des Rotisseurs; National Restaurant Association.

AREAS OF STUDY
Baking; beverage management; buffet catering; controlling costs in food service; culinary skill development; food preparation; food purchasing; food

service communication; food service math; garde-manger; international cuisine; introduction to food service; management and human resources; menu and facilities design; nutrition; patisserie; restaurant opportunities; sanitation; soup, stock, sauce, and starch production; wines and spirits.

FACILITIES
Bake shop; cafeteria; catering service; classroom; computer laboratory; food production kitchen; garden; gourmet dining room; laboratory; lecture room; library; public restaurant; snack shop; teaching kitchen.

TYPICAL STUDENT PROFILE
155 total: 130 full-time; 25 part-time.

SPECIAL PROGRAMS
Culinary competitions, field experiences, fellowships.

FINANCIAL AID
Employment placement assistance is available. Employment opportunities within the program are available.

HOUSING
Coed housing available.

APPLICATION INFORMATION
Students may begin participation in January, June, and August. Applications are accepted continuously. Applicants must submit a formal application.

CONTACT
Director of Admissions, Food Service Program, 310 Kaahumanu Avenue, Kahului, HI 96732. Telephone: 808-984-3225. Fax: 808-984-3314. World Wide Web: http://www.hawaii.edu/mcc/.

TRAVEL INSTITUTE OF THE PACIFIC

Honolulu, Hawaii

GENERAL INFORMATION
Private, coeducational, culinary institute. Urban campus. Founded in 1974. Accredited by Accrediting Commission of Career Schools and Colleges of Technology.

PROGRAM INFORMATION
Offered since 1974. Program calendar is continuous. 1-year diploma in bakery/patisserie. 1-year diploma in culinary arts.

PROGRAM AFFILIATION
American Culinary Federation; Confrerie de la Chaine des Rotisseurs.

AREAS OF STUDY
Baking; culinary French; culinary skill development; garde-manger; patisserie; saucier; soup, stock, sauce, and starch production.

FACILITIES
Bake shop; bakery; 3 classrooms; computer laboratory; demonstration laboratory; 2 food production kitchens; gourmet dining room; 2 teaching kitchens.

STUDENT PROFILE
80 full-time. 16 are under 25 years old; 58 are between 25 and 44 years old; 6 are over 44 years old.

FACULTY
10 total: 4 full-time; 6 part-time. 2 are industry professionals; 4 are master chefs; 2 are master bakers; 2 are culinary-certified teachers. Faculty-student ratio: 1:10.

TYPICAL EXPENSES
Application fee: $100. Tuition: $14,191 per year.

HOUSING
Average off-campus housing cost per month: $800.

APPLICATION INFORMATION
Students may begin participation in January, April, July, and October. Applications are accepted continuously. In 2006, 110 applied; 92 were accepted. Applicants must interview; submit a formal application.

CONTACT
Frank Green, Director, 1314 South King Street, Suite 1164, Honolulu, HI 96814. Telephone: 808-591-2708. Fax: 808-591-2709. E-mail: tip@aloha.net. World Wide Web: http://www.tiphawaii.com.

UNIVERSITY OF HAWAII–KAPIOLANI COMMUNITY COLLEGE

Culinary Institute of the Pacific

Honolulu, Hawaii

GENERAL INFORMATION
Public, coeducational, two-year college. Urban campus. Founded in 1957. Accredited by Western Association of Schools and Colleges.

PROGRAM INFORMATION
Offered since 1965. Accredited by American Culinary Federation Accrediting Commission, Commission on Accreditation of Hospitality Management Programs (CAHM). Program calendar is divided into semesters. 18-month certificate in culinary arts. 2-year associate

University of Hawaii–Kapiolani Community College (*continued*)

degree in culinary arts. 2-year associate degree in patisserie. 4-month certificate in patisserie. 4-month certificate in culinary arts.

PROGRAM AFFILIATION
American Culinary Federation; American Dietetic Association; Confrerie de la Chaine des Rotisseurs; Council on Hotel, Restaurant, and Institutional Education; International Food Service Executives Association; National Restaurant Association; National Restaurant Association Educational Foundation.

AREAS OF STUDY
Asian Pacific cookery; baking; beverage management; confectionery show pieces; controlling costs in food service; food preparation; food service math; garde-manger; international cuisine; introduction to culinary arts; introduction to food service; management and human resources; meal planning; menu and facilities design; nutrition and food service; patisserie; sanitation; soup, stock, sauce, and starch production.

FACILITIES
2 bake shops; bakery; cafeteria; 12 classrooms; coffee shop; computer laboratory; demonstration laboratory; 4 food production kitchens; garden; 2 gourmet dining rooms; learning resource center; lecture room; library; 3 public restaurants; snack shop; student lounge; teaching kitchen.

STUDENT PROFILE
400 total: 200 full-time; 200 part-time. 150 are under 25 years old; 200 are between 25 and 44 years old; 50 are over 44 years old.

FACULTY
22 total: 14 full-time; 8 part-time. 15 are industry professionals; 7 are culinary-certified teachers. Faculty-student ratio: 1:35 lecture; 1:24 lab.

SPECIAL PROGRAMS
2-week (Christmas break) paid internships on neighbor islands, Walt Disney World College internship.

TYPICAL EXPENSES
Application fee: $25. In-state tuition: $63 per credit hour. Out-of-state tuition: $256 per credit hour. Program-related fee includes $300 for uniforms and cutlery.

FINANCIAL AID
In 2006, 45 scholarships were awarded (average award was $600); 250 loans were granted (average loan was $1200). Program-specific awards include Native Hawaiian student scholarships, culinary recipe

scholarships. Employment placement assistance is available. Employment opportunities within the program are available.

HOUSING
Coed and apartment-style housing available. Average on-campus housing cost per month: $1000. Average off-campus housing cost per month: $900.

APPLICATION INFORMATION
Students may begin participation in January, March, May, July, August, and October. Application deadline for fall is July 1. Application deadline for spring is November 15. Application deadline for summer is April 15. In 2006, 400 applied; 400 were accepted. Applicants must submit a formal application.

CONTACT
Lori Maehara, Associate Professor/Counselor, Culinary Institute of the Pacific, 4303 Diamond Head Road, Honolulu, HI 96816. Telephone: 808-734-9466. Fax: 808-734-9212. E-mail: lmaehara@hawaii.edu. World Wide Web: http://www.kcc.hawaii.edu.

IDAHO

BOISE STATE UNIVERSITY

Culinary Arts Program

Boise, Idaho

GENERAL INFORMATION
Public, coeducational, comprehensive institution. Urban campus. Founded in 1932. Accredited by Northwest Commission on Colleges and Universities.

PROGRAM INFORMATION
Offered since 1979. Accredited by American Culinary Federation Accrediting Commission. Program calendar is divided into semesters. 12-month certificate in culinary arts. 18-month certificate in culinary arts. 2-year associate degree in culinary arts. 6-month certificate in culinary arts.

PROGRAM AFFILIATION
American Culinary Federation.

AREAS OF STUDY
Baking; beverage management; controlling costs in food service; culinary skill development; food preparation; food purchasing; food service math; garde-manger; international cuisine; kitchen management; meat fabrication; nutrition; patisserie; sanitation; soup, stock, sauce, and starch production; wines and spirits.

FACILITIES

Bake shop; bakery; catering service; 3 classrooms; 2 demonstration laboratories; food production kitchen; 3 laboratories; learning resource center; 3 lecture rooms; library; public restaurant; snack shop; student lounge; teaching kitchen.

STUDENT PROFILE

46 total: 40 full-time; 6 part-time.

FACULTY

5 total: 4 full-time; 1 part-time. 2 are industry professionals; 2 are culinary-certified teachers. Prominent faculty: Julie Hosman-Kulm, CEC, CCE; Vern Hickman, CCC, CCE; Kelli Dever; Marie Edwards. Faculty-student ratio: 1:8.

SPECIAL PROGRAMS

One-semester paid internship.

TYPICAL EXPENSES

Application fee: $20. In-state tuition: $1765 per semester. Out-of-state tuition: $4365 per semester. Program-related fees include $30 for lab fee; $60 for uniform fee.

FINANCIAL AID

In 2006, 4 scholarships were awarded (average award was $300).

HOUSING

Coed, apartment-style, and single-sex housing available.

APPLICATION INFORMATION

Students may begin participation in January and August. Applications are accepted continuously. Applicants must submit a formal application and complete an entrance test.

CONTACT

Student Services Department, Culinary Arts Program, 1910 University Drive, Boise, ID 83725-0399. Telephone: 208-426-1431. World Wide Web: http://www.idbsu.edu/.

IDAHO STATE UNIVERSITY

Culinary Arts Technology Program

Pocatello, Idaho

GENERAL INFORMATION

Public, coeducational, university. Rural campus. Founded in 1901. Accredited by Northwest Commission on Colleges and Universities.

PROGRAM INFORMATION

Offered since 1967. Accredited by American Culinary Federation Accrediting Commission. Program calendar is divided into semesters. 1-year certificate in culinary management. 1-year certificate in culinary arts. 2-year associate degree in restaurant management. 2-year associate degree in culinary management. 2-year associate degree in culinary arts.

PROGRAM AFFILIATION

American Culinary Federation; Council on Hotel, Restaurant, and Institutional Education.

AREAS OF STUDY

Baking; beverage management; buffet catering; controlling costs in food service; convenience cookery; culinary skill development; food preparation; food purchasing; food service math; garde-manger; international cuisine; introduction to food service; kitchen management; management and human resources; meal planning; meat cutting; menu and facilities design; nutrition and food service; patisserie; restaurant opportunities; sanitation; saucier; seafood processing; soup, stock, sauce, and starch production; wines and spirits.

FACILITIES

Bake shop; catering service; classroom; coffee shop; computer laboratory; food production kitchen; learning resource center; lecture room; library.

STUDENT PROFILE

27 total: 26 full-time; 1 part-time.

FACULTY

2 total: 2 full-time. 2 are industry professionals. Prominent faculty: David B. Miller; Garrett Peters. Faculty-student ratio: 1:13.

SPECIAL PROGRAMS

One-semester internship, culinary competitions.

TYPICAL EXPENSES

Application fee: $40. In-state tuition: $2075 per semester full-time (in district), $200 per credit part-time. Out-of-state tuition: $5925 per semester full-time, $310 per credit part-time. Program-related fees include $125 for lab fee (15+ semester), product used and uniforms; $75 for demonstration.

FINANCIAL AID

Employment placement assistance is available.

HOUSING

Coed housing available. Average on-campus housing cost per month: $300. Average off-campus housing cost per month: $500.

Idaho State University *(continued)*

APPLICATION INFORMATION

Students may begin participation in January and August. Application deadline for fall is August 20. Application deadline for spring is January 10. Applicants must submit a formal application.

CONTACT

David B. Miller, Coordinator, Culinary Arts Technology Program, Box 8380, Pocatello, ID 83209. Telephone: 208-282-3327. Fax: 208-282-2105. E-mail: milldav1@isu.edu. World Wide Web: http://www.isu.edu.

ILLINOIS

BLACK HAWK COLLEGE

Culinary Arts

Moline, Illinois

GENERAL INFORMATION

Public, coeducational, two-year college. Founded in 1946. Accredited by North Central Association of Colleges and Schools.

PROGRAM INFORMATION

Program calendar is divided into semesters. 3-year associate degree in culinary arts.

FACULTY

3 total: 1 full-time; 2 part-time.

TYPICAL EXPENSES

In-state tuition: $1275 per year (in district), $3500 per year (out-of-district). Out-of-state tuition: $6475 per year.

APPLICATION INFORMATION

Students may begin participation in January and August. Applications are accepted continuously. Applicants must interview; submit a formal application.

CONTACT

Coleman Harris, Counselor, Culinary Arts, 6600 34th Avenue, Moline, IL 61265-5899. Telephone: 309-796-5179. Fax: 309-792-5976. E-mail: harrisc@bhc.edu. World Wide Web: http://www.bhc.edu.

COLLEGE OF DUPAGE

Culinary Arts/Pastry Arts

Glen Ellyn, Illinois

GENERAL INFORMATION

Public, coeducational, two-year college. Suburban campus. Founded in 1967. Accredited by North Central Association of Colleges and Schools.

PROGRAM INFORMATION

Offered since 1967. Accredited by American Culinary Federation Accrediting Commission. Program calendar is divided into semesters. 1-year certificate in food service administration. 1-year certificate in beverage management. 1-year certificate in pastry. 1-year certificate in culinary arts. 2-year associate degree in baking and pastry. 2-year associate degree in culinary arts. 2-year associate degree in food service administration.

PROGRAM AFFILIATION

American Culinary Federation; American Institute of Baking; Council on Hotel, Restaurant, and Institutional Education; International Food Service Executives Association; National Restaurant Association; National Restaurant Association Educational Foundation; Retailer's Bakery Association.

AREAS OF STUDY

Asian cuisine; baking; beverage management; buffet catering; confectionery show pieces; controlling costs in food service; culinary skill development; food preparation; food purchasing; food service math; garde-manger; international cuisine; introduction to food service; kitchen management; management and human resources; menu and facilities design; nutrition; nutrition and food service; patisserie; sanitation; saucier; seafood processing; soup, stock, sauce, and starch production; wines and spirits.

FACILITIES

Bake shop; cafeteria; 2 classrooms; 3 computer laboratories; demonstration laboratory; food production kitchen; gourmet dining room; 2 laboratories; learning resource center; 2 lecture rooms; library; public restaurant; snack shop; student lounge; teaching kitchen.

STUDENT PROFILE

400 total: 160 full-time; 240 part-time. 160 are under 25 years old; 200 are between 25 and 44 years old; 40 are over 44 years old.

FACULTY

25 total: 5 full-time; 20 part-time. 13 are industry professionals; 6 are culinary-certified teachers. Prominent faculty: George Macht, CHA, CFE, FMP; Chris Thielman, CEC, CCE; David Kramer, CEC; Timothy Meyers, CCC, CCE. Faculty-student ratio: 1:18.

SPECIAL PROGRAMS

2-week culinary tour in Tuscany (Italy), one-week summer culinary tour in France, one-week wine and food tour of France.

TYPICAL EXPENSES

Application fee: $10. In-state tuition: $103 per credit hour full-time (in district), $103 per credit hour part-time (in district), $292 per credit hour full-time (out-of-district), $292 per credit hour part-time (out-of-district). Out-of-state tuition: $350 per credit hour full-time, $350 per credit hour part-time. Tuition for international students: $350 per credit hour full-time, $350 per credit hour part-time. Program-related fees include $70 for knives; $75 for uniforms; $50 for supplies; $75 for class-specific tools; $50 for lab fees.

FINANCIAL AID

In 2006, 3 scholarships were awarded. Employment placement assistance is available. Employment opportunities within the program are available.

HOUSING

Average off-campus housing cost per month: $1000.

APPLICATION INFORMATION

Students may begin participation in January, May, and August. Applications are accepted continuously. In 2006, 200 applied; 200 were accepted. Applicants must submit a formal application.

CONTACT

George Macht, Coordinator, Culinary Arts/Pastry Arts, College of DuPage, 425 Fawell Boulevard, Glen Ellyn, IL 60126. Telephone: 630-942-2315. Fax: 630-858-9399. E-mail: machtg@cod.edu. World Wide Web: http://www.cod.edu/.

COLLEGE OF LAKE COUNTY

Food Service Program

Grayslake, Illinois

GENERAL INFORMATION

Public, coeducational, two-year college. Suburban campus. Founded in 1967. Accredited by North Central Association of Colleges and Schools.

PROGRAM INFORMATION

Offered since 1987. National Restaurant Association Educational Foundation ManageFirst certificates available. Program calendar is divided into semesters. 1-semester certificate in cooking. 1-year certificate in food service management. 1-year certificate in culinary arts. 2-year associate degree in food service management.

PROGRAM AFFILIATION

American Culinary Federation; American Dietetic Association; Council on Hotel, Restaurant, and Institutional Education; National Restaurant Association; National Restaurant Association Educational Foundation.

AREAS OF STUDY

Baking; buffet catering; controlling costs in food service; convenience cookery; culinary skill development; food preparation; food purchasing; food service communication; food service math; garde-manger; international cuisine; introduction to food service; kitchen management; management and human resources; meal planning; menu and facilities design; nutrition; restaurant opportunities; sanitation; saucier; soup, stock, sauce, and starch production.

FACILITIES

Bake shop; cafeteria; catering service; 4 classrooms; 12 computer laboratories; 2 demonstration laboratories; 2 food production kitchens; learning resource center; library; 2 public restaurants; snack shop.

STUDENT PROFILE

175 total: 50 full-time; 125 part-time.

FACULTY

9 total: 1 full-time; 8 part-time. 4 are industry professionals; 3 are culinary-certified teachers. Prominent faculty: Tom Maguire; Jeanette Keyes; Jack Bress; Cliff Wener. Faculty-student ratio: 1:18.

SPECIAL PROGRAMS

Applied Food Service Sanitation Refresher Course, Basset Course.

TYPICAL EXPENSES

In-state tuition: $90 per credit hour full-time (in district), $90 per credit hour part-time (in district), $250 per credit hour full-time (out-of-district), $250 per credit hour part-time (out-of-district). Out-of-state tuition: $350 per credit hour full-time, $350 per credit hour part-time. Program-related fees include $150 for tools and equipment; $50 for uniforms; $50 for lab fee.

College of Lake County *(continued)*

FINANCIAL AID

In 2006, 2 scholarships were awarded (average award was $1000); 50 loans were granted (average loan was $500). Employment placement assistance is available. Employment opportunities within the program are available.

HOUSING

Average off-campus housing cost per month: $600.

APPLICATION INFORMATION

Students may begin participation in January, June, and August. Applications are accepted continuously. In 2006, 50 applied; 50 were accepted. Applicants must submit a formal application.

CONTACT

Cliff Wener, FSM Department Chair, Food Service Program, 19351 West Washington, Grayslake, IL 60030. Telephone: 847-543-2823. Fax: 847-223-7248. E-mail: crwener-fsm@clcillinois.edu. World Wide Web: http://www.clcillinois.edu.

THE COOKING AND HOSPITALITY INSTITUTE OF CHICAGO

Le Cordon Bleu Program

Chicago, Illinois

GENERAL INFORMATION

Private, coeducational, culinary institute. Urban campus. Founded in 1983. Accredited by North Central Association of Colleges and Schools.

PROGRAM INFORMATION

Offered since 1991. Accredited by American Culinary Federation Accrediting Commission. Program calendar is continuous. 15-month associate degree in patisserie and baking. 15-month associate degree in culinary arts. 8-month certificate in culinary arts.

PROGRAM AFFILIATION

American Culinary Federation; American Institute of Wine & Food; International Association of Culinary Professionals; National Restaurant Association; National Restaurant Association Educational Foundation.

AREAS OF STUDY

Baking; beverage management; confectionery show pieces; controlling costs in food service; culinary French; culinary skill development; food preparation; food purchasing; food service math; garde-manger; international cuisine; introduction to food service; kitchen management; management and human resources; meal planning; meat cutting; meat fabrication; menu and facilities design; nutrition; patisserie; restaurant opportunities; sanitation; saucier; seafood processing; soup, stock, sauce, and starch production; wines and spirits.

FACILITIES

13 classrooms; 2 computer laboratories; 4 demonstration laboratories; 13 food production kitchens; learning resource center; library; public restaurant; student lounge.

STUDENT PROFILE

898 total: 721 full-time; 177 part-time. 574 are under 25 years old; 272 are between 25 and 44 years old; 52 are over 44 years old.

FACULTY

68 total: 28 full-time; 40 part-time. 28 are culinary-certified teachers. Faculty-student ratio: 1:20.

SPECIAL PROGRAMS

Graduates with AAS receive Le Cordon Bleu Diplôme.

TYPICAL EXPENSES

Application fee: $100. Tuition: $9987.50 per 15 weeks for associate program in culinary arts; $9625 per 15 weeks for associate program in patisserie and baking; $6100 per 15 weeks for certificate program in culinary arts. Program-related fee includes $400 for activity fee.

FINANCIAL AID

In 2006, 56 scholarships were awarded (average award was $580); 230 loans were granted (average loan was $9855). Program-specific awards include Alternative Educational Loans. Employment placement assistance is available. Employment opportunities within the program are available.

HOUSING

Average off-campus housing cost per month: $800.

APPLICATION INFORMATION

Students may begin participation in January, February, April, May, July, August, September, and November. Applications are accepted continuously. Applicants must submit a formal application.

CONTACT

Matthew Verratti, Vice President of Admissions and Marketing, Le Cordon Bleu Program, 361 West Chestnut, Chicago, IL 60610-3050. Telephone: 312-873-2064. Fax: 312-798-2903. E-mail: mverratti@chicnet.org. World Wide Web: http://www.chic.edu.

ELGIN COMMUNITY COLLEGE

Culinary Arts and Hospitality Institute of Elgin

Elgin, Illinois

GENERAL INFORMATION

Public, coeducational, two-year college. Suburban campus. Founded in 1949. Accredited by North Central Association of Colleges and Schools.

PROGRAM INFORMATION

Offered since 1971. Accredited by American Culinary Federation Accrediting Commission. National Restaurant Association Educational Foundation ManageFirst certificates available. Program calendar is divided into semesters. 1-semester certificate in baking assistant. 1-semester certificate in lead baker. 1-year certificate in cook's helper. 2-semester certificate in hospitality. 2-semester certificate in prep cook. 2-year associate degree in hotel/motel management. 2-year associate degree in pastry chef. 2-year associate degree in culinary arts. 2-year associate degree in restaurant management. 3-semester certificate in restaurant operations. 3-semester certificate in first cook. 3-semester certificate in pastry chef assistant.

PROGRAM AFFILIATION

American Culinary Federation; American Institute of Baking; Council on Hotel, Restaurant, and Institutional Education; National Restaurant Association; National Restaurant Association Educational Foundation.

AREAS OF STUDY

Baking; beverage management; controlling costs in food service; culinary French; culinary skill development; food preparation; food purchasing; food service math; garde-manger; introduction to food service; management and human resources; meat cutting; meat fabrication; menu and facilities design; nutrition; patisserie; restaurant opportunities; sanitation; saucier; seafood processing; soup, stock, sauce, and starch production.

FACILITIES

2 bakeries; cafeteria; catering service; 4 classrooms; 4 demonstration laboratories; 5 food production kitchens; gourmet dining room; 5 laboratories; learning resource center; 5 lecture rooms; library; public restaurant; snack shop; student lounge; business conference center.

Elgin Community College *(continued)*

STUDENT PROFILE
450 total: 300 full-time; 150 part-time.

FACULTY
15 total: 5 full-time; 10 part-time. 9 are industry professionals; 8 are culinary-certified teachers. Prominent faculty: Michael Zema, CCE, FMP; Stephanie Johnson, FMP, CEPC; Mark Bosanac, CEC; Kimberly Rother. Faculty-student ratio: 1:30 lectures; 1:15 production classes.

SPECIAL PROGRAMS
International exchange with The Tourism School of Simmering Austria, internship opportunities, employment at BMW Championship Golf Tournament, culinary internships with Disney World.

TYPICAL EXPENSES
In-state tuition: $77 per credit hour part-time (in district), $359.30 per credit hour part-time (out-of-district). Out-of-state tuition: $437.22 per credit hour part-time. Program-related fees include $100 for lab fees; $200 for smallwares, toolbox, uniforms.

FINANCIAL AID
Program-specific awards include 5 National Restaurant Association scholarships per semester. Employment placement assistance is available. Employment opportunities within the program are available.

HOUSING
Average off-campus housing cost per month: $300.

APPLICATION INFORMATION
Students may begin participation in January, May, and August. Applications are accepted continuously. In 2006, 300 applied. Applicants must submit a formal application and have a high school diploma or GED.

CONTACT
Michael Zema, Coordinator, Culinary Arts and Hospitality Institute of Elgin, 1700 Spartan Drive, Room C AC 105A, Elgin, IL 60123. Telephone: 847-214-7461. Fax: 847-214-7510. E-mail: mzema@elgin.edu. World Wide Web: http://www.elgin.edu.

THE ILLINOIS INSTITUTE OF ART–CHICAGO

The International Culinary School at The Illinois Institute of Art–Chicago

Chicago, Illinois

GENERAL INFORMATION
Private, coeducational institution.

PROGRAM INFORMATION
Associate degree in Culinary Arts. Bachelor's degree in Culinary Management.

CONTACT
Office of Admissions, The International Culinary School at The Illinois Institute of Art–Chicago, 350 N. Orleans Street, Chicago, IL 60654-1593. Telephone: 312-280-3500. World Wide Web: http://www.artinstitutes.edu/chicago/.

See color display following page 186.

JOLIET JUNIOR COLLEGE

Culinary Arts/Hospitality Management

Joliet, Illinois

GENERAL INFORMATION
Public, coeducational, two-year college. Suburban campus. Founded in 1901. Accredited by North Central Association of Colleges and Schools.

PROGRAM INFORMATION
Offered since 1970. Accredited by American Culinary Federation Accrediting Commission. Program calendar is divided into semesters. 1-year certificate in pastry arts. 1-year certificate in baking. 1-year certificate in culinary arts. 2-year associate degree in hospitality management. 2-year associate degree in culinary arts.

PROGRAM AFFILIATION
American Culinary Federation; American Institute of Wine & Food; Council on Hotel, Restaurant, and Institutional Education; International Association of Culinary Professionals; National Restaurant Association; National Restaurant Association Educational Foundation; Women Chefs and Restaurateurs.

AREAS OF STUDY
Baking; controlling costs in food service; culinary French; culinary skill development; food preparation; garde-manger; ice carving; management and human resources; sanitation; wines and spirits.

FACILITIES

3 bake shops; bakery; 2 cafeterias; 2 catering services; 10 classrooms; 2 coffee shops; computer laboratory; 2 demonstration laboratories; 3 food production kitchens; 2 gourmet dining rooms; learning resource center; 5 lecture rooms; 2 libraries; 2 public restaurants; snack shop; student lounge; 2 teaching kitchens; ice carving room.

STUDENT PROFILE

217 total: 118 full-time; 99 part-time. 144 are under 25 years old; 55 are between 25 and 44 years old; 18 are over 44 years old.

FACULTY

9 total: 7 full-time; 2 part-time. Prominent faculty: Michael J. McGreal, CEC, CCE, CHE, FMP, CHA, MCFE; Keith Vonhoff, CEPC, CCE, CHE, FMP, CCP, CHA; Tim Bucci, CEC, CHE, CCE, MCFE, CCJ; Kyle Richardson, CEC, CHE, CCE. Faculty-student ratio: 1:16.

PROMINENT ALUMNI AND CURRENT AFFILIATION

Scott Hunnel, Walt Disney World; David Russell, Unilever Best Foods; Myk Banas, Marriott Chicago.

SPECIAL PROGRAMS

Culinary competitions, 1-year paid internships in U.S. and Germany, two-week trip to Europe to visit food and hotel venues.

TYPICAL EXPENSES

In-state tuition: $1320 per year full-time (in district), $44 per credit hour part-time (in district), $4579 per year full-time (out-of-district), $153 per credit hour part-time (out-of-district). Out-of-state tuition: $5648 per year full-time, $188 per credit hour part-time. Program-related fee includes $200 for knives and uniforms.

FINANCIAL AID

In 2006, 35 scholarships were awarded (average award was $996); 210 loans were granted (average loan was $2869). Employment placement assistance is available. Employment opportunities within the program are available.

HOUSING

Coed and apartment-style housing available. Average on-campus housing cost per month: $350. Average off-campus housing cost per month: $650.

APPLICATION INFORMATION

Students may begin participation in January, May, and August. Applications are accepted continuously. In 2006, 78 applied; 78 were accepted. Applicants must have a high school diploma or GED.

CONTACT

Michael J. McGreal, Department Chair, Culinary Arts/Hospitality Management, 1215 Houbolt Road, Joliet, IL 60431. Telephone: 815-280-2639. Fax: 815-280-2696. E-mail: mmcgreal@jjc.edu. World Wide Web: http://www.jjc.edu.

KENDALL COLLEGE

School of Culinary Arts and School of Hotel Management

Chicago, Illinois

GENERAL INFORMATION

Private, coeducational, four-year college. Urban campus. Founded in 1934. Accredited by North Central Association of Colleges and Schools.

PROGRAM INFORMATION

Offered since 1985. Accredited by American Culinary Federation Accrediting Commission, Higher Learning Commission of NCA. Program calendar is divided into quarters. 13-quarter bachelor's degree in culinary arts. 15-quarter bachelor's degree in hospitality management. 4-quarter certificate in catering. 4-quarter certificate in personal chef. 4-quarter certificate in baking and pastry arts. 4-quarter certificate in culinary arts/professional cookery. 5-quarter associate degree in culinary arts accelerated program. 6-quarter associate degree in baking and pastry arts. 7-quarter associate degree in culinary arts.

PROGRAM AFFILIATION

American Culinary Federation; American Institute of Baking; American Institute of Wine & Food; Council on Hotel, Restaurant, and Institutional Education; Hospitality Business Alliance; Illinois Restaurant Association; International Association of Culinary Professionals; National Restaurant Association; National Restaurant Association Educational Foundation; Northern Illinois Food Service Executives Association; Northern Illinois Hospitality Educators Association; The Bread Bakers Guild of America; Women Chefs and Restaurateurs.

AREAS OF STUDY

Baking; beverage management; buffet catering; confectionery show pieces; controlling costs in food service; convenience cookery; culinary French; culinary skill development; food preparation; food purchasing; food service communication; food service math; garde-manger; international cuisine; introduction to food service; kitchen management; management and human resources; meal planning; meat cutting; meat fabrication; menu and facilities design; nutrition;

Kendall College Offers Bachelor and Associate Degrees in:

- Culinary Arts

- Baking and Pastry

- Hospitality Management

- Business Management

- Early Childhood Education

For More Information call:

877-588-8860

SCHOOL OF CULINARY ARTS • LES ROCHES SCHOOL OF HOTEL MANAGEMENT

Kendall College
RIVERWORKS CAMPUS • CHICAGO

900 N. NORTH BRANCH STREET • CHICAGO, ILLINOIS 60622 • 866-667-3344 • www.kendall.edu

nutrition and food service; patisserie; restaurant opportunities; sanitation; saucier; seafood processing; soup, stock, sauce, and starch production; techniques of healthy cooking; wines and spirits.

FACILITIES
2 bake shops; cafeteria; catering service; 25 classrooms; coffee shop; 2 computer laboratories; 3 demonstration laboratories; 11 food production kitchens; garden; gourmet dining room; 4 laboratories; learning resource center; 25 lecture rooms; library; public restaurant; snack shop; student lounge; 11 teaching kitchens.

STUDENT PROFILE
1,448 total: 929 full-time; 519 part-time.

FACULTY
65 total: 50 full-time; 15 part-time. Prominent faculty: Christopher Koetke, CEC, CCE; Mike Artlip, CEC, CCE; Melina Kelson; Jeffrey Catrett. Faculty-student ratio: 1:20.

PROMINENT ALUMNI AND CURRENT AFFILIATION
Shawn McClain, Custom House/Spring Restaurants.

SPECIAL PROGRAMS
Internships (1–5 quarters), Culinary Competition Team, exchange programs in Marseille and Nice (France), Bluche (Switzerland), Montreal (Canada) and Tel Aviv (Israel).

TYPICAL EXPENSES
Application fee: $30. Tuition: $28,600 per year full-time, $600 per credit hour part-time. Program-related fees include $400 for knife kit; $300 for uniforms; $250 for book fees (per quarter).

FINANCIAL AID
Program-specific awards include graduate assistant appointments, college work-study positions in Culinary Arts Department, Hospitality Department and others. Employment placement assistance is available. Employment opportunities within the program are available.

HOUSING
Apartment-style housing available. Average on-campus housing cost per month: $1000. Average off-campus housing cost per month: $1200.

APPLICATION INFORMATION
Students may begin participation in January, March, July, and September. Applications are accepted continuously. In 2006, 816 applied; 780 were accepted. Applicants must interview; submit a formal application, an essay, official transcripts, and ACT/SAT scores (freshmen).

CONTACT
Richard Kriofsky, Director of Admissions, School of Culinary Arts and School of Hotel Management, 900 N. North Branch Street, Chicago, IL 60622. Telephone: 877-588-8860. Fax: 312-752-2021. E-mail: admissions@ kendall.edu. World Wide Web: http://www.kendall.edu/. **See display on page 158.**

LEXINGTON COLLEGE
Chicago, Illinois

GENERAL INFORMATION
Private, four-year college. Urban campus. Founded in 1977. Accredited by North Central Association of Colleges and Schools.

PROGRAM INFORMATION
Offered since 1977. Accredited by American Culinary Federation Accrediting Commission. Program calendar is divided into semesters. 2-year associate degree in hospitality management. 4-year bachelor's degree in hospitality management.

PROGRAM AFFILIATION
American Culinary Federation; Council on Hotel, Restaurant, and Institutional Education; Illinois Restaurant Association; National Restaurant Association; National Restaurant Association Educational Foundation; Women Chefs and Restaurateurs; Women's Foodservice Forum.

AREAS OF STUDY
Culinary skill development; events management; hotel and restaurant management; management and human resources.

FACILITIES
4 classrooms; computer laboratory; demonstration laboratory; library; student lounge; teaching kitchen.

STUDENT PROFILE
57 total: 48 full-time; 9 part-time. 41 are under 25 years old; 15 are between 25 and 44 years old; 1 is over 44 years old.

FACULTY
16 total: 4 full-time; 12 part-time. 8 are industry professionals; 2 are master chefs. Prominent faculty: Linda Rosner, CEC; Marta Elvira, PhD; Ines Cipriani, PhD. Faculty-student ratio: 1:8.

PROMINENT ALUMNI AND CURRENT AFFILIATION
Kristie Ranieri, Owner, Chive Catering; Alice Wheelwright, Vice President, Industry Marketing, Ecolab; Lisa Gervasio, Owner, Car Wash.

Lexington College *(continued)*

SPECIAL PROGRAMS
Summer internships (paid).

TYPICAL EXPENSES
Application fee: $30. Tuition: $9760 per semester full-time, $800 per credit hour part-time. Program-related fee includes $350 for culinary lab.

FINANCIAL AID
In 2006, 14 scholarships were awarded (average award was $30,000); 50 loans were granted (average loan was $3000). Program-specific awards include Lexington Academic Grants. Employment placement assistance is available. Employment opportunities within the program are available.

HOUSING
Average off-campus housing cost per month: $800.

APPLICATION INFORMATION
Students may begin participation in January and August. Applications are accepted continuously. In 2006, 48 applied; 46 were accepted. Applicants must submit a formal application, letters of reference, an essay, ACT or SAT scores.

CONTACT
Nina Palligrino, High School Representative, 310 South Peoria Street, Chicago, IL 60607. Telephone: 312-226-6294 Ext. 226. Fax: 312-226-6405. E-mail: admissions@lexingtoncollege.edu. World Wide Web: http://www.lexingtoncollege.edu.

LINCOLN LAND COMMUNITY COLLEGE

Hospitality Management

Springfield, Illinois

GENERAL INFORMATION
Public, coeducational, two-year college. Urban campus. Founded in 1967. Accredited by North Central Association of Colleges and Schools.

PROGRAM INFORMATION
Offered since 1994. Accredited by Council on Hotel, Restaurant and Institutional Education. National Restaurant Association Educational Foundation ManageFirst certificates available. Program calendar is divided into semesters. 1-year certificate in certified dietary manager. 1-year certificate in lodging management. 1-year certificate in culinary arts. 1-year certificate in pastry. 2-year associate degree in hospitality management.

PROGRAM AFFILIATION
American Culinary Federation; American Dietetic Association; American Vegan Society; Confrerie de la Chaine des Rotisseurs; Council on Hotel, Restaurant, and Institutional Education; Dietary Managers Association; Illinois Restaurant Association; National Restaurant Association; National Restaurant Association Educational Foundation.

AREAS OF STUDY
Baking; buffet catering; controlling costs in food service; culinary French; culinary skill development; food preparation; food purchasing; food service communication; food service math; garde-manger; international cuisine; introduction to food service; kitchen management; management and human resources; meal planning; meat cutting; nutrition; nutrition and food service; patisserie; restaurant opportunities; sanitation; seafood processing; soup, stock, sauce, and starch production; wines and spirits.

FACILITIES
Bake shop; bakery; cafeteria; catering service; classroom; computer laboratory; demonstration laboratory; food production kitchen; garden; laboratory; learning resource center; lecture room; library; public restaurant; snack shop; student lounge; teaching kitchen.

STUDENT PROFILE
130 total: 30 full-time; 100 part-time. 45 are under 25 years old; 45 are between 25 and 44 years old; 40 are over 44 years old.

FACULTY
13 total: 1 full-time; 12 part-time. 12 are industry professionals; 3 are master chefs; 1 is a master baker; 4 are culinary-certified teachers. Prominent faculty: David Radwine; Howard Seidel, CEC; Raven Pulliam, CEC; Michael Higgins. Faculty-student ratio: 1:18.

SPECIAL PROGRAMS
Paid internships, participation in culinary society events, membership in ACF chapter.

TYPICAL EXPENSES
Tuition: $900 per semester full-time (in district), $225 per semester part-time. Program-related fees include $20 for materials; $25 for chef's jacket.

FINANCIAL AID
In 2006, 6 scholarships were awarded (average award was $500); 10 loans were granted (average loan was $1000). Employment placement assistance is available. Employment opportunities within the program are available.

HOUSING
Average off-campus housing cost per month: $400.

APPLICATION INFORMATION

Students may begin participation in January, June, and August. Applications are accepted continuously. Applicants must submit a formal application.

CONTACT

Jay Kitterman, Program Director, Hospitality Management, 5250 Shepherd Road, Springfield, IL 62794. Telephone: 217-786-2772. Fax: 217-786-2339. E-mail: jay.kitterman@llcc.edu. World Wide Web: http://www.llcc.edu.

PARKLAND COLLEGE

Hospitality Industry

Champaign, Illinois

GENERAL INFORMATION

Public, coeducational, two-year college. Small-town setting. Founded in 1967. Accredited by North Central Association of Colleges and Schools.

PROGRAM INFORMATION

Offered since 1981. Accredited by Council on Hotel, Restaurant and Institutional Education, Commission on Accreditation of Hospitality Management Programs. National Restaurant Association Educational Foundation ManageFirst certificates available. Program calendar is divided into semesters. 1-year certificate in hospitality industry: food service. 2-year associate degree in hospitality industry: restaurant management.

PROGRAM AFFILIATION

Council on Hotel, Restaurant, and Institutional Education; International Executive Food Association; International Food Service Executives Association; National Restaurant Association; National Restaurant Association Educational Foundation.

AREAS OF STUDY

Baking; beverage management; buffet catering; controlling costs in food service; convenience cookery; culinary skill development; food preparation; food purchasing; food service communication; food service math; international cuisine; introduction to food service; kitchen management; management and human resources; meal planning; meat fabrication; menu and facilities design; nutrition; nutrition and food service; restaurant opportunities; sanitation; soup, stock, sauce, and starch production; wines and spirits.

FACILITIES

Catering service; classroom; computer laboratory; demonstration laboratory; food production kitchen; learning resource center; lecture room; teaching kitchen.

STUDENT PROFILE

71 total: 34 full-time; 37 part-time. 41 are under 25 years old; 26 are between 25 and 44 years old; 4 are over 44 years old.

FACULTY

5 total: 1 full-time; 4 part-time. 3 are industry professionals. Prominent faculty: Marshall Huffman, FMP, CFE; Brad Pierson; Sue Summerville; Mark Kesler. Faculty-student ratio: 1:15.

SPECIAL PROGRAMS

Food Service Sanitation Certification, semester or summer internships.

TYPICAL EXPENSES

In-state tuition: $82 per credit hour (in district), $219 per credit hour (out-of-district). Out-of-state tuition: $338 per credit hour. Tuition for international students: $338 per credit hour. Program-related fee includes $54 for lab fee for food production class.

FINANCIAL AID

In 2006, 5 scholarships were awarded (average award was $900). Program-specific awards include Arby's Foodservice/Restaurant Management Career Grant ($1000), William P. Myers Foundation Awards ($1000). Employment placement assistance is available. Employment opportunities within the program are available.

HOUSING

Average off-campus housing cost per month: $350.

APPLICATION INFORMATION

Students may begin participation in January and August. Applications are accepted continuously. In 2006, 17 applied; 17 were accepted. Applicants must submit a formal application.

CONTACT

Marshall Huffman, Hospitality Program Director, Hospitality Industry, 2400 West Bradley Avenue, Champaign, IL 61821-1806. Telephone: 217-351-2378. Fax: 217-373-3896. E-mail: mhuffman@parkland.edu. World Wide Web: http://www.parkland.edu.

ROBERT MORRIS COLLEGE

Institute of Culinary Arts

Aurora, Chicago, and Orland Park, Illinois

GENERAL INFORMATION

Private, coeducational, four-year college. Urban campus. Founded in 1913. Accredited by North Central Association of Colleges and Schools.

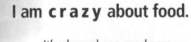

PROGRAM INFORMATION

Offered since 2003. National Restaurant Association Educational Foundation ManageFirst certificates available. Program calendar is divided into quarters, 5 ten-week academic sessions per year. 15-month associate degree in culinary arts. 3-year bachelor's degree in hospitality management.

PROGRAM AFFILIATION

American Culinary Federation; American Dietetic Association; American Institute of Wine & Food; American Wine Society; International Association of Culinary Professionals; National Restaurant Association; National Restaurant Association Educational Foundation; Women Chefs and Restaurateurs.

AREAS OF STUDY

Baking; beverage management; buffet catering; controlling costs in food service; convenience cookery; culinary French; culinary skill development; food preparation; food purchasing; food service communication; food service math; garde-manger; international cuisine; introduction to food service; kitchen management; management and human resources; meal planning; meat cutting; meat fabrication; menu and facilities design; nutrition; restaurant opportunities; sanitation; saucier; seafood processing; soup, stock, sauce, and starch production; wines and spirits.

FACILITIES

32 computer laboratories; 3 learning resource centers; 32 lecture rooms; 6 teaching kitchens.

STUDENT PROFILE

350 total: 325 full-time; 25 part-time.

FACULTY

42 total: 6 full-time; 36 part-time. Prominent faculty: Brian Flower; Jennifer Bucko; John Hudac; Scott Nitsche, CEC. Faculty-student ratio: 1:16.

SPECIAL PROGRAMS

Culinary competitions, paid internships, international experience with Italian and French culinary schools.

TYPICAL EXPENSES

Application fee: $30. Tuition: $16,800 per year full-time, $1700 per course part-time. Program-related fees include $850 for lab fee (per session); $275 for knife kit; $180 for 3 uniforms.

FINANCIAL AID

In 2006, 20 scholarships were awarded. Program-specific awards include 85% of students receive some type of financial aid. Employment placement assistance is available. Employment opportunities within the program are available.

HOUSING

Coed and apartment-style housing available. Average on-campus housing cost per month: $800.

APPLICATION INFORMATION

Students may begin participation in February, July, September, and December. Applications are accepted continuously. In 2006, 495 applied; 373 were accepted. Applicants must interview; submit a formal application and proof of high school graduation or GED completion.

CONTACT

Nancy Rotunno, Executive Director, Institute of Culinary Arts, 401 South State Street, Chicago, IL 60605. Telephone: 312-935-6800. Fax: 312-935-6930. E-mail: nrotunno@robertmorris.edu. World Wide Web: http://www.robertmorris.edu/.

See display on page 162.

SOUTHWESTERN ILLINOIS COLLEGE

Culinary Arts and Food Management

Granite City, Illinois

GENERAL INFORMATION

Public, coeducational, two-year college. Suburban campus. Founded in 1946. Accredited by North Central Association of Colleges and Schools.

PROGRAM INFORMATION

Accredited by American Culinary Federation Accrediting Commission. Program calendar is divided into semesters. 1-semester certificate in culinary arts. 1-year certificate in food service and management. 2-year associate degree in culinary arts and food management.

PROGRAM AFFILIATION

American Culinary Federation; National Restaurant Association.

AREAS OF STUDY

Baking; beverage management; controlling costs in food service; culinary skill development; food preparation; food purchasing; food service math; garde-manger; international cuisine; introduction to food service; kitchen management; meal planning; meat cutting; nutrition; nutrition and food service; restaurant opportunities; sanitation; soup, stock, sauce, and starch production.

Southwestern Illinois College *(continued)*

FACILITIES
2 bake shops; 2 bakeries; 2 cafeterias; 2 classrooms; coffee shop; 4 computer laboratories; 2 demonstration laboratories; 2 food production kitchens; 2 laboratories; 2 learning resource centers; 2 lecture rooms; 2 libraries; 2 student lounges; 2 teaching kitchens.

STUDENT PROFILE
150 total: 50 full-time; 100 part-time.

FACULTY
10 total: 1 full-time; 9 part-time. Prominent faculty: Ollie Sommer, CEC, AAC; Tom Noonan, CEC; Lee Conway; Leisa Brockman. Faculty-student ratio: 1:12.

SPECIAL PROGRAMS
Semester internships, trip to National Restaurant Association show.

TYPICAL EXPENSES
In-state tuition: $68 per credit hour (for certificate) part-time (in district), $174 per credit hour (for certificate) part-time (out-of-district). Out-of-state tuition: $275 per credit hour (for certificate) part-time. Program-related fee includes $1200 for supplies.

FINANCIAL AID
In 2006, 2 scholarships were awarded (average award was $500). Program-specific awards include National Restaurant Association scholarships. Employment placement assistance is available. Employment opportunities within the program are available.

APPLICATION INFORMATION
Students may begin participation in January, June, and August. Applications are accepted continuously. Applicants must submit a formal application; have high school diploma or GED and food service sanitation license.

CONTACT
Janice Sanders, Admissions, Culinary Arts and Food Management, 2500 Carlyle Road, Belleville, IL 62221. Telephone: 618-222-5436. Fax: 618-222-8964. E-mail: janice.sanders@swic.edu. World Wide Web: http://www.swic.edu.

TRITON COLLEGE

Hospitality Industry Administration

River Grove, Illinois

GENERAL INFORMATION
Public, coeducational, two-year college. Urban campus. Founded in 1964. Accredited by North Central Association of Colleges and Schools.

PROGRAM INFORMATION
Offered since 1972. Accredited by American Culinary Federation Accrediting Commission. Program calendar is divided into semesters. 1-year certificate in hotel management. 1-year certificate in baking and pastry. 1-year certificate in restaurant management. 1-year certificate in culinary arts. 2-year associate degree in hotel management. 2-year associate degree in restaurant management. 2-year associate degree in culinary arts.

PROGRAM AFFILIATION
American Culinary Federation; American Institute of Baking; American Institute of Wine & Food; Council on Hotel, Restaurant, and Institutional Education; International Association of Culinary Professionals; National Restaurant Association; National Restaurant Association Educational Foundation.

AREAS OF STUDY
Baking; beverage management; food preparation; food purchasing; garde-manger; international cuisine; nutrition; sanitation; wines and spirits.

FACILITIES
Bake shop; bakery; cafeteria; catering service; 7 classrooms; coffee shop; computer laboratory; demonstration laboratory; food production kitchen; garden; gourmet dining room; learning resource center; 7 lecture rooms; 2 libraries; public restaurant; snack shop; student lounge; teaching kitchen; vineyard.

STUDENT PROFILE
250 total: 150 full-time; 100 part-time. 75 are under 25 years old; 100 are between 25 and 44 years old; 75 are over 44 years old.

FACULTY
24 total: 4 full-time; 20 part-time. 2 are industry professionals; 2 are culinary-certified teachers. Prominent faculty: Jerome Drosos, CEC; Denise Smith, CEPC; Chod Pagtakhan, CEC. Faculty-student ratio: 1:15.

PROMINENT ALUMNI AND CURRENT AFFILIATION
Jim Banos; Steven Langois; Vito Barbarante.

SPECIAL PROGRAMS
Wine making class includes tours in southwest Michigan, culinary competition.

TYPICAL EXPENSES

Application fee: $10. In-state tuition: $900 per semester full-time (in district), $56 per credit hour part-time (in district), $2700 per semester full-time (out-of-district), $181 per credit hour part-time (out-of-district). Out-of-state tuition: $2700 per semester full-time, $181 per credit hour part-time. Tuition for international students: $2700 per semester full-time, $181 per credit hour part-time. Program-related fees include $100 for cutlery; $50 for uniform; $150 for lab fees.

FINANCIAL AID

In 2006, 8 scholarships were awarded (average award was $2000). Employment placement assistance is available. Employment opportunities within the program are available.

HOUSING

Average off-campus housing cost per month: $600.

APPLICATION INFORMATION

Students may begin participation in January, June, and August. Applications are accepted continuously. In 2006, 150 applied; 150 were accepted. Applicants must submit a formal application.

CONTACT

Jerome Drosos, Coordinator, Chef Instructor, Hospitality Industry Administration, 2000 Fifth Avenue, River Grove, IL 60171. Telephone: 708-456-0300 Ext. 3624. E-mail: jdrosos@triton.edu. World Wide Web: http://www.triton.edu.

UNIVERSITY OF ILLINOIS AT URBANA–CHAMPAIGN

Hospitality Management/Department of Food Science and Human Nutrition

Urbana, Illinois

GENERAL INFORMATION

Public, coeducational, university. Urban campus. Founded in 1867. Accredited by North Central Association of Colleges and Schools.

PROGRAM INFORMATION

Offered since 1952. Accredited by American Dietetic Association. Program calendar is divided into semesters. 4-year bachelor's degree in hospitality management.

PROGRAM AFFILIATION

American Dietetic Association; Council on Hotel, Restaurant, and Institutional Education; Illinois Restaurant Association; Institute of Food Technologists.

AREAS OF STUDY

Buffet catering; controlling costs in food service; food preparation; food purchasing; food science; kitchen management; management and human resources; meat cutting; meat fabrication; nutrition; restaurant opportunities; sanitation.

FACILITIES

Cafeteria; catering service; classroom; computer laboratory; food production kitchen; gourmet dining room; laboratory; lecture room; student lounge; teaching kitchen.

TYPICAL STUDENT PROFILE

106 full-time. 106 are under 25 years old.

SPECIAL PROGRAMS

Practical work experience, professional work experience.

FINANCIAL AID

Program-specific awards include two 4-year work-study scholarships ($2000 per year plus hourly wage). Employment placement assistance is available. Employment opportunities within the program are available.

HOUSING

Coed, apartment-style, and single-sex housing available.

APPLICATION INFORMATION

Students may begin participation in August. Application deadline for fall is January 1. Applicants must submit a formal application, an essay, ACT scores.

CONTACT

Director of Admissions, Hospitality Management/Department of Food Science and Human Nutrition, 901 West Illinois Street, Urbana, IL 61801. Telephone: 217-333-0302. World Wide Web: http://www.fshn.uiuc.edu/academics/undergraduate_programs/hospitality_management/.

WASHBURNE CULINARY INSTITUTE

Chicago, Illinois

GENERAL INFORMATION

Public, coeducational, culinary institute. Urban campus. Founded in 1937. Accredited by North Central Association of Colleges and Schools.

PROGRAM INFORMATION

Offered since 1937. Program calendar is divided into semesters, year-round. 48-week advanced certificate in culinary arts. 48-week advanced certificate in baking and pastry arts. 48-week advanced certificate in baking

Washburne Culinary Institute *(continued)*

and pastry arts. 48-week advanced certificate in culinary arts. 64-week associate degree in baking and pastry arts. 80-week associate degree in culinary arts.

PROGRAM AFFILIATION

American Culinary Federation; International Food Service Executives Association; National Restaurant Association Educational Foundation.

AREAS OF STUDY

Baking; buffet catering; controlling costs in food service; culinary skill development; food preparation; food purchasing; food service math; garde-manger; international cuisine; introduction to food service; kitchen management; management and human resources; meal planning; meat cutting; meat fabrication; menu and facilities design; nutrition; nutrition and food service; patisserie; restaurant opportunities; sanitation; saucier; seafood processing; soup, stock, sauce, and starch production.

FACILITIES

3 bake shops; cafeteria; catering service; 8 classrooms; coffee shop; computer laboratory; demonstration laboratory; 9 food production kitchens; garden; 8 lecture rooms; library; 2 public restaurants; snack shop; 2 student lounges; 9 teaching kitchens.

STUDENT PROFILE

150 full-time. 25 are under 25 years old; 100 are between 25 and 44 years old; 25 are over 44 years old.

FACULTY

10 total: 8 full-time; 2 part-time. 4 are industry professionals; 1 is a master chef; 3 are culinary-certified teachers. Prominent faculty: Alex Dering; Tim Coonan; Delfina Perez; Lee Jamison. Faculty-student ratio: 1:20.

PROMINENT ALUMNI AND CURRENT AFFILIATION

Jimmy Bannos, Heaven on Seven Restaurants; Mary Sue Milliken, Border Grill; Jim Singerling, CEO, Club Manager Association.

SPECIAL PROGRAMS

16-week experience in school's public restaurant, continuing education center at South Shore Cultural Center.

TYPICAL EXPENSES

In-state tuition: $13,000 per degree (in district), add $108.83 per credit hour (out-of-district). Out-of-state tuition: add $219.62 per credit hour. Program-related fees include $25 for registration fee; $100 for activity fee; $20 for graduation fee.

FINANCIAL AID

In 2006, 25 scholarships were awarded (average award was $35,000). Employment placement assistance is available. Employment opportunities within the program are available.

APPLICATION INFORMATION

Students may begin participation in January, May, and August. Application deadline for fall is August 10. Application deadline for winter is January 10. Application deadline for summer is May 1. In 2006, 400 applied; 150 were accepted. Applicants must interview; submit a formal application.

CONTACT

Rhonda Purwin, Manager, Enrollment and Industry Services, 740 West 63rd Street, Chicago, IL 60620. Telephone: 773-281-8559. Fax: 773-602-5452. E-mail: rpurwin@ccc.edu. World Wide Web: http://kennedyking.ccc.edu/washburne/index.html.

INDIANA

THE ART INSTITUTE OF INDIANAPOLIS

The International Culinary School at The Art Institute of Indianapolis

Indianapolis, Indiana

GENERAL INFORMATION

Private, coeducational institution.

PROGRAM INFORMATION

Associate degree in Culinary Arts. Bachelor's degree in Culinary Management. Certificate in Baking and Pastry. Certificate in Culinary Arts.

CONTACT

Office of Admissions, The International Culinary School at The Art Institute of Indianapolis, 3500 Depauw Boulevard, Indianapolis, IN 46268-6124. Telephone: 317-613-4800. World Wide Web: http://www.artinstitutes.edu/indianapolis/.

See color display following page 186.

BALL STATE UNIVERSITY

Department of Family and Consumer Sciences

Muncie, Indiana

GENERAL INFORMATION
Public, coeducational, university. Urban campus. Founded in 1918. Accredited by North Central Association of Colleges and Schools.

PROGRAM INFORMATION
Offered since 1975. Program calendar is divided into semesters. 2-year associate degree in hospitality and food management. 4-year bachelor's degree in hospitality and food management.

PROGRAM AFFILIATION
American Culinary Federation; Council on Hotel, Restaurant, and Institutional Education.

AREAS OF STUDY
Beverage management; buffet catering; controlling costs in food service; convenience cookery; culinary skill development; customer relations; food preparation; food purchasing; introduction to food service; kitchen management; management and human resources; meal planning; nutrition; nutrition and food service; restaurant opportunities; sanitation.

FACILITIES
5 classrooms; computer laboratory; food production kitchen; gourmet dining room; 3 laboratories; learning resource center; lecture room; library; public restaurant; student lounge; teaching kitchen.

TYPICAL STUDENT PROFILE
75 full-time. 65 are under 25 years old; 10 are between 25 and 44 years old.

SPECIAL PROGRAMS
Paid internships.

FINANCIAL AID
Program-specific awards include 5 Moore Scholarships ($10,000). Employment placement assistance is available. Employment opportunities within the program are available.

HOUSING
Coed, apartment-style, and single-sex housing available.

APPLICATION INFORMATION
Students may begin participation in January, May, and August. Applications are accepted continuously. Applicants must submit a formal application and letters of reference.

CONTACT
Director of Admissions, Department of Family and Consumer Sciences, AT 150 D, Ball State University, Muncie, IN 47306. Telephone: 765-285-5956. Fax: 765-285-2314. World Wide Web: http://www.bsu.edu/fcs/article/0,1894,35151-4865-10251,00.html.

INDIANA BUSINESS COLLEGE

Indianapolis, Indiana

GENERAL INFORMATION
Private, coeducational, two-year college. Accredited by Accrediting Council for Independent Colleges and Schools.

PROGRAM INFORMATION
2-year associate degree in pastry arts. 2-year associate degree in culinary arts.

SPECIAL PROGRAMS
Externships.

CONTACT
Admissions Office, 644 East Washington Street, Indianapolis, IN 46204. Telephone: 877-IND-CHEF. World Wide Web: http://www.thechefsacademy.com.

INDIANA UNIVERSITY–PURDUE UNIVERSITY FORT WAYNE

Hospitality Management

Fort Wayne, Indiana

GENERAL INFORMATION
Public, coeducational, comprehensive institution. Suburban campus. Founded in 1917. Accredited by North Central Association of Colleges and Schools.

PROGRAM INFORMATION
Offered since 1976. Program calendar is divided into semesters. 2-year associate degree in hotel, restaurant, and tourism management. 4-year bachelor's degree in hospitality and tourism management.

PROGRAM AFFILIATION
Confrerie de la Chaine des Rotisseurs; Council on Hotel, Restaurant, and Institutional Education; National Restaurant Association Educational Foundation.

AREAS OF STUDY
Beverage management; buffet catering; controlling costs in food service; convenience cookery; culinary French; culinary skill development; food preparation; food

Indiana University–Purdue University Fort Wayne
(continued)

purchasing; food service communication; food service math; introduction to food service; kitchen management; management and human resources; meal planning; menu and facilities design; nutrition; nutrition and food service; restaurant opportunities; sanitation; soup, stock, sauce, and starch production; tourism; wines and spirits.

FACILITIES
5 computer laboratories; demonstration laboratory; food production kitchen; learning resource center; library; 6 student lounges; ballroom.

TYPICAL STUDENT PROFILE
100 total: 80 full-time; 20 part-time.

SPECIAL PROGRAMS
Annual visits to New York, Las Vegas, Chicago, Walt Disney World, and international venues, opportunity for students to serve dining public in local hotels and restaurants.

FINANCIAL AID
Employment placement assistance is available.

HOUSING
Apartment-style housing available.

APPLICATION INFORMATION
Students may begin participation in January and August. Applications are accepted continuously. Applicants must submit a formal application.

CONTACT
Director of Admissions, Hospitality Management, Neff Hall, Room 330B, Fort Wayne, IN 46805-1499. Telephone: 260-481-6562. Fax: 260-481-5767. World Wide Web: http://www.ipfw.edu/cfs/undergrad/bshtm.shtml.

IVY TECH COMMUNITY COLLEGE– CENTRAL INDIANA

Hospitality Administration Program

Indianapolis, Indiana

GENERAL INFORMATION
Public, coeducational, two-year college. Urban campus. Founded in 1963. Accredited by North Central Association of Colleges and Schools.

PROGRAM INFORMATION
Offered since 1981. Accredited by Council on Hotel, Restaurant and Institutional Education, Commission on Accreditation on Hospitality Management (CAHM). National Restaurant Association Educational Foundation ManageFirst certificates available. Program calendar is divided into semesters. 2-year associate degree in restaurant management. 2-year associate degree in hotel management specialty. 2-year associate degree in event management specialty. 2-year associate degree in hospitality administration degree. 2-year associate degree in baking and pastry arts specialty. 2-year associate degree in culinary arts specialty. 3-year associate degree in culinary arts (with apprenticeship). 8-month certificate in baking/pastry arts. 8-month certificate in culinary arts. 8-month certificate in hospitality management.

PROGRAM AFFILIATION
American Culinary Federation; Council on Hotel, Restaurant, and Institutional Education; International Wine & Food Society; National Restaurant Association; National Restaurant Association Educational Foundation; Retailer's Bakery Association; Society of Wine Educators; Women Chefs and Restaurateurs.

AREAS OF STUDY
Baking; beverage management; controlling costs in food service; culinary French; culinary skill development; food preparation; food purchasing; food service communication; food service math; garde-manger; international cuisine; introduction to food service; kitchen management; management and human resources; meat cutting; meat fabrication; menu and facilities design; nutrition; nutrition and food service; patisserie; restaurant opportunities; sanitation; saucier; seafood processing; soup, stock, sauce, and starch production; wines and spirits.

FACILITIES
Cafeteria; catering service; 20 classrooms; 3 computer laboratories; 2 food production kitchens; 2 laboratories; 3 lecture rooms; library; student lounge; 2 teaching kitchens.

STUDENT PROFILE
450 total: 180 full-time; 270 part-time.

FACULTY
25 total: 4 full-time; 21 part-time. 20 are industry professionals; 16 are culinary-certified teachers. Prominent faculty: Lauri Griffin, CEC; Jeff Bricker, CEC; Thom England; Paul Vida. Faculty-student ratio: 1:25 lectures; 1:15 labs.

SPECIAL PROGRAMS
2-week program at cooking school in Europe, culinary competitions, ACF student chapter-club.

TYPICAL EXPENSES

In-state tuition: $83.95 per credit hour full-time (in district), $83.95 per credit hour part-time. Out-of-state tuition: $170.25 per credit hour full-time, $170.25 per credit hour part-time. Program-related fees include $245 for culinary/baking tool kit; $85 for student uniform.

FINANCIAL AID

Employment placement assistance is available. Employment opportunities within the program are available.

HOUSING

Average off-campus housing cost per month: $425.

APPLICATION INFORMATION

Students may begin participation in January, May, and August. Applications are accepted continuously. Applicants must submit a formal application and have a high school diploma, GED, or equivalent.

CONTACT

Jeff Bricker, Chairperson, Hospitality Administration Program, 50 West Fall Creek Parkway, N. Drive, Indianapolis, IN 46208. Telephone: 317-921-4516. Fax: 317-921-4203. E-mail: jbricker@ivytech.edu. World Wide Web: http://www.ivytech.edu/indianapolis.

IVY TECH COMMUNITY COLLEGE– NORTH CENTRAL

South Bend, Indiana

GENERAL INFORMATION

Public, coeducational, two-year college. Urban campus. Founded in 1963. Accredited by North Central Association of Colleges and Schools.

PROGRAM INFORMATION

Offered since 2000. Accredited by American Culinary Federation Accrediting Commission. Program calendar is divided into semesters. 2-year associate degree in hospitality administration: restaurant management. 2-year associate degree in hospitality administration: culinary arts. 2-year associate degree in hospitality administration: baking and pastry.

PROGRAM AFFILIATION

American Culinary Federation.

AREAS OF STUDY

Baking.

FACILITIES

Bake shop; classroom; demonstration laboratory; food production kitchen; garden.

STUDENT PROFILE

180 total: 60 full-time; 120 part-time. 80 are under 25 years old; 80 are between 25 and 44 years old; 20 are over 44 years old.

FACULTY

8 total: 2 full-time; 6 part-time. Prominent faculty: Tim Carrigan; Patsy Wyman. Faculty-student ratio: 1:20.

SPECIAL PROGRAMS

Annual trip (different every year with some scholarships available).

TYPICAL EXPENSES

In-state tuition: $91.30 per credit hour full-time (in district), $91.30 per credit hour part-time. Out-of-state tuition: $185.75 per credit hour full-time, $185.75 per credit hour part-time. Program-related fees include $200 for cutlery; $40–$50 for uniforms.

FINANCIAL AID

In 2006, 10 scholarships were awarded (average award was $500). Employment placement assistance is available.

HOUSING

Average off-campus housing cost per month: $600–$800.

APPLICATION INFORMATION

Students may begin participation in January and August. Applications are accepted continuously. In 2006, 60 applied; 60 were accepted. Applicants must submit a formal application and placement/assessment testing.

CONTACT

Timothy Carrigan, Chair, Hospitality Administration Program, 220 Dean Johnson Boulevard, South Bend, IN 46601. Telephone: 574-289-7001 Ext. 5440. Fax: 574-245-7102. E-mail: tcarriga@ivytech.edu. World Wide Web: http://www.ivytech.edu.

IVY TECH COMMUNITY COLLEGE– NORTHEAST

Hospitality Administration

Fort Wayne, Indiana

GENERAL INFORMATION

Public, coeducational, two-year college. Suburban campus. Founded in 1969. Accredited by North Central Association of Colleges and Schools.

Ivy Tech Community College–Northeast *(continued)*

PROGRAM INFORMATION
Offered since 1969. Accredited by American Culinary Federation Accrediting Commission. Program calendar is divided into semesters. 2-year associate degree in baking/pastry arts. 2-year associate degree in culinary arts.

PROGRAM AFFILIATION
American Culinary Federation.

AREAS OF STUDY
Baking; confectionery show pieces; controlling costs in food service; food preparation; food purchasing; garde-manger; international cuisine; kitchen management; management and human resources; meat cutting; meat fabrication; nutrition; patisserie; sanitation; seafood processing; soup, stock, sauce, and starch production; wines and spirits.

FACILITIES
Bake shop; bakery; catering service; 4 classrooms; 2 computer laboratories; demonstration laboratory; food production kitchen; gourmet dining room; 3 laboratories; 3 lecture rooms; library; 2 student lounges; teaching kitchen.

FACULTY
15 total: 3 full-time; 12 part-time. 10 are industry professionals; 1 is a master chef; 1 is a master baker; 3 are culinary-certified teachers. Prominent faculty: Robert Kelty, CCE; Meshele Wyneken, RD; G. Alan Eyler, CFBE; Jeff Bunting. Faculty-student ratio: 1:13.

PROMINENT ALUMNI AND CURRENT AFFILIATION
Renee Endres, Joseph Dugus; Kyle Hockomeyer, Back Forty; James House, Parkview Hospital.

SPECIAL PROGRAMS
10-day European culinary study tour.

TYPICAL EXPENSES
In-state tuition: $91.30 per credit hour. Out-of-state tuition: $186 per credit hour. Program-related fees include $175 for knife kit, cutlery; $185 for baking kit, knives/baking supplies.

FINANCIAL AID
In 2006, 8 scholarships were awarded (average award was $2600). Program-specific awards include scholarships funded by Boiardi Endowment, Gordons Scholarship. Employment placement assistance is available.

HOUSING
Average off-campus housing cost per month: $600.

APPLICATION INFORMATION
Students may begin participation in January, May, and August. Application deadline for fall is August 15. Application deadline for spring is December 15. Application deadline for summer is April 30. Applicants must submit a formal application.

CONTACT
Alan Eyler, Program Chairperson, Hospitality Administration, 3800 North Anthony Boulevard, Ft. Wayne, IN 46805. Telephone: 260-480-4240. Fax: 260-480-2051. E-mail: aeyler@ivytech.edu. World Wide Web: http://www.ivytech.edu.

IVY TECH COMMUNITY COLLEGE–NORTHWEST

Hospitality Administration

Gary, Indiana

GENERAL INFORMATION
Public, coeducational, two-year college. Urban campus. Founded in 1963. Accredited by North Central Association of Colleges and Schools.

PROGRAM INFORMATION
Offered since 1985. Accredited by American Culinary Federation Accrediting Commission. Program calendar is divided into semesters. 1-year certificate in culinary arts. 2-year associate degree in convention management. 2-year associate degree in restaurant management. 2-year associate degree in hotel/restaurant management. 2-year associate degree in bakery and pastry arts. 2-year associate degree in culinary arts.

PROGRAM AFFILIATION
American Culinary Federation; National Restaurant Association; National Restaurant Association Educational Foundation; Women Chefs and Restaurateurs.

AREAS OF STUDY
Baking; buffet catering; controlling costs in food service; culinary French; culinary skill development; food preparation; food purchasing; garde-manger; international cuisine; introduction to food service; management and human resources; meal planning; meat cutting; meat fabrication; menu and facilities design; nutrition; patisserie; sanitation; saucier; seafood processing; soup, stock, sauce, and starch production; wines and spirits.

FACILITIES
Bake shop; 2 computer laboratories; 2 demonstration laboratories; gourmet dining room; learning resource center; library; student lounge; teaching kitchen.

STUDENT PROFILE
96 total: 75 full-time; 21 part-time.

FACULTY
9 total: 3 full-time; 6 part-time. Prominent faculty: Jo Anne Garvey; Elida Abeyta; Richard Delby.

SPECIAL PROGRAMS
National Restaurant Association shows, 2-week trip to France, National Convention for the American Culinary Education.

TYPICAL EXPENSES
In-state tuition: $87.75 per credit hour. Out-of-state tuition: $178.50 per credit hour. Program-related fees include $347 for knife set; $60 for lab uniform; $167 for baking kit; $50 for garde manager.

FINANCIAL AID
In 2006, 8 scholarships were awarded (average award was $752). Employment placement assistance is available.

APPLICATION INFORMATION
Students may begin participation in January, May, and August. Applications are accepted continuously. Applicants must submit a formal application and have a high school diploma or GED.

CONTACT
Terry Zych, Program Chair/School Chair, Hospitality Administration, 3714 Franklin Street, Michigan City, IN 46360. Telephone: 219-981-1111 Ext. 4400. Fax: 219-981-4415. E-mail: tzych@ivytech.edu. World Wide Web: http://www.ivytech.edu.

IOWA

DES MOINES AREA COMMUNITY COLLEGE

Iowa Culinary Institute (ICI)

Ankeny, Iowa

GENERAL INFORMATION
Public, coeducational, two-year college. Urban campus. Founded in 1966. Accredited by North Central Association of Colleges and Schools.

PROGRAM INFORMATION
Offered since 1975. Accredited by American Culinary Federation Accrediting Commission. Program calendar is divided into semesters. 2-year associate degree in hotel/restaurant management. 2-year associate degree in culinary arts.

PROGRAM AFFILIATION
American Culinary Federation; National Restaurant Association.

AREAS OF STUDY
Baking; beverage management; buffet catering; culinary French; culinary skill development; food preparation; food purchasing; garde-manger; international cuisine; introduction to food service; menu and facilities design; nutrition; sanitation; soup, stock, sauce, and starch production; wines and spirits.

FACILITIES
Bake shop; cafeteria; 3 classrooms; computer laboratory; demonstration laboratory; 2 food production kitchens; gourmet dining room; learning resource center; lecture room; library.

STUDENT PROFILE
95 total: 90 full-time; 5 part-time. 48 are under 25 years old; 47 are between 25 and 44 years old.

FACULTY
11 total: 6 full-time; 5 part-time. 8 are industry professionals; 1 is a culinary-certified teacher. Prominent faculty: Robert L. Anderson, CEC, CCE; Chris Palar; Lori Dowie.

SPECIAL PROGRAMS
French culinary exchange, field study tour of Chicago.

TYPICAL EXPENSES
In-state tuition: $904 per semester full-time (in district), $75.40 per credit part-time. Out-of-state tuition: $1800 per semester full-time, $150.80 per credit part-time. Program-related fees include $250 for cutlery; $250 for uniforms; $200 for books.

FINANCIAL AID
Employment placement assistance is available.

HOUSING
Apartment-style housing available. Average on-campus housing cost per month: $400. Average off-campus housing cost per month: $400.

APPLICATION INFORMATION
Students may begin participation in January and September. Application deadline for spring is January 5. Application deadline for fall is August 1. In 2006, 120 applied; 90 were accepted. Applicants must submit a formal application.

Des Moines Area Community College *(continued)*

CONTACT

Robert L. Anderson, Program Chair, Iowa Culinary Institute (ICI), 2006 South Ankeny Boulevard, Building #7, Ankeny, IA 50023. Telephone: 515-964-6532. Fax: 515-965-7129. E-mail: rlanderson@dmacc.edu. World Wide Web: http://www.dmacc.edu/.

IOWA LAKES COMMUNITY COLLEGE

Hotel and Restaurant Management Program

Emmetsburg, Iowa

GENERAL INFORMATION

Public, coeducational, two-year college. Rural campus. Founded in 1967. Accredited by North Central Association of Colleges and Schools.

PROGRAM INFORMATION

Offered since 1973. Accredited by Council on Hotel, Restaurant and Institutional Education. Program calendar is divided into semesters. 1-year diploma in hospitality technology program. 2-year associate degree in dietary management program. 2-year associate degree in hotel and restaurant management program.

PROGRAM AFFILIATION

American Hotel and Lodging Association; Council on Hotel, Restaurant, and Institutional Education; Dietary Managers Association; Iowa Hospitality Association; Iowa Lodging Association; National Restaurant Association; National Restaurant Association Educational Foundation.

AREAS OF STUDY

Baking; beverage management; buffet catering; controlling costs in food service; convenience cookery; culinary skill development; food preparation; food purchasing; food service communication; food service math; garde-manger; hospitality law; international cuisine; introduction to food service; kitchen management; management and human resources; marketing; meal planning; menu and facilities design; nutrition; nutrition and food service; restaurant opportunities; sanitation; saucier; soup, stock, sauce, and starch production; wines and spirits.

FACILITIES

Bakery; 2 cafeterias; 3 catering services; 3 classrooms; coffee shop; 5 computer laboratories; demonstration laboratory; 2 food production kitchens; gourmet dining room; 2 laboratories; 3 learning resource centers; 2 lecture rooms; 3 libraries; public restaurant; snack shop; student lounge; teaching kitchen.

STUDENT PROFILE

45 total: 40 full-time; 5 part-time.

FACULTY

3 total: 1 full-time; 2 part-time. 2 are industry professionals; 2 are culinary-certified teachers. Prominent faculty: Robert Halverson; Kerry Erickson, ED. Faculty-student ratio: 1:20.

SPECIAL PROGRAMS

Iowa Hospitality Show in Des Moines, Midwest Hospitality Show in Minneapolis, Las Vegas Hospitality Show.

TYPICAL EXPENSES

In-state tuition: $130 per credit part-time. Out-of-state tuition: $132 per credit part-time. Program-related fees include $100 for lab fee; $150 for trip fees.

FINANCIAL AID

In 2006, 5 scholarships were awarded (average award was $850); 35 loans were granted (average loan was $2600). Program-specific awards include National Restaurant Association scholarships, scholarships for freshmen and sophomores ($150), American Hotel and Lodging Association Scholarship. Employment placement assistance is available. Employment opportunities within the program are available.

HOUSING

Coed and apartment-style housing available. Average on-campus housing cost per month: $675.

APPLICATION INFORMATION

Students may begin participation in January, May, and August. Application deadline for fall is August 1. Application deadline for spring is January 1. Application deadline for summer is May 1. Applicants must interview; submit a formal application.

CONTACT

Mr. Robert Halverson, Coordinator/Professor, Hotel and Restaurant Management Program, 3200 College Drive, Emmetsburg, IA 50536-1098. Telephone: 712-852-5256. Fax: 712-852-2152. E-mail: rhalverson@ iowalakes.edu. World Wide Web: http://www.iowalakes. edu.

Iowa State University of Science and Technology

Hotel, Restaurant, and Institution Management

Ames, Iowa

GENERAL INFORMATION
Public, coeducational, university. Small-town setting. Founded in 1858. Accredited by North Central Association of Colleges and Schools.

PROGRAM INFORMATION
Offered since 1924. Accredited by Accreditation Commission for Programs in Hospitality Administration. National Restaurant Association Educational Foundation ManageFirst certificates available. Program calendar is divided into semesters. 2-year master's degree in hotel and restaurant management. 3-year doctoral degree in hotel and restaurant management. 4-year bachelor's degree in hotel and restaurant management.

PROGRAM AFFILIATION
American Dietetic Association; Council on Hotel, Restaurant, and Institutional Education; National Restaurant Association; National Restaurant Association Educational Foundation.

AREAS OF STUDY
Beverage management; controlling costs in food service; food preparation; food purchasing; introduction to food service; management and human resources; nutrition and food service; sanitation; wines and spirits.

FACILITIES
2 classrooms; computer laboratory; food production kitchen; laboratory; learning resource center; lecture room; library; public restaurant; student lounge; teaching kitchen.

STUDENT PROFILE
235 total: 225 full-time; 10 part-time.

FACULTY
11 total: 8 full-time; 3 part-time. Prominent faculty: Robert Bosselman, PhD; Haemoon Oh, PhD; Miyoung Jeong, PhD; Susan Arendt, PhD. Faculty-student ratio: 1:20.

SPECIAL PROGRAMS
Summer study abroad in Thailand, internships.

TYPICAL EXPENSES
Application fee: $30. In-state tuition: $2445 per semester (undergraduate); $2854 per semester (graduate); $4890 per year. Out-of-state tuition: $7490 per semester (undergraduate); $7860 per semester (graduate); $14,980 year.

FINANCIAL AID
In 2006, 27 scholarships were awarded (average award was $1000). Employment placement assistance is available. Employment opportunities within the program are available.

HOUSING
Coed, apartment-style, and single-sex housing available.

APPLICATION INFORMATION
Students may begin participation in January, June, and August. Applications are accepted continuously. In 2006, 65 applied; 50 were accepted. Applicants must submit a formal application, SAT or ACT scores, TOEFL scores (international applicants), and academic transcripts.

CONTACT
Dr. Robert Bosselman, Professor and Chair, Hotel, Restaurant, and Institution Management, 31 Mackay Hall, Ames, IA 50011-1121. Telephone: 515-294-7474. Fax: 515-294-6364. E-mail: drbob@iastate.edu. World Wide Web: http://www.iastate.edu.

Kirkwood Community College

Hospitality Programs

Cedar Rapids, Iowa

GENERAL INFORMATION
Public, coeducational, two-year college. Urban campus. Founded in 1966. Accredited by North Central Association of Colleges and Schools.

PROGRAM INFORMATION
Offered since 1968. Accredited by American Culinary Federation Accrediting Commission. Program calendar is divided into semesters. 1-year certificate in bakery. 1-year diploma in food service training. 2-year associate degree in lodging management. 2-year associate degree in restaurant management. 2-year associate degree in culinary arts.

PROGRAM AFFILIATION
National Restaurant Association; National Restaurant Association Educational Foundation.

AREAS OF STUDY
Baking; beverage management; buffet catering; controlling costs in food service; culinary competition; culinary skill development; food and culture; food preparation; food purchasing; food service communication; food service math; garde-manger; international cuisine; kitchen management; management

Kirkwood Community College *(continued)*

and human resources; meal planning; meat fabrication; menu and facilities design; nutrition; sanitation; soup, stock, sauce, and starch production; wines and spirits.

FACILITIES
Bakery; catering service; 2 classrooms; computer laboratory; demonstration laboratory; food production kitchen; gourmet dining room; 2 laboratories; learning resource center; 2 lecture rooms; library; public restaurant.

TYPICAL STUDENT PROFILE
230 total: 165 full-time; 65 part-time.

SPECIAL PROGRAMS
Professional meetings and conventions (local, state, national), international study tours (offered periodically), culinary competition.

FINANCIAL AID
Program-specific awards include study abroad travel scholarships. Employment opportunities within the program are available.

APPLICATION INFORMATION
Students may begin participation in January and August. Applications are accepted continuously. Applicants must submit a formal application, take placement tests, and attend a program conference.

CONTACT
Director of Admissions, Hospitality Programs, 6301 Kirkwood Boulevard SW, Cedar Rapids, IA 52403. Telephone: 319-398-4981. Fax: 319-398-1244. World Wide Web: http://www.kirkwood.edu.

KANSAS

AMERICAN INSTITUTE OF BAKING

Baking Science and Technology

Manhattan, Kansas

GENERAL INFORMATION
Private, coeducational institution. Small-town setting. Founded in 1919. Accredited by North Central Association of Colleges and Schools.

PROGRAM INFORMATION
Offered since 1919. Program calendar is divided into semesters. 2.5-month certificate in maintenance engineering. 5-month certificate in baking science and technology.

PROGRAM AFFILIATION
American Institute of Baking.

AREAS OF STUDY
Baking; maintenance engineering.

FACILITIES
4 bake shops; bakery; 4 classrooms; computer laboratory; 4 demonstration laboratories; laboratory; library; student lounge; cookie-cracker production line.

STUDENT PROFILE
150 full-time.

FACULTY
10 total: 8 full-time; 2 part-time. 8 are industry professionals; 1 is a master baker. Prominent faculty: Michael Moore; Jeff Rootring; Kirk O'Donnell, PhD; Debi Rogers, PhD, AACC. Faculty-student ratio: 1:5.

SPECIAL PROGRAMS
Half-day tours of grain elevator, flour mill, and Kansas wheat farm, half-day tours of commercial wholesale bakeries, 50-lesson correspondence course in science of baking.

TYPICAL EXPENSES
Application fee: $45. Tuition: $7200 per certificate (baking science); $4600 per certificate (maintenance engineering).

FINANCIAL AID
In 2006, 25 scholarships were awarded (average award was $2500); 15 loans were granted (average loan was $2000). Program-specific awards include full-tuition scholarships for food science graduates. Employment placement assistance is available.

HOUSING
Coed housing available. Average off-campus housing cost per month: $550.

APPLICATION INFORMATION
Students may begin participation in February, July, August, and September. Applications are accepted continuously. Applicants must submit a formal application, letters of reference, an essay; have a college degree, or 2 years of work experience, or completed a baking science course.

CONTACT
Ken Embers, Director of Admissions and Financial Aid, Baking Science and Technology, 1213 Bakers Way, Manhattan, KS 66502. Telephone: 800-633-5137. Fax: 785-537-1493. E-mail: kembers@aibonline.org. World Wide Web: http://www.aibonline.org.

JOHNSON COUNTY COMMUNITY COLLEGE

Hospitality Management/Chef Apprenticeship

Overland Park, Kansas

GENERAL INFORMATION
Public, coeducational, two-year college. Suburban campus. Founded in 1967. Accredited by North Central Association of Colleges and Schools.

PROGRAM INFORMATION
Offered since 1975. Accredited by American Culinary Federation Accrediting Commission. Program calendar is divided into semesters. 1-year certificate in baking and pastry. 2-year associate degree in hotel management. 2-year associate degree in food and beverage management. 3-year associate degree in chef apprenticeship.

PROGRAM AFFILIATION
American Culinary Federation; American Institute of Wine & Food; Council on Hotel, Restaurant, and Institutional Education; Hotel/Motel Association of Kansas City; Kansas Restaurant Hospitality Association; Missouri Restaurant Association; National Restaurant Association; National Restaurant Association Educational Foundation.

AREAS OF STUDY
Baking; beverage management; buffet catering; confectionery show pieces; controlling costs in food service; convenience cookery; culinary skill development; food preparation; food purchasing; food service math; garde-manger; international cuisine; introduction to food service; kitchen management; management and human resources; meal planning; menu and facilities design; nutrition; nutrition and food service; sanitation; saucier; seafood processing; soup, stock, sauce, and starch production; wines and spirits.

FACILITIES
Bake shop; 2 demonstration laboratories; food production kitchen; gourmet dining room; learning resource center; 4 lecture rooms; library; 2 teaching kitchens.

STUDENT PROFILE
473 total: 191 full-time; 282 part-time. 287 are under 25 years old; 35 are between 25 and 44 years old; 151 are over 44 years old.

FACULTY
19 total: 10 full-time; 9 part-time. 5 are industry professionals; 5 are culinary-certified teachers; 2 are certified hospitality educators. Prominent faculty: Jerry Marcellus, CEC, CCE; Felix Sturmer; John Head, CCC; Robert Sobierja. Faculty-student ratio: 1:16.

SPECIAL PROGRAMS
National culinary competitions, ACF Knowledge Bowl competitions, trips to New York Hotel Show and NRA show in Chicago.

TYPICAL EXPENSES
In-state tuition: $63 per credit hour full-time (in district), $63 per credit hour part-time. Out-of-state tuition: $144 per credit hour full-time, $144 per credit hour part-time.

FINANCIAL AID
In 2006, 20 scholarships were awarded (average award was $500). Program-specific awards include paid apprenticeship program. Employment placement assistance is available.

HOUSING
Average off-campus housing cost per month: $600.

APPLICATION INFORMATION
Students may begin participation in January, June, and August. Application deadline for fall is August 15. Application deadline for spring is January 15. Application deadline for summer is May 1. In 2006, 144 applied; 144 were accepted. Applicants must submit a formal application.

CONTACT
Lindy Robinson, Assistant Dean, Hospitality Management/Chef Apprenticeship, 12345 College Boulevard, Overland Park, KS 66210. Telephone: 913-469-8500 Ext. 3250. Fax: 913-469-2560. E-mail: lrobinsn@jccc.edu. World Wide Web: http://www.johnco.cc.ks.us/.

KANSAS CITY KANSAS AREA TECHNICAL SCHOOL

Professional Cooking

Kansas City, Kansas

GENERAL INFORMATION
Public, coeducational, adult vocational school. Urban campus. Founded in 1972. Accredited by North Central Association of Colleges and Schools.

Kansas City Kansas Area Technical School *(continued)*

PROGRAM INFORMATION
Offered since 1972. Program calendar is continuous, year-round. 6-month certificate in food service.

AREAS OF STUDY
Baking; catering; culinary skill development; dining room service; food preparation; food purchasing; food service management; garde-manger; introduction to food service; meal planning; patisserie; restaurant opportunities; sanitation; soup, stock, sauce, and starch production.

FACILITIES
Cafeteria; classroom; computer laboratory; food production kitchen; gourmet dining room; learning resource center; lecture room; library; snack shop.

TYPICAL STUDENT PROFILE
22 total: 10 full-time; 12 part-time.

FINANCIAL AID
Employment placement assistance is available. Employment opportunities within the program are available.

APPLICATION INFORMATION
Students may begin participation in January, February, March, April, May, June, August, September, October, November, and December. Applications are accepted continuously. Applicants must have a high school diploma or GED.

CONTACT
Director of Admissions, Professional Cooking, 2220 North 59th Street, Kansas City, KS 66104. Telephone: 913-627-4100. World Wide Web: http://www.kckats.com/.

KENTUCKY

ELIZABETHTOWN COMMUNITY AND TECHNICAL COLLEGE

Culinary Arts

Elizabethtown, Kentucky

GENERAL INFORMATION
Public, coeducational, two-year college. Small-town setting. Founded in 1966. Accredited by Southern Association of Colleges and Schools.

PROGRAM INFORMATION
Offered since 1975. Program calendar is divided into semesters. 12-month degree in food and beverage management. 12-month degree in culinary arts. 12-month degree in catering. 18-month diploma in food and beverage management. 18-month diploma in culinary arts. 18-month diploma in catering. 6- to 12-month certificate in professional development. 6- to 12-month certificate in culinary arts. 6- to 12-month certificate in catering.

PROGRAM AFFILIATION
International Association of Culinary Professionals; National Restaurant Association; National Restaurant Association Educational Foundation; Retailer's Bakery Association.

AREAS OF STUDY
Baking; beverage management; buffet catering; confectionery show pieces; controlling costs in food service; culinary skill development; food preparation; food purchasing; food service communication; food service math; garde-manger; international cuisine; introduction to food service; kitchen management; management and human resources; meal planning; menu and facilities design; nutrition; nutrition and food service; restaurant opportunities; sanitation; soup, stock, sauce, and starch production.

FACILITIES
Bake shop; cafeteria; catering service; classroom; computer laboratory; food production kitchen; learning resource center; library; teaching kitchen.

TYPICAL STUDENT PROFILE
38 total: 28 full-time; 10 part-time. 20 are under 25 years old; 18 are between 25 and 44 years old.

SPECIAL PROGRAMS
Field trips, public food demonstrations, culinary competitions.

FINANCIAL AID
Program-specific awards include scholarships available through local organizations. Employment placement assistance is available. Employment opportunities within the program are available.

APPLICATION INFORMATION
Students may begin participation in January and August. Application deadline for fall is July 1. Application deadline for spring is November 30. Applicants must submit a formal application and academic transcripts; take the COMPASS Test.

CONTACT
Director of Admissions, Culinary Arts, 620 College Street Road, Elizabethtown, KY 42701. Telephone: 270-706-8732. Fax: 270-766-5131. World Wide Web: http://www.elizabethtown.kctcs.edu/index.cfm.

SULLIVAN UNIVERSITY

National Center for Hospitality Studies

Louisville, Kentucky

GENERAL INFORMATION
Private, coeducational, comprehensive institution. Suburban campus. Founded in 1962. Accredited by Southern Association of Colleges and Schools.

PROGRAM INFORMATION
Offered since 1987. Accredited by American Culinary Federation Accrediting Commission. Program calendar is divided into quarters. 12-month diploma in professional cook. 18-month associate degree in travel and tourism. 18-month associate degree in professional catering. 18-month associate degree in hotel and restaurant management. 18-month associate degree in baking and pastry arts. 18-month associate degree in culinary arts. 36-month bachelor's degree in hospitality management. 9-month diploma in travel and tourism. 9-month diploma in professional baker.

PROGRAM AFFILIATION
American Culinary Federation; American Dietetic Association; American Institute of Wine & Food; Confrerie de la Chaine des Rotisseurs; Council on Hotel, Restaurant, and Institutional Education; International Association of Culinary Professionals; International Food Service Executives Association; James Beard Foundation, Inc.; Kentucky Restaurant Association; National Restaurant Association; National Restaurant Association Educational Foundation; United States Personal Chef Association; Women Chefs and Restaurateurs.

AREAS OF STUDY
Baking; beverage management; buffet catering; confectionery show pieces; controlling costs in food service; culinary French; culinary skill development; food preparation; food purchasing; food service math; garde-manger; hotel restaurant management; international cuisine; introduction to food service; kitchen management; management and human resources; meat cutting; menu and facilities design; nutrition; patisserie; professional catering; restaurant opportunities; sanitation; saucier; seafood processing; soup, stock, sauce, and starch production; travel and tourism; wines and spirits.

FACILITIES
5 bake shops; bakery; cafeteria; catering service; 41 classrooms; 7 computer laboratories; demonstration laboratory; 13 food production kitchens; garden; gourmet dining room; 3 laboratories; library; public restaurant; student lounge.

STUDENT PROFILE
960 total: 850 full-time; 110 part-time. 375 are under 25 years old; 375 are between 25 and 44 years old; 210 are over 44 years old.

FACULTY
28 total: 26 full-time; 2 part-time. 26 are industry professionals; 1 is a master chef; 12 are culinary-certified teachers. Prominent faculty: Thomas Hickey, CEC, CCE, CFE, CHE; Derek Spendlove, CEPC, CCE, AAC; David H. Dodd, MBE, CEC, CCE; Walter Rhea, CMPC, CCE, CEC, AAC. Faculty-student ratio: 1:19.

SPECIAL PROGRAMS
3-month restaurant practicum, culinary competitions, trip to Boston, MA and one-week cruise for hospitality (hotel-restaurant) majors.

TYPICAL EXPENSES
Application fee: $90. Tuition: $27,900 per 18 months. Program-related fee includes $845 for general fees.

FINANCIAL AID
In 2006, 8 scholarships were awarded (average award was $6000). Employment placement assistance is available. Employment opportunities within the program are available.

HOUSING
Apartment-style housing available. Average on-campus housing cost per month: $440.

APPLICATION INFORMATION
Students may begin participation in January, March, June, and September. Application deadline for fall is September 15. Application deadline for winter is December 15. Application deadline for spring is March 15. Application deadline for summer is June 15. In 2006, 940 applied; 860 were accepted. Applicants must interview; submit a formal application and CPAT, SAT, or ACT scores and TOEFL scores for international applicants.

CONTACT
Terri Thomas, Director of Admissions, National Center for Hospitality Studies, 3101 Bardstown Road, Louisville, KY 40205. Telephone: 502-456-6505. Fax: 502-456-0040. E-mail: admissions@sullivan.edu. World Wide Web: http://www.sullivan.edu.

See color display following page 186.

Western Kentucky University

Hospitality Management and Dietetics

Bowling Green, Kentucky

General Information
Public, coeducational, comprehensive institution. Small-town setting. Founded in 1906. Accredited by Southern Association of Colleges and Schools.

Program Information
Offered since 1969. Accredited by American Dietetic Association. Program calendar is divided into semesters. 4-year bachelor's degree in hotel, restaurant, and tourism management.

Program Affiliation
American Dietetic Association; Council on Hotel, Restaurant, and Institutional Education; National Restaurant Association; National Restaurant Association Educational Foundation.

Areas of Study
Beverage management; buffet catering; controlling costs in food service; food preparation; food purchasing; international cuisine; introduction to food service; kitchen management; management and human resources; meal planning; nutrition; nutrition and food service; restaurant management; restaurant opportunities; sanitation.

Facilities
2 classrooms; computer laboratory; demonstration laboratory; food production kitchen; gourmet dining room; laboratory; learning resource center; 2 libraries; teaching kitchen.

Student Profile
164 total: 153 full-time; 11 part-time. 144 are under 25 years old; 20 are between 25 and 44 years old.

Faculty
7 total: 6 full-time; 1 part-time. 6 are industry professionals. Prominent faculty: Richard F. Patterson, EdD, RD; Patty J. Silfies, MHRIM; Danita Kelley, PhD, RD; Julie Lee, MBA, CEC.

Prominent Alumni and Current Affiliation
John Anderson, Senior Vice President, Hilton Hotels Corporation; Jeff Anderson, Regional Vice President, Hilton Hotels Corporation; Joe Micatrotto, Micatrotto Restaurant Group.

Special Programs
2 semesters of paid internships.

Typical Expenses
Application fee: $35. In-state tuition: $3208 per semester full-time (in district), $267 per credit hour part-time. Out-of-state tuition: $7735 per semester full-time, $645 per credit hour part-time. Program-related fee includes $75 for food preparation lab fee.

Financial Aid
In 2006, 3 scholarships were awarded (average award was $500). Program-specific awards include Rafferty Restaurant Scholarship, Kentucky Restaurant Association Scholarship, Bowling Green/Warren County Lodging Scholarship. Employment placement assistance is available. Employment opportunities within the program are available.

Housing
Coed and single-sex housing available. Average on-campus housing cost per month: $340. Average off-campus housing cost per month: $425.

Application Information
Students may begin participation in January and August. Application deadline for fall is August 1. Application deadline for spring is January 1. In 2006, 60 applied; 55 were accepted. Applicants must submit a formal application.

Contact
Dr. Richard F. Patterson, Associate Professor, Hospitality Management and Dietetics, Department of Consumer and Family Sciences, 1906 College Heights Boulevard, #11037, Bowling Green, KY 42101-1037. Telephone: 270-745-4031. Fax: 270-745-3999. E-mail: rich.patterson@wku.edu. World Wide Web: http://www.wku.edu/hospitality.

Louisiana

Delgado Community College

Culinary Arts and Hospitality

New Orleans, Louisiana

General Information
Public, coeducational, two-year college. Urban campus. Accredited by Southern Association of Colleges and Schools.

Program Information
Offered since 1925. Accredited by American Culinary Federation Accrediting Commission. National Restaurant Association Educational Foundation ManageFirst certificates available. Program calendar is divided into semesters. 2-semester certificate in pastry

arts. 3-semester certificate in hospitality management. 4-semester certificate in culinary arts. 6-semester associate degree in hospitality management. 6-semester associate degree in culinary arts. 6-semester associate degree in catering.

PROGRAM AFFILIATION
American Culinary Federation; American Institute of Wine & Food; Confrerie de la Chaine des Rotisseurs; International Association of Culinary Professionals; James Beard Foundation, Inc.; National Association of Catering Professionals; National Restaurant Association; National Restaurant Association Educational Foundation; Society of Wine Educators.

AREAS OF STUDY
Baking; buffet catering; confectionery show pieces; controlling costs in food service; food purchasing; garde-manger; management and human resources; nutrition; patisserie; sanitation; saucier; soup, stock, sauce, and starch production; wines and spirits.

FACILITIES
Bake shop; classroom; computer laboratory; garden; laboratory; lecture room; library; teaching kitchen.

STUDENT PROFILE
170 total: 120 full-time; 50 part-time.

FACULTY
9 total: 5 full-time; 4 part-time. 1 is an industry professional; 4 are culinary-certified teachers. Prominent faculty: Karl Tipton, CEC, CCE, MBA, AAC; Vance Roux, CCC, CCE; Nancy Burback, CEC, CCE; Jon Petrie, CEPC. Faculty-student ratio: 1:16.

PROMINENT ALUMNI AND CURRENT AFFILIATION
Tom DiGiovanni, Arnaud's; Anthony Spizale, Royal Orleans Rib Room; Greg Piccola, The Bistro and Maison de Ville.

SPECIAL PROGRAMS
4000-hour chef apprenticeship.

TYPICAL EXPENSES
Application fee: $15. In-state tuition: $768 per semester. Out-of-state tuition: $2258 per semester. Tuition for international students: $2258 per semester. Program-related fees include $300 for tool kit; $100 for uniform; $75 for ACF fee; $115 for log book fee.

FINANCIAL AID
Employment placement assistance is available.

APPLICATION INFORMATION
Students may begin participation in August. Application deadline for fall is May 30. In 2006, 100 applied; 60 were accepted. Applicants must submit a formal application, letters of reference, placement test.

CONTACT
Dr. Mary Bartholomew, Director, Culinary Arts and Hospitality, 615 City Park Avenue, New Orleans, LA 70119. Telephone: 504-671-6199. Fax: 504-483-4893. E-mail: mbart@dcc.edu. World Wide Web: http://www.dcc.edu.

GRAMBLING STATE UNIVERSITY

Hotel/Restaurant Management

Grambling, Louisiana

GENERAL INFORMATION
Public, coeducational, university. Rural campus. Founded in 1901. Accredited by Southern Association of Colleges and Schools.

PROGRAM INFORMATION
Offered since 1985. National Restaurant Association Educational Foundation ManageFirst certificates available. Program calendar is divided into semesters. 4-year bachelor's degree in hotel/restaurant management.

PROGRAM AFFILIATION
Council on Hotel, Restaurant, and Institutional Education; National Restaurant Association; National Restaurant Association Educational Foundation.

AREAS OF STUDY
Beverage management; food preparation; kitchen management; restaurant opportunities.

FACILITIES
Cafeteria; 2 catering services; 6 classrooms; computer laboratory; 4 demonstration laboratories; 3 food production kitchens; gourmet dining room; 4 laboratories; learning resource center; 2 lecture rooms; library; public restaurant; snack shop; student lounge; 2 teaching kitchens.

STUDENT PROFILE
62 total: 59 full-time; 3 part-time. 47 are under 25 years old; 9 are between 25 and 44 years old; 6 are over 44 years old.

FACULTY
3 total: 2 full-time; 1 part-time. Prominent faculty: Joseph Naylor, MBA; Frankie Raben, Safe Serv Faculty; Dr. Willie Ford, ADA. Faculty-student ratio: 1:30.

PROMINENT ALUMNI AND CURRENT AFFILIATION
Eric Wiley, Walt Disney Management; Dr. Berkita Bradford, Associate Professor, North Carolina University; James Udela, Hyatt Hotel & Resorts.

Grambling State University *(continued)*

TYPICAL EXPENSES
Application fee: $20. In-state tuition: $3622 per year.
Out-of-state tuition: $8972 per year. Tuition for
international students: $8972 per year.

FINANCIAL AID
In 2006, individual scholarships were awarded at $500.
Employment opportunities within the program are
available.

HOUSING
Coed, apartment-style, and single-sex housing available.
Average off-campus housing cost per month: $575–
$700.

APPLICATION INFORMATION
Students may begin participation in January, May, and
August. In 2006, 33 applied; 22 were accepted.

CONTACT
Ms. Annie Moss, Director of Admissions, Hotel/
Restaurant Management, CSU Box 4200, Grambling, LA
71245. Telephone: 318-274-6183. Fax: 318-274-3292.
E-mail: mossa@gram.edu. World Wide Web: http://www.
gram.edu/.

LOUISIANA CULINARY INSTITUTE, LLC

Professional Cooking and Culinary Arts

Baton Rouge, Louisiana

GENERAL INFORMATION
Private, coeducational, culinary institute. Urban campus.
Founded in 2002. Accredited by Council on
Occupational Education.

PROGRAM INFORMATION
Offered since 2002. Accredited by Council on
Occupational Education. National Restaurant
Association Educational Foundation ManageFirst
certificates available. Program calendar is divided into
quarters. 12-month diploma in professional cooking and
culinary arts. 18-month associate degree in culinary arts
and restaurant management.

PROGRAM AFFILIATION
American Culinary Federation; International Association
of Culinary Professionals; National Restaurant
Association; National Restaurant Association
Educational Foundation.

AREAS OF STUDY

Baking; beverage management; controlling costs in food service; convenience cookery; culinary French; culinary skill development; food preparation; food purchasing; food service communication; food service math; garde-manger; international cuisine; introduction to food service; kitchen management; management and human resources; meal planning; meat cutting; meat fabrication; menu and facilities design; nutrition; nutrition and food service; patisserie; sanitation; saucier; seafood processing; soup, stock, sauce, and starch production; wines and spirits.

FACILITIES

Bake shop; 3 classrooms; computer laboratory; 2 demonstration laboratories; food production kitchen; garden; gourmet dining room; learning resource center; lecture room; library; teaching kitchen.

STUDENT PROFILE

90 full-time. 40 are under 25 years old; 40 are between 25 and 44 years old; 10 are over 44 years old.

FACULTY

7 total: 5 full-time; 2 part-time. 5 are culinary-certified teachers; 2 are academic instructors. Prominent faculty: Ross Headlee, FMP, CCP; David Tiner, CCC. Faculty-student ratio: 1:13.

PROMINENT ALUMNI AND CURRENT AFFILIATION

Ashlee Sanders, Another Broken Egg; Josh Crenshaw, Sullivan's Metropolitan Grill.

SPECIAL PROGRAMS

Two-day "stage" at Commander's Palace, externships in Hawaii, study abroad program, Home Plate Classic, state and national competitions, tours of McIlhenny's Tabasco plant, Tony Chechere's spice plant, and many others.

TYPICAL EXPENSES

Tuition: $22,500 per associate, $15,000 for diploma. Program-related fees include $100 for one-time registration (refundable); $3000 for one-time meal plan, lab fees, uniforms, knives, books.

FINANCIAL AID

In 2006, 19 scholarships were awarded (average award was $1000); 4 loans were granted (average loan was $14,750). Program-specific awards include sponsored professional education program ($2500), pro-start scholarship, Foundation for Culinary Excellence Scholarships. Employment placement assistance is available. Employment opportunities within the program are available.

HOUSING

Coed housing available. Average on-campus housing cost per month: $300. Average off-campus housing cost per month: $320.

APPLICATION INFORMATION

Students may begin participation in March, June, September, and December. Application deadline for spring is March 5. Application deadline for summer is June 11. Application deadline for fall is September 10. Application deadline for winter is December 10. In 2006, 180 applied; 60 were accepted. Applicants must interview; submit a formal application, letters of reference, an essay, high school diploma or GED, state required skills test (if no college transcripts).

CONTACT

Erin Perdue, Admissions, Professional Cooking and Culinary Arts, 5837 Essen Lane, Baton Rouge, LA 70810. Telephone: 877-769-8820. Fax: 225-769-8792. E-mail: admissions@louisianaculinary.com. World Wide Web: http://www.louisianaculinary.com.

LOUISIANA TECHNICAL COLLEGE–BATON ROUGE CAMPUS

Culinary Arts and Occupations

Baton Rouge, Louisiana

GENERAL INFORMATION

Public, coeducational, two-year college. Urban campus. Founded in 1974. Accredited by Southern Association of Colleges and Schools.

PROGRAM INFORMATION

Offered since 1974. Accredited by American Culinary Federation Accrediting Commission. Program calendar is divided into semesters. 18-month diploma in culinary arts and occupations. 3-month certificate in nutrition. 3-month certificate in supervision. 3-month certificate in sanitation.

PROGRAM AFFILIATION

American Culinary Federation; Louisiana Restaurant Association; National Restaurant Association Educational Foundation.

AREAS OF STUDY

Baking; controlling costs in food service; culinary skill development; food preparation; food purchasing; food service communication; food service math; garde-manger; kitchen management; management and human resources; meat fabrication; nutrition; nutrition and food service; sanitation; saucier; soup, stock, sauce, and starch production.

FACILITIES

Bake shop; 2 classrooms; computer laboratory; food production kitchen; garden; 2 public restaurants.

Louisiana Technical College–Baton Rouge Campus
(continued)

STUDENT PROFILE
45 total: 35 full-time; 10 part-time. 43 are under 25 years old; 2 are between 25 and 44 years old.

FACULTY
4 total: 2 full-time; 2 part-time. 2 are industry professionals; 1 is a culinary-certified teacher. Prominent faculty: Michael Travasos, CCE; Jean Frances, CEC, AAC, FMP. Faculty-student ratio: 1:15.

SPECIAL PROGRAMS
Culinary competitions.

TYPICAL EXPENSES
Application fee: $20. Tuition: $2500 per diploma. Program-related fees include $100 for uniforms; $400 for textbooks.

FINANCIAL AID
Employment placement assistance is available. Employment opportunities within the program are available.

HOUSING
Average off-campus housing cost per month: $400.

APPLICATION INFORMATION
Students may begin participation in January and August. Applications are accepted continuously. Applicants must submit a formal application and complete an entrance test.

CONTACT
Michael Travasos, Instructor, Culinary Arts and Occupations, 3250 North Acadian Thruway, East, Baton Rouge, LA 70805. Telephone: 225-359-9226. Fax: 225-359-9296. E-mail: mtravasos@ltc.edu. World Wide Web: http://www.region2.ltc.edu/.

NICHOLLS STATE UNIVERSITY

Chef John Folse Culinary Institute

Thibodaux, Louisiana

GENERAL INFORMATION
Public, coeducational, comprehensive institution. Rural campus. Founded in 1948. Accredited by Southern Association of Colleges and Schools.

PROGRAM INFORMATION
Offered since 1994. Program calendar is divided into semesters. 2-year associate degree in culinary arts. 4-year bachelor's degree in culinary arts.

PROGRAM AFFILIATION
American Culinary Federation; Confrerie de la Chaine des Rotisseurs; Council on Hotel, Restaurant, and Institutional Education; Institut Paul Bocuse World Wide Alliance; National Restaurant Association; Research Chefs Association; Society for the Advancement of Food Service Research.

AREAS OF STUDY
Baking; beverage management; buffet catering; confectionery show pieces; controlling costs in food service; convenience cookery; culinary entrepreneurship; culinary French; culinary skill development; food preparation; food purchasing; garde-manger; international cuisine; introduction to food service; kitchen management; management and human resources; meal planning; meat cutting; meat fabrication; menu and facilities design; nutrition; nutrition and food service; patisserie; restaurant opportunities; sanitation; saucier; seafood processing; soup, stock, sauce, and starch production; wines and spirits.

FACILITIES
Bakery; cafeteria; catering service; 3 classrooms; 2 computer laboratories; demonstration laboratory; food production kitchen; gourmet dining room; 3 laboratories; 2 learning resource centers; 3 lecture rooms; library; public restaurant; snack shop; student lounge; 2 teaching kitchens.

STUDENT PROFILE
198 full-time. 169 are under 25 years old; 25 are between 25 and 44 years old; 4 are over 44 years old.

FACULTY
9 total: 6 full-time; 3 part-time. 5 are industry professionals; 1 is a master chef; 2 are culinary-certified teachers. Prominent faculty: Alton Frederick Doody, Jr.; John Folse, CEC, AAC. Faculty-student ratio: 1:20.

PROMINENT ALUMNI AND CURRENT AFFILIATION
Amanda Heffelfinger, Product Development, Ventura Foods; Michael Gullotta, Chef De Cuisine, Restaurant August, New Orleans, LA; Kevin Bordelon, Research and Development, Bruce Foods.

SPECIAL PROGRAMS
State and regional culinary competitions, summer study at Institut Paul Bocuse in Lyon, France.

TYPICAL EXPENSES
Application fee: $20. In-state tuition: $1777.25 per semester full-time (in district), $524 per 3 hour credit part-time. Out-of-state tuition: $4501.25 per semester full-time, $524 per 3 hour credit part-time. Program-related fees include $335 for knives; $300 for uniforms; $250 for lab fees (per lab class).

FINANCIAL AID
In 2006, 30 scholarships were awarded (average award was $800). Employment placement assistance is available.

HOUSING
Coed, apartment-style, and single-sex housing available. Average on-campus housing cost per month: $435. Average off-campus housing cost per month: $600.

APPLICATION INFORMATION
Students may begin participation in January and August. Application deadline for fall is July 15. Application deadline for spring is November 15. In 2006, 65 applied; 62 were accepted. Applicants must submit a formal application and high school transcript, minimum 2.5 high school GPA, ACT composite score of 20 or higher.

CONTACT
Randolph J. Cheramie, Associate Dean, Chef John Folse Culinary Institute, PO Box 2099, Thibodaux, LA 70310. Telephone: 985-449-7091. Fax: 985-449-7089. E-mail: Randy.Cheramie@nicholls.edu. World Wide Web: http://www.nicholls.edu/jfolse.

SCLAFANI COOKING SCHOOL, INC.

Commercial Cook/Baker Certificate

Metairie, Louisiana

GENERAL INFORMATION
Private, coeducational, culinary institute. Suburban campus. Founded in 1987.

PROGRAM INFORMATION
Offered since 1987. Accredited by Licensed by the Louisiana State Board of Regents as a Post Secondary Proprietary School. Program calendar is continuous, monthly. 4-week certificate in commercial cook/baker. 8-hour certificate in NRAEF ServSafe certificate.

PROGRAM AFFILIATION
American Culinary Federation; Foodservice Management Professionals; Louisiana Restaurant Association; National Restaurant Association; National Restaurant Association Educational Foundation.

AREAS OF STUDY
Baking; controlling costs in food service; culinary skill development; food preparation; food service math; garde-manger; introduction to food service; kitchen management; management and human resources; meal planning; restaurant opportunities; sanitation; saucier; soup, stock, sauce, and starch production.

FACILITIES
Bake shop; bakery; classroom; computer laboratory; demonstration laboratory; food production kitchen; lecture room; library; teaching kitchen; dining room.

STUDENT PROFILE
110 full-time.

FACULTY
3 total: 2 full-time; 1 part-time. 2 are industry professionals. Prominent faculty: Frank P. Sclafani Sr., CEC, FMP. Faculty-student ratio: 1:9.

PROMINENT ALUMNI AND CURRENT AFFILIATION
David Guas, Executive Pastry Chef, DC Coast Restaurant, Washington, DC; Russell Green, Certified Executive Sous Chef, Harrah's Casino.

SPECIAL PROGRAMS
Culinary SoftSkill Training (culinary interview, resume), Commercial Kitchen Management Systems.

TYPICAL EXPENSES
Application fee: $150. Tuition: $3995 per 4 weeks.

FINANCIAL AID
In 2006, 55 scholarships were awarded (average award was $4000). Program-specific awards include Workforce Investment Agency 100% Grants, Louisiana Department of Labor Incumbent Worker Training. Employment placement assistance is available.

HOUSING
Average off-campus housing cost per month: $1500.

APPLICATION INFORMATION
Students may begin participation year-round. Applications are accepted continuously. In 2006, 120 applied; 108 were accepted. Applicants must interview; submit a formal application; pass the Wonderlic aptitude test.

CONTACT
Frank P. Sclafani, President, Commercial Cook/Baker Certificate, 107 Gennaro Place, Metairie, LA 70001. Telephone: 504-833-7861. Fax: 504-833-7872. E-mail: info@sclafanicookingschool.com. World Wide Web: http://www.sclafanicookingschool.com.

SOUTHERN UNIVERSITY AT SHREVEPORT

Shreveport, Louisiana

GENERAL INFORMATION
Public, coeducational, two-year college. Urban campus. Founded in 1964. Accredited by Southern Association of Colleges and Schools.

Southern University at Shreveport *(continued)*

PROGRAM INFORMATION

Offered since 1984. Accredited by Student can earn an industry certificate in hospitality from the Educational Institute of the American Hotel and Motel Association for each course in hospitality. Program calendar is divided into semesters. 1-year certificate in food and beverage management. 1-year certificate in hospitality operation. 2-year associate degree in hospitality.

PROGRAM AFFILIATION

Council on Hotel, Restaurant, and Institutional Education; Educational Institute American Hotel and Motel Association.

AREAS OF STUDY

Baking; beverage management; controlling costs in food service; convenience cookery; culinary French; food preparation; food purchasing; food service communication; food service math; international cuisine; kitchen management; management and human resources; meal planning; menu and facilities design; nutrition and food service; restaurant opportunities; sanitation.

FACILITIES

Catering service; classroom; computer laboratory; demonstration laboratory; gourmet dining room; laboratory; lecture room; library; snack shop; vineyard.

TYPICAL STUDENT PROFILE

16 full-time. 3 are under 25 years old; 9 are between 25 and 44 years old; 4 are over 44 years old.

SPECIAL PROGRAMS

Field trips to area food shows, internships with hospitality partners.

FINANCIAL AID

Program-specific awards include industry scholarships. Employment placement assistance is available.

APPLICATION INFORMATION

Students may begin participation in January, June, and August. Application deadline for fall is August 30. Application deadline for spring is January 15. Application deadline for summer is June 6. Applicants must submit a formal application and high school transcript/diploma or equivalent.

CONTACT

Director of Admissions, Division of Business Studies, Shreveport, LA 71107. Telephone: 318-429-7236. Fax: 318-674-3313. World Wide Web: http://www.susla.edu.

UNIVERSITY OF LOUISIANA AT LAFAYETTE

College of Applied Life Sciences

Lafayette, Louisiana

GENERAL INFORMATION

Public, coeducational, university. Urban campus. Founded in 1898. Accredited by Southern Association of Colleges and Schools.

PROGRAM INFORMATION

Offered since 1950. Accredited by American Dietetic Association. Program calendar is divided into semesters. 4-year bachelor's degree in hospitality management.

PROGRAM AFFILIATION

American Culinary Federation; American Dietetic Association; Confrerie de la Chaine des Rotisseurs; Council on Hotel, Restaurant, and Institutional Education; National Restaurant Association; National Restaurant Association Educational Foundation.

AREAS OF STUDY

Beverage management; controlling costs in food service; food purchasing; food service communication; hotel and restaurant management; kitchen management; management and human resources; meal planning; tourism management.

FACILITIES

Catering service; computer laboratory; food production kitchen; gourmet dining room; laboratory; library; public restaurant; teaching kitchen.

TYPICAL STUDENT PROFILE

95 total: 86 full-time; 9 part-time. 76 are under 25 years old; 18 are between 25 and 44 years old; 1 is over 44 years old.

SPECIAL PROGRAMS

Senior level 15-week internship, required 1500 hours of work experience, trips to NRA and AMLA shows in New York, Chicago, and New Orleans.

FINANCIAL AID

Employment placement assistance is available. Employment opportunities within the program are available.

HOUSING

Apartment-style and single-sex housing available.

APPLICATION INFORMATION

Students may begin participation in January, June, and August. Applications are accepted continuously. Applicants must submit a formal application and ACT or SAT scores.

CONTACT
Director of Admissions, College of Applied Life Sciences, PO Box 40399, Lafayette, LA 70504. Telephone: 337-482-5724. Fax: 337-482-5395. World Wide Web: http://www.louisiana.edu.

MAINE

EASTERN MAINE COMMUNITY COLLEGE

Culinary Arts Department

Bangor, Maine

GENERAL INFORMATION
Public, coeducational, two-year college. Small-town setting. Founded in 1966. Accredited by New England Association of Schools and Colleges.

PROGRAM INFORMATION
Program calendar is divided into semesters. 1-year certificate in food service specialist. 2-year associate degree in culinary arts.

PROGRAM AFFILIATION
American Culinary Federation; International Association of Culinary Professionals; Maine Restaurant Association; National Restaurant Association; National Restaurant Association Educational Foundation.

FACILITIES
Bake shop; 2 bakeries; cafeteria; catering service; 2 classrooms; 5 computer laboratories; food production kitchen; garden; gourmet dining room; learning resource center; 2 lecture rooms; 2 libraries; public restaurant; snack shop; 3 student lounges; teaching kitchen.

STUDENT PROFILE
69 total: 64 full-time; 5 part-time.

FACULTY
3 total: 2 full-time; 1 part-time. 1 is an industry professional; 2 are culinary-certified teachers. Prominent faculty: Mark Janicki; Jay Demers. Faculty-student ratio: 1:15.

SPECIAL PROGRAMS
Exchange program, culinary competitions, food shows.

TYPICAL EXPENSES
Application fee: $20. In-state tuition: $1890 per semester full-time (in district), $80 per credit part-time. Out-of-state tuition: $3105 per semester full-time, $161 per credit part-time. Program-related fee includes $350 for food and other program costs (per semester).

FINANCIAL AID
In 2006, 2 scholarships were awarded (average award was $300). Employment placement assistance is available.

HOUSING
Coed housing available.

APPLICATION INFORMATION
Students may begin participation in January and August. Applications are accepted continuously. In 2006, 82 applied; 38 were accepted. Applicants must interview; submit a formal application and an essay.

CONTACT
Elizabeth Russell, Director of Admissions, Culinary Arts Department, 354 Hogan Road, Bangor, ME 04401. Telephone: 207-974-4680. Fax: 207-974-4683. E-mail: admissions@emtc.edu. World Wide Web: http://www.emcc.edu.

SOUTHERN MAINE COMMUNITY COLLEGE

Culinary Arts

South Portland, Maine

GENERAL INFORMATION
Public, coeducational, two-year college. Suburban campus. Founded in 1946. Accredited by New England Association of Schools and Colleges.

PROGRAM INFORMATION
Offered since 1958. Program calendar is divided into semesters. 2-year associate degree in culinary arts/applied science.

PROGRAM AFFILIATION
American Culinary Federation; American Institute of Baking; Council on Hotel, Restaurant, and Institutional Education; Foodservice Educators Network International; International Association of Culinary Professionals; Maine Restaurant Association; National Restaurant Association; National Restaurant Association Educational Foundation.

Southern Maine Community College *(continued)*

AREAS OF STUDY

Baking; beverage management; buffet catering; confectionery show pieces; controlling costs in food service; culinary skill development; food preparation; food purchasing; food service communication; food service math; garde-manger; international cuisine; introduction to food service; kitchen management; management and human resources; meal planning; meat cutting; meat fabrication; menu and facilities design; nutrition; nutrition and food service; restaurant opportunities; sanitation; saucier; seafood processing; soup, stock, sauce, and starch production.

FACILITIES

Bake shop; bakery; 7 classrooms; computer laboratory; demonstration laboratory; 4 food production kitchens; gourmet dining room; 3 laboratories; learning resource center; lecture room; library; public restaurant; 2 teaching kitchens.

STUDENT PROFILE

150 total: 98 full-time; 52 part-time. 114 are under 25 years old; 34 are between 25 and 44 years old; 2 are over 44 years old.

FACULTY

8 total: 4 full-time; 4 part-time. 4 are industry professionals; 2 are culinary-certified teachers. Prominent faculty: David Libby, MSEd; Paul Charpentier, MS, CCE, CEC; Wilfred Beriau, MS, CCE, CEC, AAC. Faculty-student ratio: 1:15.

SPECIAL PROGRAMS

Tours of food service establishments, guest lectures, study abroad program in Austria/Italy.

TYPICAL EXPENSES

Application fee: $20. In-state tuition: $1648 per semester. Out-of-state tuition: $2863 per semester. Program-related fees include $400 for uniforms, knives, and equipment; $900–$1000 for texts (for two years).

FINANCIAL AID

In 2006, 8 scholarships were awarded (average award was $500). Employment placement assistance is available. Employment opportunities within the program are available.

HOUSING

Coed housing available. Average on-campus housing cost per month: $350–$650. Average off-campus housing cost per month: $550.

APPLICATION INFORMATION

Students may begin participation in January and August. Applications are accepted continuously. In 2006, 151 applied; 89 were accepted. Applicants must submit a formal application.

CONTACT

Staci Grasky, Associate Dean of Information and Enrollment Services/Registrar, Culinary Arts, Fort Road, South Portland, ME 04106. Telephone: 207-741-5500. Fax: 207-741-5760. E-mail: menrollmentservices@smccme.edu. World Wide Web: http://www.smccme.edu.

YORK COUNTY COMMUNITY COLLEGE

Wells, Maine

GENERAL INFORMATION

Public, coeducational, two-year college. Small-town setting. Founded in 1994. Accredited by New England Association of Schools and Colleges.

PROGRAM INFORMATION

Offered since 1995. Program calendar is divided into semesters. 1-year certificate in food and beverage operations. 2-year associate degree in culinary arts.

PROGRAM AFFILIATION

Council on Hotel, Restaurant, and Institutional Education; National Restaurant Association; National Restaurant Association Educational Foundation.

AREAS OF STUDY

Baking; beverage management; controlling costs in food service; culinary skill development; food preparation; food purchasing; food service communication; food service math; garde-manger; international cuisine; kitchen management; management and human resources; meal planning; meat fabrication; menu and facilities design; nutrition and food service; sanitation; saucier; seafood processing; soup, stock, sauce, and starch production; wines and spirits.

FACILITIES

Bake shop; catering service; classroom; computer laboratory; demonstration laboratory; food production kitchen; learning resource center; library; student lounge; teaching kitchen.

STUDENT PROFILE

52 total: 26 full-time; 26 part-time.

FACULTY

8 total: 1 full-time; 7 part-time. 1 is an industry professional; 1 is a culinary-certified teacher. Prominent faculty: Norman Hebert, CHE, FMP; Jack Davis; Dale Mowery; Doreen Adler. Faculty-student ratio: 1:10.

SPECIAL PROGRAMS

Culinary competitions through the Maine Restaurant Association, Austria Exchange Program through Maine Community College System.

TYPICAL EXPENSES
Application fee: $20. In-state tuition: $4000 per year full-time (in district), $80 per credit part-time. Out-of-state tuition: $6000 per year full-time, $161 per credit part-time. Program-related fees include $150 for cutlery; $200 for uniforms.

FINANCIAL AID
In 2006, 3 scholarships were awarded (average award was $1200). Employment placement assistance is available.

HOUSING
Average off-campus housing cost per month: $300–$500.

APPLICATION INFORMATION
Students may begin participation in January, May, and September. Applications are accepted continuously. In 2006, 50 applied; 50 were accepted. Applicants must submit a formal application, an essay, high school transcript or GED; take assessment test (administered by college).

CONTACT
Fred Quistgard, Director of Admissions, 112 College Drive, Wells, ME 04090. Telephone: 207-646-9282. Fax: 207-641-0837. E-mail: admissions@yccc.edu. World Wide Web: http://www.yccc.edu.

MARYLAND

ALLEGANY COLLEGE OF MARYLAND

School of Hospitality, Tourism, and Culinary Arts

Cumberland, Maryland

GENERAL INFORMATION
Public, coeducational, two-year college. Suburban campus. Founded in 1961. Accredited by Middle States Association of Colleges and Schools.

PROGRAM INFORMATION
Offered since 1998. Program calendar is divided into semesters. 2-term/11 credit letter of recognition in baking essentials. 2-term/11 credit letter of recognition in culinary essential. 2-year associate degree in culinary arts.

PROGRAM AFFILIATION
American Dietetic Association.

AREAS OF STUDY
Baking; culinary skill development; kitchen management; restaurant opportunities; sanitation.

FACILITIES
Bake shop; 3 classrooms; 2 computer laboratories; food production kitchen; gourmet dining room; learning resource center; library; public restaurant; student lounge; teaching kitchen.

STUDENT PROFILE
40 total: 16 full-time; 24 part-time. 34 are under 25 years old; 5 are between 25 and 44 years old; 1 is over 44 years old.

FACULTY
8 total: 3 full-time; 5 part-time. 3 are industry professionals. Prominent faculty: Debra Frank, RD; David L. Sanford, CCC; Bill Hand; Debbie Schurg. Faculty-student ratio: 1:13.

SPECIAL PROGRAMS
Responsibility for student-operated restaurant, ServSafe Certification with National Restaurant Association.

TYPICAL EXPENSES
In-state tuition: $3168 per year full-time (in district), $96 per credit hour part-time (in district), $5874 per year full-time (out-of-district), $178 per credit hour part-time (out-of-district). Out-of-state tuition: $6864 per year full-time, $208 per credit hour part-time. Program-related fees include $135 for cutlery kit; $72 for lab fee (per course); $100 for uniform.

FINANCIAL AID
In 2006, 1 scholarship was awarded (award was $1000). Program-specific awards include Culinary Arts is a statewide designated program. Employment placement assistance is available.

HOUSING
Apartment-style housing available. Average on-campus housing cost per month: $500. Average off-campus housing cost per month: $350.

APPLICATION INFORMATION
Students may begin participation in January and August. Applications are accepted continuously. In 2006, 77 applied; 74 were accepted. Applicants must interview; submit a formal application, an essay, a separate culinary arts application.

CONTACT
Mrs. Cathy Nolan, Director of Admissions and Registration, School of Hospitality, Tourism, and Culinary Arts, 12401 Willowbrook Road, SE, Cumberland, MD 21502. Telephone: 301-784-5000. Fax: 301-784-5027. E-mail: cnolan@allegany.edu. World Wide Web: http://www.allegany.edu.

ANNE ARUNDEL COMMUNITY COLLEGE

Hospitality, Culinary Arts, and Tourism Institute

Arnold, Maryland

GENERAL INFORMATION
Public, coeducational, two-year college. Suburban campus. Founded in 1961. Accredited by Middle States Association of Colleges and Schools.

PROGRAM INFORMATION
Offered since 1988. Accredited by American Culinary Federation Accrediting Commission. Program calendar is divided into semesters. Associate degree in hotel/restaurant management-hospitality business management. Associate degree in hotel/restaurant management-culinary arts operations. Certificate in hotel/restaurant management-food service operations. Certificate in hotel/restaurant management-culinary arts operations. Certificate in hotel/lodging management. Certificate in catering operations. Certificate in baking and pastry arts operations.

PROGRAM AFFILIATION
American Culinary Federation; Council on Hotel, Restaurant, and Institutional Education; International Association of Culinary Professionals; International Food Service Executives Association; National Restaurant Association; National Restaurant Association Educational Foundation; Women Chefs and Restaurateurs.

AREAS OF STUDY
Baking; beverage management; buffet catering; confectionery show pieces; controlling costs in food service; convenience cookery; culinary French; culinary skill development; food preparation; food purchasing; food service math; garde-manger; international cuisine; introduction to food service; kitchen management; management and human resources; meal planning; meat fabrication; menu and facilities design; nutrition; nutrition and food service; patisserie; sanitation; saucier; soup, stock, sauce, and starch production; wines and spirits.

FACILITIES
Bake shop; 5 classrooms; computer laboratory; demonstration laboratory; 4 food production kitchens; learning resource center; student lounge.

STUDENT PROFILE
467 total: 169 full-time; 298 part-time. 282 are under 25 years old; 142 are between 25 and 44 years old; 43 are over 44 years old.

FACULTY
18 total: 6 full-time; 12 part-time. 13 are industry professionals; 5 are culinary-certified teachers. Prominent faculty: Shawn Harlan, CEC, CHE; David Ludwig, CEPC, CHE; Ken Jarvis, CEC, CCE, CHE; Lou Woods, CEC, CLE, CHE, FMP. Faculty-student ratio: 1:16.

SPECIAL PROGRAMS
Student culinary team, international internship to Amalfi coast of Italy, internship in Hawaii, Student Chef's Club, ACF chef certification testing.

TYPICAL EXPENSES
Application fee: $20. In-state tuition: $86 per credit hour full-time (in district), $86 per credit hour part-time (in district), $165 per credit hour full-time (out-of-district), $165 per credit hour part-time (out-of-district). Out-of-state tuition: $292 per credit hour full-time, $292 per credit hour part-time. Tuition for international students: $292 per credit hour full-time, $292 per credit hour part-time. Program-related fees include $100 for uniform; $200 for knife kit; $35–$270 for lab fees (vary per course).

FINANCIAL AID
In 2006, 9 scholarships were awarded. Employment placement assistance is available. Employment opportunities within the program are available.

APPLICATION INFORMATION
Students may begin participation in January, June, and September. Applications are accepted continuously. Applicants must submit a formal application.

CONTACT
Mary Ellen Mason, Director, Hospitality, Culinary Arts, and Tourism Institute, 101 College Parkway, CALT 129, Arnold, MD 21012. World Wide Web: http://www.aacc.edu.

BALTIMORE INTERNATIONAL COLLEGE

School of Culinary Arts

Baltimore, Maryland

GENERAL INFORMATION
Private, coeducational, four-year college. Urban campus. Founded in 1972. Accredited by Middle States Association of Colleges and Schools.

PROGRAM INFORMATION
Offered since 1972. Accredited by American Culinary Federation Accrediting Commission. Program calendar is divided into semesters. 12-month certificate in

professional culinary arts. 2-year associate degree in professional cooking and baking. 2-year associate degree in professional cooking. 2-year associate degree in professional baking and pastry. 2-year master's degree in hospitality management. 22-month certificate in culinary arts-evening program. 4-year bachelor's degree in hospitality management. 4-year bachelor's degree in hospitality management with marketing concentration. 4-year bachelor's degree in culinary management.

PROGRAM AFFILIATION
American Culinary Federation; Council on Hotel, Restaurant, and Institutional Education; International Association of Culinary Professionals; National Restaurant Association.

AREAS OF STUDY
Baking; beverage management; buffet catering; classical cuisine; confectionery show pieces; controlling costs in food service; convenience cookery; culinary skill development; food preparation; food purchasing; food service communication; garde-manger; hotel operations; international cuisine; introduction to food service; kitchen management; management and human resources; marketing; meal planning; meat fabrication; menu and facilities design; nutrition; patisserie; restaurant operations; sanitation; saucier; seafood processing; soup, stock, sauce, and starch production; wines and spirits.

FACILITIES
21 classrooms; 2 computer laboratories; garden; gourmet dining room; learning resource center; library; public restaurant; snack shop; student lounge; 7 teaching kitchens; 2 public hotels; auditorium.

STUDENT PROFILE
800 full-time.

FACULTY
35 total: 15 full-time; 20 part-time. 5 are industry professionals; 1 is a master baker; 9 are culinary-certified teachers. Prominent faculty: Jan Bandula, CMPC, CCE, AAC; Charles Talucci, CEC; Greg Wentz, CEC; Faith Kling, CEC. Faculty-student ratio: 1:18.

SPECIAL PROGRAMS
Externships, five-week course at campus in Ireland for associate and bachelor's students, accelerated programs.

TYPICAL EXPENSES
Application fee: $35. Tuition: $7744 per semester.

FINANCIAL AID
In 2006, 582 scholarships were awarded (average award was $3862). Program-specific awards include scholarships for alumni returning to complete

bachelor's degree, Career Opportunity Grant, Leadership Grant. Employment placement assistance is available. Employment opportunities within the program are available.

HOUSING
Coed housing available.

APPLICATION INFORMATION
Students may begin participation in January, May, July, and September. Applications are accepted continuously. Applicants must submit a formal application, academic transcripts, SAT or ACT scores.

CONTACT
Kristin Ciarlo, Director of Admissions, School of Culinary Arts, 17 Commerce Street, Baltimore, MD 21202-3230. Telephone: 410-752-4710 Ext. 120. Fax: 410-752-3730. E-mail: admissions@bic.edu. World Wide Web: http://www.bic.edu.

See color display following page 186.

L'ACADEMIE DE CUISINE

Gaithersburg, Maryland

GENERAL INFORMATION
Private, coeducational, culinary institute. Suburban campus. Founded in 1976. Accredited by Accrediting Council for Continuing Education and Training.

PROGRAM INFORMATION
Offered since 1976. Program calendar is continuous, year-round. 34-week certificate in pastry arts. 48-week certificate in culinary arts.

PROGRAM AFFILIATION
American Institute of Wine & Food; Confrerie de la Chaine des Rotisseurs; International Association of Culinary Professionals; Les Dames d'Escoffier; National Restaurant Association; National Restaurant Association Educational Foundation; The Bread Bakers Guild of America; Women Chefs and Restaurateurs.

AREAS OF STUDY
Baking; buffet catering; controlling costs in food service; culinary French; culinary skill development; food preparation; food purchasing; food service math; garde-manger; international cuisine; kitchen management; meal planning; meat cutting; meat fabrication; menu and facilities design; nutrition; nutrition and food service; patisserie; sanitation; saucier; seafood processing; soup, stock, sauce, and starch production; wines and spirits.

FACILITIES
2 demonstration laboratories; 4 food production kitchens; library; student lounge.

L'Academie de Cuisine *(continued)*

STUDENT PROFILE
130 full-time.

FACULTY
18 total: 11 full-time; 7 part-time. 9 are industry professionals; 2 are culinary-certified teachers. Prominent faculty: Francois Dionot; Mark Ramsdell; Gerard Paugaud; Somchet Chumpapo. Faculty-student ratio: 1:13.

PROMINENT ALUMNI AND CURRENT AFFILIATION
Damian Salvatore, Persimmon; Jeff Heineman, Grapeseed.

SPECIAL PROGRAMS
1-week culinary tour in Gascony, France.

TYPICAL EXPENSES
Application fee: $75. Tuition: $26,635 for culinary arts certificate; $18,375 for pastry arts certificate. Program-related fees include $810 for books, cutlery, uniforms, and pastry equipment (culinary arts program); $525 for books, cutlery, uniforms, and pastry equipment (pastry arts program).

FINANCIAL AID
In 2006, 2 scholarships were awarded (average award was $4500). Employment placement assistance is available.

HOUSING
Average off-campus housing cost per month: $750.

APPLICATION INFORMATION
Students may begin participation in January, April, July, and October. Applications are accepted continuously. In 2006, 160 applied; 140 were accepted. Applicants must interview; submit a formal application, letters of reference, an essay, resume, proof of high school graduation, and proof of age (18 or older).

CONTACT
Barbara Cullen, Admissions Director, 16006 Industrial Drive, Gaithersburg, MD 20877. Telephone: 301-670-8670. Fax: 301-670-0450. E-mail: info@lacademie.com. World Wide Web: http://www.lacademie.com.

LINCOLN TECH

Center for Culinary Arts

Columbia, Maryland

GENERAL INFORMATION
Private, coeducational institution. Accredited by Accrediting Commission of Career Schools and Colleges of Technology.

PROGRAM INFORMATION
Offered since 2007. Diploma in culinary arts.

CONTACT
Admissions Department, Center for Culinary Arts, 9325 Snowden River Parkway, Columbia, MD 21046. Telephone: 410-290-7100.

WOR-WIC COMMUNITY COLLEGE

Hotel/Motel/Restaurant Management

Salisbury, Maryland

GENERAL INFORMATION
Public, coeducational, two-year college. Small-town setting. Founded in 1975. Accredited by Middle States Association of Colleges and Schools.

PROGRAM INFORMATION
Offered since 1976. Program calendar is divided into semesters. 1-year certificate in culinary arts. 1-year certificate in restaurant management. 1-year certificate in hotel/motel management. 2-year associate degree in culinary arts. 2-year associate degree in hotel/motel/restaurant management.

PROGRAM AFFILIATION
American Culinary Federation; Council on Hotel, Restaurant, and Institutional Education; National Restaurant Association; Ocean City Hotel-Motel-Restaurant Association.

AREAS OF STUDY
Baking; beverage management; controlling costs in food service; culinary French; culinary skill development; food preparation; food purchasing; garde-manger; international cuisine; introduction to food service; management and human resources; menu and facilities design; nutrition; patisserie; sanitation.

FACILITIES
Classroom; computer laboratory; gourmet dining room; teaching kitchen.

STUDENT PROFILE
49 total: 16 full-time; 33 part-time. 30 are under 25 years old; 17 are between 25 and 44 years old; 2 are over 44 years old.

FACULTY
2 total: 2 full-time; 0 part-time. Prominent faculty: Scott D. Dahlberg, EdD; Ricardo H. Aragon. Faculty-student ratio: 1:24.

SPECIAL PROGRAMS
Trade shows, guest chefs, access to many resort hotels in Ocean City and Salisbury for tours.

TYPICAL EXPENSES
In-state tuition: $912 per semester full-time (in district), $76 per credit hour part-time (in district), $2304 per semester full-time (out-of-district), $192 per credit hour part-time (out-of-district). Out-of-state tuition: $2688 per semester full-time, $224 per credit hour part-time. Program-related fee includes $50–$75 for materials for various courses.

FINANCIAL AID
In 2006, 3 scholarships were awarded (average award was $1000).

HOUSING
Average off-campus housing cost per month: $750.

APPLICATION INFORMATION
Students may begin participation in January, May, July, and September. Applications are accepted continuously. In 2006, 101 applied; 101 were accepted. Applicants must submit a formal application.

CONTACT
Richard C. Webster, Director of Admissions, Hotel/Motel/Restaurant Management, 32000 Campus Drive, Salisbury, MD 21804. Telephone: 410-334-2895. Fax: 410-334-2954. E-mail: admissions@worwic.edu. World Wide Web: http://www.worwic.edu.

MASSACHUSETTS

BRANFORD HALL CAREER INSTITUTE

Springfield, Massachusetts

GENERAL INFORMATION
Private institution. Accredited by Accrediting Council for Independent Colleges and Schools.

PROGRAM INFORMATION
Certificate in culinary arts.

SPECIAL PROGRAMS
Externships.

CONTACT
Admissions Department, Technical Training Center, 189 Brookdale Drive, Springfield, MA 01104. Telephone: 800-959-7599. World Wide Web: http://www.branfordhall.com.

BRISTOL COMMUNITY COLLEGE

Culinary Arts Department

Fall River, Massachusetts

GENERAL INFORMATION
Public, coeducational, two-year college. Suburban campus. Founded in 1965. Accredited by New England Association of Schools and Colleges.

PROGRAM INFORMATION
Offered since 1985. Program calendar is divided into semesters. 2-year associate degree in baking/pastry arts. 2-year associate degree in culinary arts.

AREAS OF STUDY
Baking; beverage management; buffet catering; confectionery show pieces; controlling costs in food service; culinary skill development; food preparation; food purchasing; food service math; garde-manger; international cuisine; introduction to food service; meal planning; nutrition; patisserie; sanitation; saucier; seafood processing; soup, stock, sauce, and starch production; wines and spirits.

FACILITIES
Bake shop; cafeteria; catering service; classroom; computer laboratory; food production kitchen; gourmet dining room; learning resource center; lecture room; library; teaching kitchen; bar/lounge.

STUDENT PROFILE
52 total: 50 full-time; 2 part-time. 40 are under 25 years old; 10 are between 25 and 44 years old; 2 are over 44 years old.

FACULTY
6 total: 2 full-time; 4 part-time. 4 are industry professionals; 2 are culinary-certified teachers. Prominent faculty: John Caressimo, AAC, CCE, CCC. Faculty-student ratio: 1:9.

PROMINENT ALUMNI AND CURRENT AFFILIATION
Craig Lewis, Sous Chef, White Horse Tavern, Newport, RI.

SPECIAL PROGRAMS
College-wide Honors Program, Skills USA.

Bristol Community College *(continued)*

TYPICAL EXPENSES
Application fee: $10. In-state tuition: $123 per credit hour. Students from Rhode Island pay in-state tuition. Out-of-state tuition: $329 per credit hour. Program-related fee includes $10 for high course cost fee (per credit).

FINANCIAL AID
In 2006, 4 scholarships were awarded (average award was $500); 5 loans were granted (average loan was $150–$200). Program-specific awards include scholarships for second-year students. Employment placement assistance is available. Employment opportunities within the program are available.

HOUSING
Average off-campus housing cost per month: $750.

APPLICATION INFORMATION
Students may begin participation in September. Applications are accepted continuously. In 2006, 82 applied; 65 were accepted. Applicants must interview; submit a formal application.

CONTACT
John Caressimo, Director, Culinary Arts Department, 777 Elsbree Street, Fall River, MA 02720. Telephone: 508-678-2811 Ext. 2111. Fax: 508-730-3290. E-mail: jcaressi@bristol.mass.edu. World Wide Web: http://www.bristol.mass.edu.

BUNKER HILL COMMUNITY COLLEGE

Culinary Arts Program

Boston, Massachusetts

GENERAL INFORMATION
Public, coeducational, two-year college. Urban campus. Founded in 1973. Accredited by New England Association of Schools and Colleges.

PROGRAM INFORMATION
Offered since 1978. Program calendar is divided into semesters. 1-year certificate in culinary arts. 2-year associate degree in culinary arts.

PROGRAM AFFILIATION
American Culinary Federation; Council on Hotel, Restaurant, and Institutional Education; Food Service Consultants International; National Restaurant Association; National Restaurant Association Educational Foundation.

AREAS OF STUDY
Baking; bar and beverage management; beverage management; buffet catering; café/bistro cuisine; controlling costs in food service; convenience cookery; culinary French; culinary skill development; dining room management; dining room service; food preparation; food purchasing; food service communication; food service math; garde-manger; hospitality law; international cuisine; introduction to food service; kitchen management; management and human resources; meal planning; meat cutting; menu and facilities design; nutrition; nutrition and food service; patisserie; sanitation; saucier; seafood processing; soup, stock, sauce, and starch production; wines and spirits.

FACILITIES
Bake shop; bakery; catering service; classroom; demonstration laboratory; food production kitchen; gourmet dining room; learning resource center; lecture room; library; public restaurant; teaching kitchen.

TYPICAL STUDENT PROFILE
280 total: 252 full-time; 28 part-time.

SPECIAL PROGRAMS
Culinary competitions.

FINANCIAL AID
Employment placement assistance is available. Employment opportunities within the program are available.

APPLICATION INFORMATION
Students may begin participation in January and September. Applications are accepted continuously. Applicants must submit a formal application.

CONTACT
Director of Admissions, Culinary Arts Program, 250 New Rutherford Avenue, Boston, MA 02129. Telephone: 617-228-2171. Fax: 617-228-2052. World Wide Web: http://www.bhcc.mass.edu.

THE CAMBRIDGE SCHOOL OF CULINARY ARTS

Professional Chef's Program, Professional Pastry Program

Cambridge, Massachusetts

GENERAL INFORMATION
Private, coeducational, culinary institute. Urban campus. Founded in 1974. Accredited by Accrediting Commission of Career Schools and Colleges of Technology.

PROGRAM INFORMATION

Offered since 1974. Program calendar is divided into quarters. 16-week certificate in pastry arts training. 16-week certificate in culinary training. 37-week diploma in professional pastry training. 37-week diploma in professional chef training.

PROGRAM AFFILIATION

American Institute of Wine & Food; International Association of Culinary Professionals; James Beard Foundation, Inc.; National Restaurant Association; Oldways Preservation and Exchange Trust; Women Chefs and Restaurateurs.

AREAS OF STUDY

Baking; confectionery show pieces; controlling costs in food service; culinary French; culinary skill development; food preparation; food purchasing; garde-manger; international cuisine; kitchen management; meal planning; meat cutting; nutrition; nutrition and food service; patisserie; restaurant opportunities; sanitation; saucier; soup, stock, sauce, and starch production; wines and spirits.

FACILITIES

Learning resource center; 5 lecture rooms; library; student lounge; 5 teaching kitchens.

STUDENT PROFILE

165 full-time. 36 are under 25 years old; 109 are between 25 and 44 years old; 20 are over 44 years old.

FACULTY

30 total: 10 full-time; 20 part-time. 7 are industry professionals; 1 is a master chef; 5 are culinary-certified teachers. Prominent faculty: Roberta Dowling, CCP; Jan Schiff, CCP; Stephan Viau, CCP; Deb Drinker, CCP. Faculty-student ratio: 1:12.

PROMINENT ALUMNI AND CURRENT AFFILIATION

Craig "Andy" Beardslee, Hash House A Go Go, San Diego, CA; Steve DiFillipo, Davio's, Boston, MA; Lisa Rappael, Delicious Desserts, Falmouth, MA.

SPECIAL PROGRAMS

International culinary excursions, culinary competitions, externships and internships.

TYPICAL EXPENSES

Application fee: $45. Tuition: $22,412 for diploma; $10,416 for certificate. Program-related fees include $290 for books; $450 for materials (diploma program); $225 for materials (certificate program); $950 for kitchen equipment and uniforms.

The Cambridge School of Culinary Arts *(continued)*

FINANCIAL AID

In 2006, 5 scholarships were awarded (average award was $1000); 30 loans were granted (average loan was $15,000). Program-specific awards include The Anthony Spinazzola Foundation Awards. Employment placement assistance is available. Employment opportunities within the program are available.

HOUSING

Average off-campus housing cost per month: $1000.

APPLICATION INFORMATION

Students may begin participation in January, May, and September. Application deadline for fall is August 1. Application deadline for winter is December 1. Application deadline for spring (certificate) is April 1. In 2006, 178 applied; 168 were accepted. Applicants must interview; submit a formal application, letters of reference, an essay, resume, educational records.

CONTACT

Lilly Ascenzo, Admissions Representative, Professional Chef's Program, Professional Pastry Program, 2020 Massachusetts Avenue, Cambridge, MA 02140. Telephone: 617-354-2020. Fax: 617-576-1963. E-mail: admissions@cambridgeculinary.com. World Wide Web: http://www.cambridgeculinary.com.

ENDICOTT COLLEGE

Hotel and Tourism Administration

Beverly, Massachusetts

GENERAL INFORMATION

Private, coeducational, comprehensive institution. Suburban campus. Founded in 1939. Accredited by New England Association of Schools and Colleges.

PROGRAM INFORMATION

Offered since 1994. Program calendar is divided into semesters. Bachelor's degree in spa and resort management. Bachelor's degree in senior community management. Bachelor's degree in events management. 4-year bachelor's degree in hospitality and tourism administration.

PROGRAM AFFILIATION

American Culinary Federation; American Hotel and Lodging Association; Club Managers Association of America; Council on Hotel, Restaurant, and Institutional Education; Massachusetts Restaurant Association; National Restaurant Association; National Restaurant Association Educational Foundation.

AREAS OF STUDY

Beverage management; buffet catering; controlling costs in food service; culinary French; culinary skill development; food preparation; food purchasing; food service communication; garde-manger; international cuisine; introduction to food service; kitchen management; management and human resources; meal planning; menu and facilities design; nutrition; restaurant opportunities; sanitation; soup, stock, sauce, and starch production; wines and spirits.

FACILITIES

Cafeteria; 3 classrooms; computer laboratory; food production kitchen; gourmet dining room; learning resource center; public restaurant; student lounge; teaching kitchen.

STUDENT PROFILE

155 full-time. 148 are under 25 years old; 7 are between 25 and 44 years old.

FACULTY

11 total: 6 full-time; 5 part-time. 5 are industry professionals; 1 is a master chef; 1 is a culinary-certified teacher. Prominent faculty: Brendan Cronin; Peter Jenner; Patricia McCaughey; William H. Samerfink. Faculty-student ratio: 1:15.

SPECIAL PROGRAMS

Community service activities, 1-semester internship, study abroad opportunities.

TYPICAL EXPENSES

Application fee: $40. Tuition: $22,550 per year full-time, $654 per credit part-time. Program-related fee includes $50–$65 for food and wine.

FINANCIAL AID

In 2006, 4 scholarships were awarded (average award was $1500-$2000). Employment placement assistance is available.

HOUSING

Coed, apartment-style, and single-sex housing available. Average on-campus housing cost per month: $856.

APPLICATION INFORMATION

Students may begin participation in February and September. Applications are accepted continuously. In 2006, 213 applied; 120 were accepted. Applicants must submit a formal application, an essay, letters of reference, academic transcripts, and SAT scores.

CONTACT

Thomas Redman, Vice President of Admission and Financial Aid, Hotel and Tourism Administration, 376 Hale Street, Beverly, MA 01915-2096. Telephone: 978-921-1000. Fax: 978-232-2520. E-mail: admissio@endicott.edu. World Wide Web: http://www.endicott.edu/.

INTERNATIONAL INSTITUTE OF CULINARY ARTS

Fall River, Massachusetts

GENERAL INFORMATION
Private, coeducational, culinary institute. Urban campus. Founded in 1997.

PROGRAM INFORMATION
Offered since 1997. Program calendar is divided into semesters. 1-year certificate in culinary. 1-year diploma in baking. 2-year grand diploma in baking/pastry arts. 2-year grand diploma in culinary arts/restaurant hospitality.

PROGRAM AFFILIATION
The Bread Bakers Guild of America.

AREAS OF STUDY
Baking; beverage management; buffet catering; confectionery show pieces; controlling costs in food service; convenience cookery; culinary French; culinary skill development; food preparation; food purchasing; food service communication; food service math; garde-manger; international cuisine; introduction to food service; kitchen management; management and human resources; meal planning; meat cutting; meat fabrication; menu and facilities design; nutrition; nutrition and food service; patisserie; restaurant opportunities; sanitation; saucier; seafood processing; soup, stock, sauce, and starch production; wines and spirits.

FACILITIES
Bake shop; 4 classrooms; computer laboratory; 6 food production kitchens; garden; 4 gourmet dining rooms; 5 lecture rooms; 2 libraries; 5 public restaurants; snack shop; student lounge.

STUDENT PROFILE
20 full-time. 18 are under 25 years old; 2 are over 44 years old.

FACULTY
6 total: 5 full-time; 1 part-time. Prominent faculty: George Karousos, Master Chef; Theodore Karousos; Mark Bennison; Robert Castagna. Faculty-student ratio: 1:10.

TYPICAL EXPENSES
Application fee: $45. Tuition: $11,500 per year for grand diploma, diploma, or certificate. Program-related fee includes $1800 for uniform, equipment, fees, publications, commencement and labs.

FINANCIAL AID
In 2006, 3 scholarships were awarded (average award was $11,500); 9 loans were granted (average loan was $11,000). Employment placement assistance is available. Employment opportunities within the program are available.

HOUSING
Average off-campus housing cost per month: $500–$750.

APPLICATION INFORMATION
Students may begin participation in January and September. Applications are accepted continuously. In 2006, 70 applied; 25 were accepted. Applicants must interview; submit letters of reference, an essay, formal application, and academic transcripts.

CONTACT
Theodore Karousas, Director of Admissions, 100 Rock Street, Fall River, MA 02720. Telephone: 508-675-9305. Fax: 508-678-5214. E-mail: culinaryarts@meganet.net. World Wide Web: http://www.iicaculinary.com.

MASSASOIT COMMUNITY COLLEGE

Culinary Arts Program

Brockton, Massachusetts

GENERAL INFORMATION
Public, coeducational, two-year college. Urban campus. Founded in 1966. Accredited by New England Association of Schools and Colleges.

PROGRAM INFORMATION
Offered since 1982. Program calendar is divided into semesters. 2-semester certificate in food production. 2-year associate degree in culinary arts.

PROGRAM AFFILIATION
National Restaurant Association; National Restaurant Association Educational Foundation.

AREAS OF STUDY
Baking; introduction to food service; soup, stock, sauce, and starch production; storeroom and inventory procedures.

FACILITIES
Bakery; classroom; computer laboratory; demonstration laboratory; food production kitchen; gourmet dining room; lecture room; library; student lounge; teaching kitchen.

STUDENT PROFILE
89 total: 54 full-time; 35 part-time.

Massasoit Community College *(continued)*

FACULTY
4 total: 4 full-time. Faculty-student ratio: 1:13.

TYPICAL EXPENSES
In-state tuition: $1332 per 12 credits full-time (in district), $111 per credit part-time. Out-of-state tuition: $3804 per 12 credits full-time, $317 per credit part-time. Tuition for international students: $3804 per 12 credits full-time, $317 per credit part-time. Program-related fees include $70 for uniforms; $100 for knives.

FINANCIAL AID
Employment placement assistance is available.

APPLICATION INFORMATION
Students may begin participation in January and September. Applications are accepted continuously. Applicants must submit a formal application.

CONTACT
Michelle Hughes, Director of Admissions, Culinary Arts Program, One Massasoit Boulevard, Brockton, MA 02402-3996. Telephone: 508-588-9100 Ext. 1411. E-mail: admoffice@massasoit.mass.edu. World Wide Web: http://www.massasoit.mass.edu.

MIDDLESEX COMMUNITY COLLEGE
Lowell, Massachusetts

GENERAL INFORMATION
Public, coeducational, two-year college. Urban campus. Founded in 1970. Accredited by New England Association of Schools and Colleges.

PROGRAM INFORMATION
Accredited by NEASC. Program calendar is divided into semesters. 1-year certificate in culinary arts. 2-year associate degree in hospitality management-culinary arts option.

PROGRAM AFFILIATION
Council on Hotel, Restaurant, and Institutional Education; National Restaurant Association; National Restaurant Association Educational Foundation.

AREAS OF STUDY
Baking; beverage management; buffet catering; confectionery show pieces; culinary skill development; food preparation; food purchasing; food service math; introduction to food service; kitchen management; management and human resources; menu and facilities design; nutrition and food service; patisserie; sanitation; soup, stock, sauce, and starch production; wines and spirits.

FACILITIES
Bake shop; bakery; classroom; computer laboratory; demonstration laboratory; food production kitchen; lecture room; library.

TYPICAL STUDENT PROFILE
25 total: 20 full-time; 5 part-time. 20 are under 25 years old; 5 are between 25 and 44 years old.

FINANCIAL AID
Program-specific awards include local industry scholarships-through the Massachusetts Lodging Association. Employment placement assistance is available. Employment opportunities within the program are available.

APPLICATION INFORMATION
Students may begin participation in January and September. Application deadline for fall is September 6. Applicants must submit a formal application.

CONTACT
Director of Admissions, 33, Kearney Square, Lowell, MA 01852-1987. Telephone: 978-656-3170. Fax: 978-656-3150. World Wide Web: http://www.middlesex.mass.edu.

NEWBURY COLLEGE
Brookline, Massachusetts

GENERAL INFORMATION
Private, coeducational, four-year college. Suburban campus. Founded in 1962. Accredited by New England Association of Schools and Colleges.

PROGRAM INFORMATION
Program calendar is divided into semesters. 11-month certificate in meeting management. 11-month certificate in hotel and resort management. 11-month certificate in pastry arts. 11-month certificate in buffet catering. 11-month certificate in food service and restaurant management. 2-year associate degree in food service and restaurant management. 2-year associate degree in hotel and resort management. 2-year associate degree in culinary arts. 4-year bachelor's degree in hotel, restaurant, and service management/culinary management concentration. 4-year bachelor's degree in hotel, restaurant, and service management/hotel administration concentration.

PROGRAM AFFILIATION
National Restaurant Association Educational Foundation.

SPECIAL PROGRAMS
Internships, operation of college's own restaurant.

TYPICAL EXPENSES
Application fee: $50. Tuition: $18,900 per year. Program-related fee includes $105 for credit hour (food, equipment, utilities and supplies).

FINANCIAL AID
Employment placement assistance is available.

HOUSING
Coed housing available.

APPLICATION INFORMATION
Students may begin participation in January and September. Applications are accepted continuously. Applicants must submit a formal application, letters of reference, an essay, transcripts.

CONTACT
Salvadore Liberto, Vice President of Enrollment, 129 Fisher Avenue, Brookline, MA 02445. Telephone: 617-730-7007. Fax: 617-731-9618. E-mail: info@newbury.edu. World Wide Web: http://www.newbury.edu.

UNIVERSITY OF MASSACHUSETTS AMHERST

Hospitality and Tourism Management

Amherst, Massachusetts

GENERAL INFORMATION
Public, coeducational, university. Small-town setting. Founded in 1863. Accredited by New England Association of Schools and Colleges.

PROGRAM INFORMATION
Offered since 1938. Accredited by Council on Hotel, Restaurant and Institutional Education. National Restaurant Association Educational Foundation ManageFirst certificates available. Program calendar is divided into semesters. 2-year master's degree in hospitality and tourism management (MS/MBA joint degree). 2-year master's degree in hospitality and tourism management. 4-year bachelor's degree in hospitality and tourism management. 5-course certificate in casino management. 5-course certificate in event and tourism management.

University of Massachusetts Amherst *(continued)*

Program Affiliation
Club Managers Association of America; Council on Hotel, Restaurant, and Institutional Education; National Restaurant Association; National Restaurant Association Educational Foundation.

Areas of Study
Beverage management; casino management; club management; events management; food service management; lodging; management and human resources; restaurant opportunities.

Facilities
Catering service; 5 classrooms; 3 coffee shops; computer laboratory; demonstration laboratory; food production kitchen; gourmet dining room; learning resource center; 3 lecture rooms; library; student lounge; teaching kitchen.

Student Profile
639 full-time.

Faculty
19 total: 16 full-time; 3 part-time.

Special Programs
600 hour work experience requirement, internships available, domestic, international and study abroad options.

Typical Expenses
In-state tuition: $15,795 per year. Out-of-state tuition: $24,914 per year.

Financial Aid
Employment placement assistance is available. Employment opportunities within the program are available.

Housing
Coed and apartment-style housing available.

Application Information
Students may begin participation in January and September. Applications are accepted continuously. Applicants must submit a formal application, letters of reference, and an essay.

Contact
Derek Bratton, Academic Advisor, Hospitality and Tourism Management, 101 Flint Lab, 90 Campus Center Way, Amherst, MA 01003. Telephone: 413-545-4049. E-mail: dbratton@ht.umass.edu. World Wide Web: http://www.umass.edu.

Michigan

The Art Institute of Michigan

The International Culinary School at The Art Institute of Michigan

Novi, Michigan

General Information
Private, coeducational institution.

Program Information
Associate degree in Culinary Arts. Bachelor's degree in Culinary Management. Certificate in Professional Baking and Pastry.

Contact
Office of Admissions, The International Culinary School at The Art Institute of Michigan, 28125 Cabot Drive, Suite 100, Novi, MI 48377. Telephone: 248-675-3800. Fax: 248-675-3830. World Wide Web: http://www.artinstitutes.edu/detroit.

See color display following page 186.

Baker College of Muskegon

Culinary Arts and Food and Beverage Management

Muskegon, Michigan

General Information
Private, coeducational, four-year college. Suburban campus. Founded in 1888. Accredited by North Central Association of Colleges and Schools.

Program Information
Offered since 1997. Accredited by American Culinary Federation Accrediting Commission. Program calendar is divided into quarters. 1-year certificate in baking and pastry. 2-year associate degree in food and beverage management. 2-year associate degree in culinary arts. 4-year bachelor's degree in food and beverage management.

Program Affiliation
American Culinary Federation; Council on Hotel, Restaurant, and Institutional Education; National Restaurant Association; National Restaurant Association Educational Foundation; Tasters Guild International.

AREAS OF STUDY

Baking; beverage management; buffet catering; confectionery show pieces; controlling costs in food service; convenience cookery; culinary French; culinary skill development; food preparation; food purchasing; food service math; garde-manger; international cuisine; introduction to food service; kitchen management; management and human resources; meal planning; meat cutting; meat fabrication; menu and facilities design; nutrition; nutrition and food service; patisserie; restaurant opportunities; sanitation; saucier; seafood processing; soup, stock, sauce, and starch production; wines and spirits.

FACILITIES

Bake shop; catering service; 5 classrooms; 10 computer laboratories; demonstration laboratory; food production kitchen; garden; gourmet dining room; learning resource center; 105 lecture rooms; library; public restaurant; student lounge; teaching kitchen.

TYPICAL STUDENT PROFILE

330 full-time.

SPECIAL PROGRAMS

Culinary competitions, ice carving, international competitions and overseas excursions.

FINANCIAL AID

Program-specific awards include National Restaurant Association scholarships ($2000), Warren A. Husid Memorial Scholarships ($2000). Employment placement assistance is available. Employment opportunities within the program are available.

HOUSING

Coed and apartment-style housing available.

APPLICATION INFORMATION

Students may begin participation in January, April, and September. Applications are accepted continuously. Applicants must submit a formal application and have high school diploma or GED.

CONTACT

Director of Admissions, Culinary Arts and Food and Beverage Management, 1903 Marquette Avenue, Muskegon, MT 49442. Telephone: 231-777-5207. Fax: 231-777-5256. World Wide Web: http://www.baker.edu.

CENTRAL MICHIGAN UNIVERSITY

Foodservice Administration

Mount Pleasant, Michigan

GENERAL INFORMATION

Public, coeducational, university. Small-town setting. Founded in 1892. Accredited by North Central Association of Colleges and Schools.

PROGRAM INFORMATION

Accredited by American Dietetic Association. Program calendar is divided into semesters. 4-year bachelor's degree in dietetics. 4-year bachelor's degree in food service administration.

PROGRAM AFFILIATION

American Dietetic Association.

AREAS OF STUDY

Beverage management; culinary skill development; food preparation; food purchasing; menu and facilities design; nutrition and food service; sanitation.

FACILITIES

Demonstration laboratory.

STUDENT PROFILE

126 total: 111 full-time; 15 part-time. 111 are under 25 years old; 12 are between 25 and 44 years old; 3 are over 44 years old.

FACULTY

7 total: 7 full-time. 7 are registered dietitians. Prominent faculty: Wesley Luckhardt, MBA, RD; Christine Henries-Zerbe, MS, RD. Faculty-student ratio: 1:18.

SPECIAL PROGRAMS

Food service internship.

TYPICAL EXPENSES

Application fee: $35. In-state tuition: $9120 per 2 semesters full-time (in district), $304 per credit hour part-time. Out-of-state tuition: $21,210 per 2 semesters full-time, $707 per credit hour part-time. Tuition for international students: $21,210 per 2 semesters full-time, $707 per credit hour part-time. Program-related fees include $40 for lab fee (procurement of ingredients); $15 for lab fee (procurement of ingredients).

FINANCIAL AID

Program-specific awards include Rose J. Hogue Scholarship (junior or senior with 3.0 or higher GPA). Employment placement assistance is available. Employment opportunities within the program are available.

Central Michigan University *(continued)*

HOUSING
Coed housing available. Average on-campus housing cost per month: $804.

APPLICATION INFORMATION
Students may begin participation in January and August. Applications are accepted continuously. Applicants must submit a formal application.

CONTACT
Wesley Luckhardt, Faculty, Human Environmental Studies, Foodservice Administration, Wightman Hall 109, Mt. Pleasant, MI 48859. Telephone: 989-774-5591. E-mail: luckh1we@cmich.edu. World Wide Web: http://nutrition.cmich.edu/.

GRAND RAPIDS COMMUNITY COLLEGE

Hospitality Education Department

Grand Rapids, Michigan

GENERAL INFORMATION
Public, coeducational, two-year college. Urban campus. Founded in 1914. Accredited by North Central Association of Colleges and Schools.

PROGRAM INFORMATION
Offered since 1980. Accredited by American Culinary Federation Accrediting Commission. Program calendar is divided into semesters. 12-month certificate in baking and pastry arts. 21-month associate degree in culinary arts. 21-month associate degree in culinary management.

PROGRAM AFFILIATION
American Culinary Federation; American Institute of Baking; American Vegan Society; Confrerie de la Chaine des Rotisseurs; Council on Hotel, Restaurant, and Institutional Education; Foodservice Educators Network International; International Food Service Executives Association; National Restaurant Association; National Restaurant Association Educational Foundation; North American Vegetarian Society; Retailer's Bakery Association; Society of Wine Educators; Tasters Guild International.

AREAS OF STUDY
Baking; beverage management; buffet catering; cake decorating; confectionery show pieces; controlling costs in food service; culinary skill development; deli-bakery operations; food preparation; food purchasing; food service math; garde-manger; ice carving; international cuisine; introduction to food service; kitchen management; management and human resources; meat fabrication; menu and facilities design; nutrition; nutrition and food service; patisserie; restaurant opportunities; sanitation; saucier; seafood processing; soup, stock, sauce, and starch production; table service; vegetarian and vegan cooking; wines and spirits.

FACILITIES
3 bake shops; cafeteria; catering service; 3 classrooms; coffee shop; computer laboratory; 2 demonstration laboratories; 3 food production kitchens; garden; 3 gourmet dining rooms; learning resource center; 3 lecture rooms; library; public restaurant; snack shop; student lounge; 6 teaching kitchens; 6 banquet rooms; beverage lab; wine education classroom.

STUDENT PROFILE
495 total: 300 full-time; 195 part-time. 352 are under 25 years old; 118 are between 25 and 44 years old; 25 are over 44 years old.

FACULTY
22 total: 12 full-time; 10 part-time. 17 are industry professionals; 2 are master chefs; 2 are culinary-certified teachers. Prominent faculty: Robert Garlough; Jim Muth; Angus Campbell; Kevin Dunn. Faculty-student ratio: 1:18.

SPECIAL PROGRAMS
International exchange program, international culinary study tours, culinary competition.

TYPICAL EXPENSES
Application fee: $20. In-state tuition: $79.50 per contact hour full-time (in district), $79.50 per contact hour part-time (in district), $157 per contact hour full-time (out-of-district), $157 per contact hour part-time (out-of-district). Out-of-state tuition: $227 per contact hour full-time, $227 per contact hour part-time. Program-related fees include $260 for knife kit; $350 for uniforms; $1000 for textbooks.

FINANCIAL AID
In 2006, 19 scholarships were awarded (average award was $1000). Employment placement assistance is available. Employment opportunities within the program are available.

HOUSING
Average off-campus housing cost per month: $400.

APPLICATION INFORMATION
Students may begin participation in January and September. Applications are accepted continuously. In 2006, 170 applied; 160 were accepted. Applicants must submit a formal application and ACT scores or Accuplacer Test.

Grand Rapids Community College Hospitality Education

the choice is yours...

Hospitality Education students choose from among three programs:

Baking and Pastry Arts

Our certificate-granting program can prepare you for a rewarding career as a baker, pastry chef, deli-bakery manager or the proprietor of your own bakery.

Culinary Arts or Culinary Management

Our associate degree-granting programs in Applied Arts and Sciences can prepare you for an exciting career as a food and beverage director, executive chef, caterer, or the proprietor of your own foodservice operation.

- See our listing in this edition of *Peterson's Culinary Schools*
- Visit our Web Site – www.grcc.edu
- Contact us for more information at (616) 234-3690
- Visit our Center for Culinary Education, 151 Fountain St, NE Grand Rapids, MI 49503-3263

Grand Rapids Community College is an equal opportunity institution.

Grand Rapids Community College *(continued)*

CONTACT

Mr. Randy Sahajdack, Program Director, Hospitality Education Department, 143 Bostwick, NE, Grand Rapids, MI 49503. Telephone: 616-234-3690. Fax: 616-234-3698. E-mail: marp@grcc.edu. World Wide Web: http://www.grcc.edu/hospitality.

See display on page 201.

GRAND VALLEY STATE UNIVERSITY

Hospitality and Tourism Management

Allendale, Michigan

GENERAL INFORMATION

Public, coeducational, comprehensive institution. Suburban campus. Founded in 1960. Accredited by North Central Association of Colleges and Schools.

PROGRAM INFORMATION

Offered since 1977. Program calendar is divided into semesters. 4-year bachelor's degree in hospitality and tourism management.

PROGRAM AFFILIATION

American Dietetic Association; Council on Hotel, Restaurant, and Institutional Education; National Restaurant Association; Professional Convention Management Association.

AREAS OF STUDY

Beverage management; food and beverage service management; kitchen management; lodging; meeting and event planning; tourism.

FACILITIES

Classroom; computer laboratory; lecture room; library.

STUDENT PROFILE

407 total: 349 full-time; 58 part-time. 380 are under 25 years old; 25 are between 25 and 44 years old; 2 are over 44 years old.

FACULTY

17 total: 8 full-time; 9 part-time. Prominent faculty: Paul Stansbie; Allison Adams; Dr. Charles Baker-Clark; Kristen Jack. Faculty-student ratio: 1:16.

SPECIAL PROGRAMS

4-week study abroad in Italy, semester abroad opportunities in Australia and New Zealand, 1000 hours of coordinated internships.

TYPICAL EXPENSES

Application fee: $20. In-state tuition: $2528 per semester full-time (in district), $221 per credit part-time. Out-of-state tuition: $5468 per semester full-time, $466 per credit part-time.

FINANCIAL AID

Employment placement assistance is available. Employment opportunities within the program are available.

HOUSING

Coed and apartment-style housing available.

APPLICATION INFORMATION

Students may begin participation in January, May, and September. Application deadline for fall is July 30. Application deadline for winter is November 30. Application deadline for summer is April 15. Applicants must submit a formal application, ACT scores, and minimum GPA.

CONTACT

Director of Admissions, Hospitality and Tourism Management, 1 Campus Drive, Allendale, MI 49401. Telephone: 616-895-2025. Fax: 616-895-2000. E-mail: go2gvsu@gvsu.edu. World Wide Web: http://gvsu.edu.

GREAT LAKES CULINARY INSTITUTE AT NORTHWESTERN MICHIGAN COLLEGE

Great Lakes Culinary Institute

Traverse City, Michigan

GENERAL INFORMATION

Public, coeducational, culinary institute. Small-town setting. Founded in 1951. Accredited by North Central Association of Colleges and Schools.

PROGRAM INFORMATION

Offered since 1992. Accredited by American Culinary Federation Accrediting Commission. Program calendar is divided into semesters. 2-year associate degree in culinary arts. 2-year certificate in culinary arts.

PROGRAM AFFILIATION

American Culinary Federation; American Institute of Baking; Council on Hotel, Restaurant, and Institutional Education; National Restaurant Association; National Restaurant Association Educational Foundation; Tasters Guild International; The Bread Bakers Guild of America.

AREAS OF STUDY
Baking; buffet catering; controlling costs in food service; culinary skill development; food preparation; food purchasing; food service communication; food service math; garde-manger; international cuisine; introduction to food service; kitchen management; management and human resources; meal planning; nutrition; nutrition and food service; patisserie; restaurant opportunities; sanitation; soup, stock, sauce, and starch production.

FACILITIES
Bake shop; bakery; cafeteria; catering service; 3 classrooms; 2 computer laboratories; demonstration laboratory; food production kitchen; laboratory; 2 learning resource centers; 2 lecture rooms; library; public restaurant; student lounge; teaching kitchen; vineyard.

STUDENT PROFILE
190 total: 150 full-time; 40 part-time. 70 are under 25 years old; 110 are between 25 and 44 years old; 10 are over 44 years old.

FACULTY
15 total: 6 full-time; 9 part-time. 9 are industry professionals; 5 are culinary-certified teachers. Prominent faculty: Fred Laughlin, CCE; Lucy House, CCE; Joe Papcun; Michael Skarupinski. Faculty-student ratio: 1:15.

SPECIAL PROGRAMS
6-month paid internship.

TYPICAL EXPENSES
Application fee: $15. In-state tuition: $77 per contact hour (in district), $127 per contact hour (out-of-district). Out-of-state tuition: $156 per contact hour. Tuition for international students: $156 per contact hour. Program-related fee includes $350 for knives and uniforms.

FINANCIAL AID
In 2006, 8 scholarships were awarded (average award was $1500); 60 loans were granted (average loan was $2500). Program-specific awards include industry scholarships. Employment placement assistance is available. Employment opportunities within the program are available.

HOUSING
Coed, apartment-style, and single-sex housing available. Average on-campus housing cost per month: $250. Average off-campus housing cost per month: $350.

APPLICATION INFORMATION
Students may begin participation in January and August. Application deadline for fall is August 15. Application deadline for spring is December 15. In 2006, 160 applied; 120 were accepted. Applicants must submit a formal application.

CONTACT
Fred Laughlin, Director, Great Lakes Culinary Institute, 1701 East Front Street, Traverse City, MI 49686. Telephone: 800-748-0566 Ext. 51197. Fax: 231-995-1134. E-mail: flaughlin@nmc.edu. World Wide Web: http://www.nmc.edu/.

HENRY FORD COMMUNITY COLLEGE
Hospitality Studies/Culinary Arts and Hotel Restaurant Management

Dearborn, Michigan

GENERAL INFORMATION
Public, coeducational, two-year college. Suburban campus. Founded in 1938. Accredited by North Central Association of Colleges and Schools.

PROGRAM INFORMATION
Offered since 1972. Accredited by American Culinary Federation Accrediting Commission. Program calendar is divided into semesters. 1-year certificate in hospitality professional management. 1-year certificate in hospitality service career. 1-year certificate in culinary arts supervisor. 1-year certificate in culinary skills. 1-year certificate in culinary/baking. 2-year associate degree in culinary arts. 2-year associate degree in hotel/restaurant management.

PROGRAM AFFILIATION
American Culinary Federation; American Institute of Baking; Council on Hotel, Restaurant, and Institutional Education; International Food Service Executives Association; Michigan Lodging and Tourism Association; Michigan Restaurant Association; National Restaurant Association; National Restaurant Association Educational Foundation.

AREAS OF STUDY
Baking; beverage management; confectionery show pieces; controlling costs in food service; culinary skill development; food preparation; food purchasing; food service communication; food service math; garde-manger; international cuisine; introduction to food service; kitchen management; management and human resources; meal planning; meat cutting; meat fabrication; menu and facilities design; nutrition; patisserie; sanitation; saucier; seafood processing; soup, stock, sauce, and starch production; wines and spirits.

FACILITIES
Bake shop; bakery; cafeteria; catering service; classroom; computer laboratory; 2 food production kitchens; gourmet dining room; laboratory; learning resource center; lecture room; library; public restaurant; snack shop; student lounge; teaching kitchen.

Henry Ford Community College *(continued)*

TYPICAL STUDENT PROFILE
225 full-time.

SPECIAL PROGRAMS
Culinary competitions, ice carving.

FINANCIAL AID
Employment placement assistance is available. Employment opportunities within the program are available.

APPLICATION INFORMATION
Students may begin participation in January, May, July, and August. Applications are accepted continuously. Applicants must submit a formal application and have a high school diploma or GED.

CONTACT
Director of Admissions, Hospitality Studies/Culinary Arts and Hotel Restaurant Management, 5101 Evergreen Road, Dearborn, MI 48128-1495. Telephone: 313-845-6390. Fax: 313-845-9784. World Wide Web: http://www.hfcc.edu/.

MACOMB COMMUNITY COLLEGE

Macomb Culinary Institute

Clinton Township, Michigan

GENERAL INFORMATION
Public, coeducational, two-year college. Suburban campus. Founded in 1954. Accredited by North Central Association of Colleges and Schools.

PROGRAM INFORMATION
Offered since 1969. Accredited by American Culinary Federation Accrediting Commission. National Restaurant Association Educational Foundation ManageFirst certificates available. Program calendar is divided into semesters. 1-year certificate in culinary management. 1-year certificate in pastry arts. 2-year associate degree in hospitality management. 2-year associate degree in culinary arts. 2-year associate degree in pastry arts. 2-year associate degree in restaurant management.

PROGRAM AFFILIATION
American Culinary Federation; Council on Hotel, Restaurant, and Institutional Education; Michigan Restaurant Association; National Restaurant Association; National Restaurant Association Educational Foundation.

AREAS OF STUDY
Baking; beverage management; buffet catering; confectionery show pieces; controlling costs in food service; culinary skill development; food preparation; food purchasing; food service communication; food service math; garde-manger; international cuisine; kitchen management; management and human resources; meal planning; meat cutting; meat fabrication; menu and facilities design; nutrition; nutrition and food service; patisserie; restaurant opportunities; sanitation; saucier; seafood processing; soup, stock, sauce, and starch production; wines and spirits.

FACILITIES
Bake shop; 4 classrooms; computer laboratory; demonstration laboratory; food production kitchen; gourmet dining room; learning resource center; lecture room; library; public restaurant; student lounge; 3 teaching kitchens.

STUDENT PROFILE
320 total: 160 full-time; 160 part-time.

FACULTY
15 total: 4 full-time; 11 part-time. 7 are industry professionals; 8 are culinary-certified teachers; 1 is a ServSafe-Alcohol. Prominent faculty: David F. Schneider, CEC, CCE; Francois Faloppa, CEPC, CCE; Jeff Wolf; Scott O'Farrell, CEC, CEPC, CCA. Faculty-student ratio: 1:30 lecture; 1:15 lab.

PROMINENT ALUMNI AND CURRENT AFFILIATION
Charles Deeby, Kristofer's; Todd Engel, Beaumont Hospital; Pat Dinco/Carol John-Walezy, Ambiance Catering by Cee-Jay Z.

SPECIAL PROGRAMS
Apprenticeship program with ACF Blue Water Chefs Association, IKA Culinary Olympics (every 4 years); Hot/Cold/Ice/Gingerbread/Skills USA competitions, culinary tour of France.

TYPICAL EXPENSES
In-state tuition: $70 per credit hour full-time (in district), $70 per credit hour part-time (in district), $107 per credit hour full-time (out-of-district), $107 per credit hour part-time (out-of-district). Out-of-state tuition: $139 per credit hour full-time, $139 per credit hour part-time. Program-related fees include $134 for kitchen classes; $150 for cutlery; $60 for uniforms.

FINANCIAL AID
In 2006, 3 scholarships were awarded (average award was $300). Employment placement assistance is available. Employment opportunities within the program are available.

HOUSING

Average off-campus housing cost per month: $800–$900.

APPLICATION INFORMATION

Students may begin participation in January and August. Applications are accepted continuously. Applicants must submit a formal application.

CONTACT

David F. Schneider, Department Coordinator, Macomb Culinary Institute, 44575 Garfield Road, Clinton Township, MI 48038. Telephone: 586-286-2088. Fax: 586-226-4725. World Wide Web: http://www.macomb.edu.

MICHIGAN STATE UNIVERSITY

The School of Hospitality Business

East Lansing, Michigan

GENERAL INFORMATION

Public, coeducational, university. Suburban campus. Founded in 1855. Accredited by North Central Association of Colleges and Schools.

PROGRAM INFORMATION

Offered since 1927. Program calendar is divided into semesters. 1- to 2-year master's degree in hospitality business. 1- to 2-year master's degree in foodservice management. 2-year master of business administration in hospitality business. 4-year bachelor's degree in hospitality business.

PROGRAM AFFILIATION

American Culinary Federation; American Hotel and Lodging Association; Council on Hotel, Restaurant, and Institutional Education; National Restaurant Association; National Restaurant Association Educational Foundation; Society for Foodservice Management.

AREAS OF STUDY

Accounting; beverage management; controlling costs in food service; finance; food preparation; foodservice management; human resource management; introduction to food service; management and human resources; marketing; nutrition and food service; restaurant opportunities; sanitation; wines and spirits.

FACILITIES

6 classrooms; 4 computer laboratories; demonstration laboratory; 2 food production kitchens; gourmet dining room; learning resource center; lecture room; 2 libraries.

STUDENT PROFILE

800 full-time.

FACULTY

21 total: 11 full-time; 10 part-time. 1 is an industry professional; 2 are culinary-certified teachers; 2 are certified food and beverage executives; 1 certified chef. Prominent faculty: Allan Sherwin,CEC, CCE, FMP; Michael Kasavana, PhD; Ray Schmidgall, PhD; Ronald Cichy, PhD, CFBE. Faculty-student ratio: 1:30.

PROMINENT ALUMNI AND CURRENT AFFILIATION

Phil Hickey, CEO and Chairman, RARE Hospitality, Inc.; Dave Geroge, President, LongHorn Steakhouses; Kevin Brown, President and CEO, Lettuce Entertain You Enterprises, Inc..

SPECIAL PROGRAMS

Paid internships, student club visits to program-related venues, leadership development in 10 clubs and 4 events.

TYPICAL EXPENSES

Application fee: $30. In-state tuition: $280–$379 per credit hour. Out-of-state tuition: $742–$800 per credit hour.

FINANCIAL AID

In 2006, 150 scholarships were awarded. Program-specific awards include industry-sponsored scholarships, need-based scholarships. Employment placement assistance is available. Employment opportunities within the program are available.

HOUSING

Coed, apartment-style, and single-sex housing available. Average on-campus housing cost per month: $587–$740.

APPLICATION INFORMATION

Students may begin participation in January, May, and August. Applications are accepted continuously. Applicants must submit a formal application, an essay, letters of reference, and SAT, GRE, or GMAT scores.

CONTACT

Authella Collins Hawks, Director, Student and Industry Resource Center, The School of Hospitality Business, The School of Hospitality Business, MSU, 227 Eppley Center, East Lansing, MI 48824. Telephone: 517-353-9747. Fax: 517-432-1170. E-mail: hawks@msu.edu. World Wide Web: http://www.bus.msu.edu/shb/.

MOTT COMMUNITY COLLEGE

Culinary Arts Program

Flint, Michigan

GENERAL INFORMATION
Public, coeducational, two-year college. Urban campus. Founded in 1923. Accredited by North Central Association of Colleges and Schools.

PROGRAM INFORMATION
Offered since 1984. National Restaurant Association Educational Foundation ManageFirst certificates available. Program calendar is divided into semesters. 2-year associate degree in baking and pastry arts. 2-year associate degree in culinary arts. 2-year associate degree in food service management.

PROGRAM AFFILIATION
Flint/Saginaw Valley Chefs Association; National Restaurant Association; National Restaurant Association Educational Foundation.

AREAS OF STUDY
À la carte dining; baking; beverage management; buffet catering; confectionery show pieces; controlling costs in food service; culinary skill development; food preparation; food purchasing; food service math; garde-manger; international cuisine; introduction to food service; kitchen management; management and human resources; meal planning; meat cutting; meat fabrication; menu and facilities design; nutrition; patisserie; sanitation; specialty desserts.

FACILITIES
Bake shop; cafeteria; catering service; 5 classrooms; computer laboratory; demonstration laboratory; food production kitchen; gourmet dining room; laboratory; 2 public restaurants; 2 student lounges.

STUDENT PROFILE
207 total: 142 full-time; 65 part-time.

FACULTY
8 total: 3 full-time; 5 part-time. 2 are industry professionals; 1 is a master baker; 3 are culinary-certified teachers. Prominent faculty: E. Grace Washington; William Crawford, CEC; David Miller, EPC; Matt Cooper, CEC. Faculty-student ratio: 1:11.

SPECIAL PROGRAMS
Internships, culinary competitions.

TYPICAL EXPENSES
In-state tuition: $82.05 per contact hour full-time (in district), $82.05 per contact hour part-time (in district), $122.85 per contact hour full-time (out-of-district), $122.85 per contact hour part-time (out-of-district). Out-of-state tuition: $163.95 per contact hour full-time,

$163.95 per contact hour part-time. Program-related fees include $120 for lab fee (per class); $100 for uniforms; $150 for cutlery.

FINANCIAL AID
In 2006, individual scholarships were awarded at $1000. Employment placement assistance is available. Employment opportunities within the program are available.

APPLICATION INFORMATION
Students may begin participation in January and September. Applications are accepted continuously. Applicants must submit a formal application.

CONTACT
Grace Washington, Coordinator, Culinary Arts Program, 1401 East Court Street, Flint, MI 48501. Telephone: 810-232-7845. Fax: 810-232-6744. E-mail: galexand@mcc.edu. World Wide Web: http://www.mcc.edu/.

NORTHERN MICHIGAN UNIVERSITY

Hospitality Management

Marquette, Michigan

GENERAL INFORMATION
Public, coeducational, comprehensive institution. Rural campus. Founded in 1899. Accredited by North Central Association of Colleges and Schools.

PROGRAM INFORMATION
Offered since 1980. Program calendar is divided into semesters. 2-year associate degree in food service management. 4-year bachelor's degree in hospitality management.

PROGRAM AFFILIATION
American Culinary Federation; American Institute of Baking; Council on Hotel, Restaurant, and Institutional Education; National Restaurant Association; National Restaurant Association Educational Foundation.

AREAS OF STUDY
Hotel and restaurant management; kitchen management.

FACILITIES
Bake shop; cafeteria; catering service; 4 classrooms; computer laboratory; food production kitchen; garden; 3 laboratories; learning resource center; library; public restaurant; teaching kitchen.

STUDENT PROFILE
160 total: 140 full-time; 20 part-time. 120 are under 25 years old; 40 are between 25 and 44 years old.

FACULTY

4 total: 3 full-time; 1 part-time. 4 are industry professionals; 2 are culinary-certified teachers. Prominent faculty: Christopher Kibit, CCE, CHE; Yvonne Lee, CHE; Leslie Cory; Deborah Pearce. Faculty-student ratio: 1:20.

SPECIAL PROGRAMS

Paid internships, international study.

TYPICAL EXPENSES

Application fee: $25. In-state tuition: $256 per credit hour. Out-of-state tuition: $420 per credit hour. Program-related fee includes $100 for uniforms.

FINANCIAL AID

In 2006, 6 scholarships were awarded (average award was $500). Program-specific awards include ProMgmt. Scholarships, ACF Upper Michigan Chapter scholarships, Thaddeus Bogdan scholarships. Employment placement assistance is available. Employment opportunities within the program are available.

HOUSING

Coed, apartment-style, and single-sex housing available. Average off-campus housing cost per month: $350.

APPLICATION INFORMATION

Students may begin participation in January and August. Application deadline for fall is July 1. Application deadline for spring is November 1. In 2006, 47 applied; 47 were accepted. Applicants must submit a formal application.

CONTACT

Kathy Solka, Administrative Assistant, Hospitality Management, 1401 Presque Isle Avenue, Marquette, MI 49855-5366. Telephone: 906-227-2135. Fax: 906-227-1549. E-mail: ksolka@nmu.edu. World Wide Web: http://www.nmu.edu/.

NORTHWOOD UNIVERSITY

Hotel, Restaurant, and Resort Management

Midland, Michigan

GENERAL INFORMATION

Private, coeducational, four-year college. Suburban campus. Founded in 1959. Accredited by North Central Association of Colleges and Schools.

PROGRAM INFORMATION

Offered since 1966. Program calendar is divided into quarters. 2-year associate degree in hotel/restaurant/resort management. 4-year bachelor's degree in hotel/restaurant/resort management.

PROGRAM AFFILIATION

Council on Hotel, Restaurant, and Institutional Education; Institute of Food Technologists; National Restaurant Association; National Restaurant Association Educational Foundation.

AREAS OF STUDY

Beverage management; controlling costs in food service; food preparation; food purchasing; introduction to food service; kitchen management; management and human resources; meal planning; menu and facilities design; nutrition; sanitation; wines and spirits.

FACILITIES

Classroom; demonstration laboratory; food production kitchen; gourmet dining room; lecture room; teaching kitchen.

STUDENT PROFILE

91 full-time. 89 are under 25 years old; 2 are between 25 and 44 years old.

FACULTY

5 total: 2 full-time; 3 part-time. 2 are industry professionals. Prominent faculty: William E. Spaulding, MBA, CHA; Karla H. Shaw, MBA. Faculty-student ratio: 1:20.

SPECIAL PROGRAMS

3-month faculty-supervised internships, trips to AHLA show in New York and NRA show in Chicago, annual "live-in weekend" at Zehnders of Frankemuth.

TYPICAL EXPENSES

Tuition: $15,825 per year full-time, $330 per credit hour part-time. Program-related fees include $50 for wine/beverage seminars fees; $50 for food lab fees; $25 for paper application fee, no application fee to apply online.

FINANCIAL AID

In 2006, 34 scholarships were awarded (average award was $400). Employment placement assistance is available. Employment opportunities within the program are available.

HOUSING

Single-sex housing available. Average on-campus housing cost per month: $413.

APPLICATION INFORMATION

Students may begin participation in March, September, and December. Applications are accepted continuously. In 2006, 109 applied; 75 were accepted. Applicants must submit a formal application and an essay.

Northwood University *(continued)*

CONTACT
Dan Toland, Dean of Admissions, Hotel, Restaurant, and Resort Management, 4000 Whiting Drive, Midland, MI 48640. Telephone: 989-837-4273. Fax: 989-837-4490. E-mail: miadmit@northwood.edu. World Wide Web: http://www.northwood.edu.

OAKLAND COMMUNITY COLLEGE

Culinary Studies Institute

Farmington Hills, Michigan

GENERAL INFORMATION
Public, coeducational, two-year college. Suburban campus. Founded in 1964. Accredited by North Central Association of Colleges and Schools.

PROGRAM INFORMATION
Offered since 1965. Accredited by American Culinary Federation Accrediting Commission. Program calendar is divided into semesters. 1-year certificate in baking and pastry arts. 2-year associate degree in hotel management. 2-year associate degree in restaurant management. 2-year associate degree in culinary arts. 3-year certificate in culinary apprentice.

PROGRAM AFFILIATION
American Culinary Federation; American Dietetic Association; American Institute of Baking; Council on Hotel, Restaurant, and Institutional Education; National Restaurant Association; National Restaurant Association Educational Foundation; Tasters Guild International.

AREAS OF STUDY
Baking; beverage management; buffet catering; confectionery show pieces; controlling costs in food service; culinary skill development; food preparation; food purchasing; garde-manger; international cuisine; management and human resources; meat cutting; meat fabrication; menu and facilities design; nutrition; patisserie; sanitation; saucier; seafood processing; soup, stock, sauce, and starch production; wines and spirits.

FACILITIES
2 bake shops; cafeteria; catering service; 3 classrooms; computer laboratory; demonstration laboratory; 3 food production kitchens; 2 gourmet dining rooms; 4 laboratories; learning resource center; 2 lecture rooms; library; public restaurant; teaching kitchen; bakery retail center.

STUDENT PROFILE
225 total: 150 full-time; 75 part-time.

FACULTY
18 total: 8 full-time; 10 part-time. 5 are culinary-certified teachers; 2 are food management professionals. Prominent faculty: Kevin Enright, CEC, CCE; Doug Ganhs, CEC; Roger Holden, CEPC, CCE; Darlene Levinson, FMP. Faculty-student ratio: 1:12.

SPECIAL PROGRAMS
Ice carving/sugar artistry/culinary competitions.

TYPICAL EXPENSES
In-state tuition: $55.15 per credit hour part-time. Out-of-state tuition: $93.35 per credit hour part-time. Tuition for international students: $130.90 per credit hour part-time. Program-related fee includes $50–$100 for lab fee (per course), food product used in classes, small equipment.

FINANCIAL AID
In 2006, 5 scholarships were awarded (average award was $500). Employment placement assistance is available. Employment opportunities within the program are available.

APPLICATION INFORMATION
Students may begin participation in January, May, and September. Application deadline for fall is July 15. Application deadline for winter is November 15. Application deadline for spring is April 15. Applicants must interview; submit a formal application.

CONTACT
Susan Baier, Program Coordinator, Culinary Studies Institute, 27055 Orchard Lake Road, Farmington Hills, MI 48334. Telephone: 248-522-3700. Fax: 248-522-3706. E-mail: smbaier@oaklandcc.edu. World Wide Web: http://www.oaklandcc.edu.

SCHOOLCRAFT COLLEGE

Culinary Arts

Livonia, Michigan

GENERAL INFORMATION
Public, coeducational, two-year college. Suburban campus. Founded in 1961. Accredited by North Central Association of Colleges and Schools.

PROGRAM INFORMATION
Program calendar is divided into semesters. 1-year certificate in culinary arts. 2-year associate degree in culinary arts. 30-week certificate in baking and pastry.

PROGRAM AFFILIATION
American Culinary Federation.

Everything about our program is world-class.

The faculty

- Six Certified Master and Executive Chefs, each an industry leader in his own right.

The facility

- Part of a $27 million culinary education/business training/ conference center.

- Six specialized teaching kitchens: Restaurant, Production, Charcuterie, Bake Shop, Pastry, and Demonstration.

- Student-run gourmet restaurant and retail café.

The students

- American Culinary Federation National Champions in Salon Hot Food and Culinary Knowledge Bowl competitions.

The curriculum

- Certificate and associate degree programs have trained hundreds of graduates who now enjoy career success in America and abroad.

- New Baking and Pastry one-year certificate program.

Schoolcraft College
18600 Haggerty Road
Livonia, MI 48152-2696
734-462-4426
admissions@schoolcraft.edu

Schoolcraft College *(continued)*

FACULTY
4 are master chefs; 2 are certified executive chefs. Faculty-student ratio: 1:16.

SPECIAL PROGRAMS
Salon competitions, local culinary competitions.

TYPICAL EXPENSES
In-state tuition: $70 per credit hour (in district), $103 per credit hour (out-of-district). Out-of-state tuition: $154 per credit hour. Program-related fees include $1900 for lab fees for instruction; $225 for uniforms; $350 for knife set; $982 for books.

FINANCIAL AID
Employment placement assistance is available. Employment opportunities within the program are available.

APPLICATION INFORMATION
Students may begin participation in January and August. Applications are accepted continuously. Applicants must submit a formal application and transcripts; complete prerequisite course and placement test or ACT.

CONTACT
Office of Admissions, Culinary Arts, 18600 Haggerty Road, Livonia, MI 48152-2696. Telephone: 734-462-4426. Fax: 734-462-4553. E-mail: admissions@ schoolcraft.edu. World Wide Web: http://www. schoolcraft.edu.

See display on page 209.

WASHTENAW COMMUNITY COLLEGE

Culinary and Hospitality Management

Ann Arbor, Michigan

GENERAL INFORMATION
Public, coeducational, two-year college. Suburban campus. Founded in 1965. Accredited by North Central Association of Colleges and Schools.

PROGRAM INFORMATION
Offered since 1971. Accredited by American Culinary Federation Accrediting Commission. Program calendar is divided into semesters. 1-year certificate in hospitality management. 1-year certificate in culinary arts. 1-year certificate in baking and pastry. 2-year associate degree in culinary and hospitality management.

PROGRAM AFFILIATION
American Culinary Federation; Council on Hotel, Restaurant, and Institutional Education; National Restaurant Association; National Restaurant Association Educational Foundation.

AREAS OF STUDY
Baking; beverage management; buffet catering; controlling costs in food service; culinary skill development; food preparation; food purchasing; food service math; garde-manger; international cuisine; introduction to food service; kitchen management; management and human resources; meal planning; menu and facilities design; nutrition; nutrition and food service; patisserie; restaurant opportunities; sanitation; saucier; seafood processing; soup, stock, sauce, and starch production.

FACILITIES
Bake shop; cafeteria; catering service; 5 classrooms; coffee shop; 3 computer laboratories; 2 demonstration laboratories; food production kitchen; gourmet dining room; 3 laboratories; learning resource center; 5 lecture rooms; library; public restaurant; snack shop; 5 student lounges; 3 teaching kitchens.

STUDENT PROFILE
160 total: 110 full-time; 50 part-time.

FACULTY
12 total: 4 full-time; 8 part-time. 8 are industry professionals; 4 are culinary-certified teachers. Prominent faculty: Terry Herrera; Jill Beauchamp; Paul McPherson CCE, CCC; Carol Caulder Dienzer, CEPC. Faculty-student ratio: 1:15.

SPECIAL PROGRAMS
Culinary competitions, paid internships.

TYPICAL EXPENSES
Application fee: $23. In-state tuition: $60 per credit hour (in district), $101 per credit hour (out-of-district). Out-of-state tuition: $134 per credit hour. Program-related fees include $75 for uniforms; $100 for equipment.

FINANCIAL AID
In 2006, 12 scholarships were awarded (average award was $500). Employment placement assistance is available.

APPLICATION INFORMATION
Students may begin participation in January, May, and September. Application deadline for fall is September 8. Application deadline for winter is January 6. Application deadline for spring/summer is May 5. Applicants must submit a formal application.

CONTACT

Paul McPherson, Chef Instructor, Culinary and Hospitality Management, 4800 East Huron River Drive, PO Box D-1, Ann Arbor, MI 48106. Telephone: 734-973-3531. Fax: 734-477-8523. E-mail: pauldo@wccnet.org. World Wide Web: http://www.washtenaw.cc.mi.us/.

MINNESOTA

THE ART INSTITUTES INTERNATIONAL MINNESOTA

The International Culinary School at The Art Institutes International Minnesota

Minneapolis, Minnesota

GENERAL INFORMATION

Private, coeducational institution.

PROGRAM INFORMATION

Associate degree in Baking and Pastry. Associate degree in Culinary Arts. Bachelor's degree in Hospitality Management. Bachelor's degree in Culinary Management. Certificate in Baking and Pastry. Certificate in The Art of Cooking.

CONTACT

Office of Admissions, The International Culinary School at The Art Institutes International Minnesota, 15 South 9th Street, Minneapolis, MN 55402-3105. Telephone: 612-332-3361. World Wide Web: http://www.artinstitutes.edu/minneapolis/.

See color display following page 186.

HENNEPIN TECHNICAL COLLEGE

Culinary Arts Department

Brooklyn Park, Minnesota

GENERAL INFORMATION

Public, coeducational, two-year college. Suburban campus. Founded in 1972. Accredited by North Central Association of Colleges and Schools.

PROGRAM INFORMATION

Offered since 1972. Accredited by American Culinary Federation Accrediting Commission. National Restaurant Association Educational Foundation ManageFirst certificates available. Program calendar is divided into semesters. 1.5-year diploma in culinary arts. 15-month certificate in culinary arts. 2-year associate degree in culinary arts.

PROGRAM AFFILIATION

American Culinary Federation; American Institute of Baking.

AREAS OF STUDY

Baking; bar and beverage management; beverage management; buffet catering; confectionery show pieces; controlling costs in food service; convenience cookery; culinary French; culinary skill development; food preparation; food purchasing; food service communication; food service math; garde-manger; hospitality law; hospitality marketing; international cuisine; introduction to food service; kitchen management; meal planning; meat cutting; meat fabrication; menu and facilities design; nutrition; nutrition and food service; restaurant opportunities; sanitation; saucier; seafood processing; soup, stock, sauce, and starch production; sugar work; wines and spirits.

FACILITIES

4 bake shops; 4 bakeries; 4 cafeterias; 4 catering services; 4 classrooms; coffee shop; 6 computer laboratories; 2 demonstration laboratories; 2 food production kitchens; 5 gourmet dining rooms; 4 laboratories; 20 learning resource centers; 25 lecture rooms; 20 libraries; 5 public restaurants; 4 snack shops; 2 student lounges; 20 teaching kitchens.

STUDENT PROFILE

120 full-time.

FACULTY

9 total: 5 full-time; 4 part-time. Prominent faculty: Carlo Castagneri; Rich Forphal, CEC; David Eisenreich, CEC; Donald Woods. Faculty-student ratio: 1:20.

SPECIAL PROGRAMS

Specialized labs with individual students, culinary competitions, 1-year paid internships.

TYPICAL EXPENSES

Application fee: $20. Tuition: $137 per credit. Program-related fees include $100 for knives; $300 for books; $20 for food shows; $100 for uniforms.

FINANCIAL AID

In 2006, 5 scholarships were awarded (average award was $300); 4 loans were granted (average loan was $300). Program-specific awards include 3 Minneapolis ACF Scholarships ($500), Toby Landgraf Scholarships ($500). Employment placement assistance is available. Employment opportunities within the program are available.

Hennepin Technical College *(continued)*

APPLICATION INFORMATION
Students may begin participation in January and August. Application deadline for fall is October 1. Application deadline for spring is February 1. In 2006, 25 applied; 25 were accepted. Applicants must interview; submit a formal application.

CONTACT
Gini Beran, Counselor, Culinary Arts Department, 9000 Brooklyn Boulevard, Brooklyn Park, MN 55445. Telephone: 763-488-2412. Fax: 763-488-2938. E-mail: gini.beran@hennepintech.edu. World Wide Web: http://www.hennepintech.edu/.

HIBBING COMMUNITY COLLEGE

Culinary Arts

Hibbing, Minnesota

GENERAL INFORMATION
Public, coeducational, two-year college. Small-town setting. Founded in 1916. Accredited by North Central Association of Colleges and Schools.

PROGRAM INFORMATION
Offered since 1965. Program calendar is divided into semesters. 1-year diploma in culinary arts. 2-year diploma in food service and management. 5-semester associate degree in culinary arts.

PROGRAM AFFILIATION
National Restaurant Association.

AREAS OF STUDY
Baking; buffet catering; controlling costs in food service; culinary skill development; food preparation; food purchasing; food service management; food service math; international cuisine; introduction to food service; kitchen management; management and human resources; meal planning; meat cutting; meat fabrication; menu and facilities design; nutrition and food service; restaurant opportunities; sanitation; saucier; seafood processing; soup, stock, sauce, and starch production.

FACILITIES
Bake shop; bakery; cafeteria; 2 classrooms; coffee shop; 3 computer laboratories; demonstration laboratory; 2 food production kitchens; gourmet dining room; 2 laboratories; 3 learning resource centers; lecture room; 2 libraries; public restaurant; 3 student lounges; teaching kitchen.

FACULTY
Prominent faculty: Victor Bagan; Daniel E.Lidholm.

SPECIAL PROGRAMS
Upper Midwest Hospitality Show, tours of food service distribution facilities (Sysco, Upper Lakes Foods, Fraboni Wholesalers).

TYPICAL EXPENSES
Tuition: $2172 per semester part-time.

CONTACT
Admissions Department, Culinary Arts, 1515 East 25th Street, Hibbing, MN 55746. Telephone: 218-262-7228. E-mail: admissions@hibbing.edu. World Wide Web: http://www.hibbing.edu.

LE CORDON BLEU MINNEAPOLIS/ ST. PAUL

Le Cordon Bleu Culinary Program

Mendota Heights, Minnesota

GENERAL INFORMATION
Private, coeducational, culinary institute. Suburban campus. Founded in 1999. Accredited by Accrediting Commission of Career Schools and Colleges of Technology.

PROGRAM INFORMATION
Offered since 1999. Accredited by American Culinary Federation. Program calendar is divided into quarters. 15-month associate degree in patisserie and baking. 15-month associate degree in Le Cordon Bleu culinary program. 6-month certificate in Le Cordon Bleu culinary.

PROGRAM AFFILIATION
American Culinary Federation.

AREAS OF STUDY
Baking; beverage management; controlling costs in food service; culinary French; culinary skill development; food preparation; food purchasing; food service math; garde-manger; international cuisine; introduction to food service; kitchen management; management and human resources; meal planning; meat cutting; meat fabrication; menu and facilities design; nutrition; patisserie; restaurant opportunities; sanitation; saucier; soup, stock, sauce, and starch production; wines and spirits.

FACILITIES

3 bakeries; cafeteria; 7 classrooms; 3 computer laboratories; 3 demonstration laboratories; 4 food production kitchens; gourmet dining room; learning resource center; 8 lecture rooms; library; public restaurant; 2 snack shops; student lounge; 6 teaching kitchens.

STUDENT PROFILE

710 full-time.

FACULTY

49 total: 35 full-time; 14 part-time. 29 are industry professionals; 1 is a master chef; 1 is a master baker; 1 is a culinary-certified teacher. Prominent faculty: Chef Toufik Halimi; Chef Walter Whitwen; Chef Gil Gaiton; Chef Steven Shapley, CCE. Faculty-student ratio: 1:20.

SPECIAL PROGRAMS

Culinary competitions, internship opportunities, clubs and organizations.

TYPICAL EXPENSES

Application fee: $50. Tuition: $37,500 per program. Program-related fee includes $2700 for knife kits, uniforms, books, and supplies.

FINANCIAL AID

In 2006, 25 scholarships were awarded (average award was $2000). Employment placement assistance is available. Employment opportunities within the program are available.

HOUSING

Average off-campus housing cost per month: $600.

APPLICATION INFORMATION

Students may begin participation in January, February, April, June, July, August, October, and November. Applications are accepted continuously. Applicants must interview; submit a formal application.

CONTACT

Abby Norbin, Director of Admissions, Le Cordon Bleu Culinary Program, 1315 Mendota Heights Road, Mendota Heights, MN 55120. Telephone: 651-675-4700. Fax: 651-452-5282. E-mail: info@twincitiesculinary.com. World Wide Web: http://www.twincitiesculinary.com/.

SOUTH CENTRAL COLLEGE

Culinary Arts

North Mankato, Minnesota

GENERAL INFORMATION

Public, coeducational, two-year college. Urban campus. Founded in 1947. Accredited by North Central Association of Colleges and Schools.

PROGRAM INFORMATION

Offered since 1968. Program calendar is divided into semesters. 16-month diploma in restaurant management. 16-month diploma in culinary arts. 24-month associate degree in restaurant management. 24-month associate degree in culinary arts.

PROGRAM AFFILIATION

American Institute of Baking; National Restaurant Association Educational Foundation.

AREAS OF STUDY

Baking; food preparation; kitchen management.

FACILITIES

Bake shop; cafeteria; catering service; 4 classrooms; coffee shop; demonstration laboratory; food production kitchen; garden; lecture room; library; student lounge.

STUDENT PROFILE

22 total: 18 full-time; 4 part-time. 10 are under 25 years old; 8 are between 25 and 44 years old; 4 are over 44 years old.

FACULTY

2 total: 1 full-time; 1 part-time. 1 is an industry professional; 1 is a culinary-certified teacher. Prominent faculty: James R. Hanson, MBA; Rebecca Hagebak, CFM. Faculty-student ratio: 1:15.

PROMINENT ALUMNI AND CURRENT AFFILIATION

Mike Broughton, Corporate Chef, Grand Hotels.

SPECIAL PROGRAMS

Culinary competitions, paid internships in restaurant management.

TYPICAL EXPENSES

Application fee: $20. In-state tuition: $8000 per 16 months full-time (in district), $140 per credit part-time. Out-of-state tuition: $16,000 per 16 months full-time, $280 per credit part-time. Program-related fees include $200 for cutlery fee; $400 for textbooks.

FINANCIAL AID

In 2006, 10 scholarships were awarded (average award was $500); 18 loans were granted (average loan was $5000). Program-specific awards include Toby-Landgraf Scholarship ($700). Employment placement assistance is available.

South Central College *(continued)*

HOUSING
Average off-campus housing cost per month: $500.

APPLICATION INFORMATION
Students may begin participation in January, May, and August. Applications are accepted continuously. In 2006, 25 applied; 25 were accepted. Applicants must submit a formal application.

CONTACT
James R. Hanson, Instructor, Culinary Arts, 1920 Lee Boulevard, North Mankato, MN 56003. Telephone: 507-389-7229. Fax: 507-389-8950. E-mail: jimh@southcentral.edu. World Wide Web: http://www.southcentral.edu.

MISSISSIPPI

COAHOMA COMMUNITY COLLEGE

Department of Culinary Arts

Clarksdale, Mississippi

GENERAL INFORMATION
Public, coeducational, two-year college. Rural campus. Founded in 1949. Accredited by Southern Association of Colleges and Schools.

PROGRAM INFORMATION
Offered since 2006. National Restaurant Association Educational Foundation ManageFirst certificates available. Program calendar is divided into semesters. 1-year certificate in culinary arts. 2-year associate degree in restaurant management. 2-year associate degree in culinary arts.

AREAS OF STUDY
Baking; buffet catering; culinary French; food preparation; garde-manger; international cuisine; management and human resources; menu and facilities design; restaurant opportunities; sanitation.

FACILITIES
Catering service; 2 classrooms; computer laboratory; food production kitchen; gourmet dining room; learning resource center; 2 lecture rooms; library; teaching kitchen.

STUDENT PROFILE
50 full-time. 20 are under 25 years old; 27 are between 25 and 44 years old; 3 are over 44 years old.

FACULTY
4 total: 4 full-time; 0 part-time. 2 are industry professionals. Faculty-student ratio: 1:12.

SPECIAL PROGRAMS
Regional culinary tours/dining tours (Louisiana, the Carolinas, etc.).

TYPICAL EXPENSES
In-state tuition: $1900 per year. Out-of-state tuition: $2900 per year. Program-related fees include $275 for uniform costs; $250 for culinary equipment kit; $150 for membership in Epicurean Society.

FINANCIAL AID
Employment opportunities within the program are available.

HOUSING
Coed and single-sex housing available. Average off-campus housing cost per month: $400.

APPLICATION INFORMATION
Students may begin participation in January and August. Application deadline for fall is April 1. Application deadline for spring is October 1. In 2006, 50 applied; 50 were accepted. Applicants must submit a formal application and satisfactory scores on ACT and/or Accuplacer tests.

CONTACT
Wanda Holmes, Director of Admissions, Department of Culinary Arts, 3240 Friars Point Road, Clarksdale, MS 38614. Telephone: 662-621-4205. Fax: 662-621-4297. E-mail: wholmes@coahomacc.edu. World Wide Web: http://www.coahomacc.edu.

MERIDIAN COMMUNITY COLLEGE

Hotel and Restaurant Management Technology

Meridian, Mississippi

GENERAL INFORMATION
Public, coeducational, two-year college. Small-town setting. Founded in 1937. Accredited by Southern Association of Colleges and Schools.

PROGRAM INFORMATION
Offered since 1970. Program calendar is divided into semesters. 2-year associate degree in hotel and restaurant management.

PROGRAM AFFILIATION
American Hotel and Lodging Association; Mississippi Hotel and Motel Association; National Restaurant Association.

AREAS OF STUDY

Baking; beverage management; buffet catering; controlling costs in food service; convenience cookery; culinary skill development; food preparation; food purchasing; food service communication; food service math; garde-manger; international cuisine; introduction to food service; kitchen management; management and human resources; meal planning; meat cutting; meat fabrication; menu and facilities design; nutrition and food service; restaurant opportunities; sanitation; saucier; soup, stock, sauce, and starch production; wines and spirits.

FACILITIES

Classroom; computer laboratory; demonstration laboratory; food production kitchen; learning resource center; lecture room; teaching kitchen.

STUDENT PROFILE

33 full-time. 19 are under 25 years old; 12 are between 25 and 44 years old; 2 are over 44 years old.

FACULTY

1 total: 1 full-time. 1 is an industry professional. Prominent faculty: Mark A. Chandler. Faculty-student ratio: 1:33.

SPECIAL PROGRAMS

Mississippi Hotel and Lodging Association Convention and Trade Show, DEX-DECA Management Skills Competition.

TYPICAL EXPENSES

Application fee: $73. In-state tuition: $725 per semester full-time (in district), $80 per semester hour part-time. Out-of-state tuition: $1320 per semester full-time, $137 per semester hour part-time. Tuition for international students: $1570 per semester full-time, $157 per semester hour part-time. Program-related fee includes $15 for DEX-DECA membership (optional).

FINANCIAL AID

In 2006, 1 scholarship was awarded (award was $1500). Employment placement assistance is available.

HOUSING

Coed, apartment-style, and single-sex housing available. Average on-campus housing cost per month: $300. Average off-campus housing cost per month: $450.

APPLICATION INFORMATION

Students may begin participation in January and August. Application deadline for fall is August 30. Application deadline for spring is January 12. In 2006, 28 applied; 28 were accepted. Applicants must submit a formal application.

CONTACT

Mark A. Chandler, Coordinator/Instructor, Hotel and Restaurant Management Technology, 910 Highway 19 North, Meridan, MS 39307. Telephone: 601-484-8825. Fax: 601-484-8824. E-mail: mchandle@mcc.cc.ms.us. World Wide Web: http://www.mcc.cc.ms.us.

MISSISSIPPI GULF COAST COMMUNITY COLLEGE

Culinary Arts and Related Food Technology

Perkinston, Mississippi

GENERAL INFORMATION

Public, coeducational, two-year college. Suburban campus. Founded in 1911. Accredited by Southern Association of Colleges and Schools.

PROGRAM INFORMATION

Program calendar is divided into semesters. 1-year diploma in food production and management technology.

PROGRAM AFFILIATION

American Culinary Federation.

AREAS OF STUDY

Baking; buffet catering; controlling costs in food service; fast foods; food preparation; food purchasing; food service math; meal planning; nutrition; quantity foods; sanitation.

FACILITIES

2 cafeterias; 2 classrooms; 2 food production kitchens.

STUDENT PROFILE

25 total: 23 full-time; 2 part-time.

FACULTY

2 total: 1 full-time; 1 part-time. 2 are industry professionals. Faculty-student ratio: 1:25.

SPECIAL PROGRAMS

Internship (up to 3 semesters).

TYPICAL EXPENSES

In-state tuition: $745 per semester full-time (in district), $75 per semester hour part-time. Out-of-state tuition: $1718 per semester full-time, $152 per semester hour part-time. Program-related fee includes $75 for student membership.

FINANCIAL AID

Employment placement assistance is available.

HOUSING

Single-sex housing available.

Mississippi Gulf Coast Community College
(continued)

APPLICATION INFORMATION
Students may begin participation in January and August. Applications are accepted continuously. In 2006, 25 applied; 25 were accepted. Applicants must submit a formal application.

CONTACT
Shelly Caro, Recruiter, Culinary Arts and Related Food Technology, PO Box 609, Perkinston, MS 39573. Telephone: 601-928-6381. Fax: 601-928-6279. E-mail: shelly.caro@mgccc.edu. World Wide Web: http://www.mgccc.cc.ms.us.

MISSISSIPPI UNIVERSITY FOR WOMEN

Culinary Arts Institute

Columbus, Mississippi

GENERAL INFORMATION
Public, coeducational, comprehensive institution. Small-town setting. Founded in 1884. Accredited by Southern Association of Colleges and Schools.

PROGRAM INFORMATION
Offered since 1997. Program calendar is divided into semesters. 4-year bachelor's degree in culinary arts.

PROGRAM AFFILIATION
International Association of Culinary Professionals; National Restaurant Association; Research Chefs Association; Southern Foodways Alliance; Women Chefs and Restaurateurs.

AREAS OF STUDY
Baking; buffet catering; controlling costs in food service; culinary skill development; food for special diets; food preparation; food purchasing; food service communication; food service math; garde-manger; international cuisine; introduction to food service; kitchen management; meal planning; meat fabrication; nutrition; nutrition and food service; patisserie; sanitation; saucier; soup, stock, sauce, and starch production.

FACILITIES
Bake shop; cafeteria; classroom; computer laboratory; demonstration laboratory; 2 food production kitchens; garden; learning resource center; 10 lecture rooms; library; teaching kitchen; food photography kitchen.

STUDENT PROFILE
100 full-time. 70 are under 25 years old; 25 are between 25 and 44 years old; 5 are over 44 years old.

FACULTY
15 total: 4 full-time; 11 part-time. 3 are culinary-certified teachers; 1 is a RD, LD. Prominent faculty: James Fitzgerald, PhD, CCP, CRC; W. Scott McKenzie; Amanda Al-Turk; Erich Ogle. Faculty-student ratio: 1:12.

PROMINENT ALUMNI AND CURRENT AFFILIATION
Sarah Wood, K-Paul's Louisiana Kitchen; Augustus Argrett, Sanderson Farms Test Kitchen; Misty Prather Siadek, Sharp Test Kitchen.

SPECIAL PROGRAMS
3-month paid internship, international internship.

TYPICAL EXPENSES
In-state tuition: $2104 per semester full-time (in district), $157 per credit hour part-time. Out-of-state tuition: $2896 per semester full-time, $446 per credit hour part-time. Program-related fee includes $125 for food for each food preparation course.

FINANCIAL AID
In 2006, 3 scholarships were awarded (average award was $500); 2 loans were granted (average loan was $500). Program-specific awards include internship grant stipend ($1000-2500). Employment placement assistance is available. Employment opportunities within the program are available.

HOUSING
Coed, apartment-style, and single-sex housing available. Average on-campus housing cost per month: $378. Average off-campus housing cost per month: $450.

APPLICATION INFORMATION
Students may begin participation in January, June, and August. Applications are accepted continuously. In 2006, 95 applied; 33 were accepted. Applicants must submit a formal application, SAT or ACT scores, and academic transcripts.

CONTACT
James A. Fitzgerald, Director, Culinary Arts Institute, 1100 College Street MUW 1639, Columbus, MS 39701-5800. Telephone: 662-241-7472. Fax: 662-241-7627. E-mail: cbrown@ca.muw.edu. World Wide Web: http://www.muw.edu/culinary.

MISSOURI

COLLEGE OF THE OZARKS

Hotel and Restaurant Management

Point Lookout, Missouri

GENERAL INFORMATION
Private, coeducational, four-year college. Small-town setting. Founded in 1906. Accredited by North Central Association of Colleges and Schools.

PROGRAM INFORMATION
Offered since 1993. Accredited by American Dietetic Association. National Restaurant Association Educational Foundation ManageFirst certificates available. Program calendar is divided into semesters. 4-year bachelor's degree in hotel and restaurant management: meeting and special event management emphasis. 4-year bachelor's degree in hotel and restaurant management: professional food service emphasis. 4-year bachelor's degree in food and nutrition. 4-year bachelor's degree in dietetics. 4-year bachelor's degree in hotel and restaurant management.

PROGRAM AFFILIATION
American Culinary Federation; American Dietetic Association; Council on Hotel, Restaurant, and Institutional Education; Missouri Hotel and Motel Association; National Restaurant Association; National Restaurant Association Educational Foundation.

AREAS OF STUDY
Baking; controlling costs in food service; culinary skill development; food preparation; food purchasing; garde-manger; international cuisine; introduction to food service; kitchen management; management and human resources; meal planning; menu and facilities design; nutrition; nutrition and food service; restaurant opportunities; sanitation; seafood processing; soup, stock, sauce, and starch production.

FACILITIES
Bake shop; cafeteria; catering service; 5 classrooms; computer laboratory; demonstration laboratory; food production kitchen; laboratory; learning resource center; lecture room; public restaurant; snack shop; student lounge; teaching kitchen.

STUDENT PROFILE
54 full-time. 52 are under 25 years old; 1 is between 25 and 44 years old; 1 is over 44 years old.

FACULTY
5 total: 2 full-time; 3 part-time. 3 are industry professionals; 2 are culinary-certified teachers. Faculty-student ratio: 1:14.

SPECIAL PROGRAMS
Paid internships, travel to regional program-related events and shows, leadership opportunities through student organizations.

TYPICAL EXPENSES
Tuition: Use Pell or other grants and college scholarships full-time, $295 per credit hour part-time.

FINANCIAL AID
Employment placement assistance is available.

HOUSING
Single-sex housing available. Average on-campus housing cost per month: $500.

APPLICATION INFORMATION
Students may begin participation in August. Application deadline for fall is February 15. Application deadline for spring a year in advance is January 1. Applicants must interview; submit a formal application, letters of reference, an essay, ACT score, financial information (FAFSA form).

CONTACT
Jerry J. Shackette, Associate Professor, Hotel/Restaurant Management, Hotel and Restaurant Management, PO Box 17, Point Lookout, MO 65726. Telephone: 417-239-1900 Ext. 119. Fax: 417-335-8140. E-mail: shackette@cofo.edu. World Wide Web: http://www.cofo.edu.

JEFFERSON COLLEGE

Culinary Arts

Hillsboro, Missouri

GENERAL INFORMATION
Public, coeducational, two-year college. Rural campus. Founded in 1963. Accredited by North Central Association of Colleges and Schools.

PROGRAM INFORMATION
Offered since 1999. Program calendar is divided into semesters. 1-semester certificate in NRA ServSafe certification. 2-year associate degree in culinary arts. 2-year certificate in culinary arts.

PROGRAM AFFILIATION
National Restaurant Association; National Restaurant Association Educational Foundation.

AREAS OF STUDY
Baking; beverage management; buffet catering; controlling costs in food service; culinary skill development; food preparation; food service communication; food service math; garde-manger; international cuisine; introduction to food service;

Jefferson College *(continued)*

kitchen management; management and human resources; meal planning; meat fabrication; menu and facilities design; nutrition; restaurant opportunities; sanitation; saucier; seafood processing; soup, stock, sauce, and starch production.

FACILITIES
Classroom; computer laboratory; demonstration laboratory; 2 food production kitchens; learning resource center; library; teaching kitchen.

STUDENT PROFILE
115 total: 75 full-time; 40 part-time. 40 are under 25 years old; 75 are between 25 and 44 years old.

FACULTY
3 total: 3 full-time. 2 are industry professionals; 1 is a culinary-certified teacher. Prominent faculty: Steve Berkel; Jeff Hunt; Laura Albach. Faculty-student ratio: 1:18.

SPECIAL PROGRAMS
Culinary competitions.

TYPICAL EXPENSES
Application fee: $15. In-state tuition: $3008 per degree full-time (in district), $47 per credit hour part-time (in district), $61 per credit hour part-time (out-of-district). Out-of-state tuition: $76 per credit hour part-time.

HOUSING
Apartment-style housing available. Average on-campus housing cost per month: $400. Average off-campus housing cost per month: $400.

APPLICATION INFORMATION
Students may begin participation in January and August. Applications are accepted continuously. In 2006, 210 applied; 105 were accepted. Applicants must submit a formal application.

CONTACT
Julie Pierce, Director of Admissions and Financial Aid, Culinary Arts, 1000 Viking Drive, Hillsboro, MO 63050. Telephone: 636-797-3000. Fax: 636-789-3535. E-mail: jpierce@gateway.jeffco.edu. World Wide Web: http://www.jeffco.edu.

PENN VALLEY COMMUNITY COLLEGE

Lodging and Food Service Department

Kansas City, Missouri

GENERAL INFORMATION
Public, coeducational, two-year college. Urban campus. Founded in 1975. Accredited by North Central Association of Colleges and Schools.

PROGRAM INFORMATION
Offered since 1975. Program calendar is divided into semesters. 4-semester associate degree in food and beverage. 6-semester associate degree in chef apprenticeship (both programs offered jointly with Johnson County Community College).

STUDENT PROFILE
9 total: 1 full-time; 8 part-time.

TYPICAL EXPENSES
In-state tuition: $2250 per 1 year full-time (in district), $75 per credit hour part-time (in district), $4110 per 1 year full-time (out-of-district), $137 per credit hour part-time (out-of-district). Out-of-state tuition: $5550 per 1 year full-time, $185 per credit hour part-time. Tuition for international students: $5550 per 1 year full-time, $185 per credit hour part-time.

APPLICATION INFORMATION
Students may begin participation in January and August. Applications are accepted continuously. In 2006, 12 applied; 12 were accepted. Applicants must submit a formal application.

CONTACT
Johnson County Community College, Lodging and Food Service Department, 12345 College Boulevard, Overland Park, KS 66210. Telephone: 913-469-8500. E-mail: jhaas@jccc.edu. World Wide Web: http://www.mcckc.edu.

ST. LOUIS COMMUNITY COLLEGE

Hospitality Studies

St. Louis, Missouri

GENERAL INFORMATION
Public, coeducational, two-year college. Urban campus. Founded in 1964. Accredited by North Central Association of Colleges and Schools.

PROGRAM INFORMATION

Offered since 1964. Accredited by American Culinary Federation Accrediting Commission. National Restaurant Association Educational Foundation ManageFirst certificates available. Program calendar is divided into semesters. 1-year certificate in travel and tourism. 1-year certificate in hotel management. 1-year certificate in restaurant management. 1-year certificate in baking and pastry. 2-year associate degree in travel and tourism. 2-year associate degree in hospitality, baking and pastry. 2-year associate degree in hospitality management. 2-year associate degree in hospitality culinary.

PROGRAM AFFILIATION

American Culinary Federation; National Restaurant Association; National Restaurant Association Educational Foundation.

AREAS OF STUDY

Baking; culinary skill development.

FACILITIES

Bake shop; 3 classrooms; computer laboratory; demonstration laboratory; food production kitchen; garden; gourmet dining room; library.

STUDENT PROFILE

486 total: 227 full-time; 259 part-time.

FACULTY

38 total: 7 full-time; 31 part-time. Prominent faculty: Charles Rossi, CEC; Michael Downey, CCC, CCE; Robert Hertel, CEC, CCE, AAC. Faculty-student ratio: 1:14 lab; 1:28 lecture.

PROMINENT ALUMNI AND CURRENT AFFILIATION

John Bogacki, CEC, CCE, AAC, Westwood Country Club; Jeffrey Seaborne, CEC, Scottrade Center.

SPECIAL PROGRAMS

Continuing education.

TYPICAL EXPENSES

Tuition: $83 per credit hour full-time (in district), $83 per credit hour part-time.

FINANCIAL AID

Employment opportunities within the program are available.

APPLICATION INFORMATION

Students may begin participation in January, May, and August. Applications are accepted continuously.

CONTACT

Robert B. Hertel, Associate Professor, Hospitality Studies, 5600 Oakland Avenue, St. Louis, MO 63110. Telephone: 314-644-9617. E-mail: rhertel@stlcc.edu. World Wide Web: http://www.stlcc.edu.

UNIVERSITY OF MISSOURI–COLUMBIA

Hotel and Restaurant Management

Columbia, Missouri

GENERAL INFORMATION

Public, coeducational, university. Small-town setting. Founded in 1839. Accredited by North Central Association of Colleges and Schools.

PROGRAM INFORMATION

Offered since 1971. Accredited by Council on Hotel, Restaurant and Institutional Education. Program calendar is divided into semesters. 2-Year master's degree in food science/hotel and restaurant management. 4-Year bachelor's degree in hotel and restaurant management.

PROGRAM AFFILIATION

Council on Hotel, Restaurant, and Institutional Education; Educational Institute-American Hotel and Motel Association; Institute of Food Technologists; National Restaurant Association; National Restaurant Association Educational Foundation.

AREAS OF STUDY

Beverage management; controlling costs in food service; food preparation; food purchasing; management and human resources; restaurant opportunities; sanitation.

FACILITIES

3 classrooms; 2 computer laboratories; 2 demonstration laboratories; 2 food production kitchens; lecture room; library; public restaurant; student lounge; 2 teaching kitchens.

STUDENT PROFILE

315 total: 290 full-time; 25 part-time. 300 are under 25 years old; 14 are between 25 and 44 years old; 1 is over 44 years old.

FACULTY

7 total: 5 full-time; 2 part-time. Prominent faculty: Leslie Jett, CEC. Faculty-student ratio: 1:42.

SPECIAL PROGRAMS

600-hour internship (paid by industry), self-designed internship.

TYPICAL EXPENSES

Application fee: $45. In-state tuition: $7077 per 30 semester credit hours full-time (in district), $235.90 per semester credit hour part-time. Out-of-state tuition: $17,733 per 30 semester credit hours full-time, $591.10 per semester credit hour part-time. Program-related fee includes $37.50 for undergraduate upgrading education (per credit hour).

University of Missouri–Columbia *(continued)*

FINANCIAL AID

In 2006, 11 scholarships were awarded (average award was $1000). Employment placement assistance is available.

HOUSING

Coed, apartment-style, and single-sex housing available. Average on-campus housing cost per month: $489–$550.

APPLICATION INFORMATION

Students may begin participation in January, June, and August. Applications are accepted continuously. Applicants must submit a formal application.

CONTACT

James Groves, Chair, Undergraduate Program, Hotel and Restaurant Management, 122 Eckles Hall, Columbia, MO 65211. Telephone: 573-884-7816. E-mail: grovesj@missouri.edu. World Wide Web: http://hrm.missouri.edu.

MONTANA

FLATHEAD VALLEY COMMUNITY COLLEGE

Culinary Arts

Kalispell, Montana

GENERAL INFORMATION

Public, coeducational, two-year college. Rural campus. Founded in 1967. Accredited by Northwest Commission on Colleges and Universities.

PROGRAM INFORMATION

Offered since 2005. Program calendar is divided into semesters. 2-year associate degree in culinary arts.

PROGRAM AFFILIATION

American Culinary Federation.

AREAS OF STUDY

Baking; beverage management; controlling costs in food service; culinary skill development; food preparation; food purchasing; food service communication; kitchen management; meal planning; meat cutting; meat fabrication; menu and facilities design; nutrition; nutrition and food service; patisserie; restaurant opportunities; sanitation; saucier; seafood processing; soup, stock, sauce, and starch production; wines and spirits.

FACILITIES

Classroom; 5 computer laboratories; demonstration laboratory; food production kitchen; laboratory; learning resource center; library; teaching kitchen.

STUDENT PROFILE

27 total: 22 full-time; 5 part-time. 22 are under 25 years old; 5 are between 25 and 44 years old.

FACULTY

3 total: 1 full-time; 2 part-time. 1 is a culinary-certified teacher. Prominent faculty: Hillary Ginepra; Andy Blanton; Ted Chapell. Faculty-student ratio: 1:20.

SPECIAL PROGRAMS

140-hour internships (2), ten-day cooking tour of France and Italy (2nd year students).

TYPICAL EXPENSES

Application fee: $15. In-state tuition: $1120 per semester full-time (in district), $80 per credit part-time (in district), $1708 per semester full-time (out-of-district), $122 per credit part-time (out-of-district). Out-of-state tuition: $4200 per semester full-time, $300 per credit part-time. Program-related fee includes $225 for supplies.

FINANCIAL AID

In 2006, 3 scholarships were awarded (average award was $583). Employment placement assistance is available.

APPLICATION INFORMATION

Students may begin participation in January, June, and September. Applications are accepted continuously. Applicants must submit a formal application.

CONTACT

Phil MacGregor, Division Chair, Culinary Arts, 777 Grandview Drive, Kalispell, MT 59901. Telephone: 406-756-3865. Fax: 406-756-3815. E-mail: pmacgreg@fvcc.edu. World Wide Web: http://www.fvcc.edu.

THE UNIVERSITY OF MONTANA– MISSOULA

Culinary Arts Department/Food Service Management

Missoula, Montana

GENERAL INFORMATION

Public, coeducational, university. Suburban campus. Founded in 1893. Accredited by Northwest Commission on Colleges and Universities.

PROGRAM INFORMATION

Offered since 1974. Accredited by American Culinary Federation Accrediting Commission. Program calendar is divided into semesters. 1-year certificate in culinary arts. 2-year associate degree in food service management.

PROGRAM AFFILIATION

American Culinary Federation; Council on Hotel, Restaurant, and Institutional Education; International Food Service Executives Association; National Association of College and University Food Service; National Restaurant Association; National Restaurant Association Educational Foundation.

AREAS OF STUDY

Baking; beverage management; buffet catering; confectionery show pieces; controlling costs in food service; convenience cookery; culinary French; culinary skill development; food preparation; food purchasing; food service communication; food service math; garde-manger; international cuisine; introduction to food service; kitchen management; management and human resources; meal planning; meat fabrication; menu and facilities design; nutrition and food service; patisserie; restaurant opportunities; sanitation; saucier; seafood processing; soup, stock, sauce, and starch production; wines and spirits.

FACILITIES

Bake shop; cafeteria; 3 classrooms; 4 computer laboratories; food production kitchen; gourmet dining room; learning resource center; 4 lecture rooms; 2 libraries; student lounge.

STUDENT PROFILE

30 full-time. 20 are under 25 years old; 7 are between 25 and 44 years old; 3 are over 44 years old.

FACULTY

3 total: 2 full-time; 1 part-time. 2 are industry professionals; 1 is a culinary-certified teacher. Prominent faculty: Ross W. Lodahl; Thomas Campbell, CEC; Laura Swanson, CC. Faculty-student ratio: 1:10.

PROMINENT ALUMNI AND CURRENT AFFILIATION

Thomas Siegal, CEC, UM Dining Services; Travis Schlader, Ciao Mambo.

SPECIAL PROGRAMS

Specialized internships at local, regional, and national sites, individual culinary competitions (ACF), ACF Junior Team culinary competitions.

TYPICAL EXPENSES

Application fee: $30. In-state tuition: $1649 per semester. Out-of-state tuition: $4480 per semester. Program-related fee includes $2600 for student fees per semester (food supplies, book, and uniforms).

FINANCIAL AID

In 2006, 2 scholarships were awarded (average award was $1500); 20 loans were granted (average loan was $6000). Employment placement assistance is available. Employment opportunities within the program are available.

HOUSING

Coed, apartment-style, and single-sex housing available. Average off-campus housing cost per month: $400.

APPLICATION INFORMATION

Students may begin participation in January and September. Applications are accepted continuously. In 2006, 50 applied; 30 were accepted. Applicants must submit a formal application.

CONTACT

Alan Fugleberg, Admissions Representative, Culinary Arts Department/Food Service Management, 909 South Avenue West, Missoula, MT 59801. Telephone: 406-243-7888. Fax: 406-243-7899. E-mail: alan. fugleberg@umontana.edu. World Wide Web: http://www.cte.umt.edu.

NEBRASKA

CENTRAL COMMUNITY COLLEGE-HASTINGS CAMPUS

Hospitality Management and Culinary Arts

Hastings, Nebraska

GENERAL INFORMATION

Public, coeducational, two-year college. Small-town setting. Founded in 1966. Accredited by North Central Association of Colleges and Schools.

PROGRAM INFORMATION

Offered since 1970. Program calendar is semester plus summer session. 1-year diploma in hospitality services. 1-year diploma in culinary arts. 2-year associate degree in hotel management. 2-year associate degree in culinary arts. 2-year associate degree in restaurant management.

PROGRAM AFFILIATION

Council on Hotel, Restaurant, and Institutional Education; National Restaurant Association.

AREAS OF STUDY

Baking; beverage management; confectionery show pieces; controlling costs in food service; culinary skill development; food preparation; food purchasing; food service math; garde-manger; international cuisine;

Central Community College–Hastings Campus
(continued)

introduction to food service; kitchen management; management and human resources; meal planning; menu and facilities design; nutrition and food service; patisserie; sanitation; saucier; soup, stock, sauce, and starch production.

FACILITIES
Bake shop; cafeteria; catering service; 3 classrooms; 2 computer laboratories; food production kitchen; learning resource center; 2 lecture rooms; library; public restaurant; teaching kitchen.

STUDENT PROFILE
45 total: 30 full-time; 15 part-time. 30 are under 25 years old; 10 are between 25 and 44 years old; 5 are over 44 years old.

FACULTY
3 total: 2 full-time; 1 part-time. 2 are industry professionals. Prominent faculty: Jaye Kieselhorst; Rhonda Herrington. Faculty-student ratio: 1:15.

PROMINENT ALUMNI AND CURRENT AFFILIATION
Ryan Fahey, Assistant Executive Chef, Paris Hotel; Jerry Allen, Delmonico Steakhouse, Venetian Hotel.

SPECIAL PROGRAMS
Annual field trip for club members (Las Vegas, Seattle, Chicago).

TYPICAL EXPENSES
In-state tuition: $66 per credit hour full-time (in district), $66 per credit hour part-time. Out-of-state tuition: $99 per credit hour full-time, $99 per credit hour part-time. Program-related fee includes $150 for uniforms, technical manuals, thermometer, timer, recipe book.

FINANCIAL AID
In 2006, 3 scholarships were awarded (average award was $350). Employment placement assistance is available.

HOUSING
Coed, apartment-style, and single-sex housing available. Average on-campus housing cost per month: $438. Average off-campus housing cost per month: $450.

APPLICATION INFORMATION
Students may begin participation in January, February, March, April, May, June, August, September, October, November, and December. Applications are accepted continuously. In 2006, 25 applied; 25 were accepted. Applicants must submit a formal application.

CONTACT
Bob Glenn, Admissions Officer, Hospitality Management and Culinary Arts, Box 1024, Hastings, NE 68803. Telephone: 402-463-9811. Fax: 402-461-2506. E-mail: rglenn@cccneb.edu. World Wide Web: http://www.cccneb.edu/igsbase/igstemplate.cfm?SRC=DB&SRCN=&GnavID=134.

METROPOLITAN COMMUNITY COLLEGE

Institute for the Culinary Arts

Omaha, Nebraska

GENERAL INFORMATION
Public, coeducational, two-year college. Urban campus. Founded in 1974. Accredited by North Central Association of Colleges and Schools.

PROGRAM INFORMATION
Offered since 1974. Accredited by American Culinary Federation Accrediting Commission, Council on Hotel, Restaurant and Institutional Education. National Restaurant Association Educational Foundation ManageFirst certificates available. Program calendar is divided into quarters. 2-year associate degree in small business practices. 2-year associate degree in convention and meeting planning. 2-year associate degree in lodging transfer. 2-year associate degree in food and beverage management. 2-year associate degree in culinary management. 2-year associate degree in bakery arts. 2-year associate degree in Culinology (TM). 2-year associate degree in culinary arts. 3-year associate degree in chef apprentice.

PROGRAM AFFILIATION
American Culinary Federation; American Institute of Baking; American Wine Society; Council on Hotel, Restaurant, and Institutional Education; International Association of Culinary Professionals; International Wine & Food Society; National Restaurant Association; National Restaurant Association Educational Foundation; Research Chefs Association; The Bread Bakers Guild of America; United States Personal Chef Association.

AREAS OF STUDY
Baking; beverage management; buffet catering; controlling costs in food service; convenience cookery; culinary skill development; food preparation; food purchasing; food service communication; food service math; garde-manger; international cuisine; introduction to food service; kitchen management; management and human resources; meal planning; meat fabrication; menu and facilities design; nutrition; nutrition and food

service; patisserie; restaurant opportunities; sanitation; saucier; seafood processing; soup, stock, sauce, and starch production; wines and spirits.

FACILITIES
Bake shop; bakery; cafeteria; catering service; 4 classrooms; 2 coffee shops; computer laboratory; demonstration laboratory; food production kitchen; garden; 2 gourmet dining rooms; 2 laboratories; learning resource center; 4 lecture rooms; library; public restaurant; teaching kitchen.

STUDENT PROFILE
625 total: 325 full-time; 300 part-time. 300 are under 25 years old; 275 are between 25 and 44 years old; 50 are over 44 years old.

FACULTY
31 total: 6 full-time; 25 part-time. 20 are industry professionals; 5 are culinary-certified teachers. Prominent faculty: James E. Trebbien, CCE; Janet Mar, PhD; Brian O'Malley; Michael Roddey. Faculty-student ratio: 1:12.

SPECIAL PROGRAMS
Study tour to annual NRA convention in Chicago, participation in local, regional, and national SkillsUSA competition, paid research and development projects for local food manufacturing companies.

TYPICAL EXPENSES
In-state tuition: $43 per credit hour part-time. Out-of-state tuition: $58 per credit hour part-time. Tuition for international students: $100 per credit hour part-time. Program-related fee includes $300 for uniforms and knives.

FINANCIAL AID
In 2006, 40 scholarships were awarded (average award was $750). Program-specific awards include Omaha Restaurant Association scholarships (up to $1000), Con Agra scholarships ($1000), International Food & Wine Society Scholarship (up to $1000). Employment placement assistance is available. Employment opportunities within the program are available.

HOUSING
Coed housing available. Average on-campus housing cost per month: $450. Average off-campus housing cost per month: $450–$600.

APPLICATION INFORMATION
Students may begin participation in March, June, September, and December. Applications are accepted continuously. In 2006, 985 applied; 710 were accepted. Applicants must submit a formal application.

CONTACT
James Trebbien, Director, ICA, Institute for the Culinary Arts, PO Box 3777, Omaha, NE 68103-0777. Telephone: 402-457-2510. Fax: 402-457-2984. E-mail: jtrebbien@mccneb.edu. World Wide Web: http://www.mccneb.edu/culinary.

SOUTHEAST COMMUNITY COLLEGE, LINCOLN CAMPUS
Food Service/Hospitality
Lincoln, Nebraska

GENERAL INFORMATION
Public, coeducational, two-year college. Urban campus. Founded in 1973. Accredited by North Central Association of Colleges and Schools.

PROGRAM INFORMATION
Offered since 1973. Accredited by American Culinary Federation Accrediting Commission, American Dietetic Association. National Restaurant Association Educational Foundation ManageFirst certificates available. Program calendar is divided into quarters. 18-month associate degree in lodging. 18-month associate degree in food service management. 18-month associate degree in culinary arts. 18-month associate degree in dietetic technology.

PROGRAM AFFILIATION
American Culinary Federation; American Dietetic Association; Council on Hotel, Restaurant, and Institutional Education; Dietary Managers Association; National Restaurant Association; National Restaurant Association Educational Foundation.

AREAS OF STUDY
Baking; beverage management; buffet catering; controlling costs in food service; culinary French; culinary skill development; food preparation; food purchasing; food service math; garde-manger; introduction to food service; kitchen management; management and human resources; meal planning; meat fabrication; menu and facilities design; nutrition; sanitation; saucier; soup, stock, sauce, and starch production.

FACILITIES
Bakery; cafeteria; catering service; 5 classrooms; computer laboratory; food production kitchen; gourmet dining room; learning resource center; 2 lecture rooms; library; public restaurant; student lounge; teaching kitchen.

Southeast Community College, Lincoln Campus
(continued)

STUDENT PROFILE
125 total: 90 full-time; 35 part-time. 90 are under 25 years old; 31 are between 25 and 44 years old; 4 are over 44 years old.

FACULTY
8 total: 3 full-time; 5 part-time. 4 are industry professionals; 1 is a culinary-certified teacher; 2 are registered dietitians. Prominent faculty: Jo Taylor, RD, LMNT; Gerrine Schrek Kirby, CEC, CCE; Lois Cockerham, CDM; Erin Caudill, RD, LMNT. Faculty-student ratio: 1:18.

PROMINENT ALUMNI AND CURRENT AFFILIATION
Rob Epps, Sweeter Side Bakery; Jarred Beckman, Olive Garden; Travis Evans, Venue.

SPECIAL PROGRAMS
Trip to the National Restaurant Association show, culinary competitions.

TYPICAL EXPENSES
Application fee: $25. In-state tuition: $46 per credit hour part-time. Out-of-state tuition: $56 per credit hour part-time. Program-related fee includes $330 for uniform, knives, and shoes.

FINANCIAL AID
In 2006, 4 scholarships were awarded (average award was $300). Employment placement assistance is available. Employment opportunities within the program are available.

HOUSING
Average off-campus housing cost per month: $350.

APPLICATION INFORMATION
Students may begin participation in January, March, July, and October. Application deadline for fall is September 1. Application deadline for winter is November 23. Application deadline for spring is February 22. Application deadline for summer is May 17. In 2006, 57 applied; 57 were accepted. Applicants must submit a formal application and have high school diploma or GED.

CONTACT
Jo Taylor, Program Chair, Food Service/Hospitality, 8800 O Street, Southeast Community College, Lincoln, NE 68520. Telephone: 402-437-2465. Fax: 402-437-2404. E-mail: jtaylor@southeast.edu. World Wide Web: http://www.southeast.edu/discover/lincoln.asp.

NEVADA

THE ART INSTITUTE OF LAS VEGAS

The International Culinary School at The Art Institute of Las Vegas

Henderson, Nevada

GENERAL INFORMATION
Private, coeducational institution.

PROGRAM INFORMATION
Associate degree in Baking and Pastry. Associate degree in Culinary Arts. Bachelor's degree in Culinary Management.

CONTACT
Office of Admissions, The International Culinary School at The Art Institute of Las Vegas, 2350 Corporate Circle, Las Vegas, NV 89074-7737. Telephone: 702-369-9944. World Wide Web: http://www.artinstitutes.edu/lasvegas/.

See color display following page 186.

LE CORDON BLEU COLLEGE OF CULINARY ARTS, LAS VEGAS

Las Vegas, Nevada

GENERAL INFORMATION
Private, coeducational, culinary institute. Suburban campus. Founded in 2003. Accredited by Accrediting Commission of Career Schools and Colleges of Technology.

PROGRAM INFORMATION
Offered since 2003. Program calendar is continuous. 15-month associate degree in culinary arts. 9-month certificate in patisserie and baking.

TYPICAL EXPENSES
Application fee: $50.

APPLICATION INFORMATION
Students may begin participation in January, February, April, May, June, August, September, and November.

CONTACT
Director of Admissions, 1451 Center Crossing Road, Las Vegas, NV 89144.

UNIVERSITY OF NEVADA, LAS VEGAS

Department of Food and Beverage Management

Las Vegas, Nevada

GENERAL INFORMATION
Public, coeducational, university. Urban campus. Founded in 1957. Accredited by Northwest Commission on Colleges and Universities.

PROGRAM INFORMATION
Offered since 1967. Program calendar is divided into semesters. 4-year bachelor's degree in culinary arts management.

PROGRAM AFFILIATION
American Culinary Federation; American Dietetic Association; Council on Hotel, Restaurant, and Institutional Education; International Food Service Executives Association; National Restaurant Association; National Restaurant Association Educational Foundation; Nevada Restaurant Association; Research Chefs Association; Women Chefs and Restaurateurs.

AREAS OF STUDY
Baking; beers; beverage management; buffet catering; controlling costs in food service; culinary skill development; culture and cuisine; food preparation; food purchasing; food science; food service communication; food service math; garde-manger; introduction to food service; kitchen management; management and human resources; meal planning; menu and facilities design; noncommercial food service; nutrition; nutrition and food service; operations management; quantity foods; quick service; restaurant opportunities; sanitation; saucier; soup, stock, sauce, and starch production; wines and spirits.

FACILITIES
Bake shop; catering service; 25 classrooms; computer laboratory; demonstration laboratory; 2 food production kitchens; 3 gourmet dining rooms; 4 laboratories; 25 lecture rooms; library; public restaurant; 2 teaching kitchens; 2 bar/lounges.

STUDENT PROFILE
185 total: 160 full-time; 25 part-time.

FACULTY
87 total: 55 full-time; 32 part-time. 12 are industry professionals; 1 is a master baker; 5 are culinary-certified teachers. Prominent faculty: Claude Lambertz, CHE; John Stefanelli, PhD; Jean Hertzman, CCE, PhD; Don Bell, PhD. Faculty-student ratio: 1:24.

SPECIAL PROGRAMS
5-week summer studies in Switzerland and Australia, local and national internships, local and national conferences and trade shows.

TYPICAL EXPENSES
Application fee: $90. In-state tuition: $117 per semester hour full-time (in district), $117 per semester hour (up to 6 hours) part-time. Out-of-state tuition: $5405 per semester; $117 per semester hour full-time, $247 per semester hour (up to 6 hours) part-time. Tuition for international students: $5405 per semester; $117 per semester hour full-time, $247 per semester hour (up to 6 hours) part-time. Program-related fees include $30–$125 for supplies-per class for lab classes; $20 for internship administration; $173 for student activities fee per semester; $100 for international student fee per semester; $15 for distance education course fee per course.

FINANCIAL AID
In 2006, 140 scholarships were awarded (average award was $1500). Program-specific awards include Banfi Research Scholarship. Employment placement assistance is available.

HOUSING
Coed housing available. Average on-campus housing cost per month: $485. Average off-campus housing cost per month: $650.

APPLICATION INFORMATION
Students may begin participation in January, May, and August. Application deadline for fall is February 1. Application deadline for spring is October 1. Application deadline for summer is February 1. Applicants must submit a formal application.

CONTACT
Sherri Theriault, Advising Coordinator, Department of Food and Beverage Management, Harrah Hotel College, Office for Student Advising, Las Vegas, NV 89154-6039. Telephone: 702-895-3616. Fax: 702-895-3127. E-mail: hoaadviz@ncvada.edu. World Wide Web: http://www.unlv.edu.

NEW HAMPSHIRE

MCINTOSH COLLEGE

Dover, New Hampshire

GENERAL INFORMATION
Private, coeducational, two-year college. Small-town setting. Founded in 1896. Accredited by New England Association of Schools and Colleges.

McIntosh College *(continued)*

PROGRAM INFORMATION
Offered since 2000. Accredited by American Culinary Federation Accrediting Commission. National Restaurant Association Educational Foundation ManageFirst certificates available. Program calendar is divided into quarters. 18-month associate degree in culinary arts.

PROGRAM AFFILIATION
American Culinary Federation; National Restaurant Association.

AREAS OF STUDY
Culinary skill development.

FACILITIES
Bake shop; cafeteria; computer laboratory; 5 demonstration laboratories; garden; gourmet dining room; learning resource center; library; public restaurant.

STUDENT PROFILE
202 full-time. 142 are under 25 years old; 54 are between 25 and 44 years old; 6 are over 44 years old.

FACULTY
17 total: 15 full-time; 2 part-time. 13 are industry professionals; 1 is a culinary-certified teacher. Prominent faculty: Michael Graves, CCP; Michael Ciuffetti, CEC; Julienne Guyette, MG (Master Gardner); Murray Long, CCE, CEC. Faculty-student ratio: 1:16.

PROMINENT ALUMNI AND CURRENT AFFILIATION
Ben Hasty, Executive Chef, Dunaway Restaurant, Porthsouth NH; James Fowler, Director Food Service, Portland, OR Public School; Teresa Cleary, Assistant Innkeeper, Silver Fountain Inn, Dover, NH.

SPECIAL PROGRAMS
320-hour externship.

TYPICAL EXPENSES
Application fee: $50. Tuition: $34,000 per 18 months. Program-related fees include $617 for uniforms and shoes; $825 for knife kit; $800 for books.

FINANCIAL AID
In 2006, 42 scholarships were awarded (average award was $1600). Program-specific awards include extended loan financing. Employment placement assistance is available. Employment opportunities within the program are available.

HOUSING
Coed housing available. Average on-campus housing cost per month: $880.

APPLICATION INFORMATION
Students may begin participation in January, April, July, and October. Applications are accepted continuously. In 2006, 756 applied; 756 were accepted. Applicants must interview; submit a formal application.

CONTACT
Mary Lou Ross, Assistant Director of Admissions, 23 Cataract Avenue, Dover, NH 03820. Telephone: 800-624-6867 Ext. 1443. Fax: 603-742-3755. E-mail: mross@mcintoshcollege.edu. World Wide Web: http://www.mcintoshcollege.edu.

NEW HAMPSHIRE COMMUNITY TECHNICAL COLLEGE

New Hampshire Culinary Institute

Berlin, New Hampshire

GENERAL INFORMATION
Public, coeducational, two-year college. Rural campus. Founded in 1966. Accredited by New England Association of Schools and Colleges.

PROGRAM INFORMATION
Offered since 1965. Program calendar is divided into semesters. 1-year certificate in culinary arts. 1-year diploma in culinary arts (basic). 2-year associate degree in baking. 2-year associate degree in culinary arts.

PROGRAM AFFILIATION
American Culinary Federation; Institute of Food Technologists; National Restaurant Association.

AREAS OF STUDY
Baking; beverage management; buffet catering; confectionery show pieces; controlling costs in food service; culinary skill development; food preparation; food purchasing; food service communication; food service math; garde-manger; international cuisine; introduction to food service; kitchen management; management and human resources; meal planning; meat cutting; meat fabrication; menu and facilities design; nutrition; nutrition and food service; patisserie; restaurant opportunities; sanitation; saucier; seafood processing; soup, stock, sauce, and starch production; wines and spirits.

FACILITIES
Bakery; cafeteria; catering service; 5 computer laboratories; 2 demonstration laboratories; 3 food production kitchens; garden; gourmet dining room; 2 laboratories; learning resource center; 3 lecture rooms; library; public restaurant; snack shop; student lounge; 2 teaching kitchens.

STUDENT PROFILE
54 total: 48 full-time; 6 part-time. 51 are under 25 years old; 3 are between 25 and 44 years old.

FACULTY
9 total: 3 full-time; 6 part-time. 3 are industry professionals. Prominent faculty: Kurt Hohmeister; Travis Giles; Angela Brassard. Faculty-student ratio: 1:10.

SPECIAL PROGRAMS
2-course externship at area restaurants, apprenticeship with Balsams Hotel.

TYPICAL EXPENSES
Application fee: $10. In-state tuition: $175 per credit (in district), $199.50 per credit (out-of-district). Out-of-state tuition: $400 per credit. Program-related fees include $150 for knives; $145 for uniforms (3 sets).

FINANCIAL AID
Employment placement assistance is available.

HOUSING
Average off-campus housing cost per month: $350.

APPLICATION INFORMATION
Students may begin participation in January and September. Applications are accepted continuously. Applicants must submit a formal application and high school transcript.

CONTACT
Kurt Hohmeister, Professor, New Hampshire Culinary Institute, 2020 Riverside Drive, Berlin, NH 03570-3717. Telephone: 603-752-1113. Fax: 603-752-6335. E-mail: khohmeister@nhctc.edu. World Wide Web: http://www.berlin.nhctc.edu/.

SOUTHERN NEW HAMPSHIRE UNIVERSITY

The School of Professional and Continuing Education

Manchester, New Hampshire

GENERAL INFORMATION
Private, coeducational, university. Suburban campus. Founded in 1932. Accredited by New England Association of Schools and Colleges.

PROGRAM INFORMATION
Offered since 1983. Accredited by American Culinary Federation Accrediting Commission. Program calendar is divided into semesters. 2-year associate degree in baking and pastry arts. 2-year associate degree in culinary arts. 2-year master of business administration in hospitality concentration. 4-year bachelor's degree in culinary arts. 4-year bachelor's degree in food and beverage management. 4-year bachelor's degree in hospitality administration. 9-month certificate in culinary arts. 9-month certificate in baking and pastry arts.

PROGRAM AFFILIATION
American Culinary Federation; Council on Hotel, Restaurant, and Institutional Education; International Association of Culinary Professionals; National Restaurant Association; Retailer's Bakery Association; Women Chefs and Restaurateurs.

AREAS OF STUDY
Advanced pastry; bakery management; bakeshop; baking; beverage management; buffet catering; classic cuisine; confectionery show pieces; controlling costs in food service; culinary competition; culinary French; culinary skill development; food preparation; food purchasing; food service communication; food service math; garde-manger; holiday baking; international baking; international cuisine; introduction to culinary arts; introduction to food service; kitchen management; meal planning; meat cutting; menu and facilities design; new American cuisine; nutrition; nutrition and food service; patisserie; principles of supervision; regional American cooking; restaurant opportunities; sanitation; saucier; soup, stock, sauce, and starch production; spa cuisine; table service; wines and spirits.

FACILITIES
2 bake shops; bakery; cafeteria; catering service; 5 classrooms; coffee shop; 2 computer laboratories; 5 demonstration laboratories; 4 food production kitchens; garden; gourmet dining room; 2 laboratories; learning resource center; 9 lecture rooms; library; public restaurant; snack shop; student lounge; 4 teaching kitchens.

STUDENT PROFILE
107 total: 105 full-time; 2 part-time. 101 are under 25 years old; 5 are between 25 and 44 years old; 1 is over 44 years old.

FACULTY
12 total: 5 full-time; 7 part-time. 6 are industry professionals; 1 is a master baker; 5 are culinary-certified teachers. Prominent faculty: J. Desmond Keefe, III, CHE; Mary Brigid Flanigan, CHE. Faculty-student ratio: 1:10.

PROMINENT ALUMNI AND CURRENT AFFILIATION
William Kovel, Four Seasons, Boston; John Coleman, Ritz Carlton, Dallas.

Some call it "the freshman 15."
We call it "going the extra mile."

Before you can create the perfect chocolate soufflé, you need to know what it should taste like. Compare recipes. Order it at your favorite restaurant. And practice, practice, practice. At SNHU, it's a sacrifice our culinary arts students are all too happy to make.

From basic baking to cost control, our culinary arts program preps you for every aspect of the industry, with on-campus facilities like our full-service restaurant and our cozy café.

By the way, you'll also have access to our 5,500 square-foot fitness center. (Just in case!)

For more information call 1.800.642.4968
or e-mail admission@snhu.edu.

SPECIAL PROGRAMS

Internships at various locations in the United States, 12 month paid internship, 3 week culinary tour/class in Spain, culinary competitions, semester abroad in Italy.

TYPICAL EXPENSES

Application fee: $35. Tuition: $23,106 per year full-time, $738 per credit part-time. Program-related fees include $125 for uniforms; $300 for knives; $550 for books (2 semesters).

FINANCIAL AID

In 2006, 22 scholarships were awarded (average award was $7000). Employment placement assistance is available. Employment opportunities within the program are available.

HOUSING

Coed, apartment-style, and single-sex housing available. Average on-campus housing cost per month: $1150.

APPLICATION INFORMATION

Students may begin participation in September. Applications are accepted continuously. In 2006, 159 applied; 121 were accepted. Applicants must submit a formal application, letters of reference, an essay, academic transcripts.

CONTACT

Sam Mahra, Senior Assistant Director of Admission/ Coordinator for Culinary Recruitment, The School of Professional and Continuing Education, 2500 North River Road, Manchester, NH 03106-1045. Telephone: 603-645-9611. Fax: 603-645-9693. E-mail: s.mahra@ snhu.edu. World Wide Web: http://www.snhu.edu.

See display on page 228.

UNIVERSITY OF NEW HAMPSHIRE

Food Services Management

Durham, New Hampshire

GENERAL INFORMATION

Public, coeducational institution. Small-town setting. Founded in 1895. Accredited by New England Association of Schools and Colleges.

PROGRAM INFORMATION

Offered since 1967. Accredited by American Dietetic Association. National Restaurant Association Educational Foundation ManageFirst certificates available. Program calendar is divided into semesters. 2-year associate degree in dietetic technician. 2-year associate degree in restaurant management.

PROGRAM AFFILIATION

American Dietetic Association; Council on Hotel, Restaurant, and Institutional Education; National Restaurant Association; National Restaurant Association Educational Foundation.

AREAS OF STUDY

Baking; beverage management; buffet catering; controlling costs in food service; convenience cookery; culinary skill development; food preparation; food purchasing; food service communication; garde-manger; international cuisine; introduction to food service; kitchen management; management and human resources; meal planning; nutrition; nutrition and food service; restaurant opportunities; sanitation; saucier; soup, stock, sauce, and starch production; wines and spirits.

FACILITIES

3 cafeterias; catering service; 5 classrooms; computer laboratory; 2 demonstration laboratories; 2 food production kitchens; 2 gardens; learning resource center; 3 lecture rooms; library; 3 public restaurants; student lounge; teaching kitchen.

STUDENT PROFILE

450 total: 425 full-time; 25 part-time.

FACULTY

4 total: 3 full-time; 1 part-time. 3 are industry professionals; 1 is a culinary-certified teacher; 1 is a certified hospitality educator. Prominent faculty: Gino Alibrio, MS, CHE; Charlie Caramihalis, MCE, CCE; Nancy Johnson, MED, RD, LD. Faculty-student ratio: 1:8.

PROMINENT ALUMNI AND CURRENT AFFILIATION

A. J. Bruno, 4 Seasons, Boston; Steven Dixon, GM, Applebee's Inc.; Renee Barstow, District Manager, Golbon Foods.

SPECIAL PROGRAMS

3-month paid internship.

TYPICAL EXPENSES

Application fee: $45. In-state tuition: $8810 per year full-time (in district), $367 per credit part-time. Out-of-state tuition: $10,885 per year full-time, $907 per credit part-time. Program-related fees include $425 for one time fee covering field trips, food related labs and computer use; $2200 for yearly fees.

FINANCIAL AID

Employment placement assistance is available.

HOUSING

Coed, apartment-style, and single-sex housing available. Average off-campus housing cost per month: $800–$1000.

University of New Hampshire *(continued)*

APPLICATION INFORMATION
Students may begin participation in January and September. Application deadline for fall (early action) is November 15. Application deadline for fall (regular admission) is February 1. Application deadline for spring is October 15. In 2006, 500 applied; 350 were accepted. Applicants must submit a formal application, letters of reference, an essay, ACT/SAT scores.

CONTACT
Deb Pack, Admissions Coordinator, Food Services Management, Cole Hall, 291 Mast Road, Durham, NII 03824. Telephone: 603-862-3115. Fax: 603-862-2915. E-mail: deborah.pack@unh.edu. World Wide Web: http://www.thompsonschool.unh.edu.

NEW JERSEY

ATLANTIC CAPE COMMUNITY COLLEGE

Academy of Culinary Arts

Mays Landing, New Jersey

GENERAL INFORMATION
Public, coeducational, two-year college. Small-town setting. Founded in 1964. Accredited by Middle States Association of Colleges and Schools.

PROGRAM INFORMATION
Offered since 1981. Program calendar is divided into semesters. 2-year associate degree in pastry/baking. 2-year associate degree in food service management. 2-year associate degree in culinary arts. 3-semester certificate in food service management. 3-semester certificate in baking/pastry. 3-semester certificate in culinary arts. 9-month certificate of specialization in catering. 9-month certificate of specialization in food service management. 9-month certificate of specialization in hot foods. 9-month certificate of specialization in pastry/baking.

PROGRAM AFFILIATION

American Culinary Federation; Center for the Advancement of Food Service Education; Foodservice Educators Network International; International Association of Culinary Professionals; National Restaurant Association; National Restaurant Association Educational Foundation; New Jersey Restaurant Association; Retailer's Bakery Association.

AREAS OF STUDY

American regional; baking; buffet catering; charcuterie; confectionery show pieces; controlling costs in food service; culinary skill development; food preparation; food purchasing; food service math; garde-manger; international cuisine; introduction to food service; Italian regional and traditional cooking; kitchen management; meal planning; meat cutting; meat fabrication; menu and facilities design; nutrition; patisserie; restaurant operations; sanitation; saucier; soup, stock, sauce, and starch production; vegetarian cooking; wines and spirits.

FACILITIES

2 bake shops; 4 classrooms; computer laboratory; food production kitchen; gourmet dining room; learning resource center; 4 lecture rooms; library; public restaurant; 5 teaching kitchens; banquet room.

STUDENT PROFILE

370 total: 231 full-time; 139 part-time. 260 are under 25 years old; 80 are between 25 and 44 years old; 30 are over 44 years old.

FACULTY

18 total: 13 full-time; 5 part-time. 18 are industry professionals; 6 are culinary-certified teachers. Prominent faculty: Mary Theresa McCann, CEPC; Marsha Patrick, RD; Philip Cragg, CEC, CCE, AAC; Annmarie Chelius, CCE, CWPC. Faculty-student ratio: 1:20.

PROMINENT ALUMNI AND CURRENT AFFILIATION

Michael Schlow, Chef/Owner, Radius, Via Matta, Great Bay, Alta Strada (in Boston); Bill McCarrick, Pastry Chef, Sir Hans Sloane Chocolate & Champagne House of London; Patricia Nash, Pastry Chef, Westchester Country Club, 2007 ACF Pastry Chef of the Year.

SPECIAL PROGRAMS

400-hour cooperative education program, culinary competitions, study abroad.

TYPICAL EXPENSES

Application fee: $35. In-state tuition: $5844 per semester full-time (in district), $1461 per course part-time (in district), $6840 per semester full-time (out-of-district), $1710 per course part-time (out-of-district). Out-of-state tuition: $8832 per semester

full-time, $2208 per course part-time. Program-related fees include $300 for knives and specialty tools; $400 for textbooks; $350 for uniforms.

FINANCIAL AID

In 2006, 131 scholarships were awarded (average award was $1101). Program-specific awards include Press of Atlantic City Restaurant Gala Scholarships. Employment placement assistance is available. Employment opportunities within the program are available.

APPLICATION INFORMATION

Students may begin participation in January and August. Applications are accepted continuously. In 2006, 395 applied; 395 were accepted. Applicants must submit a formal application.

CONTACT

Linda McLeod, Assistant Director for College Recruitment, Academy of Culinary Arts, 5100 Black Horse Pike, Mays Landing, NJ 08330-2699. Telephone: 609-343-5009. Fax: 609-343-4921. E-mail: accadmit@ atlantic.edu. World Wide Web: http://www.atlantic.edu/aca.

BERGEN COMMUNITY COLLEGE

Hotel/Restaurant/Hospitality

Paramus, New Jersey

GENERAL INFORMATION

Public, coeducational, two-year college. Suburban campus. Founded in 1965. Accredited by Middle States Association of Colleges and Schools.

PROGRAM INFORMATION

Offered since 1974. Program calendar is divided into semesters. 1-semester certificate of achievement in professional cooking. 1-year certificate in hospitality management. 1-year certificate in culinary arts. 2-year associate degree in catering/ banquet management. 2-year associate degree in hospitality management.

PROGRAM AFFILIATION

Council on Hotel, Restaurant, and Institutional Education; National Restaurant Association; National Restaurant Association Educational Foundation; New Jersey Restaurant Association.

AREAS OF STUDY

Baking; beverage management; buffet catering; controlling costs in food service; culinary skill development; food preparation; food purchasing; garde-manger; international cuisine; introduction to food service; kitchen management; meal planning; nutrition; sanitation; soup, stock, sauce, and starch production; wines and spirits.

Bergen Community College *(continued)*

FACILITIES

Cafeteria; 6 classrooms; 2 computer laboratories; 2 food production kitchens; gourmet dining room; learning resource center; library; public restaurant; snack shop; 2 student lounges; teaching kitchen.

STUDENT PROFILE

230 total: 170 full-time; 60 part-time. 70 are under 25 years old; 100 are between 25 and 44 years old; 60 are over 44 years old.

FACULTY

4 total: 4 full-time. Prominent faculty: Arthur P. Tolve, Coordinator. Faculty-student ratio: 1:57.

SPECIAL PROGRAMS

Co-op work experience.

TYPICAL EXPENSES

Application fee: $25. In-state tuition: $98.40 per credit hour (in district), $203 per credit hour (out-of-district). Out-of-state tuition: $213 per credit hour. Tuition for international students: $203 per credit hour. Program-related fees include $30 for lab fees (per course); $17 for general fee (per credit hour).

FINANCIAL AID

Employment placement assistance is available. Employment opportunities within the program are available.

HOUSING

Average off-campus housing cost per month: $750–$1300.

APPLICATION INFORMATION

Students may begin participation in January, June, July, and September. Application deadline for fall is August 31. Application deadline for spring is January 14. In 2006, 241 applied; 241 were accepted. Applicants must interview; submit a formal application.

CONTACT

Arthur P. Tolve, Coordinator Hotel, Restaurant, Hospitality, Hotel/Restaurant/Hospitality, 400 Paramus Road-E185A, Paramus, NJ 07052-1595. Telephone: 201-447-7192. Fax: 201-612-5240. E-mail: atolve@bergen.edu. World Wide Web: http://www.bergen.edu.

BROOKDALE COMMUNITY COLLEGE

Asbury Park, New Jersey

GENERAL INFORMATION

Public, coeducational, two-year college. Founded in 1967. Accredited by Middle States Association of Colleges and Schools.

PROGRAM INFORMATION

Program calendar is divided into semesters. Certificate in culinary arts. 2-year associate degree in food service management. 2-year associate degree in culinary arts.

FACILITIES

2 bakeries; 5 classrooms; computer laboratory; 3 food production kitchens; learning resource center; 2 public restaurants.

SPECIAL PROGRAMS

Externships.

TYPICAL EXPENSES

Tuition: $13,529 per associates degree. Program-related fee includes $2055 for books and supplies.

APPLICATION INFORMATION

Applicants must interview; submit a formal application, high school diploma or equivalent, health screen form.

CONTACT

Enrollment Services, 765 Newman Springs Road, Lincroft, NJ 07738. Telephone: 732-224-2371. E-mail: recruitment@brookdalecc.edu. World Wide Web: http://www.brookdalecc.edu/fac/culinary.

BURLINGTON COUNTY COLLEGE

Food Service and Hospitality Management

Pemberton, New Jersey

GENERAL INFORMATION

Public, coeducational, two-year college. Suburban campus. Founded in 1966. Accredited by Middle States Association of Colleges and Schools.

PROGRAM INFORMATION

Offered since 1997. Program calendar is semester plus 2 summer terms. 1-year certificate in food service and hospitality management. 1.5-year certificate in cooking and baking. 2-year associate degree in food service and hospitality management.

PROGRAM AFFILIATION

National Restaurant Association Educational Foundation.

AREAS OF STUDY

Baking; controlling costs in food service; food preparation; food purchasing; food service math; introduction to food service; management and human resources; managing quantity food service; marketing for hospitality; menu and facilities design; nutrition; nutrition and food service; quality service; sanitation.

FACILITIES

Classroom; food production kitchen; lecture room.

TYPICAL STUDENT PROFILE

30 total: 10 full-time; 20 part-time. 10 are under 25 years old; 20 are between 25 and 44 years old.

FINANCIAL AID

Employment placement assistance is available. Employment opportunities within the program are available.

APPLICATION INFORMATION

Students may begin participation in January, May, July, and September. Application deadline for fall is August 25. Application deadline for spring is January 25. Application deadline for summer is May 25. Applicants must submit a formal application.

CONTACT

Director of Admissions, Food Service and Hospitality Management, Route 530, Pemberton, NJ 08068-1599. Telephone: 609-894-9311 Ext. 2750. Fax: 609-726-0442. World Wide Web: http://staff.bcc.edu/fsm/Index.htm.

HUDSON COUNTY COMMUNITY COLLEGE

Culinary Arts Institute

Jersey City, New Jersey

GENERAL INFORMATION

Public, coeducational, two-year college. Urban campus. Founded in 1974. Accredited by Middle States Association of Colleges and Schools.

PROGRAM INFORMATION

Accredited by American Culinary Federation Accrediting Commission. Program calendar is divided into semesters. 1-semester certificate in hot food production. 1-semester certificate in garde manger. 1-semester certificate in baking. 1-year certificate in hospitality management. 1-year certificate in culinary arts. 2-year associate degree in hospitality management. 2-year associate degree in culinary arts.

PROGRAM AFFILIATION

American Culinary Federation.

TYPICAL EXPENSES

Application fee: $15. In-state tuition: $5740 per associate degree; $2706 per certificate full-time (in district), $82 per credit part-time (in district), $11,480 per associate degree; $5442 per certificate full-time (out-of-district), $164 per credit part-time (out-of-district). Out-of-state tuition: $17,220 per associate degree; $8118 per certificate full-time, $246 per credit part-time. Program-related fees include $233 for culinary fee (per course); $206 for knife kit; $258 for uniforms.

APPLICATION INFORMATION

Applicants must submit a formal application and transcripts.

CONTACT

Recruiter, Culinary Arts Institute, 161 Newkirk Street, Jersey City, NJ 07306. Telephone: 201-360-4640. Fax: 201-795-4641. E-mail: cai@hccc.edu. World Wide Web: http://www.hccc.edu.

See display on page 234.

MERCER COUNTY COMMUNITY COLLEGE

Hotel and Restaurant Management

Trenton, New Jersey

GENERAL INFORMATION

Public, coeducational, two-year college. Suburban campus. Founded in 1966. Accredited by Middle States Association of Colleges and Schools.

PROGRAM INFORMATION

Offered since 1988. Program calendar is divided into semesters. 1-year certificate in catering management. 1-year certificate in professional baking. 1-year certificate in professional cooking. 2-year associate degree in culinology. 2-year associate degree in hotel, restaurant, and institution management. 3-year associate degree in chef apprenticeship.

FACULTY

Prominent faculty: Douglas Fee.

TYPICAL EXPENSES

In-state tuition: $102 per credit (in district), $136.50 per credit (out-of-district). Out-of-state tuition: $208.50 per credit.

Award-Winning Culinary Program

ASSOCIATE IN APPLIED SCIENCE & CERTIFICATE PROGRAMS OFFERED

- New Culinary Arts Institute/Business Conference Center/ Classroom Building with state-of-the-art classrooms and elegant banquet facilities
- Fully accredited by the American Culinary Federation
- Award-winning chef instructors
- Extensive externship requirement with some of the most prominent hotels, country clubs, restaurants, and other food service establishments in the country
- Student to faculty ratio of 12:1
- Individualized instruction
- "Hands-On" classroom instruction
- Exchange programs available overseas
- Culinary education providing the total dining experience
- Operating restaurant as a part of the curriculum
- State-of-the-art equipment and kitchen designs
- 99% job placement
- Several articulation agreements with four-year college and universities
- Culinary Arts Club - Winner of several awards in food competitions

Specialized Programs offered at The Culinary Arts Institute

- **Bakeshop**
- **Garde Manger**
- **Hot Food Production**

- **10 minutes by PATH to NYC**

- **1 block from Journal Square PATH Station**

- **Financial Aid Available**

- **Full-time and Part-time options**

CULINARY ARTS INSTITUTE OF HUDSON COUNTY COMMUNITY COLLEGE

161 Newkirk Street • Jersey City, NJ • 201-360-4639
www.hccc.edu

APPLICATION INFORMATION

Students may begin participation in January, May, and August. Applications are accepted continuously. Applicants must submit a formal application, high school transcripts or GED, immunization form.

CONTACT

Douglas Fee, Coordinator, Hotel and Restaurant Management, PO Box B, Trenton, NJ 08690. Telephone: 609-586-4800 Ext. 3447. E-mail: feed@mccc.edu. World Wide Web: http://www.mccc.edu.

MIDDLESEX COUNTY COLLEGE

Hotel Restaurant and Institution Management

Edison, New Jersey

GENERAL INFORMATION

Public, coeducational, two-year college. Suburban campus. Founded in 1964. Accredited by Middle States Association of Colleges and Schools.

PROGRAM INFORMATION

Offered since 1964. Program calendar is divided into semesters. Certificate of achievement in culinary arts. 2-year associate degree in hotel, restaurant, and institution management (with culinary arts option).

PROGRAM AFFILIATION

American Dietetic Association; American Hotel and Lodging Association; Council on Hotel, Restaurant, and Institutional Education; Institute of Food Technologists; National Association for the Specialty Food Trade, Inc.; National Restaurant Association; National Restaurant Association Educational Foundation.

AREAS OF STUDY

Baking; beverage management; controlling costs in food service; culinary skill development; facilities layout and design; food preparation; food purchasing; food service communication; food service math; garde-manger; international cuisine; introduction to food service; kitchen management; management and human resources; meal planning; meat fabrication; menu and facilities design; nutrition; nutrition and food service; restaurant opportunities; sanitation; soup, stock, sauce, and starch production; wines and spirits.

FACILITIES

Bake shop; cafeteria; catering service; 2 classrooms; computer laboratory; demonstration laboratory; food production kitchen; laboratory; learning resource center; 2 lecture rooms; library; public restaurant; teaching kitchen.

TYPICAL STUDENT PROFILE

200 total: 125 full-time; 75 part-time.

SPECIAL PROGRAMS

Externships, cooperative work experiences, Walt Disney World College Program (practicum).

FINANCIAL AID

Employment placement assistance is available. Employment opportunities within the program are available.

APPLICATION INFORMATION

Students may begin participation in January, May, and August. Application deadline for fall is August 1. Application deadline for spring is December 31. Application deadline for summer is May 1. Applicants must submit a formal application.

CONTACT

Director of Admissions, Hotel Restaurant and Institution Management, 2600 Woodbridge Avenue, PO Box 3050, Edison, NJ 08818-3050. Telephone: 732-906-2538. Fax: 732-906-7745. World Wide Web: http://www.middlesexcc.edu.

TECHNICAL INSTITUTE OF CAMDEN COUNTY

Culinary Arts

Sicklerville, New Jersey

GENERAL INFORMATION

Public, coeducational, technical institute. Rural campus. Founded in 1927.

PROGRAM INFORMATION

Offered since 1927. Accredited by New Jersey Department of Education. Program calendar is divided into semesters. 1-year diploma in culinary arts.

PROGRAM AFFILIATION

National Restaurant Association Educational Foundation.

AREAS OF STUDY

Buffet catering; convenience cookery; culinary French; culinary skill development; food preparation; food purchasing; food service communication; food service math; garde-manger; international cuisine; introduction to food service; meal planning; meat cutting; meat fabrication; menu and facilities design; nutrition; nutrition and food service; sanitation; saucier; seafood processing; soup, stock, sauce, and starch production.

Technical Institute of Camden County *(continued)*

FACILITIES
Cafeteria; 2 classrooms; coffee shop; demonstration laboratory; food production kitchen; gourmet dining room; lecture room; public restaurant; 2 teaching kitchens.

STUDENT PROFILE
21 full-time. 10 are under 25 years old; 9 are between 25 and 44 years old; 2 are over 44 years old.

FACULTY
3 total: 3 part-time. 3 are culinary-certified teachers. Prominent faculty: Barry Galasso; Anthony Marrocco; William Washart. Faculty-student ratio: 1:10.

TYPICAL EXPENSES
Application fee: $25. In-state tuition: $1975 per year (in district), $2075 per year (out-of-district). Out-of-state tuition: $3222 per year. Program-related fees include $400 for uniforms and books; $100 for administrative fee.

FINANCIAL AID
Employment placement assistance is available.

APPLICATION INFORMATION
Students may begin participation in September. Application deadline for fall is October 15. In 2006, 52 applied; 30 were accepted. Applicants must submit a formal application.

CONTACT
Gayle S. Butler, Director of Student Personnel Services, Culinary Arts, 343 Berlin Cross Keys Road, Sicklerville, NJ 08081. Telephone: 856-767-7002. Fax: 856-767-4278. E-mail: gbutler@ccts.tec.nj.us. World Wide Web: http://www.ticareers.com.

THOMAS EDISON STATE COLLEGE

Hospitality Management

Trenton, New Jersey

GENERAL INFORMATION
Public, coeducational, comprehensive institution. Urban campus. Founded in 1972. Accredited by Middle States Association of Colleges and Schools.

PROGRAM INFORMATION
Offered since 1981. Program calendar is continuous. Bachelor's degree in hospitality management.

STUDENT PROFILE
37 part-time.

PROMINENT ALUMNI AND CURRENT AFFILIATION
Ernest Wooden, Jr., Executive Vice President of Brand Management at Hilton Hotel Corporation.

TYPICAL EXPENSES
Application fee: $75. In-state tuition: $4300 per year part-time. Out-of-state tuition: $6150 per year part-time. Tuition for international students: $6150 per year part-time.

APPLICATION INFORMATION
Students may begin participation year-round. Applications are accepted continuously. In 2006, 28 applied. Applicants must submit a formal application.

CONTACT
Director of Admissions, Hospitality Management, 101 West State Street, Trenton, NJ 08608. Telephone: 888-442-8372. Fax: 609-984-8447. E-mail: admissions@tesc.edu. World Wide Web: http://www.tesc.edu.

UNION COUNTY COLLEGE

Cranford, New Jersey

GENERAL INFORMATION
Public, coeducational, two-year college. Suburban campus. Founded in 1933. Accredited by Middle States Association of Colleges and Schools.

PROGRAM INFORMATION
Offered since 1996. Program calendar is divided into semesters. 2-year associate degree in hospitality management. 2-year associate degree in restaurant management (offered jointly with Fairleigh Dickinson University).

AREAS OF STUDY
Beverage management; food preparation; food purchasing; food service communication; kitchen management; management and human resources; sanitation.

STUDENT PROFILE
30 total: 21 full-time; 9 part-time. 23 are under 25 years old; 7 are between 25 and 44 years old.

SPECIAL PROGRAMS
Opportunity to transfer to a four-year program in hospitality management.

TYPICAL EXPENSES
Application fee: $35. In-state tuition: $87 per credit. Out-of-state tuition: $174 per credit. Program-related fees include $26 for per credit, required fees; $415.50 for restaurant management course fees.

APPLICATION INFORMATION

Applications are accepted continuously. In 2006, 31 applied; 31 were accepted. Applicants must submit a formal application.

CONTACT

Ms. Joann Davis, Director of Admissions/Records/Registration, 1033 Springfield Avenue, Cranford, NJ 07016. Telephone: 908-709-7596. Fax: 908-709-7131. E-mail: davis@ucc.edu. World Wide Web: http://www.ucc.edu.

NEW MEXICO

CULINARY BUSINESS ACADEMY

Rio Rancho, New Mexico

GENERAL INFORMATION

Private, coeducational institution. Urban campus. Founded in 1991.

PROGRAM INFORMATION

Offered since 1991. Program calendar is continuous. 100-hour certificate in personal chef (quick start). 100-hour certificate in personal chef (home study). 50-hour certificate in personal chef (mentorship).

PROGRAM AFFILIATION

United States Personal Chef Association.

AREAS OF STUDY

Controlling costs in food service; food purchasing; kitchen management; meal planning; sanitation.

FACILITIES

Classroom; food production kitchen.

STUDENT PROFILE

500 full-time. 25 are under 25 years old; 275 are between 25 and 44 years old; 200 are over 44 years old.

FACULTY

8 total: 8 part-time. 8 are industry professionals. Faculty-student ratio: 1:3.

SPECIAL PROGRAMS

USPCA National Conference.

TYPICAL EXPENSES

Tuition: $2695 per course.

APPLICATION INFORMATION

Students may begin participation year-round. Applications are accepted continuously. In 2006, 500 applied; 500 were accepted. Applicants must have ability to cook.

CONTACT

Phil Ellison, Director of Admissions, 610 Quantum Road, Rio Rancho, NM 87124. Telephone: 505-994-6392. Fax: 505-994-6399. E-mail: info@culinarybusiness.com. World Wide Web: http://www.culinarybusiness.com.

LUNA COMMUNITY COLLEGE

Culinary Arts Program

Las Vegas, New Mexico

GENERAL INFORMATION

Public, coeducational, two-year college. Small-town setting. Founded in 1969. Accredited by North Central Association of Colleges and Schools.

PROGRAM INFORMATION

Offered since 1970. Program calendar is divided into semesters. 18-month certificate in culinary. 2.5-year associate degree in culinary arts. 4-month certificate in NRA ServSafe certification.

AREAS OF STUDY

Baking; culinary skill development; nutrition.

FACILITIES

Bake shop; 7 cafeterias; 5 catering services; 6 computer laboratories; 4 food production kitchens; 7 learning resource centers; 3 lecture rooms; 2 teaching kitchens.

STUDENT PROFILE

38 total: 15 full-time; 23 part-time. 7 are under 25 years old; 21 are between 25 and 44 years old; 10 are over 44 years old.

FACULTY

3 total: 2 full-time; 1 part-time. 1 is an industry professional. Prominent faculty: Adrienne M. O'Brien; Kathleen Leger. Faculty-student ratio: 1:10.

SPECIAL PROGRAMS

Culinary Arts Club monthly activities, Skills USA/VICA competition.

TYPICAL EXPENSES

In-state tuition: $300 per semester full-time (in district), $25 per credit hour (up to 6 credit hours) part-time (in district), $408 per semester full-time (out-of-district), $25 per credit hour (up to 6 credit hours) part-time (out-of-district). Out-of-state tuition: $804 per semester full-time, $25 per credit hour (up to 6 credit hours) part-time. Tuition for international students: $804 per semester full-time, $25 per credit hour (up to 6 credit hours) part-time. Program-related fees include $13 for registration/activity fee; $10 for lab fee.

Luna Community College *(continued)*

FINANCIAL AID

In 2006, 5 scholarships were awarded (average award was $750); 3 loans were granted (average loan was $1500). Employment placement assistance is available.

HOUSING

Average off-campus housing cost per month: $400.

APPLICATION INFORMATION

Students may begin participation in January, June, and August. Applications are accepted continuously. Applicants must submit an application, a transcript.

CONTACT

Adrienne O'Brien, Lead Instructor, Culinary Arts Program, 366 Luna Drive, Las Vegas, NM 87701. Telephone: 505-454-5346. Fax: 505-454-2588. E-mail: aobrien@luna.edu. World Wide Web: http://www.luna.edu.

NEW MEXICO STATE UNIVERSITY

Hotel, Restaurant, and Tourism Management

Las Cruces, New Mexico

GENERAL INFORMATION

Public, coeducational, university. Suburban campus. Founded in 1888. Accredited by North Central Association of Colleges and Schools.

PROGRAM INFORMATION

Offered since 1988. Program calendar is divided into semesters. 4-year bachelor's degree in hotel, restaurant, and tourism management.

PROGRAM AFFILIATION

Council on Hotel, Restaurant, and Institutional Education; National Restaurant Association; National Restaurant Association Educational Foundation.

AREAS OF STUDY

Beverage management; controlling costs in food service; culinary skill development; food preparation; food purchasing; food service math; introduction to food service; management and human resources; meal planning; restaurant opportunities; sanitation; soup, stock, sauce, and starch production; wines and spirits.

FACILITIES

3 classrooms; computer laboratory; demonstration laboratory; food production kitchen.

STUDENT PROFILE

366 total: 338 full-time; 28 part-time. 305 are under 25 years old; 56 are between 25 and 44 years old; 5 are over 44 years old.

FACULTY

11 total: 8 full-time; 3 part-time. 1 is an industry professional; 2 are master chefs; 2 are culinary-certified teachers. Prominent faculty: Keith Mandabach, EdD; Maurice Zeck, CEC, AAC.

PROMINENT ALUMNI AND CURRENT AFFILIATION

Dominic Sanchez, The Mayflower, Washington, DC.

SPECIAL PROGRAMS

International Hotel Motel Restaurant Show, New York City, NY, National Restaurant Association Restaurant Hotel Motel Show, Chicago, IL, summer internships (paid by industry).

TYPICAL EXPENSES

Application fee: $15. In-state tuition: $4452 per year full-time (in district), $185.50 per credit part-time. Out-of-state tuition: $14,180 per year full-time, $590.85 per credit part-time. Program-related fees include $40 for cutlery, lab coats; $30 for sanitation fee for certification; $30 for additional booklets.

FINANCIAL AID

In 2006, 35 scholarships were awarded (average award was $500). Program-specific awards include industry scholarships outside of university. Employment placement assistance is available. Employment opportunities within the program are available.

HOUSING

Coed, apartment-style, and single-sex housing available.

APPLICATION INFORMATION

Students may begin participation in January and August. Applicants must submit a formal application.

CONTACT

Tyler Pruett, Office of Admissions, Hotel, Restaurant, and Tourism Management, PO Box 30001, MSC 3A, Las Cruces, NM 88003-8001. Telephone: 505-646-3121. Fax: 505-646-6330. E-mail: hrtm@nmsu.edu. World Wide Web: http://cahe.nmsu.edu/academics/shrtm/index.html.

THE ROSWELL JOB CORPS CENTER

Culinary Arts

Roswell, New Mexico

GENERAL INFORMATION
Public, coeducational, culinary institute. Rural campus. Founded in 1979. Accredited by North Central Association of Colleges and Schools.

PROGRAM INFORMATION
Offered since 1979. Program calendar is continuous. 12-month certificate in culinary arts.

AREAS OF STUDY
Baking; buffet catering; food preparation; introduction to food service; meal planning; sanitation.

FACILITIES
12 cafeterias; 8 catering services; 12 classrooms; 12 computer laboratories; 12 food production kitchens; gourmet dining room; student lounge; teaching kitchen.

STUDENT PROFILE
24 full-time.

FACULTY
104 total: 98 full-time; 6 part-time. 1 is an industry professional; 1 is a master baker. Prominent faculty: Joseph Naguin; Troy Gibson; Milburn Dolen. Faculty-student ratio: 1:12.

SPECIAL PROGRAMS
Food shows, advanced training at Treasure Island, San Francisco, CA, local and distant catering opportunities.

TYPICAL EXPENSES
Tuition: $27,000 per year (every student has full federal scholarship).

FINANCIAL AID
In 2006, individual scholarships were awarded at $27,500. Employment placement assistance is available.

HOUSING
Coed and single-sex housing available. Average off-campus housing cost per month: $550.

APPLICATION INFORMATION
Students may begin participation year-round. Applications are accepted continuously. Applicants must interview; submit a formal application; have a comprehensive background check; be legal U.S. resident.

CONTACT
Milburn Dolen, Admissions Counselor, Culinary Arts, PO Box 5633, Roswell, NM 88202. Telephone: 505-347-7419. World Wide Web: http://roswell.jobcorps.gov/.

NEW YORK

THE ART INSTITUTE OF NEW YORK CITY

The International Culinary School at The Art Institute of New York City

New York, New York

GENERAL INFORMATION
Private, coeducational institution.

PROGRAM INFORMATION
Associate degree in Culinary Arts and Restaurant Management. Certificate in Restaurant Management. Certificate in Culinary Arts. Certificate in Pastry Arts.

CONTACT
Office of Admissions, The International Culinary School at The Art Institute of New York City, 75 Varick Street, 16th Floor, New York, NY 10013-1917. Telephone: 212-226-5500. World Wide Web: http://www.artinstitutes.edu/newyork/.

See color display following page 186.

BROOME COMMUNITY COLLEGE

Hotel Restaurant Management

Binghamton, New York

GENERAL INFORMATION
Public, coeducational, two-year college. Suburban campus. Founded in 1946. Accredited by Middle States Association of Colleges and Schools.

PROGRAM INFORMATION
Offered since 1986. Program calendar is divided into semesters. 2-year associate degree in hotel restaurant management.

PROGRAM AFFILIATION
Council on Hotel, Restaurant, and Institutional Education; National Restaurant Association; National Restaurant Association Educational Foundation; New York State Hospitality and Tourism Association.

AREAS OF STUDY
Controlling costs in food service; convenience cookery; culinary skill development; food preparation; food service math; management and human resources.

Broome Community College *(continued)*

FACILITIES
3 classrooms; computer laboratory; demonstration laboratory; food production kitchen; laboratory; lecture room; teaching kitchen.

STUDENT PROFILE
78 total: 63 full-time; 15 part-time. 57 are under 25 years old; 19 are between 25 and 44 years old; 2 are over 44 years old.

FACULTY
1 total: 1 full-time. 1 is an industry professional; 2 are culinary-certified teachers. Faculty-student ratio: 1:78.

SPECIAL PROGRAMS
American Hotel and Lodging Association and food service trade shows, internship opportunities for credit (one year), study abroad and international internship opportunities.

TYPICAL EXPENSES
In-state tuition: $3058 per year full-time (in district), $128 per credit hour part-time. Out-of-state tuition: $6116 per year full-time, $256 per credit hour part-time.

FINANCIAL AID
Employment placement assistance is available.

HOUSING
Average off-campus housing cost per month: $300–$400.

APPLICATION INFORMATION
Students may begin participation in January and September. Applications are accepted continuously. In 2006, 78 applied; 78 were accepted.

CONTACT
Gregory Saracero, Dean, Division of Business and Public Services, Hotel Restaurant Management, PO Box 1017, Binghamton, NY 13902. Telephone: 607-778-5008. E-mail: saracero_g@sunybroome.edu. World Wide Web: http://www.sunybroome.edu.

CAREER ACADEMY OF NEW YORK

New York, New York

GENERAL INFORMATION
Founded in 1935. Accredited by Accrediting Commission of Career Schools and Colleges of Technology.

PROGRAM INFORMATION
Certificate in baking and pastry arts II. Certificate in baking and pastry arts I. 600-hour certificate in commercial cooking. 900-hour certificate in hotel management. 900-hour certificate in commercial cooking. 900-hour certificate in commercial cooking and catering.

SPECIAL PROGRAMS
Externship.

APPLICATION INFORMATION
Applicants must interview; submit a formal application and high school diploma or equivalent.

CONTACT
Director of Student Services, 154 West 14th Street, New York, NY 10011-7307. Telephone: 212-675-6655. World Wide Web: http://www.culinaryacademy.edu.

CULINARY ACADEMY OF LONG ISLAND

Syosset, New York

GENERAL INFORMATION
Private, coeducational, culinary institute. Suburban campus. Founded in 1996. Accredited by Accrediting Commission of Career Schools and Colleges of Technology.

PROGRAM INFORMATION
Offered since 1996. Program calendar is continuous. Certificate in commercial cooking. 13-session certificate in advanced baking/pastry arts. 13-session certificate in basic baking pastry arts. 9-month certificate in hotel management (evening courses available). 900-hour certificate in professional cooking.

PROGRAM AFFILIATION
American Culinary Federation; American Hotel and Lodging Association; National Restaurant Association Educational Foundation.

FINANCIAL AID
Employment placement assistance is available.

APPLICATION INFORMATION
Applications are accepted continuously. Applicants must interview.

CONTACT
Director of Admissions, 125 Michael Drive, Syosset, NY 11791. Telephone: 516-364-4344. Fax: 516-846-8488. E-mail: admissions@culinaryacademy.com. World Wide Web: http://www.culinaryacademyli.com.

THE CULINARY INSTITUTE OF AMERICA

Hyde Park, New York

GENERAL INFORMATION
Private, coeducational, four-year college. Small-town setting. Founded in 1946. Accredited by Middle States Association of Colleges and Schools.

PROGRAM INFORMATION
Offered since 1946. Program calendar is continuous. 2-year associate degree in baking and pastry arts. 2-year associate degree in culinary arts. 4-year bachelor's degree in baking and pastry arts management. 4-year bachelor's degree in culinary arts management.

FACILITIES
9 bake shops; library; 5 public restaurants; 32 teaching kitchens.

STUDENT PROFILE
2700 full-time.

FACULTY
Prominent faculty: Thomas Vaccaro, CEPC; Eve Felder, CEC, CHC; Oliver Andreini, CMC, CHE.

TYPICAL EXPENSES
Application fee: $50. Tuition: $21,280 per full academic year. Program-related fees include $995–$1180 for books and supplies; $495 for general fee; $1120 for board (mandatory).

FINANCIAL AID
Employment placement assistance is available. Employment opportunities within the program are available.

HOUSING
Coed housing available.

APPLICATION INFORMATION
Applicants must submit a formal application, letters of reference, an essay, academic transcript; have an interview (for bachelor's degree); take an assessment test.

CONTACT
Director of Admissions, 1946 Campus Drive, Hyde Park, NY 12538. Telephone: 845-452-9600. Fax: 845-451-1068. E-mail: admissions@culinary.edu. World Wide Web: http://www.ciachef.edu.

See display on page 242.

ERIE COMMUNITY COLLEGE, CITY CAMPUS

Culinary Arts

Buffalo, New York

GENERAL INFORMATION
Public, coeducational, two-year college. Urban campus. Founded in 1971. Accredited by Middle States Association of Colleges and Schools.

PROGRAM INFORMATION
Offered since 1984. Program calendar is divided into semesters. 1-year certificate in baking and pastry arts. 2-year associate degree in culinary arts.

PROGRAM AFFILIATION
American Culinary Federation; National Restaurant Association; National Restaurant Association Educational Foundation.

AREAS OF STUDY
Baking; beverage management; buffet catering; confectionery show pieces; controlling costs in food service; culinary skill development; food preparation; food purchasing; food service math; garde-manger; international cuisine; introduction to food service; kitchen management; management and human resources; meal planning; menu and facilities design; nutrition; sanitation; soup, stock, sauce, and starch production; wines and spirits.

FACILITIES
Bake shop; bakery; cafeteria; classroom; coffee shop; computer laboratory; 2 food production kitchens; gourmet dining room; learning resource center; library; 3 teaching kitchens.

STUDENT PROFILE
83 total: 71 full-time; 12 part-time. 46 are under 25 years old; 31 are between 25 and 44 years old; 6 are over 44 years old.

FACULTY
12 total: 4 full-time; 8 part-time. 10 are industry professionals; 2 are culinary-certified teachers. Prominent faculty: Paul J. Cannamela, CCE, AAC; Anthony Songin. Faculty-student ratio: 1:16.

TYPICAL EXPENSES
Application fee: $25. In-state tuition: $1493.50 per semester full-time (in district), $125 per credit hour part-time (in district), $2987 per semester full-time (out-of-district), $250 per credit hour part-time (out-of-district). Out-of-state tuition: $2987 per semester full-time, $250 per credit hour part-time.

Tuition for international students: $2987 per semester full-time, $250 per credit hour part-time. Program-related fees include $185 for knives; $600 for books; $175 for uniforms.

FINANCIAL AID

In 2006, 50 scholarships were awarded (average award was $700); 40 loans were granted (average loan was $1500). Program-specific awards include Statler Foundation Scholarship. Employment placement assistance is available. Employment opportunities within the program are available.

APPLICATION INFORMATION

Students may begin participation in January and September. Applications are accepted continuously. In 2006, 126 applied; 92 were accepted. Applicants must submit a formal application.

CONTACT

Richard Mills, Professor, Culinary Arts, 121 Ellicott Street, Buffalo, NY 14203-2698. Telephone: 716-851-1034. Fax: 716-851-1133. E-mail: millsr@ecc.edu. World Wide Web: http://www.ecc.edu.

ERIE COMMUNITY COLLEGE, NORTH CAMPUS

Food Service Administration/Restaurant Management

Williamsville, New York

GENERAL INFORMATION

Public, coeducational, two-year college. Suburban campus. Founded in 1946. Accredited by Middle States Association of Colleges and Schools.

PROGRAM INFORMATION

Offered since 1953. Accredited by American Dietetic Association, Council on Hotel, Restaurant and Institutional Education, Commission on Accreditation of Hospitality Management Programs. Program calendar is divided into semesters. 2-year associate degree in culinary arts. 2-year associate degree in food service administration: dietetic technology/nutrition. 2-year associate degree in hotel/restaurant management.

PROGRAM AFFILIATION

American Culinary Federation; American Dietetic Association; Confrerie de la Chaine des Rotisseurs; Council on Hotel, Restaurant, and Institutional Education; International Food Service Executives Association; International Foodservice Editorial Council;

National Restaurant Association; National Restaurant Association Educational Foundation; New York State Restaurant Association.

AREAS OF STUDY

Baking; beverage management; buffet catering; controlling costs in food service; culinary skill development; food preparation; food purchasing; food service communication; food service math; garde-manger; international cuisine; introduction to food service; kitchen management; management and human resources; meal planning; menu and facilities design; nutrition; nutrition and food service; sanitation; soup, stock, sauce, and starch production; wines and spirits.

FACILITIES

Bake shop; bakery; cafeteria; 2 classrooms; computer laboratory; demonstration laboratory; 3 food production kitchens; gourmet dining room; laboratory; lecture room; library; 2 public restaurants; student lounge; teaching kitchen.

STUDENT PROFILE

250 total: 201 full-time; 49 part-time. 169 are under 25 years old; 65 are between 25 and 44 years old; 16 are over 44 years old.

FACULTY

36 total: 8 full-time; 28 part-time. 18 are industry professionals; 2 are master chefs; 1 is a master baker; 4 are culinary-certified teachers. Prominent faculty: Terance McDonough; Jane Myers-Reitmeier; Mark Wright, CEC; Donald Spasiano. Faculty-student ratio: 1:16.

SPECIAL PROGRAMS

8-week off-campus internship, culinary competitions.

TYPICAL EXPENSES

Application fee: $25. In-state tuition: $1493.50 per semester full-time (in district), $125 per credit hour part-time (in district), $2987 per semester full-time (out-of-district), $250 per credit hour part-time (out-of-district). Out-of-state tuition: $2987 per semester full-time, $250 per credit hour part-time. Tuition for international students: $2987 per semester full-time, $250 per credit hour part-time. Program-related fees include $70 for lab fee (per semester); $150 for cutlery; $100 for uniforms.

FINANCIAL AID

In 2006, 50 scholarships were awarded (average award was $500–$750). Program-specific awards include Erie Community College Foundation scholarships; American Dietetic Association Scholarship, Gertrude Chrymko Memorial Scholarship, Statler Foundation Scholarships, New York State Restaurant Association Scholarships. Employment placement assistance is available. Employment opportunities within the program are available.

Erie Community College, North Campus *(continued)*

APPLICATION INFORMATION
Students may begin participation in January and September. Applications are accepted continuously. In 2006, 207 applied; 181 were accepted. Applicants must submit a formal application.

CONTACT
Mark Wright (culinary arts/hotel restaurant), Margaret Garfoot (dietetics), Food Service Administration/ Restaurant Management, 6205 Main Street, Williamsville, NY 14221. Telephone: 716-851-1391. Fax: 716-851-1429. E-mail: wrightm@ecc.edu or garfoot@ecc. edu. World Wide Web: http://www.ecc.edu.

THE FRENCH CULINARY INSTITUTE AT THE INTERNATIONAL CULINARY CENTER

Classic Culinary Arts

New York, New York

GENERAL INFORMATION
Private, coeducational, culinary institute. Urban campus. Founded in 1984. Accredited by Accrediting Commission of Career Schools and Colleges of Technology.

PROGRAM INFORMATION
Offered since 1984. Accredited by Accrediting Commission of Career Schools and Colleges of Technology. Program calendar is continuous, six-week cycles. 10-hour certificate in plating and food styling. 100-hour certificate in pastry techniques. 110-hour certificate in culinary techniques. 12-hour certificate in magic potions: hydrocolloids. 12-hour certificate in whole grain breads. 120-hour certificate in restaurant bread baking. 15-hour certificate in knife skills, deboning, & filleting. 15-hour certificate in chocolate desserts. 15-week certificate in restaurant management. 20-hour certificate in sous vide & low temperature cooking. 25-hour certificate in breakfast breads, pastries, and more. 25-hour certificate in fondant & royal icing. 29-week diploma in The Italian Culinary Academy-Italian culinary experience. 30-hour certificate in artisanal bread baking. 35-hour certificate in The Italian Culinary Academy-Italian fish and shellfish. 35-hour certificate in The Italian Culinary Academy-Italian meat and poultry. 35-hour certificate in The Italian Culinary Academy-Italian cheese, wine and vegetables. 35-hour certificate in The Italian Culinary Academy-Italian pastries, gelato and more. 35-hour certificate in The Italian Culinary Academy-pasta, pizza, polenta and more. 40-hour certificate in The Italian Culinary Academy-essentials of Italian cooking. 6-hour certificate in magic potions: transglutaminase. 6-month diploma in classic culinary arts. 6-month diploma in classic pastry arts. 6-week certificate in food & wine pairing. 6-week certificate in the craft of food writing. 6-week diploma in the art of international bread baking. 60-hour certificate in culinary techniques 2. 8-week certificate in essentials of fine cooking. 8-week certificate in fundamentals of wine.

PROGRAM AFFILIATION
American Institute of Baking; American Institute of Wine & Food; Chefs Collaborative 2000; Council on Hotel, Restaurant, and Institutional Education; Federation of Dining Rooms Professionals; International Association of Culinary Professionals; James Beard Foundation, Inc.; National Restaurant Association; National Restaurant Association Educational Foundation; Slow Food International; The Bread Bakers Guild of America; Women Chefs and Restaurateurs.

AREAS OF STUDY
Baking; beverage management; buffet catering; confectionery show pieces; culinary French; culinary skill development; food preparation; food purchasing; garde-manger; introduction to food service; kitchen management; management and human resources; meal planning; meat cutting; menu and facilities design; nutrition and food service; patisserie; restaurant opportunities; sanitation; saucier; seafood processing; soup, stock, sauce, and starch production; wines and spirits.

FACILITIES
4 classrooms; computer laboratory; demonstration laboratory; food production kitchen; gourmet dining room; 4 lecture rooms; library; public restaurant; student lounge; 13 teaching kitchens.

STUDENT PROFILE
1,098 total: 463 full-time; 635 part-time. 443 are under 25 years old; 613 are between 25 and 44 years old; 42 are over 44 years old.

FACULTY
52 total: 52 full-time. Prominent faculty: Jacques Pépin; André Soltner; Alain Sailhac; Jacques Torres; Andrea Robinson; Alan Richman. Faculty-student ratio: 1:12.

PROMINENT ALUMNI AND CURRENT AFFILIATION
Bobby Flay, Mesa Grill, Bolo, Bar Americain; Dan Barber, Blue Hill and Blue Hill of Stone Barns; Wylie Dufresne, wd~50.

SPECIAL PROGRAMS
Demonstrations in International Culinary Theater, internships, student clubs and activities: Supper Club, Wine Club, Career Avenues, Forager Club, International Student Club.

TYPICAL EXPENSES
Application fee: $100. Tuition: Tuition varies by program. Contact school directly for current costs. Program-related fees include $10 for insurance; $40–$700 for books, tools, and uniforms.

FINANCIAL AID
In 2006, 41 scholarships were awarded (average award was $4756.05); 518 loans were granted (average loan was $38,697.12). Employment placement assistance is available. Employment opportunities within the program are available.

HOUSING
Coed and apartment-style housing available. Average on-campus housing cost per month: $1060. Average off-campus housing cost per month: $2000.

APPLICATION INFORMATION
Students may begin participation year-round. Applications are accepted continuously. In 2006, 2008 applied; 1985 were accepted. Applicants must interview; submit a formal application, an essay, proof of high school graduation or equivalent, and resume (career programs only).

CONTACT
Claudia Ramone, Director of Admission, Classic Culinary Arts, 462 Broadway, 4th Floor, New York, NY 10013. Telephone: 888-324-CHEF. Fax: 212-431-3065. E-mail: info@frenchculinary.com. World Wide Web: http://www.frenchculinary.com.

See color display following page 234.

GENESEE COMMUNITY COLLEGE
Tourism and Hospitality Management
Batavia, New York

GENERAL INFORMATION
Public, coeducational, two-year college. Small-town setting. Founded in 1967. Accredited by Middle States Association of Colleges and Schools.

PROGRAM INFORMATION
Offered since 1967. Program calendar is divided into semesters. 2-year associate degree in tourism and hospitality management. 2-year certificate in hospitality management.

AREAS OF STUDY
Management and human resources.

STUDENT PROFILE
17 total: 14 full-time; 3 part-time.

FACULTY
3 total: 1 full-time; 2 part-time. 3 are industry professionals. Faculty-student ratio: 1:17.

TYPICAL EXPENSES
In-state tuition: $3300 per year full-time (in district), $136 per credit hour part-time. Out-of-state tuition: $3900 per year full-time, $154 per credit hour part-time. Tuition for international students: $3900 per year full-time, $154 per credit hour part-time.

HOUSING
Coed housing available. Average on-campus housing cost per month: $544. Average off-campus housing cost per month: $500.

APPLICATION INFORMATION
Students may begin participation in January and August. In 2006, 42 applied.

CONTACT
Tanya Lane-Martin, Admission Office, Tourism and Hospitality Management, 1 College Road, Batavia, NY 14020. Telephone: 866-CALLGCC. Fax: 585-345-6842. E-mail: tmlanemartin@genesee.edu. World Wide Web: http://www.genesee.edu.

THE INSTITUTE OF CULINARY EDUCATION
New York, New York

GENERAL INFORMATION
Private, coeducational, culinary institute. Urban campus. Founded in 1975. Accredited by Accrediting Commission of Career Schools and Colleges of Technology.

PROGRAM INFORMATION
Offered since 1975. Accredited by Accrediting Commission of Career Schools and Colleges of Technology (ACCSCT). Program calendar is continuous. 26-week diploma in full-time career Culinary Management. 26-week diploma in full-time career Pastry and Baking Arts. 28-week diploma in full-time career Culinary Arts. 31-week diploma in part-time career Pastry and Baking Arts. 34-week diploma in part-time career Culinary Arts. 39-week diploma in weekend part-time career Pastry and Baking Arts. 39-week diploma in weekend part-time Culinary Arts.

The Institute of Culinary Education *(continued)*

PROGRAM AFFILIATION

American Institute of Wine & Food; International Association of Culinary Professionals; International Wine & Food Society; James Beard Foundation, Inc.; National Restaurant Association; National Restaurant Association Educational Foundation; Society of Wine Educators; Sommelier Society of America; The Bread Bakers Guild of America; United States Personal Chef Association; Women Chefs and Restaurateurs.

AREAS OF STUDY

Baking; beverage management; buffet catering; controlling costs in food service; culinary French; culinary skill development; food preparation; food purchasing; food service communication; food service math; garde-manger; international cuisine; introduction to food service; kitchen management; management and human resources; meal planning; meat cutting; meat fabrication; menu and facilities design; nutrition; nutrition and food service; patisserie; restaurant opportunities; sanitation; seafood processing; soup, stock, sauce, and starch production; wines and spirits.

FACILITIES

Bake shop; catering service; 3 classrooms; 2 demonstration laboratories; food production kitchen; lecture room; library; 2 student lounges; 12 teaching kitchens.

STUDENT PROFILE

750 total: 586 full-time; 164 part-time. 101 are under 25 years old; 577 are between 25 and 44 years old; 72 are over 44 years old.

FACULTY

32 total: 24 full-time; 8 part-time. Prominent faculty: Nick Malgieri; Toba Garrett; Michael Handel, CCC, CCE; Chris Gesaldi. Faculty-student ratio: 1:14.

PROMINENT ALUMNI AND CURRENT AFFILIATION

Marc Murphy, Chef/Owner, Landmarc; Gina DePalma, Executive Pastry Chef, Babbo; Susan Stockton, Vice President of Culinary Production, Food Network,.

SPECIAL PROGRAMS

210-hours in critically-acclaimed restaurants, hotels, pastry or catering facilities. Sites include: Union Square Café, Le Bernadin, Gramercy Tavern, Daniel, Mesa Grill, and Nobu, 9-day student trip to France including cooking and baking classes, market visits and vineyard tours, elective classes on specialized wine, baking, and cooking topics. Advanced pastry program with visiting masters are available for alumni via ICE's Center for Advance Pastry Studies (CAPS).

TYPICAL EXPENSES

Application fee: $25. Tuition: $28,017 for Culinary Arts Diploma program, including supplies; $12,000 for Culinary Management program; $26,334 for Pastry & Baking Arts Diploma program, including supplies.

FINANCIAL AID

In 2006, 47 scholarships were awarded (average award was $4000); 450 loans were granted (average loan was $27,000). Program-specific awards include career placement services are available.

APPLICATION INFORMATION

Students may begin participation year-round. Applications are accepted continuously. In 2006, 1856 applied; 750 were accepted. Applicants must interview; submit a formal application and schedule a personal school tour.

CONTACT

Stephen Tave, Admissions Department, Institute of Culinary Education, 50 West 23rd Street—5th Floor, New York, NY 10010. Telephone: 888-861-CHEF. E-mail: stave@iceculinary.com. World Wide Web: http://www.ICEculinary.com.

See color display following page 234.

JULIE SAHNI'S SCHOOL OF INDIAN COOKING

Brooklyn, New York

GENERAL INFORMATION

Private, coeducational, culinary institute. Urban campus. Founded in 1974.

PROGRAM INFORMATION

Offered since 1974. Program calendar is divided into weekends, weekends. 3-day diploma in vegetarian cooking. 3-day diploma in Indian cooking. 3-day diploma in spices and herbs.

PROGRAM AFFILIATION

International Association of Culinary Professionals.

AREAS OF STUDY

Indian cooking; international cuisine; spices and herbs.

FACULTY

1 total: 1 full-time. 1 is a master chef. Prominent faculty: Julie Sahni.

TYPICAL EXPENSES

Application fee: $35. Tuition: $1295–$1795 per $1295 (2 day program) and $1795 (4 day program).

APPLICATION INFORMATION

Students may begin participation in January, February, March, April, May, June, September, October, November, and December. Applications are accepted continuously. Applicants must submit a formal application.

CONTACT

Julie Sahni, President, PO Box 023792, Brooklyn, NY 11202-3792. Telephone: 718-772-5600. Fax: 718-625-3958. E-mail: jsicooking@aol.com.

MOHAWK VALLEY COMMUNITY COLLEGE

Hospitality Programs

Rome, New York

GENERAL INFORMATION

Public, coeducational, two-year college. Urban campus. Founded in 1946. Accredited by Middle States Association of Colleges and Schools.

PROGRAM INFORMATION

Offered since 1980. Program calendar is divided into semesters. 1-year certificate in chef training. 2-year associate degree in hotel technology: meeting services management. 2-year associate degree in culinary arts management. 2-year associate degree in food service administration: restaurant management.

PROGRAM AFFILIATION

American Culinary Federation; Council on Hotel, Restaurant, and Institutional Education; International Food Service Executives Association; National Restaurant Association; National Restaurant Association Educational Foundation.

AREAS OF STUDY

Baking; beverage management; buffet catering; controlling costs in food service; culinary skill development; food preparation; food purchasing; food service math; garde-manger; international cuisine; kitchen management; management and human resources; meal planning; meat cutting; meat fabrication; menu and facilities design; nutrition; patisserie; restaurant opportunities; sanitation; saucier; seafood processing; soup, stock, sauce, and starch production; wines and spirits.

FACILITIES

Bake shop; catering service; 6 classrooms; computer laboratory; demonstration laboratory; 2 food production kitchens; gourmet dining room; learning resource center; library; public restaurant; snack shop; student lounge; teaching kitchen; banquet room.

TYPICAL STUDENT PROFILE

120 total: 80 full-time; 40 part-time.

SPECIAL PROGRAMS

Annual participation in National Restaurant Association and International Hotel and Motel Association shows, semester-long internship/co-op experience.

FINANCIAL AID

Employment placement assistance is available. Employment opportunities within the program are available.

APPLICATION INFORMATION

Students may begin participation in January, May, and August. Applications are accepted continuously. Applicants must submit a formal application.

CONTACT

Director of Admissions, Hospitality Programs, 1101 Floyd Avenue, Rome, NY 13440. Telephone: 315-334-7702. World Wide Web: http://www.mvcc.edu.

MONROE COLLEGE

Hospitality Management

New Rochelle, New York

GENERAL INFORMATION

Private, coeducational, four-year college. Suburban campus. Founded in 1933. Accredited by Middle States Association of Colleges and Schools.

PROGRAM INFORMATION

Offered since 1993. Program calendar is divided into trimesters. 16-month associate degree in baking and pastry arts. 16-month associate degree in culinary arts. 16-month associate degree in hotel/restaurant management. 32-month bachelor's degree in hotel/restaurant management.

PROGRAM AFFILIATION

American Culinary Federation; American Hotel and Lodging Association; Caribbean Tourism Association; Council on Hotel, Restaurant, and Institutional Education; International Association of Culinary Professionals; James Beard Foundation, Inc.; National

Monroe College *(continued)*

Restaurant Association; National Restaurant Association Educational Foundation; Sommelier Society of America; The Bread Bakers Guild of America; Women Chefs and Restaurateurs.

AREAS OF STUDY

Baking; confectionery show pieces; culinary skill development; food preparation; food purchasing; food service math; garde-manger; international cuisine; introduction to food service; kitchen management; management and human resources; menu and facilities design; patisserie; restaurant opportunities; sanitation; soup, stock, sauce, and starch production.

FACILITIES

Bake shop; bakery; 10 classrooms; 6 computer laboratories; demonstration laboratory; 2 food production kitchens; garden; gourmet dining room; 3 laboratories; 2 learning resource centers; 10 lecture rooms; 2 libraries; public restaurant; student lounge; 3 teaching kitchens.

STUDENT PROFILE

658 total: 644 full-time; 14 part-time.

FACULTY

15 total: 8 full-time; 7 part-time. 15 are industry professionals. Prominent faculty: Luke Schultheis; Daniel Hinder; Michael Rothman. Faculty-student ratio: 1:20.

SPECIAL PROGRAMS

Paid internships in New York City, semester of study abroad in Italy, residential internships abroad.

TYPICAL EXPENSES

Application fee: $35. Tuition: $4992 per semester full-time, $1248 per 3 credits part-time.

FINANCIAL AID

In 2006, 10 scholarships were awarded (average award was $4500). Program-specific awards include industry scholarships, Trades Council (NYC Hotel) scholarship, AH&LA Foundation scholarship. Employment placement assistance is available. Employment opportunities within the program are available.

HOUSING

Coed, apartment-style, and single-sex housing available. Average on-campus housing cost per month: $841. Average off-campus housing cost per month: $700.

APPLICATION INFORMATION

Students may begin participation in January, May, and September. Applications are accepted continuously. In 2006, 613 applied; 179 were accepted. Applicants must interview; submit a formal application, letters of reference, and an essay.

CONTACT

Luke D. Schultheis, Dean of the School of Hospitality Management and The Culinary Arts, Hospitality Management, 434 Main Street, New Rochelle, NY 10801. Telephone: 914-632-5400. Fax: 914-632-8506. E-mail: lschultheis@monroecollege.edu. World Wide Web: http://www.monroecollege.edu.

MONROE COMMUNITY COLLEGE

Department of Hospitality Management

Rochester, New York

GENERAL INFORMATION

Public, coeducational, two-year college. Suburban campus. Founded in 1961. Accredited by Middle States Association of Colleges and Schools.

PROGRAM INFORMATION

Offered since 1967. National Restaurant Association Educational Foundation ManageFirst certificates available. Program calendar is divided into semesters. 16-month certificate in travel and tourism. 16-month certificate in hotel management. 16-month certificate in culinary arts. 16-month certificate in food management. 2-year associate degree in hospitality management-travel and tourism. 2-year associate degree in hospitality management-physical fitness. 2-year associate degree in hospitality management-golf management. 2-year associate degree in hospitality management-food service. 2-year associate degree in hospitality management-hotel.

PROGRAM AFFILIATION

American Culinary Federation; American Dietetic Association; Council on Hotel, Restaurant, and Institutional Education; International Food Service Executives Association; National Restaurant Association; National Restaurant Association Educational Foundation.

AREAS OF STUDY

Baking; beverage management; buffet catering; controlling costs in food service; culinary French; culinary skill development; food preparation; food purchasing; introduction to food service; kitchen management; management and human resources; meal planning; menu and facilities design; nutrition; nutrition and food service; restaurant opportunities; sanitation; soup, stock, sauce, and starch production.

FACILITIES

2 cafeterias; 2 catering services; coffee shop; 12 computer laboratories; 4 demonstration laboratories; 3 food production kitchens; gourmet dining room; 10 learning resource centers; 2 libraries; public restaurant; snack shop; 2 student lounges; 3 teaching kitchens.

STUDENT PROFILE
327 total: 247 full-time; 80 part-time. 164 are under 25 years old; 120 are between 25 and 44 years old; 43 are over 44 years old.

FACULTY
15 total: 5 full-time; 10 part-time. 5 are industry professionals; 2 are culinary-certified teachers. Prominent faculty: Diane Cheasty, CHA, CHE; Michelle Bartell, RD; Kim Wightman, CFE; Gerald Brinkman, Chef. Faculty-student ratio: 1:19.

SPECIAL PROGRAMS
Visits to various culinary conventions, culinary tour of Italy-Florence Culinary Institute.

TYPICAL EXPENSES
Application fee: $20. In-state tuition: $2800 per year full-time (in district), $117 per credit hour part-time. Out-of-state tuition: $5600 per year full-time, $234 per credit hour part-time. Program-related fee includes $50 for lab fees.

FINANCIAL AID
In 2006, 15 scholarships were awarded (average award was $1000). Employment placement assistance is available. Employment opportunities within the program are available.

HOUSING
Coed housing available.

APPLICATION INFORMATION
Students may begin participation in January, May, June, and September. Applications are accepted continuously. In 2006, 445 applied; 311 were accepted. Applicants must submit a formal application.

CONTACT
Prof. Diane Cheasty, Chairperson-Hospitality Management, Department of Hospitality Management, 1000 East Henrietta Road, Rochester, NY 14623. Telephone: 585-292-2580. Fax: 585-292-3826. E-mail: dcheasty@monroecc.edu. World Wide Web: http://www.monroecc.edu.

NASSAU COMMUNITY COLLEGE

Garden City, New York

GENERAL INFORMATION
Public, coeducational, two-year college. Suburban campus. Founded in 1959. Accredited by Middle States Association of Colleges and Schools.

PROGRAM INFORMATION
Offered since 1973. Program calendar is divided into semesters. 1-year certificate in food service technology. 1-year certificate in dietary management. 2-year associate degree in food service administration. 2-year associate degree in food and nutrition. 2-year associate degree in hotel technology administration.

PROGRAM AFFILIATION
American Culinary Federation; American Dietetic Association; Council on Hotel, Restaurant, and Institutional Education; National Restaurant Association; National Restaurant Association Educational Foundation.

AREAS OF STUDY
Baking; beverage management; buffet catering; controlling costs in food service; culinary skill development; food preparation; food purchasing; garde-manger; international cuisine; introduction to food service; kitchen management; management and human resources; meal planning; meat cutting; meat fabrication; menu and facilities design; nutrition and food service; restaurant opportunities; sanitation; saucier; soup, stock, sauce, and starch production; wines and spirits.

FACILITIES
Bake shop; 3 cafeterias; catering service; 3 classrooms; 3 coffee shops; 2 computer laboratories; 3 demonstration laboratories; 4 food production kitchens; 2 laboratories; 5 learning resource centers; 6 lecture rooms; library; 2 snack shops; student lounge; 2 teaching kitchens.

FACULTY
11 total: 6 full-time; 5 part-time. Prominent faculty: Christopher Argento, RD, CEC, CCE; Eric Schafler; Anthony Bruno; Tom Field. Faculty-student ratio: 1:18.

PROMINENT ALUMNI AND CURRENT AFFILIATION
John Molino, Tavern on the Green; Jonathan Nosotsky, Cheese Cake Factory.

SPECIAL PROGRAMS
6-month internship at Walt Disney World, 2-week international study abroad (Italy), 4-6 month international work co-op (England).

TYPICAL EXPENSES
Application fee: $20. In-state tuition: $1655 per semester full-time (in district), $138 per credit part-time. Out-of-state tuition: $3310 per semester full-time, $276 per credit part-time.

FINANCIAL AID
In 2006, 3 scholarships were awarded (average award was $500). Employment placement assistance is available. Employment opportunities within the program are available.

Nassau Community College *(continued)*

APPLICATION INFORMATION
Students may begin participation in January and September. Applications are accepted continuously.

CONTACT
Anne Cubeta, Chairman, Hotel/Restaurant Department, Building K, Garden City, NY 11530. Telephone: 516-572-7344. Fax: 516-572-9739. E-mail: anne.cubeta@ncc.edu. World Wide Web: http://www.sunynassau.edu.

THE NATURAL GOURMET INSTITUTE FOR HEALTH AND CULINARY ARTS

Chef's Training Program

New York, New York

GENERAL INFORMATION
Private, coeducational, culinary institute. Urban campus. Founded in 1977. Accredited by Accrediting Council for Continuing Education and Training.

PROGRAM INFORMATION
Program calendar is continuous. 5-month (full-time), 11 month (part-time) diploma in health-supportive culinary arts.

PROGRAM AFFILIATION
International Association of Culinary Professionals; James Beard Foundation, Inc.

AREAS OF STUDY
Baking; business and career skills; controlling costs in food service; culinary skill development; food preparation; food purchasing; food service math; garde-manger; international cooking; international cuisine; living foods; meal planning; nutrition; sanitation; saucier; seafood processing; soup, stock, sauce, and starch production; teaching a cooking class; theoretical approaches to diet and health.

FACILITIES
3 food production kitchens; 2 lecture rooms; library; student lounge.

STUDENT PROFILE
165 total: 100 full-time; 65 part-time. 20 are under 25 years old; 125 are between 25 and 44 years old; 20 are over 44 years old.

FACULTY
19 total: 7 full-time; 12 part-time. Faculty-student ratio: 1:16.

SPECIAL PROGRAMS
Individualized internships, culinary tours of New York City.

TYPICAL EXPENSES
Application fee: $100. Tuition: $19,350 per full program (5 months, full-time; 11 months, part-time). Tuition for international students: $19,350 per full program (5 months, full-time; 11 months, part-time). Program-related fees include $325 for knife and tool kit; $75 for uniform items; $25 for pastry and baking kit.

FINANCIAL AID
In 2006, 2 scholarships were awarded (average award was $1000). Employment placement assistance is available.

HOUSING
Average off-campus housing cost per month: $800.

APPLICATION INFORMATION
Students may begin participation year-round. Applications are accepted continuously. In 2006, 190 applied; 165 were accepted. Applicants must interview; submit a formal application, letters of reference, an essay, documentation of education.

CONTACT
Merle Brown, Vice President/Director of Admissions, Chef's Training Program, 48 West 21st Street, 2nd Floor, New York, NY 10010. Telephone: 212-645-5170 Ext. 109. Fax: 212-989-1493. E-mail: admissions@naturalgourmetschool.com. World Wide Web: http://www.naturalgourmetschool.com.

NEW YORK CITY COLLEGE OF TECHNOLOGY OF THE CITY UNIVERSITY OF NEW YORK

Hospitality Management

Brooklyn, New York

GENERAL INFORMATION
Public, coeducational, four-year college. Urban campus. Founded in 1946. Accredited by Middle States Association of Colleges and Schools.

PROGRAM INFORMATION
Offered since 1947. Accredited by Council on Hotel, Restaurant and Institutional Education, ACPHA-Accrediting Commission for Programs in Hospitality Administration. Program calendar is divided into semesters. 2-year associate degree in hospitality management. 4-year bachelor's degree in hospitality management.

PROGRAM AFFILIATION

American Culinary Federation; American Institute of Wine & Food; Council on Hotel, Restaurant, and Institutional Education; International Association of Culinary Professionals; James Beard Foundation, Inc.; National Restaurant Association; National Restaurant Association Educational Foundation; Women Chefs and Restaurateurs.

AREAS OF STUDY

Baking; beverage management; confectionery show pieces; controlling costs in food service; culinary French; food preparation; food purchasing; garde-manger; introduction to food service; management and human resources; meal planning; menu and facilities design; nutrition; patisserie; sanitation; saucier; seafood processing; soup, stock, sauce, and starch production; wines and spirits.

FACILITIES

2 bake shops; 4 classrooms; 2 computer laboratories; demonstration laboratory; food production kitchen; gourmet dining room; laboratory; learning resource center; 3 lecture rooms; library; teaching kitchen.

STUDENT PROFILE

740 total: 630 full-time; 110 part-time.

FACULTY

35 total: 15 full-time; 20 part-time. 11 are industry professionals; 2 are master bakers; 2 are culinary-certified teachers. Prominent faculty: Jean Claude, CCE, CHE; Julia V. Jordan; Elizabeth Schaible, CHE; Louise Hoffman. Faculty-student ratio: 1:18.

PROMINENT ALUMNI AND CURRENT AFFILIATION

Michael Lomanaco, Porterhouse.

SPECIAL PROGRAMS

Summer work abroad (hotels and restaurants in France, Germany, Italy, and Spain), study abroad in Paris, Disney internships.

TYPICAL EXPENSES

Application fee: $50. In-state tuition: $2000 per semester full-time (in district), $170 per credit part-time. Out-of-state tuition: $360 per credit full-time, $360 per credit part-time.

FINANCIAL AID

In 2006, 30 scholarships were awarded (average award was $1500). Employment placement assistance is available.

HOUSING

Average off-campus housing cost per month: $1200.

APPLICATION INFORMATION

Students may begin participation in February and September. Applications are accepted continuously. Applicants must submit a formal application.

CONTACT

Elizabeth Schaible, Chairperson, Hospitality Management, 300 Jay Street N220, Brooklyn, NY 11201. Telephone: 718-260-5630. Fax: 718-254-8682. E-mail: hospitalitymgmt@citytech.cuny.edu. World Wide Web: http://www.citytech.cuny.edu.

NEW YORK INSTITUTE OF TECHNOLOGY

Center for Hospitality and Culinary Arts

Central Islip, New York

GENERAL INFORMATION

Private, coeducational, comprehensive institution. Suburban campus. Founded in 1955. Accredited by Middle States Association of Colleges and Schools.

PROGRAM INFORMATION

Offered since 1985. Accredited by American Culinary Federation Accrediting Commission. Program calendar is divided into semesters. 2-year associate degree in culinary arts. 4-year bachelor's degree in hospitality management. 500-hour certificate in baking and pastry arts. 500-hour certificate in culinary arts.

PROGRAM AFFILIATION

American Culinary Federation; American Institute of Wine & Food; Council on Hotel, Restaurant, and Institutional Education; International Association of Culinary Professionals; National Restaurant Association; National Restaurant Association Educational Foundation; Oldways Preservation and Exchange Trust; Women Chefs and Restaurateurs.

AREAS OF STUDY

Allergy specific foods and service; artisanal breads; baking; beverage management; buffet catering; confectionery show pieces; controlling costs in food service; convenience cookery; culinary horticulture; culinary skill development; food preparation; food purchasing; food service communication; food service math; garde-manger; international cuisine; kitchen management; management and human resources; meal planning; meat cutting; meat fabrication; menu and facilities design; nutrition; patisserie; restaurant opportunities; sanitation; saucier; seafood processing; soup, stock, sauce, and starch production; wines and spirits.

FACILITIES

Bake shop; bakery; 2 cafeterias; catering service; 10 classrooms; coffee shop; 3 computer laboratories; demonstration laboratory; 2 food production kitchens;

New York Institute of Technology *(continued)*

garden; gourmet dining room; learning resource center; library; public restaurant; snack shop; student lounge; 3 teaching kitchens; sugar and chocolate room; interactive synchronistic lab.

TYPICAL STUDENT PROFILE
142 total: 127 full-time; 15 part-time. 33 are under 25 years old; 101 are between 25 and 44 years old; 8 are over 44 years old.

SPECIAL PROGRAMS
Summer program in Switzerland and Italy, 3-month paid externship, culinary competitions.

FINANCIAL AID
Program-specific awards include Whitson's Scholarship ($500), J. King Scholarship ($1000), James Lewis Scholarship ($1000); Scotto Brothers Scholarship. Employment opportunities within the program are available.

HOUSING
Coed housing available.

APPLICATION INFORMATION
Students may begin participation in January and September. Application deadline for fall is June 1. Application deadline for spring is December 1. Applicants must submit a formal application, an essay; have a high school diploma; minimum combined SAT score of 800.

CONTACT
Director of Admissions, Center for Hospitality and Culinary Arts, PO Box 8000, Old Westbury, NY 11568-8000. Telephone: 800-345-NYIT. Fax: 516-686-7516. World Wide Web: http://iris.nyit.edu/culinary/.

NEW YORK UNIVERSITY

Steinhardt School of Culture, Education, and Human Development; Department of Nutrition, Food Studies, and Public Health

New York, New York

GENERAL INFORMATION
Private, coeducational, university. Urban campus. Founded in 1831. Accredited by Middle States Association of Colleges and Schools.

PROGRAM INFORMATION
Offered since 1926. Accredited by American Dietetic Association, Council on the Education of Public Health (CEPH). Program calendar is divided into semesters. 24-month master's degree in nutrition and dietetics.

24-month master's degree in food studies: food culture. 24-month master's degree in food studies: food systems. 4-year bachelor's degree in nutrition and dietetics. 4-year bachelor's degree in food and restaurant management. 4-year bachelor's degree in food studies. 5-year doctoral degree in nutrition and dietetics. 5-year doctoral degree in food studies and food management.

PROGRAM AFFILIATION
American Dietetic Association; Association for the Study of Food and Society.

AREAS OF STUDY
Community public health; food history and culture; food writing; introduction to food service; management and human resources; nutrition; nutrition and food service; public health nutrition.

FACILITIES
Classroom; computer laboratory; demonstration laboratory; food production kitchen; lecture room; library; teaching kitchen.

STUDENT PROFILE
501 total: 256 full-time; 245 part-time. 125 are under 25 years old; 313 are between 25 and 44 years old; 63 are over 44 years old.

FACULTY
59 total: 14 full-time; 45 part-time. 20 are industry professionals; 5 are culinary-certified teachers. Prominent faculty: Marion Nestle, PhD, MPH; Amy Bentley, PhD; Judith Gilbride PhD, RD; Sally Guttmacher, PhD; Beth Dixon, PhD. Faculty-student ratio: 1:7.

PROMINENT ALUMNI AND CURRENT AFFILIATION
Rose Levy Beranbaum, cookbook author; Julie O'Sullivan Maillet, PhD, RD, University of Medicine and Dentistry of New Jersey; Catherine Cowell, Ph.D, Former Director, Bureau of Nutrition.

SPECIAL PROGRAMS
Internships in every program, summer graduate study in Italy and South Africa, intersession courses.

TYPICAL EXPENSES
Application fee: $50–$65. Tuition: $17,645 per semester (undergraduate); $1097 per credit (graduate) full-time, $980 per credit (undergraduate); $1097 per credit (graduate) part-time. Program-related fees include $347 for fall 2007 registration fee; $362 for spring 2008 registration fee.

FINANCIAL AID

In 2006, 200 scholarships were awarded. Program-specific awards include food studies scholarships, graduate assistantships, teaching fellowships. Employment placement assistance is available. Employment opportunities within the program are available.

HOUSING

Coed, apartment-style, and single-sex housing available. Average on-campus housing cost per month: $1300. Average off-campus housing cost per month: $1500.

APPLICATION INFORMATION

Students may begin participation in January, May, June, July, and September. Application deadline for fall (doctoral) is December 15. Application deadline for fall (bachelor's) is January 15. Application deadline for fall (master's) is February 1. Application deadline for spring (bachelor's and master's) is November 1. In 2006, 314 applied; 233 were accepted. Applicants must submit a formal application, letters of reference, GRE score (MPH and doctoral applicants), MCAT score (alternate for MPH applicants), transcripts.

CONTACT

Kelli Ranieri, Department Administrator, Steinhardt School of Culture, Education, and Human Development; Department of Nutrition, Food Studies, and Public Health, 35 West 4th Street, Room 1077 I, New York, NY 10012. Telephone: 212-998-5580. Fax: 212-995-4194. E-mail: nutrition@nyu.edu. World Wide Web: http://www.steinhardt.nyu.edu.

NIAGARA COUNTY COMMUNITY COLLEGE

Culinary Arts Program

Sanborn, New York

GENERAL INFORMATION

Public, coeducational, two-year college. Founded in 1962. Accredited by Middle States Association of Colleges and Schools.

PROGRAM INFORMATION

Offered since 1976. Accredited by American Culinary Federation Accrediting Commission. Program calendar is divided into semesters. Associate degree in hospitality operations. 1-year certificate in casino operations. 1-year certificate in hospitality operations. 1-year certificate in food service. 1-year certificate in baking and pastry arts. 2-year associate degree in baking and pastry arts. 2-year associate degree in food services. 2-year associate degree in gaming and casino management. 2-year associate degree in hospitality management. 2-year associate degree in culinary arts.

PROGRAM AFFILIATION

American Culinary Federation; American Dietetic Association; National Restaurant Association.

AREAS OF STUDY

Baking; beverage management; casino management; controlling costs in food service; culinary French; food preparation; food purchasing; food service math; garde-manger; hospitality; international cuisine; introduction to food service; management and human resources; meat cutting; menu and facilities design; nutrition; patisserie; sanitation; saucier; soup, stock, sauce, and starch production; wines and spirits.

FACILITIES

Bake shop; cafeteria; 3 classrooms; coffee shop; computer laboratory; demonstration laboratory; food production kitchen; 3 laboratories; learning resource center; 5 lecture rooms; library; snack shop; 2 food preparation laboratories; baking laboratory.

STUDENT PROFILE

176 total: 150 full-time; 26 part-time. 85 are under 25 years old; 69 are between 25 and 44 years old; 22 are over 44 years old.

FACULTY

12 total: 6 full-time; 6 part-time. 6 are industry professionals; 2 are culinary-certified teachers; 1 is a registered dietitian. Prominent faculty: Carl B. Heintz, Professor; Sam Sheusi, Professor, CEC, CCE; Mark Mistriner, Associate Professor, CCC. Faculty-student ratio: 1:16 lab; 1:30 lecture.

SPECIAL PROGRAMS

Two 6-month internships/cooperative education, study abroad (Italy and France).

TYPICAL EXPENSES

In-state tuition: $2976 per year full-time (in district), $124 per credit hour part-time. Out-of-state tuition: $4464 per year full-time, $186 per credit hour part-time. Program-related fees include $60 for uniform; $150 for knives; $150–$200 for books.

FINANCIAL AID

In 2006, 3 scholarships were awarded (average award was $1000). Program-specific awards include Statler Foundation Scholarship, Antoncci scholarship. Employment placement assistance is available. Employment opportunities within the program are available.

Niagara County Community College *(continued)*

APPLICATION INFORMATION
Students may begin participation in January, May, and September. Application deadline for fall is August 29. Application deadline for spring is January 16. Application deadline for summer is June 9. In 2006, 200 applied. Applicants must submit a formal application.

CONTACT
Kathy Saunders, Director of Admissions, Culinary Arts Program, 3111 Saunders Settlement Road, Sanborn, NY 14132-9460. Telephone: 716-614-6201. Fax: 716-614-6820. E-mail: saunders@niagaracc.suny.edu. World Wide Web: http://www.niagaracc.suny.edu.

NIAGARA UNIVERSITY

College of Hospitality and Tourism Management

Niagara University, New York

GENERAL INFORMATION
Private, coeducational, comprehensive institution. Suburban campus. Founded in 1856. Accredited by Middle States Association of Colleges and Schools.

PROGRAM INFORMATION
Offered since 1968. Accredited by Council on Hotel, Restaurant and Institutional Education. Program calendar is divided into semesters. 4-year bachelor's degree in hotel and restaurant management-food service management. 4-year bachelor's degree in hotel and restaurant management-hotel planning and control. 4-year bachelor's degree in hotel and restaurant management-restaurant entrepreneurship.

PROGRAM AFFILIATION
Council on Hotel, Restaurant, and Institutional Education; National Restaurant Association; National Restaurant Association Educational Foundation.

AREAS OF STUDY
Beverage management; controlling costs in food service; food preparation; food purchasing; kitchen management; management and human resources; restaurant opportunities.

FACILITIES
2 cafeterias; catering service; 4 classrooms; 2 coffee shops; 5 computer laboratories; demonstration laboratory; food production kitchen; gourmet dining room; learning resource center; lecture room; library; snack shop; 2 student lounges; teaching kitchen.

STUDENT PROFILE
460 total: 450 full-time; 10 part-time. 425 are under 25 years old; 30 are between 25 and 44 years old; 5 are over 44 years old.

FACULTY
15 total: 9 full-time; 6 part-time. 6 are industry professionals. Prominent faculty: Edward Friel, Expert in Residence; William Frye; Steven H. Siegal; Deborah Curtis. Faculty-student ratio: 1:35.

PROMINENT ALUMNI AND CURRENT AFFILIATION
Paul McManus, President/CEO, Leading Hotels of the World; Douglas Artusro, Chairman, Dellisart Lodging; Amanda Marsh, Waldorf-Astoria Hotel.

SPECIAL PROGRAMS
Work-based program in Como, Italy and co-ops across the country, 60 industry speakers/demonstrations per year, cruise course.

TYPICAL EXPENSES
Application fee: $30. Tuition: $20,500 per year full-time, $700 per credit hour part-time. Tuition for international students: $20,500 per year full-time, $700 per credit hour part-time.

FINANCIAL AID
Program-specific awards include 1-3 Statler Foundation Scholarships of Excellence ($20,000), Statler Scholarships (up to $2000 per year), transfer scholarships. Employment placement assistance is available. Employment opportunities within the program are available.

HOUSING
Coed, apartment-style, and single-sex housing available.

APPLICATION INFORMATION
Students may begin participation in January, May, and September. Applications are accepted continuously. In 2006, 450 applied; 200 were accepted. Applicants must submit a formal application, letters of reference, and an essay.

CONTACT
Dr. Gary D. Praetzel, Dean, College of Hospitality and Tourism Management, College of Hospitality and Tourism Management, Niagara University, NY 14109-2012. Telephone: 716-286-8272. Fax: 716-286-8277. E-mail: gdp@niagara.edu. World Wide Web: http://www.niagara.edu/hospitality.

ONONDAGA COMMUNITY COLLEGE

Food Service Administration/Restaurant Management/Professional Cooking

Syracuse, New York

GENERAL INFORMATION
Public, coeducational, two-year college. Suburban campus. Founded in 1962. Accredited by Middle States Association of Colleges and Schools.

PROGRAM INFORMATION
Offered since 1979. Program calendar is divided into semesters. 1-year certificate in professional cooking. 2-year associate degree in food service administration/restaurant management. 2-year associate degree in hotel technology.

PROGRAM AFFILIATION
American Culinary Federation; Council on Hotel, Restaurant, and Institutional Education; International Food Service Executives Association; National Restaurant Association; National Restaurant Association Educational Foundation.

AREAS OF STUDY
Buffet catering; controlling costs in food service; food preparation; food purchasing; food service math; international cuisine; management and human resources; meal planning; menu and facilities design; nutrition; nutrition and food service; patisserie; sanitation.

FACILITIES
Catering service; computer laboratory; 2 food production kitchens; garden; gourmet dining room; 2 laboratories; learning resource center; library; student lounge; 2 teaching kitchens.

TYPICAL STUDENT PROFILE
100 total: 80 full-time; 20 part-time.

SPECIAL PROGRAMS
2-day trip to New York City, 5-day tour of restaurants, hotels, and casinos in Las Vegas, Walt Disney World College Program (internship).

FINANCIAL AID
Employment placement assistance is available.

APPLICATION INFORMATION
Students may begin participation in January and August. Applicants must submit a formal application.

CONTACT
Director of Admissions, Food Service Administration/Restaurant Management/Professional Cooking, 4941 Onondaga Road, Syracuse, NY 13215. Telephone: 315-498-2232. Fax: 315-498-2703. World Wide Web: http://www.sunyocc.edu/.

PAUL SMITH'S COLLEGE OF ARTS AND SCIENCES

Hotel, Resort and Culinary Management

Paul Smiths, New York

GENERAL INFORMATION
Private, coeducational, four-year college. Rural campus. Founded in 1937. Accredited by Middle States Association of Colleges and Schools.

PROGRAM INFORMATION
Offered since 1982. Accredited by American Culinary Federation Accrediting Commission, Council on Hotel, Restaurant and Institutional Education. Program calendar is divided into semesters. 1-year certificate in baking and pastry arts. 2-year associate degree in hotel and restaurant management. 2-year associate degree in culinary arts. 2-year associate degree in culinary arts–baking track. 4-year bachelor's degree in hotel, resort, and tourism management. 4-year bachelor's degree in culinary arts and service management.

PROGRAM AFFILIATION
American Culinary Federation; Council on Hotel, Restaurant, and Institutional Education; National Restaurant Association; National Restaurant Association Educational Foundation; Retailer's Bakery Association.

AREAS OF STUDY
Baking; beverage management; buffet catering; confectionery show pieces; controlling costs in food service; culinary French; culinary skill development; food preparation; food purchasing; food service communication; food service math; garde-manger; international cuisine; introduction to food service; kitchen management; management and human resources; meal planning; meat cutting; meat fabrication; menu and facilities design; nutrition; nutrition and food service; patisserie; restaurant opportunities; sanitation; saucier; seafood processing; soup, stock, sauce, and starch production; wines and spirits.

FACILITIES
Bake shop; bakery; 15 classrooms; 5 computer laboratories; demonstration laboratory; gourmet dining room; 5 laboratories; learning resource center; lecture

Paul Smith's College of Arts and Sciences *(continued)*

room; library; 2 public restaurants; snack shop; student lounge; 5 teaching kitchens; on-campus retail bakery; new Wally Ganzi, Jr. Restaurant Training Center (modeled after legendary Palm Restaurant Steakhouse).

FACULTY

23 total: 15 full-time; 8 part-time. 1 is a master baker; 3 are culinary-certified teachers. Prominent faculty: Ernest Wilson; Robert Brown, CMB; Dave Gotzmer. Faculty-student ratio: 1:14.

PROMINENT ALUMNI AND CURRENT AFFILIATION

Wally Ganzi, Jr., Owner, The Palm Restaurant; John Luther, CEO, Dunkin' Brands.

SPECIAL PROGRAMS

International Student Exchange Program, bakery operated 22 weeks a year, over 1100 externship opportunities.

TYPICAL EXPENSES

Application fee: $30. Tuition: $16,100 per year. Program-related fee includes $730 for uniforms, clothing, and equipment.

FINANCIAL AID

In 2006, 4 scholarships were awarded. Program-specific awards include Cooking for Scholarships competition. Employment placement assistance is available. Employment opportunities within the program are available.

HOUSING

Coed and single-sex housing available.

APPLICATION INFORMATION

Students may begin participation in January and September. Applications are accepted continuously. Applicants must submit a formal application, high school or college transcripts, SAT/ACT scores, and letters of recommendation and a personal essay are recommended.

CONTACT

Admissions Office, Hotel, Resort and Culinary Management, Routes 86 and 30, PO Box 265, Paul Smiths, NY 12970. Telephone: 800-421-2605. Fax: 518-327-6016. E-mail: admiss@paulsmiths.edu. World Wide Web: http://www.paulsmiths.edu/.

PLATTSBURGH STATE UNIVERSITY OF NEW YORK

Hotel, Restaurant, and Tourism Management

Plattsburgh, New York

GENERAL INFORMATION
Public, coeducational, university. Small-town setting. Founded in 1889. Accredited by Middle States Association of Colleges and Schools.

PROGRAM INFORMATION
Offered since 1988. Accredited by Council on Hotel, Restaurant and Institutional Education. Program calendar is divided into semesters. 4-year bachelor's degree in hotel, restaurant, and tourism management.

PROGRAM AFFILIATION
American Hotel and Lodging Association; Council on Hotel, Restaurant, and Institutional Education; National Restaurant Association; National Restaurant Association Educational Foundation; New York State Hospitality and Tourism Association.

AREAS OF STUDY
Beverage management; food preparation; introduction to food service; lodging; restaurant opportunities; tourism.

FACILITIES
Classroom; coffee shop; computer laboratory; demonstration laboratory; food production kitchen; laboratory; lecture room; public restaurant; student lounge; teaching kitchen.

STUDENT PROFILE
219 total: 210 full-time; 9 part-time.

FACULTY
7 total: 6 full-time; 1 part-time. 7 are industry professionals. Prominent faculty: Ray Guydosh, PhD; Kimberly Emery, CIA; Robert Rolf, MA; Mark Gultek, PhD. Faculty-student ratio: 1:26.

SPECIAL PROGRAMS
800 hours of field work, community-related projects, special dinners for nonprofit organizations.

TYPICAL EXPENSES
Application fee: $30. In-state tuition: $4350 per year full-time (in district), $181 per credit hour part-time. Out-of-state tuition: $10,610 per year full-time, $442 per credit hour part-time. Program-related fees include $100 for food labs; $50 for wine courses.

FINANCIAL AID
In 2006, 15 scholarships were awarded (average award was $883.06); 141 loans were granted (average loan was $4015.30). Program-specific awards include Marriott Corporation Award, Sodexo Award, Restaurants of New York Foundations Awards. Employment opportunities within the program are available.

HOUSING
Coed housing available. Average on-campus housing cost per month: $400. Average off-campus housing cost per month: $400.

APPLICATION INFORMATION
Students may begin participation in January and September. Application deadline for fall is August 1. Application deadline for spring is January 1. In 2006, 91 applied. Applicants must interview; submit a formal application and essay (recommended).

CONTACT
Richard Higgins, Director of Admissions, Hotel, Restaurant, and Tourism Management, Kehoe Building, Plattsburgh, NY 12901. Telephone: 518-564-2040. Fax: 518-564-2045. E-mail: higginrj@plattsburgh.edu. World Wide Web: http://www.plattsburgh.edu.

ROCHESTER INSTITUTE OF TECHNOLOGY

School of Hospitality and Service Management

Rochester, New York

GENERAL INFORMATION
Private, coeducational, comprehensive institution. Suburban campus. Founded in 1829. Accredited by Middle States Association of Colleges and Schools.

PROGRAM INFORMATION
Offered since 1891. Accredited by American Dietetic Association. Program calendar is divided into quarters. 12-month master's degree in service management. 12-month master's degree in hospitality and tourism management. 4-year bachelor's degree in nutrition management. 4-year bachelor's degree in hospitality and service management.

PROGRAM AFFILIATION
American Dietetic Association; Council on Hotel, Restaurant, and Institutional Education; Institute of Food Technologists; International Food Service Executives Association; National Restaurant Association; National Restaurant Association Educational Foundation.

AREAS OF STUDY
Beverage management; controlling costs in food service; food preparation; food purchasing; food service communication; food service math; international cuisine; introduction to food service; kitchen

Rochester Institute of Technology *(continued)*

management; management and human resources; meal planning; menu and facilities design; nutrition; nutrition and food service; restaurant opportunities; sanitation; wines and spirits.

FACILITIES
Bakery; 3 classrooms; computer laboratory; demonstration laboratory; food production kitchen; gourmet dining room; laboratory; learning resource center; lecture room; library; public restaurant; teaching kitchen.

STUDENT PROFILE
225 total: 200 full-time; 25 part-time.

FACULTY
45 total: 15 full-time; 30 part-time. 10 are industry professionals; 1 is a master chef. Prominent faculty: Carol Whitlock, PhD, RD; Barbra Cerio-Iocco, RN, CDN; Elizabeth Kmiecinski, RD. Faculty-student ratio: 1:13.

SPECIAL PROGRAMS
Required cooperative education plan (provides periods of salaried employment alternated with periods of full-time study), operation of hotel and conference center on campus, international hospitality and food management program in Croatia.

TYPICAL EXPENSES
Application fee: $50. Tuition: $26,085 per year (undergraduate); $28,491 per year (graduate) full-time, $580 per credit hour (undergraduate); $800 per credit hour (graduate) part-time.

FINANCIAL AID
Program-specific awards include RIT achievement scholarship for hospitality and service management ($5000/year). Employment placement assistance is available. Employment opportunities within the program are available.

HOUSING
Coed, apartment-style, and single-sex housing available. Average on-campus housing cost per month: $540. Average off-campus housing cost per month: $550.

APPLICATION INFORMATION
Students may begin participation in March, June, September, and December. Applications are accepted continuously. In 2006, 177 applied; 119 were accepted. Applicants must submit a formal application and high school and/or college transcripts.

CONTACT
Daniel Shelley, Director of Undergraduate Admissions, School of Hospitality and Service Management, 60 Lomb Memorial Drive, Rochester, NY 14624. Telephone: 585-475-6631. Fax: 585-475-7428. E-mail: admissions@rit.edu. World Wide Web: http://www.rit.edu.

ST. JOHN'S UNIVERSITY

Division of Hotel, Restaurant, Sports, Travel, and Tourism

Queens and Staten Island, New York

GENERAL INFORMATION
Private, coeducational, university. Urban campus. Founded in 1870. Accredited by Middle States Association of Colleges and Schools.

PROGRAM INFORMATION
Offered since 1997. Accredited by Council on Hotel, Restaurant and Institutional Education, International Society of Travel and Tourism Edu, American Hotel and Lodging Association. Program calendar is divided into semesters. 4-year bachelor's degree in hospitality management.

PROGRAM AFFILIATION
Council on Hotel, Restaurant, and Institutional Education; National Restaurant Association.

AREAS OF STUDY
Beverage management; confectionery show pieces; food purchasing; international cuisine; introduction to food service; management and human resources; menu and facilities design; restaurant opportunities.

FACILITIES
2 cafeterias; catering service; 2 coffee shops; 2 computer laboratories; 2 gardens; learning resource center; lecture room; 2 libraries; student lounge.

TYPICAL STUDENT PROFILE
99 total: 95 full-time; 4 part-time. 89 are under 25 years old; 10 are between 25 and 44 years old.

SPECIAL PROGRAMS
Certificate Program in "Tourism Italy" at Perugia University (5 weeks summer), study abroad program in "Event Management" at Leeds Metropolitan University UK.

HOUSING
Coed housing available.

APPLICATION INFORMATION

Students may begin participation in January, June, and September. Applications are accepted continuously. Applicants must submit a formal application, letters of reference, an essay, SAT or ACT scores, high school transcript.

CONTACT

Director of Admissions, Division of Hotel, Restaurant, Sports, Travel, and Tourism, 8000 Utopia Parkway, Queens, NY 11439. Telephone: 718-990-2000. Fax: 718-990-5728. World Wide Web: http://www.stjohns.edu.

STATE UNIVERSITY OF NEW YORK
COLLEGE AT COBLESKILL

Culinary Arts, Hospitality, and Tourism

Cobleskill, New York

GENERAL INFORMATION

Public, coeducational, four-year college. Rural campus. Founded in 1916. Accredited by Middle States Association of Colleges and Schools.

PROGRAM INFORMATION

Offered since 1971. Accredited by American Culinary Federation Accrediting Commission. Program calendar is divided into semesters. 1-year certificate in commercial cooking. 2-year associate degree in travel and resort marketing. 2-year associate degree in restaurant management. 2-year associate degree in institutional foods. 2-year associate degree in hotel technology. 2-year associate degree in culinary arts. 4-year bachelor's degree in culinary arts/technology management.

PROGRAM AFFILIATION

American Culinary Federation; American Dietetic Association; Chefs Collaborative 2000; Council on Hotel, Restaurant, and Institutional Education; Institute of Food Technologists; National Restaurant Association; National Restaurant Association Educational Foundation; The Bread Bakers Guild of America; Women Chefs and Restaurateurs.

AREAS OF STUDY

Beverage management; buffet catering; confectionery show pieces; controlling costs in food service; culinary French; culinary skill development; food preparation; food purchasing; food service math; garde-manger; hospitality law; international cuisine; management; management and human resources; marketing; meat cutting; menu and facilities design; nutrition; sanitation; wines and spirits.

FACILITIES

Catering service; 15 classrooms; 4 computer laboratories; demonstration laboratory; food production kitchen; gourmet dining room; learning resource center; 15 lecture rooms; library; public restaurant; 3 teaching kitchens; vineyard.

TYPICAL STUDENT PROFILE

132 total: 120 full-time; 12 part-time.

SPECIAL PROGRAMS

Culinary competitions, student-run restaurant and catering facilities, internship in bachelor's program.

FINANCIAL AID

Program-specific awards include on-campus work-study programs. Employment placement assistance is available.

HOUSING

Coed and single-sex housing available.

APPLICATION INFORMATION

Students may begin participation in January and August. Applications are accepted continuously. Applicants must submit a formal application.

CONTACT

Director of Admissions, Culinary Arts, Hospitality, and Tourism, Knapp Hall, Cobleskill, NY 12043. Telephone: 800-295-8988. Fax: 518-255-6769. World Wide Web: http://www.cobleskill.edu/.

STATE UNIVERSITY OF NEW YORK
COLLEGE AT ONEONTA

Food Service and Restaurant Administration

Oneonta, New York

GENERAL INFORMATION

Public, coeducational, comprehensive institution. Small-town setting. Founded in 1889. Accredited by Middle States Association of Colleges and Schools.

PROGRAM INFORMATION

Offered since 1974. Accredited by American Association of Family and Consumer Sciences. Program calendar is divided into semesters. 4-year bachelor's degree in food service/restaurant administration.

PROGRAM AFFILIATION

American Dietetic Association; Council on Hotel, Restaurant, and Institutional Education; National Restaurant Association; National Restaurant Association Educational Foundation.

State University of New York College at Oneonta
(continued)

AREAS OF STUDY
Buffet catering; controlling costs in food service; food preparation; food purchasing; food service communication; food service math; introduction to food service; kitchen management; management and human resources; meal planning; menu and facilities design; nutrition; nutrition and food service; restaurant opportunities; sanitation; wines and spirits.

FACILITIES
3 classrooms; computer laboratory; demonstration laboratory; food production kitchen; gourmet dining room; laboratory; learning resource center; 3 lecture rooms; library; student lounge; teaching kitchen.

STUDENT PROFILE
58 total: 53 full-time; 5 part-time. 57 are under 25 years old; 1 is between 25 and 44 years old.

FACULTY
5 total: 5 full-time. Prominent faculty: Oscar Oberkircher, CHE; Mary Ann Dowdell, PhD, RD, CDN; Shih Ming Hu, PhD, CHE; Jennifer Bueche, PhD, RD. Faculty-student ratio: 1:21.

PROMINENT ALUMNI AND CURRENT AFFILIATION
Christine Sandstedt, Restaurant Associates, Harvard University; Mark Vogel, Red Lobster Restaurants; Kim Whisher, Sagamore Hotel and Resort.

SPECIAL PROGRAMS
Food and Nutrition Association, field trips to food shows in the Northeast and speakers from the profession, Nutrition Awareness Week.

TYPICAL EXPENSES
Application fee: $30. In-state tuition: $2175 per semester full-time (in district), $181 per semester hour part-time. Out-of-state tuition: $5305 per semester full-time, $429 per semester hour part-time. Program-related fee includes $1097 for comprehensive student fee.

FINANCIAL AID
In 2006, 7 scholarships were awarded (average award was $500). Employment placement assistance is available. Employment opportunities within the program are available.

HOUSING
Coed housing available.

APPLICATION INFORMATION
Students may begin participation in January and August. Applications are accepted continuously. In 2006, 60 applied; 30 were accepted. Applicants must submit a formal application and an essay.

CONTACT
Mr. Oscar L. Oberkircher, Foodservice Management Instructor, Food Service and Restaurant Administration, 142 B. Human Ecology Building, Oneonta, NY 13820. Telephone: 607-436-2071. Fax: 607-436-2051. E-mail: oberkioj@oneonta.edu. World Wide Web: http://www.oneonta.edu.

STATE UNIVERSITY OF NEW YORK COLLEGE OF AGRICULTURE AND TECHNOLOGY AT MORRISVILLE

Restaurant Management

Morrisville, New York

GENERAL INFORMATION
Public, coeducational, two-year college. Small-town setting. Founded in 1908. Accredited by Middle States Association of Colleges and Schools.

PROGRAM INFORMATION
Offered since 1908. Accredited by American Dietetic Association. Program calendar is divided into semesters. 2-year associate degree in food service administration. 2-year associate degree in restaurant management. 4-year bachelor's degree in resort and recreation service management.

PROGRAM AFFILIATION
Council on Hotel, Restaurant, and Institutional Education; International Food Service Executives Association; National Restaurant Association; National Restaurant Association Educational Foundation.

AREAS OF STUDY
Beverage management; buffet catering; controlling costs in food service; culinary skill development; food preparation; food purchasing; food service math; international cuisine; introduction to food service; kitchen management; management and human resources; meal planning; menu and facilities design; nutrition; nutrition and food service; sanitation; soup, stock, sauce, and starch production.

FACILITIES
Bake shop; cafeteria; catering service; classroom; computer laboratory; demonstration laboratory; food production kitchen; laboratory; learning resource center; lecture room; library; public restaurant; snack shop; student lounge; teaching kitchen.

STUDENT PROFILE
125 total: 100 full-time; 25 part-time. 80 are under 25 years old; 30 are between 25 and 44 years old; 15 are over 44 years old.

FACULTY

8 total: 5 full-time; 3 part-time. 3 are industry professionals; 1 is a culinary-certified teacher. Prominent faculty: Joan Johnson, CFE; Kerry Beadle, CEC, CFE; Bert Hundredmark, CFE; Bill Moore, CEC, AAC. Faculty-student ratio: 1:15.

SPECIAL PROGRAMS

320-hour paid internship, attendance at International Food Service Executives Association Conference.

TYPICAL EXPENSES

In-state tuition: $4350 per year full-time (in district), $181 per credit hour part-time. Out-of-state tuition: $7000 per year full-time, $300 per credit hour part-time. Program-related fees include $500 for computer required for curriculum (per semester); $75 for uniform.

FINANCIAL AID

In 2006, 12 scholarships were awarded (average award was $350). Employment placement assistance is available. Employment opportunities within the program are available.

HOUSING

Coed housing available. Average off-campus housing cost per month: $500.

APPLICATION INFORMATION

Students may begin participation in January and August. Applications are accepted continuously. In 2006, 60 applied; 40 were accepted. Applicants must submit a formal application.

CONTACT

Kerry Beadle, Department Chair, Restaurant Management, Brooks Hall, Morrisville, NY 13408. Telephone: 315-684-6232. Fax: 315-684-6225. E-mail: beadlekj@morrisville.edu. World Wide Web: http://www.morrisville.edu.

STATE UNIVERSITY OF NEW YORK COLLEGE OF TECHNOLOGY AT ALFRED

Culinary Arts Program

Wellsville, New York

GENERAL INFORMATION

Public, coeducational, two-year college. Small-town setting. Founded in 1908. Accredited by Middle States Association of Colleges and Schools.

PROGRAM INFORMATION

Offered since 1966. Program calendar is divided into semesters. 2-year associate degree in baking and pastry arts. 2-year associate degree in culinary arts.

PROGRAM AFFILIATION

American Culinary Federation; Council on Hotel, Restaurant, and Institutional Education; National Restaurant Association; National Restaurant Association Educational Foundation; New York State Restaurant Association.

AREAS OF STUDY

Baking; beverage management; buffet catering; confectionery show pieces; controlling costs in food service; culinary French; culinary skill development; food preparation; food purchasing; food service math; garde-manger; international cuisine; introduction to food service; kitchen management; management and human resources; meal planning; meat cutting; menu and facilities design; nutrition; nutrition and food service; sanitation; seafood processing; soup, stock, sauce, and starch production; wines and spirits.

FACILITIES

2 bake shops; bakery; cafeteria; catering service; 3 classrooms; coffee shop; computer laboratory; 3 demonstration laboratories; 2 food production kitchens; gourmet dining room; laboratory; learning resource center; 3 lecture rooms; 2 libraries; public restaurant; student lounge; 2 teaching kitchens.

STUDENT PROFILE

72 full-time. 69 are under 25 years old; 3 are between 25 and 44 years old.

FACULTY

3 total: 3 full-time. Faculty-student ratio: 1:24.

PROMINENT ALUMNI AND CURRENT AFFILIATION

Michael Olday, Brookfield Country Club (ACF Chef of the Year, Buffalo Chapter); Jason Walker, Executive Chef, Locust Hill Country Club; Jamie H. Wells, Owner, Sweet Beginnings Bakery, Kenmore, NY.

SPECIAL PROGRAMS

Annual Culinary Arts Food Show, regional ACF Hot Foods and Team Competitions at SUNY Delhi, senior class fine dining excursion and training seminar.

TYPICAL EXPENSES

Application fee: $40. In-state tuition: $4350 per year full-time (in district), $181 per credit hour part-time. Out-of-state tuition: $7200 per year full-time, $300 per credit hour part-time. Program-related fees include $225 for uniforms; $400 for books.

State University of New York College of Technology at Alfred *(continued)*

FINANCIAL AID

In 2006, 7 scholarships were awarded (average award was $1700). Employment placement assistance is available.

HOUSING

Coed housing available. Average on-campus housing cost per month: $448.

APPLICATION INFORMATION

Students may begin participation in August. Applications are accepted continuously. In 2006, 180 applied; 103 were accepted. Applicants must submit a formal application.

CONTACT

John M. Santora, Department Chairman, Culinary Arts Program, 2530 South Brooklyn Avenue, Wellsville, NY 14895. Telephone: 800-4-ALFRED. Fax: 607-587-3171. E-mail: santorjm@alfredstate.edu. World Wide Web: http://www.alfredstate.edu.

STATE UNIVERSITY OF NEW YORK COLLEGE OF TECHNOLOGY AT DELHI

Hospitality Management

Delhi, New York

GENERAL INFORMATION

Public, coeducational, two-year college. Rural campus. Founded in 1913. Accredited by Middle States Association of Colleges and Schools.

PROGRAM INFORMATION

Offered since 1994. Accredited by American Culinary Federation Accrediting Commission. Program calendar is divided into semesters. 2-year associate degree in restaurant management. 2-year associate degree in culinary arts. 4-year bachelor's degree in restaurant management. 4-year bachelor's degree in culinary arts management.

PROGRAM AFFILIATION

American Culinary Federation; Council on Hotel, Restaurant, and Institutional Education; International Food Service Executives Association; International Hotel and Motel Association; National Restaurant Association; New York State Hospitality and Tourism Association; Society of Wine Educators.

AREAS OF STUDY

Baking; beverage management; buffet catering; confectionery show pieces; controlling costs in food service; convenience cookery; culinary competition; culinary French; culinary skill development; food preparation; food purchasing; food service communication; food service math; garde-manger; ice carving; international cuisine; introduction to food service; kitchen management; management and human resources; meal planning; meat cutting; meat fabrication; menu and facilities design; nutrition; patisserie; restaurant management; restaurant opportunities; salt carving; sanitation; saucier; seafood processing; soup, stock, sauce, and starch production; wines and spirits.

FACILITIES

Bakery; catering service; 2 classrooms; computer laboratory; demonstration laboratory; 2 food production kitchens; gourmet dining room; laboratory; learning resource center; 2 lecture rooms; library; public restaurant; 2 teaching kitchens; beverage lounge; charcuterie.

STUDENT PROFILE

173 full-time. 158 are under 25 years old; 15 are between 25 and 44 years old.

FACULTY

12 total: 11 full-time; 1 part-time. 8 are industry professionals; 3 are culinary-certified teachers. Prominent faculty: Thomas Recinella, CEC; Michael Petrillose, PhD; Julee Miller,CEC; Jamie Rotter, CEC.

PROMINENT ALUMNI AND CURRENT AFFILIATION

John Caparella, COO, Gaylord Hotels.

SPECIAL PROGRAMS

Culinary competitions, organized trips to food shows and businesses.

TYPICAL EXPENSES

Application fee: $30. In-state tuition: $2175 per semester full-time (in district), $181 per credit hour part-time. Out-of-state tuition: $3605 per semester full-time, $300 per credit hour part-time. Program-related fee includes $130 for lab fees.

FINANCIAL AID

In 2006, 6 scholarships were awarded (average award was $300). Employment placement assistance is available. Employment opportunities within the program are available.

HOUSING

Coed and single-sex housing available. Average on-campus housing cost per month: $350. Average off-campus housing cost per month: $350.

APPLICATION INFORMATION

Students may begin participation in January and September. Applications are accepted continuously. In 2006, 334 applied; 218 were accepted. Applicants must submit a formal application.

CONTACT

Craig Wesley, Dean of Enrollment Services, Hospitality Management, 119 Bush Hall, Main Street, Delhi, NY 13753. Telephone: 607-746-4556. Fax: 607-746-4104. E-mail: enroll@delhi.edu. World Wide Web: http://www.delhi.edu/.

SULLIVAN COUNTY COMMUNITY COLLEGE

Culinary Arts Division

Loch Sheldrake, New York

GENERAL INFORMATION

Public, coeducational, two-year college. Rural campus. Founded in 1962. Accredited by Middle States Association of Colleges and Schools.

PROGRAM INFORMATION

Offered since 1965. Accredited by American Culinary Federation Accrediting Commission. Program calendar is divided into semesters. 1-year certificate in food service. 2-year associate degree in pastry arts. 2-year associate degree in culinary arts. 2-year associate degree in hospitality management. 2-year associate degree in professional chef.

PROGRAM AFFILIATION

American Culinary Federation; Council on Hotel, Restaurant, and Institutional Education; National Restaurant Association; National Restaurant Association Educational Foundation; The Bread Bakers Guild of America.

AREAS OF STUDY

Baking; beverage management; buffet catering; confectionery show pieces; controlling costs in food service; convenience cookery; culinary French; culinary skill development; food preparation; food purchasing; food service math; garde-manger; international cuisine; introduction to food service; kitchen management; management and human resources; meal planning; meat cutting; meat fabrication; menu and facilities design; nutrition; nutrition and food service; patisserie; restaurant opportunities; sanitation; saucier; seafood processing; soup, stock, sauce, and starch production; wines and spirits.

FACILITIES

2 bake shops; classroom; 3 demonstration laboratories; 2 food production kitchens; gourmet dining room.

STUDENT PROFILE

100 total: 75 full-time; 25 part-time. 80 are under 25 years old; 15 are between 25 and 44 years old; 5 are over 44 years old.

FACULTY

6 total: 4 full-time; 2 part-time. 3 are culinary-certified teachers. Prominent faculty: Mark A. Sanok; Michael Bel; Scott Vitulli. Faculty-student ratio: 1:16.

SPECIAL PROGRAMS

Societe Culinaire Philanthropique Salon of Culinary Arts.

TYPICAL EXPENSES

Application fee: $30. In-state tuition: $2900 per year full-time (in district), $105 per credit hour part-time. Out-of-state tuition: $5800 per year full-time, $139 per credit hour part-time. Program-related fees include $210 for knife set; $90 for uniforms.

FINANCIAL AID

In 2006, 12 scholarships were awarded (average award was $2000). Employment placement assistance is available. Employment opportunities within the program are available.

HOUSING

Coed housing available. Average on-campus housing cost per month: $475.

APPLICATION INFORMATION

Students may begin participation in January and August. Applications are accepted continuously. Applicants must submit a formal application.

CONTACT

Sari Rosenheck, Director of Admissions and Registration Services, Culinary Arts Division, 112 College Road, Loch Sheldrake, NY 12759. Telephone: 800-577-5243. Fax: 845-434-4806. E-mail: sarir@sullivan.suny.edu. World Wide Web: http://www.sullivan.suny.edu/.

SYRACUSE UNIVERSITY

Department of Hospitality Management

Syracuse, New York

GENERAL INFORMATION

Private, coeducational, university. Urban campus. Founded in 1870. Accredited by Middle States Association of Colleges and Schools.

Syracuse University *(continued)*

PROGRAM INFORMATION
Offered since 1986. Accredited by Council on Hotel, Restaurant and Institutional Education. Program calendar is divided into semesters. 4-year bachelor's degree in hospitality management.

PROGRAM AFFILIATION
Council on Hotel, Restaurant, and Institutional Education; National Restaurant Association; National Restaurant Association Educational Foundation.

AREAS OF STUDY
Baking; beverage management; buffet catering; controlling costs in food service; culinary skill development; food preparation; food purchasing; introduction to food service; kitchen management; management and human resources; menu and facilities design; nutrition; nutrition and food service; restaurant development; sanitation; wines and spirits.

FACILITIES
Bake shop; bakery; 8 cafeterias; catering service; 25 classrooms; coffee shop; 5 computer laboratories; 2 demonstration laboratories; 2 food production kitchens; 2 gardens; gourmet dining room; 5 learning resource centers; 12 lecture rooms; 8 libraries; 2 public restaurants; 6 snack shops; 9 student lounges; 2 teaching kitchens.

STUDENT PROFILE
168 total: 165 full-time; 3 part-time.

FACULTY
14 total: 6 full-time; 8 part-time. 3 are industry professionals; 1 is a master chef; 1 is a master baker; 2 are culinary-certified teachers. Prominent faculty: Norm Faiola, PhD, MPS; Mary Ann Kiernan, PCII, CCC; Kimberly Johnson, RD; Debra Connolly, RD. Faculty-student ratio: 1:10.

PROMINENT ALUMNI AND CURRENT AFFILIATION
Daniel Kluger, Core Club, New York City; Timothy MacTurk, Aramark, Rochester, NY; Jeff Rosenthal, Staples Center, San Diego, CA.

SPECIAL PROGRAMS
ServSafe Program.

TYPICAL EXPENSES
Application fee: $75. Tuition: $30,470 per year. Program-related fees include $200 for communication fee (housing); $240 for co-curricular fee; $247 for health fee; $500 for course fees (approximate).

FINANCIAL AID
In 2006, 2 scholarships were awarded (average award was $500). Employment placement assistance is available.

HOUSING
Coed, apartment-style, and single-sex housing available.

APPLICATION INFORMATION
Students may begin participation in January and August. Application deadline for fall is January 15. Application deadline for spring is November 15. Applicants must submit a formal application and letters of reference.

CONTACT
Norman Faiola, Director/Associate Dean, Department of Hospitality Management, 302 Lyman Hall, Syracuse, NY 13244. Telephone: 315-443-4550. Fax: 315-443-2735. E-mail: nafaiola@syr.edu. World Wide Web: http://www.syr.edu/.

TOMPKINS CORTLAND COMMUNITY COLLEGE

Hotel and Restaurant Management

Dryden, New York

GENERAL INFORMATION
Public, coeducational, two-year college. Small-town setting. Founded in 1969. Accredited by Middle States Association of Colleges and Schools.

PROGRAM INFORMATION
Offered since 1970. Program calendar is divided into semesters. 2-year associate degree in hotel and restaurant management.

PROGRAM AFFILIATION
Council on Hotel, Restaurant, and Institutional Education; National Restaurant Association.

AREAS OF STUDY
Beverage management; food preparation; food purchasing; food service math; introduction to food service; management and human resources; nutrition; sanitation; soup, stock, sauce, and starch production; wines and spirits.

FACILITIES
5 classrooms; 3 computer laboratories; demonstration laboratory; learning resource center; lecture room.

TYPICAL STUDENT PROFILE
42 total: 33 full-time; 9 part-time. 28 are under 25 years old; 9 are between 25 and 44 years old; 5 are over 44 years old.

SPECIAL PROGRAMS
AAS degree program available online.

FINANCIAL AID
Employment placement assistance is available. Employment opportunities within the program are available.

HOUSING
Apartment-style housing available.

APPLICATION INFORMATION
Students may begin participation in January and August. Applications are accepted continuously. Applicants must submit a formal application.

CONTACT
Director of Admissions, Hotel and Restaurant Management, 170 North Street, PO Box 139, Dryden, NY 13053-0139. Telephone: 607-844-6580. Fax: 607-844-6541. World Wide Web: http://www.sunytccc.edu.

WESTCHESTER COMMUNITY COLLEGE

Culinary Arts and Management

Valhalla, New York

GENERAL INFORMATION
Public, coeducational, two-year college. Suburban campus. Founded in 1946. Accredited by Middle States Association of Colleges and Schools.

PROGRAM INFORMATION
Offered since 1946. National Restaurant Association Educational Foundation ManageFirst certificates available. Program calendar is divided into semesters. 2-year associate degree in food service administration: culinary arts and management.

PROGRAM AFFILIATION
American Dietetic Association; Council on Hotel, Restaurant, and Institutional Education; National Restaurant Association; National Restaurant Association Educational Foundation.

AREAS OF STUDY
Baking; beverage management; buffet catering; controlling costs in food service; convenience cookery; culinary French; culinary skill development; food preparation; food purchasing; food service math; garde-manger; international cuisine; introduction to food service; kitchen management; management and human resources; meal planning; menu and facilities design; nutrition; nutrition and food service; patisserie; restaurant opportunities; sanitation; soup, stock, sauce, and starch production; wines and spirits.

FACILITIES
Catering service; classroom; computer laboratory; demonstration laboratory; 2 food production kitchens; gourmet dining room; 2 laboratories; learning resource center; lecture room; library; public restaurant; student lounge; 2 teaching kitchens.

STUDENT PROFILE
120 total: 70 full-time; 50 part-time. 60 are under 25 years old; 48 are between 25 and 44 years old; 12 are over 44 years old.

FACULTY
6 total: 2 full-time; 4 part-time. 2 are industry professionals; 2 are culinary-certified teachers. Prominent faculty: Daryl Nosek, FMP; Desi Colón, CEC; Theresa Cousins, RD, MS, CDN; Teresa Schlanger, RD, MS, CDN. Faculty-student ratio: 1:35 class; 1:15 labs.

SPECIAL PROGRAMS
Culinary competitions, 3-4 day trip to Chicago in May for NRA Trade Show, industry fund raising events for charity.

TYPICAL EXPENSES
Application fee: $25. In-state tuition: $1225 per semester full-time (in district), $103 per credit part-time. Out-of-state tuition: $3063 per semester full-time, $256 per credit part-time. Program-related fee includes $10 for lab fees.

FINANCIAL AID
In 2006, 7 scholarships were awarded (average award was $1000). Employment placement assistance is available. Employment opportunities within the program are available.

APPLICATION INFORMATION
Students may begin participation in January, May, and September. Applications are accepted continuously. Applicants must submit a formal application.

CONTACT
Daryl Nosek, Curriculum Chair, Culinary Arts and Management, 75 Grasslands Road, Valhalla, NY 10595. Telephone: 914-606-6551. Fax: 914-606-7989. E-mail: daryl.nosek@sunywcc.edu. World Wide Web: http://www.sunywcc.edu.

WILSON TECHNOLOGICAL CENTER

Culinary Arts

Dix Hills, New York

GENERAL INFORMATION
Public, coeducational, career school. Suburban campus. Founded in 1948.

PROGRAM INFORMATION
Offered since 1948. Accredited by American Culinary Federation Accrediting Commission, National Restaurant Association Education Foundation. Program calendar is divided into semesters. 1-year certificate in Culinary Arts I. 1-year certificate in Culinary Arts II.

PROGRAM AFFILIATION
American Culinary Federation; Council on Hotel, Restaurant, and Institutional Education; National Restaurant Association; National Restaurant Association Educational Foundation.

AREAS OF STUDY
Baking; buffet catering; confectionery show pieces; controlling costs in food service; culinary skill development; food preparation; food purchasing; food service communication; food service math; garde-manger; international cuisine; introduction to food service; kitchen management; meal planning; meat cutting; meat fabrication; nutrition; nutrition and food service; patisserie; restaurant opportunities; sanitation; saucier; soup, stock, sauce, and starch production.

FACILITIES
Bake shop; cafeteria; 3 classrooms; computer laboratory; demonstration laboratory; 3 food production kitchens.

STUDENT PROFILE
185 total: 125 full-time; 60 part-time. 125 are under 25 years old; 40 are between 25 and 44 years old; 20 are over 44 years old.

FACULTY
8 total: 4 full-time; 4 part-time. 3 are industry professionals; 3 are culinary-certified teachers. Prominent faculty: Lawrence Weiss, CEC, CSC, AAC; Nancy Kombert, CEC; Pam Caputo; Robert Scavo. Faculty-student ratio: 1:22.

PROMINENT ALUMNI AND CURRENT AFFILIATION
John Doherty, Executive Chef, Waldorf Astoria; Harold Dieterle, winner of season 1 of "Top Chef".

SPECIAL PROGRAMS
Individual continuing education courses, Skills USA Food Preparation Assistant Cooking Competition.

TYPICAL EXPENSES
Tuition: $6330 per certificate full-time (in district), $8470 per certificate (1/2 day) part-time. Program-related fee includes $58 for student uniform package.

FINANCIAL AID
In 2006, 3 scholarships were awarded (average award was $2000). Employment placement assistance is available.

APPLICATION INFORMATION
Students may begin participation in January and September. Applications are accepted continuously. Applicants must have referral by school district or Continuing Education application.

CONTACT
Debra Tenenbaum, Administrator, Career and Technical Education, Culinary Arts, 17 Westminster Avenue, Dix Hills, NY 11746. Telephone: 631-667-6000 Ext. 320. Fax: 631-667-1519. E-mail: dtenenba@wsboces.org. World Wide Web: http://www.wilsontech.org.

NORTH CAROLINA

THE ART INSTITUTE OF CHARLOTTE

The International Culinary School at The Art Institute of Charlotte

Charlotte, North Carolina

GENERAL INFORMATION
Private, coeducational institution.

PROGRAM INFORMATION
Associate degree in Culinary Arts. Bachelor's degree in Culinary Arts Management. Certificate in The Art of Cooking.

CONTACT
Office of Admissions, The International Culinary School at The Art Institute of Charlotte, Three Lake Pointe Plaza, 2110 Water Ridge Parkway, Charlotte, NC 28217-4536. Telephone: 704-357-8020. World Wide Web: http://www.artinstitutes.edu/charlotte/.

See color display following page 186.

ASHEVILLE-BUNCOMBE TECHNICAL COMMUNITY COLLEGE

Culinary Technology

Asheville, North Carolina

GENERAL INFORMATION
Public, coeducational, two-year college. Urban campus. Founded in 1959. Accredited by Southern Association of Colleges and Schools.

PROGRAM INFORMATION
Offered since 1967. Accredited by Culinary Technology program accredited by the American Culinary Federation. Program calendar is divided into semesters. 2-year associate degree in baking and pastry arts. 2-year associate degree in culinary technology. 2-year associate degree in hotel and restaurant management.

PROGRAM AFFILIATION
American Culinary Federation; Council on Hotel, Restaurant, and Institutional Education; National Restaurant Association; National Restaurant Association Educational Foundation; Women Chefs and Restaurateurs.

AREAS OF STUDY
American regional cuisine; baking; beverage management; classical cuisine; confectionery show pieces; controlling costs in food service; culinary skill development; food preparation; food purchasing; food service math; garde-manger; international cuisine; introduction to food service; management and human resources; meal planning; meat cutting; meat fabrication; menu and facilities design; nutrition; nutrition and food service; patisserie; restaurant opportunities; sanitation; saucier; seafood processing; soup, stock, sauce, and starch production; wines and spirits.

FACILITIES
Bake shop; 4 classrooms; computer laboratory; demonstration laboratory; food production kitchen; 2 gourmet dining rooms; laboratory; learning resource center; 4 lecture rooms; library; public restaurant; student lounge; 2 teaching kitchens; hotel.

STUDENT PROFILE
110 total: 70 full-time; 40 part-time.

FACULTY
15 total: 9 full-time; 6 part-time. 2 are industry professionals; 7 are culinary-certified teachers. Prominent faculty: John Hofland; Vincent Donatelli; Sheila Tillman; Gary Schwartz, JD. Faculty-student ratio: 1:10.

SPECIAL PROGRAMS
Culinary competitions, paid internship.

TYPICAL EXPENSES
In-state tuition: $672 per semester full-time (in district), $42 per credit part-time. Out-of-state tuition: $3512 per semester full-time, $233 per credit part-time.

FINANCIAL AID
In 2006, 10 scholarships were awarded (average award was $500). Employment placement assistance is available. Employment opportunities within the program are available.

HOUSING
Average off-campus housing cost per month: $900.

APPLICATION INFORMATION
Students may begin participation in January, May, and August. Applications are accepted continuously. In 2006, 120 applied; 60 were accepted. Applicants must submit a formal application and computerized placement test scores.

CONTACT
Sheila Tillman, Associate Dean, Culinary Technology, 340 Victoria Road, Asheville, NC 28801. Telephone: 828-254-1921 Ext. 232. Fax: 828-281-9794. E-mail: stillman@abtech.edu. World Wide Web: http://www.abtech.edu.

CENTRAL PIEDMONT COMMUNITY COLLEGE

Hospitality Education Division

Charlotte, North Carolina

GENERAL INFORMATION
Public, coeducational, two-year college. Urban campus. Founded in 1963. Accredited by Southern Association of Colleges and Schools.

PROGRAM INFORMATION
Offered since 1977. Accredited by American Culinary Federation Accrediting Commission. National Restaurant Association Educational Foundation ManageFirst certificates available. Program calendar is divided into semesters. 1-year certificate in service. 1-year certificate in sales and events. 1-year certificate in hotel management. 1-year certificate in management skills. 1-year certificate in restaurant management. 1-year certificate in garde manger. 1-year certificate in hot foods. 1-year certificate in baking. 1-year certificate in culinary. 1- to 2-year diploma in restaurant management. 1- to 2-year diploma in hotel management. 2-year associate degree in baking and

Central Piedmont Community College *(continued)*

pastry arts. 2-year associate degree in hotel and restaurant management. 2-year associate degree in culinary technology.

PROGRAM AFFILIATION
American Culinary Federation; National Association of Catering Executives; National Restaurant Association; National Restaurant Association Educational Foundation.

AREAS OF STUDY
Baking; beverage management; buffet catering; confectionery show pieces; controlling costs in food service; culinary skill development; food preparation; food purchasing; food service communication; garde-manger; international cuisine; introduction to food service; kitchen management; management and human resources; meal planning; meat cutting; nutrition; patisserie; restaurant opportunities; sanitation; soup, stock, sauce, and starch production; wines and spirits.

FACILITIES
2 bake shops; 4 classrooms; demonstration laboratory; 2 food production kitchens; gourmet dining room; learning resource center; 2 lecture rooms; library; public restaurant.

STUDENT PROFILE
390 full-time.

FACULTY
13 total: 7 full-time; 6 part-time. 7 are industry professionals; 6 are culinary-certified teachers. Prominent faculty: Jeff LaBarge, CEC; Bill Lassiter, CCE, CEC; Jim Bowen, CEC, CFBE; Don Cheatham, CEC. Faculty-student ratio: 1:16.

PROMINENT ALUMNI AND CURRENT AFFILIATION
Gene Kato, Japonais.

SPECIAL PROGRAMS
Culinary tour of France.

TYPICAL EXPENSES
In-state tuition: $672 per semester full-time (in district), $42 per semester hour part-time. Out-of-state tuition: $3733 per semester full-time, $233 per semester hour part-time. Program-related fees include $300 for cutlery, uniforms; $48 for lab fees.

FINANCIAL AID
Employment placement assistance is available.

APPLICATION INFORMATION
Students may begin participation in January and August. Applications are accepted continuously. Applicants must submit a formal application, have a high school diploma or GED, and take placement test.

CONTACT
Robert G. Boll, Division Director, Hospitality Education Division, PO Box 35009, Charlotte, NC 28235. Telephone: 704-330-6721. Fax: 704-330-6581. E-mail: bob_boll@cpcc.edu. World Wide Web: http://www.cpcc.edu.

EAST CAROLINA UNIVERSITY

Department of Hospitality Management

Greenville, North Carolina

GENERAL INFORMATION
Public, coeducational, university. Small-town setting. Founded in 1907. Accredited by Southern Association of Colleges and Schools.

PROGRAM INFORMATION
Offered since 1988. Program calendar is divided into semesters. 1- to 2-year master of business administration in hospitality management (concentration). 4-year bachelor's degree in hospitality management (lodging, food and beverage, conventions and special events).

PROGRAM AFFILIATION
American Dietetic Association; American Hotel and Lodging Association; Council on Hotel, Restaurant, and Institutional Education; Culinary Hospitality and Tourism Educators Association of North Carolina; Educational Association of the AH & LA; Hospitality Sales and Marketing Association International; National Restaurant Association; National Restaurant Association Educational Foundation; North Carolina Hotel and Lodging Association; North Carolina Tourism Educational Foundation.

AREAS OF STUDY
Food and beverage service; hotel and restaurant management; lodging; Meetings and Conventions; restaurant opportunities.

FACILITIES
4 classrooms; computer laboratory; demonstration laboratory; food production kitchen; 2 teaching kitchens.

STUDENT PROFILE
149 total: 133 full-time; 16 part-time. 133 are under 25 years old; 15 are between 25 and 44 years old; 1 is over 44 years old.

FACULTY
14 total: 10 full-time; 4 part-time. 1 is a master chef. Prominent faculty: Dori Finley, PhD, RD, LDN; Jim Chandler, PhD, CHA, CHE; Mel Weber, PhD; David Rivera, PhD. Faculty-student ratio: 1:13.

PROMINENT ALUMNI AND CURRENT AFFILIATION
Perry Dunbar, Marriott; John LaMarche, Bettcher Industries, Inc.; Jeff Bass, MBM Corporation.

SPECIAL PROGRAMS
Paid internship, international study abroad program, tours of North Carolina wineries, including Biltmore Estates and Childres wineries, attend national professional conferences.

TYPICAL EXPENSES
Application fee: $50. In-state tuition: $2431 per year full-time (in district), $608 per 1 to 5 hours; $1215 for 6 to 8 hours; $1823 for 9 to 11 hours part-time. Out-of-state tuition: $12,945 per year full-time, $3236 per 1 to 5 hours; $6473 for 6 to 8 hours; $9709 for 9 to 11 hours part-time. Tuition for international students: $12,945 per year full-time, $3236 per 1 to 5 hours; $6473 for 6 to 8 hours; $9709 for 9 to 11 hours part-time. Program-related fee includes $100 for kitchen uniforms (paid externally).

FINANCIAL AID
In 2006, 12 scholarships were awarded (average award was $1500). Program-specific awards include paid internship with Red Lobster, ARAMARK, Biltmore Estates, Pinehurst Resorts, Kingsmill Resort and more. Employment placement assistance is available. Employment opportunities within the program are available.

HOUSING
Coed, apartment-style, and single-sex housing available. Average on-campus housing cost per month: $352. Average off-campus housing cost per month: $485.

APPLICATION INFORMATION
Students may begin participation in January, May, July, and August. Application deadline for summer and fall is March 15. Application deadline for spring is November 1. Application deadline for transfers (summer and fall) is April 15. Applicants must submit a formal application and letters of reference.

CONTACT
Robert M. O'Halloran, Chair, Department of Hospitality Management, Rivers Building Room 152, Greenville, NC 27858. Telephone: 252-737-1604. Fax: 252-328-4276. E-mail: ohalloranr@ecu.edu. World Wide Web: http://www.ecu.edu/che/hmgt/index.html.

JOHNSON & WALES UNIVERSITY–CHARLOTTE

College of Culinary Arts

Charlotte, North Carolina

GENERAL INFORMATION
Private, coeducational, university. Urban campus. Founded in 1914. Accredited by New England Association of Schools and Colleges.

PROGRAM INFORMATION
Offered since 2004. Program calendar is divided into quarters. Associate degree in baking and pastry arts. Associate degree in culinary arts. Bachelor's degree in culinary arts and food service management (joint degree with the College of Culinary Arts and The Hospitality College). Bachelor's degree in pastry arts and food service management (joint degree with the College of Culinary Arts and The Hospitality College). Bachelor's degree in restaurant, food and beverage management. Bachelor's degree in hotel and lodging management.

PROGRAM AFFILIATION
American Culinary Federation; American Institute of Wine & Food; Institute of Food Technologists; International Association of Culinary Professionals; National Restaurant Association; National Restaurant Association Educational Foundation; Research Chefs Association; The Bread Bakers Guild of America; Women Chefs and Restaurateurs.

AREAS OF STUDY
Baking; beverage management; confectionery show pieces; controlling costs in food service; culinary skill development; food preparation; food purchasing; food service math; garde-manger; international cuisine; introduction to food service; meat cutting; meat fabrication; menu and facilities design; nutrition; patisserie; sanitation; saucier; seafood processing; soup, stock, sauce, and starch production; wines and spirits.

FACILITIES
6 bake shops; cafeteria; 12 classrooms; 4 computer laboratories; demonstration laboratory; food production kitchen; 3 gourmet dining rooms; learning resource center; lecture room; library; snack shop; 2 student lounges; 11 teaching kitchens; storeroom.

STUDENT PROFILE
1,264 total: 1232 full-time; 32 part-time. 1069 are under 25 years old; 186 are between 25 and 44 years old; 9 are over 44 years old.

Johnson & Wales University–Charlotte *(continued)*

FACULTY
39 total: 38 full-time; 1 part-time. Prominent faculty: Ed Batten, CEC, CCE, FMP, CCI; Susan Batten, CEC, CCE, FMP, CCI; Frances Burnett, CMB, CEPC; Michael Calenda, CEC. Faculty-student ratio: 1:32.

SPECIAL PROGRAMS
Summer tour abroad (Germany, France, or Singapore), Inter-Campus Hot Food Competition.

TYPICAL EXPENSES
Tuition: $20,478 per year. Program-related fees include $984 for general fee; $255 for orientation fee; $987 for optional weekend meal plan; $300 for room and board reservation deposit.

FINANCIAL AID
In 2006, individual scholarships were awarded at $3771; 571 loans were granted (average loan was $3735.91). Employment placement assistance is available.

HOUSING
Coed housing available. Average on-campus housing cost per month: $1000.

APPLICATION INFORMATION
Students may begin participation in March, September, and December. Applications are accepted continuously. In 2006, 2536 applied; 1841 were accepted. Applicants must submit a formal application.

CONTACT
Brian Stanley, Director of Admissions, College of Culinary Arts, 901 West Trade Street, Charlotte, NC 28202. Telephone: 980-598-1100. Fax: 980-598-1111. E-mail: charlotte.admissions@jwu.edu. World Wide Web: http://culinary.jwu.edu.

See color display following page 90.

SOUTHWESTERN COMMUNITY COLLEGE

Culinary Technology

Sylva, North Carolina

GENERAL INFORMATION
Public, coeducational, two-year college. Small-town setting. Founded in 1964. Accredited by Southern Association of Colleges and Schools.

PROGRAM INFORMATION
Offered since 1973. Program calendar is divided into semesters. 2-semester certificate in culinary technology. 5-semester associate degree in culinary technology.

PROGRAM AFFILIATION
National Restaurant Association Educational Foundation.

FACILITIES
Classroom; teaching kitchen.

STUDENT PROFILE
43 total: 30 full-time; 13 part-time. 26 are under 25 years old; 14 are between 25 and 44 years old; 3 are over 44 years old.

FACULTY
1 total: 1 full-time. Prominent faculty: Ceretta Davis. Faculty-student ratio: 1:35.

SPECIAL PROGRAMS
Annual gingerbread house competition at Grove Park Inn.

TYPICAL EXPENSES
In-state tuition: $672 per semester full-time (in district), $42 per credit hour part-time. Out-of-state tuition: $3732 per semester full-time, $233.30 per credit hour part-time.

FINANCIAL AID
Program-specific awards include E.M. Moulton scholarships ($200).

HOUSING
Average off-campus housing cost per month: $450.

APPLICATION INFORMATION
Students may begin participation in January, May, and August. Applications are accepted continuously. Applicants must submit a formal application.

CONTACT
Matthew Chadwick, Admissions Officer, Culinary Technology, 447 College Drive, Sylva, NC 28779. Telephone: 828-586-4091 Ext. 217. Fax: 828-586-3129. E-mail: mchadwick@southwesterncc.edu. World Wide Web: http://www.southwesterncc.edu.

THE UNIVERSITY OF NORTH CAROLINA AT GREENSBORO

Greensboro, North Carolina

GENERAL INFORMATION
Public, coeducational, university. Urban campus. Founded in 1891. Accredited by Southern Association of Colleges and Schools.

PROGRAM INFORMATION

Accredited by American Dietetic Association. Program calendar is divided into semesters. 122-hour bachelor's degree in nutrition. 37- to 40-hour master's degree in nutrition. 37- to 40-hour master's degree in nutrition and food service systems. 4-year bachelor's degree in restaurant and institution management. 63-hour doctoral degree in nutrition.

PROGRAM AFFILIATION

American Dietetic Association.

AREAS OF STUDY

Hospitality management; nutrition; nutrition and food service; restaurant opportunities.

FACILITIES

Classroom; computer laboratory; demonstration laboratory; lecture room; library; student lounge.

STUDENT PROFILE

207 total: 165 full-time; 42 part-time. 146 are under 25 years old; 55 are between 25 and 44 years old; 6 are over 44 years old.

FACULTY

12 total: 10 full-time; 2 part-time. Faculty-student ratio: 1:17.

SPECIAL PROGRAMS

Dietetic internship.

TYPICAL EXPENSES

Application fee: $35. In-state tuition: $4029 per year full-time (in district), $476.39 per 3 hours part-time. Out-of-state tuition: $15,297 per year full-time, $1884.89 per 3 hours part-time. Tuition for international students: $15,297 per year full-time, $1884.89 per 3 hours part-time.

HOUSING

Coed, apartment-style, and single-sex housing available. Average on-campus housing cost per month: $428. Average off-campus housing cost per month: $576.

APPLICATION INFORMATION

Students may begin participation in January and August. Application deadline for fall is March 1. Application deadline for spring is December 1. Applicants must submit a formal application and SAT or ACT scores.

CONTACT

Office of Admissions, 1400 Spring Garden Street, PO Box 26170, Greensboro, NC 27402. Telephone: 336-334-5243. Fax: 336-334-4180. E-mail: undergrad_admissions@uncg.edu. World Wide Web: http://www.uncg.edu.

WAKE TECHNICAL COMMUNITY COLLEGE

Culinary Technology, Hotel/Restaurant Management

Raleigh, North Carolina

GENERAL INFORMATION

Public, coeducational, two-year college. Suburban campus. Founded in 1958. Accredited by Southern Association of Colleges and Schools.

PROGRAM INFORMATION

Offered since 1983. Accredited by American Culinary Federation Accrediting Commission. National Restaurant Association Educational Foundation ManageFirst certificates available. Program calendar is divided into semesters. 1-year certificate in hotel management. 1-year certificate in restaurant management. 1-year certificate in baking and pastry arts. 1-year certificate in culinary technology. 2-year associate degree in hotel/restaurant management. 2-year associate degree in culinary technology.

PROGRAM AFFILIATION

American Culinary Federation; American Hotel and Lodging Association; American Institute of Baking; American Institute of Wine & Food; Council on Hotel, Restaurant, and Institutional Education; National Restaurant Association; National Restaurant Association Educational Foundation; North Carolina Culinary, Hospitality, and Tourism Alliance; North Carolina Restaurant and Hotel Management Association; Triangle Area Hotel/Motel Association (TAHMA).

AREAS OF STUDY

Baking; beverage management; buffet catering; confectionery show pieces; controlling costs in food service; culinary French; culinary skill development; food preparation; food purchasing; food service communication; food service math; garde-manger; hotel operations; international cuisine; introduction to food service; kitchen management; management and human resources; meal planning; meat cutting; meat fabrication; menu and facilities design; nutrition; nutrition and food service; patisserie; restaurant opportunities; sanitation; saucier; seafood processing; soup, stock, sauce, and starch production; table service; wines and spirits.

FACILITIES

Bake shop; 2 classrooms; computer laboratory; demonstration laboratory; 4 food production kitchens; gourmet dining room; learning resource center; 2 lecture rooms; library; public restaurant; student lounge; 7 teaching kitchens.

Wake Technical Community College *(continued)*

STUDENT PROFILE
210 total: 160 full-time; 50 part-time. 130 are under 25 years old; 50 are between 25 and 44 years old; 30 are over 44 years old.

FACULTY
11 total: 7 full-time; 4 part-time. Prominent faculty: Fredi Mort; Caralyn House; Penny Prichard; Jane Broden. Faculty-student ratio: 1:15.

SPECIAL PROGRAMS
3-week work-study in France, American Culinary Federation Hot Food Competition, pastry show and competition.

TYPICAL EXPENSES
In-state tuition: $35.50 per credit hour. Out-of-state tuition: $197 per credit hour.

FINANCIAL AID
In 2006, 4 scholarships were awarded (average award was $1500); 1 loan was granted (loan was $1500). Employment placement assistance is available. Employment opportunities within the program are available.

APPLICATION INFORMATION
Students may begin participation in January, May, and August. Applications are accepted continuously. In 2006, 125 applied; 90 were accepted. Applicants must submit a formal application and SAT scores or equivalent.

CONTACT
Admissions, Culinary Technology, Hotel/Restaurant Management, 9101 Fayetteville Road, Raleigh, NC 27603. Telephone: 919-866-5957. E-mail: plprichard@ waketech.edu. World Wide Web: http://www.waketech. edu.

WILKES COMMUNITY COLLEGE

Culinary Technology and Baking and Pastry Arts

Wilkesboro, North Carolina

GENERAL INFORMATION
Public, coeducational, two-year college. Rural campus. Founded in 1965. Accredited by Southern Association of Colleges and Schools.

PROGRAM INFORMATION
Offered since 1997. Program calendar is divided into semesters. 2-year associate degree in baking and pastry arts. 2-year associate degree in culinary technology. 4-month certificate in line cook.

PROGRAM AFFILIATION
Chefs Collaborative 2000.

AREAS OF STUDY
Artisanal breads; baking; beverage management; buffet catering; controlling costs in food service; convenience cookery; culinary skill development; food preparation; food purchasing; garde-manger; international cuisine; introduction to food service; kitchen management; nutrition; pastry cooking; sanitation.

FACILITIES
Bake shop; classroom; food production kitchen; public restaurant; teaching kitchen.

STUDENT PROFILE
32 total: 22 full-time; 10 part-time. 16 are under 25 years old; 10 are between 25 and 44 years old; 6 are over 44 years old.

FACULTY
3 total: 1 full-time; 2 part-time. 1 is an industry professional; 2 are culinary-certified teachers. Prominent faculty: Kimrey Jordan; William Bullock; Celena Nilo. Faculty-student ratio: 1:10.

SPECIAL PROGRAMS
Participation in providing food for Merlefest (bluegrass festival), student-run Tory Oak Restaurant on campus, trip to Paris to work in Alain Ducasse, Michael Rostang, and Grand Cascade restaurants.

TYPICAL EXPENSES
In-state tuition: $1423 per year full-time (in district), $42.00 per credit hour part-time. Out-of-state tuition: $7545 per year full-time, $233.30 per credit hour part-time. Program-related fee includes $200 for uniforms and cutlery.

FINANCIAL AID
In 2006, 10 scholarships were awarded (average award was $1000). Program-specific awards include participation in Ye Host Culinary Club (provides full tuition for up to four semesters). Employment placement assistance is available. Employment opportunities within the program are available.

HOUSING
Average off-campus housing cost per month: $600.

APPLICATION INFORMATION
Students may begin participation in January and August. Applications are accepted continuously. In 2006, 20 applied; 20 were accepted. Applicants must submit a formal application.

CONTACT
C. Mac Warren, Director of Admissions, Culinary Technology and Baking and Pastry Arts, PO Box 120, Wilkesboro, NC 28677. Telephone: 336-838-6141. Fax: 336-838-6547. E-mail: mac.warren@wilkescc.edu. World Wide Web: http://www.wilkescc.edu.

NORTH DAKOTA

NORTH DAKOTA STATE COLLEGE OF SCIENCE

Culinary Arts

Wahpeton, North Dakota

GENERAL INFORMATION
Public, coeducational, two-year college. Small-town setting. Founded in 1903. Accredited by North Central Association of Colleges and Schools.

PROGRAM INFORMATION
Offered since 1971. Program calendar is divided into semesters. 2-year associate degree in restaurant management. 2-year associate degree in chef training and management technology. 2-year diploma in chef training and management technology.

PROGRAM AFFILIATION
American Culinary Federation; National Restaurant Association; North Dakota Hospitality Association.

AREAS OF STUDY
Baking; buffet catering; controlling costs in food service; culinary skill development; food preparation; food purchasing; food service math; garde-manger; introduction to food service; kitchen management; management and human resources; meal planning; meat cutting; meat fabrication; menu and facilities design; nutrition and food service; patisserie; sanitation; saucier; seafood processing; soup, stock, sauce, and starch production.

FACILITIES
Bake shop; bakery; cafeteria; catering service; classroom; coffee shop; 7 computer laboratories; demonstration laboratory; food production kitchen; laboratory; learning resource center; lecture room; 2 libraries; public restaurant; snack shop; 3 student lounges; teaching kitchen.

STUDENT PROFILE
30 full-time. 25 are under 25 years old; 5 are between 25 and 44 years old.

FACULTY
2 total: 2 full-time. 2 are industry professionals. Prominent faculty: Kyle Armitage; Mary Uhren. Faculty-student ratio: 1:15.

SPECIAL PROGRAMS
Cooperative education program (paid internship).

TYPICAL EXPENSES
Application fee: $25. In-state tuition: $3920 per year full-time (in district), $128.66 per credit part-time (in district), $4776–$5631 per year depending upon reciprocity arrangement full-time (out-of-district), $155.39–$182.11 per credit depending upon reciprocity arrangement part-time (out-of-district). Out-of-state tuition: $9632 per year full-time, $307.18 per credit part-time. Program-related fees include $290 for uniforms; $170 for cutlery; $150 for laboratory supply fees (per semester); $300 for program fees.

FINANCIAL AID
In 2006, 6 scholarships were awarded (average award was $500). Employment placement assistance is available.

HOUSING
Coed, apartment-style, and single-sex housing available. Average on-campus housing cost per month: $96. Average off-campus housing cost per month: $250.

APPLICATION INFORMATION
Students may begin participation in January and August. Application deadline for fall is August 24. Application deadline for spring is January 8. In 2006, 45 applied; 25 were accepted. Applicants must submit a formal application and ACT scores.

CONTACT
Mary Uhren, Director, Culinary Arts, 800 North Sixth Street, Wahpeton, ND 58076. Telephone: 701-671-2842. Fax: 701-671-2774. E-mail: mary.uhren@ndscs.nodak. edu. World Wide Web: http://www.ndscs.nodak.edu/ departments/culinary-arts/index.jsp.

OHIO

THE ART INSTITUTE OF OHIO– CINCINNATI

The International Culinary School at The Art Institute of Ohio–Cincinnati

Cincinnati, Ohio

GENERAL INFORMATION
Private, coeducational institution.

The Art Institute of Ohio–Cincinnati *(continued)*

PROGRAM INFORMATION
Associate degree in Culinary Arts.

CONTACT
Office of Admissions, The International Culinary School at The Art Institute of Ohio–Cincinnati, 8845 Governors Hill Drive, Suite 100, Cincinnati, OH 45249-3317. Telephone: 513-833-2400. World Wide Web: http://www.artinstitutes.edu/cincinnati/.
See color display following page 186.

ASHLAND UNIVERSITY

Ashland, Ohio

GENERAL INFORMATION
Private, coeducational, comprehensive institution. Rural campus. Founded in 1878. Accredited by North Central Association of Colleges and Schools.

PROGRAM INFORMATION
Accredited by Council on Hotel, Restaurant and Institutional Education. Program calendar is divided into semesters. 4-year bachelor's degree in hotel and restaurant management.

PROGRAM AFFILIATION
American Culinary Federation; Council on Hotel, Restaurant, and Institutional Education; Gold and Silver Plate Society; National Association of College and University Food Service; National Restaurant Association; Ohio Hotel/Motel Association.

AREAS OF STUDY
Beverage management; food purchasing; management and human resources.

FACILITIES
Bakery; cafeteria; catering service; classroom; coffee shop; computer laboratory; demonstration laboratory; food production kitchen; lecture room; public restaurant; snack shop; teaching kitchen.

STUDENT PROFILE
26 total: 24 full-time; 2 part-time. 24 are under 25 years old; 2 are between 25 and 44 years old.

FACULTY
4 total: 3 full-time; 1 part-time. 2 are industry professionals; 1 is a culinary-certified teacher. Prominent faculty: Diane Moretz; Rene Rawraway, CHE. Faculty-student ratio: 1:12.

SPECIAL PROGRAMS
640-hour internship, semester at Disney (for credit), international internship opportunities, on-campus internships.

TYPICAL EXPENSES
Application fee: $25. Tuition: $22,216 per year full-time, $682 per semester hour part-time. Tuition for international students: $22,216 per year.

FINANCIAL AID
In 2006, 4 scholarships were awarded (average award was $1000); 20 loans were granted (average loan was $2600). Employment placement assistance is available. Employment opportunities within the program are available.

HOUSING
Coed, apartment-style, and single-sex housing available.

APPLICATION INFORMATION
Students may begin participation in January and August. Application deadline for fall is August 25. Application deadline for spring is January 15. In 2006, 20 applied; 18 were accepted. Applicants must submit a formal application, an essay, high school transcripts, ACT or SAT score.

CONTACT
Thomas Mansperger, Director of Admission, 401 College Avenue, Ashland, OH 44805. Telephone: 800-882-1548. Fax: 419-289-5999. E-mail: auadmsn@ashland.edu. World Wide Web: http://www.exploreashland.com.

CINCINNATI STATE TECHNICAL AND COMMUNITY COLLEGE

Business Division

Cincinnati, Ohio

GENERAL INFORMATION
Public, coeducational, two-year college. Urban campus. Founded in 1966. Accredited by North Central Association of Colleges and Schools.

PROGRAM INFORMATION
Offered since 1978. Accredited by American Culinary Federation Accrediting Commission. National Restaurant Association Educational Foundation ManageFirst certificates available. Program calendar is 5 ten-week terms. 1-year certificate in culinary arts. 2-year associate degree in hotel management. 2-year associate degree in restaurant management. 2-year associate degree in culinary arts.

PROGRAM AFFILIATION
American Culinary Federation; Council on Hotel, Restaurant, and Institutional Education; National Restaurant Association; National Restaurant Association Educational Foundation.

AREAS OF STUDY
Baking; beverage management; buffet catering; controlling costs in food service; culinary skill development; food preparation; food purchasing; food service math; garde-manger; international cuisine; management and human resources; meat cutting; meat fabrication; nutrition; nutrition and food service; restaurant opportunities; sanitation; seafood processing; soup, stock, sauce, and starch production; wines and spirits.

FACILITIES
Computer laboratory; demonstration laboratory; food production kitchen; gourmet dining room; 4 lecture rooms; 6 teaching kitchens.

STUDENT PROFILE
400 total: 300 full-time; 100 part-time.

FACULTY
22 total: 7 full-time; 15 part-time. 5 are industry professionals; 1 is a master chef; 4 are culinary-certified teachers. Prominent faculty: John Kinsella, CMC. Faculty-student ratio: 1:20.

SPECIAL PROGRAMS
Cooperative education experience.

TYPICAL EXPENSES
In-state tuition: $80 per credit hour full-time (in district), $80 per credit hour part-time. Out-of-state tuition: $160 per credit hour full-time, $160 per credit hour part-time. Program-related fees include $260 for knives; $1000 for lab fees; $300 for uniforms.

FINANCIAL AID
In 2006, 20 scholarships were awarded (average award was $1000). Employment placement assistance is available. Employment opportunities within the program are available.

HOUSING
Average off-campus housing cost per month: $350–$600.

APPLICATION INFORMATION
Students may begin participation in February, April, June, September, and November. Applications are accepted continuously. Applicants must submit a formal application and take entrance exam.

CONTACT
Jeff Sheldon, Program Chair, Business Division, 3520 Central Parkway, Cincinnati, OH 45223-2690. Telephone: 513-569-1637. Fax: 513-569-1467. E-mail: jeffery.sheldon@cincinnatistate.edu. World Wide Web: http://www.cincinnatistate.edu/.

COLUMBUS STATE COMMUNITY COLLEGE

Hospitality, Massage Therapy, Sport and Exercise Studies

Columbus, Ohio

GENERAL INFORMATION
Public, coeducational, two-year college. Urban campus. Founded in 1963. Accredited by North Central Association of Colleges and Schools.

PROGRAM INFORMATION
Offered since 1966. Accredited by American Culinary Federation Accrediting Commission, American Dietetic Association, Commission on Accreditation of Hospitality Management Programs. National Restaurant Association Educational Foundation ManageFirst certificates available. Program calendar is divided into quarters. 1-year certificate in baking. 2-year associate degree in travel/tourism hotel management. 2-year associate degree in dietetic technician. 2-year associate degree in food service/restaurant management. 3-year associate degree in chef apprenticeship. 9-month certificate in dietary manager.

PROGRAM AFFILIATION
American Dietetic Association; Council on Hotel, Restaurant, and Institutional Education; National Restaurant Association; National Restaurant Association Educational Foundation; Ohio Hotel and Lodging Association; Retailer's Bakery Association.

AREAS OF STUDY
Baking; beverage management; catering services; controlling costs in food service; food preparation; food purchasing; food service math; garde-manger; introduction to food service; kitchen management; management and human resources; meal planning; menu and facilities design; nutrition; nutrition and food service; restaurant opportunities; sanitation; soup, stock, sauce, and starch production; wines and spirits.

FACILITIES
Catering service; 3 classrooms; computer laboratory; demonstration laboratory; 2 food production kitchens; 2 laboratories; learning resource center; 3 lecture rooms; library; 2 teaching kitchens.

Columbus State Community College *(continued)*

STUDENT PROFILE
450 total: 200 full-time; 250 part-time.

FACULTY
13 total: 5 full-time; 8 part-time. 3 are industry professionals; 2 are culinary-certified teachers. Prominent faculty: Mokie Steiskal, PhD, CCE, RD, FMP; James Taylor, CEC, AAC; Jan Van Horn, RDLD. Faculty-student ratio: 1:25 lecture; 1:15 lab.

PROMINENT ALUMNI AND CURRENT AFFILIATION
Thom Coffman, Thom's on Grandview, The Clarmont; Brian Hinshaw, Cameron Mitchell's Restaurants; Chuck Kline, Cameron Mitchell's Restaurants.

SPECIAL PROGRAMS
Wine-food pairing competition-2 winners get trip to California wine country, culinary competitions and demonstrations, paid apprenticeship and cooperative work experiences.

TYPICAL EXPENSES
Application fee: $50. In-state tuition: $79 per quarter credit hour full-time (in district), $79 per quarter credit hour part-time. Out-of-state tuition: $175 per quarter credit hour full-time, $175 per quarter credit hour part-time. Tuition for international students: $210 per quarter credit hour full-time, $210 per quarter credit hour part-time. Program-related fees include $150 for average food and non-food lab supplies (per year); $75 for ACF Junior Membership for Chef Apprentice.

FINANCIAL AID
In 2006, 10 scholarships were awarded (average award was $1000). Employment placement assistance is available. Employment opportunities within the program are available.

HOUSING
Average off-campus housing cost per month: $375.

APPLICATION INFORMATION
Students may begin participation in January, March, June, and September. Application deadline for fall chef apprenticeships is May 15. Application deadline for spring chef apprenticeships; continuous for other majors is November 15. In 2006, 225 applied; 200 were accepted. Applicants must submit a formal application, 2 letters of reference, essay and have an interview (chef apprentice option only).

CONTACT
Mokie Steiskal, Chairperson, Hospitality Management, Hospitality, Massage Therapy, Sport and Exercise Studies, 550 East Spring Street, Columbus, OH 43215. Telephone: 614-287-5126. Fax: 614-287-5973. E-mail: msteiska@cscc.edu. World Wide Web: http://www.cscc.edu/.

CUYAHOGA COMMUNITY COLLEGE, METROPOLITAN CAMPUS

Hospitality Management Department

Cleveland, Ohio

GENERAL INFORMATION
Public, coeducational, two-year college. Urban campus. Founded in 1963. Accredited by North Central Association of Colleges and Schools.

PROGRAM INFORMATION
Offered since 1976. Accredited by American Culinary Federation Accrediting Commission, Commission on Accreditation of Hospitality Management Programs. National Restaurant Association Educational Foundation ManageFirst certificates available. Program calendar is divided into semesters. 1-year certificate in food and beverage operations. 1-year certificate in culinarian/cook. 1-year certificate in professional baker. 2-year associate degree in restaurant/food service management. 2-year associate degree in culinary arts.

PROGRAM AFFILIATION
American Culinary Federation; American Personal Chef Institute & Association; Council on Hotel, Restaurant, and Institutional Education; International Food Service Executives Association; National Restaurant Association; National Restaurant Association Educational Foundation.

AREAS OF STUDY
Baking; beverage management; buffet catering; controlling costs in food service; culinary skill development; food preparation; food purchasing; food service math; garde-manger; international cuisine; introduction to food service; kitchen management; management and human resources; meal planning; meat cutting; menu and facilities design; nutrition; nutrition and food service; restaurant opportunities; sanitation; saucier; seafood processing; soup, stock, sauce, and starch production; wines and spirits.

FACILITIES
Bake shop; 4 classrooms; computer laboratory; demonstration laboratory; 2 food production kitchens; gourmet dining room; learning resource center; lecture room; library; public restaurant; student lounge; 2 teaching kitchens.

STUDENT PROFILE
150 total: 85 full-time; 65 part-time.

FACULTY

7 total: 6 full-time; 1 part-time. Prominent faculty: Richard Fulchiron, CEC, CCE, M.Ed.; Thomas Capretta, M.Ed., CEC, CCE; Paul Glatt, MBA; Kim Susbauer, MED. Faculty-student ratio: 1:14.

SPECIAL PROGRAMS

210-hour required practicum and 210-hours management (associate degree), culinary competitions, personal chef, service leaving experience.

TYPICAL EXPENSES

In-state tuition: $5235 per associate degree full-time (in district), $80.54 per credit hour part-time (in district), $6721 per associate degree full-time (out-of-district), $106.48 per credit hour part-time (out-of-district). Out-of-state tuition: $14,172 per associate degree full-time, $218.04 per credit hour part-time. Tuition for international students: $14,172 per associate degree full-time, $218.04 per credit hour part-time. Program-related fees include $165 for lab fees (cooking/baking classes) (2 years); $80 for uniforms (2 years); $2000 for books (2 years).

FINANCIAL AID

In 2006, 20 scholarships were awarded (average award was $600). Program-specific awards include Chef Boirdee Scholarship, A. LoPresti Scholarship, Hospitality Student Club Scholarship-for books only. Employment placement assistance is available. Employment opportunities within the program are available.

HOUSING

Average off-campus housing cost per month: $500.

APPLICATION INFORMATION

Students may begin participation in January, March, May, August, and October. Applications are accepted continuously. In 2006, 231 applied; 231 were accepted. Applicants must interview; submit a formal application; be high school graduate or have GED, take college math and English placements tests.

CONTACT

Julia Patterson, Program Assistant, Hospitality Management Department, Hospitality Management, 2900 Community College Avenue, Cleveland, OH 44115. Telephone: 216-987-4081. Fax: 216-987-4086. E-mail: julia.patterson@tri-c.edu. World Wide Web: http://www.tri-c.edu/infoaccess.

THE INTERNATIONAL CULINARY ARTS & SCIENCES INSTITUTE (ICASI)

Chesterland, Ohio

GENERAL INFORMATION

Private, coeducational, culinary institute. Suburban campus. Founded in 2002.

PROGRAM INFORMATION

Offered since 2002. Program calendar is divided into quarters. 18-month diploma in pastry arts. 18-month diploma in culinary arts. 6-month certificate in pastry arts. 6-month certificate in culinary arts.

PROGRAM AFFILIATION

American Culinary Federation; American Institute of Wine & Food; International Association of Culinary Professionals.

AREAS OF STUDY

Baking; buffet catering; confectionery show pieces; culinary skill development; food preparation; food purchasing; food service math; garde-manger; international cuisine; introduction to food service; kitchen management; meal planning; meat fabrication; menu and facilities design; nutrition; nutrition and food service; patisserie; restaurant opportunities; sanitation; saucier; seafood processing; soup, stock, sauce, and starch production; wines and spirits.

FACILITIES

Bake shop; classroom; computer laboratory; food production kitchen; garden; lecture room; library; 2 teaching kitchens.

STUDENT PROFILE

50 are under 25 years old; 46 are between 25 and 44 years old; 8 are over 44 years old.

FACULTY

16 total: 4 full-time; 12 part-time. 10 are industry professionals; 6 are culinary-certified teachers. Prominent faculty: Loretta Paganini, CCP; Tim McCoy; Matthew Anderson; Neil MacKenzie. Faculty-student ratio: 1:12.

SPECIAL PROGRAMS

5-day cooking classes in Italy.

TYPICAL EXPENSES

Tuition: $19,800 per 18-month diploma; $6,400 for 6-month certificate. Program-related fees include $600 for cutlery, uniform, books, tool kit (for certificate program); $1000 for uniform, cutlery, books, tool kit (for diploma program); $100 for enrollment fee.

The International Culinary Arts & Sciences Institute (ICASI) *(continued)*

FINANCIAL AID
Employment placement assistance is available. Employment opportunities within the program are available.

HOUSING
Average off-campus housing cost per month: $500.

APPLICATION INFORMATION
Students may begin participation in January, April, July, and September. Applications are accepted continuously. In 2006, 90 applied; 90 were accepted. Applicants must interview; submit a formal application, letters of reference, an essay; have high school diploma or GED; pass entrance exam.

CONTACT
Ruthann Kostadinov, Student Services Director, 8700 Mayfield Road, Chesterland, OH 44026. Telephone: 440-729-7340. Fax: 440-729-4546. E-mail: icasi@lpscinc.com. World Wide Web: http://www.icasi.net.

OWENS COMMUNITY COLLEGE

Hotel, Restaurant, and Institution Technology

Toledo, Ohio

GENERAL INFORMATION
Public, coeducational, two-year college. Suburban campus. Founded in 1965. Accredited by North Central Association of Colleges and Schools.

PROGRAM INFORMATION
Offered since 1968. Program calendar is divided into semesters. 1-year certificate in culinary arts. 2-year associate degree in hospitality management. 2-year associate degree in food service management.

PROGRAM AFFILIATION
National Restaurant Association; Ohio Restaurant Association.

AREAS OF STUDY
Advanced food production; baking; beverage management; buffet catering; controlling costs in food service; culinary skill development; food preparation; food purchasing; garde-manger; international cuisine; introduction to food service; management and human resources; meal planning; menu and facilities design; nutrition; restaurant opportunities; sanitation; soup, stock, sauce, and starch production; wines and spirits.

FACILITIES
Classroom; food production kitchen; public restaurant.

TYPICAL STUDENT PROFILE
150 total: 50 full-time; 100 part-time. 40 are under 25 years old; 100 are between 25 and 44 years old; 10 are over 44 years old.

SPECIAL PROGRAMS
Cooperative work experience, department-run Terrace View Café.

FINANCIAL AID
Employment placement assistance is available.

APPLICATION INFORMATION
Students may begin participation in January, June, and August. Applications are accepted continuously. Applicants must submit a formal application.

CONTACT
Director of Admissions, Hotel, Restaurant, and Institution Technology, PO Box 10000, Oregon Road, Toledo, OH 43699-1947. Telephone: 567-661-7563. Fax: 567-661-7251. World Wide Web: http://www.owens.edu/academic_dept/health_tech/hri/index.html.

SINCLAIR COMMUNITY COLLEGE

Hospitality Management/Culinary Arts Option

Dayton, Ohio

GENERAL INFORMATION
Public, coeducational, two-year college. Urban campus. Founded in 1887. Accredited by North Central Association of Colleges and Schools.

PROGRAM INFORMATION
Offered since 1993. Accredited by American Culinary Federation Accrediting Commission, Commission on Accreditation of Hospitality Management Programs. Program calendar is divided into quarters. 1-year certificate in food service management. 2-year associate degree in hospitality, management and tourism. 2-year associate degree in hotel lodging. 2-year associate degree in restaurant management. 2-year associate degree in meeting and event planning. 2-year associate degree in tourism. 2-year associate degree in culinary arts option. 2-year associate degree in hospitality management.

PROGRAM AFFILIATION
American Culinary Federation; Council on Hotel, Restaurant, and Institutional Education; National Restaurant Association; National Restaurant Association Educational Foundation.

AREAS OF STUDY
Baking; beverage management; buffet catering; controlling costs in food service; culinary skill development; food preparation; food purchasing;

garde-manger; international cuisine; introduction to food service; management and human resources; meat cutting; meat fabrication; menu and facilities design; nutrition; patisserie; restaurant opportunities; sanitation; saucier; seafood processing; soup, stock, sauce, and starch production; wines and spirits.

FACILITIES
Catering service; 5 classrooms; 5 computer laboratories; demonstration laboratory; food production kitchen; gourmet dining room; 3 laboratories; learning resource center; library; public restaurant; 3 snack shops; student lounge; 3 teaching kitchens.

STUDENT PROFILE
400 total: 100 full-time; 300 part-time.

FACULTY
15 total: 4 full-time; 11 part-time. 8 are industry professionals; 4 are culinary-certified teachers. Prominent faculty: Steven K. Cornelius, CCE, FMP, CEC; Frank Leibold, CEC, CWPC, CCE; Derek Allen, CHE, MBA; Gabriel Gardner. Faculty-student ratio: 1:20.

PROMINENT ALUMNI AND CURRENT AFFILIATION
Karen Harmon, CC, Cameron Mitchell Restaurants, Columbus, OH; James Chantansombot, CC, Canterbury Hotel, Indianapolis, IN; Randy Hixon, CC, Faculty/Sinclair Community College.

SPECIAL PROGRAMS
Disney World Internship Program.

TYPICAL EXPENSES
Application fee: $10. In-state tuition: $45 per credit hour full-time (in district), $45 per credit hour part-time (in district), $73.50 per credit hour full-time (out-of-district), $73.50 per credit hour part-time (out-of-district). Out-of-state tuition: $145 per credit hour full-time, $145 per credit hour part-time. Tuition for international students: $145 per credit hour full-time, $145 per credit hour part-time. Program-related fees include $60–$120 for lab fees for products used in demonstrations and training; $200 for uniforms and knives.

FINANCIAL AID
In 2006, 7 scholarships were awarded (average award was $400). Employment placement assistance is available. Employment opportunities within the program are available.

APPLICATION INFORMATION
Students may begin participation in January, March, June, and September. Applications are accepted continuously. In 2006, 225 applied; 225 were accepted. Applicants must submit a formal application.

CONTACT
Steven Cornelius, Department Chair/Professor, Hospitality Management/Culinary Arts Option, 444 West Third Street, Dayton, OH 45402. Telephone: 937-512-5197. Fax: 937-512-5396. E-mail: steve.cornelius@sinclair.edu. World Wide Web: http://www.sinclair.edu/academics/bps/departments/hmt/.

THE UNIVERSITY OF AKRON
Hospitality Management
Akron, Ohio

GENERAL INFORMATION
Public, coeducational, university. Urban campus. Founded in 1870. Accredited by North Central Association of Colleges and Schools.

PROGRAM INFORMATION
Offered since 1974. Accredited by ACBSP. Program calendar is divided into semesters. 1-year certificate in restaurant management. 1-year certificate in hotel/motel management. 1-year certificate in culinary arts. 2-year associate degree in culinary arts. 2-year associate degree in restaurant management. 2-year associate degree in hotel/motel management. 2-year associate degree in hospitality marketing and sales.

PROGRAM AFFILIATION
American Culinary Federation; Council on Hotel, Restaurant, and Institutional Education; National Restaurant Association; Ohio Hotel/Motel Association.

AREAS OF STUDY
Baking; beverage management; controlling costs in food service; culinary skill development; food preparation; food purchasing; food service communication; food service math; garde-manger; international cuisine; introduction to food service; kitchen management; management and human resources; meal planning; menu and facilities design; nutrition; sanitation; soup, stock, sauce, and starch production; wines and spirits.

FACILITIES
Food production kitchen; public restaurant.

STUDENT PROFILE
150 total: 75 full-time; 75 part-time. 90 are under 25 years old; 50 are between 25 and 44 years old; 10 are over 44 years old.

The University of Akron *(continued)*

FACULTY
7 total: 5 full-time; 2 part-time. 5 are industry professionals; 2 are culinary-certified teachers. Prominent faculty: Mark Kent, CEC; Lawrence Gilpatric, CEC, CCE, CHA, FMP; Jamal Feerasta; Tim Mehlberg.

PROMINENT ALUMNI AND CURRENT AFFILIATION
Aaron Costic, Olympic Champion Ice Carver.

SPECIAL PROGRAMS
Internships, field trips to local and national professional shows.

TYPICAL EXPENSES
Application fee: $30. In-state tuition: $5885 per year full-time (in district), $229 per credit part-time. Out-of-state tuition: $12,845 per year full-time, $525 per credit part-time. Program-related fees include $100 for lab fees for culinary courses; $50 for uniforms; $75 for knife set.

FINANCIAL AID
In 2006, 10 scholarships were awarded (average award was $1000). Employment placement assistance is available. Employment opportunities within the program are available.

HOUSING
Coed, apartment-style, and single-sex housing available. Average off-campus housing cost per month: $250.

APPLICATION INFORMATION
Students may begin participation in January and August. Applications are accepted continuously. In 2006, 85 applied; 85 were accepted. Applicants must submit a formal application and have a high school diploma or GED.

CONTACT
Office of Admissions, Hospitality Management, 302 Buchtel Common, Akron, OH 44325. Telephone: 800-655-4884. E-mail: admissions@uakron.edu. World Wide Web: http://www.uakron.edu/.

ZANE STATE COLLEGE

Culinary Arts Program

Zanesville, Ohio

GENERAL INFORMATION
Public, coeducational, two-year college. Suburban campus. Founded in 1970. Accredited by North Central Association of Colleges and Schools.

PROGRAM INFORMATION
Offered since 1993. Accredited by American Culinary Federation Accrediting Commission. Program calendar is divided into quarters. 1-quarter certificate in safety and sanitation. 2-year associate degree in culinary arts.

PROGRAM AFFILIATION
American Culinary Federation; National Restaurant Association; National Restaurant Association Educational Foundation.

AREAS OF STUDY
Baking; culinary French; culinary skill development; food preparation; food purchasing; food service math; garde-manger; international cuisine; meat cutting; meat fabrication; menu and facilities design; nutrition and food service; sanitation; soup, stock, sauce, and starch production.

FACILITIES
Bake shop; cafeteria; classroom; 10 computer laboratories; demonstration laboratory; food production kitchen; learning resource center; lecture room; library; 4 public restaurants; 2 student lounges; teaching kitchen.

TYPICAL STUDENT PROFILE
30 total: 20 full-time; 10 part-time. 15 are under 25 years old; 10 are between 25 and 44 years old; 5 are over 44 years old.

FINANCIAL AID
Employment placement assistance is available.

APPLICATION INFORMATION
Students may begin participation in September. Applications are accepted continuously. Applicants must submit a formal application.

CONTACT
Director of Admissions, Culinary Arts Program, 1555 Newark Road, Zanesville, OH 43701. Telephone: 740-588-1334. Fax: 740-454-0035. World Wide Web: http://www.zanestate.edu/CUL/default.htm.

OKLAHOMA

METRO AREA VOCATIONAL TECHNICAL SCHOOL DISTRICT 22

Oklahoma City, Oklahoma

GENERAL INFORMATION
Public, coeducational, technical institute. Urban campus. Founded in 1980.

PROGRAM INFORMATION

Offered since 1980. Program calendar is divided into quarters. 525- to 600-hour certificate in food service management/production. 525- to 600-hour certificate in food service production.

PROGRAM AFFILIATION

American Culinary Federation; National Restaurant Association; National Restaurant Association Educational Foundation; Oklahoma Restaurant Association.

AREAS OF STUDY

Baking; buffet catering; controlling costs in food service; food preparation; food purchasing; food service communication; food service math; introduction to food service; kitchen management; meal planning; nutrition; nutrition and food service; sanitation.

FACILITIES

Bake shop; cafeteria; classroom; demonstration laboratory; food production kitchen; learning resource center; library.

STUDENT PROFILE

34 total: 1 full-time; 33 part-time. 33 are under 25 years old; 1 is over 44 years old.

FACULTY

1 total: 1 full-time. Faculty-student ratio: 1:34.

SPECIAL PROGRAMS

400-hour paid internship.

FINANCIAL AID

Employment placement assistance is available. Employment opportunities within the program are available.

APPLICATION INFORMATION

Students may begin participation in January, February, March, April, May, August, September, October, November, and December. Applications are accepted continuously. Applicants must submit a formal application.

CONTACT

Rennie Benefield, Counselor, 4901 South Bryant, Oklahoma City, OK 73129. Telephone: 405-605-2206. Fax: 405-671-3410. World Wide Web: http://www.metrotech.org.

OKLAHOMA STATE UNIVERSITY, OKMULGEE

Hospitality Services Department

Okmulgee, Oklahoma

GENERAL INFORMATION

Public, coeducational, two-year college. Rural campus. Founded in 1946. Accredited by North Central Association of Colleges and Schools.

PROGRAM INFORMATION

Offered since 1946. Program calendar is divided into trimesters. 90-hour associate degree in culinary arts.

PROGRAM AFFILIATION

Greater Southwest Retail Bakers Association; International Food Service Executives Association; National Restaurant Association; National Restaurant Association Educational Foundation; Oklahoma Restaurant Association; Retailer's Bakery Association.

AREAS OF STUDY

Baking; buffet catering; controlling costs in food service; culinary French; culinary skill development; food preparation; food purchasing; garde-manger; international cuisine; introduction to food service; kitchen management; management and human resources; meal planning; meat cutting; meat fabrication; menu and facilities design; nutrition; patisserie; sanitation; saucier; seafood processing; soup, stock, sauce, and starch production; wines and spirits.

FACILITIES

Cafeteria; 5 classrooms; coffee shop; computer laboratory; demonstration laboratory; 2 food production kitchens; gourmet dining room; learning resource center; library; 2 public restaurants; snack shop; student lounge.

STUDENT PROFILE

180 total: 175 full-time; 5 part-time.

FACULTY

8 total: 8 full-time. 8 are industry professionals; 8 are culinary-certified teachers; 2 are certified executive chefs. Prominent faculty: René Jungo CEC; John Surmont CEC; Ronald L'Heureux. Faculty-student ratio: 1:15.

SPECIAL PROGRAMS

Class trips to wineries, San Francisco, and fine dining establishments, 8-week paid internships, culinary competitions.

Oklahoma State University, Okmulgee *(continued)*

TYPICAL EXPENSES
Application fee: $15. In-state tuition: $116 per credit hour. Out-of-state tuition: $279 per credit hour. Program-related fees include $120 for beginning knife set; $140 for 3 uniforms (hats and 4-way aprons included).

FINANCIAL AID
In 2006, 10 scholarships were awarded (average award was $500); 3 loans were granted (average loan was $2500). Program-specific awards include work-study programs, possible waiver of out-of-state tuition. Employment placement assistance is available. Employment opportunities within the program are available.

HOUSING
Coed and apartment-style housing available. Average on-campus housing cost per month: $387. Average off-campus housing cost per month: $350.

APPLICATION INFORMATION
Students may begin participation in January, April, and August. Application deadline for fall is August 30. Application deadline for spring is January 3. Application deadline for summer is April 25. In 2006, 91 applied; 91 were accepted. Applicants must submit a formal application, ACT scores; have a high school diploma or GED.

CONTACT
Mary Ashley, Senior Administrative Assistant, Hospitality Services Department, 1801 East Fourth Street, Okmulgee, OK 74447-3901. Telephone: 918-293-5030. Fax: 918-293-4618. E-mail: mary.bell@okstate.edu. World Wide Web: http://www.osu-okmulgee.edu/.

OREGON

CENTRAL OREGON COMMUNITY COLLEGE

Cascade Culinary Institute

Bend, Oregon

GENERAL INFORMATION
Public, coeducational, two-year college. Small-town setting. Founded in 1949. Accredited by Northwest Commission on Colleges and Universities.

PROGRAM INFORMATION
Offered since 1993. Accredited by American Culinary Federation Accrediting Commission. Program calendar is divided into quarters. 4-term certificate in culinary arts. 6-term associate degree in culinary management. 6-term associate degree in hospitality/tourism/recreation management.

PROGRAM AFFILIATION
American Culinary Federation; American Dietetic Association; Council on Hotel, Restaurant, and Institutional Education; International Association of Culinary Professionals.

AREAS OF STUDY
Baking; beverage management; controlling costs in food service; culinary skill development; food preparation; food purchasing; food service math; garde-manger; introduction to food service; kitchen management; management and human resources; meal planning; nutrition; nutrition and food service; restaurant opportunities; sanitation; soup, stock, sauce, and starch production; wines and spirits.

FACILITIES
Bake shop; cafeteria; catering service; 2 classrooms; computer laboratory; food production kitchen; 2 lecture rooms; library; public restaurant; snack shop; teaching kitchen.

STUDENT PROFILE
43 full-time.

FACULTY
6 total: 2 full-time; 4 part-time. 4 are industry professionals; 2 are culinary-certified teachers; 1 is a certified executive chef. Prominent faculty: Julian Darwin, CEC, CHE; Julie Hood; Maeve Perle. Faculty-student ratio: 1:18.

SPECIAL PROGRAMS
3-day tour of Napa Valley wineries and farm gardens, visit to fisheries on Oregon coast, food and cultural experience in Spain.

TYPICAL EXPENSES
Application fee: $25. In-state tuition: $63 per credit, 4 term program (in district), $86 per credit (out-of-district). Out-of-state tuition: $176 per credit. Tuition for international students: $176 per credit.

FINANCIAL AID
In 2006, 3 scholarships were awarded (average award was $1000); 18 loans were granted (average loan was $2100). Program-specific awards include Pine Tavern Award ($1800). Employment placement assistance is available. Employment opportunities within the program are available.

HOUSING

Coed housing available. Average on-campus housing cost per month: $325. Average off-campus housing cost per month: $400–$600.

APPLICATION INFORMATION

Students may begin participation in January, March, and September. Application deadline for fall is August 1. Application deadline for winter is November 1. Application deadline for spring is February 1. In 2006, 22 were accepted. Applicants must interview; submit a formal application.

CONTACT

Scott Hays, Program Coordinator, Cascade Culinary Institute, 2600 Northwest College Way, Bend, OR 97701-5998. Telephone: 541-383-7715. Fax: 541-383-7508. E-mail: shays@cocc.edu. World Wide Web: http://culinary.cocc.edu.

CHEMEKETA COMMUNITY COLLEGE

Hospitality and Tourism Management

Salem, Oregon

GENERAL INFORMATION

Public, coeducational, two-year college. Urban campus. Founded in 1955. Accredited by Northwest Commission on Colleges and Universities.

PROGRAM INFORMATION

Offered since 1974. Program calendar is divided into quarters. 1-year certificate in destination marketing. 1-year certificate in tourism and travel management. 1-year certificate in hospitality management. 1-year certificate in event management. 2-year associate degree in nutrition and food management with Oregon State University. 2-year associate degree in hotel and business management with Washington State University. 2-year associate degree in tourism and travel management. 2-year associate degree in hotel, restaurant, and resort management. 2-year associate degree in hospitality management.

PROGRAM AFFILIATION

American Hotel and Lodging Association; Council on Hotel, Restaurant, and Institutional Education; Hospitality Sales and Marketing Association International; National Restaurant Association; National Restaurant Association Educational Foundation; Oregon Lodging Association; Oregon Restaurant Educational Foundation; Portland Oregon Visitors Association.

AREAS OF STUDY

Beverage management; controlling costs in food service; cultural heritage tourism; food purchasing; gaming; introduction to food service; leisure/recreation; lodging; management and human resources; meal planning; meeting and event planning; nature-based tourism; nutrition; nutrition and food service; restaurant opportunities; sanitation; travel and tourism; wines and spirits.

FACILITIES

Classroom; computer laboratory; lecture room; library; vineyard.

STUDENT PROFILE

225 total: 125 full-time; 100 part-time.

FACULTY

9 total: 4 full-time; 5 part-time. 9 are industry professionals. Prominent faculty: Eric Aebi; Ben Gentile; Ann Raymon; Kris Powers. Faculty-student ratio: 1:25.

SPECIAL PROGRAMS

Online classes (complete degree/certificate are available online), transfer degree to Washington State University School of Hospitality Business Management.

TYPICAL EXPENSES

In-state tuition: $768–$960 per quarter, 12 to 15 credits full-time (in district), $64 per credit hour part-time. Out-of-state tuition: $2436–$3045 per quarter, 12 to 15 credits full-time, $203 per credit hour part-time. Tuition for international students: $2436–$3045 per quarter, 12 to 15 credits full-time, $203 per credit hour part-time. Program-related fee includes $50 for online fee (per course).

FINANCIAL AID

Employment placement assistance is available. Employment opportunities within the program are available.

APPLICATION INFORMATION

Students may begin participation in January, March, June, and September. Applications are accepted continuously. Applicants must submit a formal application, have high school diploma or GED, and take placement test.

CONTACT

Nancy Duncan, Program Director, Hospitality and Tourism Management, 4000 Lancaster Drive NE, Salem, OR 97305. Telephone: 503-399-5296. Fax: 503-365-4770. E-mail: nduncan@chemeketa.edu. World Wide Web: http://www.hsm.org.

CULINARY AWAKENINGS

Portland, Oregon

GENERAL INFORMATION
Private, coeducational institution. Urban campus. Founded in 1993.

PROGRAM INFORMATION
Offered since 1993. Program calendar is custom programs all year. 1—20 day certificate in vegan culinary arts.

PROGRAM AFFILIATION
American Vegan Society; Bioneers; Chefs Collaborative 2000; International Vegetarian Union; North American Vegetarian Society; Northwest VEG; Vegetarian Resource Group.

AREAS OF STUDY
Baking; culinary skill development; food preparation; introduction to food service; meal planning; menu and facilities design; sanitation.

FACILITIES
Garden; lecture room; teaching kitchen.

STUDENT PROFILE
30 part-time.

FACULTY
2 total: 2 full-time. 1 is an industry professional; 1 is a culinary-certified teacher. Prominent faculty: Albert H. Chase, Jr.; Donna Benjamin. Faculty-student ratio: 1:8.

SPECIAL PROGRAMS
20 day vegan culinary arts program, kitchen and pantry transformation, outing days to local vegan businesses, business consultations, public speaking services, workshops and training programs.

TYPICAL EXPENSES
Tuition: $2800 per 20-day program. Program-related fee includes $275 for knife kit (optional).

FINANCIAL AID
Program-specific awards include sous chef discounts. Employment placement assistance is available.

APPLICATION INFORMATION
Applications are accepted continuously. In 2006, 30 applied; 30 were accepted. Applicants must have a phone interview, client contact form.

CONTACT
Chef Albert H. Chase, Founder and Culinary Director, 4110 SE Hawthorne Boulevard #173, Portland, OR 97214. Telephone: 503-752-2588. E-mail: chefal@chefal.org. World Wide Web: http://www.chefal.org.

INTERNATIONAL SCHOOL OF BAKING

Bend, Oregon

GENERAL INFORMATION
Private, coeducational, culinary institute. Urban campus. Founded in 1986.

PROGRAM INFORMATION
Offered since 1986. Program calendar is customized to meet student needs, customized to meet students needs. 1-month certificate in start-up bakery course. 2-week certificate in European pastries. 2-week certificate in artisan breads. 3-day certificate in individualized specialization. 6-week certificate in start-up bakery course including wedding cakes.

PROGRAM AFFILIATION
American Culinary Federation; International Association of Culinary Professionals; James Beard Foundation, Inc.; Retailer's Bakery Association; The Bread Bakers Guild of America.

AREAS OF STUDY
Bakery start-up; baking; custom designed studies; kitchen management; menu and facilities design; patisserie; sanitation.

FACILITIES
Bakery; classroom; demonstration laboratory; food production kitchen; garden; learning resource center; library; teaching kitchen.

STUDENT PROFILE
21 total: 5 full-time; 16 part-time.

FACULTY
4 total: 2 full-time; 2 part-time. 1 is an industry professional; 1 is a master baker. Prominent faculty: Marda E. Stoliar; Jeri Boe; Tracy Van Oden.

SPECIAL PROGRAMS
6-month unpaid internship, 1-year unpaid internship.

TYPICAL EXPENSES
Tuition: $12,000 per month full-time, $600 per day part-time. Program-related fee includes all fees included.

FINANCIAL AID
Employment placement assistance is available.

HOUSING
Average off-campus housing cost per month: $2400.

APPLICATION INFORMATION
Students may begin participation year-round. Applications are accepted continuously. Application deadline for each course is 2 months prior to start date. In 2006, 24 applied; 21 were accepted. Applicants must submit a formal application.

CONTACT

Marda Stoliar, Director, 1971 NW Juniper Street, Bend, OR 97701. Telephone: 541-389-8553. Fax: 541-389-3736. E-mail: marda@schoolofbaking.com. World Wide Web: http://www.schoolofbaking.com.

LANE COMMUNITY COLLEGE

Culinary Arts and Hospitality Management

Eugene, Oregon

GENERAL INFORMATION

Public, coeducational, two-year college. Suburban campus. Founded in 1964. Accredited by Northwest Commission on Colleges and Universities.

PROGRAM INFORMATION

Offered since 1979. Accredited by American Culinary Federation. Program calendar is divided into quarters. 1-year certificate of completion in hospitality management. 2-year associate degree in culinary arts. 2-year associate degree in hospitality management.

PROGRAM AFFILIATION

Council on Hotel, Restaurant, and Institutional Education; Educational Institute-American Hotel and Motel Association; National Restaurant Association; National Restaurant Association Educational Foundation.

AREAS OF STUDY

Baking; beverage management; buffet catering; controlling costs in food service; culinary skill development; food preparation; food purchasing; food service math; garde-manger; international cuisine; introduction to food service; management and human resources; menu and facilities design; nutrition; sanitation; soup, stock, sauce, and starch production.

FACILITIES

3 classrooms; 3 demonstration laboratories; 2 food production kitchens; gourmet dining room; learning resource center; 3 lecture rooms; library; public restaurant; 3 teaching kitchens.

TYPICAL STUDENT PROFILE

105 total: 85 full-time; 20 part-time.

SPECIAL PROGRAMS

Culinary competition.

FINANCIAL AID

Employment placement assistance is available. Employment opportunities within the program are available.

APPLICATION INFORMATION

Students may begin participation in January, April, and September. Application deadline for fall is June 30. Applicants must interview; submit a formal application, letters of reference, test scores.

CONTACT

Director of Admissions, Culinary Arts and Hospitality Management, 4000 East 30th Avenue, Building 19 Room 202, Eugene, OR 97405. Telephone: 541-463-3510 Ext. 3510. Fax: 541-463-4738. World Wide Web: http://www.lanecc.edu.

LINN-BENTON COMMUNITY COLLEGE

Culinary Arts/Restaurant Management

Albany, Oregon

GENERAL INFORMATION

Public, coeducational, two-year college. Rural campus. Founded in 1966. Accredited by Northwest Commission on Colleges and Universities.

PROGRAM INFORMATION

Offered since 1969. Program calendar is divided into quarters. 2-year associate degree in wine and food dynamics. 2-year associate degree in chef training. 2-year associate degree in pre-restaurant management.

PROGRAM AFFILIATION

American Culinary Federation; Council on Hotel, Restaurant, and Institutional Education; National Restaurant Association; Women Chefs and Restaurateurs.

AREAS OF STUDY

Baking; beverage management; buffet catering; confectionery show pieces; controlling costs in food service; culinary French; culinary skill development; food preparation; food purchasing; food service math; garde-manger; international cuisine; introduction to food service; kitchen management; management and human resources; meal planning; meat cutting; meat fabrication; menu and facilities design; nutrition; patisserie; sanitation; saucier; seafood processing; soup, stock, sauce, and starch production; wine and food; wines and spirits.

FACILITIES

Bake shop; bakery; cafeteria; catering service; classroom; coffee shop; computer laboratory; food production kitchen; garden; gourmet dining room; laboratory; learning resource center; lecture room; library; public restaurant; snack shop; student lounge.

Linn-Benton Community College *(continued)*

STUDENT PROFILE
45 full-time. 15 are under 25 years old; 25 are between 25 and 44 years old; 5 are over 44 years old.

FACULTY
6 total: 2 full-time; 4 part-time. 6 are industry professionals; 2 are culinary-certified teachers. Prominent faculty: Scott Anselm; John Jarscke.

TYPICAL EXPENSES
In-state tuition: $792 per quarter. Out-of-state tuition: $2004 per quarter.

FINANCIAL AID
In 2006, 7 scholarships were awarded (average award was $500). Program-specific awards include 36 credits of tuition waiver per year for program club officers. Employment placement assistance is available.

HOUSING
Average off-campus housing cost per month: $300.

APPLICATION INFORMATION
Students may begin participation in September. Applications are accepted continuously. In 2006, 45 applied; 45 were accepted. Applicants must submit a formal application.

CONTACT
Scott Anselm, Department Chair, Culinary Arts/Restaurant Management, 6500 Southwest Pacific Boulevard, Albany, OR 97321. Telephone: 541-917-4388. Fax: 541-917-4395. E-mail: anselms@linnbenton.edu. World Wide Web: http://www.linnbenton.edu/.

OREGON COAST CULINARY INSTITUTE

Coos Bay, Oregon

GENERAL INFORMATION
Public, coeducational, culinary institute. Small-town setting. Founded in 2000. Accredited by Northwest Commission on Colleges and Universities.

PROGRAM INFORMATION
Offered since 2000. Accredited by American Culinary Federation Accrediting Commission. Program calendar is divided into quarters. 15-month associate degree in pastry and baking. 15-month associate degree in culinary arts management.

PROGRAM AFFILIATION
American Culinary Federation.

AREAS OF STUDY

Baking; beverage management; buffet catering; confectionery show pieces; culinary skill development; food preparation; food purchasing; food service communication; food service math; garde-manger; international cuisine; introduction to food service; kitchen management; meal planning; meat cutting; menu and facilities design; Northwest cuisine; nutrition; nutrition and food service; patisserie; restaurant opportunities; sanitation; saucier; seafood processing; soup, stock, sauce, and starch production; wines and spirits.

FACILITIES

Bakery; cafeteria; catering service; 3 classrooms; computer laboratory; demonstration laboratory; food production kitchen; gourmet dining room; learning resource center; 3 lecture rooms; library; student lounge; 2 teaching kitchens.

STUDENT PROFILE

60 full-time. 40 are under 25 years old; 20 are between 25 and 44 years old.

FACULTY

8 total: 3 full-time; 5 part-time. 3 are industry professionals; 2 are culinary-certified teachers. Prominent faculty: Kevin Shaw, CEPC. Faculty-student ratio: 1:20.

SPECIAL PROGRAMS

Internships, two-week European baking tour (optional baking and pastry program), culinary competition, including team events.

TYPICAL EXPENSES

Application fee: $30. Tuition: $19,500 per 15-month program (includes textbooks, knife set, 2 sets of chef uniforms).

FINANCIAL AID

In 2006, 15 scholarships were awarded (average award was $2470); 72 loans were granted (average loan was $6782). Program-specific awards include ProStart certificate scholarship, GPA tuition discount. Employment placement assistance is available. Employment opportunities within the program are available.

HOUSING

Coed and apartment-style housing available. Average on-campus housing cost per month: $500–$600. Average off-campus housing cost per month: $500.

APPLICATION INFORMATION

Students may begin participation in September. Applications are accepted continuously. In 2006, 105 applied; 60 were accepted. Applicants must submit a formal application.

CONTACT

Tom Nicholls, Admissions Representative, 1988 Newmark Avenue, Coos Bay, OR 97420. Telephone: 877-895-CHEF. Fax: 541-888-7195. E-mail: tnicholls@socc.edu. World Wide Web: http://www.occi.net.

OREGON CULINARY INSTITUTE

Portland, Oregon

GENERAL INFORMATION

Private, coeducational, culinary institute. Founded in 2006. Accredited by Accrediting Council for Independent Colleges and Schools.

PROGRAM INFORMATION

Program calendar is continuous. Associate degree in culinary arts. Certificate in baking and pastry. Diploma in culinary arts.

FACILITIES

Computer laboratory; 3 food production kitchens; gourmet dining room.

TYPICAL EXPENSES

Application fee: $50. Tuition: $16,200 for the diploma program; $23,400 for the Associate of Applied Science (AAS) degree program, $9550 for baking and pastry certificate program. Program-related fees include $50 for graduation fee; $300 for registration fee; $550 for lab fee, uniforms, and knives.

FINANCIAL AID

Employment placement assistance is available. Employment opportunities within the program are available.

APPLICATION INFORMATION

Applications are accepted continuously. Applicants must interview; submit a formal application, high school diploma or GED, ACT Career Programs Assessment or one year post-secondary education (minimum 2.5 GPA).

CONTACT

Director of Admissions, 1717 SW Madison Street, Portland, OR 97205. Telephone: 888-OCI-CHEF. Fax: 503-961-6240. E-mail: oci-info@pioneerpacific.edu. World Wide Web: http://www.oregonculinaryinstitute.com.

SOUTHERN OREGON UNIVERSITY

Hospitality and Tourism Management

Ashland, Oregon

GENERAL INFORMATION
Public, coeducational, four-year college. Small-town setting. Founded in 1926. Accredited by Northwest Commission on Colleges and Universities.

PROGRAM INFORMATION
Offered since 1992. Program calendar is divided into quarters. 4-year bachelor's degree in business administration (hospitality and tourism management).

AREAS OF STUDY
Beverage management; controlling costs in food service; food purchasing; food service communication; food service math; introduction to food service; management and human resources; restaurant opportunities; wines and spirits.

FACILITIES
Cafeteria; catering service; 10 classrooms; coffee shop; 2 computer laboratories; food production kitchen; learning resource center; lecture room; library; public restaurant; student lounge; vineyard.

STUDENT PROFILE
40 full-time.

FACULTY
4 total: 1 full-time; 3 part-time. Prominent faculty: Dennis Slattery, MBA, CPA. Faculty-student ratio: 1:15.

SPECIAL PROGRAMS
Internships with industry leaders, hands on event planning and execution.

TYPICAL EXPENSES
Application fee: $50. In-state tuition: $5135 per year full-time (in district), $1289 per quarter part-time. Out-of-state tuition: $15,478 per year.

FINANCIAL AID
Employment placement assistance is available. Employment opportunities within the program are available.

HOUSING
Coed housing available. Average off-campus housing cost per month: $450.

APPLICATION INFORMATION
Students may begin participation in January, April, June, and September. Applications are accepted continuously. In 2006, 40 applied; 40 were accepted. Applicants must submit a formal application.

CONTACT
Dr. Dave Harris, Dean, School of Business, Hospitality and Tourism Management, 1250 Siskiyou Boulevard, Ashland, OR 97520. Telephone: 541-552-6483. E-mail: harrisda@sou.edu. World Wide Web: http://www.sou.edu/business.

WESTERN CULINARY INSTITUTE

Le Cordon Bleu Programs at Western Culinary Institute

Portland, Oregon

GENERAL INFORMATION
Private, coeducational, culinary institute. Urban campus. Founded in 1983. Accredited by Accrediting Commission of Career Schools and Colleges of Technology.

PROGRAM INFORMATION
Offered since 1983. Accredited by American Culinary Federation Accrediting Commission. Program calendar is divided into six-week cycles, six-week cycles. 15-month associate degree in patisserie and baking. 15-month associate degree in hospitality and restaurant management. 15-month associate degree in culinary arts. 9-month diploma in culinary arts. 9-month diploma in patisserie and baking.

PROGRAM AFFILIATION
American Culinary Federation; California Restaurant Association; International Sommelier Guild; James Beard Foundation, Inc.; National Restaurant Association; National Restaurant Association Educational Foundation; Ontario Restaurant Association; Washington Restaurant Association; Women Chefs and Restaurateurs.

AREAS OF STUDY
Baking; beverage management; buffet catering; confectionery show pieces; controlling costs in food service; convenience cookery; culinary French; culinary skill development; food preparation; food purchasing; food service communication; food service math; garde-manger; international cuisine; introduction to food service; kitchen management; management and human resources; meal planning; meat cutting; meat fabrication; menu and facilities design; nutrition; nutrition and food service; patisserie; restaurant opportunities; sanitation; saucier; soup, stock, sauce, and starch production; wines and spirits.

FACILITIES
Bake shop; bakery; cafeteria; catering service; 7 classrooms; coffee shop; 3 computer laboratories; 2 demonstration laboratories; 13 food production

kitchens; gourmet dining room; learning resource center; 7 lecture rooms; library; 2 public restaurants; 2 student lounges; bakery/delicatessen.

STUDENT PROFILE
950 full-time.

FACULTY
51 total: 48 full-time; 3 part-time. 40 are industry professionals; 1 is a master baker; 7 are culinary-certified teachers. Prominent faculty: Jacky Bonnet, CCE, CEC; Ron Costa, CC; Tina Powers, CEC, CLE, CMB. Faculty-student ratio: 1:18 in culinary labs.

PROMINENT ALUMNI AND CURRENT AFFILIATION
Homaro Cantu, Executive Chef, Moto, Chicago; Brian Malarkey, Executive Chef, Oceanaire, San Diego.

SPECIAL PROGRAMS
6 to 12 week internship required at U.S. or international location, culinary competitions.

TYPICAL EXPENSES
Application fee: $50. Tuition: Contact school for costs.

FINANCIAL AID
In 2006, 93 scholarships were awarded. Employment placement assistance is available. Employment opportunities within the program are available.

APPLICATION INFORMATION
Students may begin participation in January, February, April, May, July, August, October, and November. Applications are accepted continuously. Applicants must submit a formal application and have a high school diploma.

CONTACT
Director of Admissions, Le Cordon Bleu Programs at Western Culinary Institute, 921 SW Morrison Street, Suite 400, Portland, OR 97205. Telephone: 888-848-3202. Fax: 503-223-5554. E-mail: info@wci.edu. World Wide Web: http://www.wci.edu.

See color display following page 282.

PENNSYLVANIA

THE ART INSTITUTE OF PHILADELPHIA
The International Culinary School at The Art Institute of Philadelphia

Philadelphia, Pennsylvania

GENERAL INFORMATION
Private, coeducational institution.

PROGRAM INFORMATION
Associate degree in Culinary Arts. Bachelor's degree in Culinary Management. Diploma in Culinary Arts. Diploma in Baking and Pastry.

CONTACT
Office of Admissions, The International Culinary School at The Art Institute of Philadelphia, 1622 Chestnut Street, Philadelphia, PA 19103-5119. Telephone: 215-567-7080. World Wide Web: http://www.artinstitutes.edu/philadelphia/.

See color display following page 186.

THE ART INSTITUTE OF PITTSBURGH
The International Culinary School at The Art Institute of Pittsburgh

Pittsburgh, Pennsylvania

GENERAL INFORMATION
Private, coeducational institution.

PROGRAM INFORMATION
Associate degree in Restaurant and Catering Operations. Associate degree in Culinary Arts. Bachelor's degree in Hotel and Restaurant Management. Bachelor's degree in Culinary Management. Diploma in The Art of Cooking.

CONTACT
Office of Admissions, The International Culinary School at The Art Institute of Pittsburgh, 420 Boulevard of the Allies, Pittsburgh, PA 15219-1301. Telephone: 412-263-6600. World Wide Web: http://www.artinstitutes.edu/pittsburgh/.

See color display following page 186.

THE ART INSTITUTE ONLINE

The International Culinary School at The Art Institute Online

Pittsburgh, Pennsylvania

GENERAL INFORMATION
Private, coeducational institution.

PROGRAM INFORMATION
Bachelor's degree in Hotel and Restaurant Management. Bachelor's degree in Culinary Management.

CONTACT
Office of Admissions, The International Culinary School at The Art Institute Online, 1400 Penn Avenue, Pittsburgh, PA 15222-4332. Telephone: 412-291-5100. World Wide Web: http://www.artinstitutes.edu/.
See color display following page 186.

BUCKS COUNTY COMMUNITY COLLEGE

Business Department

Newtown, Pennsylvania

GENERAL INFORMATION
Public, coeducational, two-year college. Suburban campus. Founded in 1964. Accredited by Middle States Association of Colleges and Schools.

PROGRAM INFORMATION
Offered since 1967. Program calendar is divided into semesters. 1-year associate degree in travel and event planning. 1-year certificate in travel and event planning. 1-year certificate in culinary/pastry and catering arts. 1-year certificate in hospitality/restaurant/institutional supervision. 2-year associate degree in tourism/hospitality/restaurant management. 3-year associate degree in chef apprenticeship-pastry emphasis. 3-year associate degree in chef apprenticeship-foods emphasis.

PROGRAM AFFILIATION
American Culinary Federation; Confrerie de la Chaine des Rotisseurs; International Association of Culinary Professionals; International Food Service Executives Association; National Restaurant Association; National Restaurant Association Educational Foundation.

AREAS OF STUDY
Baking; buffet catering; confectionery show pieces; controlling costs in food service; culinary skill development; food preparation; food purchasing; food service communication; food service math; garde-manger; introduction to food service; kitchen management; management and human resources; meal planning; meat cutting; meat fabrication; menu and facilities design; nutrition; nutrition and food service; patisserie; restaurant opportunities; sanitation; saucier; seafood processing; soup, stock, sauce, and starch production.

FACILITIES
Cafeteria; 5 classrooms; computer laboratory; demonstration laboratory; 2 food production kitchens; gourmet dining room; laboratory; learning resource center; library; snack shop; student lounge; teaching kitchen; greenhouse.

SPECIAL PROGRAMS
Required paid cooperative education and paid summer internship in management.

FINANCIAL AID
Employment placement assistance is available. Employment opportunities within the program are available.

APPLICATION INFORMATION
Students may begin participation in January and August. Applicants must submit a formal application and an essay.

CONTACT
Director of Admissions, Business Department, 275 Swamp Road, Newton, PA 18901-4106. Telephone: 215-968-8241. Fax: 215-504-8509. World Wide Web: http://www.bucks.edu.

BUTLER COUNTY COMMUNITY COLLEGE

Hospitality Management/Dietary Management

Butler, Pennsylvania

GENERAL INFORMATION
Public, coeducational, two-year college. Small-town setting. Founded in 1965. Accredited by Middle States Association of Colleges and Schools.

PROGRAM INFORMATION
Offered since 1988. Program calendar is divided into semesters. 1-year certificate in hospitality management. 2-year associate degree in hospitality management/dietary manager. 2-year associate degree in hospitality management.

PROGRAM AFFILIATION
Dietary Managers Association; National Restaurant Association Educational Foundation.

AREAS OF STUDY

Buffet catering; controlling costs in food service; diet therapy; food preparation; food purchasing; food service communication; food service math; international cuisine; kitchen management; lodging; management and human resources; meal planning; nutrition; nutrition and food service; sanitation; travel and tourism.

FACILITIES

Cafeteria; classroom; 2 computer laboratories; demonstration laboratory; food production kitchen; laboratory; learning resource center; lecture room; library.

STUDENT PROFILE

34 total: 24 full-time; 10 part-time.

FACULTY

3 total: 1 full-time; 2 part-time. Prominent faculty: Mary Ellen Smith, RD, LD. Faculty-student ratio: 1:15.

SPECIAL PROGRAMS

Attendance at NRA show and local food shows.

TYPICAL EXPENSES

Application fee: $25. In-state tuition: $93 per credit hour full-time (in district), $93 per credit hour part-time (in district), $166 per credit hour full-time (out-of-district), $166 per credit hour part-time (out-of-district). Out-of-state tuition: $239 per credit hour full-time, $239 per credit hour part-time. Tuition for international students: $239 per credit hour full-time, $239 per credit hour part-time.

FINANCIAL AID

Program-specific awards include National Restaurant Association scholarships ($2000), Hoss's Steak House scholarship ($500). Employment placement assistance is available. Employment opportunities within the program are available.

HOUSING

Average off-campus housing cost per month: $300.

APPLICATION INFORMATION

Students may begin participation in January, May, and August. Applications are accepted continuously. In 2006, 22 were accepted. Applicants must submit a formal application and have a high school transcript.

CONTACT

Mary Ellen Smith, Coordinator/Associate Professor, Hospitality Management/Dietary Management, PO Box 1203, Butler, PA 16003-1203. Telephone: 724-287-8711 Ext. 388. Fax: 724-285-6047. E-mail: marye.smith@bc3.cc.pa.us. World Wide Web: http://bc3.cc.pa.us/.

CHEYNEY UNIVERSITY OF PENNSYLVANIA

Hotel and Restaurant Management

Cheyney, Pennsylvania

GENERAL INFORMATION

Public, coeducational, comprehensive institution. Rural campus. Founded in 1837. Accredited by Middle States Association of Colleges and Schools.

PROGRAM INFORMATION

Offered since 1976. Program calendar is divided into 4-1-4. 4-year bachelor's degree in hotel and restaurant management.

PROGRAM AFFILIATION

Council on Hotel, Restaurant, and Institutional Education; National Restaurant Association; National Restaurant Association Educational Foundation; Pennsylvania Travel Council.

AREAS OF STUDY

Beverage management; buffet catering; controlling costs in food service; culinary skill development; food preparation; food purchasing; food service math; international cuisine; kitchen management; management and human resources; menu and facilities design; nutrition; sanitation.

FACILITIES

Cafeteria; catering service; 4 classrooms; computer laboratory; demonstration laboratory; food production kitchen; laboratory; learning resource center; 4 lecture rooms; library; 2 teaching kitchens.

STUDENT PROFILE

40 total: 37 full-time; 3 part-time. 35 are under 25 years old; 3 are between 25 and 44 years old; 2 are over 44 years old.

FACULTY

2 total: 2 full-time; 0 part-time. Faculty-student ratio: 1:12.

SPECIAL PROGRAMS

One-year internship, student-operated dining facility.

TYPICAL EXPENSES

Application fee: $20. In-state tuition: $5177 per year full-time (in district), $216 per credit part-time. Out-of-state tuition: $12,944 per year full-time, $539 per credit part-time.

FINANCIAL AID

In 2006, 1 scholarship was awarded. Program-specific awards include Walt Disney Scholarship Endowment. Employment placement assistance is available.

Cheyney University of Pennsylvania *(continued)*

HOUSING
Coed and single-sex housing available.

APPLICATION INFORMATION
Students may begin participation in January and September. Applications are accepted continuously. Applicants must interview; submit a formal application, letters of reference, an essay, academic transcript.

CONTACT
Ms. Gemma Stemley, Director of Admissions, Hotel and Restaurant Management, 1837 University Circle, PO Box 200, Cheyney, PA 19319. Telephone: 610-399-2275. Fax: 610-399-2099. E-mail: gstemley@cheyney.edu. World Wide Web: http://www.cheyney.edu.

COMMONWEALTH TECHNICAL INSTITUTE

Culinary Arts Program

Johnstown, Pennsylvania

GENERAL INFORMATION
Private, coeducational, technical institute. Suburban campus. Founded in 1959. Accredited by Accrediting Commission of Career Schools and Colleges of Technology.

PROGRAM INFORMATION
Offered since 1974. Program calendar is divided into trimesters. 16-month associate degree in culinary arts. 8-month diploma in kitchen helper.

PROGRAM AFFILIATION
Council on Hotel, Restaurant, and Institutional Education.

AREAS OF STUDY
Baking; controlling costs in food service; food preparation; food purchasing; food service math; introduction to food service; management and human resources; meal planning; menu and facilities design; nutrition; sanitation; soup, stock, sauce, and starch production.

FACILITIES
Bake shop; cafeteria; 3 classrooms; 2 computer laboratories; food production kitchen; 2 laboratories; learning resource center; library; snack shop; teaching kitchen.

STUDENT PROFILE
74 full-time. 66 are under 25 years old; 8 are between 25 and 44 years old.

FACULTY
4 total: 4 full-time. 1 is an industry professional; 2 are culinary-certified teachers. Prominent faculty: Noel B. Graham; Robert Forquer, CEC, AAC; Alexander M. McLachlan, CVI; Kim Fox, AST.

TYPICAL EXPENSES
Tuition: $5612 per 16 weeks.

FINANCIAL AID
Employment placement assistance is available.

HOUSING
Single-sex housing available.

APPLICATION INFORMATION
Students may begin participation in January, May, and September. Applications are accepted continuously. In 2006, 39 applied; 35 were accepted. Applicants must submit a formal application.

CONTACT
Rebecca Halza, Supervisor of Admissions, Culinary Arts Program, 727 Goucher Street, Johnstown, PA 15905. Telephone: 814-255-8256. E-mail: rhalza@state.pa.us. World Wide Web: http://www.hgac.org.

DELAWARE VALLEY COLLEGE

Food Science and Management

Doylestown, Pennsylvania

GENERAL INFORMATION
Private, coeducational, four-year college. Suburban campus. Founded in 1896. Accredited by Middle States Association of Colleges and Schools.

PROGRAM INFORMATION
Offered since 1961. Program calendar is divided into semesters. 2-year associate degree in culinary arts. 4-year bachelor's degree in food management.

PROGRAM AFFILIATION
American Institute of Wine & Food; American Wine Society; Institute of Food Technologists; National Restaurant Association Educational Foundation; Slow Food International; Society of Wine Educators; United States Personal Chef Association.

AREAS OF STUDY
Baking; beverage management; confectionery show pieces; controlling costs in food service; convenience cookery; culinary skill development; food preparation; food purchasing; food service communication; garde-manger; international cuisine; introduction to food service; kitchen management; management and human resources; meal planning; meat cutting; meat

fabrication; menu and facilities design; nutrition; nutrition and food service; patisserie; restaurant opportunities; sanitation; saucier; soup, stock, sauce, and starch production; wines and spirits.

FACILITIES
Bake shop; bakery; cafeteria; classroom; computer laboratory; demonstration laboratory; food production kitchen; garden; gourmet dining room; laboratory; learning resource center; lecture room; library; student lounge; teaching kitchen.

STUDENT PROFILE
30 total: 23 full-time; 7 part-time.

FACULTY
2 are culinary-certified teachers. Faculty-student ratio: 1:18.

SPECIAL PROGRAMS
Tour of International Experiences, access to 500-acre operating farm, access to beef on the dairy farm.

TYPICAL EXPENSES
Application fee: $35. Tuition: $24,710 per year full-time, $636 per credit part-time. Program-related fees include $200 for technology; $300 for experiential learning; $150 for new student fee.

HOUSING
Coed housing available. Average on-campus housing cost per month: $451. Average off-campus housing cost per month: $700.

APPLICATION INFORMATION
Students may begin participation in January and September. Applications are accepted continuously. In 2006, 9 applied; 2 were accepted. Applicants must submit a formal application and an essay.

CONTACT
Mr. Steve Zenko, Director of Admissions, Food Science and Management, 700 East Butler Avenue, Doylestown, PA 18901. Telephone: 800-2DELVAL. Fax: 215-230-2968. E-mail: admitme@delval.edu.

DREXEL UNIVERSITY

Hospitality Management, Culinary Arts, Culinary Science and Food Science

Philadelphia, Pennsylvania

GENERAL INFORMATION
Private, coeducational, university. Urban campus. Founded in 1891. Accredited by Middle States Association of Colleges and Schools.

PROGRAM INFORMATION
Offered since 1988. Accredited by Council on Hotel, Restaurant and Institutional Education, Commission on Accreditation of Hospitality Management Programs. Program calendar is divided into quarters. 4-year bachelor's degree in culinary science. 4-year bachelor's degree in culinary arts. 4-year bachelor's degree in hospitality management.

PROGRAM AFFILIATION
American Culinary Federation; American Dietetic Association; American Institute of Wine & Food; American Vegan Society; American Wine Society; Confrerie de la Chaine des Rotisseurs; Council on Hotel, Restaurant, and Institutional Education; International Association of Culinary Professionals; International Wine & Food Society; James Beard Foundation, Inc.; National Restaurant Association; National Restaurant Association Educational Foundation; Society of Wine Educators; Women Chefs and Restaurateurs.

AREAS OF STUDY
Baking; beverage management; buffet catering; confectionery show pieces; controlling costs in food service; convenience cookery; culinary French; culinary skill development; food preparation; food purchasing; food service communication; garde-manger; international cuisine; kitchen management; management and human resources; meal planning; meat cutting; meat fabrication; menu and facilities design; nutrition; nutrition and food service; patisserie; restaurant opportunities; sanitation; saucier; seafood processing; soup, stock, sauce, and starch production; wines and spirits.

FACILITIES
Bake shop; bakery; catering service; 10 classrooms; coffee shop; 7 computer laboratories; demonstration laboratory; 3 food production kitchens; garden; 2 gourmet dining rooms; 4 laboratories; learning resource center; 2 lecture rooms; 2 libraries; public restaurant; snack shop; student lounge; 2 teaching kitchens.

STUDENT PROFILE
156 total: 127 full-time; 29 part-time. 146 are under 25 years old; 10 are between 25 and 44 years old.

FACULTY
22 total: 7 full-time; 15 part-time. Prominent faculty: Charles Ziccardi; Adrienne Hall; Edward Bottone; Christina Pirello. Faculty-student ratio: 1:12.

PROMINENT ALUMNI AND CURRENT AFFILIATION
Celina Tio, The American Restaurant, Kansas City, MO; Charles Roman, Blackfish, Philadelphia, PA; Corinne Trang.

CULINARY ARTS AND HOSPITALITY MANAGEMENT

The Department of Hospitality Management at Goodwin College, Drexel University offers the following undergraduate degrees:

- **BS in Hospitality Management (HM) with concentrations in**
  - ○ **Lodging Administration**
  - ○ **Food & Beverage Management**
  - ○ **Travel and Tourism Consulting**
- **BS in Culinary Arts (CULA) with a Business minor**

Both programs prepare students for leadership positions with a global perspective and offer the option of a BS/MBA.

Drexel's programs, among the technology-oriented leaders in the country, offer students exposure to cutting edge problem solving techniques and ideas. Distinguishing features include a 14,000 square-foot state-of-the-art commercial kitchen, The Academic Bistro (student run restaurant & lounge), Goodwin Technology Center, The Culinary Reference Library, The Center for the Study of Wine and Food and the Ross Commons Advisement Center, as well as a student-run kitchen garden.

Centrally located in the heart of Philadelphia, the campus is close to New York City, Baltimore, Washington and the Atlantic seacoast. This region includes hundreds of five star/diamond hotels, award-winning restaurants and resorts, many of which are active partners in our curriculum and in Drexel's Co-Operative Education Program. Programs offer the option to study at the London Campus for three months in the sophomore, junior or senior year.

Contact:
Drexel University
Department of Hospitality
229 N. 34th Street
Philadelphia, PA 19104
215-895-2411
hospitality.mgt@drexel.edu
www.drexel.edu/goodwin

SPECIAL PROGRAMS

Study abroad in London, cooperative employment experience.

TYPICAL EXPENSES

Application fee: $50. Tuition: $32,000 per year full-time, $480 per credit part-time. Program-related fees include $200 for uniform; $350 for cutlery.

FINANCIAL AID

In 2006, 10 scholarships were awarded (average award was $4000). Employment placement assistance is available. Employment opportunities within the program are available.

HOUSING

Coed and apartment-style housing available. Average on-campus housing cost per month: $1000. Average off-campus housing cost per month: $700.

APPLICATION INFORMATION

Students may begin participation in January, April, June, and September. Application deadline for fall is March 1. In 2006, 353 applied; 173 were accepted. Applicants must submit a formal application, letters of reference, and an essay.

CONTACT

Maria McNichols, Program Manager, Hospitality Management, Culinary Arts, Culinary Science and Food Science, 33rd and Arch Street, Suite 110, Philadelphia, PA 19104. Telephone: 215-895-2836. Fax: 215-895-2426. E-mail: hospitality.mgt@drexel.edu. World Wide Web: http://www.drexel.edu.

See display on page 294.

EAST STROUDSBURG UNIVERSITY OF PENNSYLVANIA

Hotel, Restaurant and Tourism Management

East Stroudsburg, Pennsylvania

GENERAL INFORMATION

Public, coeducational, four-year college. Founded in 1893. Accredited by Middle States Association of Colleges and Schools.

PROGRAM INFORMATION

Offered since 1980. Program calendar is divided into semesters. 4-year bachelor's degree in tourism management. 4-year bachelor's degree in hotel management. 4-year bachelor's degree in restaurant management.

PROGRAM AFFILIATION

Council on Hotel, Restaurant, and Institutional Education; International Special Events Society; Meeting Professionals International; National Restaurant Association; National Restaurant Association Educational Foundation; National Tour Association; Society of Travel and Tourism Educators.

AREAS OF STUDY

Controlling costs in food service; food preparation; food purchasing; food service communication; international cuisine; introduction to food service; kitchen management; management and human resources; marketing; meal planning; menu and facilities design; restaurant opportunities; sanitation.

FACILITIES

3 classrooms; computer laboratory; demonstration laboratory; 2 food production kitchens; gourmet dining room; laboratory; 2 lecture rooms; library; public restaurant; teaching kitchen.

STUDENT PROFILE

216 total: 208 full-time; 8 part-time. 208 are under 25 years old; 8 are between 25 and 44 years old.

FACULTY

6 total: 6 full-time; 0 part-time. Faculty-student ratio: 1:18.

PROMINENT ALUMNI AND CURRENT AFFILIATION

Jodi Shapiro, Director Marketing, Courtyard Marriott, Washington, DC; Paul Farnell, Manager, Valley Forge Suites, Wayne, PA; Gerald Beaver, Food & Beverage Director: Bally's Resort and Casino, Atlantic City.

SPECIAL PROGRAMS

2 day casino tour focusing on food and beverage management, 12-15 week internship.

TYPICAL EXPENSES

Application fee: $35. In-state tuition: $5178 per academic year full-time (in district), $216 per credit part-time. Out-of-state tuition: $12,944 per academic year full-time, $539 per credit part-time.

FINANCIAL AID

In 2006, 13 scholarships were awarded (average award was $1500). Employment placement assistance is available. Employment opportunities within the program are available.

HOUSING

Coed housing available. Average on-campus housing cost per month: $473.50. Average off-campus housing cost per month: $504.75.

East Stroudsburg University of Pennsylvania
(continued)

APPLICATION INFORMATION
Students may begin participation in January and August. Application deadline for fall is April 1. Application deadline for spring is November 15. In 2006, 120 applied; 84 were accepted. Applicants must submit a formal application.

CONTACT
Associate Director, Admissions Office, Hotel, Restaurant and Tourism Management, East Stroudsburg University, East Stroudsburg, PA 18301. Telephone: 877-230-5547. Fax: 570-422-3933. E-mail: undergrads@po-box.esu.edu. World Wide Web: http://www.esu.edu/hrtm.

GREATER ALTOONA CAREER AND TECHNOLOGY CENTER

Altoona, Pennsylvania

GENERAL INFORMATION
Public, coeducational, adult vocational school. Founded in 1970. Accredited by Council on Occupational Education, Middle States Association of Colleges and Schools.

PROGRAM INFORMATION
Offered since 2000. National Restaurant Association Educational Foundation ManageFirst certificates available. Program calendar is divided into semesters. 9-month diploma in baker/pastry cook. 9-month diploma in culinary arts.

PROGRAM AFFILIATION
American Culinary Federation.

AREAS OF STUDY
Baking; culinary skill development.

FACILITIES
Bake shop; bakery; 2 classrooms; computer laboratory; food production kitchen; public restaurant; teaching kitchen.

STUDENT PROFILE
6 full-time. 5 are under 25 years old; 1 is between 25 and 44 years old.

FACULTY
1 total: 1 full-time. 1 is a culinary-certified teacher. Faculty-student ratio: 1:10.

TYPICAL EXPENSES
Application fee: $10. In-state tuition: $6000 per 9 months. Out-of-state tuition: $6000 per 9 months. Program-related fees include $1400 for textbooks; $200 for uniforms/shoes.

FINANCIAL AID
Employment placement assistance is available. Employment opportunities within the program are available.

HOUSING
Average off-campus housing cost per month: $400.

APPLICATION INFORMATION
Students may begin participation in August. Application deadline for fall is August 25. In 2006, 6 applied; 6 were accepted. Applicants must interview; submit a formal application, and take Test of Adult Basic Education.

CONTACT
Coordinator, Continuing Education Office, 1500 Fourth Avenue, Altoona, PA 16602. Telephone: 814-946-8469. Fax: 814-941-4690. E-mail: cont-ed@gacto.com. World Wide Web: http://www.gactc.com/cont-ed.

HARRISBURG AREA COMMUNITY COLLEGE

Hospitality, Restaurant, and Institutional Management Department

Harrisburg, Pennsylvania

GENERAL INFORMATION
Public, coeducational, two-year college. Suburban campus. Founded in 1964. Accredited by Middle States Association of Colleges and Schools.

PROGRAM INFORMATION
Offered since 1989. National Restaurant Association Educational Foundation ManageFirst certificates available. Program calendar is divided into semesters. 1-year diploma in institutional food service. 1-year diploma in culinary arts/catering. 10-month diploma in dietary manager. 12-month certificate in baking and pastry arts. 16-month certificate in restaurant food service management. 17-month certificate in culinary arts. 21-month associate degree in hotel and motel management. 21-month associate degree in health care food service. 21-month associate degree in restaurant food service management. 21-month associate degree in culinary arts.

PROGRAM AFFILIATION

American Culinary Federation; American Dietetic Association; College Restaurant Hospitality Institute Educators; Council on Hotel, Restaurant, and Institutional Education; National Restaurant Association; National Restaurant Association Educational Foundation.

AREAS OF STUDY

Baking; controlling costs in food service; culinary skill development; food preparation; food purchasing; introduction to hospitality; kitchen management; management and human resources; meal planning; meat cutting; menu and facilities design; nutrition; sanitation; soup, stock, sauce, and starch production.

FACILITIES

Bake shop; classroom; computer laboratory; demonstration laboratory; food production kitchen; gourmet dining room; learning resource center; lecture room; library; public restaurant; teaching kitchen; herb garden; public meat and artisan cheese shop.

STUDENT PROFILE

150 total: 75 full-time; 75 part-time. 83 are under 25 years old; 45 are between 25 and 44 years old; 22 are over 44 years old.

FACULTY

8 total: 5 full-time; 3 part-time. 2 are industry professionals; 1 is a culinary-certified teacher. Prominent faculty: Michael A. Finch, CEC; Ruth Anne McGinley, RD; Getach W. Kassahun, CHM; James Switzenberg, CEC. Faculty-student ratio: 1:15.

SPECIAL PROGRAMS

4-month paid internship, culinary competitions, participation in community charity events.

TYPICAL EXPENSES

Application fee: $25. In-state tuition: $73 per credit hour part-time (in district), $146 per credit hour part-time (out-of-district). Out-of-state tuition: $219 per credit hour part-time. Program-related fees include $300 for knives, garnishing tools, and uniforms; $12 for lab fees (per lab hour).

FINANCIAL AID

In 2006, 4 scholarships were awarded (average award was $1200). Employment placement assistance is available.

APPLICATION INFORMATION

Students may begin participation in January, May, and August. Application deadline for fall is May 1. Application deadline for spring is November 1. In 2006, 175 applied; 50 were accepted. Applicants must interview; submit a formal application, an essay, letters of reference; and have a health certificate.

CONTACT

Michael A. Finch, Chef Instructor, Hospitality, Restaurant, and Institutional Management Department, 125-E One HACC Drive, Harrisburg, PA 17110-2999. Telephone: 717-780-2674. Fax: 717-780-1130. E-mail: mafinch@hacc.edu. World Wide Web: http://www.hacc.edu/.

INDIANA UNIVERSITY OF PENNSYLVANIA

Academy of Culinary Arts

Punxsutawney, Pennsylvania

GENERAL INFORMATION

Public, coeducational, university. Rural campus. Founded in 1875. Accredited by Middle States Association of Colleges and Schools.

PROGRAM INFORMATION

Offered since 1989. Accredited by American Culinary Federation Accrediting Commission. Program calendar is divided into semesters. 12-month certificate in baking and pastry arts. 16-month certificate in culinary arts. 2-year certificate in culinary arts and baking and pastry arts. 4-year bachelor's degree in food and nutrition. 4-year bachelor's degree in hotel, restaurant, and institutional management.

PROGRAM AFFILIATION

American Culinary Federation; American Dietetic Association; Confrerie de la Chaine des Rotisseurs; Council on Hotel, Restaurant, and Institutional Education; International Association of Culinary Professionals; National Restaurant Association; National Restaurant Association Educational Foundation.

AREAS OF STUDY

Baking; beverage management; buffet catering; confectionery show pieces; controlling costs in food service; convenience cookery; culinary French; culinary skill development; food preparation; food purchasing; food service communication; food service math; garde-manger; international cuisine; introduction to food service; kitchen management; management and human resources; meal planning; meat cutting; meat fabrication; menu and facilities design; nutrition; nutrition and food service; patisserie; restaurant opportunities; sanitation; saucier; seafood processing; soup, stock, sauce, and starch production; wines and spirits.

Indiana University of Pennsylvania *(continued)*

FACILITIES
Bake shop; cafeteria; 6 classrooms; computer laboratory; 2 demonstration laboratories; food production kitchen; garden; gourmet dining room; learning resource center; lecture room; library; student lounge; 2 teaching kitchens.

STUDENT PROFILE
127 full-time. 115 are under 25 years old; 11 are between 25 and 44 years old; 1 is over 44 years old.

FACULTY
11 total: 10 full-time; 1 part-time. Prominent faculty: Albert Wutsch, CEC, CCE; Hilary DeMane, CEPC, CCE; Clifford Klinger, CEC, CCE; Gary Fitting, CEC, CCE, CCA. Faculty-student ratio: 1:14.

PROMINENT ALUMNI AND CURRENT AFFILIATION
Jeremy Critchfield, Nemacolin Woodlands; Michael Herr, Ritz Carlton; Sean Echman, Breakers, Palm Beach.

SPECIAL PROGRAMS
International externship option, international study tours, advanced baking and pastry arts instruction.

TYPICAL EXPENSES
Application fee: $30. Tuition: $6606 per semester. Program-related fees include $1500 for supply package (culinary arts); $500 for supply package (baking and pastry arts).

FINANCIAL AID
In 2006, 16 scholarships were awarded (average award was $2300). Program-specific awards include private scholarship support for program students. Employment placement assistance is available. Employment opportunities within the program are available.

HOUSING
Coed, apartment-style, and single-sex housing available. Average on-campus housing cost per month: $750. Average off-campus housing cost per month: $350.

APPLICATION INFORMATION
Students may begin participation in September. Applications are accepted continuously. In 2006, 294 applied; 176 were accepted. Applicants must submit a formal application, letters of reference, an essay, official high school transcript or GED certificate and visit the school.

CONTACT
Teresa Brownlee, Admissions Counselor, Academy of Culinary Arts, 1012 Winslow Street, Punxsutawney, PA 15767. Telephone: 800-438-6424. Fax: 814-938-1158. E-mail: culinary-arts@iup.edu. World Wide Web: http://www.iup.edu/culinary.

JNA INSTITUTE OF CULINARY ARTS
Philadelphia, Pennsylvania

GENERAL INFORMATION
Private, coeducational, culinary institute. Urban campus. Founded in 1988. Accredited by Accrediting Commission of Career Schools and Colleges of Technology.

PROGRAM INFORMATION
Offered since 1988. Program calendar is divided into quarters, ten-week cycles. 30-week diploma in specialized food service management. 30-week diploma in food service training/professional cooking. 60-week associate degree in culinary arts/restaurant management.

PROGRAM AFFILIATION
American Culinary Federation; Foodservice Educators Network International; International Food Service Executives Association; National Restaurant Association; National Restaurant Association Educational Foundation.

AREAS OF STUDY
Baking; beverage management; buffet catering; controlling costs in food service; culinary French; culinary skill development; food preparation; food purchasing; food service communication; food service math; garde-manger; international cuisine; introduction to food service; kitchen management; management and human resources; meal planning; meat cutting; menu and facilities design; nutrition; nutrition and food service; patisserie; restaurant opportunities; sanitation; saucier; seafood processing; soup, stock, sauce, and starch production; wines and spirits.

FACILITIES
Bake shop; cafeteria; catering service; 4 classrooms; computer laboratory; demonstration laboratory; food production kitchen; learning resource center; lecture room; library; public restaurant; student lounge; teaching kitchen.

STUDENT PROFILE
71 total: 68 full-time; 3 part-time.

FACULTY
10 total: 7 full-time; 3 part-time. 10 are industry professionals. Prominent faculty: Joseph DiGironimo, CFE, FMP; Michael DeLuca, FMP; Roland Pasche; Michael Gilletto, MCFE, FMP. Faculty-student ratio: 1:12.

SPECIAL PROGRAMS
Paid externships, student clubs (wine club, culinary club), culinary competitions.

TYPICAL EXPENSES

Tuition: $8500 per diploma; $17,000 per degree full-time, $188 per credit part-time. Program-related fees include $75 for registration; $150 for knives.

FINANCIAL AID

In 2006, 4 scholarships were awarded (average award was $8500); 51 loans were granted (average loan was $3000). Employment placement assistance is available. Employment opportunities within the program are available.

HOUSING

Average off-campus housing cost per month: $650.

APPLICATION INFORMATION

Students may begin participation in January, March, April, June, July, September, October, and December. Applications are accepted continuously. In 2006, 103 applied; 75 were accepted. Applicants must submit a formal application and schedule an interview or provide letters of reference.

CONTACT

Darrence DuBose, Admissions Department, 1212 South Broad Street, Philadelphia, PA 19146. Telephone: 215-468-8800. Fax: 215-468-8838. E-mail: admissions@ culinaryarts.com. World Wide Web: http://www. culinaryarts.com.

KEYSTONE TECHNICAL INSTITUTE

Harrisburg, Pennsylvania

GENERAL INFORMATION

Private, coeducational, culinary institute. Suburban campus. Founded in 1980. Accredited by Accrediting Commission of Career Schools and Colleges of Technology.

PROGRAM INFORMATION

Program calendar is continuous. 15-month degree in culinary arts.

PROGRAM AFFILIATION

American Culinary Federation.

AREAS OF STUDY

Baking; buffet catering; controlling costs in food service; culinary skill development; food preparation; food purchasing; food service communication; food service math; garde-manger; introduction to food service; kitchen management; meal planning; meat cutting; menu and facilities design; nutrition; nutrition and food service; sanitation; saucier; seafood processing; soup, stock, sauce, and starch production.

Keystone Technical Institute *(continued)*

FACILITIES

10 classrooms; 3 computer laboratories; learning resource center; library; snack shop; student lounge; teaching kitchen.

STUDENT PROFILE

15 full-time.

FACULTY

3 total: 1 full-time; 2 part-time. 1 is a culinary-certified teacher. Prominent faculty: Richard Stiffler, Chef. Faculty-student ratio: 1:8.

TYPICAL EXPENSES

Application fee: $20. Tuition: $24,885 per entire program. Program-related fees include $1500 for lab; $160 for certification; $75 for graduation; $400 for lab kit; $100 for technology fee.

FINANCIAL AID

In 2006, 2 scholarships were awarded (average award was $12,000). Employment placement assistance is available.

APPLICATION INFORMATION

Applications are accepted continuously. Applicants must interview; submit a formal application.

CONTACT

Tom Bogush, Director of Admissions, 2301 Academy Drive, Harrisburg, PA 17112. Telephone: 717-545-4747. Fax: 717-901-9090. E-mail: tbogush@kti.edu. World Wide Web: http://www.kti.edu.

LEHIGH CARBON COMMUNITY COLLEGE

Hotel/Restaurant Management–Foodservice Management

Schnecksville, Pennsylvania

GENERAL INFORMATION

Public, coeducational, two-year college. Suburban campus. Founded in 1967. Accredited by Middle States Association of Colleges and Schools.

PROGRAM INFORMATION

Offered since 1986. National Restaurant Association Educational Foundation ManageFirst certificates available. Program calendar is divided into semesters. 2-year associate degree in foodservice management. 2-year associate degree in hotel/resort management.

PROGRAM AFFILIATION

American Culinary Federation; Council on Hotel, Restaurant, and Institutional Education; National Restaurant Association; National Restaurant Association Educational Foundation.

AREAS OF STUDY

Baking; beverage management; controlling costs in food service; culinary skill development; dining room operation; food preparation; food purchasing; food service math; international cuisine; introduction to food service; management and human resources; meal planning; menu and facilities design; nutrition; nutrition and food service; sanitation; soup, stock, sauce, and starch production.

FACILITIES

Classroom; computer laboratory; lecture room; student lounge; teaching kitchen.

STUDENT PROFILE

116 total: 31 full-time; 85 part-time. 78 are under 25 years old; 31 are between 25 and 44 years old; 7 are over 44 years old.

FACULTY

4 total: 2 full-time; 2 part-time. 3 are industry professionals; 1 is a culinary-certified teacher. Prominent faculty: Timothy Gibbons, HTHM, CHE; Pamela Weldon, MEd, CHE. Faculty-student ratio: 1:15.

PROMINENT ALUMNI AND CURRENT AFFILIATION

Erica Ziegler, Walt Disney World; Joshua Strobl, Boston's Restaurants.

SPECIAL PROGRAMS

Paid internships in all degree programs, for-credit participation in Walt Disney World College program.

TYPICAL EXPENSES

Application fee: $30. In-state tuition: $1425 per semester full-time (in district), $95 per credit part-time (in district), $2760 per semester full-time (out-of-district), $184 per credit part-time (out-of-district). Out-of-state tuition: $4095 per semester full-time, $273 per credit part-time. Tuition for international students: $4095 per semester full-time, $273 per credit part-time. Program-related fee includes $75 for lab fee (food costs for specific courses).

FINANCIAL AID

Employment placement assistance is available.

APPLICATION INFORMATION

Students may begin participation in January and August. Applications are accepted continuously. In 2006, 77 applied. Applicants must submit a formal application.

CONTACT
Timothy J. Gibbons, Assistant Professor, Hospitality Education, Hotel/Restaurant Management–Foodservice Management, 4525 Education Park Drive, Schnecksville, PA 18078. Telephone: 610-794-1852. E-mail: tgibbons@lccc.edu. World Wide Web: http://www.lccc.edu.

MERCYHURST COLLEGE

The Culinary and Wine Institute of Mercyhurst North East

North East, Pennsylvania

GENERAL INFORMATION
Private, coeducational, comprehensive institution. Small-town setting. Founded in 1926. Accredited by Middle States Association of Colleges and Schools.

PROGRAM INFORMATION
Offered since 1995. Accredited by Accreditation Commission for Programs in Hospitality Administration (ACPHA). Program calendar is term 4-3-3. 2-year associate degree in culinary arts. 2-year associate degree in hospitality management. 4-year bachelor's degree in hotel, restaurant, and institutional management (culinary arts concentration).

PROGRAM AFFILIATION
American Culinary Federation; Council on Hotel, Restaurant, and Institutional Education; National Restaurant Association.

AREAS OF STUDY
Baking; beverage management; buffet catering; controlling costs in food service; culinary skill development; food preparation; food purchasing; food service communication; food service math; garde-manger; international cuisine; introduction to food service; kitchen management; management and human resources; meal planning; meat cutting; meat fabrication; menu and facilities design; nutrition; nutrition and food service; patisserie; restaurant opportunities; sanitation; saucier; seafood processing; soup, stock, sauce, and starch production; wine making; wines and spirits.

FACILITIES
Bake shop; cafeteria; 4 classrooms; 2 computer laboratories; 3 demonstration laboratories; 3 food production kitchens; garden; gourmet dining room; learning resource center; 2 lecture rooms; library; student lounge; 2 teaching kitchens; vineyard.

STUDENT PROFILE
55 total: 53 full-time; 2 part-time. 44 are under 25 years old; 10 are between 25 and 44 years old; 1 is over 44 years old.

FACULTY
7 total: 3 full-time; 4 part-time. 3 are industry professionals; 1 is a culinary-certified teacher; 2 are ServSafe instructors, 1 registered dietitian. Prominent faculty: Brian Stahlsmith; Beth Ann Sheldon, RD, LDN; Daryl Georger; Dennis Dunne. Faculty-student ratio: 1:15.

PROMINENT ALUMNI AND CURRENT AFFILIATION
Alan Bickel, Gaylord Opreland; Cory Brown, Pompano Beach Club.

SPECIAL PROGRAMS
400-hour culinary externship, 120 hour culinar service hour component, food distribution/food show participant.

TYPICAL EXPENSES
Application fee: $25. Tuition: $12,123 per year full-time, $367 per credit part-time. Program-related fee includes $425 for culinary fee per term (knives, uniforms, and baking kit).

FINANCIAL AID
Program-specific awards include institution grants. Employment placement assistance is available.

HOUSING
Coed, apartment-style, and single-sex housing available. Average on-campus housing cost per month: $622. Average off-campus housing cost per month: $450.

APPLICATION INFORMATION
Students may begin participation in March, September, and November. Applications are accepted continuously. In 2006, 116 applied; 112 were accepted. Applicants must submit a formal application and high school diploma or GED.

CONTACT
Travis Lindahl, Director of Admission, The Culinary and Wine Institute of Mercyhurst North East, 16 West Division Street, North East, PA 16428. Telephone: 814-725-6144. Fax: 814-725-6251. E-mail: neadmiss@mercyhurst.edu. World Wide Web: http://northeast.mercyhurst.edu.

NORTHAMPTON COUNTY AREA COMMUNITY COLLEGE

Culinary Arts

Bethlehem, Pennsylvania

GENERAL INFORMATION
Public, coeducational, two-year college. Suburban campus. Founded in 1967. Accredited by Middle States Association of Colleges and Schools.

PROGRAM INFORMATION
Offered since 1993. National Restaurant Association Educational Foundation ManageFirst certificates available. Program calendar is divided into semesters. 2-year associate degree in culinary arts. 2-year associate degree in restaurant/hotel management. 45-week diploma in culinary arts.

AREAS OF STUDY
Baking; beverage management; controlling costs in food service; culinary skill development; food preparation; food purchasing; garde-manger; introduction to food service; meat cutting; meat fabrication; nutrition; restaurant opportunities; sanitation; seafood processing; soup, stock, sauce, and starch production; wines and spirits.

FACILITIES
Bakery; cafeteria; catering service; 10 computer laboratories; food production kitchen; gourmet dining room; learning resource center; lecture room; library; public restaurant; snack shop; student lounge; teaching kitchen.

STUDENT PROFILE
60 full-time.

FACULTY
9 total: 5 full-time; 4 part-time. 4 are industry professionals; 3 are culinary-certified teachers. Prominent faculty: Duncan Howden; Scott Kalamar; Susan Roth. Faculty-student ratio: 1:28.

TYPICAL EXPENSES
Application fee: $20. In-state tuition: $100 per credit (in district), $200 per credit (out-of-district). Out-of-state tuition: $300 per credit. Program-related fee includes $172.50 for meal fee.

FINANCIAL AID
In 2006, 1 scholarship was awarded (award was $250); 10 loans were granted (average loan was $2000). Employment placement assistance is available.

HOUSING
Coed and apartment-style housing available. Average on-campus housing cost per month: $600. Average off-campus housing cost per month: $600.

APPLICATION INFORMATION
Students may begin participation in March and September. Applications are accepted continuously. In 2006, 100 applied; 56 were accepted. Applicants must submit a formal application.

CONTACT
Duncan Howden, Director of Hospitality Programs, Culinary Arts, 3835 Green Pond Road, Bethlehem, PA 18020. Telephone: 610-861-5593. Fax: 610-861-5487. E-mail: dhowden@northampton.edu. World Wide Web: http://www.northampton.edu/academics/departments/culinary/.

PENNSYLVANIA COLLEGE OF TECHNOLOGY

School of Hospitality

Williamsport, Pennsylvania

GENERAL INFORMATION
Public, coeducational, two-year college. Urban campus. Founded in 1965. Accredited by Middle States Association of Colleges and Schools.

PROGRAM INFORMATION
Offered since 1965. Accredited by American Culinary Federation Accrediting Commission, Commission on Accreditation of Hospitality Management Programs. Program calendar is divided into semesters. 2-year associate degree in hospitality management. 2-year associate degree in baking/pastry arts. 2-year associate degree in culinary arts technology. 4-year bachelor's degree in culinary arts & systems. 8-month competency credential in professional cooking. 8-month competency credential in professional baking. 8-month competency credential in dining room service.

PROGRAM AFFILIATION
American Culinary Federation; American Institute of Baking; Council on Hotel, Restaurant, and Institutional Education; National Restaurant Association; National Restaurant Association Educational Foundation; Pennsylvania Travel Council; Retailer's Bakery Association; Sommelier Society of America; The Bread Bakers Guild of America; Women Chefs and Restaurateurs.

AREAS OF STUDY

Baking; beverage management; catering; confectionery show pieces; controlling costs in food service; culinary French; culinary skill development; food preparation; food purchasing; garde-manger; international cuisine; introduction to food service; kitchen management; management and human resources; meal planning; meat cutting; meat fabrication; menu and facilities design; nutrition; nutrition and food service; patisserie; restaurant opportunities; sanitation; seafood processing; wines and spirits.

FACILITIES

Catering service; 3 classrooms; computer laboratory; 4 food production kitchens; garden; 2 gourmet dining rooms; learning resource center; lecture room; library; public restaurant; teaching kitchen; conference center; performing arts center; culinary, baking, and pastry skills lab.

STUDENT PROFILE

204 total: 183 full-time; 21 part-time. 185 are under 25 years old; 14 are between 25 and 44 years old; 5 are over 44 years old.

FACULTY

22 total: 9 full-time; 13 part-time. 18 are industry professionals; 2 are culinary-certified teachers; 1 is a certified hospitality educator. Prominent faculty: Paul Mach, CHE; Mike Ditchfield, CEC, CCE; Judith Shimp, CEC, CCE. Faculty-student ratio: 1:24 lecture; 1:12 lab.

PROMINENT ALUMNI AND CURRENT AFFILIATION

James Parker.

SPECIAL PROGRAMS

Semi-annual Visiting Chefs Series, Hunt County Vineyards, Finger Lakes Harvest Festival, Kentucky Derby Experience.

TYPICAL EXPENSES

Application fee: $50. In-state tuition: $11,250 per year full-time (in district), $375 per credit part-time. Out-of-state tuition: $14,130 per year full-time, $471 per credit part-time. Tuition for international students: $14,130 per year full-time, $471 per credit part-time. Program-related fees include $190 for knife kit; $320 for uniforms; $250 for tools.

FINANCIAL AID

In 2006, 42 scholarships were awarded (average award was $1535). Program-specific awards include D.L. Stroehmann Culinary Scholarship, Hector Boiardi Scholarship, Penn College Visiting Chef Scholarship,, David B. Person Memorial Scholarship, Ann Miglio Scholarship, Louis A. Miele Sr. Memorial Scholarship,, Labels by Pulizzi Scholarship, Girio Family Scholarship,

Burger King Scholarship. Employment placement assistance is available. Employment opportunities within the program are available.

HOUSING

Coed and apartment-style housing available.

APPLICATION INFORMATION

Students may begin participation in January and August. Applications are accepted continuously. In 2006, 228 applied; 215 were accepted. Applicants must submit a formal application and high school transcript.

CONTACT

Chester D. Schuman, Director of Admissions, School of Hospitality, One College Avenue, Williamsport, PA 17701. Telephone: 800-367-9222. Fax: 570-321-5551. World Wide Web: http://www.pct.edu/peter.

See color display following page 282.

PENNSYLVANIA CULINARY INSTITUTE

Le Cordon Bleu Culinary Arts

Pittsburgh, Pennsylvania

GENERAL INFORMATION

Private, coeducational, culinary institute. Urban campus. Founded in 1986. Accredited by Accrediting Commission of Career Schools and Colleges of Technology.

PROGRAM INFORMATION

Offered since 1986. Associate degree in Le Cordon Bleu Hospitality and Restaurant Management. Associate degree in Le Cordon Bleu Patisserie and Baking. Associate degree in Le Cordon Bleu culinary arts. Diploma in Le Cordon Bleu culinary techniques.

SPECIAL PROGRAMS

Externships, culinary competitions.

HOUSING

Coed and apartment-style housing available.

APPLICATION INFORMATION

Applications are accepted continuously. Applicants must interview; submit a formal application and high school diploma/GED.

CONTACT

Admissions Department, Le Cordon Bleu Culinary Arts, 717 Liberty Avenue, Pittsburgh, PA 15222-3500. Telephone: 888-314-8222. World Wide Web: http://www.pci.edu.

THE PENNSYLVANIA STATE UNIVERSITY–UNIVERSITY PARK CAMPUS

School of Hospitality Management

University Park, Pennsylvania

GENERAL INFORMATION
Public, coeducational, university. Small-town setting. Founded in 1855. Accredited by Middle States Association of Colleges and Schools.

PROGRAM INFORMATION
Offered since 1937. Program calendar is divided into semesters. 18-month master's degree in hospitality management. 2-year associate degree in hospitality management. 4-year bachelor's degree in hospitality management. 4-year doctoral degree in hospitality management.

PROGRAM AFFILIATION
Council on Hotel, Restaurant, and Institutional Education; National Restaurant Association; National Restaurant Association Educational Foundation.

FACILITIES
Cafeteria; 4 classrooms; 2 computer laboratories; demonstration laboratory; food production kitchen; gourmet dining room; learning resource center; lecture room; public restaurant; teaching kitchen.

STUDENT PROFILE
800 total: 740 full-time; 60 part-time.

FACULTY
33 total: 30 full-time; 3 part-time. Prominent faculty: Anna Mattila, PhD; Arun Upneja, PhD; David Cranage, PhD; John O'Neill, PhD. Faculty-student ratio: 1:30.

PROMINENT ALUMNI AND CURRENT AFFILIATION
Walter Conti.

SPECIAL PROGRAMS
Spring break trips to Italy, Greece, Spain, culinary program in Lyon, France, 6-week trip to Switzerland.

TYPICAL EXPENSES
In-state tuition: $12,284 per year. Out-of-state tuition: $23,284 per year.

FINANCIAL AID
In 2006, individual scholarships were awarded at $180. Employment placement assistance is available.

HOUSING
Coed and apartment-style housing available. Average on-campus housing cost per month: $350. Average off-campus housing cost per month: $500.

APPLICATION INFORMATION
Students may begin participation in January and August. Applicants must submit a formal application.

CONTACT
Mr. David Rachau, Academic Advisor, School of Hospitality Management, 201 Mateer Building, University Park, PA 16802. Telephone: 814-865-7033. Fax: 814-863-4257. E-mail: dqr5@psu.edu. World Wide Web: http://www.hhdev.psu.edu/shm.

THE RESTAURANT SCHOOL AT WALNUT HILL COLLEGE

School of Hospitality Management/School of Culinary and Pastry Arts

Philadelphia, Pennsylvania

GENERAL INFORMATION
Private, coeducational, four-year college. Urban campus. Founded in 1974. Accredited by Accrediting Commission of Career Schools and Colleges of Technology.

PROGRAM INFORMATION
Program calendar is divided into semesters. 18-month associate degree in hotel management. 18-month associate degree in restaurant management. 18-month associate degree in pastry arts. 18-month associate degree in culinary arts. 36-month bachelor's degree in hotel management. 36-month bachelor's degree in restaurant management. 36-month bachelor's degree in pastry arts. 36-month bachelor's degree in culinary arts.

PROGRAM AFFILIATION
American Culinary Federation; American Institute of Wine & Food; Council on Hotel, Restaurant, and Institutional Education; International Association of Culinary Professionals; National Restaurant Association; National Restaurant Association Educational Foundation.

FACULTY
Prominent faculty: Manfred Bast, CMPC, CEC, AAC; John Gallagher, CEPC.

SPECIAL PROGRAMS
8-day gastronomic tour of France (culinary students), 8-day Florida and Bahamas cruise and resort tour (management students), culinary competitions.

TYPICAL EXPENSES
Application fee: $50.

FINANCIAL AID

Employment placement assistance is available. Employment opportunities within the program are available.

HOUSING

Coed and apartment-style housing available. Average on-campus housing cost per month: $580. Average off-campus housing cost per month: $800.

APPLICATION INFORMATION

Students may begin participation in January, May, September, and November. Applications are accepted continuously. Applicants must interview; submit a formal application, letters of reference, and an essay.

CONTACT

Director of Admissions, School of Hospitality Management/School of Culinary and Pastry Arts, 4207 Walnut Street, Philadelphia, PA 19104-3518. Telephone: 215-222-4200 Ext. 3011. Fax: 215-222-2811. E-mail: info@walnuthillcollege.edu. World Wide Web: http://www.walnuthillcollege.edu.

SETON HILL UNIVERSITY

Hospitality and Tourism; Dietetics

Greensburg, Pennsylvania

GENERAL INFORMATION

Private, coeducational, comprehensive institution. Small-town setting. Founded in 1883. Accredited by Middle States Association of Colleges and Schools.

PROGRAM INFORMATION

Accredited by American Dietetic Association. Program calendar is divided into semesters. 4-year bachelor's degree in dietetics. 4-year bachelor's degree in hospitality and tourism.

PROGRAM AFFILIATION

American Dietetic Association; Council on Hotel, Restaurant, and Institutional Education; National Restaurant Association; National Restaurant Association Educational Foundation.

Seton Hill University *(continued)*

AREAS OF STUDY

Controlling costs in food service; food preparation; food purchasing; food service math; introduction to food service; management and human resources; meal planning; menu and facilities design; nutrition; nutrition and food service; sanitation.

FACILITIES

Computer laboratory; demonstration laboratory; food production kitchen; 2 laboratories; learning resource center; teaching kitchen.

STUDENT PROFILE

50 full-time. 48 are under 25 years old; 2 are between 25 and 44 years old.

FACULTY

4 total: 4 full-time; 0 part-time. 2 are registered dietitians, 1 certified sous-chef. Prominent faculty: Doreen Tracy, RD; Victoria M. Gribshaw, SC, PhD; Jan Sandrick, PhD, RD; Daniel Bernstein, EdD. Faculty-student ratio: 1:10.

PROMINENT ALUMNI AND CURRENT AFFILIATION

Aimee St. Clair, Nemarolin Woodlands Resort; Nancy R. Hudson, University of California at Berkley; Rosemary C. Tobelman, General Mills.

SPECIAL PROGRAMS

Internship (required), coordinated supervised practice.

TYPICAL EXPENSES

Application fee: $30. Tuition: $24,806 per year full-time, $660 per credit part-time.

FINANCIAL AID

Program-specific awards include dedicated scholarship for dietetics students. Employment placement assistance is available.

HOUSING

Coed and single-sex housing available. Average on-campus housing cost per month: $850.

APPLICATION INFORMATION

Students may begin participation in January and August. Application deadline for spring is December 1. Application deadline for fall is August 1. In 2006, 42 applied; 31 were accepted. Applicants must submit letters of reference, an essay, transcripts, SAT or ACT scores.

CONTACT

Sherri Bett, Director of Admissions, Hospitality and Tourism; Dietetics, Seton Hill Drive, Greensburg, PA 15601. Telephone: 724-838-4255. Fax: 724-830-1294. E-mail: admit@setonhill.edu. World Wide Web: http://www.setonhill.edu.

WESTMORELAND COUNTY COMMUNITY COLLEGE

Hospitality Programs Department

Youngwood, Pennsylvania

GENERAL INFORMATION

Public, coeducational, two-year college. Rural campus. Founded in 1970. Accredited by Middle States Association of Colleges and Schools.

PROGRAM INFORMATION

Offered since 1980. Accredited by American Culinary Federation Accrediting Commission, American Dietetic Association. Program calendar is divided into semesters. 16-month associate degree in culinary arts-nonapprenticeship. 2-year associate degree in baking and pastry nonapprenticeship. 2-year associate degree in culinary-nonapprenticeship. 2-year associate degree in travel and tourism. 2-year associate degree in hotel/motel management. 2-year associate degree in restaurant and culinary management. 2-year associate degree in dietetic technician. 3-year associate degree in baking and pastry apprenticeship. 3-year associate degree in culinary arts-apprenticeship. 5-month certificate in hotel/motel management. 5-month certificate in dining room management. 5-month certificate in culinary arts. 5-month certificate in baking and pastry.

PROGRAM AFFILIATION

American Culinary Federation; American Dietetic Association; Council on Hotel, Restaurant, and Institutional Education; National Restaurant Association.

AREAS OF STUDY

Baking; beverage management; buffet catering; confectionery show pieces; controlling costs in food service; convenience cookery; culinary French; culinary skill development; food preparation; food purchasing; food service communication; food service math; garde-manger; international cuisine; introduction to food service; kitchen management; management and human resources; meal planning; menu and facilities design; nutrition; nutrition and food service; patisserie; restaurant opportunities; sanitation; saucier; seafood processing; soup, stock, sauce, and starch production; wines and spirits.

FACILITIES

2 bake shops; cafeteria; 10 classrooms; 4 computer laboratories; demonstration laboratory; food production kitchen; gourmet dining room; laboratory; learning resource center; lecture room; library; 2 student lounges; teaching kitchen.

TYPICAL STUDENT PROFILE
201 total: 131 full-time; 70 part-time. 135 are under 25 years old; 42 are between 25 and 44 years old; 24 are over 44 years old.

SPECIAL PROGRAMS
10-day hospitality study tour of Italy, culinary competition, paid apprenticeship.

FINANCIAL AID
Employment placement assistance is available. Employment opportunities within the program are available.

APPLICATION INFORMATION
Students may begin participation in January, May, and August. Applications are accepted continuously. Applicants must submit a formal application and take a physical exam.

CONTACT
Director of Admissions, Hospitality Programs Department, 400 Armbrust Road, Youngwood, PA 15697. Telephone: 724-925-4123. Fax: 724-925-5802. World Wide Web: http://wccc.edu/ac/programpages/culinary/index.html.

WIDENER UNIVERSITY
School of Hospitality Management
Chester, Pennsylvania

GENERAL INFORMATION
Private, coeducational, university. Suburban campus. Founded in 1821. Accredited by Middle States Association of Colleges and Schools.

PROGRAM INFORMATION
Offered since 1981. Accredited by Council on Hotel, Restaurant and Institutional Education, Accreditation Commission for Programs in Hospitality Administration (ACPHA). Program calendar is divided into semesters. 2-year master's degree in hospitality management. 4-year bachelor's degree in hospitality management.

PROGRAM AFFILIATION
American Dietetic Association; Council on Hotel, Restaurant, and Institutional Education; International Food Service Executives Association; National Restaurant Association; National Restaurant Association Educational Foundation; Society for Foodservice Management.

AREAS OF STUDY
Beverage management; club management; contract services management; controlling costs in food service; food preparation; food purchasing; gaming and racing management; hotel management; introduction to food service; kitchen management; management and human resources; menu and facilities design; nutrition; nutrition and food service; resort management; restaurant opportunities; sanitation; wines and spirits.

FACILITIES
5 classrooms; computer laboratory; demonstration laboratory; food production kitchen; gourmet dining room; laboratory; lecture room; library; public restaurant; student lounge; teaching kitchen; hotel technology laboratory.

STUDENT PROFILE
180 total: 175 full-time; 5 part-time.

FACULTY
9 total: 6 full-time; 3 part-time. 1 is an industry professional; 1 is a registered dietitian. Prominent faculty: David Tucker, FMP; Shiang-Lih Chen McCain, PhD; John Mahoney, PhD; Joy Dickerson, EdD. Faculty-student ratio: 1:12.

PROMINENT ALUMNI AND CURRENT AFFILIATION
D. Chip Wade, Senior Vice President, Red Lobster Restaurants; Luke A. O'Boyle, General Manager, Chevy Chase Club; Kevin Kenney, District Manager, Aramark Corporation.

SPECIAL PROGRAMS
2 paid summer internships, paid cooperative education semester, study abroad program.

TYPICAL EXPENSES
Application fee: $35. Tuition: $28,180 per year full-time, $939 per credit hour part-time. Program-related fee includes $50 for uniform.

FINANCIAL AID
In 2006, 6 scholarships were awarded (average award was $1000). Employment placement assistance is available. Employment opportunities within the program are available.

HOUSING
Coed, apartment-style, and single-sex housing available. Average off-campus housing cost per month: $400.

APPLICATION INFORMATION
Students may begin participation in January and September. Applications are accepted continuously. In 2006, 125 applied; 82 were accepted. Applicants must submit a formal application, an essay, SAT or ACT scores, and high school transcripts.

Widener University *(continued)*

CONTACT
Courtney Kelly, Associate Director of Admissions, School of Hospitality Management, Widener University, One University Place, Chester, PA 19013. Telephone: 610-499-4126. Fax: 610-499-4676. E-mail: chkelly@widener.edu. World Wide Web: http://www.widener.edu/shm/.

WINNER INSTITUTE OF ARTS & SCIENCES CULINARY EDUCATION

Culinary Arts Program

Transfer, Pennsylvania

GENERAL INFORMATION
Private, coeducational, culinary institute. Rural campus. Founded in 1997. Accredited by Council on Occupational Education.

PROGRAM INFORMATION
Accredited by American Culinary Federation Accrediting Commission. 15-month associate degree in culinary arts.

PROGRAM AFFILIATION
American Culinary Federation.

HOUSING
Apartment-style housing available.

APPLICATION INFORMATION
Students may begin participation in January, April, July, and October. Applications are accepted continuously. Applicants must interview, submit a formal application and take an entrance exam.

CONTACT
Director of Admissions, Culinary Arts Program, One Winner Place, Transfer, PA 16154. Telephone: 724-646-2433. Fax: 724-646-0218. E-mail: info@winner-institute.edu. World Wide Web: http://www.winner-institute.edu.

YORKTOWNE BUSINESS INSTITUTE

School of Culinary Arts

York, Pennsylvania

Turn Your *Zest For Cooking* Into A Career!

Our Professional Culinary Arts Training Offers:

- 16-month Culinary Arts Degree Program
- Professional Baking & Pastry Program
- Professional Bartending Course
- Student-run Restaurant & Lunch Shop
- Financial Aid Available to Those Who Qualify
- Located in Historic Central PA!

The School of Culinary Arts at Yorktowne Business Institute

1063 North George Street • York, PA 17404
1-800-840-1004 • www.yorkchef.com

GENERAL INFORMATION

Private, coeducational, two-year college. Founded in 1976. Accredited by Accrediting Council for Independent Colleges and Schools.

PROGRAM INFORMATION

Offered since 1998. 12-month diploma in professional baking and pastry. 12-month diploma in food service. 16-month associate degree in culinary arts. 5-week certificate in professional bartending.

SPECIAL PROGRAMS

6-week externship (including European locations), culinary competitions, participation in student-run restaurant.

TYPICAL EXPENSES

Application fee: $55.

FINANCIAL AID

Employment placement assistance is available. Employment opportunities within the program are available.

APPLICATION INFORMATION

Applicants must interview, submit a formal application, and take entrance exam.

CONTACT

Director of Admissions, School of Culinary Arts, West 7th Avenue, York, PA 17404. Telephone: 800-840-1004. Fax: 717-848-4584. E-mail: chef@ybi.edu. World Wide Web: http://www.yorkchef.com.

YTI CAREER INSTITUTE

Lancaster, Pennsylvania

GENERAL INFORMATION

Private, coeducational, two-year college. Suburban campus. Founded in 1967. Accredited by Accrediting Commission of Career Schools and Colleges of Technology.

PROGRAM INFORMATION

Offered since 1999. Program calendar is continuous. 12-month diploma in pastry arts. 21-month associate degree in culinary arts/restaurant management.

PROGRAM AFFILIATION

American Culinary Federation; National Restaurant Association Educational Foundation; Pennsylvania Restaurant Association.

AREAS OF STUDY

Baking; beverage management; buffet catering; confectionery show pieces; controlling costs in food service; culinary skill development; food preparation; food purchasing; food service communication; food service math; garde-manger; international cuisine; introduction to food service; kitchen management; management and human resources; meal planning; meat fabrication; menu and facilities design; nutrition; patisserie; restaurant opportunities; sanitation; saucier; seafood processing; soup, stock, sauce, and starch production; wines and spirits.

FACILITIES

Bakery; 7 classrooms; computer laboratory; demonstration laboratory; 4 food production kitchens; gourmet dining room; learning resource center; 7 lecture rooms; library; student lounge.

TYPICAL STUDENT PROFILE

200 full-time.

FINANCIAL AID

Employment placement assistance is available. Employment opportunities within the program are available.

APPLICATION INFORMATION

Students may begin participation in January, July, and October. Applications are accepted continuously. Applicants must interview; submit a formal application and transcript.

CONTACT

Director of Admissions, Lancaster Campus, 3050 Hempland Road, Lancaster, PA 17601. Telephone: 866-984-4723. Fax: 717-295-1135. World Wide Web: http://cuisine.yti.edu.

RHODE ISLAND

JOHNSON & WALES UNIVERSITY

College of Culinary Arts

Providence, Rhode Island

GENERAL INFORMATION

Private, coeducational, comprehensive institution. Urban campus. Founded in 1914. Accredited by New England Association of Schools and Colleges.

PROGRAM INFORMATION

Offered since 1973. Accredited by American Dietetic Association. Program calendar is divided into quarters. Associate degree in culinary arts. Associate degree in

Johnson & Wales University *(continued)*

baking and pastry arts. Bachelor's degree in culinary arts and food service management (joint degree with the College of Culinary Arts and The Hospitality College). Bachelor's degree in pastry arts and food service management (joint degree with the College of Culinary Arts and The Hospitality College). Bachelor's degree in restaurant, food and beverage management. Bachelor's degree in hotel and lodging management. Bachelor's degree in baking and pastry arts. Bachelor's degree in culinary nutrition. Bachelor's degree in food marketing (offered through the College of Business). Bachelor's degree in food service entrepreneurship (offered through the College of Business).

PROGRAM AFFILIATION
American Culinary Federation; American Dietetic Association; American Institute of Baking; American Institute of Wine & Food; Confrerie de la Chaine des Rotisseurs; Council on Hotel, Restaurant, and Institutional Education; Institute of Food Technologists; International Association of Culinary Professionals; International Food Service Executives Association; International Foodservice Editorial Council; James Beard Foundation, Inc.; National Restaurant Association; National Restaurant Association Educational Foundation; Oldways Preservation and Exchange Trust; Society of Wine Educators; The Bread Bakers Guild of America; Women Chefs and Restaurateurs.

AREAS OF STUDY
Baking; beverage management; buffet catering; confectionery show pieces; controlling costs in food service; convenience cookery; culinary French; culinary skill development; food preparation; food purchasing; food service communication; food service math; garde-manger; international cuisine; introduction to food service; kitchen management; management and human resources; meal planning; meat cutting; meat fabrication; menu and facilities design; nutrition; nutrition and food service; patisserie; sanitation; saucier; seafood processing; soup, stock, sauce, and starch production; wines and spirits.

FACILITIES
4 bake shops; bakery; 4 cafeterias; catering service; 22 classrooms; coffee shop; 4 computer laboratories; demonstration laboratory; 21 food production kitchens; 2 gardens; 4 gourmet dining rooms; 4 laboratories; learning resource center; 22 lecture rooms; 2 libraries; 10 public restaurants; snack shop; student lounge.

STUDENT PROFILE
2,458 total: 2246 full-time; 212 part-time. 2178 are under 25 years old; 240 are between 25 and 44 years old; 40 are over 44 years old.

FACULTY
80 total: 77 full-time; 3 part-time. Prominent faculty: Frank Terranova, CEC, CCE; Robert Lucier, CEC; George O'Palenick, CEC, CCE, AAC; Stephen Scaife, CEC, CCE, CFE. Faculty-student ratio: 1:29.

SPECIAL PROGRAMS
Customized corporate and commercial training programs, every culinary student gets a real life, career-building work experience through internship/co-op, ACF certification and one year membership for all completing associates degree.

TYPICAL EXPENSES
Tuition: $20,478 per year. Program-related fees include $984 for general fee; $255 for orientation; $987 for optional weekend meal plan; $300 for room and board reservation deposit.

FINANCIAL AID
In 2006, individual scholarships were awarded at $4024.81; 1032 loans were granted (average loan was $3792). Employment placement assistance is available. Employment opportunities within the program are available.

HOUSING
Coed housing available. Average on-campus housing cost per month: $1030.

APPLICATION INFORMATION
Students may begin participation in March, June, September, and December. Applications are accepted continuously. In 2006, 3438 applied; 2684 were accepted. Applicants must submit a formal application and high school and/or college transcripts.

CONTACT
Amy Podbelski, Assistant Director of Admissions, College of Culinary Arts, 8 Abbott Park Place, Providence, RI 02903-3703. Telephone: 800-342-5598 Ext. 2370. Fax: 401-598-2948. E-mail: admissions.pvd@jwu.edu. World Wide Web: http://culinary.jwu.edu.
See color display following page 90.

SOUTH CAROLINA

THE ART INSTITUTE OF CHARLESTON

The International Culinary School at The Art Institute of Charleston

Charleston, South Carolina

GENERAL INFORMATION
Private, coeducational institution.

PROGRAM INFORMATION
Associate degree in Culinary Arts with a concentration in Baking and Pastry. Associate degree in Culinary Arts. Bachelor's degree in Culinary Arts Management.

CONTACT
Office of Admissions, The International Culinary School at The Art Institute of Charleston, 24 North Market Street, Charleston, SC 29401-2623. Telephone: 843-727-3500. World Wide Web: http://www.artinstitutes.edu/charleston/.

See color display following page 186.

THE CULINARY INSTITUTE OF CHARLESTON

The Culinary Institute of Charleston at Trident Technical College

Charleston, South Carolina

GENERAL INFORMATION
Public, coeducational, two-year college. Urban campus. Founded in 1964. Accredited by Southern Association of Colleges and Schools.

PROGRAM INFORMATION
Offered since 1988. Accredited by American Culinary Federation Accrediting Commission, Council on Hotel, Restaurant and Institutional Education, Commission on Accreditation of Hospitality Management Programs. Program calendar is divided into semesters. 1-year certificate in catering. 1-year certificate in hospitality industry service. 1-year certificate in baking and pastry. 1-year diploma in culinary arts. 2-year associate degree in culinary arts technology. 2-year associate degree in hospitality and tourism management.

PROGRAM AFFILIATION
American Culinary Federation; American Institute of Wine & Food; Council on Hotel, Restaurant, and Institutional Education; Federation of Dining Rooms Professionals; International Association of Culinary Professionals; Les Dames d'Escoffier; National Association of Catering Executives; National Restaurant Association; National Restaurant Association Educational Foundation; Serve Safe Sanitation National Certification Association; Southeast Council in Hotel, Restaurant and Institutional Education.

AREAS OF STUDY
Baking; beverage management; buffet catering; controlling costs in food service; convenience cookery; culinary skill development; food preparation; food purchasing; food service math; garde-manger; ice carving; introduction to food service; kitchen management; management and human resources; meal planning; meat cutting; meat fabrication; menu and facilities design; nutrition; nutrition and food service; patisserie; restaurant opportunities; sanitation; saucier; seafood processing; soup, stock, sauce, and starch production; wines and spirits.

FACILITIES
2 bake shops; catering service; 10 classrooms; computer laboratory; 5 demonstration laboratories; food production kitchen; garden; gourmet dining room; learning resource center; 6 lecture rooms; library; public restaurant; student lounge; 2 teaching kitchens; broadcast kitchen amphitheater.

STUDENT PROFILE
629 total: 436 full-time; 193 part-time. 377 are under 25 years old; 219 are between 25 and 44 years old; 33 are over 44 years old.

FACULTY
25 total: 11 full-time; 14 part-time. 11 are industry professionals; 1 is a master baker; 7 are culinary-certified teachers. Prominent faculty: Michael Carmel, CEC, CCE; Benjamin Black, CCC; Berndt Gronert, CMPC; Ward Morgan, CWC, CCE. Faculty-student ratio: 1:16.

PROMINENT ALUMNI AND CURRENT AFFILIATION
Cory Elliott, Cordavi Restaurant; Trey Dutton, The Cloister; Lucas Smith, Charleston Place Hotel.

SPECIAL PROGRAMS
Participation in Annual Chef's Fest Benefit for Lowcountry Food Bank for 900 guests, participation in formal, black tie Vintners Dinner for 600 guests, participation in annual Wine Expo with 1800 guests and 40 vintners, participation in annual Charleston Food & Wine Festival weekend.

The Culinary Institute of Charleston *(continued)*

TYPICAL EXPENSES

Application fee: $25. In-state tuition: $1557 per semester full-time (in district), $127 per credit hour part-time (in district), $1729 per semester full-time (out-of-district), $141 per credit hour part-time (out-of-district). Out-of-state tuition: $2949 per semester full-time, $243 per credit hour part-time. Program-related fees include $123–$139 for uniforms culinary; $231 for knife kit; $188 for pastry kit; $154–$194 for uniforms (dining room).

FINANCIAL AID

In 2006, 8 scholarships were awarded (average award was $1000). Program-specific awards include Hotel and Restaurant Association scholarships, Women in Wine organization scholarship, Franz Meier scholarship, scholarships sponsored by College Foundation, baking and pastry scholarship, Stolze scholarship, NACE scholarship, Concierge Association of Charleston scholarship, Nathalie Dupree Culinary scholarship. Employment placement assistance is available. Employment opportunities within the program are available.

HOUSING

Average off-campus housing cost per month: $720.

APPLICATION INFORMATION

Students may begin participation in January, May, and August. Application deadline for spring is December 7. Application deadline for summer is May 9. Applicants must submit a formal application, placement tests, high school diploma or GED.

CONTACT

Chef Michael Carmel, Department Head, The Culinary Institute of Charleston at Trident Technical College, PO Box 118067, HT-M, Charleston, SC 29423-8067. Telephone: 843-820-5096. Fax: 843-820-5060. E-mail: michael.carmel@tridenttech.edu. World Wide Web: http://www.culinaryinstituteofcharleston.com/.

See color display following page 378.

GREENVILLE TECHNICAL COLLEGE

Culinary Arts/Hospitality Education

Greenville, South Carolina

GENERAL INFORMATION

Public, coeducational, two-year college. Suburban campus. Founded in 1962. Accredited by Southern Association of Colleges and Schools.

PROGRAM INFORMATION

Accredited by American Culinary Federation Accrediting Commission, American Dietetic Association, Association of Collegiate Business Schools and Programs. Program calendar is divided into semesters. 1-year certificate in sales/catering and events management. 1-year certificate in hospitality management. 1-year certificate in baking and pastry arts. 1-year certificate in catering. 1-year certificate in culinary education. 2-year associate degree in culinary arts/food service management.

PROGRAM AFFILIATION

American Culinary Federation; American Dietetic Association; Council on Hotel, Restaurant, and Institutional Education; National Restaurant Association; South Carolina Hospitality Association.

AREAS OF STUDY

Baking; beverage management; buffet catering; confectionery show pieces; controlling costs in food service; convenience cookery; culinary skill development; food preparation; food purchasing; food service communication; food service math; garde-manger; international cuisine; introduction to food service; kitchen management; management and human resources; meal planning; meat cutting; meat fabrication; menu and facilities design; nutrition; nutrition and food service; sanitation; saucier; seafood processing; soup, stock, sauce, and starch production.

FACILITIES

Bake shop; 3 classrooms; computer laboratory; 5 demonstration laboratories; 2 food production kitchens; garden; gourmet dining room; 5 laboratories; learning resource center; 3 lecture rooms; library; student lounge; 5 teaching kitchens.

FACULTY

4 total: 4 full-time. Prominent faculty: Alan J. Scheidhauer, CEC; Sybil Davis, CHE; Patrick Wagner; Mark Bergstrom. Faculty-student ratio: 1:17.

TYPICAL EXPENSES

Application fee: $35. Program-related fee includes $150 for knife set.

FINANCIAL AID

Employment placement assistance is available.

HOUSING

Apartment-style and single-sex housing available.

APPLICATION INFORMATION

Students may begin participation in January, May, and August. Applications are accepted continuously. Applicants must submit a formal application.

CONTACT
Allen Scheidhauer, Department Head, Culinary Arts/
Hospitality Education, Culinary Arts/Hospitality
Education, PO Box 5616, Greenville, SC 29606-5616.
Telephone: 864-250-8404. Fax: 864-250-8455. E-mail:
alan.scheidhauer@gvltec.edu. World Wide Web: http://
www.culinaryartsatgtc.com.

HORRY-GEORGETOWN TECHNICAL COLLEGE

Culinary Arts Department

Conway, South Carolina

GENERAL INFORMATION
Public, coeducational, two-year college. Suburban
campus. Founded in 1965. Accredited by Southern
Association of Colleges and Schools.

PROGRAM INFORMATION
Offered since 1987. Accredited by American Culinary
Federation Accrediting Commission. Program calendar
is divided into semesters. 1-semester certificate in
culinary arts certification. 2-semester certificate in
baking and pastry arts. 5-semester associate degree in
culinary arts technology-business major.

PROGRAM AFFILIATION
American Culinary Federation; Council on Hotel,
Restaurant, and Institutional Education; National
Restaurant Association Educational Foundation.

AREAS OF STUDY
Baking; beverage management; buffet catering;
controlling costs in food service; culinary French; food
preparation; food purchasing; food service
communication; food service math; garde-manger;
international cuisine; introduction to food service;
kitchen management; management and human
resources; meat fabrication; menu and facilities design;
nutrition; sanitation; saucier; seafood processing; soup,
stock, sauce, and starch production.

FACILITIES
2 bake shops; cafeteria; 3 classrooms; computer
laboratory; 2 demonstration laboratories; 4 food
production kitchens; garden; 3 gourmet dining rooms; 2
learning resource centers; 2 lecture rooms; 2 libraries; 2
public restaurants; 2 student lounges; teaching kitchen.

STUDENT PROFILE
140 full-time.

FACULTY
12 total: 3 full-time; 9 part-time. 1 is an industry
professional; 2 are culinary-certified teachers; 1 is a
registered dietitian. Prominent faculty: Kathleen Gerba,
CCE; Lindsey McInville; Eric Wagner, CEC. Faculty-
student ratio: 1:25 lecture; 1:10 lab.

SPECIAL PROGRAMS
Student exchange program with Bahamas Hotel
Training College, Nassau, Bahamas.

TYPICAL EXPENSES
Application fee: $25. In-state tuition: $1460 per
semester (in district), $1844 per semester (out-of-
district). Out-of-state tuition: $2360 per semester.
Program-related fees include $185 for knives; $80 for
uniforms; $250 for books (per semester); $60 for
technology fee (per semester).

FINANCIAL AID
In 2006, 50 scholarships were awarded (average award
was $680); 3 loans were granted (average loan was
$300). Employment placement assistance is available.

APPLICATION INFORMATION
Students may begin participation in January, May, and
August. Applications are accepted continuously. In
2006, 70 applied. Applicants must submit a formal
application and SAT, CPT, or ACT scores.

CONTACT
Carmen Catino, Academic Coordinator, Culinary Arts
Department, 2050 Hwy 501 East, Conway, SC 29526.
Telephone: 843-349-5333. Fax: 843-349-7577. E-mail:
catino@hor.tec.sc.us. World Wide Web: http://www.hgtc.
edu/.

SOUTH DAKOTA

MITCHELL TECHNICAL INSTITUTE

Culinary Arts Program

Mitchell, South Dakota

GENERAL INFORMATION
Coeducational, two-year college. Rural campus.
Founded in 1968. Accredited by North Central
Association of Colleges and Schools.

PROGRAM INFORMATION
Offered since 1968. Program calendar is divided into
semesters. 1-year diploma in culinary arts. 2-year
associate degree in culinary arts.

SPECIAL PROGRAMS
Paid internship.

Mitchell Technical Institute *(continued)*

TYPICAL EXPENSES
Application fee: $35. Tuition: $3885 for diploma; $5994 for associates degree. Program-related fees include $1175–$2038 for program fees; $900–$1250 for books and tools (estimated); $90–$180 for uniform fee.

FINANCIAL AID
Employment placement assistance is available.

APPLICATION INFORMATION
Students may begin participation in January and August. Applications are accepted continuously. Applicants must submit a formal application, high school/college transcripts.

CONTACT
Tim Edwards, Student Services, Culinary Arts Program, 821 North Capital Street, Mitchell, SD 57301. Telephone: 605-995-3025. E-mail: tim.edwards@ mitchelltech.edu. World Wide Web: http://www. mitchelltech.com.

SOUTH DAKOTA STATE UNIVERSITY

Hotel and Foodservice Management

Brookings, South Dakota

GENERAL INFORMATION
Public, coeducational, university. Small-town setting. Founded in 1881. Accredited by North Central Association of Colleges and Schools.

PROGRAM INFORMATION
Program calendar is divided into semesters. 30-month master's degree in nutrition and food science. 4-year bachelor's degree in hotel and foodservice management/hotel and hospitality management specialization. 4-year bachelor's degree in nutrition and food science/nutritional sciences specialization. 4-year bachelor's degree in nutrition and food science/food science specialization. 4-year bachelor's degree in nutrition and food science/dietetics specialization. 4-year bachelor's degree in hotel and foodservice management/foodservice management specialization. 48-month doctoral degree in nutrition and food science.

TYPICAL EXPENSES
Application fee: $20. Tuition: $83 per credit.

FINANCIAL AID
Employment placement assistance is available.

HOUSING
Coed and apartment-style housing available.

APPLICATION INFORMATION
Students may begin participation in January and September. Applications are accepted continuously. Applicants must submit a formal application and high school transcript.

CONTACT
Admissions Counselor, Hotel and Foodservice Management, Box 2201, Brookings, SD 57007. Telephone: 800-952-3541. Fax: 605-688-6891. E-mail: sdsu_admissions@sdstate.edu. World Wide Web: http://www3.sdstate.edu.

TENNESSEE

THE ART INSTITUTE OF TENNESSEE–NASHVILLE

The International Culinary School at The Art Institute of Tennessee–Nashville

Nashville, Tennessee

GENERAL INFORMATION
Private, coeducational institution.

PROGRAM INFORMATION
Associate degree in Culinary Arts. Bachelor's degree in Culinary Arts Management. Diploma in Culinary Arts–Baking and Pastry. Diploma in Culinary Arts–Culinary Skills.

CONTACT
Office of Admissions, The International Culinary School at The Art Institute of Tennessee–Nashville, 100 Centerview Drive, Suite 250, Nashville, TN 37214-3439. Telephone: 615-874-1067. World Wide Web: http://www.artinstitutes.edu/nashville/.
See color display following page 186.

NASHVILLE STATE TECHNICAL COMMUNITY COLLEGE

Culinary Arts

Nashville, Tennessee

GENERAL INFORMATION
Public, coeducational, two-year college. Suburban campus. Founded in 1970. Accredited by Southern Association of Colleges and Schools.

PROGRAM INFORMATION
Offered since 1996. Program calendar is divided into semesters. 1-year technical certificate in culinary arts. 2-year associate degree in culinary arts.

AREAS OF STUDY
Baking; beverage management; buffet catering; culinary French; culinary skill development; food preparation; food purchasing; food service communication; food service math; garde-manger; international cuisine; kitchen management; management and human resources; meal planning; meat cutting; menu and facilities design; nutrition; patisserie; sanitation; saucier; soup, stock, sauce, and starch production.

FACILITIES
Demonstration laboratory; food production kitchen; learning resource center; library; teaching kitchen.

TYPICAL STUDENT PROFILE
120 total: 70 full-time; 50 part-time.

SPECIAL PROGRAMS
Paid internship.

FINANCIAL AID
Employment placement assistance is available.

APPLICATION INFORMATION
Students may begin participation in January and August. Applications are accepted continuously. Applicants must submit a formal application.

CONTACT
Director of Admissions, Culinary Arts, 120 White Bridge Road, Nashville, TN 37209. Telephone: 615-353-3419. Fax: 615-353-3428. World Wide Web: http://www.nscc.edu.

PELLISSIPPI STATE TECHNICAL COMMUNITY COLLEGE

Hospitality and Tourism

Knoxville, Tennessee

GENERAL INFORMATION
Public, coeducational, two-year college. Suburban campus. Founded in 1974. Accredited by Southern Association of Colleges and Schools.

PROGRAM INFORMATION
Offered since 1998. Accredited by Council on Hotel, Restaurant and Institutional Education, Association of Collegiate Business Schools and Programs. Program calendar is divided into semesters. 12-month certificate in travel and tourism. 12-month certificate in lodging. 12-month certificate in food and beverage. 2-year associate degree in hospitality.

PROGRAM AFFILIATION
Council on Hotel, Restaurant, and Institutional Education.

AREAS OF STUDY
Beverage management; buffet catering; controlling costs in food service; food preparation; food purchasing; introduction to food service; wines and spirits.

FACILITIES
2 cafeterias; 10 computer laboratories; demonstration laboratory; food production kitchen; laboratory; 4 learning resource centers; library; 3 snack shops; 4 student lounges; teaching kitchen.

STUDENT PROFILE
84 total: 63 full-time; 21 part-time.

FACULTY
4 total: 1 full-time; 3 part-time. 2 are industry professionals. Prominent faculty: T. F. Gaddis, PhD; J. Alunni; E. Smith. Faculty-student ratio: 1:15.

SPECIAL PROGRAMS
600-hour paid internship, Knoxville Tourism Alliance student membership.

TYPICAL EXPENSES
Application fee: $5. In-state tuition: $885 per semester full-time (in district), $91 per credit hour part-time. Out-of-state tuition: $3281 per semester full-time, $298 per credit hour part-time.

FINANCIAL AID
In 2006, 4 scholarships were awarded (average award was $500). Employment placement assistance is available.

HOUSING
Average off-campus housing cost per month: $500.

APPLICATION INFORMATION
Students may begin participation in January and August. Application deadline for fall is August 20. Application deadline for spring is January 10. In 2006, 42 applied; 42 were accepted. Applicants must submit a formal application.

CONTACT
Leigh Anne Touzeau, Director of Admissions, Hospitality and Tourism, PO Box 22990, Knoxville, TN 37933-0990. Telephone: 865-694-6572. Fax: 865-539-7217. E-mail: latouzeau@pstcc.cc.tn.us. World Wide Web: http://www.pstcc.edu/.

WALTERS STATE COMMUNITY COLLEGE

Hospitality Business/Rel Maples Institute for Culinary Arts

Sevierville, Tennessee

GENERAL INFORMATION
Public, coeducational, two-year college. Small-town setting. Founded in 1970. Accredited by Southern Association of Colleges and Schools.

PROGRAM INFORMATION
Offered since 1997. Accredited by American Culinary Federation Accrediting Commission. Program calendar is divided into semesters. 1-year certificate in culinary arts. 2-year associate degree in hotel/restaurant management. 2-year associate degree in culinary arts.

PROGRAM AFFILIATION
American Culinary Federation; National Restaurant Association; Sevier County Hospitality Association; Tennessee Restaurant Association.

AREAS OF STUDY
Baking; beverage management; buffet catering; confectionery show pieces; controlling costs in food service; culinary French; culinary skill development; food preparation; food purchasing; food service communication; food service math; garde-manger; international cuisine; introduction to food service; kitchen management; management and human resources; meal planning; meat cutting; meat fabrication; menu and facilities design; nutrition; nutrition and food service; patisserie; restaurant opportunities; sanitation; saucier; seafood processing; soup, stock, sauce, and starch production.

FACILITIES
Bake shop; cafeteria; catering service; 4 classrooms; 2 computer laboratories; demonstration laboratory; food production kitchen; garden; gourmet dining room; learning resource center; lecture room; library; student lounge; teaching kitchen; herb garden.

STUDENT PROFILE
115 total: 75 full-time; 40 part-time. 67 are under 25 years old; 30 are between 25 and 44 years old; 18 are over 44 years old.

FACULTY
10 total: 4 full-time; 6 part-time. 7 are industry professionals; 3 are culinary-certified teachers. Prominent faculty: Vanda Porter, Chef Instructor; Catherine Hallman, CEPC; David Colburn, CEC. Faculty-student ratio: 1:13.

PROMINENT ALUMNI AND CURRENT AFFILIATION
Aaron Ward, Taulbee's, Sevierville, TN; Aaron Dawson, General Morgan Inn, Greeneville, TN; Danielle McGinnis, Wolf Gang Puck Catering Company, Los Angeles, CA.

SPECIAL PROGRAMS
Culinary Competition Team, annual visit to National Restaurant Show (Chicago), biennial trips emphasizing the culinary industry.

TYPICAL EXPENSES
Application fee: $10. In-state tuition: $1313.50 per semester full-time (in district), $358 per 3 credit hours part-time. Out-of-state tuition: $4851.50 per semester full-time, $1276 per 3 credit hours part-time. Program-related fees include $70 for uniform (1); $175 for knife kit; $75 for American Culinary Federation membership.

FINANCIAL AID
In 2006, 6 scholarships were awarded (average award was $500). Program-specific awards include state and local tourism association scholarships. Employment placement assistance is available. Employment opportunities within the program are available.

HOUSING
Average off-campus housing cost per month: $550.

APPLICATION INFORMATION
Students may begin participation in January and August. Applications are accepted continuously. In 2006, 50 applied; 45 were accepted. Applicants must submit a formal application.

CONTACT
Marvin Curnutt, Office of Enrollment Development, Hospitality Business/Rel Maples Institute for Culinary Arts, 500 South Davy Crockett Parkway, Morristown, TN 37813. Telephone: 423-585-2691. Fax: 423-585-6786. E-mail: marvin.curnutt@ws.edu. World Wide Web: http://www.ws.edu.

TEXAS

AIMS ACADEMY

Carrollton, Texas

GENERAL INFORMATION
Private, coeducational, culinary institute. Suburban campus. Founded in 1987. Accredited by Council on Occupational Education.

PROGRAM INFORMATION

Offered since 1987. Accredited by Council On Occupation Education. Program calendar is continuous. 9-month diploma in culinary.

AREAS OF STUDY

Baking; food preparation; food purchasing; introduction to food service; meat fabrication; nutrition; nutrition and food service; restaurant opportunities; sanitation; seafood processing; soup, stock, sauce, and starch production.

FACILITIES

3 classrooms; food production kitchen; 2 lecture rooms; library; 2 public restaurants; snack shop; student lounge; teaching kitchen.

STUDENT PROFILE

81 full-time. 14 are under 25 years old; 59 are between 25 and 44 years old; 8 are over 44 years old.

FACULTY

4 total: 4 full-time. 4 are culinary-certified teachers. Prominent faculty: Russell Hodges; Jerry Cangemi; Jason Chavez; Sheila Larson. Faculty-student ratio: 1:20.

PROMINENT ALUMNI AND CURRENT AFFILIATION

Sheila Larson, The Mediterranean Villa, Arlington, TX; Birkley Johnson; Tommy Jones, Abacus, Dallas, TX.

SPECIAL PROGRAMS

Certified Food Protection Certificate, TABC certifications.

TYPICAL EXPENSES

Application fee: $100. Tuition: $19,985 per 9 month period.

FINANCIAL AID

Program-specific awards include Title Four Funding. Employment placement assistance is available.

APPLICATION INFORMATION

Students may begin participation in January, February, March, April, May, June, July, August, September, October, and November. Applications are accepted continuously. In 2006, 109 applied; 81 were accepted. Applicants must interview and submit a high school diploma or GED.

CONTACT

Ricky Watkins, Director of Admissions, 1711 I35 East, Carrollton, TX 75006. Telephone: 972-323-6333. E-mail: rwatkins@aimsacademy.com.

AIMS ACADEMY SCHOOL OF CULINARY ARTS

School of Culinary Arts/School of Professional Bartending

Dallas, Texas

GENERAL INFORMATION

Private, coeducational, culinary institute. Urban campus. Founded in 1987.

PROGRAM INFORMATION

Offered since 1987. Program calendar is continuous. 14-day diploma in professional bartending. 9-month diploma in culinary arts.

FINANCIAL AID

Employment placement assistance is available.

APPLICATION INFORMATION

Applications are accepted continuously. Applicants must interview, submit a formal application, and have a high school diploma or GED.

CONTACT

Admissions Department, School of Culinary Arts/School of Professional Bartending, SMU 6116, North Central Expressway, Suite 140, Dallas, TX 75206. Telephone: 972-988-3202. E-mail: aimsinfo@aimsacademy.com. World Wide Web: http://aimsacademy.com.

THE ART INSTITUTE OF DALLAS

The International Culinary School at The Art Institute of Dallas

Dallas, Texas

GENERAL INFORMATION

Private, coeducational institution.

PROGRAM INFORMATION

Associate degree in Restaurant and Catering Management. Associate degree in Culinary Arts. Certificate in Art of Cooking.

CONTACT

Office of Admissions, The International Culinary School at The Art Institute of Dallas, Two North Park East, 8080 Park Lane, Suite 100, Dallas, TX 75231-5993. Telephone: 214-692-8080. World Wide Web: http://www.artinstitutes.edu/dallas/.

See color display following page 186.

THE ART INSTITUTE OF HOUSTON

The International Culinary School at The Art Institute of Houston

Houston, Texas

GENERAL INFORMATION
Private, coeducational institution.

PROGRAM INFORMATION
Associate degree in Baking and Pastry. Associate degree in Culinary Arts. Associate degree in Restaurant and Catering Management. Bachelor's degree in Culinary Management. Diploma in Culinary Arts.

CONTACT
Office of Admissions, The International Culinary School at The Art Institute of Houston, 1900 Yorktown Street, Houston, TX 77056-4197. Telephone: 713-623-2040. World Wide Web: http://www.artinstitutes.edu/houston/.
See color display following page 186.

AUSTIN COMMUNITY COLLEGE

Culinary Arts

Austin, Texas

GENERAL INFORMATION
Public, coeducational, two-year college. Urban campus. Founded in 1972. Accredited by Southern Association of Colleges and Schools.

PROGRAM INFORMATION
Accredited by American Culinary Federation Accrediting Commission. Program calendar is divided into semesters. 1-year certificate in hospitality management. 12-month certificate in culinary arts. 2-year associate degree in hospitality management. 2-year associate degree in culinary arts.

PROGRAM AFFILIATION
American Culinary Federation; American Institute of Baking; Council on Hotel, Restaurant, and Institutional Education; International Association of Culinary Professionals; International Foodservice Editorial Council; International Sommelier Guild; National Restaurant Association; National Restaurant Association Educational Foundation; Society of Wine Educators; The Bread Bakers Guild of America; Women Chefs and Restaurateurs.

AREAS OF STUDY
Beverage management; controlling costs in food service; culinary skill development; food service math; international cuisine; kitchen management; management and human resources; meat cutting; meat fabrication; nutrition; restaurant opportunities; sanitation; wines and spirits.

FACILITIES
10 classrooms; 4 computer laboratories; demonstration laboratory; food production kitchen; gourmet dining room; learning resource center; library; snack shop; student lounge.

STUDENT PROFILE
150 total: 50 full-time; 100 part-time.

FACULTY
12 total: 4 full-time; 8 part-time. 7 are industry professionals; 2 are culinary-certified teachers. Faculty-student ratio: 1:12.

SPECIAL PROGRAMS
School trips (Napa Valley, New York), culinary competitions, internships/practicums.

TYPICAL EXPENSES
In-state tuition: $1800 per year full-time (in district), $160 per 3 credit hour class part-time. Out-of-state tuition: $3200 per year full-time, $280 per 3 credit hour class part-time. Program-related fees include $200 for equipment and uniforms; $150 for books (per semester).

FINANCIAL AID
In 2006, 5 scholarships were awarded (average award was $425). Employment opportunities within the program are available.

HOUSING
Average off-campus housing cost per month: $700.

APPLICATION INFORMATION
Students may begin participation in January, May, and August. Applications are accepted continuously. In 2006, 60 applied; 45 were accepted.

CONTACT
Brian Hay, Program Coordinator, Culinary Arts, 3401 Webberville Road, Austin, TX 78702. Telephone: 512-223-5173. Fax: 512-223-5125. E-mail: bhay@ austincc.edu. World Wide Web: http://www2.austincc. edu/hospmgmt.

Central Texas College

Hospitality Management/Culinary Arts

Killeen, Texas

General Information
Public, coeducational, two-year college. Small-town setting. Founded in 1965. Accredited by Southern Association of Colleges and Schools.

Program Information
Offered since 1970. Program calendar is divided into semesters. 16-month certificate in culinary arts. 16-month certificate in institutional food service operations. 2-year associate degree in food and beverage management. 2-year associate degree in food service management. 2-year associate degree in restaurant and culinary management. 9-month certificate in food and beverage management. 9-month certificate in restaurant skills.

Program Affiliation
American Culinary Federation; American Hotel and Lodging Association; Council on Hotel, Restaurant, and Institutional Education; Institute of Food Technologists; National Restaurant Association; National Restaurant Association Educational Foundation; Texas Restaurant Association; Texas State Food Servers Association.

Areas of Study
Baking; beverage management; buffet catering; confectionery show pieces; controlling costs in food service; culinary French; culinary skill development; food preparation; food purchasing; food service math; garde-manger; international cuisine; introduction to food service; kitchen management; management and human resources; meal planning; meat cutting; menu and facilities design; nutrition; nutrition and food service; restaurant opportunities; sanitation; saucier; seafood processing; soup, stock, sauce, and starch production; wines and spirits.

Facilities
Bake shop; bakery; cafeteria; catering service; 6 classrooms; 2 computer laboratories; demonstration laboratory; food production kitchen; gourmet dining room; laboratory; learning resource center; lecture room; library; snack shop; student lounge; teaching kitchen.

Student Profile
300 total: 100 full-time; 200 part-time. 120 are under 25 years old; 120 are between 25 and 44 years old; 60 are over 44 years old.

Faculty
5 total: 3 full-time; 2 part-time. 4 are industry professionals; 1 is a culinary-certified teacher. Prominent faculty: Richard Brownlee, CFE; Ramona Lezo, ACF; Rick Hindman. Faculty-student ratio: 1:12.

Special Programs
Dual credit program for high school students.

Typical Expenses
In-state tuition: $2940 per 2 years full-time (in district), $36 per semester hour part-time (in district), $3036 per 2 years full-time (out-of-district), $46 per semester hour part-time (out-of-district). Out-of-state tuition: $8580 per 2 years full-time, $130 per semester hour part-time. Program-related fees include $150 for cutlery; $100 for uniforms; $100–$150 for lab (cooking classes).

Financial Aid
In 2006, 8 scholarships were awarded (average award was $500). Program-specific awards include Charles Leopard Scholarship.

Housing
Coed housing available. Average on-campus housing cost per month: $243. Average off-campus housing cost per month: $427.

Application Information
Students may begin participation in January, May, and August. Applications are accepted continuously. In 2006, 300 applied. Applicants must interview; submit a formal application.

Contact
Richard Hindman, Director, Hospitality Management/ Culinary Arts, PO Box 1800, Killeen, TX 76540-1800. Telephone: 800-792-3348 Ext. 1539. Fax: 254-526 1841. E-mail: rick.hindman@ctc-disted.net. World Wide Web: http://www.ctcd.edu.

Culinary Academy of Austin, Inc.

Austin, Texas

General Information
Private, coeducational, culinary institute. Urban campus. Founded in 1998. Accredited by Council on Occupational Education.

Program Information
Offered since 1998. Program calendar is divided into quarters. 15-month diploma in professional culinary arts. 6-month diploma in professional pastry arts.

Culinary Academy of Austin, Inc. *(continued)*

PROGRAM AFFILIATION
American Culinary Federation; Foodservice Educators Network International; National Restaurant Association; Texas Restaurant Association; The Bread Bakers Guild of America.

AREAS OF STUDY
Baking; buffet catering; controlling costs in food service; convenience cookery; culinary skill development; food history and culture; food preparation; food service math; garde-manger; international cuisine; introduction to food service; kitchen management; meal planning; meat cutting; menu and facilities design; nutrition; nutrition and food service; patisserie; restaurant opportunities; sanitation; saucier; seafood processing; soup, stock, sauce, and starch production; wines and spirits.

FACILITIES
Bake shop; catering service; 2 classrooms; computer laboratory; food production kitchen; learning resource center; library.

STUDENT PROFILE
15 are under 25 years old; 12 are between 25 and 44 years old; 7 are over 44 years old.

FACULTY
5 total: 4 full-time; 1 part-time. 4 are industry professionals; 1 is a culinary professional. Prominent faculty: Steve Mannion, CEC, CEPC; Stephen Rafferty, CEC. Faculty-student ratio: 1:12.

PROMINENT ALUMNI AND CURRENT AFFILIATION
Stephen Sicola, Sicola Catering and Events; Jennifer Moore, All in One, Austin, TX.

SPECIAL PROGRAMS
International culinary programs in Italy, culinary competitions, food and drink symposium.

TYPICAL EXPENSES
Application fee: $75. Tuition: $23,000 per year. Program-related fees include $302 for lab fees (aprons, towels, food); $30 for media services.

FINANCIAL AID
In 2006, 2 scholarships were awarded (average award was $1000); 2 loans were granted (average loan was $2200). Program-specific awards include work-study with professional catering company. Employment placement assistance is available. Employment opportunities within the program are available.

HOUSING
Average off-campus housing cost per month: $500.

APPLICATION INFORMATION
Students may begin participation in January, April, July, and October. Applications are accepted continuously. In 2006, 48 applied; 42 were accepted. Applicants must interview; submit a formal application, letters of reference, an essay, high school diploma.

CONTACT
Steve Mannion, Director, 6020 B. Dillard Circle, Austin, TX 78752. Telephone: 512-451-5743. Fax: 512-467-9120. E-mail: info@culinaryacademyofaustin.com. World Wide Web: http://www.culinaryacademyofaustin.com/.

CULINARY INSTITUTE ALAIN AND MARIE LENÔTRE

Houston, Texas

GENERAL INFORMATION
Private, coeducational, culinary institute. Urban campus. Founded in 1998. Accredited by Accrediting Commission of Career Schools and Colleges of Technology.

PROGRAM INFORMATION
Offered since 1998. Accredited by Accrediting Commission of Career Schools and Colleges of Technology (ACCSCT). Endorsed for quality education by the American Culinary Federation Foundation. National Restaurant Association Educational Foundation ManageFirst certificates available. Program calendar is continuous, with a new cycle every 10 weeks. 20- to 40-week diploma in sous-chef patissier. 20- to 40-week diploma in sous-chef de cuisine. 30- to 60-week diploma in culinary arts: specialty in baking and pastry. 30- to 60-week diploma in culinary arts: specialty in cooking and catering. 60- to 100-week associate degree in baking and pastry arts. 60- to 100-week associate degree in culinary arts.

PROGRAM AFFILIATION
American Culinary Federation; Houston Professional Chef Association; National Restaurant Association; Texas Chefs Association; Texas Restaurant Association.

AREAS OF STUDY
Bakery Operations; baking; beverage management; buffet catering; cakes; Career Exploration and Planning; chocolate candy making; chocolate décor; confectionery show pieces; controlling costs in food service; croissant; culinary French; culinary skill development; danishes; Dining Room service; Food and Beverage Control; food and beverage management; food preparation; food purchasing; food service math; garde-manger; Hospitality Marketing/Sales; human resource management; ice cream and sorbet; international

cuisine; introduction to hospitality; Italian, Sushi, Regional American and French Cuisine; kitchen management; management and human resources; meat cutting; menu and facilities design; Menu Management; nutrition; nutrition and food service; Nutrition for Food Service Professionals; pastry; patisserie; pies; purchasing; rotisserie; sanitation; Sanitation and Safety; saucier; seafood; seafood processing; soup; soup, stock, sauce, and starch production; stock & sauce; tarts; wines and spirits.

FACILITIES

Classroom; computer laboratory; gourmet dining room; learning resource center; library; student lounge; 6 teaching kitchens.

STUDENT PROFILE

156 total: 94 full-time; 62 part-time. 68 are under 25 years old; 70 are between 25 and 44 years old; 18 are over 44 years old.

FACULTY

16 total: 7 full-time; 9 part-time. xperience. Prominent faculty: Chef Phillippe Richard, CEPC; Chef Bertrand Goutelon, CEC; Chef Jean Rene Thiery; Chef Dominique Bocquier. Faculty-student ratio: 1:12.

SPECIAL PROGRAMS

Culinary internships in France, externships in US, team building, culinary competitions, summer camp for teenagers and adults, monthly Chef Club cooking classes, alumni workshops, etc..

TYPICAL EXPENSES

Application fee: $50. Tuition: $17,325 to $22,000 per 20 to 30 weeks morning classes and 40 to 60 weeks evening classes for the Diploma programs; $33,530 to $33,950 per 60 to 100 weeks for each of the Associate degree programs. Program-related fees include $1718 for culinary arts program (tools, uniforms, textbooks and lab fee); $1286 for sous-chef de cuisine program (tools, uniforms, textbooks and lab fee); $1297 for sous-chef Pâtissier program (tools, uniforms, textbooks and lab fee); $3542–$3653 for Associate degree programs (tools, uniform, textbooks and lab fee); $50 for enrollment fee.

FINANCIAL AID

Program-specific awards include many in-house and outside scholarships for those who qualify. Employment placement assistance is available. Employment opportunities within the program are available.

HOUSING

Average off-campus housing cost per month: $600–$800.

Culinary Institute Alain and Marie LeNôtre
(continued)

APPLICATION INFORMATION
Students may begin participation year-round. Applications are accepted continuously. In 2006, 174 applied; 156 were accepted. Applicants must submit a formal application, an essay, a high school diploma or GED, essay for scholarship consideration for those who qualify.

CONTACT
Jean Luc Hauvillier, School Representative, 7070 Allensby, Houston, TX 77022. Telephone: 713-692-0077. Fax: 713-692-7399. E-mail: admission@culinaryinstitute. edu. World Wide Web: http://www.ciaml.com.

DEL MAR COLLEGE

Department of Hospitality Management

Corpus Christi, Texas

GENERAL INFORMATION
Public, coeducational, two-year college. Urban campus. Founded in 1935. Accredited by Southern Association of Colleges and Schools.

PROGRAM INFORMATION
Offered since 1963. Accredited by American Culinary Federation Accrediting Commission. Program calendar is divided into semesters. 1-year certificate in kitchen supervisor. 1-year certificate in restaurant supervisor. 2-year associate degree in baking pastry specialization. 2-year associate degree in culinary arts. 2-year associate degree in restaurant management specialization. 9-month certificate in cook/baker.

PROGRAM AFFILIATION
American Culinary Federation; Coastal Bend Hotel Motel Condominium Association; Coastal Bend Restaurant Association; Council on Hotel, Restaurant, and Institutional Education; National Restaurant Association; Texas Chefs Association; Texas Restaurant Association.

AREAS OF STUDY
Baking; beverage management; buffet catering; confectionery show pieces; controlling costs in food service; culinary skill development; food preparation; food purchasing; garde-manger; international cuisine; introduction to food service; kitchen management; management and human resources; menu and facilities design; nutrition; nutrition and food service; patisserie; restaurant opportunities; sanitation; saucier; soup, stock, sauce, and starch production.

FACILITIES
Bake shop; cafeteria; catering service; 4 classrooms; computer laboratory; 2 demonstration laboratories; 2 food production kitchens; gourmet dining room; 2 laboratories; learning resource center; 4 lecture rooms; 2 libraries; public restaurant; 2 teaching kitchens; herb garden; ice carving room.

TYPICAL STUDENT PROFILE
120 total: 24 full-time; 96 part-time. 24 are under 25 years old; 84 are between 25 and 44 years old; 12 are over 44 years old.

SPECIAL PROGRAMS
Paid internships in local restaurants, hotels, and clubs, annual pastry and garde manger competition.

FINANCIAL AID
Employment placement assistance is available. Employment opportunities within the program are available.

APPLICATION INFORMATION
Students may begin participation in January, June, and September. Application deadline for fall is August 18. Application deadline for spring is January 15. Application deadline for summer is May 25. Applicants must submit a formal application, academic transcripts, and test scores.

CONTACT
Director of Admissions, Department of Hospitality Management, 101 Baldwin Boulevard, Corpus Christi, TX 78404-3897. Telephone: 361-698-1734. Fax: 361-698-1829. World Wide Web: http://www.delmar.edu/hospmgmt.

EL PASO COMMUNITY COLLEGE

Culinary Arts and Related Sciences

El Paso, Texas

GENERAL INFORMATION
Public, coeducational, two-year college. Urban campus. Founded in 1969. Accredited by Southern Association of Colleges and Schools.

PROGRAM INFORMATION
Offered since 1989. National Restaurant Association Educational Foundation ManageFirst certificates available. Program calendar is divided into semesters. 1-year certificate of completion in pastry. 1-year certificate of completion in restaurant/food service management. 1-year certificate of completion in

culinary arts. 2-year associate degree in pastry. 2-year associate degree in culinary arts. 2-year associate degree in restaurant/food service management.

PROGRAM AFFILIATION

American Culinary Federation; American Hotel and Lodging Association Educational Institute; Council on Hotel, Restaurant, and Institutional Education; National Restaurant Association Educational Foundation.

AREAS OF STUDY

Baking; beverage management; buffet catering; confectionery show pieces; controlling costs in food service; culinary French; culinary skill development; food and beverage management; food and beverage service; food preparation; food purchasing; garde-manger; international cuisine; introduction to food service; kitchen management; management and human resources; meal planning; meat cutting; menu and facilities design; nutrition; patisserie; sanitation; saucier; soup, stock, sauce, and starch production.

FACILITIES

Bake shop; 3 classrooms; computer laboratory; 2 food production kitchens; 2 gardens; gourmet dining room; 6 lecture rooms; library; teaching kitchen.

STUDENT PROFILE

218 total: 176 full-time; 42 part-time. 34 are under 25 years old; 148 are between 25 and 44 years old; 36 are over 44 years old.

FACULTY

7 total: 2 full-time; 5 part-time. 5 are industry professionals; 2 are culinary-certified teachers. Prominent faculty: Richard Webb, CCE; Jesus Lugo, CEC.

PROMINENT ALUMNI AND CURRENT AFFILIATION

Daniel Guerra, Executive Chef, Mesa Street Bar & Grill; Armando Pomales, Executive Chef, Cafe Centrale; Natalia Harrera, Corporate Chef, Helen of Troy.

TYPICAL EXPENSES

Application fee: $10. In-state tuition: $7400 per 2 year degree full-time (in district), $150 per credit hour part-time. Out-of-state tuition: $275 per credit hour part-time.

FINANCIAL AID

In 2006, 6 scholarships were awarded (average award was $1000). Employment placement assistance is available. Employment opportunities within the program are available.

HOUSING

Average off-campus housing cost per month: $400.

APPLICATION INFORMATION

Students may begin participation in January, June, and September. Application deadline for fall is July 22. Application deadline for spring is November 18. Application deadline for summer is May 4. Applicants must submit a formal application and have a high school diploma or GED.

CONTACT

Richard Webb, Curriculum Coordinator, Culinary Arts and Related Sciences, 9570 Gateway North, El Paso, TX 79924. Telephone: 915-831-5148. Fax: 915-831-5017. E-mail: ewebb1@epcc.edu. World Wide Web: http://www.epcc.edu/.

GALVESTON COLLEGE

Culinary Arts Academy

Galveston, Texas

GENERAL INFORMATION

Public, coeducational, two-year college. Urban campus. Founded in 1967. Accredited by Southern Association of Colleges and Schools.

PROGRAM INFORMATION

Offered since 1987. National Restaurant Association Educational Foundation ManageFirst certificates available. Program calendar is divided into semesters. 1-year certificate in culinary/hospitality management. 1-year certificate in culinary arts. 2-year associate degree in culinary arts/hospitality.

PROGRAM AFFILIATION

American Culinary Federation; Confrerie de la Chaine des Rotisseurs; International Association of Culinary Professionals; National Restaurant Association; National Restaurant Association Educational Foundation; Texas Chefs Association; Texas Restaurant Association.

AREAS OF STUDY

Baking; beverage management; culinary skill development; food preparation; food purchasing; garde-manger; international cuisine; kitchen management; menu and facilities design; nutrition; sanitation; soup, stock, sauce, and starch production.

FACILITIES

Bake shop; 3 classrooms; 2 computer laboratories; food production kitchen; learning resource center; library; snack shop; student lounge; teaching kitchen.

STUDENT PROFILE

40 total: 25 full-time; 15 part-time.

Galveston College *(continued)*

FACULTY
3 total: 1 full-time; 2 part-time. 2 are industry professionals; 1 is a culinary-certified teacher. Prominent faculty: Paul Mendoza; Kaye Gable; Peter Mitchell, MHM. Faculty-student ratio: 1:15.

SPECIAL PROGRAMS
320-hour paid internships, ServSafe certification.

TYPICAL EXPENSES
In-state tuition: $750 per semester. Out-of-state tuition: $1230 per semester. Program-related fees include $275 for knives; $600 for books; $100 for uniforms; $192 for lab fee.

FINANCIAL AID
In 2006, 2 scholarships were awarded (average award was $500); 15 loans were granted (average loan was $750). Employment placement assistance is available.

HOUSING
Average off-campus housing cost per month: $500.

APPLICATION INFORMATION
Students may begin participation in January, February, March, April, May, June, July, August, September, October, and November. Applications are accepted continuously. In 2006, 40 applied; 40 were accepted. Applicants must submit a formal application.

CONTACT
Paul Mendoza, Director, Culinary Arts Academy, 4015 Avenue Q, Galveston, TX 77550. Telephone: 409-944-1304. Fax: 409-944-1511. E-mail: chef@gc.edu. World Wide Web: http://www.gc.edu/gc/Culinary_Arts.asp?SnID=1069165685.

HOUSTON COMMUNITY COLLEGE SYSTEM

Culinary Services and Hospitality Services

Houston, Texas

GENERAL INFORMATION
Public, coeducational, two-year college. Urban campus. Founded in 1972. Accredited by Southern Association of Colleges and Schools.

PROGRAM INFORMATION
Offered since 1980. National Restaurant Association Educational Foundation ManageFirst certificates available. Program calendar is divided into semesters. 1-semester certificate in travel and tourism. 2-semester certificate in restaurant management. 2-semester certificate in hotel management. 3-semester certificate in pastry arts. 3-semester certificate in culinary arts. 4-semester associate degree in travel and tourism. 4-semester associate degree in culinary arts. 4-semester associate degree in pastry arts. 4-semester associate degree in hotel and restaurant management.

PROGRAM AFFILIATION
American Institute of Baking; Council on Hotel, Restaurant, and Institutional Education; Foodservice Educators Network International; Les Dames d'Escoffier; National Restaurant Association.

AREAS OF STUDY
Baking; beverage management; breads; confectionery show pieces; controlling costs in food service; croissant, Danish, and puff pastry; culinary skill development; food preparation; food purchasing; food service math; garde-manger; international cuisine; introduction to food service; kitchen management; management and human resources; nutrition; patisserie; restaurant opportunities; sanitation; saucier; soup, stock, sauce, and starch production.

FACILITIES
2 bake shops; cafeteria; 5 classrooms; 2 computer laboratories; demonstration laboratory; 2 food production kitchens; gourmet dining room; learning resource center; 2 lecture rooms; library; public restaurant; student lounge.

STUDENT PROFILE
700 total: 350 full-time; 350 part-time. 150 are under 25 years old; 400 are between 25 and 44 years old; 150 are over 44 years old.

FACULTY
15 total: 7 full-time; 8 part-time. 8 are industry professionals; 4 are culinary-certified teachers. Prominent faculty: Eddy Van Damme; Ezat Moradi, CHA; Troy King; Judith Boykin. Faculty-student ratio: 1:16.

PROMINENT ALUMNI AND CURRENT AFFILIATION
Joseph Massa, Massa's Restaurant; Hugo Ortega, Backstreet Café; Nancy Walsh, World Catering.

SPECIAL PROGRAMS
5-day classes with Lenôtre in France -day classes with Lenôtre in France, 7-8 day European trips, marketable skills courses for individuals working in the industry who want to upgrade their skills.

TYPICAL EXPENSES
In-state tuition: $798.75 per semester (in district), $1608.75 per semester (out-of-district). Out-of-state tuition: $1908.75 per semester. Tuition for international students: $1908.75 per semester. Program-related fees include $6 for lab fees; $80 for travel and tourism fee (for computer automated reservation system).

FINANCIAL AID
In 2006, 2 scholarships were awarded (average award was $5000). Employment placement assistance is available. Employment opportunities within the program are available.

HOUSING
Average off-campus housing cost per month: $600–$700.

APPLICATION INFORMATION
Students may begin participation in January, May, and August. Applications are accepted continuously. Applicants must take Test of Adult Basic Education.

CONTACT
Ezat Moradi, Hospitality and Culinary Arts Department Chair, Culinary Services and Hospitality Services, 1300 Holman, Room 302-A, Houston, TX 77004. Telephone: 713-718-6072. Fax: 713-718-6044. E-mail: ezat.moradi@ hccs.edu. World Wide Web: http://www.hccs.edu.

LAMAR UNIVERSITY

Family and Consumer Sciences–Hospitality Management

Beaumont, Texas

GENERAL INFORMATION
Public, coeducational, university. Urban campus. Founded in 1923. Accredited by Southern Association of Colleges and Schools.

PROGRAM INFORMATION
Offered since 1986. Accredited by American Culinary Federation Accrediting Commission, American Dietetic Association. Program calendar is divided into semesters. 2-year certificate in lodging. 2-year certificate in restaurant management. 2-year certificate in culinary arts. 2-year master's degree in family and consumer sciences. 4-year bachelor's degree in hospitality management.

PROGRAM AFFILIATION
American Dietetic Association; American Hotel and Lodging Association; Confrerie de la Chaine des Rotisseurs; Council on Hotel, Restaurant, and Institutional Education; International Food Service Executives Association; National Restaurant Association; National Restaurant Association Educational Foundation.

AREAS OF STUDY
Baking; beverage management; buffet catering; controlling costs in food service; culinary French; culinary skill development; food preparation; food purchasing; food service math; garde-manger; introduction to food service; kitchen management; management and human resources; meal planning; meat cutting; menu and facilities design; nutrition; nutrition and food service; patisserie; restaurant opportunities; sanitation; saucier; soup, stock, sauce, and starch production; wines and spirits.

FACILITIES
2 cafeterias; catering service; 6 classrooms; 2 computer laboratories; demonstration laboratory; food production kitchen; laboratory; 2 learning resource centers; 6 lecture rooms; library; teaching kitchen.

TYPICAL STUDENT PROFILE
70 total: 50 full-time; 20 part-time.

SPECIAL PROGRAMS
Culinary competitions, paid internships with local properties.

FINANCIAL AID
Employment placement assistance is available. Employment opportunities within the program are available.

HOUSING
Coed housing available.

APPLICATION INFORMATION
Students may begin participation in January and August. Applications are accepted continuously. Applicants must submit a formal application and an essay.

CONTACT
Director of Admissions, Family and Consumer Sciences - Hospitality Management, 211 Redbird Lane, Box 10035, Beaumont, TX 77710. Telephone: 409-880-1744. Fax: 409-880-8666. World Wide Web: http://www.lamar.edu.

LE CORDON BLEU INSTITUTE OF CULINARY ARTS

Dallas, Texas

GENERAL INFORMATION
Coeducational, culinary institute. Founded in 1999.

PROGRAM INFORMATION
15-month diploma in Le Cordon Bleu Culinary Arts.

SPECIAL PROGRAMS
3-month externship.

FINANCIAL AID
Employment placement assistance is available.

Le Cordon Bleu Institute of Culinary Arts *(continued)*

APPLICATION INFORMATION
Applications are accepted continuously.

CONTACT
Admissions Office, 11830 Webb Chapel Road, Dallas, TX 75234. Telephone: 888-495-5222. World Wide Web: http://www.dallasculinary.com/programs.

NORTHWOOD UNIVERSITY, TEXAS CAMPUS

Hotel, Restaurant, and Resort Management

Cedar Hill, Texas

GENERAL INFORMATION
Private, coeducational, four-year college. Suburban campus. Founded in 1965. Accredited by North Central Association of Colleges and Schools.

PROGRAM INFORMATION
Offered since 1966. National Restaurant Association Educational Foundation ManageFirst certificates available. Program calendar is divided into quarters. 2-year associate degree in hotel, restaurant, resort management. 4-year bachelor's degree in hotel, restaurant, resort management.

PROGRAM AFFILIATION
Council on Hotel, Restaurant, and Institutional Education; Institute of Food Technologists; National Restaurant Association; National Restaurant Association Educational Foundation.

AREAS OF STUDY
Beverage management; food preparation; food purchasing; food service communication; food service math; introduction to food service; kitchen management; management and human resources; meal planning; menu and facilities design; nutrition; nutrition and food service; restaurant opportunities; sanitation.

FACILITIES
Classroom; demonstration laboratory; lecture room.

STUDENT PROFILE
32 total: 31 full-time; 1 part-time. 31 are under 25 years old; 1 is between 25 and 44 years old.

FACULTY
2 total: 1 full-time; 1 part-time. 1 is an industry professional. Prominent faculty: Michael Lansing. Faculty-student ratio: 1:18.

SPECIAL PROGRAMS
Trip to NRA trade show in Chicago.

TYPICAL EXPENSES
Application fee: $25. Tuition: $15,825 per year full-time, $330 per credit hour part-time.

FINANCIAL AID
In 2006, 1 scholarship was awarded (award was $1250). Employment placement assistance is available. Employment opportunities within the program are available.

HOUSING
Single-sex housing available. Average on-campus housing cost per month: $413.

APPLICATION INFORMATION
Students may begin participation in March, September, and December. Applications are accepted continuously. In 2006, 49 applied; 21 were accepted. Applicants must submit a formal application and an essay.

CONTACT
Sylvia Correa, Director of Admissions, Hotel, Restaurant, and Resort Management, 1114 West FM 1382, Cedar Hill, TX 75104. Telephone: 800-927-9663. Fax: 972-291-3824. E-mail: xadmit@northwood.edu. World Wide Web: http://www.northwood.edu.

REMINGTON COLLEGE–DALLAS CAMPUS

Garland, Texas

GENERAL INFORMATION
Private, two-year college. Founded in 1987. Accredited by Accrediting Council for Independent Colleges and Schools.

PROGRAM INFORMATION
Associate degree in culinary arts.

APPLICATION INFORMATION
Applicants must high school diploma or equivalent.

CONTACT
Admissions Department, 1800 Eastgate Drive, Garland, TX 75041-5513. Telephone: 800-725-1327.

San Jacinto College–Central Campus

Culinary Arts/Restaurant Management/Dietetic Technology

Pasadena, Texas

GENERAL INFORMATION
Public, coeducational, two-year college. Suburban campus. Founded in 1961. Accredited by Southern Association of Colleges and Schools.

PROGRAM INFORMATION
Accredited by American Dietetic Association. Program calendar is divided into semesters. 1-year certificate in dietetic technology. 1-year certificate in restaurant management. 1-year certificate in culinary arts. 2-year associate degree in dietetic technology. 2-year associate degree in culinary arts. 2-year associate degree in restaurant management.

PROGRAM AFFILIATION
National Restaurant Association; Texas Restaurant Association.

AREAS OF STUDY
Baking; beverage management; buffet catering; confectionery show pieces; controlling costs in food service; convenience cookery; culinary French; culinary skill development; food preparation; food purchasing; food service communication; food service math; garde-manger; international cuisine; introduction to food service; kitchen management; management and human resources; meal planning; meat cutting; meat fabrication; menu and facilities design; nutrition; nutrition and food service; patisserie; restaurant opportunities; sanitation; saucier; seafood processing; soup, stock, sauce, and starch production; wines and spirits.

FACILITIES
Cafeteria; catering service; 4 classrooms; food production kitchen; learning resource center; lecture room; library; public restaurant; snack shop; student lounge.

STUDENT PROFILE
110 total: 50 full-time; 60 part-time.

FACULTY
9 total: 3 full-time; 6 part-time. 9 are industry professionals. Prominent faculty: Leonard Pringle, DTR; Ernest Becerra; Adrienne Sonnier, RD. Faculty-student ratio: 1:15.

SPECIAL PROGRAMS
Paid internships.

TYPICAL EXPENSES
In-state tuition: $352 per semester full-time (in district), $22 per hour part-time (in district), $720 per semester full-time (out-of-district), $45 per hour part-time (out-of-district). Out-of-state tuition: $1088 per semester full-time, $68 per hour part-time. Program-related fees include $200 for equipment; $26 for lab fee (per class).

FINANCIAL AID
Employment placement assistance is available.

APPLICATION INFORMATION
Students may begin participation in January, June, and September. Applications are accepted continuously. Applicants must interview, submit a formal application, and take the Texas Academic Skills Program test.

CONTACT
Mr. Leonard Pringle, Department Chair, Culinary Arts/Restaurant Management/Dietetic Technology, 8060 Spencer Highway, Pasadena, TX 77505. Telephone: 281-542-2099. Fax: 281-478-2790. E-mail: leonard.pringle@sjcd.edu. World Wide Web: http://www.sjcd.edu.

Texas Culinary Academy

Austin, Texas

GENERAL INFORMATION
Private, coeducational, culinary institute. Urban campus. Founded in 1981. Accredited by Accrediting Council for Independent Colleges and Schools.

PROGRAM INFORMATION
Program calendar is continuous. Associate degree in Le Cordon Bleu Culinary Arts. Certificate in Le Cordon Bleu Patisserie and Baking.

SPECIAL PROGRAMS
Externships, culinary competitions.

APPLICATION INFORMATION
Applications are accepted continuously. Applicants must interview; submit a formal application, and have a high school diploma or GED.

CONTACT
Admissions Department, 11400 Burnet Road, Suite 2100, Austin, TX 78758. Telephone: 888-559-7222. World Wide Web: http://www.tca.com.

UNIVERSITY OF HOUSTON

Conrad N. Hilton College of Hotel and Restaurant Management

Houston, Texas

GENERAL INFORMATION
Public, coeducational, university. Urban campus. Founded in 1927. Accredited by Southern Association of Colleges and Schools.

PROGRAM INFORMATION
Offered since 1969. Accredited by Council on Hotel, Restaurant and Institutional Education. Program calendar is divided into semesters. 1- to 2-year master's degree in hospitality management. 4-year bachelor's degree in hotel and restaurant management.

PROGRAM AFFILIATION
American Hotel and Lodging Association; Confrerie de la Chaine des Rotisseurs; Council on Hotel, Restaurant, and Institutional Education; Greater Houston Restaurant Association; International Food Service Executives Association; International Hotel and Restaurant Association; National Restaurant Association; National Restaurant Association Educational Foundation; Society of Wine Educators; Texas Restaurant Association.

AREAS OF STUDY
Beverage management; buffet catering; catering (management); controlling costs in food service; culinary skill development; facilities layout and design; food and beverage management; food and beverage of gaming operation; food and beverage service; food preparation; food purchasing; food service communication; food service math; hotel food and beverage management; international cuisine; introduction to food service; kitchen management; management and human resources; meal planning; menu and facilities design; nutrition and food service; restaurant development; restaurant management; restaurant opportunities; sanitation; wines and spirits.

FACILITIES
Bake shop; cafeteria; catering service; 6 classrooms; coffee shop; 4 computer laboratories; 2 demonstration laboratories; 8 food production kitchens; gourmet dining room; 2 laboratories; learning resource center; library; 2 public restaurants; snack shop; student lounge; 2 teaching kitchens.

STUDENT PROFILE
841 total: 681 full-time; 160 part-time. 676 are under 25 years old; 158 are between 25 and 44 years old; 7 are over 44 years old.

FACULTY
36 total: 23 full-time; 13 part-time. 39 are industry professionals; 3 are culinary-certified teachers; 24 are certified hospitality educators; 1 registered dietitian; 2 certified hotel administrators; 1 certified lodging security director. Prominent faculty: John Bowen, PhD, CHE; Agnes L. DeFranco, EdD, CHE, CHAE; Carl A. Boger, Jr., PhD; Ronald Nykiel, PhD, CHE, CHA. Faculty-student ratio: 1:27.

PROMINENT ALUMNI AND CURRENT AFFILIATION
Joseph Jackson, Vice President of Inclusion, Outback Steakhouses; Nick Massad, President, American Liberty Hospitality; Doug Brooks, President, Brinker International.

SPECIAL PROGRAMS
Paid internships, international programs in France, Mexico and Hong Kong, domestic programs in casino operations in Nevada, New Jersey, and Mississippi, wine program in California, marking programs in New York and Chicago.

TYPICAL EXPENSES
Application fee: $50. In-state tuition: $4826 per year full-time (in district), $161 per credit hour (undergraduate); $262 per credit hour for graduate part-time. Out-of-state tuition: $13,166 per year full-time, $439 per credit hour (undergraduate); $540 per credit hour (graduate) part-time. Program-related fees include $15–$90 for fees for food and beverage purchases in selected courses; $450 for college fees.

FINANCIAL AID
In 2006, 139 scholarships were awarded (average award was $2500). Program-specific awards include Conrad N. Hilton College Scholarships, teaching and research assistantships for graduate students. Employment placement assistance is available. Employment opportunities within the program are available.

HOUSING
Coed and apartment-style housing available. Average on-campus housing cost per month: $337–$450. Average off-campus housing cost per month: $350–$700.

APPLICATION INFORMATION
Students may begin participation in January, May, and August. Application deadline for summer/fall is May 1. Application deadline for spring is December 1. In 2006, 302 applied; 247 were accepted. Applicants must submit a formal application and letters of reference and essay (for master's program only).

CONTACT

Danny Arocha, Enrollment Manager, Conrad N. Hilton College of Hotel and Restaurant Management, 229 C. N. Hilton Hotel-College, Houston, TX 77204-3028. Telephone: 713-743-2446. Fax: 713-743-2581. E-mail: darocha@uh.edu. World Wide Web: http://www.hrm.uh. edu/.

UNIVERSITY OF NORTH TEXAS

Hospitality Management

Denton, Texas

GENERAL INFORMATION

Public, coeducational, university. Urban campus. Founded in 1890. Accredited by Southern Association of Colleges and Schools.

PROGRAM INFORMATION

Offered since 1985. Accredited by Council on Hotel, Restaurant and Institutional Education. Program calendar is divided into semesters. 2-year master's degree in hospitality management. 4-year bachelor's degree in hospitality management.

PROGRAM AFFILIATION

American Dietetic Association; American Hotel and Lodging Association; Council on Hotel, Restaurant, and Institutional Education; International Wine & Food Society; National Restaurant Association; National Restaurant Association Educational Foundation.

AREAS OF STUDY

Controlling costs in food service; food preparation; food purchasing; international cuisine; introduction to food service; kitchen management; management and human resources; menu and facilities design; nutrition; nutrition and food service; restaurant opportunities; sanitation; wines and spirits.

FACILITIES

4 classrooms; 6 computer laboratories; 2 demonstration laboratories; 2 food production kitchens; gourmet dining room; 2 laboratories; learning resource center; 4 lecture rooms; 2 libraries; public restaurant; 2 teaching kitchens.

TYPICAL STUDENT PROFILE

450 full-time.

SPECIAL PROGRAMS

Faculty-supervised internships, student-operated laboratory restaurant.

FINANCIAL AID

Employment placement assistance is available.

HOUSING

Coed and apartment-style housing available.

APPLICATION INFORMATION

Students may begin participation in January, May, June, July, and August. Applications are accepted continuously. Applicants must submit a formal application.

CONTACT

Director of Admissions, Hospitality Management, PO Box 311100, Denton, TX 75057. Telephone: 940-565-2436. Fax: 940-565-4348. World Wide Web: http://www. smhm.unt.edu.

UTAH

THE ART INSTITUTE OF SALT LAKE CITY

The International Culinary School at The Art Institute of Salt Lake City

Draper, Utah

GENERAL INFORMATION

Private, coeducational institution.

PROGRAM INFORMATION

Associate degree in Baking and Pastry. Associate degree in Culinary Arts. Bachelor's degree in Culinary Management. Diploma in Baking and Pastry. Diploma in The Art of Cooking.

CONTACT

Office of Admissions, The International Culinary School at The Art Institute of Salt Lake City, 121 West Election Road, Suite 100, Salt Lake City, UT 84020-9492. Telephone: 801-601-4700. World Wide Web: http:// www.artinstitutes.edu/saltlakecity/.

See color display following page 186.

UTAH VALLEY STATE COLLEGE

Culinary Arts Institute

Orem, Utah

GENERAL INFORMATION

Public, coeducational, four-year college. Urban campus. Founded in 1941. Accredited by Northwest Commission on Colleges and Universities.

Utah Valley State College *(continued)*

PROGRAM INFORMATION
Offered since 1990. Program calendar is divided into semesters. Associate degree in culinary arts.

PROGRAM AFFILIATION
American Culinary Federation; National Restaurant Association; National Restaurant Association Educational Foundation.

AREAS OF STUDY
Baking; beverage management; buffet catering; controlling costs in food service; culinary skill development; food preparation; food purchasing; garde-manger; international cuisine; introduction to food service; meal planning; menu and facilities design; nutrition and food service; patisserie; restaurant opportunities; sanitation; saucier; seafood processing; soup, stock, sauce, and starch production; wines and spirits.

FACILITIES
Bake shop; cafeteria; catering service; classroom; computer laboratory; demonstration laboratory; food production kitchen; gourmet dining room; public restaurant; teaching kitchen.

FACULTY
8 total: 5 full-time; 3 part-time. Prominent faculty: Diane Fallis, CEPC; Troy Wilson, CEC; Franz X. Kubak, CEC; Todd Leonard, CEC. Faculty-student ratio: 1:15.

PROMINENT ALUMNI AND CURRENT AFFILIATION
Kenny Snapp, Typhoon Restaurant, Manhattan.

SPECIAL PROGRAMS
Culinary competitions, international internships, large group catering.

TYPICAL EXPENSES
Application fee: $35. In-state tuition: $1500 per semester full-time (in district), $156 per 3 credits; $804 for 6 credits; $1152 for 9 credits part-time. Out-of-state tuition: $5250 per semester full-time, $1596 per 3 credits; $2814 for 6 credits; $4032 for 9 credits part-time. Tuition for international students: $5250 per semester full-time, $1596 per 3 credits; $2814 for 6 credits; $4032 for 9 credits part-time. Program-related fees include $500 for tool kit; $200 for uniforms (approximately); $750 for cooking course fee per semester.

FINANCIAL AID
In 2006, individual scholarships were awarded at $800. Program-specific awards include privately funded scholarships, Culinary Arts program scholarships. Employment placement assistance is available. Employment opportunities within the program are available.

HOUSING
Average off-campus housing cost per month: $300.

APPLICATION INFORMATION
Students may begin participation in January and August. Application deadline for fall semester is August 1. Application deadline for spring semester is February 1. In 2006, 168 applied; 20 were accepted. Applicants must submit a formal application, pre-requisite courses (2), and college level math, English and reading skills as determined by ACT scores or Compass exam.

CONTACT
Julie Slocum, Academic Advisor-154, Culinary Arts Institute, 800 West University Parkway, Orem, UT 84058. Telephone: 801-863-8914. Fax: 801-863-6103. E-mail: slocumju@uvsc.edu. World Wide Web: http://www.uvsc.edu.

VERMONT

CHAMPLAIN COLLEGE

Hospitality Industry Management

Burlington, Vermont

GENERAL INFORMATION
Private, coeducational, four-year college. Urban campus. Founded in 1878. Accredited by New England Association of Schools and Colleges.

PROGRAM INFORMATION
Offered since 1979. Program calendar is divided into semesters. 1-year certificate in event management. 1-year certificate in hotel/restaurant management. 4-year bachelor's degree in event management. 4-year bachelor's degree in hotel/restaurant management.

PROGRAM AFFILIATION
American Culinary Federation; American Hotel and Lodging Association; Council on Hotel, Restaurant, and Institutional Education; National Restaurant Association; National Restaurant Association Educational Foundation; Vermont Lodging and Restaurant Association.

AREAS OF STUDY
Controlling costs in food service; culinary skill development; food preparation; food purchasing; food service math; introduction to food service; kitchen management; management and human resources; nutrition; nutrition and food service; restaurant opportunities; sanitation; soup, stock, sauce, and starch production.

FACILITIES

5 classrooms; 2 computer laboratories; 2 demonstration laboratories; food production kitchen; gourmet dining room; 2 laboratories; learning resource center; lecture room; library; public restaurant; snack shop; student lounge; teaching kitchen; bistro.

STUDENT PROFILE

90 total: 80 full-time; 10 part-time. 84 are under 25 years old; 6 are between 25 and 44 years old.

FACULTY

9 total: 5 full-time; 4 part-time. 5 are industry professionals. Prominent faculty: Peter Straube, MSA; Charles Amey, MSA. Faculty-student ratio: 1:16.

SPECIAL PROGRAMS

10-day spring break European tour, paid internship, resort management apprenticeship (during senior year).

TYPICAL EXPENSES

Application fee: $35. Tuition: $22,550 per year full-time, $465 per credit part-time.

FINANCIAL AID

In 2006, 3 scholarships were awarded (average award was $1000). Employment placement assistance is available. Employment opportunities within the program are available.

HOUSING

Coed, apartment-style, and single-sex housing available.

APPLICATION INFORMATION

Students may begin participation in January and September. Application deadline for fall is January 31. Applicants must submit a formal application, letters of reference, an essay, SAT or ACT scores, TOEFL scores for international applicants.

CONTACT

Laryn Runco, Director of Admissions, Hospitality Industry Management, 163 South Willard Street, Burlington, VT 05401. Telephone: 802-860-2727. Fax: 802-860-2767. E-mail: admission@champlain.edu. World Wide Web: http://www.champlain.edu.

JOHNSON STATE COLLEGE

Hospitality and Tourism Management

Johnson, Vermont

GENERAL INFORMATION

Public, coeducational, four-year college. Rural campus. Founded in 1828. Accredited by New England Association of Schools and Colleges.

PROGRAM INFORMATION

Offered since 1986. Program calendar is divided into semesters. 4-year bachelor's degree in tourism management. 4-year bachelor's degree in food service management. 4-year bachelor's degree in lodging management.

PROGRAM AFFILIATION

American Hotel and Lodging Association; Council on Hotel, Restaurant, and Institutional Education; National Restaurant Association; National Restaurant Association Educational Foundation; Vermont Lodging and Restaurant Association.

AREAS OF STUDY

Beverage management; controlling costs in food service; dining room management; food preparation; food purchasing; introduction to food service; kitchen management; management and human resources; menu and facilities design; menu explosion analysis; restaurant opportunities; sanitation; wines and spirits.

FACILITIES

Cafeteria; catering service; 6 classrooms; coffee shop; 3 computer laboratories; food production kitchen; learning resource center; 2 lecture rooms; library; snack shop; student lounge.

TYPICAL STUDENT PROFILE

71 full-time. 58 are under 25 years old; 13 are between 25 and 44 years old.

SPECIAL PROGRAMS

Paid internships and General Manager Mentorship Program, trip to the New York Hotel Show, 4-day tour of hotel and restaurant facilities in Canada.

FINANCIAL AID

Employment placement assistance is available.

HOUSING

Coed, apartment-style, and single-sex housing available.

APPLICATION INFORMATION

Students may begin participation in January and August. Applications are accepted continuously. Applicants must submit a formal application, letters of reference, an essay, interview (recommended).

CONTACT

Director of Admissions, Hospitality and Tourism Management, 337 College Hill, Johnson, VT 05656. Telephone: 802-635-1219. Fax: 802-635-1230. World Wide Web: http://www.jsc.vsc.edu.

NEW ENGLAND CULINARY INSTITUTE

Montpelier and Essex Junction, Vermont

GENERAL INFORMATION

Private, coeducational, culinary institute. Founded in 1980. Accredited by Accrediting Commission of Career Schools and Colleges of Technology.

PROGRAM INFORMATION

Offered since 1980. Accredited by Accrediting Commission of Career Schools and Colleges of Technology. Program calendar is divided into quarters. 10-month certificate in pastry. 10-month certificate in baking. 10-month certificate in basic cooking. 15-month associate degree in hospitality and restaurant management. 18-month bachelor's degree in hospitality and restaurant management (must have 60 prior credits). 2-year associate degree in baking and pastry arts. 2-year associate degree in culinary arts. 39-month bachelor's degree in culinary arts.

PROGRAM AFFILIATION

American Culinary Federation; American Institute of Wine & Food; Council on Hotel, Restaurant, and Institutional Education; International Association of Culinary Professionals; James Beard Foundation, Inc.; National Restaurant Association; National Restaurant Association Educational Foundation; Vermont Fresh Network; Women Chefs and Restaurateurs.

AREAS OF STUDY

Baking; beverage management; buffet catering; controlling costs in food service; culinary skill development; financial analysis; food preparation; food purchasing; food service communication; food service math; garde-manger; introduction to food service; kitchen knife skills management; management and human resources; meal planning; meat cutting; meat fabrication; menu and facilities design; non-commercial preparation; nutrition; patisserie; restaurant service and operations management; sanitation; saucier; seafood processing; soup, stock, sauce, and starch production; sustainability in food service; technology applications; wines and spirits.

FACILITIES

2 bake shops; bakery; 3 cafeterias; 2 catering services; 20 classrooms; 2 computer laboratories; 12 food production kitchens; 2 gardens; 2 gourmet dining rooms; 2 laboratories; 2 learning resource centers; 2 libraries; 5 public restaurants; student lounge; non-commercial food kitchen; wireless dorms.

STUDENT PROFILE

842 full-time.

FACULTY

86 total: 60 full-time; 26 part-time. Faculty-student ratio: 1:10 culinary arts; 1:8 basic cooking; 1:15 in food and beverage management.

SPECIAL PROGRAMS

6-month paid internship following 6-month residency in culinary arts or baking and pastry arts, 6-month paid internship following calendar year in residency in hospitality and restaurant management, 6-month paid internship following 15-week residency in basic cooking or baking and pastry arts, 9-month paid internship following an additional 6-month residency for BA in Culinary Arts.

TYPICAL EXPENSES

Tuition: $18,236–$24,788 per year for associates and bachelors degree programs; $10,338 per year for certificate programs. Program-related fees include $350 for books (culinary arts); $475 for knives (culinary arts and basic cooking); $675 for books (hospitality and restaurant management); $300 for books (certificate programs); $300 for knives (hospitality and restaurant management).

FINANCIAL AID

Program-specific awards include more than 95% of NECI students receive financial aid in the form of scholarships, grants, loans, and Federal work-study.

HOUSING

Coed, apartment-style, and single-sex housing available. Average on-campus housing cost per month: $717.

APPLICATION INFORMATION

Students may begin participation in January, March, June, September, and December. Applications are accepted continuously. In 2006, 1116 applied; 787 were accepted. Applicants must interview; submit a formal application, letters of reference, an essay, high school transcripts or GED.

CONTACT

Jan Knutsen, Vice President of Enrollment & Marketing, 56 College Street, Montpelier, VT 05602-3115. Telephone: 802-225-3241. Fax: 802-225-3280. E-mail: janknutsen@neci.edu. World Wide Web: http://www.neci.edu/home.html.

See display on page 333.

Our Graduates Say it Best.

"When I came up with the idea for 'Good Eats,' I was directing commercials for a living, not cooking, so I figured I needed to get some serious learnin'. That's what New England Culinary Institute is. If you're considering a culinary education, give these folks a call before you make your move."

Alton Brown, Creator of *Good Eats* on the Food Network
James Beard Award Winner
Graduate — New England Culinary Institute

- **Hands-on**
- **Small class sizes — average 7:1 student/ teacher ratio with maximum of 10 in production classes**
- **Paid internships**
- **Enrollments in March, June, September, and December**
- **Scholarships available**
- **Degrees available in Culinary Arts, Baking & Pastry Arts and Hospitality & Restaurant Management**
- **Accredited Member, ACCSCT**

Transform your passion into a rewarding profession at NECI. Call us today at **877.223.6324** or visit us us at **www.neci.edu** to start your journey.

Where you learn it by living it
www.neci.edu

NEW ENGLAND CULINARY INSTITUTE ®

VIRGINIA

THE ART INSTITUTE OF WASHINGTON

The International Culinary School at The Art Institute of Washington

Arlington, Virginia

GENERAL INFORMATION
Private, coeducational institution.

PROGRAM INFORMATION
Associate degree in Wines, Spirits and Beverage Management. Associate degree in Culinary Arts. Bachelor's degree in Food and Beverage Management. Bachelor's degree in Culinary Management. Diploma in Culinary Arts–Culinary Skills. Diploma in Culinary Arts–Baking and Pastry.

CONTACT
Office of Admissions, The International Culinary School at The Art Institute of Washington, 1820 North Fort Myer Drive, Arlington, VA 22209-1802. Telephone: 703-358-9550. World Wide Web: http://www.artinstitutes.edu/arlington/.
See color display following page 186.

JAMES MADISON UNIVERSITY

Hospitality and Tourism Management

Harrisonburg, Virginia

GENERAL INFORMATION
Public, coeducational, comprehensive institution. Small-town setting. Founded in 1908. Accredited by Southern Association of Colleges and Schools.

PROGRAM INFORMATION
Offered since 1974. Accredited by Council on Hotel, Restaurant and Institutional Education, The Association to Advance Collegiate Schools of Business. Program calendar is divided into semesters. 4-year bachelor's degree in entertainment. 4-year bachelor's degree in meeting planning. 4-year bachelor's degree in food and beverage management. 4-year bachelor's degree in club and resort management. 4-year bachelor's degree in hospitality and tourism management.

PROGRAM AFFILIATION
Club Managers Association of America; Council on Hotel, Restaurant, and Institutional Education; National Restaurant Association; National Restaurant Association Educational Foundation.

AREAS OF STUDY
Beverage management; buffet catering; culinary skill development; food preparation; food purchasing; gastronomy; introduction to food service; management and human resources; restaurant opportunities.

FACILITIES
Classroom; computer laboratory; demonstration laboratory; lecture room; snack shop.

STUDENT PROFILE
350 total: 340 full-time; 10 part-time. 340 are under 25 years old; 10 are between 25 and 44 years old.

FACULTY
8 total: 8 full-time; 0 part-time. 8 are industry professionals. Prominent faculty: Brett Horton; Reg Foucar-Szocki; Michael O'Fallon; Ronald Cereola, MBA, JD. Faculty-student ratio: 1:40.

SPECIAL PROGRAMS
Six-day tour of California wineries, culinary project with The Greenbrier, paid internships.

TYPICAL EXPENSES
Application fee: $50. In-state tuition: $16,090 per year full-time (in district), $246 per credit hour part-time. Out-of-state tuition: $25,526 per year full-time, $701 per credit hour part-time.

FINANCIAL AID
In 2006, 7 scholarships were awarded (average award was $1000). Employment placement assistance is available. Employment opportunities within the program are available.

HOUSING
Coed and single-sex housing available. Average off-campus housing cost per month: $400.

APPLICATION INFORMATION
Students may begin participation in January, May, and August. Application deadline for fall is March 1. Application deadline for spring is October 15. In 2006, 100 applied; 70 were accepted. Applicants must submit a formal application, an essay, SAT/ACT scores.

CONTACT
Brett Horton, J.W. & Alice S. Marriott Foundation Professor, Hospitality and Tourism Management, James Madison University, MSC 0202, Harrisonburg, VA 22807. Telephone: 540-568-3037. Fax: 540-568-3273. E-mail: hortonbw@jmu.edu. World Wide Web: http://www.jmu.edu/hospitality.

J. SARGEANT REYNOLDS COMMUNITY COLLEGE

School of Culinary Arts, Tourism, and Hospitality

Richmond, Virginia

GENERAL INFORMATION
Public, coeducational, two-year college. Urban campus. Founded in 1972. Accredited by Southern Association of Colleges and Schools.

PROGRAM INFORMATION
Offered since 1973. Accredited by American Culinary Federation Accrediting Commission. Program calendar is divided into semesters. 2-semester certificate in pastry arts. 2-year associate degree in hospitality management. 2-year associate degree in culinary arts.

PROGRAM AFFILIATION
American Culinary Federation; Confrerie de la Chaine des Rotisseurs; Council on Hotel, Restaurant, and Institutional Education; Foodservice Educators Network International; International Society of Travel and Tourism Educators; National Restaurant Association; National Restaurant Association Educational Foundation; Society of Wine Educators.

AREAS OF STUDY
Baking; beverage management; buffet catering; controlling costs in food service; culinary skill development; food and beverage service management; food preparation; food purchasing; garde-manger; international cuisine; introduction to food service; kitchen management; management and human resources; meat cutting; meat fabrication; menu and facilities design; nutrition; nutrition and food service; patisserie; restaurant opportunities; sanitation; saucier; seafood processing; soup, stock, sauce, and starch production; total quality management for hospitality; wines and spirits.

FACILITIES
Bake shop; bakery; cafeteria; catering service; 5 classrooms; 4 computer laboratories; demonstration laboratory; food production kitchen; laboratory; 3 learning resource centers; 3 lecture rooms; 3 libraries; snack shop; student lounge; 2 teaching kitchens.

STUDENT PROFILE
143 total: 55 full-time; 88 part-time. 80 are under 25 years old; 41 are between 25 and 44 years old; 22 are over 44 years old.

FACULTY
13 total: 3 full-time; 10 part-time. 9 are industry professionals; 1 is a culinary-certified teacher; 4 are registered dietitians; 1 certified hotel administrator.

Prominent faculty: David J. Barrish, CHA; Eric Breckoff; Joseph Formica, PhD; John Maxwell, CCE, CEC. Faculty-student ratio: 1:18.

SPECIAL PROGRAMS
Semi-annual "President's Dinner" (multi-course, white glove gastronomic event), mentorship with Virginia Chefs Association professional chefs, advanced placement for previous experience.

TYPICAL EXPENSES
In-state tuition: $86.65 per credit hour full-time (in district), $86.65 per credit hour part-time. Out-of-state tuition: $261.80 per credit hour full-time, $261.80 per credit hour part-time. Program-related fee includes $1000 for textbooks.

FINANCIAL AID
In 2006, 6 scholarships were awarded (average award was $500); 60 loans were granted (average loan was $2000). Program-specific awards include Virginia Hospitality and Travel Association Scholarship, American Hotel Foundation Scholarship. Employment placement assistance is available.

HOUSING
Average off-campus housing cost per month: $600.

APPLICATION INFORMATION
Students may begin participation in January, May, and August. Applications are accepted continuously. In 2006, 57 applied; 57 were accepted. Applicants must interview; submit a formal application and academic transcripts.

CONTACT
David J. Barrish, Director, School of Culinary Arts, Tourism, and Hospitality, 701 East Jackson Street, Richmond, VA 23219. Telephone: 804-523-5069. Fax: 804-786-5465. E-mail: dbarrish@jsr.vcc.edu. World Wide Web: http://www.reynolds.edu/hospitality.

NORTHERN VIRGINIA COMMUNITY COLLEGE

Hospitality Management/Culinary Arts

Annandale, Virginia

GENERAL INFORMATION
Public, coeducational, two-year college. Suburban campus. Founded in 1965. Accredited by Southern Association of Colleges and Schools.

Northern Virginia Community College *(continued)*

PROGRAM INFORMATION
Offered since 1965. Accredited by American Culinary Federation Accrediting Commission. Program calendar is divided into semesters. 1-year certificate in hotel management. 1-year certificate in culinary arts. 1-year certificate in food service management. 2-year associate degree in hotel management. 2-year associate degree in hospitality management. 2-year associate degree in nutrition management. 2-year associate degree in food service management.

PROGRAM AFFILIATION
American Culinary Federation; American Dietetic Association; Council on Hotel, Restaurant, and Institutional Education; National Restaurant Association.

AREAS OF STUDY
Baking; buffet catering; controlling costs in food service; food preparation; food purchasing; food service communication; food service math; garde-manger; introduction to food service; management and human resources; meal planning; menu and facilities design; nutrition; nutrition and food service; patisserie; restaurant opportunities; sanitation.

FACILITIES
Cafeteria; 3 classrooms; 2 computer laboratories; demonstration laboratory; food production kitchen; garden; gourmet dining room; learning resource center; 3 lecture rooms; library; student lounge; teaching kitchen.

STUDENT PROFILE
350 total: 125 full-time; 225 part-time. 75 are under 25 years old; 225 are between 25 and 44 years old; 50 are over 44 years old.

FACULTY
10 total: 3 full-time; 7 part-time. 3 are industry professionals; 1 is a master chef; 1 is a culinary-certified teacher; 3 are registered dietitians. Prominent faculty: Bonita Wong, CCC, CCE; Janet Sass, RD; Howard Reichbart; Mark Stillions, MBA. Faculty-student ratio: 1:20.

SPECIAL PROGRAMS
ACF apprenticeship program, ACF regional student hot food competitions, New York international hotel/restaurant show and tour.

TYPICAL EXPENSES
In-state tuition: $88 per credit hour part-time. Out-of-state tuition: $265 per credit hour part-time. Program-related fees include $50–$75 for uniform; $50–$100 for knives and equipment case; $100–$300 for books.

FINANCIAL AID
In 2006, 4 scholarships were awarded (average award was $6000). Program-specific awards include industry internships (paid). Employment placement assistance is available.

HOUSING
Average off-campus housing cost per month: $900.

APPLICATION INFORMATION
Students may begin participation in January, May, and August. Application deadline for spring is January 15. Application deadline for fall is August 15. Application deadline for summer is May 15. In 2006, 87 applied; 87 were accepted. Applicants must submit a formal application.

CONTACT
Janet M. Sass, Assistant Dean, Hospitality Management, Hospitality Management/Culinary Arts, 8333 Little River Turnpike, Annandale, VA 22003. Telephone: 703-323-3458. Fax: 703-323-3509. E-mail: jsass@nvcc.edu. World Wide Web: http://www.nvcc.edu.

STRATFORD UNIVERSITY

School of Culinary Arts and Hospitality Management

Falls Church, Virginia

GENERAL INFORMATION
Private, coeducational, four-year college. Suburban campus. Founded in 1976. Accredited by Accrediting Council for Independent Colleges and Schools.

PROGRAM INFORMATION
Offered since 1991. Accredited by American Culinary Federation Foundation Accrediting Commission. Program calendar is continuous. 12-month diploma in culinary arts. 15-month associate degree in baking and pastry arts. 15-month associate degree in hotel and restaurant management. 15-month associate degree in culinary arts. 30-month bachelor's degree in hospitality management.

PROGRAM AFFILIATION
American Culinary Federation; American Dietetic Association; American Institute of Wine & Food; Council on Hotel, Restaurant, and Institutional Education; International Association of Culinary Professionals; National Restaurant Association.

AREAS OF STUDY
Baking; culinary skill development; introduction to food service; management and human resources.

FACILITIES

Bake shop; 10 classrooms; 4 computer laboratories; 4 food production kitchens; gourmet dining room; lecture room; library; public restaurant; snack shop; 3 student lounges; 5 teaching kitchens.

STUDENT PROFILE

290 total: 200 full-time; 90 part-time. 90 are under 25 years old; 150 are between 25 and 44 years old; 50 are over 44 years old.

FACULTY

20 total: 12 full-time; 8 part-time. Prominent faculty: James Sinopoli, CEPC; Richard King, CEC, CCE; Paul Hutchinson, CEC, CCE, CCA, CPFM; Mitchell Watford, CEC, CCE. Faculty-student ratio: 1:18.

PROMINENT ALUMNI AND CURRENT AFFILIATION

Jason Lage, Lansdowne Conference Resort.

SPECIAL PROGRAMS

Paid externships, culinary competitions, AH&LA certification.

TYPICAL EXPENSES

Application fee: $50. Tuition: $32,000 per 2 years. Program-related fee includes $2560 for uniform and lab fee.

FINANCIAL AID

In 2006, 5 scholarships were awarded (average award was $1000); 5 loans were granted (average loan was $3500). Program-specific awards include ACG Grant, Smart Grant. Employment placement assistance is available.

HOUSING

Apartment-style housing available. Average on-campus housing cost per month: $600.

APPLICATION INFORMATION

Students may begin participation in January, February, March, April, May, June, July, August, September, October, and November. Applications are accepted continuously. In 2006, 500 applied; 495 were accepted. Applicants must interview; submit a formal application and written essay for scholarships (HS senior only).

CONTACT

Keith Evans, Director of Admissions, School of Culinary Arts and Hospitality Management, 7777 Leesburg Pike, Falls Church, VA 22043. Telephone: 703-734-5326. Fax: 703-734-5336. E-mail: kevans@stratford.edu. World Wide Web: http://www.stratford.edu.

TIDEWATER COMMUNITY COLLEGE

Culinary Arts

Norfolk, Virginia

GENERAL INFORMATION
Public, coeducational, two-year college. Urban campus. Founded in 1968. Accredited by Southern Association of Colleges and Schools.

PROGRAM INFORMATION
Offered since 1997. Program calendar is divided into semesters. 1-year certificate in catering. 1-year certificate in classical cooking. 1-year certificate in kitchen management. 2-year associate degree in lodging management. 2-year associate degree in food and beverage management. 2-year associate degree in hospitality management culinary arts specialization.

PROGRAM AFFILIATION
American Culinary Federation; National Restaurant Association; National Restaurant Association Educational Foundation.

AREAS OF STUDY
Baking; buffet catering; controlling costs in food service; culinary French; culinary skill development; food purchasing; garde-manger; international cuisine; meat cutting; meat fabrication; nutrition; sanitation; seafood processing; soup, stock, sauce, and starch production; wines and spirits.

FACILITIES
2 classrooms; 2 food production kitchens; gourmet dining room; library.

STUDENT PROFILE
307 total: 162 full-time; 145 part-time.

FACULTY
10 total: 2 full-time; 8 part-time. 6 are industry professionals; 2 are culinary-certified teachers. Faculty-student ratio: 1:12.

SPECIAL PROGRAMS
Culinary competitions, cooperative education (apprenticeship).

TYPICAL EXPENSES
Application fee: $10. In-state tuition: $68.10 per credit hour full-time (in district), $68.10 per credit hour part-time. Out-of-state tuition: $215.55 per credit hour full-time, $215.55 per credit hour part-time.

FINANCIAL AID
In 2006, 2 scholarships were awarded (average award was $1500). Employment placement assistance is available. Employment opportunities within the program are available.

APPLICATION INFORMATION
Students may begin participation in January, May, and August. Applications are accepted continuously. Applicants must submit a formal application.

CONTACT
Information Center, Culinary Arts, 300 Granby Street, Norfolk, VA 23510-9956. Telephone: 757-822-1122. Fax: 757-822-1060. World Wide Web: http://www.tcc.edu/.

VIRGINIA STATE UNIVERSITY

Hospitality Management

Petersburg, Virginia

GENERAL INFORMATION
Public, coeducational, university. Small-town setting. Founded in 1882. Accredited by Southern Association of Colleges and Schools.

PROGRAM INFORMATION
Offered since 1981. Accredited by Council on Hotel, Restaurant and Institutional Education, Accreditation Commission for Programs in Hospitality Administration (ACPHA). National Restaurant Association Educational Foundation ManageFirst certificates available. Program calendar is divided into semesters. 4-year bachelor's degree in hospitality management.

PROGRAM AFFILIATION
American Culinary Federation; American Dietetic Association; Council on Hotel, Restaurant, and Institutional Education; International Food Service Executives Association; National Restaurant Association; National Restaurant Association Educational Foundation.

AREAS OF STUDY
Beverage management; food and beverage management; food preparation; food purchasing; lodging; meal planning; nutrition and food service; restaurant management.

FACILITIES
2 classrooms; computer laboratory; food production kitchen; gourmet dining room; lecture room; public restaurant; snack shop; teaching kitchen; lodging labs; automated front desk.

STUDENT PROFILE
80 total: 75 full-time; 5 part-time.

FACULTY

4 total: 3 full-time; 1 part-time. 3 are industry professionals; 1 is a culinary-certified teacher. Prominent faculty: Deanne Williams, EdD, CHE; Yan Zhong, PhD; Cary Snow, CEC. Faculty-student ratio: 1:20.

SPECIAL PROGRAMS

Paid internships, conferences relating to the hospitality industry, professional development seminars, international study tour, annual food show and exhibition.

TYPICAL EXPENSES

Application fee: $25. In-state tuition: $2827.50 per semester. Out-of-state tuition: $6653.50 per semester.

FINANCIAL AID

In 2006, 8 scholarships were awarded (average award was $200). Program-specific awards include assistance with trip costs, industry sponsorships. Employment placement assistance is available. Employment opportunities within the program are available.

HOUSING

Coed and apartment-style housing available. Average off-campus housing cost per month: $400.

APPLICATION INFORMATION

Students may begin participation in January and August. Applications are accepted continuously. Applicants must submit an essay, a formal application, and letters of reference.

CONTACT

Deanne Williams, Program Director, Hospitality Management, PO Box 9211, Petersburg, VA 23806. Telephone: 804-524-6753. Fax: 804-524-6843. E-mail: dwilliam@vsu.edu. World Wide Web: http://www.vsu.edu/pages/751.asp.

VIRGIN ISLANDS (U.S.)

UNIVERSITY OF THE VIRGIN ISLANDS

Hotel and Restaurant Management Program

St. Thomas, Virgin Islands (U.S.)

GENERAL INFORMATION

Public, coeducational, comprehensive institution. Small-town setting. Founded in 1962. Accredited by Middle States Association of Colleges and Schools.

University of the Virgin Islands *(continued)*

PROGRAM INFORMATION
Offered since 1962. Program calendar is divided into semesters. 2-year associate degree in hotel and restaurant management.

PROGRAM AFFILIATION
Educational Institute American Hotel and Motel Association.

AREAS OF STUDY
Food and beverage management; rooms division management.

STUDENT PROFILE
6 total: 4 full-time; 2 part-time. 5 are under 25 years old; 1 is between 25 and 44 years old.

FACULTY
2 total: 2 part-time. 1 is a certified hospitality educator. Prominent faculty: Samuel A. Rey, CHE. Faculty-student ratio: 1:3.

TYPICAL EXPENSES
Application fee: $30. In-state tuition: $110 per credit part-time. Out-of-state tuition: $330 per credit part-time.

FINANCIAL AID
Employment placement assistance is available.

HOUSING
Single-sex housing available. Average on-campus housing cost per month: $270. Average off-campus housing cost per month: $630.

APPLICATION INFORMATION
Students may begin participation in January and August. Application deadline for fall is April 30. Application deadline for spring is October 30. In 2006, 5 applied; 3 were accepted. Applicants must submit a formal application and an essay.

CONTACT
Dr. Judith Edwins, Vice Provost for Access and Enrollment, Hotel and Restaurant Management Program, 2 John Brewers Bay, St. Thomas, VI 00802. Telephone: 340-693-1152. Fax: 340-693-1227. E-mail: jedwin@uvi.edu. World Wide Web: http://www.uvi.edu.

WASHINGTON

THE ART INSTITUTE OF SEATTLE

The International Culinary School at The Art Institute of Seattle

Seattle, Washington

GENERAL INFORMATION
Private, coeducational institution.

PROGRAM INFORMATION
Diploma in Culinary Arts. 1-year diploma in The Art of Cooking. 1-year diploma in Baking and Pastry. 2-year associate degree in Culinary Arts.

CONTACT
Office of Admissions, The International Culinary School at The Art Institute of Seattle, 2323 Elliott Avenue, Seattle, WA 98121-1642. Telephone: 206-448-6600. World Wide Web: http://www.artinstitutes.edu/seattle/.

See color display following page 186.

BELLINGHAM TECHNICAL COLLEGE

Culinary Arts

Bellingham, Washington

GENERAL INFORMATION
Public, coeducational, two-year college. Small-town setting. Founded in 1957. Accredited by Northwest Commission on Colleges and Universities.

PROGRAM INFORMATION
Offered since 1957. Accredited by American Culinary Federation Accrediting Commission. Program calendar is divided into quarters. 1-quarter certificate in pastry. 1-year certificate in culinary arts. 2-year associate degree in culinary arts.

PROGRAM AFFILIATION
American Culinary Federation; National Restaurant Association Educational Foundation; Sustainable Connections.

AREAS OF STUDY
Baking; management and human resources; nutrition and food service; sanitation.

FACILITIES

Bake shop; bakery; cafeteria; catering service; classroom; coffee shop; computer laboratory; demonstration laboratory; food production kitchen; garden; gourmet dining room; learning resource center; lecture room; library; public restaurant; snack shop; student lounge.

STUDENT PROFILE

50 full-time.

FACULTY

8 total: 3 full-time; 5 part-time. 5 are industry professionals; 2 are culinary-certified teachers. Prominent faculty: Michael S. Baldwin, CEC, CCE; Hilde Korsmo; Brian McDonald, CCE, CEC. Faculty-student ratio: 1:24.

SPECIAL PROGRAMS

ACF culinary competitions, 6-week internship.

TYPICAL EXPENSES

Application fee: $35. Tuition: $3000 per year. Program-related fees include $1000 for books; $250 for cutlery; $100 for supplies; $350 for uniforms.

FINANCIAL AID

In 2006, 8 scholarships were awarded (average award was $750); 11 loans were granted (average loan was $4500). Program-specific awards include work-study. Employment placement assistance is available. Employment opportunities within the program are available.

HOUSING

Average off-campus housing cost per month: $350–$800.

APPLICATION INFORMATION

Students may begin participation in April and September. Application deadline for fall is September 5. Application deadline for spring is April 1. In 2006, 50 applied; 50 were accepted. Applicants must submit a formal application, be at least 16 years of age, and complete an entrance exam.

CONTACT

Michael Baldwin, Chef Instructor, Culinary Arts, 3028 Lindbergh Avenue, Bellingham, WA 98225. Telephone: 360-752-8400. Fax: 360-752-7400. E-mail: mbaldwin@btc.ctc.edu.

OLYMPIC COLLEGE

Culinary Arts and Hospitality Management

Bremerton, Washington

GENERAL INFORMATION

Public, coeducational, two-year college. Suburban campus. Founded in 1946. Accredited by Northwest Commission on Colleges and Universities.

PROGRAM INFORMATION

Offered since 1978. Program calendar is divided into quarters. 12-month associate degree in hospitality management. 12-month associate degree in sous chef. 3-month certificate in cook's helper. 6-month certificate of completion in hospitality supervisor. 6-month certificate of completion in prep cook. 9-month certificate of specialization in hospitality operations. 9-month certificate of specialization in lead cook.

PROGRAM AFFILIATION

American Culinary Federation; Council on Hotel, Restaurant, and Institutional Education; National Association of College Services; National Restaurant Association; National Restaurant Association Educational Foundation; United States Personal Chef Association; Washington State Chefs Association.

AREAS OF STUDY

Baking; beverage management; buffet catering; controlling costs in food service; convenience cookery; culinary French; culinary skill development; food preparation; food purchasing; food service communication; food service math; garde-manger; international cuisine; introduction to food service; kitchen management; management and human resources; meal planning; meat cutting; meat fabrication; menu and facilities design; nutrition; nutrition and food service; sanitation; saucier; seafood processing; soup, stock, sauce, and starch production.

FACILITIES

Cafeteria; catering service; classroom; food production kitchen; gourmet dining room; learning resource center; lecture room; library; public restaurant; snack shop; student lounge; teaching kitchen; banquet hall.

STUDENT PROFILE

54 total: 37 full-time; 17 part-time.

FACULTY

3 total: 2 full-time; 1 part-time. 1 is an industry professional; 2 are culinary-certified teachers. Prominent faculty: Nick Giovanni; Steve Lammers, CCE; Christopher Plemmons, CEC. Faculty-student ratio: 1:12.

Olympic College *(continued)*

PROMINENT ALUMNI AND CURRENT AFFILIATION
Tina Nys, Chef, Trophy Lake Country Club; Chris Haberstock, Chef, Oyster Bay Inn; Elton Vath, Lakeside Inn.

SPECIAL PROGRAMS
5-day gourmet cooking class, specialty training in specific cuisine areas, 6-week internships.

TYPICAL EXPENSES
In-state tuition: $981 per quarter full-time (in district), $74.30 per credit part-time. Out-of-state tuition: $1411 per quarter full-time, $117.10 per credit part-time. Program-related fees include $100 for lab fees (includes lunch); $300 for uniforms and tools; $165 for textbooks.

FINANCIAL AID
In 2006, 4 scholarships were awarded (average award was $500); 33 loans were granted (average loan was $5000). Program-specific awards include afternoon employment opportunities in food service. Employment placement assistance is available. Employment opportunities within the program are available.

HOUSING
Average off-campus housing cost per month: $600.

APPLICATION INFORMATION
Students may begin participation in January, April, and September. Application deadline for fall is September 20. Application deadline for winter is December 30. Application deadline for spring is March 28. In 2006, 75 applied; 60 were accepted. Applicants must interview and take pre-admission test.

CONTACT
Steve T. Lammers, Chef Instructor, Culinary Arts and Hospitality Management, 1600 Chester Avenue, Bremerton, WA 98337-1699. Telephone: 360-475-7571. Fax: 360-475-7575. E-mail: slammers@oc.ctc.edu. World Wide Web: http://www.oc.ctc.edu/~oc/.

SEATTLE CENTRAL COMMUNITY COLLEGE

Seattle Culinary Academy

Seattle, Washington

GENERAL INFORMATION
Public, coeducational, two-year college. Urban campus. Founded in 1941. Accredited by Northwest Commission on Colleges and Universities.

PROGRAM INFORMATION
Offered since 1941. Accredited by American Culinary Federation Accrediting Commission. Program calendar is divided into quarters. 5-quarter certificate of completion in specialty desserts and breads. 6-quarter associate degree in specialty desserts and breads. 6-quarter certificate of completion in culinary arts. 7-quarter associate degree in culinary arts.

PROGRAM AFFILIATION
American Culinary Federation; Council on Hotel, Restaurant, and Institutional Education; National Restaurant Association Educational Foundation; Slow Food International; The Bread Bakers Guild of America; Washington Restaurant Association; Women Chefs and Restaurateurs.

AREAS OF STUDY
Baking; buffet catering; confectionery show pieces; controlling costs in food service; culinary skill development; food preparation; food purchasing; food service math; garde-manger; international cuisine; introduction to food service; management and human resources; menu design; nutrition; nutrition and food service; patisserie; restaurant opportunities; sanitation; saucier; soup, stock, sauce, and starch production; wines and spirits.

FACILITIES
Bake shop; bakery; cafeteria; catering service; 5 classrooms; computer laboratory; demonstration laboratory; 5 food production kitchens; garden; gourmet dining room; 3 lecture rooms; library; 2 public restaurants; snack shop; student lounge; teaching kitchen; student activity center.

STUDENT PROFILE
150 full-time. 40 are under 25 years old; 90 are between 25 and 44 years old; 20 are over 44 years old.

FACULTY
14 total: 9 full-time; 5 part-time. 2 are industry professionals; 6 are culinary-certified teachers; 1 is a registered dietitian. Prominent faculty: Cynthia Wilson; Keijiro Miyata, CCE, CEC, AAC; Scott Samuel; Linda Chauncey. Faculty-student ratio: 1:18.

PROMINENT ALUMNI AND CURRENT AFFILIATION
Alex Nemeth, Purple; Kathy Casey, Kathy Casey Food Studios; Josh Green, Ponti.

SPECIAL PROGRAMS
Chef-of-the-Day (students create a menu and oversee its production for the restaurant), newly developed sustainable course, 20-hour externship and culinary competitions.

TYPICAL EXPENSES

In-state tuition: $900 per quarter (approximately). Out-of-state tuition: $2600 per quarter (approximately). Program-related fees include $100 for food lab fees; $10 for food handler's permit; $30 for technology fee (per quarter); $300 for hand tools; $200 for uniform.

FINANCIAL AID

In 2006, 9 scholarships were awarded (average award was $300–$800). Program-specific awards include Les Dames D'Escoffier scholarship (full-tuition), 2-3 food-related scholarships ($700), Quillisasau Farm School Scholarships.

HOUSING

Average off-campus housing cost per month: $700.

APPLICATION INFORMATION

Students may begin participation in January, April, and September. Applications are accepted continuously. In 2006, 180 applied; 150 were accepted. Applicants must submit a formal application, an essay, COMPASS scores or college transcripts that reflect the students level of math and English.

CONTACT

Joy Gulmon-Huri, Program Manager, Seattle Culinary Academy, Mailstop 2BE2120, 1701 Broadway, Seattle, WA 98122. Telephone: 206-587-5424. Fax: 206-344-4323. E-mail: cularts@sccd.ctc.edu. World Wide Web: http://seattlecentral.edu/seattleculinary/.

SOUTH PUGET SOUND COMMUNITY COLLEGE

Food and Hospitality Services

Olympia, Washington

GENERAL INFORMATION

Public, coeducational, two-year college. Suburban campus. Founded in 1970. Accredited by Northwest Commission on Colleges and Universities.

PROGRAM INFORMATION

Offered since 1990. Program calendar is divided into quarters. Associate degree in culinary arts. 1-year certificate in culinary arts.

PROGRAM AFFILIATION

American Culinary Federation.

STUDENT PROFILE

46 total: 35 full-time; 11 part-time.

FACULTY

3 total: 2 full-time; 1 part-time. 2 are industry professionals; 2 are master chefs; 2 are culinary-certified teachers. Prominent faculty: Bill Wiklendt, CEC, CCE; Dan Martinson; Debra Smith. Faculty-student ratio: 1:10.

TYPICAL EXPENSES

Program-related fees include $200 for books; $200 for assistant chef equipment; $120 for uniforms.

FINANCIAL AID

In 2006, 10 scholarships were awarded (average award was $500); 3 loans were granted (average loan was $2000). Program-specific awards include scholarships from endowment. Employment placement assistance is available. Employment opportunities within the program are available.

HOUSING

Average off-campus housing cost per month: $300.

APPLICATION INFORMATION

Students may begin participation in January, April, and September. Applications are accepted continuously. Applicants must submit a formal application.

CONTACT

Debbie Van Camp, Dean, Food and Hospitality Services, 2011 Mottman Road, SW, Olympia, WA 98512-6292. Telephone: 360-754-7711 Ext. 5347. World Wide Web: http://www.spscc.ctc.edu.

WEST VIRGINIA

WEST VIRGINIA NORTHERN COMMUNITY COLLEGE

Culinary Arts Department

Wheeling, West Virginia

GENERAL INFORMATION

Public, coeducational, two-year college. Small-town setting. Founded in 1972. Accredited by North Central Association of Colleges and Schools.

PROGRAM INFORMATION

Offered since 1974. Accredited by American Culinary Federation Accrediting Commission. Program calendar is divided into semesters. 1-year certificate in culinary arts. 2-year associate degree in culinary arts.

West Virginia Northern Community College
(continued)

PROGRAM AFFILIATION
American Culinary Federation; National Restaurant Association; National Restaurant Association Educational Foundation.

AREAS OF STUDY
Baking; confectionery show pieces; controlling costs in food service; culinary skill development; food preparation; food purchasing; garde-manger; international cuisine; management and human resources; meal planning; menu and facilities design; nutrition; patisserie; sanitation; saucier; seafood processing; soup, stock, sauce, and starch production; wines and spirits.

FACILITIES
Bake shop; 3 classrooms; 4 computer laboratories; 3 demonstration laboratories; 3 food production kitchens; gourmet dining room; 3 laboratories; 3 learning resource centers; 3 lecture rooms; 3 libraries; public restaurant; 3 student lounges; teaching kitchen.

STUDENT PROFILE
57 total: 45 full-time; 12 part-time.

FACULTY
6 total: 3 full-time; 3 part-time. 3 are industry professionals; 1 is a culinary-certified teacher. Prominent faculty: Christian Kefauver; Marian Grubor, CCE; Eugene Evans. Faculty-student ratio: 1:12.

PROMINENT ALUMNI AND CURRENT AFFILIATION
Jason Whitecotton, Nemacolin Woodlands; Steven Rujak, Hyatt Grand Cyprus/2006 Pastry Chef of the Year.

TYPICAL EXPENSES
In-state tuition: $948 per semester full-time (in district), $79 per credit hour part-time. Out-of-state tuition: $3200 per semester full-time, $250 per credit hour part-time. Program-related fees include $150 for books; $150 for uniforms; $100 for lab fee; $100 for knives; $75 for certification.

FINANCIAL AID
Employment placement assistance is available. Employment opportunities within the program are available.

HOUSING
Average off-campus housing cost per month: $400.

APPLICATION INFORMATION
Students may begin participation in January and August. Applications are accepted continuously. In 2006, 40 applied; 40 were accepted. Applicants must submit a formal application.

CONTACT
Lucy Kefauver, Admissions Counselor, Culinary Arts Department, 1704 Market Street, Wheeling, WV 26003. Telephone: 304-233-5900 Ext. 4243. E-mail: lkefauver@ northern.wunet.edu. World Wide Web: http://www. wvnorthern.edu/programs/cartsprog/index.cfm?.

WISCONSIN

BLACKHAWK TECHNICAL COLLEGE

Culinary Arts Program

Janesville, Wisconsin

GENERAL INFORMATION
Public, coeducational, two-year college. Rural campus. Founded in 1968. Accredited by North Central Association of Colleges and Schools.

PROGRAM INFORMATION
Offered since 1980. Accredited by American Culinary Federation Accrediting Commission, American Culinary Federation. Program calendar is divided into semesters. 2-year associate degree in culinary arts. 4-month certificate in quantity production. 4-month certificate in baking.

PROGRAM AFFILIATION
American Culinary Federation; National Restaurant Association.

AREAS OF STUDY
Baking; beverage management; buffet catering; confectionery show pieces; controlling costs in food service; culinary French; culinary skill development; food preparation; food purchasing; food service math; garde-manger; international cuisine; introduction to food service; kitchen management; management and human resources; meal planning; meat cutting; menu and facilities design; nutrition; restaurant opportunities; sanitation; saucier; seafood processing; soup, stock, sauce, and starch production; wines and spirits.

FACILITIES
Bake shop; bakery; cafeteria; 2 classrooms; computer laboratory; demonstration laboratory; food production kitchen; gourmet dining room; laboratory; learning resource center; lecture room; library; public restaurant; teaching kitchen.

TYPICAL STUDENT PROFILE
83 total: 62 full-time; 21 part-time. 60 are under 25 years old; 15 are between 25 and 44 years old; 8 are over 44 years old.

SPECIAL PROGRAMS

Culinary competitions, externships, National Restaurant Association show in Chicago.

FINANCIAL AID

Employment placement assistance is available.

APPLICATION INFORMATION

Students may begin participation in January and August. Application deadline for fall is August 25. Application deadline for spring is January 6. Applicants must submit a formal application.

CONTACT

Director of Admissions, Culinary Arts Program, 6004 Prairie Road, Jamesville, WI 53547. Telephone: 608-757-7696. Fax: 608-743-4407. World Wide Web: http://www.blackhawk.edu/programs/associates/culinary_arts.htm.

FOX VALLEY TECHNICAL COLLEGE

Culinary Arts and Hospitality Department

Appleton, Wisconsin

GENERAL INFORMATION

Public, coeducational, two-year college. Urban campus. Founded in 1913. Accredited by North Central Association of Colleges and Schools.

PROGRAM INFORMATION

Offered since 1973. Accredited by American Culinary Federation Accrediting Commission. Program calendar is divided into semesters. 1-year certificate in hospitality supervisor. 1-year certificate in advanced baking. 1-year diploma in food service production. 2-year associate degree in hotel and restaurant management. 2-year associate degree in culinary arts.

PROGRAM AFFILIATION

American Culinary Federation; Fox Cities Lodging and Hospitality Association; Fox Valley Culinary Association; International Food Service Executives Association; National Restaurant Association; National Restaurant Association Educational Foundation; Wisconsin Restaurant Association.

AREAS OF STUDY

Baking; beverage management; buffet catering; confectionery show pieces; controlling costs in food service; convenience cookery; culinary French; culinary skill development; food preparation; food purchasing; food service communication; food service math; garde-manger; international cuisine; introduction to food service; kitchen management; management and human resources; meal planning; meat cutting; meat fabrication; menu and facilities design; nutrition;

nutrition and food service; patisserie; restaurant opportunities; sanitation; saucier; seafood processing; soup, stock, sauce, and starch production; wines and spirits.

FACILITIES

Bake shop; bakery; cafeteria; catering service; 2 classrooms; 2 computer laboratories; demonstration laboratory; 4 food production kitchens; garden; gourmet dining room; learning resource center; lecture room; library; public restaurant; snack shop; student lounge; teaching kitchen.

STUDENT PROFILE

240 total: 120 full-time; 120 part-time. 140 are under 25 years old; 50 are between 25 and 44 years old; 50 are over 44 years old.

FACULTY

16 total: 6 full-time; 10 part-time. 16 are industry professionals; 3 are culinary-certified teachers. Prominent faculty: Jeff Igel, CEC, CCE, CCA, AAC; Scott Finley, CEC; Jean Malvitz, CEPC. Faculty-student ratio: 1:36 lecture; 1:12 lab.

SPECIAL PROGRAMS

Culinary and ice carving competitions, annual 7-day culinary tour (locations vary), National Restaurant Association show in Chicago.

TYPICAL EXPENSES

Application fee: $30. In-state tuition: $2000 per semester full-time (in district), $125 per credit part-time. Out-of-state tuition: $750 per credit part-time. Program-related fees include $250 for knives (beginning set); $600 for books (per semester); $125 for uniforms (per semester).

FINANCIAL AID

In 2006, 32 scholarships were awarded (average award was $500). Employment placement assistance is available. Employment opportunities within the program are available.

HOUSING

Average off-campus housing cost per month: $400.

APPLICATION INFORMATION

Students may begin participation in January, June, and August. Applications are accepted continuously. In 2006, 120 applied; 120 were accepted. Applicants must submit a formal application.

CONTACT

Jeffrey S. Igel, Department Chair, Culinary Arts and Hospitality Department, 1825 North Bluemound, PO Box 2277, Appleton, WI 54912-2277. Telephone: 920-735-5643. Fax: 920-735-5655. E-mail: chefjeff@fvtc.edu. World Wide Web: http://www.fvtc.edu.

Madison Area Technical College

Culinary Trades Department

Madison, Wisconsin

General Information
Public, coeducational, two-year college. Urban campus. Founded in 1911. Accredited by North Central Association of Colleges and Schools.

Program Information
Offered since 1960. Accredited by American Culinary Federation Accrediting Commission. Program calendar is divided into semesters. 1-year diploma in food service production. 1-year diploma in baking/pastry arts. 2-year associate degree in culinary arts.

Program Affiliation
American Culinary Federation; International Food Service Executives Association; National Restaurant Association; National Restaurant Association Educational Foundation; Retailer's Bakery Association; The Bread Bakers Guild of America.

Areas of Study
Baking; buffet catering; controlling costs in food service; culinary French; culinary skill development; food preparation; food purchasing; food service communication; food service math; garde-manger; international cuisine; introduction to food service; management and human resources; meal planning; meat cutting; menu and facilities design; nutrition; sanitation; soup, stock, sauce, and starch production; wines and spirits.

Facilities
Bake shop; bakery; 2 cafeterias; catering service; computer laboratory; demonstration laboratory; 2 food production kitchens; gourmet dining room; learning resource center; lecture room; library; snack shop; student lounge; 2 teaching kitchens.

Typical Student Profile
105 total: 80 full-time; 25 part-time. 63 are under 25 years old; 21 are between 25 and 44 years old; 21 are over 44 years old.

Special Programs
2-credit internship, field experiences (domestic and international), culinary competitions.

Financial Aid
Employment placement assistance is available. Employment opportunities within the program are available.

Application Information
Students may begin participation in August. Application deadline for fall is July 1. Applicants must submit a formal application and academic transcripts.

Contact
Director of Admissions, Culinary Trades Department, 3550 Anderson Street, Madison, WI 53704-2599. Telephone: 608-246-6368. Fax: 608-246-6316. World Wide Web: http://matcmadison.edu.

Milwaukee Area Technical College

Culinary Arts

Milwaukee, Wisconsin

General Information
Public, coeducational, two-year college. Urban campus. Founded in 1912. Accredited by North Central Association of Colleges and Schools.

Program Information
Offered since 1954. Accredited by American Culinary Federation. Program calendar is divided into semesters. 1-year technical diploma in baking production technical diploma. 1-year technical diploma in food service technical diploma. 2-year associate degree in culinary arts.

Program Affiliation
American Culinary Federation; Council on Hotel, Restaurant, and Institutional Education; National Restaurant Association Educational Foundation; Wisconsin Restaurant Association.

Areas of Study
Baking; beverage management; buffet catering; confectionery show pieces; controlling costs in food service; culinary skill development; food preparation; food purchasing; food service math; garde-manger; international cuisine; introduction to food service; management and human resources; meal planning; menu and facilities design; nutrition; patisserie; restaurant opportunities; sanitation; soup, stock, sauce, and starch production.

Facilities
Bake shop; bakery; cafeteria; 3 classrooms; computer laboratory; demonstration laboratory; 2 food production kitchens; gourmet dining room; library; 2 teaching kitchens.

TYPICAL STUDENT PROFILE

100 total: 65 full-time; 35 part-time. 25 are under 25 years old; 60 are between 25 and 44 years old; 15 are over 44 years old.

SPECIAL PROGRAMS

Culinary competition.

FINANCIAL AID

Program-specific awards include Five Star Culinary Endowment Grant. Employment placement assistance is available. Employment opportunities within the program are available.

APPLICATION INFORMATION

Students may begin participation in January and August. Application deadline for first day of class each semester. Applicants must submit a formal application and math and reading placement tests.

CONTACT

Director of Admissions, Culinary Arts, 700 West State Street, Milwaukee, WI 53233. Telephone: 414-297-7897. Fax: 414-297-7990. World Wide Web: http://www.matc.edu/documents/catalog/culinary_arts_aas_degree.html.

MORAINE PARK TECHNICAL COLLEGE

Culinary Arts/Food Service Production

Fond du Lac, Wisconsin

GENERAL INFORMATION

Public, coeducational, two-year college. Small-town setting. Founded in 1967. Accredited by North Central Association of Colleges and Schools.

PROGRAM INFORMATION

Offered since 1976. Accredited by American Culinary Federation Accrediting Commission. Program calendar is divided into semesters. 1-semester certificate in food production. 1-semester certificate in bakery/deli. 1-year certificate in specialty baking. 1-year certificate in school food service. 1-year certificate in culinary basics. 1-year technical diploma in food service production. 2-year associate degree in culinary arts.

PROGRAM AFFILIATION

American Culinary Federation; National Restaurant Association; Wisconsin Restaurant Association.

AREAS OF STUDY

Baking; beverage management; buffet catering; controlling costs in food service; convenience cookery; culinary skill development; food preparation; food purchasing; food service communication; food service math; garde-manger; international cuisine; introduction to food service; kitchen management; meal planning; meat cutting; menu and facilities design; nutrition; nutrition and food service; restaurant opportunities; sales and service; sanitation; saucier; seafood processing; soup, stock, sauce, and starch production.

FACILITIES

Bake shop; bakery; cafeteria; catering service; 2 classrooms; 3 computer laboratories; demonstration laboratory; 2 food production kitchens; gourmet dining room; learning resource center; 2 lecture rooms; library; public restaurant; snack shop; teaching kitchen.

STUDENT PROFILE

85 total: 70 full-time; 15 part-time.

FACULTY

6 total: 3 full-time; 3 part-time. 1 is a culinary-certified teacher; 1 is a certified baker, 3 certified chefs. Prominent faculty: James Simmers; Ron Spiech; Tom Endejan. Faculty-student ratio: 1:14.

SPECIAL PROGRAMS

Culinary competitions, National Restaurant Association Convention, attendance at Wisconsin Restaurant Association and Inn Keepers Convention.

TYPICAL EXPENSES

Application fee: $30. In-state tuition: $92.05 per credit full-time (in district), $92.05 per credit part-time. Out-of-state tuition: $570.55 per credit full-time, $570.55 per credit part-time. Program-related fees include $110 for uniforms; $105 for cutlery; $96 for material fees.

FINANCIAL AID

In 2006, 9 scholarships were awarded (average award was $570); 29 loans were granted (average loan was $2735). Program-specific awards include paid internships. Employment placement assistance is available.

HOUSING

Average off-campus housing cost per month: $400.

APPLICATION INFORMATION

Students may begin participation in January, March, August, and October. Applications are accepted continuously. In 2006, 45 applied; 41 were accepted. Applicants must interview; submit a formal application.

CONTACT

Pat Olson, Dean, Business and Culinary Arts, Culinary Arts/Food Service Production, 235 North National Avenue, PO Box 1940, Fond du Lac, WI 54936-1940. Telephone: 920-924-3333. Fax: 920-924-6356. E-mail: polson@morainepark.edu. World Wide Web: http://www.morainepark.edu.

NICOLET AREA TECHNICAL COLLEGE

Culinary Arts

Rhinelander, Wisconsin

GENERAL INFORMATION
Public, coeducational, two-year college. Rural campus. Founded in 1968. Accredited by North Central Association of Colleges and Schools.

PROGRAM INFORMATION
National Restaurant Association Educational Foundation ManageFirst certificates available. Program calendar is divided into semesters. 1-year technical diploma in food service production. 13-credit certificate in catering. 14-credit certificate in baking. 2-year associate degree in culinary arts. 8-course certificate in food service management.

PROGRAM AFFILIATION
American Culinary Federation; National Restaurant Association; National Restaurant Association Educational Foundation; Wisconsin Restaurant Association.

AREAS OF STUDY
Baking; beverage management; buffet catering; controlling costs in food service; culinary skill development; food practicum; food preparation; food purchasing; food service math; garde-manger; international cuisine; introduction to food service; management and human resources; meal planning; menu and facilities design; nutrition; nutrition and food service; restaurant opportunities; restaurant practicum; sanitation; saucier; soup, stock, sauce, and starch production; wines and spirits.

FACILITIES
Cafeteria; classroom; demonstration laboratory; food production kitchen; gourmet dining room; learning resource center; lecture room; library; student lounge; teaching kitchen.

STUDENT PROFILE
40 total: 20 full-time; 20 part-time. 28 are under 25 years old; 12 are between 25 and 44 years old.

FACULTY
2 total: 2 full-time. 1 is a culinary-certified teacher. Prominent faculty: Linda Arndt; Vicky Mendham-Whitehead, CCE. Faculty-student ratio: 1:15.

PROMINENT ALUMNI AND CURRENT AFFILIATION
Jason Meinholz, Riverstone, Soda Pops; Rhonda Jilinsky, Holiday Acres.

SPECIAL PROGRAMS
Internship in culinary arts (2 credits), attendance at the Central Regional ACF conference, culinary competition at the Wisconsin Restaurant Association Show.

TYPICAL EXPENSES
Application fee: $30. Tuition: $1750 per semester full-time (in district), $75 per credit part-time. Program-related fees include $175 for books per semester; $145 for uniforms.

FINANCIAL AID
In 2006, 8 scholarships were awarded (average award was $500). Program-specific awards include Wisconsin Restaurant Association scholarships, NRA Education Foundation scholarships, NICA Manage First Program scholarships. Employment placement assistance is available. Employment opportunities within the program are available.

HOUSING
Average off-campus housing cost per month: $350.

APPLICATION INFORMATION
Students may begin participation in January and August. Application deadline for fall is August 15. Application deadline for spring is January 15. In 2006, 30 applied; 18 were accepted. Applicants must submit a formal application, academic transcripts and complete an Accuplacer test.

CONTACT
Susan Kordula, Admissions Representative, Culinary Arts, Nicolet College, Box 518, Rhinelander, WI 54501. Telephone: 715-365-4451. Fax: 715-365-4411. E-mail: skordula@nicoletcollege.edu. World Wide Web: http://www.nicoletcollege.edu.

SOUTHWEST WISCONSIN TECHNICAL COLLEGE

Culinary Management

Fennimore, Wisconsin

GENERAL INFORMATION
Public, coeducational, two-year college. Small-town setting. Founded in 1967. Accredited by North Central Association of Colleges and Schools.

PROGRAM INFORMATION
Offered since 1994. Accredited by American Dietetic Association. Program calendar is divided into semesters. 1-year technical diploma in catering. 2-year associate degree in culinary management.

PROGRAM AFFILIATION
Catersource; National Restaurant Association.

AREAS OF STUDY
Baking; buffet catering; controlling costs in food service; culinary skill development; food preparation; food purchasing; food service communication; food service math; garde-manger; introduction to food service; kitchen management; management and human resources; meat cutting; meat fabrication; menu and facilities design; nutrition; sanitation; soup, stock, sauce, and starch production; wines and spirits.

FACILITIES
Bake shop; classroom; computer laboratory; food production kitchen; gourmet dining room; laboratory; learning resource center; library.

STUDENT PROFILE
20 full-time. 16 are under 25 years old; 3 are between 25 and 44 years old; 1 is over 44 years old.

FACULTY
2 total: 2 full-time. 2 are industry professionals. Prominent faculty: Jeff Dombeck; Karen Bast. Faculty-student ratio: 1:10.

TYPICAL EXPENSES
Application fee: $25. Tuition: $5158 per degree; $2882 per diploma full-time, $82.35 per credit part-time. Program-related fees include $125 for knives; $125 for uniforms.

FINANCIAL AID
In 2006, 3 scholarships were awarded (average award was $333). Employment placement assistance is available. Employment opportunities within the program are available.

HOUSING
Apartment-style housing available. Average on-campus housing cost per month: $200. Average off-campus housing cost per month: $175.

APPLICATION INFORMATION
Students may begin participation in August. Application deadline for fall is August 15. In 2006, 18 applied; 18 were accepted. Applicants must interview, submit a formal application, and take an entrance test.

CONTACT
Peggy Koehler, Admissions/Registration, Culinary Management, 1800 Bronson Boulevard, Fennimore, WI 53809. Telephone: 608-822-3262. World Wide Web: http://www.swtc.edu/.

UNIVERSITY OF WISCONSIN–STOUT

Department of Hospitality and Tourism

Menomonie, Wisconsin

GENERAL INFORMATION
Public, coeducational, comprehensive institution. Small-town setting. Founded in 1891. Accredited by North Central Association of Colleges and Schools.

PROGRAM INFORMATION
Offered since 1969. Program calendar is divided into semesters. 2-year master's degree in hospitality and tourism. 4-year bachelor's degree in hotel, restaurant, and tourism management.

PROGRAM AFFILIATION
American Dietetic Association; Council on Hotel, Restaurant, and Institutional Education; National Restaurant Association; National Restaurant Association Educational Foundation.

AREAS OF STUDY
Beverage management; buffet catering; controlling costs in food service; food preparation; food purchasing; introduction to food service; kitchen management; management and human resources; meal planning; menu and facilities design; nutrition; nutrition and food service; restaurant opportunities; sanitation; soup, stock, sauce, and starch production; wines and spirits.

FACILITIES
Bake shop; cafeteria; catering service; 10 classrooms; computer laboratory; 2 food production kitchens; gourmet dining room; learning resource center; 5 lecture rooms; library; 2 public restaurants; 2 teaching kitchens.

STUDENT PROFILE
625 total: 550 full-time; 75 part-time. 605 are under 25 years old; 20 are between 25 and 44 years old.

FACULTY
16 total: 13 full-time; 3 part-time. 14 are industry professionals; 2 are master chefs. Prominent faculty: Jafar Jafari, PhD; Phil McGuirk; Joe Holland, JD; Peter D'Souza. Faculty-student ratio: 1:31.

PROMINENT ALUMNI AND CURRENT AFFILIATION
David Miller, GM, St. Paul Hotel, St. Paul, MN; Doug Hustad, Vice President, Biltmore Estate, NC; Kevin Hickey, Executive Chef, Four Seasons Hotel, Chicago.

SPECIAL PROGRAMS
3-week wine and food pairing course in Palmade Mallorca (Spain) and Australia, catering opportunities, culinary competitions.

University of Wisconsin–Stout *(continued)*

TYPICAL EXPENSES

Application fee: $35. In-state tuition: $6963 per year. Out-of-state tuition: $14,613 per year. Tuition for international students: $14,613 per year.

FINANCIAL AID

In 2006, 40 scholarships were awarded (average award was $500). Employment placement assistance is available. Employment opportunities within the program are available.

HOUSING

Coed housing available. Average on-campus housing cost per month: $150. Average off-campus housing cost per month: $225.

APPLICATION INFORMATION

Students may begin participation in January and August. Applications are accepted continuously. In 2006, 230 applied; 180 were accepted. Applicants must submit a formal application and letters of reference.

CONTACT

Dr. Ted Harris, Program Director, Department of Hospitality and Tourism, 432 Home Economics Building, Menomonie, WI 54751. Telephone: 715-232-2532. Fax: 715-232-2588. E-mail: harrise@uwstout.edu. World Wide Web: http://www.uwstout.edu.

WYOMING

SHERIDAN COLLEGE

Hospitality Management/Culinary Arts

Sheridan, Wyoming

GENERAL INFORMATION

Public, coeducational, two-year college. Small-town setting. Founded in 1948. Accredited by North Central Association of Colleges and Schools.

PROGRAM INFORMATION

Offered since 1994. Accredited by American Culinary Federation Accrediting Commission. National Restaurant Association Educational Foundation ManageFirst certificates available. Program calendar is divided into semesters. 1-year certificate in culinary arts. 1-year certificate in hospitality management. 2-year associate degree in culinary arts. 2-year associate degree in hospitality management.

PROGRAM AFFILIATION

American Culinary Federation; American Hotel and Lodging Association; National Restaurant Association; National Restaurant Association Educational Foundation; Wyoming Lodging and Restaurant Association; Wyoming State-Wide Consortium for Hospitality Management; Wyoming Travel Industry Coalition.

AREAS OF STUDY

Baking; beverage management; confectionery show pieces; controlling costs in food service; culinary French; culinary skill development; food preparation; food purchasing; food service math; front office operations; garde-manger; international cuisine; introduction to food service; kitchen management; law; management and human resources; marketing; meal planning; meat cutting; meat fabrication; menu and facilities design; nutrition; nutrition and food service; patisserie; restaurant opportunities; sanitation; security and loss; soup, stock, sauce, and starch production; wines and spirits.

FACILITIES

Catering service; 3 classrooms; 2 computer laboratories; demonstration laboratory; food production kitchen; garden; gourmet dining room; learning resource center; lecture room; library; public restaurant; 3 student lounges; 2 teaching kitchens; compress video classroom.

STUDENT PROFILE

35 total: 30 full-time; 5 part-time. 25 are under 25 years old; 10 are between 25 and 44 years old.

FACULTY

6 total: 2 full-time; 4 part-time. 1 is an industry professional; 1 is a culinary-certified teacher; 1 is a certified hospitality educator. Prominent faculty: Monty Blare, CHE; R.J. Rogers, CEC; Pete Serna; Trev Lee Trautman. Faculty-student ratio: 1:14.

SPECIAL PROGRAMS

Attendance at Wyoming Governor's Conference on Travel and Tourism, internships (paid only), tours of hotels, restaurants, guest ranches, ski resorts.

TYPICAL EXPENSES

In-state tuition: $670 per semester full-time (in district), $58 per credit part-time. Out-of-state tuition: $1722 per semester full-time, $150 per credit part-time. Program-related fees include $45 for online fee; $25 for shirt and name tag; $250 for cutlery/garmets; $10 for knife fees.

FINANCIAL AID

In 2006, 15 scholarships were awarded (average award was $500). Program-specific awards include Sheridan County Liquor Dealers Association Scholarship ($750), ProMgmt. Scholarship ($850), National Tourism

Foundation Scholarship-Wyoming ($500). Employment placement assistance is available. Employment opportunities within the program are available.

Housing
Coed and single-sex housing available. Average on-campus housing cost per month: $250. Average off-campus housing cost per month: $750.

Application Information
Students may begin participation in January and August. Applications are accepted continuously. In 2006, 24 applied; 24 were accepted. Applicants must interview; submit a formal application.

Contact
Monty D. Blare, Director, Hospitality Management/ Culinary Arts, Box 1500, Sheridan, WY 82801. Telephone: 307-674-6446 Ext. 3508. Fax: 307-672-2103. E-mail: mblare@sheridan.edu. World Wide Web: http://www.sheridan.edu.

CANADA

The Art Institute of Vancouver (Dubrulle Culinary Arts Location)

The International Culinary School at The Art Institute of Vancouver (Dubrulle Culinary Arts Location)

Vancouver, British Columbia, Canada

General Information
Private, coeducational institution.

Program Information
Advanced diploma in Culinary Arts and Restaurant Ownership. Certificate in Hospitality and Restaurant Business Management. Certificate in Culinary Arts. Certificate in Baking and Pastry Arts (Level 1 and 2). Diploma in Entrepreneurship and Restaurant Ownership. Diploma in Culinary Arts. Diploma in Baking and Pastry Arts. Diploma in Hospitality and Restaurant Business Management.

Contact
Office of Admissions, The International Culinary School at The Art Institute of Vancouver (Dubrulle Culinary Arts Location), PO Box 10366, 300-609 Granville Street, Vancouver, BC V7Y 1G5, Canada. Telephone: 604-738-3155. Fax: 604-738-3205. World Wide Web: http://www.artinstitutes.edu/vancouver/culinary/index.asp.

See color display following page 186.

Canadore College of Applied Arts & Technology

School of Hospitality and Tourism

North Bay, Ontario, Canada

General Information
Public, coeducational, technical college. Rural campus. Founded in 1967.

Program Information
Offered since 1967. Program calendar is divided into semesters. 1-year certificate in culinary skills/chef training. 2-year diploma in hotel, restaurant, resort management. 2-year diploma in culinary management. 3-year diploma in hotel, restaurant, resort administration. 3-year diploma in culinary administration.

Program Affiliation
American Culinary Federation; Canadian Federation of Chefs and Cooks; Canadian Restaurant Association; Council on Hotel, Restaurant, and Institutional Education.

Areas of Study
Baking; beverage management; buffet catering; confectionery show pieces; controlling costs in food service; convenience cookery; culinary French; culinary skill development; food preparation; food purchasing; food service communication; food service math; garde-manger; international cuisine; introduction to food service; kitchen management; management and human resources; meal planning; meat fabrication; menu and facilities design; nutrition; nutrition and food

Canadore College of Applied Arts & Technology
(continued)

service; patisserie; restaurant opportunities; sanitation; saucier; seafood processing; soup, stock, sauce, and starch production; wines and spirits.

FACILITIES
Bake shop; bakery; cafeteria; 4 classrooms; 2 computer laboratories; demonstration laboratory; food production kitchen; gourmet dining room; learning resource center; lecture room; library; public restaurant; student lounge; teaching kitchen; experimental food lab.

STUDENT PROFILE
95 total: 90 full-time; 5 part-time. 76 are under 25 years old; 16 are between 25 and 44 years old; 3 are over 44 years old.

FACULTY
16 total: 14 full-time; 2 part-time. 10 are industry professionals; 4 are master chefs. Prominent faculty: Daniel Esposito; Derek Lawday; Fintan Flynn; Cynthia Simpson.

PROMINENT ALUMNI AND CURRENT AFFILIATION
Joe Farrace, Hotel Ritz, Orlando.

SPECIAL PROGRAMS
Tour of culinary sites in the Caribbean region, provincial and international student competitions.

TYPICAL EXPENSES
Application fee: Can$100. Tuition: Can$2700 per year full-time, Can$150–Can$300 per course part-time. Tuition for international students: Can$11,000 per year. Program-related fees include Can$395 for knives; Can$275 for uniforms.

FINANCIAL AID
In 2006, 15 scholarships were awarded (average award was Can$250). Employment placement assistance is available. Employment opportunities within the program are available.

HOUSING
Single-sex housing available. Average on-campus housing cost per month: Can$400.

APPLICATION INFORMATION
Students may begin participation in September. Application deadline for fall is May 15. In 2006, 211 applied; 65 were accepted. Applicants must submit a formal application.

CONTACT
Daniel Esposito, Advisor/Professor, School of Hospitality and Tourism, 100 College Drive, North Bay, ON P1B 8K9, Canada. Telephone: 705-474-7600 Ext. 5218. Fax: 705-474-2384. E-mail: daniel.esposito@canadorec.on.ca. World Wide Web: http://www.canadorec.on.ca.

CULINARY INSTITUTE OF CANADA
Charlottetown, Prince Edward Island, Canada

GENERAL INFORMATION
Public, coeducational, culinary institute. Urban campus. Founded in 1983.

PROGRAM INFORMATION
Offered since 1983. Program calendar is divided into trimesters. 1-year certificate in pastry arts. 2-year diploma in hotel restaurant management. 2-year diploma in culinary arts. 4-year applied degree in culinary operations.

PROGRAM AFFILIATION
Canadian Federation of Chefs and Cooks; Confrerie de la Chaine des Rotisseurs; Council on Hotel, Restaurant, and Institutional Education; International Association of Culinary Professionals.

AREAS OF STUDY
Baking; beverage management; buffet catering; confectionery show pieces; controlling costs in food service; convenience cookery; culinary French; culinary skill development; food preparation; food purchasing; food service communication; food service math; garde-manger; international cuisine; introduction to food service; kitchen management; management and human resources; meal planning; meat cutting; meat fabrication; menu and facilities design; nutrition; nutrition and food service; patisserie; restaurant opportunities; sanitation; saucier; seafood processing; soup, stock, sauce, and starch production; wines and spirits.

FACILITIES
Bake shop; bakery; cafeteria; 5 catering services; 14 classrooms; 3 computer laboratories; demonstration laboratory; 7 food production kitchens; gourmet dining room; learning resource center; lecture room; 2 public restaurants; snack shop; 2 student lounges; 6 teaching kitchens.

STUDENT PROFILE
215 full-time.

Culinary Institute of Canada *(continued)*

FACULTY

28 total: 19 full-time; 9 part-time. 8 are industry professionals; 10 are culinary-certified teachers. Faculty-student ratio: 1:18.

SPECIAL PROGRAMS

5-month paid internship, culinary competitions.

TYPICAL EXPENSES

Application fee: Can$40. Tuition: Can$6450 per year. Program-related fees include Can$505 for book (for 2 years); Can$300 for knives; Can$1700 for lab fees (for 2 years); Can$1935 for uniforms and laundry (for 2 years); Can$490 for student union fee and health insurance fee (for 2 years).

FINANCIAL AID

In 2006, 20 scholarships were awarded (average award was Can$1000). Employment placement assistance is available.

HOUSING

Coed and apartment-style housing available. Average on-campus housing cost per month: Can$500. Average off-campus housing cost per month: Can$400.

APPLICATION INFORMATION

Students may begin participation in March and September. Application deadline for spring is January 5. Application deadline for fall is February 25. Applicants must submit a formal application and resume.

CONTACT

David Harding, Culinary Programs Manager, 4 Sydney Street, Charlottetown, PE C1A 1E9, Canada. Telephone: 902-894-6805. Fax: 902-894-6835. E-mail: dharding@hollandc.pe.ca. World Wide Web: http://www.hollandcollege.com.

See display on page 353.

GEORGE BROWN COLLEGE

Centre for Hospitality and Culinary Arts/George Brown Chef School

Toronto, Ontario, Canada

GENERAL INFORMATION

Public, coeducational, two-year college. Urban campus. Founded in 1960.

PROGRAM INFORMATION

Offered since 1967. Accredited by American Culinary Federation Accrediting Commission, Council on Hotel, Restaurant and Institutional Education. Program calendar is divided into trimesters. 1-year certificate in culinary skills. 1-year certificate in baking and pastry arts. 1-year post diploma in culinary arts (Italian). 1-year post diploma in culinary arts (Indian). 1-year post diploma in advanced food and beverage management. 1-year post diploma in culinary arts (French). 14-week certificate in Chinese cuisine. 18-week certificate in basic food preparation. 2-year diploma in baking and pastry arts management. 2-year diploma in food and beverage management. 2-year diploma in hotel management. 2-year diploma in culinary management. 3-year certificate in apprentice cook. 3-year diploma in patissier-apprentice baker.

PROGRAM AFFILIATION

American Culinary Federation; Council on Hotel, Restaurant, and Institutional Education; Institute of Food Technologists; National Restaurant Association; National Restaurant Association Educational Foundation; Society of Wine Educators; Sommelier Guild of Canada.

AREAS OF STUDY

Baking; beverage management; buffet catering; confectionery show pieces; controlling costs in food service; culinary French; culinary skill development; food preparation; food purchasing; food service communication; food service math; French cuisine; garde-manger; Indian Cuisine; international cuisine; introduction to food service; Italian cuisine; kitchen management; management and human resources; meat cutting; menu and facilities design; nutrition; nutrition and food service; patisserie; restaurant operations; sanitation; saucier; sommelier; soup, stock, sauce, and starch production; wines and spirits.

FACILITIES

4 bake shops; bakery; cafeteria; catering service; 40 classrooms; 2 computer laboratories; 4 demonstration laboratories; 12 food production kitchens; gourmet dining room; 8 laboratories; learning resource center; 8 lecture rooms; library; public restaurant; student lounge; 16 teaching kitchens; beverage mixology classroom; wine & beverage lab.

STUDENT PROFILE

8,500 total: 2500 full-time; 6000 part-time.

FACULTY

190 total: 75 full-time; 115 part-time. 125 are industry professionals; 10 are master chefs; 6 are master bakers; 45 are culinary-certified teachers. Faculty-student ratio: 1:24.

SPECIAL PROGRAMS

Culinary Arts Italian (includes 3-month internship in Italy), French Cuisine (includes international field-trip to Bocuse Institute).

TYPICAL EXPENSES

Application fee: Can$30. Tuition: Can$1700 per 1 year. Tuition for international students: Can$9000 per 1 year. Program-related fees include Can$400 for materials; Can$300 for equipment and knives; Can$150 for uniforms.

FINANCIAL AID

In 2006, 600 scholarships were awarded (average award was Can$500). Employment placement assistance is available. Employment opportunities within the program are available.

HOUSING

Average off-campus housing cost per month: Can$500.

APPLICATION INFORMATION

Students may begin participation in January, May, and October. Application deadline for fall is March 1. Application deadline for January semester is June 1. Application deadline for summer semester is January 1. In 2006, 7000 applied; 1000 were accepted. Applicants must submit a formal application and have a grade 12 high school diploma.

CONTACT

K. Müller, Chair, George Brown Chef School, Centre for Hospitality and Culinary Arts/George Brown Chef School, 300 Adelaide Street East, Toronto, ON M5A 1N1, Canada. Telephone: 416-415-5000. Fax: 416-415-2501. E-mail: kmuller@georgebrown.ca. World Wide Web: http://www.georgebrown.ca.

GEORGIAN COLLEGE OF APPLIED ARTS AND TECHNOLOGY

Culinary Management Program

Barrie, Ontario, Canada

GENERAL INFORMATION

Public, coeducational institution. Small-town setting. Founded in 1967. Accredited by Ontario Ministry of Education and Training.

PROGRAM INFORMATION

Offered since 1984. Program calendar is divided into semesters. 2-year diploma in culinary arts.

PROGRAM AFFILIATION

Muskoka & District Chefs Association.

AREAS OF STUDY

Baking; beverage management; buffet catering; controlling costs in food service; convenience cookery; culinary French; culinary skill development; food preparation; food purchasing; food service communication; food service math; garde-manger; international cuisine; introduction to food service; kitchen management; management and human resources; meal planning; meat fabrication; menu and facilities design; nutrition; patisserie; restaurant opportunities; sanitation; saucier; seafood processing; soup, stock, sauce, and starch production; wines and spirits.

FACILITIES

Bake shop; 2 computer laboratories; food production kitchen; gourmet dining room; 2 laboratories; learning resource center.

STUDENT PROFILE

50 full-time. 42 are under 25 years old; 8 are between 25 and 44 years old.

FACULTY

24 total: 12 full-time; 12 part-time. 3 are industry professionals; 3 are master chefs; 1 is a master baker; 3 are culinary-certified teachers. Faculty-student ratio: 1:24 labs; 1:45 class.

TYPICAL EXPENSES

Application fee: Can$65. Tuition: Can$1784.60 per year. Tuition for international students: Can$9215 per year. Program-related fee includes Can$1200 for text, uniforms.

FINANCIAL AID

In 2006, 8 scholarships were awarded (average award was Can$400); 30 loans were granted (average loan was Can$400). Program-specific awards include Entry Scholarship (Can$500).

HOUSING

Coed and apartment-style housing available. Average on-campus housing cost per month: Can$480. Average off-campus housing cost per month: Can$450.

APPLICATION INFORMATION

Students may begin participation in September. Application deadline for fall is March 1. In 2006, 158 applied; 146 were accepted. Applicants must submit a formal application.

CONTACT

Ontario College Application Service, Culinary Management Program, 370 Speedvale Avenue West, PO Box 810, Guelph, ON N1H 6M4, Canada. Telephone: 519-763-4725. World Wide Web: http://www.georgianc.on.ca.

HUMBER INSTITUTE OF TECHNOLOGY AND ADVANCED LEARNING

School of Hospitality, Recreation, and Tourism

Toronto, Ontario, Canada

GENERAL INFORMATION
Public, coeducational, comprehensive institution. Urban campus. Founded in 1967.

PROGRAM INFORMATION
Offered since 1982. Program calendar is divided into semesters. 1-year certificate in food and beverage. 1-year certificate in culinary skills. 2-year diploma in hospitality management/hotel and restaurant. 2-year diploma in culinary management.

PROGRAM AFFILIATION
American Vegan Society.

AREAS OF STUDY
Baking; confectionery show pieces; controlling costs in food service; culinary French; culinary skill development; food preparation; food purchasing; food service communication; food service math; garde-manger; international cuisine; introduction to food service; kitchen management; meal planning; meat cutting; meat fabrication; menu and facilities design; nutrition; patisserie; sanitation; saucier; seafood processing; soup, stock, sauce, and starch production; wines and spirits.

FACILITIES
Bake shop; bakery; 3 cafeterias; 2 catering services; 12 classrooms; 2 coffee shops; 6 computer laboratories; demonstration laboratory; 4 food production kitchens; 4 gardens; gourmet dining room; learning resource center; lecture room; library; 2 public restaurants; 2 snack shops; 3 student lounges; teaching kitchen.

STUDENT PROFILE
485 total: 400 full-time; 85 part-time.

FACULTY
30 total: 10 full-time; 20 part-time. 13 are industry professionals; 12 are master chefs; 2 are master bakers; 5 are culinary-certified teachers. Prominent faculty: Klaus Theyer, CCC; Frank Formiella, CCC; Robert McCann, CCC; Anthony Bevan, CCC. Faculty-student ratio: 1:24.

SPECIAL PROGRAMS
Study abroad opportunities, university articulation agreements, internship.

TYPICAL EXPENSES
Application fee: Can$65. Tuition: Can$2600 per year full-time, varies part-time. Tuition for international students: Can$11,150 per year. Program-related fees include Can$150–$250 for uniforms (culinary program and hospitality programs); Can$200–$390 for tool kit and knives (culinary program and hospitality programs); Can$200–$400 for textbooks; Can$150–$350 for lab fees.

FINANCIAL AID
In 2006, individual loans were awarded at Can$750. Employment placement assistance is available. Employment opportunities within the program are available.

HOUSING
Coed, apartment-style, and single-sex housing available. Average on-campus housing cost per month: Can$460. Average off-campus housing cost per month: Can$600.

APPLICATION INFORMATION
Students may begin participation in January and September. Application deadline for fall is August 1. Application deadline for winter/spring is December 1. In 2006, 2000 applied; 240 were accepted. Applicants must submit a formal application.

CONTACT
Paul McCabe, Hospitality Program Coordinator, School of Hospitality, Recreation, and Tourism, 205 Humber College Boulevard, Toronto, ON M9W 5L7, Canada. Telephone: 416-675-6622 Ext. 5276. Fax: 416-675-3062. E-mail: paul.mccabe@humber.ca. World Wide Web: http://www.humber.ca.

LE CORDON BLEU, OTTAWA CULINARY ARTS INSTITUTE

The Classic Cycle

Ottawa, Ontario, Canada

GENERAL INFORMATION
Private, coeducational, culinary institute. Urban campus. Founded in 1988. Accredited by Ministry of Training, Colleges and Universities.

PROGRAM INFORMATION
Offered since 1988. Program calendar is divided into quarters. 10- to 12-week certificate in superior pastry. 10- to 12-week certificate in superior cuisine. 10- to 12-week certificate in intermediate pastry. 10- to 12-week certificate in basic pastry. 10- to 12-week certificate in intermediate cuisine. 10- to 12-week

certificate in basic cuisine. 4-week certificate in introduction to catering. 9-month diploma in patisserie arts. 9-month diploma in culinary arts.

PROGRAM AFFILIATION
American Institute of Wine & Food; Canadian Federation of Chefs and Cooks; Canadian Restaurant and Food Services Association; Confrerie de la Chaine des Rotisseurs; Council on Hotel, Restaurant, and Institutional Education; International Association of Culinary Professionals; James Beard Foundation, Inc.; Women Chefs and Restaurateurs; World Association of Cooks Societies.

AREAS OF STUDY
Baking; buffet catering; confectionery show pieces; culinary French; culinary skill development; food preparation; garde-manger; introduction to food service; meat cutting; meat fabrication; patisserie; sanitation; saucier; soup, stock, sauce, and starch production; wines and spirits.

FACILITIES
Demonstration laboratory; food production kitchen; gourmet dining room; learning resource center; lecture room; library; public restaurant; student lounge; 3 teaching kitchens.

STUDENT PROFILE
360 full-time. 144 are under 25 years old; 189 are between 25 and 44 years old; 27 are over 44 years old.

FACULTY
10 total: 10 full-time. 10 are master chefs. Prominent faculty: Chef Philippe Guiet; Chef Christian Favre; Chef Armando Baisas; Chef Hervé Chabert.

PROMINENT ALUMNI AND CURRENT AFFILIATION
Joshua Drache, former chef to Prime Minister; Matthew Dobry, Marriott, Toronto.

SPECIAL PROGRAMS
One-week programs in cuisine and pastry topics of general interest, short workshops in boulangerie, chocolate, sugar work, and creative cakes, introduction to catering.

TYPICAL EXPENSES
Application fee: Can$500. Tuition: Can$7000–$42,000 per 10 weeks to 9 months. Program-related fees include Can$1215 for uniform and equipment; Can$100 for student activities fee.

FINANCIAL AID
In 2006, 2 scholarships were awarded (average award was Can$6000). Program-specific awards include Canadian Federation of Chefs and Cooks Awards (Can$5500), International Association of Culinary Professionals awards (Can$5500), The Culinary Trust. Employment placement assistance is available.

HOUSING
Average off-campus housing cost per month: Can$550.

APPLICATION INFORMATION
Students may begin participation in January, April, June, September, and November. Applications are accepted continuously. In 2006, 375 applied; 360 were accepted. Applicants must submit a formal application, an essay, secondary school transcript.

CONTACT
Peter Baumgart, Sales and Recruitment Coordinator, The Classic Cycle, 453 Laurier Avenue East, Ottawa, ON K1N 6R4, Canada. Telephone: 613-236-2433. Fax: 613-236-2460. E-mail: ottawa@cordonbleu.edu. World Wide Web: http://www.lcbottawa.com.

See color display following page 378.

LIAISON COLLEGE
Culinary Arts

Hamilton, Ontario, Canada

GENERAL INFORMATION
Private, coeducational, culinary institute. Urban campus. Founded in 1996. Accredited by Ontario's Ministry of Education & Training and Apprenticeship Board.

PROGRAM INFORMATION
Offered since 1996. Accredited by Ministry of Colleges and Universities. Program calendar is continuous. 300-hour diploma in cook (advanced). 300-hour diploma in cook (basic). 400-hour diploma in hospitality administration. 80-hour diploma in personal chef.

PROGRAM AFFILIATION
Canadian Association of Food Service Professionals; Canadian Chef Educators; Canadian Federation of Chefs and Cooks; Canadian Restaurant and Food Services Association; Cuisine Canada; Personal Chef Association; Women in Food Industry Management.

AREAS OF STUDY
Baking; buffet catering; controlling costs in food service; convenience cookery; culinary French; culinary skill development; food preparation; food purchasing; food service communication; food service math; garde-manger; international cuisine; introduction to food service; kitchen management; management and human resources; meal planning; menu and facilities design; nutrition; nutrition and food service; patisserie; restaurant opportunities; sanitation; saucier; seafood processing; soup, stock, sauce, and starch production.

Liaison College *(continued)*

FACILITIES
Bake shop; classroom; gourmet dining room; lecture room; teaching kitchen.

STUDENT PROFILE
800 total: 600 full-time; 200 part-time. 300 are under 25 years old; 375 are between 25 and 44 years old; 125 are over 44 years old.

FACULTY
30 total: 20 full-time; 10 part-time. 10 are industry professionals; 8 are master chefs; 22 are culinary-certified teachers. Prominent faculty: Michael Elliott, CCC; Gary Gingras; Steve Hepting; Wanda MacDonald. Faculty-student ratio: 1:15.

PROMINENT ALUMNI AND CURRENT AFFILIATION
Felix Sano, Club Links; Trevor Cadera, Casino Rama; Greg Guthrie, Springwater Golf Club.

SPECIAL PROGRAMS
Culinary competitions, day trips to culinary interest spots, co-op (optional).

TYPICAL EXPENSES
Application fee: Can$100. Tuition: Can$6495 per 300 hours-4 months full-time, Can$6495 per 300 hours-10 months part-time. Program-related fees include Can$500 for utensil/tool kit; Can$245 for uniform; Can$150 for text; Can$70 for fees/dues.

FINANCIAL AID
In 2006, 4 scholarships were awarded (average award was Can$800). Program-specific awards include full-payment discounts, tuition financing OAC. Employment placement assistance is available. Employment opportunities within the program are available.

HOUSING
Average off-campus housing cost per month: Can$500.

APPLICATION INFORMATION
Students may begin participation year-round. Applications are accepted continuously. In 2006, 1400 applied; 600 were accepted. Applicants must interview; submit a formal application, letters of reference; show mature student testing.

CONTACT

Susanne Mikler, Director of Admissions, Culinary Arts, 1047 Main St E, Hamilton, ON L8M IN5, Canada. Telephone: 800-854-0621. Fax: 905-545-1010. E-mail: liaisonhq@liaisoncollege.com. World Wide Web: http://www.liaisoncollege.com.

MALASPINA UNIVERSITY–COLLEGE

Culinary Arts and Professional Baking

Nanaimo, British Columbia, Canada

GENERAL INFORMATION

Public, coeducational, culinary institute. Small-town setting. Founded in 1968.

PROGRAM INFORMATION

Offered since 1968. Accredited by Industry Training Authority (ITA). Program calendar is continuous. 1-year certificate in professional baking. 1-year certificate in culinary arts. 2-year diploma in culinary arts.

PROGRAM AFFILIATION

British Columbia Restaurant and Foodservices Association; Canadian Federation of Chefs and Cooks; Canadian Restaurant Association; Confrerie de la Chaine des Rotisseurs; Slow Food International.

AREAS OF STUDY

Baking; beverage management; buffet catering; confectionery show pieces; controlling costs in food service; convenience cookery; culinary French; culinary skill development; food preparation; food purchasing; food service communication; food service math; garde-manger; international cuisine; kitchen management; meal planning; meat cutting; meat fabrication; menu and facilities design; nutrition; nutrition and food service; patisserie; restaurant opportunities; sanitation; saucier; seafood processing; soup, stock, sauce, and starch production; wines and spirits.

FACILITIES

Bake shop; 2 bakeries; 2 cafeterias; catering service; 4 classrooms; computer laboratory; demonstration laboratory; 2 food production kitchens; gourmet dining room; laboratory; learning resource center; 2 lecture rooms; library; 2 public restaurants; student lounge; 2 teaching kitchens; herb garden.

STUDENT PROFILE

200 total: 140 full-time; 60 part-time.

FACULTY

13 total: 10 full-time; 3 part-time. 3 are industry professionals; 1 is a master baker; 9 are culinary-certified teachers. Prominent faculty: Michael Pelletier, CCC, past Team Canada member; Ken Harper, past Team Canada member; Bill Clay, Baking Team Canada member. Faculty-student ratio: 1:18.

PROMINENT ALUMNI AND CURRENT AFFILIATION

Derek Poivier, Valrohna, Paris; David Wong, Executive Chef, Fairmont, Edmonton/Bocuse D'Or 2008; Iain Rennie, Executive Chef, Westin Bear Mountain.

SPECIAL PROGRAMS

Paid co-op/experiential learning, BC Hot Competition, Salon Culinaire Vancouver and Victoria, Feast of Fields celebration of locally produced food, apprenticeship.

TYPICAL EXPENSES

Application fee: Can$200. Tuition: Can$5000 per year full-time (in district), Can$360 per month part-time. Tuition for international students: Can$15,000 per year. Program-related fee includes Can$900 for books and knives, partial uniform.

FINANCIAL AID

In 2006, 15 scholarships were awarded (average award was Can$250). Program-specific awards include $500 entrance scholarship (essay mapping career). Employment placement assistance is available. Employment opportunities within the program are available.

HOUSING

Coed and apartment-style housing available. Average on-campus housing cost per month: Can$350.

APPLICATION INFORMATION

Students may begin participation in January and August. Applications are accepted continuously. In 2006, 196 applied; 86 were accepted. Applicants must interview; submit a formal application, an essay; complete grade 12 or provincial equivalent; take entrance examination.

CONTACT

Debbie Shore, Department Chair, Culinary Arts and Professional Baking, 900 5th Street, Nanaimo, BC V9R 555, Canada. Telephone: 250-740-6137. Fax: 250-740-6441. E-mail: shored@mala.ca. World Wide Web: http://www.mala.ca/culinary/index.asp.

Mount Saint Vincent University

Business Administration and Tourism and Hospitality Management

Halifax, Nova Scotia, Canada

General Information
Public, coeducational, comprehensive institution. Suburban campus. Founded in 1873.

Program Information
Offered since 1986. Accredited by Canadian Association for Cooperative Education. Program calendar is divided into semesters. 2-year certificate in tourism and hospitality management. 3-year diploma in tourism and hospitality management. 4-year bachelor's degree in tourism and hospitality management.

Program Affiliation
Canadian Food Service Executives Association; Council on Hotel, Restaurant, and Institutional Education; Nova Scotia Restaurant and Food Service Association; Sommelier Guild of Canada; Tourism Industry Association of Canada; Tourism Industry Association of Nova Scotia; Travel and Tourism Research Association.

Areas of Study
Beverage management; controlling costs in food service; culinary skill development; food preparation; food purchasing; food service communication; food service math; international cuisine; introduction to food service; kitchen management; management and human resources; meal planning; menu and facilities design; nutrition and food service; sanitation; wines and spirits.

Facilities
Classroom; computer laboratory; demonstration laboratory; food production kitchen; gourmet dining room; laboratory; learning resource center; lecture room; library; student lounge; teaching kitchen.

Student Profile
84 total: 63 full-time; 21 part-time. 63 are under 25 years old; 21 are between 25 and 44 years old.

Faculty
6 total: 4 full-time; 2 part-time. Prominent faculty: Nancy Chesoworth, BA, BEd, MAEHD, PhD; James Macaulay, BSc, MBA, MPS; Candace Blayney, BA, BEd, MBA. Faculty-student ratio: 1:14.

Prominent Alumni and Current Affiliation
Eric Surette, Sales Manager, Prince George Hotel; Shannon Farris, Director of Operations, Future Inn's Canada.

Special Programs
3 work terms of cooperative education, study tour.

Typical Expenses
Application fee: Can$30. In-state tuition: Can$5050 per academic year full-time (in district), Can$1010 per unit of credit part-time (in district), Can$5550 per academic year full-time (out-of-district), Can$1110 per unit of credit part-time (out-of-district). Tuition for international students: Can$10,845 per academic year full-time, Can$2169 per unit of credit part-time. Program-related fee includes Can$1010–$1110 for work term administration (per term work).

Financial Aid
In 2006, 4 scholarships were awarded (average award was Can$875). Program-specific awards include mandatory work terms. Employment placement assistance is available. Employment opportunities within the program are available.

Housing
Coed, apartment-style, and single-sex housing available. Average on-campus housing cost per month: Can$650. Average off-campus housing cost per month: Can$700.

Application Information
Students may begin participation in January and September. Applications are accepted continuously. In 2006, 92 applied; 49 were accepted. Applicants must submit a formal application.

Contact
Karl Turner, Assistant Registrar, Business Administration and Tourism and Hospitality Management, 166 Bedford Highway, Halifax, NS B3M 2J6, Canada. Telephone: 902-457-6117. Fax: 902-457-6498. E-mail: admissions@msvu.ca. World Wide Web: http://www.msvu.ca.

Niagara College Canada

Niagara Culinary Institute

Niagara-on-the-Lake, Ontario, Canada

General Information
Public, coeducational, two-year college. Small-town setting. Founded in 1967.

Program Information
Program calendar is divided into semesters. 1-year certificate in culinary skills-chef training. 1-year graduate certificate in hospitality and tourism management systems. 1-year graduate certificate in event management. 2-year diploma in hospitality management-hotel and restaurant. 2-year diploma in tourism management-business development. 2-year diploma in culinary management. 4-year bachelor's degree in applied business-hospitality operations.

AREAS OF STUDY

Baking; culinary skill development; kitchen management; patisserie; restaurant opportunities.

FACILITIES

Bake shop; catering service; 3 computer laboratories; demonstration laboratory; food production kitchen; garden; gourmet dining room; learning resource center; 30 lecture rooms; library; public restaurant; 3 teaching kitchens; vineyard; wine laboratory.

STUDENT PROFILE

1000 full-time. 800 are under 25 years old; 150 are between 25 and 44 years old; 50 are over 44 years old.

FACULTY

57 total: 22 full-time; 35 part-time. 12 are industry professionals; 9 are master chefs; 2 are master bakers; 10 are culinary-certified teachers. Prominent faculty: Peter Blakeman, MBA, CCC; Mark Picone, CCC; Michael Olson; Paul Willie, MBA, RFM, CSFM, CHA, CHAE, CMA.

SPECIAL PROGRAMS

4-month apprenticeship programs (cook 1 & 2, baker 1 & 2).

TYPICAL EXPENSES

Tuition: Can$3400–$5500 per 8 months (dependent on program). Tuition for international students: Can$10,000 per 8 months.

HOUSING

Coed housing available.

APPLICATION INFORMATION

Students may begin participation in January and September. Application deadline for fall is February 1. Application deadline for winter is October 1. Applicants must submit a formal application.

CONTACT

Al Vaughan, Registrar, Niagara Culinary Institute, 300 Woodlawn Road, Welland, ON L3C 7L3, Canada. Telephone: 905-641-2252 Ext. 7558. E-mail: avaughan@ niagarac.on.ca. World Wide Web: http://www.niagarac. on.ca/study/programs/fulltime/mmc0435/career.html.

NORTHERN ALBERTA INSTITUTE OF TECHNOLOGY

School of Hospitality and Culinary Arts

Edmonton, Alberta, Canada

GENERAL INFORMATION

Public, coeducational, two-year college. Urban campus. Founded in 1963. Accredited by Advanced Education and Technology.

PROGRAM INFORMATION

Offered since 1965. Program calendar is divided into semesters. 1-semester certificate in retail meat cutting. 1-year certificate in hospitality management. 1-year certificate in baking. 1-year certificate in culinary arts. 2-year diploma in hospitality management. 2-year diploma in culinary arts. 3-year journeyman's certificate in cooking or baking.

PROGRAM AFFILIATION

American Institute of Baking; Canadian Culinary Federation; Confrerie de la Chaine des Rotisseurs; Council on Hotel, Restaurant, and Institutional Education; Cuisine Canada; International Association of Culinary Professionals; International Sommelier Guild; International Wine & Food Society; The Bread Bakers Guild of America.

AREAS OF STUDY

Baking; beverage management; buffet catering; confectionery show pieces; controlling costs in food service; convenience cookery; culinary French; culinary skill development; food preparation; food purchasing; food service communication; food service math; garde-manger; gastronomy; international cuisine; introduction to food service; kitchen management; management and human resources; meat cutting; meat fabrication; menu and facilities design; nutrition; patisserie; sanitation; saucier; seafood processing; soup, stock, sauce, and starch production; wines and spirits.

FACILITIES

Bake shop; bakery; 2 cafeterias; catering service; 3 classrooms; 2 computer laboratories; demonstration laboratory; food production kitchen; gourmet dining room; 2 learning resource centers; lecture room; library; public restaurant; snack shop; 3 student lounges; 10 teaching kitchens; mixology laboratory.

STUDENT PROFILE

600 total: 380 full-time; 220 part-time. 460 are under 25 years old; 110 are between 25 and 44 years old; 30 are over 44 years old.

Northern Alberta Institute of Technology *(continued)*

FACULTY
33 total: 30 full-time; 3 part-time. 3 are industry professionals; 5 are master chefs; 5 are master bakers; 20 are culinary-certified teachers. Prominent faculty: Perry Michetti, CCC; Mike Gobin, CCC; Mike Maione, CCC; Alan Domonceaux, CBS. Faculty-student ratio: 1:14.

PROMINENT ALUMNI AND CURRENT AFFILIATION
Shon Oberowsky, Characters Restaurant, Edmonton; Corbin Tomaszeski, Host, Food Network Canada; Brad Horen, Catch Restaurant, Calgary, AB.

SPECIAL PROGRAMS
Culinary Team for competitions, study tours, international student exchange.

TYPICAL EXPENSES
Application fee: Can$40. Tuition: Can$3300 per 2 semesters full-time (in district), Can$8 per instructional hour (tuition differs for night and weekend courses) part-time. Tuition for international students: Can$10,000 per 2 semesters. Program-related fees include Can$250–Can$500 for student supplies; Can$350 for knives; Can$100 for lab fee (per semester).

FINANCIAL AID
In 2006, 20–25 scholarships were awarded (average award was Can$750). Employment placement assistance is available. Employment opportunities within the program are available.

HOUSING
Average off-campus housing cost per month: Can$600.

APPLICATION INFORMATION
Students may begin participation in January and September. Applications are accepted continuously. In 2006, 600 applied; 360 were accepted. Applicants must submit a formal application, an essay, transcripts from secondary-level school.

CONTACT
Perry Michetti, Manager, School of Hospitality and Culinary Arts, 11762-106 Street, Edmonton, AB T5G 2R1, Canada. Telephone: 780-471-8679. Fax: 780-471-8914. E-mail: perrym@nait.ca. World Wide Web: http://www.nait.ca/schoolofhospitality.

NORTHWEST CULINARY ACADEMY OF VANCOUVER

Vancouver, British Columbia, Canada

GENERAL INFORMATION
Private, coeducational, culinary institute. Urban campus. Founded in 2003. Accredited by Private Career Training Institutions Agency.

PROGRAM INFORMATION
Offered since 2003. Accredited by Private Career Training Institutions Agency of BC "PCTIA". Program calendar is continuous. 12—15 week certificate in practicum (work experience). 15-week diploma in professional pastry and bread. 15-week diploma in professional culinary. 42-week diploma in professional culinary and pastry/bread.

PROGRAM AFFILIATION
British Columbia Chefs' Association; British Columbia Restaurant and Foodservices Association.

AREAS OF STUDY
Baking; buffet catering; confectionery show pieces; controlling costs in food service; culinary French; culinary skill development; food preparation; food service math; garde-manger; international cuisine; kitchen management; meal planning; meat cutting; menu and facilities design; nutrition; nutrition and food service; patisserie; sanitation; saucier; seafood processing; soup, stock, sauce, and starch production; wines and spirits.

FACILITIES
Bake shop; classroom; demonstration laboratory; food production kitchen; learning resource center; library; teaching kitchen; chef's demo station; kitchen lab; chef's table and pastry shop.

STUDENT PROFILE
140 full-time. 63 are under 25 years old; 73 are between 25 and 44 years old; 4 are over 44 years old.

FACULTY
5 total: 4 full-time; 1 part-time. 3 are industry professionals; 3 are culinary-certified teachers; 1 is a pastry chef instructor. Prominent faculty: Tony Minichiello; Christophe Kwiatkowsky; Ian Lai; Timothy Muehlbauer. Faculty-student ratio: 1:12.

PROMINENT ALUMNI AND CURRENT AFFILIATION
Dan Creyke, C Restaurant; Alessandro Vianello, Fairmont Hotel; Kimberley Slobodian.

SPECIAL PROGRAMS
Culinary competitions, work experience in catering setting, edible schoolyard project.

TYPICAL EXPENSES
Application fee: Can$50–$100. Tuition: Can$6950 per culinary diploma; $6950 for pastry/bread diploma; $975 for practicum; $13,900 for all three programs. Program-related fees include Can$400–$495 for knife kit; Can$400 for chef's uniform; Can$125 for text book culinary; Can$135 for pastry toolkit (supplement); Can$132 for text book-pastry.

FINANCIAL AID
In 2006, 2 scholarships were awarded (average award was Can$2500). Employment placement assistance is available.

HOUSING
Average off-campus housing cost per month: Can$700.

APPLICATION INFORMATION
Students may begin participation in January, April, and September. Applications are accepted continuously. Applicants must interview; submit a formal application, letters of reference, an essay; have English fluency, good health (confirmed by doctor).

CONTACT
Tony Minichiello or Christophe Kwiatkowsky, Chef Instructors, Owners, 2725 Main Street, Vancouver, BC V5T 3E9, Canada. Telephone: 866-876-2433. Fax: 604-876-7023. E-mail: chefs@nwcav.com. World Wide Web: http://www.nwcav.com/.

PACIFIC INSTITUTE OF CULINARY ARTS

Culinary Arts and Baking and Pastry Arts

Vancouver, British Columbia, Canada

GENERAL INFORMATION
Private, coeducational, culinary institute. Urban campus. Founded in 1996.

PROGRAM INFORMATION
Offered since 1996. Accredited by Private Career Training Institutions Agency of British Columbia. Program calendar is divided into quarters. Certificate in restaurant management. 6-month diploma in baking and pastry arts. 6-month diploma in culinary arts.

Aspiring Chefs
You've been thinking about it...Now's the time...Follow your passion!

- Chef designed, owned & instructed
- Open Kitchen/Classroom layout
- European style Island cooking stations
- Student based teaching
- Certified Instructors
- Conveniently located in beautiful Vancouver, BC

- One Year Program
- 15 week Professional Culinary
- 15 week Advanced Pastry & Bread Making
- 15 week Practicum Program
- Start in Jan., Apr. or Sept.
- French classics & Contemporary Influences
- Emphasis placed on developing hands-on skills

2725 Main Street, Vancouver, BC
Canada, V5T 3E9
T: 604.876.7653
or: 1.866.876.2433
E: info@nwcav.com
www.nwcav.com

NORTHWEST CULINARY ACADEMY OF VANCOUVER

Pacific Institute of Culinary Arts *(continued)*

PROGRAM AFFILIATION

British Columbia Chefs' Association; British Columbia Restaurant and Foodservices Association; International Association of Culinary Professionals; National Career Colleges Association.

AREAS OF STUDY

Baking; buffet catering; confectionery show pieces; culinary French; food preparation; garde-manger; international cuisine; introduction to food service; meal planning; nutrition; patisserie; restaurant opportunities; sanitation; saucier; soup, stock, sauce, and starch production; wines and spirits.

FACILITIES

Bake shop; catering service; coffee shop; 4 food production kitchens; gourmet dining room; 3 lecture rooms; public restaurant; 4 teaching kitchens; chocolate studio; cake-decorating studio.

STUDENT PROFILE

175 full-time. 81 are under 25 years old; 77 are between 25 and 44 years old; 17 are over 44 years old.

FACULTY

12 total: 12 full-time. 3 are industry professionals; 1 is a master baker; 8 are culinary-certified teachers. Prominent faculty: Julian Bond, Executive Chef; Kurt Ebert, Master Baker.

PROMINENT ALUMNI AND CURRENT AFFILIATION

Mark Perrier, Cin Cin; James Schenk, Destino; Cheryl Wakerhauser, Pix Patisserie.

SPECIAL PROGRAMS

Industry field days at local farms, fisheries, etc., guest chef speakers, culinary competitions.

TYPICAL EXPENSES

Application fee: Can$100. Tuition: Can$12,875 per diploma. Program-related fees include Can$525 for uniforms and shoes; Can$150 for textbooks; Can$500–$900 for knives.

FINANCIAL AID

In 2006, 3 scholarships were awarded (average award was Can$500). Employment placement assistance is available. Employment opportunities within the program are available.

HOUSING

Average off-campus housing cost per month: Can$600.

APPLICATION INFORMATION
Students may begin participation in January, April, June, and September. Applications are accepted continuously. In 2006, 225 applied; 200 were accepted. Applicants must interview; submit a formal application, letters of reference, and an essay.

CONTACT
Sue Singer, President, Admissions Director, Culinary Arts and Baking and Pastry Arts, 1505 West 2nd Avenue, Vancouver, BC V6H 3Y4, Canada. Telephone: 800-416-4040. Fax: 604-734-4408. E-mail: info@picachef.com. World Wide Web: http://www.picachef.com.

ST. CLAIR COLLEGE OF APPLIED ARTS AND TECHNOLOGY

Hospitality

Windsor, Ontario, Canada

GENERAL INFORMATION
Public, coeducational, two-year college. Urban campus. Founded in 1967.

PROGRAM INFORMATION
Offered since 1994. Program calendar is divided into semesters. 1-year certificate in chef training. 2-year diploma in hotel and restaurant management. 2-year diploma in culinary management.

PROGRAM AFFILIATION
Council on Hotel, Restaurant, and Institutional Education; Ontario Restaurant, Hotel & Motel Association; Ontario Tourism Education Corporation; Windsor/Essex County Tourism and Convention Bureau.

AREAS OF STUDY
Baking; beverage management; buffet catering; confectionery show pieces; controlling costs in food service; culinary French; culinary skill development; customer service; food preparation; food purchasing; food service communication; food service math; garde-manger; hospitality marketing; international cuisine; introduction to food service; kitchen management; management and human resources; meal planning; menu and facilities design; nutrition; nutrition and food service; patisserie; restaurant opportunities; sanitation; saucier; soup, stock, sauce, and starch production; wines and spirits.

FACILITIES
Cafeteria; catering service; 2 classrooms; coffee shop; 4 computer laboratories; 2 demonstration laboratories; 2 food production kitchens; 2 gardens; gourmet dining room; learning resource center; 2 lecture rooms; library; public restaurant; 2 snack shops; student lounge; 2 teaching kitchens.

TYPICAL STUDENT PROFILE
265 total: 220 full-time; 45 part-time. 172 are under 25 years old; 53 are between 25 and 44 years old; 40 are over 44 years old.

SPECIAL PROGRAMS
Guest lecture and tours of local casinos, banquet facilities, and wineries, domestic internship opportunity, regional culinary competition (annual).

FINANCIAL AID
Program-specific awards include South Western Ontario Vintners Association bursary. Employment placement assistance is available. Employment opportunities within the program are available.

HOUSING
Apartment-style housing available.

APPLICATION INFORMATION
Students may begin participation in September. Application deadline for fall is March 1. Applicants must submit a formal application.

CONTACT
Director of Admissions, Hospitality, 2000 Talbot Road West, Windsor, ON N9A 6S4, Canada. Telephone: 519-972-2727 Ext. 4140. Fax: 519-972-2748. World Wide Web: http://www.stclaircollege.ca.

SAIT-POLYTECHNIC SCHOOL OF HOSPITALITY AND TOURISM

Professional Cooking, Baking and Pastry Arts, Hospitality Management, Travel and Tourism, Meat Operations and Management

Calgary, Alberta, Canada

GENERAL INFORMATION
Public, coeducational, two-year college. Urban campus. Founded in 1916.

PROGRAM INFORMATION
Offered since 1948. Accredited by Alberta Advanced Education. Program calendar is divided into semesters. 2-year diploma in travel and tourism. 2-year diploma in

SAIT-Polytechnic School of Hospitality and Tourism
(continued)

hospitality management. 2-year diploma in baking and pastry arts. 56-week diploma in professional cooking. 6-month certificate in meat operations and management.

PROGRAM AFFILIATION
Canadian Federation of Chefs and Cooks; Canadian Restaurant Association; Confrerie de la Chaine des Rotisseurs; Council on Hotel, Restaurant, and Institutional Education; World Association of Chefs and Cooks.

AREAS OF STUDY
Baking; beverage management; confectionery show pieces; controlling costs in food service; culinary French; culinary skill development; food preparation; food purchasing; food service communication; food service math; garde-manger; ice carving/fat sculpture; international cuisine; introduction to food service; kitchen management; management and human resources; meal planning; meat cutting; meat fabrication; menu and facilities design; nutrition; nutrition and food service; patisserie; restaurant opportunities; sanitation; saucier; seafood processing; soup, stock, sauce, and starch production; wines and spirits.

FACILITIES
2 bakeries; 3 cafeterias; catering service; 5 classrooms; 2 coffee shops; 2 computer laboratories; 3 demonstration laboratories; 4 food production kitchens; gourmet dining room; 2 laboratories; learning resource center; 3 lecture rooms; library; 2 public restaurants; 6 snack shops; student lounge; 2 teaching kitchens; test kitchen; bakery merchandizing classroom; retail shop.

STUDENT PROFILE
205 full-time. 123 are under 25 years old; 62 are between 25 and 44 years old; 20 are over 44 years old.

FACULTY
50 total: 45 full-time; 5 part-time. 20 are industry professionals; 1 is a master chef; 1 is a master baker; 25 are culinary-certified teachers. Prominent faculty: Simon Donn; Thierry Meret; Andrew Hewson; Andreas Schwarzer. Faculty-student ratio: 1:15.

PROMINENT ALUMNI AND CURRENT AFFILIATION
Paul Ragolski, The Rouge; Ron Sadowski, Bevely Hills Hotel.

SPECIAL PROGRAMS
5-day study tours to food processing and manufacturing sites, 1-month exchange programs in Scotland, Austria, Australia, 5-day study tour to selected wine areas and 14-day study tour to Thailand, Australia, and Napa Valley, France, Spain, Canada's Niagara Region, Chile.

TYPICAL EXPENSES
Application fee: Can$35. Tuition: Can$4863 per year one. Program-related fees include Can$350 for lab fee, uniforms, and food supplies (per semester); Can$900 for books and equipment.

FINANCIAL AID
In 2006, 46 scholarships were awarded (average award was Can$400); 45 loans were granted. Program-specific awards include tuition paid-guaranteed employment in industry meat operations and management. Employment placement assistance is available. Employment opportunities within the program are available.

HOUSING
Apartment-style housing available. Average on-campus housing cost per month: Can$750. Average off-campus housing cost per month: Can$650.

APPLICATION INFORMATION
Students may begin participation in January and September. Applications are accepted continuously. In 2006, 350 applied; 221 were accepted. Applicants must submit a formal application and academic transcripts.

CONTACT
June MacKinnon, Marketing Specialist, Professional Cooking, Baking and Pastry Arts, Hospitality Management, Travel and Tourism, Meat Operations and Management, 1301-16 Avenue NW, Calgary, AB T2M 0L4, Canada. Telephone: 403-210-4015. Fax: 403-284-7034. E-mail: june.mackinnon@sait.ca. World Wide Web: http://www.sait.ca/hospitalityandtourism.

STRATFORD CHEFS SCHOOL
Stratford, Ontario, Canada

GENERAL INFORMATION
Private, coeducational, culinary institute. Small-town setting. Founded in 1983. Accredited by Ontario Ministry of Education and Training.

PROGRAM INFORMATION
Offered since 1983. Accredited by Ontario Ministry of Training Colleges and Universities-Apprenticeship Branch. Program calendar is divided into trimesters. 2-year diploma in professional cookery.

PROGRAM AFFILIATION
Canadian Restaurant and Food Services Association; Ontario Hostelry Association; Slow Food International; Women's Culinary Network.

AREAS OF STUDY

Baking; controlling costs in food service; culinary French; culinary skill development; food preparation; food purchasing; food service communication; food service math; garde-manger; international cuisine; introduction to food service; kitchen management; management and human resources; meal planning; meat cutting; menu and facilities design; nutrition; nutrition and food service; patisserie; restaurant opportunities; sanitation; saucier; seafood processing; soup, stock, sauce, and starch production; wines and spirits.

FACILITIES

3 classrooms; computer laboratory; 3 demonstration laboratories; 3 food production kitchens; gourmet dining room; lecture room; library; 3 teaching kitchens.

STUDENT PROFILE

70 full-time. 20 are under 25 years old; 48 are between 25 and 44 years old; 2 are over 44 years old.

FACULTY

19 total: 16 full-time; 3 part-time. 10 are industry professionals; 3 are master chefs; 1 is a master baker; 4 are culinary-certified teachers. Prominent faculty: Neil Baxter, Master of Cookery; Bryan Steele; James Morris; Eleanor Kane. Faculty-student ratio: 1:12 practical; 1:30 theory.

PROMINENT ALUMNI AND CURRENT AFFILIATION

Winlai Wong, Morsoon, Toronto; Paul Finkelstein; Ruth Klansen, Monforte Cheese Company.

SPECIAL PROGRAMS

Apprenticeship program, international guest chefs.

TYPICAL EXPENSES

Application fee: Can$45. Tuition: Can$12,550 per 2–year apprenticeship. Tuition for international students: Can$25,000 per non-apprenticeship diploma. Program-related fees include Can$500 for books; Can$500 for knives; Can$200 for kitchen whites.

FINANCIAL AID

In 2006, 9 scholarships were awarded (average award was Can$625). Employment placement assistance is available.

APPLICATION INFORMATION

Students may begin participation in November. Applications are accepted continuously. In 2006, 123 applied; 36 were accepted. Applicants must interview; submit a formal application, an essay; have a kitchen interview, letters of reference for students who cannot attend personal interview.

CONTACT

Jennifer Laurie, Recruitment and Admissions Officer, 68 Nilest, Stratford, ON N5A 4C5, Canada. Telephone: 519-271-1414. Fax: 519-271-5679. E-mail: jlaurie@ stratfordchef.on.ca. World Wide Web: http://www. stratfordchef.on.ca.

UNIVERSITY OF GUELPH

School of Hospitality and Tourism Management

Guelph, Ontario, Canada

GENERAL INFORMATION

Public, coeducational, university. Suburban campus. Founded in 1964. Accredited by Association of Universities and Colleges of Canada.

PROGRAM INFORMATION

Offered since 1969. Program calendar is divided into trimesters. 1-year master of business administration in hospitality and tourism. 4-year bachelor of commerce in hotel and food administration.

PROGRAM AFFILIATION

American Dietetic Association; Canadian Food Service Executives Association; Council on Hotel, Restaurant, and Institutional Education.

AREAS OF STUDY

Foodservice management; hotel management; tourism management.

FACILITIES

6 cafeterias; catering service; coffee shop; 4 computer laboratories; 2 demonstration laboratories; food production kitchen; gourmet dining room; 2 laboratories; learning resource center; library; public restaurant; snack shop; student lounge; teaching kitchen.

STUDENT PROFILE

650 total: 600 full-time; 50 part-time. 550 are under 25 years old; 100 are between 25 and 44 years old.

FACULTY

24 total: 20 full-time; 4 part-time. Prominent faculty: Stephen Lynch; Don MacLaurin; Jim Pickworth. Faculty-student ratio: 1:25.

PROMINENT ALUMNI AND CURRENT AFFILIATION

Darcy Van Wyck, Hilton Hotels, London, England; Bruce McAdams, Oliver Bonacini Restaurants, Toronto.

SPECIAL PROGRAMS

Fall study abroad semester in France, semester exchange programs in Mexico, England, and Australia, Austria, Hong Kong, Finland, co-operative education program in Hotel and Food Administration.

University of Guelph *(continued)*

TYPICAL EXPENSES

Application fee: Can$80. Tuition: Can$3013.80 per semester full-time, Can$852.66 per 0.5 credit part-time. Tuition for international students: Can$9283.80 per semester full-time, Can$2742.66 per 0.5 credit part-time. Program-related fees include Can$50 for beverage management lab supplies; Can$25 for chef jacket.

FINANCIAL AID

In 2006, 35 scholarships were awarded (average award was Can$900). Employment placement assistance is available. Employment opportunities within the program are available.

HOUSING

Coed, apartment-style, and single-sex housing available. Average on-campus housing cost per month: Can$535. Average off-campus housing cost per month: Can$350.

APPLICATION INFORMATION

Students may begin participation in September. Application deadline for fall is April 1. In 2006, 800 applied; 170 were accepted. Applicants must submit a formal application and background information sheet describing previous hospitality-related work experience and reasons for applying.

CONTACT

Valerie Allen, Academic Advisor, School of Hospitality and Tourism Management, 50 Stone Road East, Guelph, ON W1G 2WI, Canada. Telephone: 519-824-4120. Fax: 519-823-5512. E-mail: vallen@uoguelph.ca. World Wide Web: http://www.htm.uoguelph.ca.

UNIVERSITY OF NEW BRUNSWICK, SAINT JOHN CAMPUS

Faculty of Business, Applied Management (Hospitality and Tourism)

Saint John, New Brunswick, Canada

GENERAL INFORMATION

Public, coeducational, university. Suburban campus. Founded in 1964.

PROGRAM INFORMATION

Offered since 1998. Program calendar is divided into semesters, Canadian standard year. 4-year bachelor's degree in hospitality and tourism.

PROGRAM AFFILIATION

Council on Hotel, Restaurant, and Institutional Education; Travel and Tourism Research Association.

AREAS OF STUDY

Culinary skill development; culinary tourism; international tourism; travel and tourism.

FACILITIES

Cafeteria; 26 classrooms; coffee shop; 6 computer laboratories; learning resource center; 10 lecture rooms; library; 3 student lounges.

STUDENT PROFILE

57 total: 50 full-time; 7 part-time. 32 are under 25 years old; 25 are between 25 and 44 years old.

FACULTY

30 total: 20 full-time; 10 part-time. 13 are industry professionals. Prominent faculty: Lee Jolliffe, PhD; R. Keith Dewar, PhD.

PROMINENT ALUMNI AND CURRENT AFFILIATION

Jie "Louise" Zhang, Delta Canmore Alberta; Sophia Martin, Delta Saint John, NB.

SPECIAL PROGRAMS

Study abroad, optional co-op program (paid), Program is articulated with New Brunswick Community College. Culinary training is completed at New Brunswick Community College while other courses are completed on-site.

TYPICAL EXPENSES

Application fee: Can$45. Tuition: Can$5485 per 2 semesters full-time (in district), Can$548 per 3-credit course part-time. Tuition for international students: Can$11,098 per 2 semesters full-time, Can$1109 per 3 credit course part-time. Program-related fees include Can$730 for co-op administration fee (per year), and professional development seminars; Can$50 for technology fee; Can$110 for student representative council fee; Can$30 for media fees; Can$175 for facilities improvement fee.

FINANCIAL AID

In 2006, 7 scholarships were awarded (average award was Can$1000). Program-specific awards include on-campus student work grants. Employment placement assistance is available. Employment opportunities within the program are available.

HOUSING

Coed and apartment-style housing available. Average on-campus housing cost per month: Can$600. Average off-campus housing cost per month: Can$400.

APPLICATION INFORMATION

Students may begin participation in January, May, and September. Applications are accepted continuously. In 2006, 63 applied; 41 were accepted. Applicants must submit a formal application, transcripts, course outlines (in some cases).

CONTACT
Registrar's Office, Faculty of Business, Applied Management (Hospitality and Tourism), University of New Brunswick, Saint John, PO Box 5050, Saint John, NB E2L 4L5, Canada. Telephone: 506-648-5670. Fax: 506-648-5691. E-mail: sjreg@unbsj.ca. World Wide Web: http://www.unbsj.ca/business.

■ I N T E R N A T I O N A L ■

AUSTRALIA

LE CORDON BLEU AUSTRALIA

Regency Park, SA, Australia

GENERAL INFORMATION
Private, coeducational, culinary institute. Suburban campus. Founded in 1998.

PROGRAM INFORMATION
Offered since 1998. Program calendar is divided into semesters. 18-month master's degree in gastronomy. 2-year advanced diploma in restaurant and catering management. 2-year diploma in professional culinary management. 2-year master's degree in International hospitality and restaurant management. Bachelor's degree in international hotel management. 2.5-year bachelor's degree in international restaurant management. 9-month certificate in commercial cooking. 9-month certificate in pastry.

PROGRAM AFFILIATION
American Culinary Federation; American Institute of Wine & Food; Confrerie de la Chaine des Rotisseurs; Council on Hotel, Restaurant, and Institutional Education; International Association of Culinary Professionals; James Beard Foundation, Inc.

AREAS OF STUDY
Accounting; beverage management; business plan development; controlling costs in food service; culinary skill development; finance; food and wine philosophy; food preparation; food purchasing; human resources; information technology; international cuisine; kitchen management; legal aspects of food service management; management and human resources; marketing; menu and facilities design; nutrition; restaurant opportunities; sanitation; soup, stock, sauce, and starch production; wines and spirits.

FACILITIES
Bakery; cafeteria; classroom; coffee shop; computer laboratory; demonstration laboratory; garden; gourmet dining room; learning resource center; lecture room; library; public restaurant; student lounge; auditorium; butchery; winery; food science laboratory.

STUDENT PROFILE
520 total: 500 full-time; 20 part-time.

FACULTY
40 total: 40 full-time. 40 are industry professionals. Prominent faculty: Paul Reynolds; Stan Szczypiorski; Brian Lawes. Faculty-student ratio: 1:15.

SPECIAL PROGRAMS
1-year paid internship for bachelor and advanced diploma programs, 6-month paid internship for diploma program.

TYPICAL EXPENSES
Application fee: A$500. Tuition: A$59,400 per 2–5 years for bachelor; A$39,600 for 2 years for advanced diploma. Program-related fee includes A$1980 for professional culinary tool kit.

FINANCIAL AID
In 2006, 25 scholarships were awarded (average award was A$10,000). Program-specific awards include required paid internship within Australia (up to 1 year). Employment opportunities within the program are available.

HOUSING
Apartment-style housing available. Average on-campus housing cost per month: A$950. Average off-campus housing cost per month: A$800.

APPLICATION INFORMATION
Students may begin participation in January and July. Application deadline for January/February intake is November 30. Application deadline for July intake is May 31. Applicants must submit a formal application, letters of reference, 2 passport photos, evidence of English fluency (if English not first language), evidence of satisfactory completion of year 12 or equivalent.

CONTACT
Nina Lucas, Manager, Client Services, Days Road, Regency Park, South Australia, Australia. Telephone: 61-8-83463700. Fax: 61-8-83463755. E-mail: australia@ cordonbleu.edu. World Wide Web: http://www. lecordonbleu.com.au.
See color display following page 378.

LE CORDON BLEU SYDNEY CULINARY ARTS INSTITUTE

Sydney, Australia

GENERAL INFORMATION
Private, coeducational, culinary institute. Suburban campus. Founded in 1996.

PROGRAM INFORMATION
Offered since 1996. Accredited by Training and Skills Commission South Australia. Program calendar is divided into quarters. 10-week certificate 1 in basic cuisine. 10-week certificate 1 in basic patisserie. 2-year diploma in professional culinary management. 22-week certificate II in intermediate cuisine. 22-week certificate II in intermediate patisserie. 36-week certificate lll in superior patisserie. 36-week certificate lll in superior cuisine.

PROGRAM AFFILIATION
Council on Hotel, Restaurant, and Institutional Education; International Association of Culinary Professionals; James Beard Foundation, Inc.

AREAS OF STUDY
Australian cuisine; baking; buffet catering; confectionery show pieces; controlling costs in food service; culinary French; culinary skill development; food preparation; food purchasing; food service math; French cuisine; garde-manger; international cuisine; kitchen management; management and human resources; meal planning; meat cutting; menu and facilities design; nutrition and food service; patisserie; sanitation; saucier; seafood processing; soup, stock, sauce, and starch production.

FACILITIES
Cafeteria; classroom; demonstration laboratory; food production kitchen; garden; gourmet dining room; learning resource center; lecture room; library; public restaurant; snack shop; student lounge; teaching kitchen.

STUDENT PROFILE
600 full-time. 350 are under 25 years old; 200 are between 25 and 44 years old; 50 are over 44 years old.

FACULTY
15 total: 15 full-time. 8 are industry professionals; 10 are master chefs; 6 are master bakers; 12 are culinary-certified teachers. Prominent faculty: Lynley Houghton; Patrick Harris; Herve Boutin. Faculty-student ratio: 1:12.

SPECIAL PROGRAMS
Post graduate opportunities through Le Cordon Bleu in Adelaide, opportunity to mix and match course components in different world-wide locations.

TYPICAL EXPENSES
Application fee: A$500. Tuition: A$7500–A$9500 per 10 weeks per certificates level course. Program-related fee includes A$1980 for uniforms and equipment tool kit.

APPLICATION INFORMATION
Students may begin participation in January, April, July, and October. Applications are accepted continuously. In 2006, 1000 applied; 600 were accepted. Applicants must submit a formal application, proof of English language proficiency (if English not first language), evidence of completion of year 11 in high school.

CONTACT
Admissions Manager, Culinary Arts Program, Days Road, Regency Park, Australia. Telephone: 61-8-83463700. Fax: 61-8- 883463755. E-mail: australia@cordonbleu.edu. World Wide Web: http://www.lecordonbleu.com.au.

See color display following page 378.

FINLAND

HAAGA-HELIA UNIVERSITY OF APPLIED SCIENCES

Hotel, Restaurant, and Tourism Management

Helsinki, Finland

GENERAL INFORMATION
Public, coeducational institution. Suburban campus. Founded in 1969.

PROGRAM INFORMATION
Offered since 1993. Accredited by Council on Hotel, Restaurant and Institutional Education, Leading Hotel Schools of the World. Program calendar is divided into terms. 1.5-year master's degree in tourism (in English). 1.5-year master's degree in hotel, restaurant and tourism management (in Finnish). 3.5-year bachelor's degree in food production management (in Finnish). 3.5-year bachelor's degree in hotel and restaurant management (in Finnish). 3.5-year bachelor's degree in tourism management (in Finnish). 3.5-year bachelor's degree in experience and wellness management (in English). 3.5-year bachelor's degree in hotel, restaurant, and tourism management (in English).

PROGRAM AFFILIATION
Council on Hotel, Restaurant, and Institutional Education; Hotel and Catering International Management Association; International Association of Hotel School; World Tourism Organization.

AREAS OF STUDY

Beverage management; controlling costs in food service; culinary French; food preparation; food purchasing; food service communication; food service math; international cuisine; introduction to food service; kitchen management; management and human resources; meal planning; menu and facilities design; nutrition; nutrition and food service; restaurant opportunities; sanitation; wines and spirits.

FACILITIES

Cafeteria; 25 classrooms; 3 computer laboratories; demonstration laboratory; food production kitchen; gourmet dining room; learning resource center; 2 lecture rooms; library; public restaurant; student lounge; teaching kitchen; wine cellar; 2 demonstration hotel rooms.

STUDENT PROFILE

1,300 total: 900 full-time; 400 part-time. 900 are under 25 years old; 350 are between 25 and 44 years old; 50 are over 44 years old.

FACULTY

105 total: 45 full-time; 60 part-time. 40 are industry professionals; 5 are culinary-certified teachers; 1 is a certified hospitality educator. Prominent faculty: Mr. Mario Ascencas, PhD; Mrs. Outi Westman; Ms. Pirkko Salo, MBA, CHE; Mrs. Pirjo Nuotio. Faculty-student ratio: 1:30.

PROMINENT ALUMNI AND CURRENT AFFILIATION

Rabbe Gronblom, Kotipizza Chain and R6-Lines; Sebastian Björksen, Wrong Noodle Bar; Mikko Heinnen, Palace-Kamp Group.

SPECIAL PROGRAMS

Specialization modules abroad (e.g. Aviation Management in Germany), paid internships in Finland and abroad, exchange semester abroad.

TYPICAL EXPENSES

Application fee: $90. Tuition: No tuition for Finnish students or foreigners. Program-related fees include $500 for books and study material; $150 for uniforms (apron, coat, pants).

FINANCIAL AID

Employment placement assistance is available. Employment opportunities within the program are available.

HOUSING

Single-sex housing available. Average on-campus housing cost per month: $400. Average off-campus housing cost per month: $500.

APPLICATION INFORMATION

Students may begin participation in August. Application deadline for spring is January 7. In 2006, 3000 applied; 260 were accepted. Applicants must submit a formal application, an essay, written exam, and TOEFL scores.

CONTACT

Ms. Pirkko Salo, Director, Hotel, Restaurant, and Tourism Management, PO Box 8, Helsinki, Finland. Telephone: 358-9-22966326. E-mail: pirkko.salo@haaga-helia.fi. World Wide Web: http://www.haaga-helia.fi.

FRANCE

ECOLE DES ARTS CULINAIRES ET DE L'HÔTELLERIE DE LYON

Hotel, Restaurant and Culinary Arts

Lyon-Ecully, Cedex, France

GENERAL INFORMATION

Private, coeducational, culinary institute. Small-town setting. Founded in 1990.

PROGRAM INFORMATION

Offered since 1990. Program calendar is divided into semesters. 2.5- to 5-year diploma in management and culinary arts. 3-month certificate in cuisine and culture. 3-year bachelor's degree in culinary arts. 3-year bachelor's degree in hotel and restaurant management. 3-year diploma in hotel management. 5-year master's degree in administration in hotel and foodservice.

PROGRAM AFFILIATION

Council on Hotel, Restaurant, and Institutional Education.

AREAS OF STUDY

Baking; beverage management; buffet catering; confectionery show pieces; controlling costs in food service; culinary French; culinary skill development; food preparation; food purchasing; food service math; garde-manger; introduction to food service; kitchen management; management and human resources; meal planning; meat cutting; meat fabrication; menu and facilities design; nutrition and food service; patisserie; sanitation; saucier; soup, stock, sauce, and starch production; wines and spirits.

Ecole des Arts Culinaires et de l'Hôtellerie de Lyon
(continued)

FACILITIES

Bakery; cafeteria; catering service; 11 classrooms; computer laboratory; 6 demonstration laboratories; 2 food production kitchens; garden; gourmet dining room; library; public restaurant; student lounge; teaching kitchen; vineyard.

STUDENT PROFILE

240 full-time. 210 are under 25 years old; 30 are between 25 and 44 years old.

FACULTY

70 total: 30 full-time; 40 part-time. 5 are industry professionals; 4 are master chefs; 1 is a master baker; 10 are culinary-certified teachers; 2 are patisserie. Prominent faculty: Alain Le Cossec, MOF; Elaine Boissy, MOF. Faculty-student ratio: 1:3.

SPECIAL PROGRAMS

Visits to area surrounding Lyons, 4-month internship each year France or abroad.

TYPICAL EXPENSES

Application fee: 950 euros. Tuition: 9600 euros per year. Program-related fee includes 1100 euros for uniforms and set of knives, 1st year only.

FINANCIAL AID

Employment placement assistance is available. Employment opportunities within the program are available.

HOUSING

Coed housing available. Average on-campus housing cost per month: 360 euros. Average off-campus housing cost per month: 500 euros.

APPLICATION INFORMATION

Students may begin participation in January, April, May, and October. Applications are accepted continuously. In 2006, 300 applied; 100 were accepted. Applicants must interview; submit an essay and a formal application.

CONTACT

Suzanne Weber, Director of Admissions, Hotel, Restaurant and Culinary Arts, Château du Viner, Ecully, France. Telephone: 33-4 72 18 02 20. Fax: 33-478-43-33-51. E-mail: suzanne.weber@institutpaulboux.com. World Wide Web: http://www.each-lyon.com.

ECOLE SUPÉRIEURE DE CUISINE FRANÇAISE GROUPE FERRANDI

Professional Bilingual Culinary, Pastry, and Bread Baking Programs

Paris, France

GENERAL INFORMATION

Coeducational, culinary institute. Urban campus. Founded in 1932.

PROGRAM INFORMATION

Offered since 1986. Accredited by United States Department of Education. Program calendar is divided into semesters. 5-month certificate in classic French pastry and bread baking (plus 3-month internship). 5-month certificate in culinary arts (plus 3-month internship).

AREAS OF STUDY

Baking; buffet catering; confectionery show pieces; controlling costs in food service; culinary French; culinary skill development; food preparation; French cuisine; garde-manger; meat cutting; patisserie; restaurant opportunities; sanitation; saucier; soup, stock, sauce, and starch production; wines and spirits.

FACILITIES

Bakery; cafeteria; catering service; 10 classrooms; 3 computer laboratories; demonstration laboratory; 4 food production kitchens; gourmet dining room; laboratory; learning resource center; 4 lecture rooms; library; public restaurant; 10 teaching kitchens.

STUDENT PROFILE

24 full-time. 8 are under 25 years old; 16 are between 25 and 44 years old.

FACULTY

20 total: 20 full-time. Prominent faculty: Eric Robert, MOF, MCF; Didier Averty; Christian Maurice; Sebastien de Massard.

SPECIAL PROGRAMS

Excursions to French wine regions, 1 end-of-year gastronomic excursion, 3-month apprenticeship program after completion of 5-month program.

TYPICAL EXPENSES

Application fee: 300 euros. Tuition: 15,000 euros for 5 months.

FINANCIAL AID

Employment opportunities within the program are available.

HOUSING
Average off-campus housing cost per month: 400–900 euros.

APPLICATION INFORMATION
Students may begin participation in February and September. Application deadline for fall is May 1. Application deadline for spring is September 15. Applicants must interview; submit a formal application, letters of reference, and an essay.

CONTACT
Stephanie Curtis, Coordinator, Professional Bilingual Culinary, Pastry, and Bread Baking Programs, 10 rue Poussin, Paris, France. Telephone: 33-1-45270909. E-mail: stecurtis@aol.com. World Wide Web: http://www.escf.ccip.fr.

LE CORDON BLEU
The Grand Diplôme, The Diploma and Certificate Program

Paris, France

GENERAL INFORMATION
Private, coeducational, culinary institute. Urban campus. Founded in 1895.

PROGRAM INFORMATION
Offered since 1895. Program calendar is divided into trimesters, terms. 1-trimester certificate in basic, intermediate, and superior pastry. 1-trimester certificate in basic, intermediate, and superior cuisine. 1-year diploma in basic, intermediate, and superior cuisine. 1-year diploma in basic, intermediate, and superior pastry. 1-year diploma in Le Grand Diplôme-cuisine and pastry. 4-day certificate in French culinary technique (regional). 4-day certificate in French pastry technique (bread baking). 4-week certificate in professional in pastry. 5-week certificate in professional in cuisine.

PROGRAM AFFILIATION
American Institute of Wine & Food; Confrerie de la Chaine des Rotisseurs; Council on Hotel, Restaurant, and Institutional Education; International Association of Culinary Professionals; James Beard Foundation, Inc.; National Association for the Specialty Food Trade, Inc.; National Restaurant Association.

AREAS OF STUDY
Baking; cheese; confectionery show pieces; culinary French; culinary skill development; food preparation; garde-manger; meal planning; meat cutting; patisserie; saucier; soup, stock, sauce, and starch production; wines and spirits.

FACILITIES
2 demonstration laboratories; food production kitchen; student lounge; 4 teaching kitchens; boutique; showroom.

STUDENT PROFILE
380 full-time. 300 are under 25 years old; 80 are between 25 and 44 years old.

FACULTY
12 total: 12 full-time. 10 are master chefs. Prominent faculty: Didier Chantefort; Nicolas Bernardé. Faculty-student ratio: 1:12.

SPECIAL PROGRAMS
4-day program in French culinary technique, Mediterranean flavors, French regional cuisine and bread baking, 1-2 day vineyard and cultural excursions, professional internships, guest chefs.

TYPICAL EXPENSES
Application fee: 500–1500 euros. Tuition: 34,570 euros per Grand Diplôme; 21,300 euros per cuisine diploma; 15,200 euros per pastry diploma full-time, 5325 euros–7500 euros for 1 trimester part-time. Program-related fees include uniform package (included in tuition); equipment package (included in tuition).

FINANCIAL AID
In 2006, 15 scholarships were awarded (average award was 10,000 euros). Program-specific awards include work-study program. Employment placement assistance is available.

HOUSING
Average off-campus housing cost per month: 800 euros.

APPLICATION INFORMATION
Students may begin participation in January, March, June, September, and November. Applications are accepted continuously. In 2006, 420 applied. Applicants must submit a formal application, an essay, application fee.

CONTACT
Christel Hernandez, Admissions Director, The Grand Diplôme, The Diploma and Certificate Program, 8, rue Léon Delhomme, Paris, France. Telephone: 33-1-53682250. Fax: 33-1-48560396. E-mail: paris@cordonbleu.edu. World Wide Web: http://www.cordonbleu.edu.

See color display following page 378.

RITZ-ESCOFFIER PARIS

Paris Cedex 01, France

GENERAL INFORMATION
Private, coeducational, culinary institute. Urban campus.
Founded in 1988.

PROGRAM INFORMATION
Offered since 1988. Program calendar is divided into
trimesters. 1-week certificate in intermediate cuisine and
pastry. 1-week certificate in baking and breakfast pastry.
1- to 2-year master of business administration in
hospitality business. 12-week diploma in advanced
cuisine and pastry. 12-week diploma in intermediate
and advanced pastry. 2-week diploma in advanced
professional course. 6-week diploma in intermediate
cuisine and pastry.

PROGRAM AFFILIATION
American Institute of Wine & Food; International
Association of Culinary Professionals.

AREAS OF STUDY
Art de vivre; baking; cours de cocktails; culinary French;
culinary skill development; flower arranging; food
preparation; garde-manger; meat cutting; patisserie;
sanitation; saucier; soup, stock, sauce, and starch
production; wines and spirits.

FACILITIES
Bakery; cafeteria; food production kitchen; lecture
room; library; public restaurant; teaching kitchen.

STUDENT PROFILE
3,000 total: 1600 full-time; 1400 part-time.

FACULTY
4 total: 4 full-time. 4 are master chefs. Prominent
faculty: Christian Forais, Pastry Master Chef; David
Goulaze, Cooking Master Chef; Christophe Povy,
Cooking Master Chef; Didier Steudler, Pastry Master
Chef. Faculty-student ratio: 1:4.

SPECIAL PROGRAMS
6-week internship for the 12-week diplomas, Saturday
workshops, wines and food pairing evening classes.

TYPICAL EXPENSES
Application fee: 80 euros. Tuition: 885 euros per week.

FINANCIAL AID
Employment placement assistance is available.

HOUSING
Average off-campus housing cost per month: 2500
euros.

APPLICATION INFORMATION
Students may begin participation year-round.
Application deadline for admission is 6 months in
advance of program start date. Applicants must submit
a formal application, medical certificate, and portfolio.

CONTACT
Mrs. Marie-Fleur de Cosnac, Admissions and
Administration Manager, 15, place Vendôme, Paris,
France. Telephone: 33-1-43163050. Fax: 33-1-43163150.
E-mail: ecole@ritzparis.com. World Wide Web: http://
www.ritzescoffier.fr/com/jp.

ITALY

APICIUS-THE CULINARY INSTITUTE AND SCHOOL OF HOSPITALITY

Florence, Italy

GENERAL INFORMATION
Private, coeducational, culinary institute. Urban campus.
Founded in 1996.

PROGRAM INFORMATION
Offered since 1996. Program calendar is divided into
semesters. 1- to 4-semester certificate in culinary arts.
2-semester certificate in master in Italian cuisine.
2-semester certificate in food communications and
publishing. 2-semester certificate in Italian baking and
pastry. 2-semester certificate in wine studies and
enology. 2-semester certificate in hospitality
management.

PROGRAM AFFILIATION
Association of Professional Italian Chefs; International
Association of Culinary Professionals.

AREAS OF STUDY
Baking; culinary skill development; food preparation;
international cuisine; meal planning; meat cutting;
patisserie; restaurant opportunities; soup, stock, sauce,
and starch production; wines and spirits.

FACILITIES
4 classrooms; computer laboratory; 3 demonstration
laboratories; 2 food production kitchens; garden; 2
lecture rooms; library; public restaurant; 3 student
lounges; 5 teaching kitchens; state of the art wine
appreciation room.

STUDENT PROFILE
100 full-time. 70 are under 25 years old; 15 are between
25 and 44 years old; 15 are over 44 years old.

FACULTY

13 total: 10 full-time; 3 part-time. 5 are master chefs; 1 is a master baker; 7 are culinary-certified teachers. Prominent faculty: Marcella Ansaldo; Duccio Bagnoli; Andrea Trapani; Diletta Frescobaldi. Faculty-student ratio: 1:8.

SPECIAL PROGRAMS

Internships in local restaurants/hotels/wineries, 10-day tours of Tuscany, private customized cooking classes.

TYPICAL EXPENSES

Application fee: $75. Tuition: $6000 per semester full-time, $3000 per monthly part-time. Program-related fee includes $350 for student service fee.

FINANCIAL AID

In 2006, 3 scholarships were awarded (average award was $1000). Employment placement assistance is available.

HOUSING

Apartment-style housing available. Average on-campus housing cost per month: $1000.

APPLICATION INFORMATION

Students may begin participation in January, June, July, and September. Application deadline for spring is November 1. Application deadline for fall is July 1.

Application deadline for summer is April 1. In 2006, 80 applied; 80 were accepted. Applicants must submit a formal application and curriculum vitae/resume for advanced-level applicants.

CONTACT

Marilyn Etchell, Admissions Officer, 7151 Wilton Avenue, Suite 202, Sebastopol, CA 95472. Telephone: 707-824-8965. Fax: 707-824-0198. E-mail: mae@ studyabroaditaly.com. World Wide Web: http://www. culinaryinstituteofflorence.com/.

THE INTERNATIONAL COOKING SCHOOL OF ITALIAN FOOD AND WINE

Bologna, Italy

GENERAL INFORMATION

Private, coeducational, culinary institute. Urban campus. Founded in 1987.

The International Cooking School of Italian Food and Wine *(continued)*

PROGRAM INFORMATION
Offered since 1987. Program calendar is divided into weeks, weeks. 1-week certificate in foundation of Italian cooking.

PROGRAM AFFILIATION
International Association of Culinary Professionals; James Beard Foundation, Inc.; New York Association of Cooking Teachers; Women Chefs and Restaurateurs.

AREAS OF STUDY
Italian cuisine.

FACILITIES
Food production kitchen; 3 gourmet dining rooms; 3 public restaurants; teaching kitchen; 2 vineyards; pasta production kitchen; pizza production kitchen.

STUDENT PROFILE
10 full-time.

FACULTY
5 total: 3 full-time; 2 part-time. 2 are industry professionals; 3 are master chefs; 1 is a culinary-certified teacher. Faculty-student ratio: 1:4.

SPECIAL PROGRAMS
Private tours and tastings in Emilia-Romagna and Piedmont regions.

TYPICAL EXPENSES
Tuition: $2195–$2495 (4 days); $3450–$3850 (6 days); $3595–$3895 (7 days); (all costs include housing).

FINANCIAL AID
In 2006, 2 scholarships were awarded (average award was $3000).

APPLICATION INFORMATION
Students may begin participation in May, June, September, and October. Applications are accepted continuously. Applicants must submit a formal application.

CONTACT
International Cooking School of Italian Food and Wine, 201 East 28th Street, Suite 15B, New York, NY 10016-8538. Telephone: 212-779-1921. Fax: 212-779-3248. E-mail: marybethclark@internationalcookingschool.com. World Wide Web: http://www.internationalcookingschool.com.

ITALIAN CULINARY INSTITUTE FOR FOREIGNERS–USA

Costigliole d'Asti, Italy

GENERAL INFORMATION
Private, coeducational, culinary institute. Small-town setting. Founded in 1991.

PROGRAM INFORMATION
Program calendar is continuous. 3-month certificate in master-culinary arts-Italian. 6-month diploma in master-culinary arts-Italian.

SPECIAL PROGRAMS
Visits to wineries and food producers, externships.

TYPICAL EXPENSES
Tuition: 8800 euros per diploma; 4000 euros for certificate.

HOUSING
Coed and apartment-style housing available.

APPLICATION INFORMATION
Applications are accepted continuously. Applicants must submit a formal application, letters of reference, and an essay.

CONTACT
Enrico Bazzoni, Director of Programs, 126 Second Place, Brooklyn, NY 11231. Telephone: 718-875-0547. Fax: 718-875-5856. E-mail: usa@icif.com. World Wide Web: http://www.icif.com.

ITALIAN FOOD ARTISANS, LLC

various regions of Italy, Italy

GENERAL INFORMATION
Private, coeducational institution. Small-town setting. Founded in 1993.

PROGRAM INFORMATION
Offered since 1993. Accredited by IACP. Program calendar is divided into weeks. 1-week certificate of completion in Italian regional cuisine.

PROGRAM AFFILIATION
American Institute of Wine & Food; International Association of Culinary Professionals; Oldways Preservation and Exchange Trust; Roundtable for Women in Foodservice; Slow Food International.

Areas of Study

Baking; culinary skill development; food preparation; food purchasing; international cuisine; Italian cuisine; Italian regional cuisine (truffles, risotto); wines and spirits.

Facilities

Garden; gourmet dining room; teaching kitchen; vineyard; farmhouse kitchen.

Student Profile

150 part-time. 30 are under 25 years old; 50 are between 25 and 44 years old; 70 are over 44 years old.

Faculty

9 total: 1 full-time; 8 part-time. 3 are industry professionals; 4 are master chefs; 1 is a master baker; 1 is a culinary-certified teacher. Prominent faculty: Pamela Sheldon Johns, Cookbook Author. Faculty-student ratio: 1:4.

Special Programs

1 week olive harvest and olive oil production in Tuscany, 1-week cheese-making workshop (pecorino, mozzarella, ricotta), 1 week grape harvest and wine-making workshop in Tuscany.

Typical Expenses

Tuition: Ç2650–Ç2950 per week (includes housing) and all meals and ground transportation part-time.

Housing

Coed and apartment-style housing available.

Application Information

Students may begin participation in March, April, May, June, July, August, September, October, and November. Applications are accepted continuously.

Contact

Pamela Sheldon Johns, Program Director, 27 West Anapamu Street #427, Santa Barbara, CA 93101. Telephone: 805-963-7289. E-mail: pamela@foodartisans.com. World Wide Web: http://www.foodartisans.com.

Italian Institute for Advanced Culinary and Pastry Arts

Satriano, Italy

General Information

Private, coeducational, culinary institute. Suburban campus. Founded in 1997. Accredited by Accrediting Commission of Career Schools and Colleges of Technology.

Program Information

Accredited by Selected Chef and Culinary Federations. 3-month certificate in regional Italian cuisine.

Program Affiliation

American Culinary Federation; Confrerie de la Chaine des Rotisseurs; International Association of Culinary Professionals; National Restaurant Association.

Areas of Study

Baking; buffet catering; confectionery show pieces; controlling costs in food service; convenience cookery; culinary skill development; food preparation; food purchasing; food service math; garde-manger; international cuisine; introduction to food service; kitchen management; meal planning; meat cutting; menu and facilities design; patisserie; sanitation; saucier; soup, stock, sauce, and starch production; wines and spirits.

Facilities

Bake shop; cafeteria; 2 classrooms; coffee shop; demonstration laboratory; food production kitchen; 3 gardens; 2 laboratories; 2 lecture rooms; public restaurant; student lounge; teaching kitchen; 2 vineyards.

Student Profile

1,100 total: 550 full-time; 550 part-time.

Faculty

25 total: 5 full-time; 20 part-time. Prominent faculty: Fabio Bertuni; Fabio Momolo; John Nocita; Walter Zasoni. Faculty-student ratio: 1:7.

Special Programs

Tour of artisan food makers in Italy, participation in international culinary competitions, 3-6 month internships in Italy.

Typical Expenses

Tuition: $8500 per 3 months full-time, $2500 per 1 week full immersions part-time.

Financial Aid

In 2006, 4 scholarships were awarded. Program-specific awards include sponsorship for selected participants to compete in international events. Employment placement assistance is available. Employment opportunities within the program are available.

Application Information

Students may begin participation in January, February, April, May, June, September, and October. Applications are accepted continuously. In 2006, 2000 applied; 550 were accepted. Applicants must submit a formal application and an essay.

Italian Institute for Advanced Culinary and Pastry Arts *(continued)*

CONTACT
Prof. John Nocita, Director, Via T. Campanella, 37, Satriano, CZ, Italy. Telephone: 39-334 333 2554. Fax: 39-0967 21189. E-mail: johnn@italianculinary.it. World Wide Web: http://www.italianculinary.it.

JAPAN

LE CORDON BLEU JAPAN

Classic Cycle Program

Tokyo, Japan

GENERAL INFORMATION
Private, coeducational, culinary institute. Urban campus. Founded in 1991.

PROGRAM INFORMATION
Offered since 1991. Program calendar is divided into trimesters. 3-month certificate in advanced bakery. 3-month certificate in basic bakery. 3-month certificate in advanced pastry. 3-month certificate in superior cuisine. 3-month certificate in advanced cuisine. 3-month certificate in intermediate cuisine. 3-month certificate in basic cuisine. 3-month certificate in basic pastry. 3-month certificate in superior pastry.

PROGRAM AFFILIATION
Confrerie de la Chaine des Rotisseurs; James Beard Foundation, Inc.

AREAS OF STUDY
Baking; buffet catering; culinary French; patisserie; wines and spirits.

FACILITIES
2 demonstration laboratories; lecture room; student lounge; 4 teaching kitchens.

STUDENT PROFILE
1237 full-time.

FACULTY
14 total: 14 full-time. 14 are master chefs. Prominent faculty: Patrick Lemesle; Olivier Oddos; Bruno Le Dert; Dominique Gros.

SPECIAL PROGRAMS
Introduction to cuisine, pâtisserie, and boulangerie, wines and spirits courses, cheese courses.

TYPICAL EXPENSES
Application fee: 52,500 yen. Tuition: 574,000 yen–728,000 yen for 3 months. Program-related fee includes 36,500 yen–90,500 yen for uniforms, knives set, pastry/cuisine tools.

APPLICATION INFORMATION
Students may begin participation in January, April, July, and October. Application deadline for winter is December 15. Application deadline for spring is March 15. Application deadline for summer is June 15. Application deadline for fall is September 15. In 2006, 1237 applied; 1237 were accepted. Applicants must submit a formal application.

CONTACT
Taeko Okabe, Student Service and Sales Manager, Classic Cycle Program, ROOB-1, 28-13 Sarugaku-cho, Shibuya-ku, Tokyo, Japan. Telephone: 81-3-54890141. Fax: 81-3-54890145. E-mail: tokyo@cordonbleu.edu. World Wide Web: http://www.cordonbleu.co.jp.
See color display following page 378.

LE CORDON BLEU KOBE

Classic Cycle Program

Kobe-city, Hyogo, Japan

GENERAL INFORMATION
Private, coeducational, culinary institute. Urban campus. Founded in 2004.

PROGRAM INFORMATION
Offered since 2004. Program calendar is divided into trimesters. 3-month certificate in advanced bakery. 3-month certificate in basic bakery. 3-month certificate in initiation cuisine. 3-month certificate in superior pastry. 3-month certificate in intermediate pastry. 3-month certificate in basic pastry. 3-month certificate in superior cuisine. 3-month certificate in intermediate cuisine. 3-month certificate in basic cuisine.

PROGRAM AFFILIATION
Confrerie de la Chaine des Rotisseurs; James Beard Foundation, Inc.

AREAS OF STUDY
Baking; buffet catering; culinary French; patisserie; wines and spirits.

FACILITIES
2 demonstration laboratories; 2 teaching kitchens.

STUDENT PROFILE
500 full-time.

FACULTY

5 total: 5 full-time. 5 are master chefs. Prominent faculty: Bruno Le Dert; Thierry Guignard; Cyril Veniat; Mihoru Nakamura.

SPECIAL PROGRAMS

Introduction to cuisine, patisserie, and boulangerie, wine and spirits courses, cheese courses.

TYPICAL EXPENSES

Tuition: 574,000 yen–728,000 yen for 3 months. Program-related fee includes 36,500 yen–90,500 yen for uniforms, knives, pastry/cuisine tools.

APPLICATION INFORMATION

Students may begin participation in January, April, July, and October. Application deadline for winter is December 15. Application deadline for spring is March 15. Application deadline for summer is June 15. Application deadline for fall is September 15. In 2006, 500 applied; 500 were accepted. Applicants must submit a formal application.

CONTACT

Yuka Hamada, Student Service and Sales Manager, Classic Cycle Program, The 45th, 6/7 Floor, 45 Harima-machi, Chou-ku, Kobe-city, Hyogo, Japan. Telephone: 81-78 393 8221. Fax: 81-78 393 8222. E-mail: kobe@cordonbleu.edu. World Wide Web: http://www.cordonbleu.co.jp.

See color display following page 378.

LEBANON

LE CORDON BLEU LIBAN

Culinary Arts

Jounieh, Lebanon

GENERAL INFORMATION

Private, culinary institute.

CONTACT

Admissions, Culinary Arts, Rectorat B.P. 446, USEK University-Kaslik, Jounieh, Lebanon. Telephone: 961-9640644. Fax: 961-9642333. E-mail: liban@cordonbleu.edu.

See color display following page 378.

MEXICO

LE CORDON BLEU MEXICO

Mexico, Mexico

GENERAL INFORMATION

Culinary institute.

PROGRAM INFORMATION

Certificate in superior patisserie (North campus). Certificate in intermediate patisserie (North campus). Certificate in basic patisserie (North campus). Certificate in superior cuisine (North campus). Certificate in intermediate cuisine (North campus). Certificate in basic cuisine (North campus). Certificate in basic patisserie (South campus). Certificate in intermediate cuisine (South campus). Certificate in basic cuisine (South campus). Diploma in Le Grand Diplome (North campus). Diploma in patisserie diplome (North campus). Diploma in cuisine diplome (North campus).

TYPICAL EXPENSES

Tuition: $12247.50–$25817.50 for diploma programs; $3852.50–$4830 for certificate programs.

CONTACT

Admissions, Universidad Anahuac, Av. Lomas Anahuac, s/n. Lomos Anahuac, Mexico, C.P., Mexico. Telephone: 52-55 5627 0210 Ext. 7132. Fax: 52-55 5627 0210 Ext. 8724. E-mail: mexico@cordonbleu.edu.

See color display following page 378.

NEW ZEALAND

NEW ZEALAND SCHOOL OF FOOD AND WINE

Foundation Cookery Skills

Christchurch, New Zealand

GENERAL INFORMATION

Private, coeducational, culinary institute. Urban campus. Founded in 1994.

PROGRAM INFORMATION

Offered since 1995. Accredited by New Zealand Qualifications Authority. Program calendar is divided into trimesters. 12-week certificate in professional wine knowledge (sommelier). 15-week certificate in cookery and hospitality (introduction). 16-week certificate in cookery.

New Zealand School of Food and Wine (*continued*)

PROGRAM AFFILIATION
Restaurant Association of New Zealand.

AREAS OF STUDY
Baking; beverage management; controlling costs in food service; culinary French; culinary skill development; food preparation; food service math; garde-manger; international cuisine; management and human resources; meal planning; meat cutting; menu and facilities design; nutrition; patisserie; sanitation; saucier; seafood processing; soup, stock, sauce, and starch production; wines and spirits.

FACILITIES
2 classrooms; computer laboratory; demonstration laboratory; food production kitchen; library; public restaurant; teaching kitchen.

STUDENT PROFILE
80 full-time. 20 are under 25 years old; 50 are between 25 and 44 years old; 10 are over 44 years old.

FACULTY
4 total: 4 full-time. 2 are industry professionals; 1 is a master chef; 1 is a culinary-certified teacher. Prominent faculty: Celia Hay, MBA; Philippe Meyer; Gabrielle Lewis; Lois Blackie. Faculty-student ratio: 1:12.

SPECIAL PROGRAMS
Local vineyard tours, trips to relevant conferences, certification in wine.

TYPICAL EXPENSES
Tuition for international students: NZ$5400 per certificate in professional wine knowledge; $6250 for certificate in cookery and hospitality; $7500 for certificate in cookery full-time, NZ$595 per WSET intermediate, $995 for WSET advanced part-time. Program-related fees include NZ$1000 for cooking equipment; NZ$245 for textbooks; NZ$850 for WSET fees and textbooks; NZ$140 for uniform (cookery students only).

HOUSING
Average off-campus housing cost per month: NZ$320.

APPLICATION INFORMATION
Students may begin participation in January, May, July, August, and September. Applications are accepted continuously. In 2006, 100 applied; 100 were accepted. Applicants must interview; submit a formal application and letters of reference.

CONTACT
Celia Hay, Director, Foundation Cookery Skills, PO Box 25217, Christchurch, New Zealand. Telephone: 064-3-3797501. Fax: 064-3-3662302. E-mail: chay@ foodandwine.co.nz. World Wide Web: http://www. foodandwine.co.nz.

PERU

LE CORDON BLEU PERU

Lima, Peru

GENERAL INFORMATION
Private, coeducational, culinary institute. Urban campus. Founded in 1994. Accredited by Accrediting Commission of Career Schools and Colleges of Technology.

PROGRAM INFORMATION
Offered since 1994. Accredited by Council on Hotel, Restaurant and Institutional Education. Program calendar is divided into semesters. 18-month diploma in administration of hotels and restaurants. 2-year diploma in bar and cocktails. 2-year diploma in pastry. 2-year diploma in cuisine. 3-year diploma in alimentary industries. 3-year diploma in gastronomy and culinary arts. 4-year diploma in hotel and restaurant administration.

PROGRAM AFFILIATION
Organizacion Mundial del Turismo; World Association of Cooks Societies.

AREAS OF STUDY
Beverage management; culinary French; culinary skill development; international cuisine; kitchen management; nutrition; patisserie; sanitation; wines and spirits.

FACILITIES
16 classrooms; coffee shop; computer laboratory; 2 demonstration laboratories; 10 laboratories; lecture room; library; public restaurant; 6 teaching kitchens.

STUDENT PROFILE
1,005 total: 785 full-time; 220 part-time.

FACULTY
120 total: 20 full-time; 100 part-time. Prominent faculty: Dr. Sixtilio Dalmau Castañon, Director; Sra. Patricia Dalmau de Galfré, Administrative Assistant; Chef Jaques Benoit, Culinary Director.

SPECIAL PROGRAMS
Practical opportunities, culinary and bar competitions.

TYPICAL EXPENSES

Tuition: $19,200 per 3 years full-time, $2700 per 18 months part-time. Program-related fee includes $1200 for uniforms, cutlery, books, and insurance (accidental).

FINANCIAL AID

Employment placement assistance is available.

HOUSING

Average off-campus housing cost per month: $200.

APPLICATION INFORMATION

Students may begin participation in March and August. Application deadline for fall is February 1. Application deadline for winter is June 1. In 2006, 350 applied; 225 were accepted. Applicants must submit a formal application.

CONTACT

Maria Laura Bentin, Admission, Av. Nunez de Balboa 530, Miraflores, Lima, Peru. Telephone: 51-1-2428222. Fax: 51-1-2429209. E-mail: admision@cordonbleuperu. edu.pe. World Wide Web: http://www.cordonbleuperu. edu.pe.

See color display following page 378.

PHILIPPINES

CENTER FOR CULINARY ARTS, MANILA

Quezon City, Philippines

GENERAL INFORMATION

Private, coeducational, culinary institute. Urban campus. Founded in 1996.

PROGRAM INFORMATION

Offered since 1996. Program calendar is divided into terms. 1-year certificate in culinary arts. 1-year certificate in baking and pastry arts. 2-year diploma in baking, pastry arts and technology management. 2-year diploma in culinary arts and technology management.

PROGRAM AFFILIATION

International Association of Culinary Professionals; National Restaurant Association.

SPECIAL PROGRAMS

Continuing education program, culinary competitions, apprenticeships.

FINANCIAL AID

Employment placement assistance is available. Employment opportunities within the program are available.

APPLICATION INFORMATION

Students may begin participation in January, June, August, and October. Applicants must interview; submit a formal application, letters of reference, an essay, academic transcripts, and results of medical examination.

CONTACT

School Director, Katipunan Avenue, Loyola Heights, Quezon City, Philippines. Telephone: 63-2 426 4840. Fax: 63-2 426 4836. E-mail: marketing@cca-manila.com. World Wide Web: http://www.cca-manila.com/.

REPUBLIC OF KOREA

LE CORDON BLEU KOREA

Seoul, Republic of Korea

GENERAL INFORMATION

Private, coeducational, culinary institute. Urban campus. Founded in 2002.

PROGRAM INFORMATION

Offered since 2002. Program calendar is divided into quarters. 1-year diploma in culinary arts. 10- to 20-week certificate in culinary arts. 2-year master of business administration in hospitality management. 4-year bachelor's degree in restaurant management.

AREAS OF STUDY

Baking; culinary French; patisserie.

FACILITIES

3 classrooms; demonstration laboratory; food production kitchen; library; student lounge; 5 teaching kitchens.

STUDENT PROFILE

500 full-time. 300 are under 25 years old; 200 are between 25 and 44 years old.

FACULTY

4 total: 4 full-time. 4 are industry professionals. Prominent faculty: Philippe Bachmann, Executive Chef; Laurent Beltoise, Cuisine Chef; Jean Pierre Gestin, Pastry Chef; Frank Colombie, Pastry Chef. Faculty-student ratio: 1:10.

SPECIAL PROGRAMS

Workshops for gourmet enthusiasts.

TYPICAL EXPENSES

Application fee: 450,000 Korean won. Tuition: 5,229,000 Korean won; 5,922,000 Korean won per session. Program-related fees include 214,000 Korean won for uniform sets; 870,000 Korean won for tool kits.

Le Cordon Bleu Korea *(continued)*

FINANCIAL AID
Employment placement assistance is available.

APPLICATION INFORMATION
Students may begin participation in February, May, September, and November. Applications are accepted continuously. In 2006, 520 applied; 480 were accepted. Applicants must submit a formal application, an essay, resume.

CONTACT
Young Hong, Academy Manager, Le Cordon Bleu Korea, 7th Floor, Social Education Building 53-12, Chungpadong 2K, Yongsan-ku, Seoul, Republic of Korea. Telephone: 82-2-719-6961. Fax: 82-2-719-7569. E-mail: korea@cordonbleu.edu. World Wide Web: http://www.cordonbleu.co.kr.

See color display following page 378.

SOUTH AFRICA

CHRISTINA MARTIN SCHOOL OF FOOD AND WINE

Durban, South Africa

GENERAL INFORMATION
Private, coeducational, culinary institute. Urban campus. Founded in 1973. Accredited by Accrediting Council for Independent Colleges and Schools.

PROGRAM INFORMATION
Offered since 1973. Accredited by American Culinary Federation Accrediting Commission. Program calendar is continuous. 1-year diploma in patisseurier. 1-year diploma in food preparation and culinary art. 6-month certificate in patisseurier. 6-month certificate in food preparation and culinary arts.

PROGRAM AFFILIATION
Confrerie de la Chaine des Rotisseurs; Council on Hotel, Restaurant, and Institutional Education; International Association of Culinary Professionals; International Wine & Food Society; Women Chefs and Restaurateurs.

AREAS OF STUDY
Baking; beverage management; buffet catering; confectionery show pieces; controlling costs in food service; convenience cookery; culinary French; culinary skill development; food preparation; food purchasing; food service communication; food service math; garde-manger; international cuisine; introduction to food service; kitchen management; management and human resources; meal planning; meat cutting; menu and facilities design; nutrition; nutrition and food service; patisserie; restaurant opportunities; sanitation; saucier; seafood processing; soup, stock, sauce, and starch production; wines and spirits.

FACILITIES
Bake shop; 2 bakeries; cafeteria; 3 catering services; 3 classrooms; coffee shop; computer laboratory; 2 demonstration laboratories; 3 food production kitchens; garden; gourmet dining room; learning resource center; lecture room; library; public restaurant; snack shop; student lounge; 5 teaching kitchens.

STUDENT PROFILE
100 total: 60 full-time; 40 part-time.

FACULTY
100 total: 60 full-time; 40 part-time. 10 are master chefs; 20 are master bakers; 10 are culinary-certified teachers. Prominent faculty: M. Barry, Chef Cuisine; E. Bewilliec, Master Patissier; D. Carl, Chef Cuisine; W. Whittaure, Chef Cuisine. Faculty-student ratio: 1:10.

SPECIAL PROGRAMS
Lindt chocolate and sugar course, culinary competitions.

TYPICAL EXPENSES
Tuition: $13,230 per year full-time, $30 per day part-time.

FINANCIAL AID
Employment placement assistance is available. Employment opportunities within the program are available.

APPLICATION INFORMATION
Students may begin participation in January. Application deadline for spring is October 1. Application deadline for summer is November 1. Application deadline for winter is July 1. Application deadline for autumn is September 1. In 2006, 60 applied. Applicants must interview; submit a formal application and letters of reference.

CONTACT
M. Barry, Director, PO Box 4601, Durban, South Africa. Telephone: 031-3032111. Fax: 031-3123342. E-mail: chrisma@iafrica.com.

SPAIN

LE CORDON BLEU MADRID

Culinary Arts

Madrid, Spain

GENERAL INFORMATION
Private, culinary institute.

CONTACT
Admissions, Culinary Arts, Univerisdad Francisco de Vitoria, Ctra. Pozuelo-Majadahonda, Km. 1,800 Pozuelo de Alarcón, Madrid, Spain. Telephone: 34-91 351 03 03. Fax: 34-91 351 1555. E-mail: madrid@cordonbleu.edu.

See color display following page 378.

SWITZERLAND

DCT HOTEL AND CULINARY ARTS SCHOOL, SWITZERLAND

European Culinary Center

Vitznau, Switzerland

GENERAL INFORMATION
Private, coeducational, two-year college. Small-town setting. Founded in 1992. Accredited by New England Association of Schools and Colleges.

PROGRAM INFORMATION
Offered since 1997. Accredited by American Culinary Federation Accrediting Commission, Council on Hotel, Restaurant and Institutional Education, Swiss Hotel Schools Association. Program calendar is divided into quarters. 11-week certificate in European food and beverage service. 11-week certificate in foundation in European cuisine. 11-week certificate in European pastry and chocolate. 11-week certificate in European gourmet cuisine. 12—18 month advanced diploma in European culinary management.

DCT Hotel and Culinary Arts School, Switzerland
(*continued*)

PROGRAM AFFILIATION

American Culinary Federation; Council on Hotel, Restaurant, and Institutional Education; International Hotel and Restaurant Association; National Restaurant Association; Swiss Chef Association; World Association of Cooks Societies.

AREAS OF STUDY

Baking; beverage management; chocolate; confectionery show pieces; controlling costs in food service; culinary skill development; European pastries; food preparation; food purchasing; food service communication; garde-manger; international cuisine; introduction to food service; kitchen management; management and human resources; menu and facilities design; nutrition; nutrition and food service; patisserie; sanitation; saucier; soup, stock, sauce, and starch production; wines and spirits.

FACILITIES

Bakery; 7 classrooms; computer laboratory; food production kitchen; laboratory; learning resource center; library; student lounge; 2 teaching kitchens.

STUDENT PROFILE

45 full-time. 40 are under 25 years old; 4 are between 25 and 44 years old; 1 is over 44 years old.

FACULTY

9 total: 3 full-time; 6 part-time. 4 are industry professionals; 2 are master chefs; 1 is a master baker; 2 are culinary-certified teachers. Prominent faculty: Dr. Birgit Black, Dean; Swiss Master Chef Patrick Diethelm; Swiss Master Chef Urs Meichtry; Chef Stacy Black, CEC. Faculty-student ratio: 1:8.

SPECIAL PROGRAMS

6-9 month paid internship in Switzerland, tours of wineries and chocolate factories, study European cuisine in Europe.

TYPICAL EXPENSES

Application fee: $80. Tuition: $9500 per 3-month term (includes room and board). Program-related fee includes $1000 for required medical and liability insurance, uniforms, texts and classroom supplies, field trips.

FINANCIAL AID

Program-specific awards include paid Swiss internships in top-ranked restaurants. Employment placement assistance is available. Employment opportunities within the program are available.

HOUSING

Coed housing available. Average off-campus housing cost per month: $500–$700.

APPLICATION INFORMATION

Students may begin participation in January, April, July, and October. Applications are accepted continuously. In 2006, 75 applied; 50 were accepted. Applicants must submit a formal application, transcripts, prior diplomas, TOEFL scores or equivalent, proof of high school graduation or professional experience.

CONTACT

Mrs. Sharon Spaltenstein, Director of Marketing and Admission, European Culinary Center, Seestrasse, Vitznau, Switzerland. Telephone: 41-413990000. Fax: 41-413990101. E-mail: culinary@dct.ch. World Wide Web: http://www.culinary.ch.

THAILAND

LE CORDON BLEU DUSIT CULINARY SCHOOL

Bangkok, Thailand

GENERAL INFORMATION

Private, coeducational, culinary institute. Urban campus. Founded in 2007.

PROGRAM INFORMATION

Offered since 2007. Accredited by Thailand Ministry of Education. Program calendar is divided into quarters. 3-month certificate in Advanced Course-English Language for Culinary and Hospitality. 3-month certificate in Intermediate Course-English Language for Culinary and Hospitality. 3-month certificate in Basic Course-English Language for Culinary and Hospitality. 3-month certificate in Certificat de Patisserie Supérieure. 3-month certificate in Certificat de Patisserie Intermédiaire. 3-month certificate in Certificat de Patisserie de Base. 3-month certificate in Certificat de Cuisine Supérieure. 3-month certificate in Certificat de Cuisine Intermédiaire. 3-month certificate in Certificat de Cuisine de Base. 6-month certificate in Certificat de Chef de Partie. 6-month diploma in Diplôme de Direction de Cuisine. 9-month diploma in Diplôme de Patisserie. 9-month diploma in Diplôme de Cuisine. 9-month grand diploma in Grand Diplôme.

AREAS OF STUDY

Culinary English; culinary French; management.

FACILITIES

2 classrooms; 2 demonstration laboratories; 4 food production kitchens; library; public restaurant; 5 teaching kitchens.

STUDENT PROFILE

81 full-time. 10 are under 25 years old; 66 are between 25 and 44 years old; 5 are over 44 years old.

FACULTY

3 total: 3 full-time. 1 is a master chef; 2 are Cuisine Chefs. Prominent faculty: Fabrice Danniel, Executive Master Chef; Cedric Maton, Cuisine Chef; Lidivat Arnaud Bernard, Cuising Chef. Faculty-student ratio: 1:16.

SPECIAL PROGRAMS

Industry placement after the completion of Superior Level-Culinary Arts Program, industry placement after the completion of Certificat de Chef de Partie.

TYPICAL EXPENSES

Application fee: 2500 Thai bahts. Tuition: 150,000 Thai bahts per 3 month term. Tuition for international students: 180,000 Thai bahts per 3 month term. Program-related fees include 6000 Thai bahts for uniform; 35,000 Thai bahts for tool kit.

FINANCIAL AID

Program-specific awards include installment payments.

HOUSING

Average off-campus housing cost per month: 25,000 Thai bahts.

APPLICATION INFORMATION

Students may begin participation in January, April, July, and October. Applications are accepted continuously. In 2006, 81 applied; 81 were accepted. Applicants must submit a formal application, copy of educational certificate/diploma, TOEFL/IELTS for non-Thai and non-English native speakers, copy of ID/passport and 4 1-inch photos.

CONTACT

Ms. Parinporn Tungkaserawong, Admission Manager, 946 The Dusit Thani Building, Rama IV Road, Silom, Bangrak, Bangkok, Thailand. Telephone: 66-2 237 8877. Fax: 66-2 237 8878. E-mail: parinporn.tk@dusit.com. World Wide Web: http://www.cordonbleudusit.com.

See color display following page 378.

UNITED KINGDOM

COOKERY AT THE GRANGE

The Essential Cookery Course

Near Frome, Somerset, United Kingdom

GENERAL INFORMATION

Private, coeducational, culinary institute. Rural campus. Founded in 1981.

PROGRAM INFORMATION

Offered since 1981. Program calendar is divided into four-week cycles, four-week cycles. 1-month certificate in cookery.

AREAS OF STUDY

Baking; culinary skill development; food preparation; general cookery; meal planning; meat cutting; menu and facilities design; soup, stock, sauce, and starch production; wines and spirits.

FACILITIES

Garden; student lounge; teaching kitchen.

STUDENT PROFILE

24 full-time.

FACULTY

8 total: 3 full-time; 5 part-time. Faculty-student ratio: 1:7.

TYPICAL EXPENSES

Tuition: £2850–£3520 per certificate (includes housing).

HOUSING

Coed housing available.

APPLICATION INFORMATION

Students may begin participation in January, February, May, June, July, August, September, October, and November. Applicants must submit a formal application.

CONTACT

William and Jane Averill, The Essential Cookery Course, The Grange, Whatley, Near Frome, Somerset, United Kingdom. Telephone: 44-1373836579. Fax: 44-1373836579. E-mail: info@cookeryatthegrange.co.uk. World Wide Web: http://www.cookeryatthegrange.co.uk.

Professional Programs
United Kingdom

LE CORDON BLEU–LONDON CULINARY INSTITUTE

Le Cordon Bleu Classic Cycle Programme

London, United Kingdom

GENERAL INFORMATION
Private, coeducational, culinary institute. Urban campus. Founded in 1895.

PROGRAM INFORMATION
Offered since 1933. Accredited by American Culinary Federation Accrediting Commission. Program calendar is divided into quarters. 10-week certificate in basic cuisine. 10-week certificate in superior patisserie. 10-week certificate in superior cuisine. 10-week certificate in basic patisserie. 10-week certificate in intermediate cuisine. 10-week certificate in intermediate patisserie. 30-week diploma in cuisine. 30-week diploma in patisserie. 30-week diploma in grand diplome.

PROGRAM AFFILIATION
American Institute of Wine & Food; Confrerie de la Chaine des Rotisseurs; Council on Hotel, Restaurant, and Institutional Education; International Association of Culinary Professionals; James Beard Foundation, Inc.

AREAS OF STUDY
Baking; buffet catering; cheese; confectionery show pieces; controlling costs in food service; culinary French; culinary skill development; food preparation; food purchasing; international cuisine; introduction to food service; kitchen management; meal planning; nutrition; nutrition and food service; patisserie; sanitation; table service; wines and spirits.

FACILITIES
2 bakeries; 2 demonstration laboratories; food production kitchen; student lounge; 4 teaching kitchens.

STUDENT PROFILE
460 full-time.

FACULTY
8 total: 8 full-time. Prominent faculty: Chef Yann Barraud; Chef Julie Walsh. Faculty-student ratio: 1:10.

SPECIAL PROGRAMS
Restaurant market tours and hotel visits, exchanges between Le Cordon Bleu Schools worldwide, culinary competitions.

TYPICAL EXPENSES
Tuition: £3190-£29,475 for 5 weeks–9 months. Program-related fees include £500 for certificate course fee; £1500 for diploma course fee.

FINANCIAL AID
In 2006, 10 scholarships were awarded (average award was £2230). Program-specific awards include International Association of Culinary Professionals scholarship, James Beard Foundation scholarship. Employment placement assistance is available. Employment opportunities within the program are available.

HOUSING
Average off-campus housing cost per month: £1400.

APPLICATION INFORMATION
Students may begin participation in January, March, April, June, July, August, September, and October. In 2006, 431 applied. Applicants must submit a formal application, curriculum vitae, and letter of motivation.

CONTACT
Admissions Officer, Le Cordon Bleu Classic Cycle Programme, 114 Marylebone Lane, London, United Kingdom. Telephone: 44-20-79353503. Fax: 44-20-79357621. E-mail: london@cordonbleu.edu. World Wide Web: http://www.cordonbleu.net.

See color display following page 378.

LEITH'S SCHOOL OF FOOD AND WINE

London, United Kingdom

GENERAL INFORMATION
Private, coeducational, culinary institute. Urban campus. Founded in 1975.

PROGRAM INFORMATION
Offered since 1975. Program calendar is divided into trimesters. 1-month certificate of completion in cookery (beginners/advanced). 1-month certificate in practical cookery. 1-term certificate in food and wine (advanced). 1-term certificate in food and wine (intermediate). 1-term certificate in food and wine (beginners). 1-week certificate of completion in advanced skills. 1-week certificate of completion in beginners' skills. 1-week certificate of completion in easy dinner parties. 1-year diploma in food and wine. 10-class (evenings) certificate of completion in intermediate skills. 10-class (evenings) certificate of completion in beginners' skills. 2-term diploma in food and wine. 5-class certificate in wine.

AREAS OF STUDY
Baking; buffet catering; chocolate; confectionery show pieces; controlling costs in food service; culinary French; culinary skill development; easy dinner party; fish cookery; food preparation; food purchasing; game; healthy eating; international cuisine; introduction to

386   *www.petersons.com*

Peterson's Culinary Schools

food service; Italian; kitchen management; meal planning; meat cutting; menu and facilities design; nutrition; nutrition and food service; patisserie; restaurant opportunities; sanitation; saucier; seafood processing; soup, stock, sauce, and starch production; wines and spirits.

FACILITIES
Demonstration laboratory; food production kitchen; lecture room; library; student lounge; 3 teaching kitchens.

TYPICAL STUDENT PROFILE
546 total: 96 full-time; 450 part-time.

SPECIAL PROGRAMS
Excursions to Billingsgate and Smithfield markets, recipe writing competition, restaurant work placements.

FINANCIAL AID
Employment placement assistance is available. Employment opportunities within the program are available.

APPLICATION INFORMATION
Students may begin participation in January, March, April, July, August, September, and December. Applications are accepted continuously. Applicants must interview (if possible); submit a formal application and letters of reference.

CONTACT
Director of Admissions, 21 St Alban's Grove, London, United Kingdom. Telephone: 44-20-72290177. Fax: 44-20-79375257. World Wide Web: http://www.leiths.com.

ROSIE DAVIES

Courses for Cooks

Frome, Somerset, United Kingdom

GENERAL INFORMATION
Private, coeducational institution. Rural campus. Founded in 1996.

PROGRAM INFORMATION
Offered since 1996. Program calendar is divided into months, months. 1-month certificate in basic cooking in chalets. 1-month certificate in basic cooking on yachts. 1-month certificate in basic cooking.

AREAS OF STUDY
Baking; beverage management; buffet catering; controlling costs in food service; convenience cookery; culinary French; culinary skill development; food preparation; food purchasing; food service

communication; food service math; international cuisine; introduction to food service; kitchen management; meal planning; meat cutting; menu and facilities design; nutrition; nutrition and food service; patisserie; sanitation; saucier; seafood processing; soup, stock, sauce, and starch production; wines and spirits.

FACILITIES
Food production kitchen; garden; gourmet dining room; library; student lounge; teaching kitchen.

STUDENT PROFILE
35 full-time. 15 are under 25 years old; 14 are between 25 and 44 years old; 6 are over 44 years old.

FACULTY
3 total: 1 full-time; 2 part-time. 1 is an industry professional; 1 is a culinary-certified teacher; 1 is a hygiene specialist. Prominent faculty: Rosie Davies. Faculty-student ratio: 1:4.

TYPICAL EXPENSES
Application fee: £500. Tuition: £3050 per 4 weeks (includes housing).

HOUSING
Coed housing available.

APPLICATION INFORMATION
Students may begin participation in January, February, April, July, September, October, and November. Applications are accepted continuously. In 2006, 100 applied; 35 were accepted. Applicants must submit a formal application.

CONTACT
Rosie Davies, Principal, Courses for Cooks, Penny's Mill, Horn Street, Nunney, Frome, SO BA11 4NP, United Kingdom. Telephone: 44-1373836210. Fax: 44-1373836018. E-mail: info@rosiedavies.co.uk. World Wide Web: http://www.rosiedavies.co.uk.

TANTE MARIE SCHOOL OF COOKERY

Woking, Surrey, United Kingdom

GENERAL INFORMATION
Private, coeducational, culinary institute. Urban campus. Founded in 1954. Accredited by Accrediting Council for Independent Colleges and Schools.

PROGRAM INFORMATION
Offered since 1954. Accredited by British Accreditation Council for Independent Further and Higher Education and The Year Out Group. Program calendar is divided into trimesters. 3-month certificate in Cordon Bleu cookery. 6-month intensive diploma in Cordon Bleu cookery. 9-month diploma in Cordon Bleu cookery.

Tante Marie School of Cookery *(continued)*

AREAS OF STUDY
Baking; buffet catering; confectionery show pieces; controlling costs in food service; convenience cookery; culinary French; culinary skill development; food preparation; food purchasing; garde-manger; international cuisine; introduction to food service; kitchen management; meal planning; meat cutting; meat fabrication; menu and facilities design; nutrition; nutrition and food service; patisserie; restaurant opportunities; sanitation; saucier; seafood processing; soup, stock, sauce, and starch production; wines and spirits.

FACILITIES
Garden; lecture room; library; student lounge; 5 teaching kitchens; vineyard; demonstration theatre.

STUDENT PROFILE
206 total: 98 full-time; 108 part-time.

FACULTY
10 total: 7 full-time; 3 part-time. 2 are industry professionals; 8 are culinary-certified teachers. Prominent faculty: Claire Alexander-Brown; Susan B. Alexander; Marcella O'Donovan. Faculty-student ratio: 1:10.

PROMINENT ALUMNI AND CURRENT AFFILIATION
Lyndy Redding, Absolute Taste Catering and Event Design Company; Dan Levy, The Wateside Inn at Bray; Richard Piombini, Salterns Harbourside Hotel.

SPECIAL PROGRAMS
3-day course on wines and spirits, 1-day course on food safety and hygiene, visits to Smithfield Market, herb farm and vegetable growers.

TYPICAL EXPENSES
Tuition: £4900 per semester (11 weeks).

FINANCIAL AID
In 2006, 5 scholarships were awarded (average award was £2000). Employment placement assistance is available. Employment opportunities within the program are available.

HOUSING
Average off-campus housing cost per month: £400.

APPLICATION INFORMATION
Students may begin participation in January, April, July, September, October, and November. Applications are accepted continuously. In 2006, 232 applied; 232 were accepted. Applicants must submit a formal application.

CONTACT
Mrs. Marcella O'Donovan, Principal, Woodham House, Carlton Road, Woking, SU GU21 4HF, United Kingdom. Telephone: 44-1483726957. Fax: 44-1483724173. E-mail: info@tantemarie.co.uk. World Wide Web: http://www.tantemarie.co.uk/press.html.

PROFILES OF APPRENTICESHIP PROGRAMS

ALABAMA

ACF GREATER MONTGOMERY CHAPTER

Montgomery, Alabama

PROGRAM INFORMATION
Approved by the American Culinary Federation. Academic requirements are met through a chef-taught curriculum and at Trenholm State Technical College (degree available). Special apprenticeships available in baking and pastries and catering; hospitality management.

PLACEMENT INFORMATION
Participants are placed in 1 of 32 locations, including full-service restaurants, hotels, private clubs, fine dining restaurants, and catering businesses. Most popular placement locations are Wyn Lakes Country Club, City Grill, and Embassy Suites.

TYPICAL APPRENTICE PROFILE
Applicants must interview; submit a formal application, an essay, and letters of reference (recommended).

CONTACT
Director of Apprenticeship Program, 1225 Airbase Boulevard, Montgomery, AL 36108. Telephone: 334-420-4495. Fax: 334-420-4491. World Wide Web: http://www.acfchefs.org/Content/presidents_portal/ACFChapter.cfm?ChapterChoice=AL032.

ARIZONA

CHEFS ASSOCIATION OF SOUTHERN ARIZONA, TUCSON

Tucson, Arizona

PROGRAM INFORMATION
Approved by the American Culinary Federation. Academic requirements are met at Pima Community College (degree available). Special apprenticeships available in pastry.

PLACEMENT INFORMATION
Participants are placed in 1 of 9 locations, including hotels, country clubs, restaurants, and casinos. Most popular placement locations are Hilton El Conquistador, Desert Diamond Casino, and Accacia Restaurant.

TYPICAL APPRENTICE PROFILE
Applicants must submit a formal application.

CONTACT
Director of Apprenticeship Program, 3438 E Bellevue Street, Tucson, AZ 85716-3910. Telephone: 520-318-3448. World Wide Web: http://www.acfchefs.org/presidents_portal/ACFChapter.cfm?ChapterChoice=AZ023.

CALIFORNIA

BARONA VALLEY RANCH RESORT & CASINO

Lakeside, California

PROGRAM INFORMATION
Approved by the American Culinary Federation. Academic requirements are met through a chef-taught curriculum at Grossmont College (degree available).

PLACEMENT INFORMATION
Participants are placed in Barona Valley Ranch (resort, hotel, and casino).

APPRENTICE PROFILE
Number of participants in 2006: 12. 2 apprentices were under 25 years old; 8 were between 25 and 44 years old; 2 were over 44 years old. Applicants must interview, submit an essay, and obtain a culinary position/Barona Gaming License.

ENTRY-LEVEL COMPENSATION
$10–$13 per hour.

CONTACT
Dean A. Thomas, Executive Chef, 1932 Wildcat Canyon Road, Lakeside, CA 92040. Telephone: 619-328-3524. Fax: 619-443-2418. E-mail: dthomas@barona.com. World Wide Web: http://www.barona.com.

SAN FRANCISCO CULINARY/PASTRY PROGRAM

San Francisco, California

PROGRAM INFORMATION
Academic requirements are met through a chef-taught curriculum and at City College of San Francisco. Special apprenticeships available in pastry (4000 hours).

PLACEMENT INFORMATION
Participants are placed in hotels/clubs/restaurants. Most popular placement locations are the Palace Hotel, the Hilton Hotel, and Michael Mina Restaurant.

APPRENTICE PROFILE
Number of participants in 2006: 13. 13 apprentices were between 25 and 44 years old. Applicants must interview; submit a formal application and letters of reference; have a high school diploma or GED.

TYPICAL EXPENSES
Program-related fees include $100 for uniforms; $150 for equipment (knives).

ENTRY-LEVEL COMPENSATION
$79.87 per 8-hour shift.

CONTACT
Joan Ortega, Director, 760 Market Street, Suite 1066, San Francisco, CA 94102. Telephone: 415-989-8726. Fax: 415-989-2920. E-mail: joanlortega@aol.com.

COLORADO

ACF COLORADO CHEFS ASSOCIATION

Denver, Colorado

PROGRAM INFORMATION
Approved by the American Culinary Federation. Academic requirements are met through a chef-taught curriculum.

PLACEMENT INFORMATION
Participants are placed in 1 of 30 locations, including hotels, restaurants, country clubs, assisted living, and universities.

APPRENTICE PROFILE
Number of participants in 2006: 30. 15 apprentices were under 25 years old; 13 were between 25 and 44 years old; 2 were over 44 years old. Applicants must submit a formal application, letters of reference, an essay; have a high school diploma or GED; must be 17 years of age.

TYPICAL EXPENSES
Application fee: $50. Basic cost of participation is $2000 per 2 years for state residents, $2000 per 2 years for nonresidents. Program-related fee includes $85 for annual ACF junior membership.

ENTRY-LEVEL COMPENSATION
$8–$12 per hour.

CONTACT
Kari Jensen, Director of Apprenticeship, Johnson&Wales University, 7150 Montview Boulevard, Denver, CO 80220. Telephone: 303-264-3005. Fax: 303-264-3007. E-mail: kari78@msn.com. World Wide Web: http://www. acfcoloradochefs.org.

COLORADO MOUNTAIN COLLEGE

Edwards, Colorado

PROGRAM INFORMATION
Approved by the American Culinary Federation. Academic requirements are met through a chef-taught curriculum and at Colorado Mountain College (degree available).

PLACEMENT INFORMATION
Participants are placed in 1 of 11 locations, including restaurants. Most popular placement locations are Beano's Cabin, Toscanini, and Zach's Cabin.

APPRENTICE PROFILE
Number of participants in 2006: 27. 17 apprentices were under 25 years old; 10 were between 25 and 44 years old. Applicants must interview; submit a formal application, letters of reference, and an essay.

TYPICAL EXPENSES
Basic cost of participation is $5043 per three year program for state residents (in-district), $6957 per three year program for state residents (out-of-district), $17,451 per three year program for nonresidents, $17,451 per three year program for international residents.

ENTRY-LEVEL COMPENSATION
$9 per hour.

CONTACT

Director of Apprenticeship Program, Colorado Mountain College, Culinary Apprenticeship Program, 831 Grand Avenue, Glenwood Springs, CO 81601. Telephone: 800-621-8559. Fax: 970-947-8324. E-mail: trymer@coloradomtn.edu. World Wide Web: http://www.coloradomtn.edu/culinary.

FLORIDA

ACF TREASURE COAST CHAPTER

Fort Pierce, Florida

PROGRAM INFORMATION

Approved by the American Culinary Federation. Academic requirements are met at Indian River Community College (degree available). Special apprenticeships available in pastry and cook's apprentice.

PLACEMENT INFORMATION

Participants are placed in 1 of 90 locations, including restaurants, hotels, country clubs, and institutional settings. Most popular placement locations are Bent Pines Golf Club, Ian's Tropical Grill, and Indian River Plantation-Marriott.

TYPICAL APPRENTICE PROFILE

Applicants must interview; submit a formal application; have a high school diploma or GED; must be 18 years of age.

CONTACT

Director of Apprenticeship Program, 3209 Virginia Avenue, Ft. Pierce, FL 34981-5596. Telephone: 772-462-7641. Fax: 772-462-4796. World Wide Web: http://www.acfchefs.org/content/chapter/fl121.html.

FORT LAUDERDALE ACF INC.

Coconut Creek, Florida

PROGRAM INFORMATION

Approved by the American Culinary Federation. Academic requirements are met through a chef-taught curriculum and at Atlantic Technical Center.

PLACEMENT INFORMATION

Participants are placed in 1 of 20 locations, including hotel and resorts, restaurants, hospitals and retirement homes, retail bakeries, and country clubs. Most popular placement locations are Westin Diplomat Hotel and Resort, Radisson Bridge Resort Hotel (Carmens), and Marriott Hotel and Resort.

APPRENTICE PROFILE

Number of participants in 2006: 20. 5 apprentices were under 25 years old; 13 were between 25 and 44 years old; 2 were over 44 years old. Applicants must interview; submit a formal application.

TYPICAL EXPENSES

Application fee: $30. Program-related fees include $80 for ACF junior dues; $41 for textbook and workbook; $39 for ACF training log.

ENTRY-LEVEL COMPENSATION

$9–$12 per hour.

CONTACT

Steve Mosley, Apprenticeship Coordinator, Atlantic Technical Center, 4700 NW Coconut Creek Parkway, Coconut Creek, FL 33063. Telephone: 954-309-3591.

INDIAN RIVER COMMUNITY COLLEGE

Fort Pierce, Florida

PROGRAM INFORMATION

Approved by the American Culinary Federation. Academic requirements are met through a chef-taught curriculum and at Indian River Community College (degree available).

PLACEMENT INFORMATION

Participants are placed in country club, institutions, and hotels. Most popular placement locations are Orchid Isle Country Club, Disney Reports, and Bent Pines Gold Club.

APPRENTICE PROFILE

40 apprentices were under 25 years old; 20 were between 25 and 44 years old; 20 were over 44 years old. Applicants must interview; submit a formal application.

TYPICAL EXPENSES

Program-related fee for $600–$800 for books, tools, uniforms, and ACF dues.

CONTACT

Jack Fredericks, Culinary Instructor, 3209 Virginia Avenue, Ft. Pierce, FL 34981. Telephone: 772-462-7641. E-mail: jfrederi@ircc.edu.

KANSAS

JOHNSON COUNTY COMMUNITY COLLEGE

Overland Park, Kansas

PROGRAM INFORMATION
Approved by the American Culinary Federation. Academic requirements are met at Johnson County Community College (degree available).

PLACEMENT INFORMATION
Participants are placed in 1 of 60 locations, including hotels, restaurants, country clubs, casinos, and health-care facilities. Most popular placement locations are the Westin Crown Center Hotel, Hyatt Regency Hotel, and Mission Hills Country Club.

APPRENTICE PROFILE
Number of participants in 2006: 243. Applicants must interview; submit a formal application.

TYPICAL EXPENSES
Basic cost of participation is $64 per credit hour for state residents, $145 per credit hour for nonresidents, $145 per credit hour for international residents. Program-related fee includes $180 for apprenticeship fee/registration of DOC and ACF.

ENTRY-LEVEL COMPENSATION
$7.50 per hour.

CONTACT
Lindy Robinson, Assistant Dean, Johnson County Community College, 12345 College Boulevard, Overland Park, KS 66210. Telephone: 913-469-8500 Ext. 3250. Fax: 913-469-2560. E-mail: lrobinsn@jccc.edu.

LOUISIANA

DELGADO COMMUNITY COLLEGE

New Orleans, Louisiana

PROGRAM INFORMATION
Approved by the American Culinary Federation. Academic requirements are met through a chef-taught curriculum and at Delgado Community College (degree available).

PLACEMENT INFORMATION
Participants are placed in 1 of 80 locations, including restaurants, hotels, hospitals, and convention centers. Most popular placement locations are Ritz-Carlton Hotel, Hilton Hotel, and Brennan's Family Restaurants.

APPRENTICE PROFILE
Number of participants in 2006: 110. 62 apprentices were under 25 years old; 41 were between 25 and 44 years old; 7 were over 44 years old. Applicants must submit a formal application, letters of reference, ACT scores; have a high school diploma or GED.

TYPICAL EXPENSES
Application fee: $25. Basic cost of participation is $800 per semester for state residents, $2200 per semester for nonresidents. Program-related fees include $350 for tool kit and student uniform; $115 for ACF logbook; $75 for annual dues for ACF membership.

ENTRY-LEVEL COMPENSATION
$8 per hour.

CONTACT
Dr. Mary P. Bartholomew, Director of Culinary Arts and Hospitality, Delgado Community College, 615 City Park Avenue, New Orleans, LA 70119. Telephone: 504-671-6199. Fax: 504-483-4893. E-mail: mbart@dcc.edu. World Wide Web: http://www.dcc.edu/.

MICHIGAN

ACF BLUE WATER CHEFS ASSOCIATION

Clinton Township, Michigan

PROGRAM INFORMATION
Approved by the American Culinary Federation. Academic requirements are met through a chef-taught curriculum and at Macomb Community College (degree available).

PLACEMENT INFORMATION
Participants are placed in restaurants and hotels.

TYPICAL APPRENTICE PROFILE
Applicants must interview; submit a formal application, letters of reference, and an essay.

CONTACT
Director of Apprenticeship Program, 44575 Garfield Road, Room K-124-1, Clinton Township, MI 48038. Telephone: 586-286-2088. Fax: 586-226-4725. World Wide Web: http://www.macomb.edu.

ACF MICHIGAN CHEFS DE CUISINE ASSOCIATION

Farmington Hills, Michigan

PROGRAM INFORMATION
Approved by the American Culinary Federation. Academic requirements are met through a chef-taught curriculum and at Oakland Community College (degree available).

PLACEMENT INFORMATION
Participants are placed in 1 of 60 locations, including restaurants, clubs, and hotels. Most popular placement locations are the Detroit Athletic Club, the Palace of Auburn Hills, and the Bloomfield Hills Country Club.

TYPICAL APPRENTICE PROFILE
Applicants must interview; submit a formal application, letters of reference, and an essay.

CONTACT
Director of Apprenticeship Program, 27055 Orchard Lake Road, Farmington Hills, MI 48334. Telephone: 248-522-3710. Fax: 248-522-3706. World Wide Web: http://www.acfchefs.org/Content/presidents_portal/ACFChapter.cfm?ChapterChoice=MI012.

MISSOURI

CHEFS DE CUISINE OF ST. LOUIS ASSOCIATION

St. Louis, Missouri

PROGRAM INFORMATION
Approved by the American Culinary Federation. Academic requirements are met at St. Louis Community College at Forest Park (degree available). Special apprenticeships available in baking and pastry.

PLACEMENT INFORMATION
Participants are placed in 1 of 42 locations, including country clubs, hotels, fine dining restaurants, and casinos. Most popular placement locations are Old Warson Country Club, Westwood Country Club, and Bellerive Country Club.

TYPICAL APPRENTICE PROFILE
Applicants must interview; submit a formal application, an essay, and letters of reference; complete one semester of studies.

CONTACT
Director of Apprenticeship Program, Gatesworth 1 McKnight Place, St. Louis, MO 63124. Telephone: 314-993-0111. World Wide Web: http://www.stlcc.edu.

COLUMBIA MISSOURI CHAPTER ACF

Columbia, Missouri

PROGRAM INFORMATION
Approved by the American Culinary Federation. Academic requirements are met through a chef-taught curriculum and at Johnson County Community College (degree available).

PLACEMENT INFORMATION
Participants are placed in 1 of 2 locations, including private clubs, hotels, and restaurants. Most popular placement locations are University Club and Capital Plaza Hotel.

TYPICAL APPRENTICE PROFILE
Applicants must interview; submit a formal application and letters of reference.

CONTACT
Director of Apprenticeship Program, University Club of Missouri, 107 Donald W. Reynolds Alumni Center, Columbia, MO 65211. Telephone: 573-882-2433. Fax: 573-884-2063. World Wide Web: http://acfchefs.missouri.org.

NEBRASKA

ACF PROFESSIONAL CHEFS AND CULINARIANS OF THE HEARTLAND

Omaha, Nebraska

PROGRAM INFORMATION
Approved by the American Culinary Federation. Academic requirements are met at Metropolitan Community College (degree available).

PLACEMENT INFORMATION
Participants are placed in 1 of 21 locations, including country clubs, hotels, restaurants, and casinos. Most popular placement locations are the Happy Hollow Country Club, Doubletree Hotel, and Ameristar.

TYPICAL APPRENTICE PROFILE
Applicants must submit a formal application.

ACF Professional Chefs and Culinarians of the Heartland *(continued)*

CONTACT
Director of Apprenticeship Program, PO Box 3777, Omaha, NE 68103. Telephone: 402-457-2510. Fax: 402-457-2833. World Wide Web: http://www.acfchefs.org/content/chapter/ne032.html.

OHIO

ACF COLUMBUS CHAPTER

Columbus, Ohio

PROGRAM INFORMATION
Approved by the American Culinary Federation. Academic requirements are met at Columbus State Community College (degree available).

PLACEMENT INFORMATION
Participants are placed in 1 of 55 locations, including hotels, catering firms, clubs, and restaurants. Most popular placement locations are Cameron Mitchell Restaurants, all Country Clubs in the Central Ohio area, and Hyatt Regency-Hyatt on Capital Square.

TYPICAL APPRENTICE PROFILE
Applicants must interview; submit a formal application, an essay, letters of reference, and academic transcripts.

CONTACT
Director of Apprenticeship Program, Columbus State Community College, 550 East Spring Street, Columbus, OH 43215. Telephone: 614-287-5061. Fax: 614-287-5973. World Wide Web: http://www.acfcolumbus.org.

PENNSYLVANIA

ACF LAUREL HIGHLANDS CHAPTER

Youngwood, Pennsylvania

PROGRAM INFORMATION
Approved by the American Culinary Federation. Academic requirements are met through a chef-taught curriculum and at Westmoreland County Community College (degree available). Special apprenticeships available in culinary arts and baking and pastry.

PLACEMENT INFORMATION
Participants are placed in 1 of 100 locations, including clubs, resorts, hotels, fine dining facilities, and institutional feeding sites.

TYPICAL APPRENTICE PROFILE
Applicants must submit a formal application and take a physical exam.

CONTACT
Director of Apprenticeship Program, Westmoreland County Community College, Youngwood, PA 15697-1898. Telephone: 724-925-4123. Fax: 724-925-5802. World Wide Web: http://chefpertise.com/Content/presidents_portal/ACFChapter.cfm?ChapterChoice=PA021.

BUCKS COUNTY COMMUNITY COLLEGE

Newtown, Pennsylvania

PROGRAM INFORMATION
Academic requirements are met through a chef-taught curriculum and at Bucks County Community College (degree available).

PLACEMENT INFORMATION
Participants are placed in 1 of 120 locations, including hotels, restaurants and country clubs, contract food services, extended-care facilities, and supermarkets.

APPRENTICE PROFILE
Number of participants in 2006: 65. Applicants must interview; submit a formal application and an essay.

TYPICAL EXPENSES
Application fee: $30. Basic cost of participation is $93 per credit hour for state residents (in-district), $186 per credit hour for state residents (out-of-district), $279 per credit hour for nonresidents. Program-related fees include $200 for knives and pastry kits; $100 for uniform.

ENTRY-LEVEL COMPENSATION
$7.80–$12.00 per hour.

CONTACT
Earl R. Arrowood, Chef Apprenticeship Program Coordinator, 275 Swamp Road, Newtown, PA 18940. Telephone: 215-968-8241. Fax: 215-504-8509. E-mail: arrowood@bucks.edu. World Wide Web: http://www.bucks.edu.

WISCONSIN

CHEFS OF MILWAUKEE

Germantown, Wisconsin

PROGRAM INFORMATION
Approved by the American Culinary Federation. Academic requirements are met at Milwaukee Area Technical College (degree available).

PLACEMENT INFORMATION
Participants are placed in 1 of 37 locations, including restaurants, hotels/resorts, caterers, private clubs, and institutional food service. Most popular placement locations are Hilton Milwaukee City Center, Coquette Café/Sanford Restaurant, and The American Club.

APPRENTICE PROFILE
Number of participants in 2006: 40. 26 apprentices were under 25 years old; 12 were between 25 and 44 years old; 2 were over 44 years old. Applicants must interview.

TYPICAL EXPENSES
Basic cost of participation is $4000 per apprenticeship (3 years). Program-related fees include $200 for uniforms; $150 for cutlery set; $300 for ACF apprentice fee and membership; $1200 for books.

ENTRY-LEVEL COMPENSATION
$7–$12 per hour.

CONTACT
John Reiss, Culinary Apprentice Coordinator, 700 West State Street, Milwaukee, WI 53233. Telephone: 414-297-6861. Fax: 414-297-7990. E-mail: reissj@matc.edu. World Wide Web: http://www.acfchefsofmilwaukee.com.

INDEXES

Certificate and Diploma Programs

U.S.

Associate Degree Programs

U.S.

Bachelor's Degree Programs

U.S.

Master's Degree Programs

U.S.

Doctoral Degree Programs

(A) = Apprenticeship Programs   (P) = Professional Programs

(A) = Apprenticeship Programs   *(P) = Professional Programs*

(A) = Apprenticeship Programs   (P) = Professional Programs

(A) = Apprenticeship Programs   (P) = Professional Programs

NOTES

NOTES

NOTES

NOTES

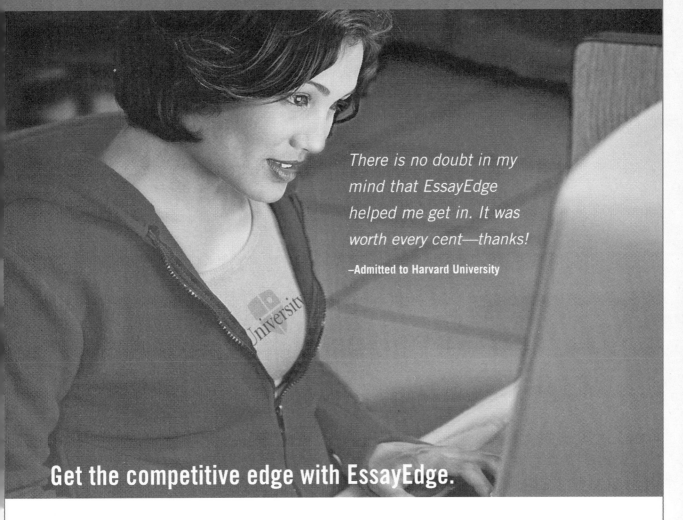

Peterson's
Book Satisfaction Survey

Give Us Your Feedback

Thank you for choosing Peterson's as your source for personalized solutions for your education and career achievement. Please take a few minutes to answer the following questions. Your answers will go a long way in helping us to produce the most user-friendly and comprehensive resources to meet your individual needs.

When completed, please tear out this page and mail it to us at:

Publishing Department
Peterson's, a Nelnet company
2000 Lenox Drive
Lawrenceville, NJ 08648

You can also complete this survey online at **www.petersons.com/booksurvey.**

1. **What is the ISBN of the book you have purchased? (The ISBN can be found on the book's back cover in the lower right-hand corner.)** _____

2. **Where did you purchase this book?**
   ❑ Retailer, such as Barnes & Noble
   ❑ Online reseller, such as Amazon.com
   ❑ Petersons.com
   ❑ Other (please specify) _____

3. **If you purchased this book on Petersons.com, please rate the following aspects of your online purchasing experience on a scale of 4 to 1 (4 = Excellent and 1 = Poor).**

	4	3	2	1
Comprehensiveness of Peterson's Online Bookstore page	❑	❑	❑	❑
Overall online customer experience	❑	❑	❑	❑

4. **Which category best describes you?**

   ❑ High school student
   ❑ Parent of high school student
   ❑ College student
   ❑ Graduate/professional student
   ❑ Returning adult student

   ❑ Teacher
   ❑ Counselor
   ❑ Working professional/military
   ❑ Other (please specify) _____

5. **Rate your overall satisfaction with this book.**

Extremely Satisfied	Satisfied	Not Satisfied
❑	❑	❑

6. **Rate each of the following aspects of this book on a scale of 4 to 1 (4 = Excellent and 1 = Poor).**

	4	3	2	1
Comprehensiveness of the information	❑	❑	❑	❑
Accuracy of the information	❑	❑	❑	❑
Usability	❑	❑	❑	❑
Cover design	❑	❑	❑	❑
Book layout	❑	❑	❑	❑
Special features (e.g., CD, flashcards, charts, etc.)	❑	❑	❑	❑
Value for the money	❑	❑	❑	❑

7. **This book was recommended by:**
   ❑ Guidance counselor
   ❑ Parent/guardian
   ❑ Family member/relative
   ❑ Friend
   ❑ Teacher
   ❑ Not recommended by anyone—I found the book on my own
   ❑ Other (please specify) _____

8. **Would you recommend this book to others?**

Yes	Not Sure	No
❑	❑	❑

9. **Please provide any additional comments.**

   _____

   _____

   _____

   _____

   _____

Remember, you can tear out this page and mail it to us at:

   Publishing Department
   Peterson's, a Nelnet company
   2000 Lenox Drive
   Lawrenceville, NJ 08648

or you can complete the survey online at **www.petersons.com/booksurvey**.

Your feedback is important to us at Peterson's, and we thank you for your time!

If you would like us to keep in touch with you about new products and services, please include your
e-mail address here: _____